THIRD EDITION

WALTER AERTS
PETER WALTON

Global Financial Accounting and Reporting: Principles and Analysis

CENGAGE
Learning™

Australia • Brazil • Japan • Korea • Mexico • Singapore • Spain • United Kingdom • United States

Global Financial Accounting and Reporting:
Principles and Analysis 3rd Edition
Walter Aerts and Peter Walton

Publishing Director: Linden Harris

Publisher: Andrew Ashwin

Commissioning Editor: Annabel Ainscow

Editorial Assistant: Lauren Darby

Project Editor: Alison Cooke

Production Controller: Eyvett Davis

Marketing Manager: Anne Renton

Typesetter: S4Carlisle Publishing Services

Cover design: Adam Renvoize

For product information and technology assistance, contact
emea.info@cengage.com.

For permission to use material from this text or product,
and for permission queries,
email **emea.permissions@cengage.com**..

British Library Cataloguing-in-Publication Data

A catalogue record for this book is available from the British Library.

ISBN: 978-1-4080-6286-9

Cengage Learning EMEA
Cheriton House, North Way, Andover, Hampshire, SP10 5BE, United Kingdom

Cengage Learning products are represented in Canada by Nelson Education Ltd.

For your lifelong learning solutions, visit
www.cengage.co.uk

Purchase your next print book, e-book or e-chapter at
www.cengagebrain.com

Printed in China by RR Donnelley
1 2 3 4 5 6 7 8 9 10 – 15 14 13

BRIEF CONTENTS

CONTENTS

Part 3 An introduction to financial statement analysis 215

Part 5 Advanced financial statement analysis   449

PREFACE

This book was conceived as a support for courses whose objective is to provide students with a working understanding of financial statements and the meaning of accounting numbers. Our intention is to place reporting in its business context, and to make it clear to managers how accounting reflects their work. We also aim to teach the conceptual foundation of accounting and how this translates into the financial statements of businesses. The book is aimed at future users of accounting information–managers and analysts – not at future auditors or accountants.

The book is sited emphatically in an intuitive approach to understanding accounting and concerns itself with the underlying logic of the corporate accounting system and its exploitation in the financial statements. It is not a book-keeping course and we have used a spreadsheet for double entry, rather than T-accounts or debits and credits, since we believe that the latter are technically unnecessary and are practically an obstacle to non-specialists.

The book does not situate itself in an individual national context. It uses International Financial Reporting Standards (IFRS) as its basis, and reflects, therefore, the rules followed by nearly all European listed companies and by an increasing number of Asian, African and American (non-US) companies. We also try to keep up with current IFRS terminology (e.g. statement of financial position, statement of profit or loss (and other comprehensive income)) in order to be consistent with the IFRS extracts used in our book.

Walter Aerts
Peter Walton

ACKNOWLEDGEMENTS

This book has evolved out of teaching materials drawn from a wide range of teaching experiences in Belgium, France, Switzerland, the UK and the USA. As a result many people, students and colleagues, have influenced the content indirectly, and we are grateful for their help and advice over the years. We should also like to thank Brendan George, Annabel Ainscow, Lauren Darby and Alison Cooke for their support and commitment in producing a new edition, as well as the rest of the publishing team at Cengage Learning.

The text contains quotations from published material and we should like to thank the following for permission to use these: Trustees of the IASC Foundation, Association of Chartered Certified Accountants (*Accounting & Business*), the International Federation of Accountants, the United Nations Conference on Trade and Development, the Organization for Economic Co-operation and Development, the US Securities and Exchange Commission and the Institute of Chartered Accountants in England and Wales. We also thank the many companies whose financial statements have supplied illustrative material.

Reviewer Acknowledgements

The publishers and author team would like to thank the following academics for their review comments which have helped shape this new edition of the book:

Chris Coles – University of Glasgow

Claus Koss – Fachhochschule Regensburg

Blain Lambert – Fontys International School of Business Economics, Venlo

Eileen Roddy – ESCP-EAP European School of Management

Mark Whittington – University of Aberdeen

Eugene Apakoh – Royal Docks Business School

STRUCTURE OF THE BOOK

The aim of this book is to provide a complete companion to financial reporting that will take business students with no knowledge of accounting through the mechanics of how financial records are structured through to being able to understand and analyze published consolidated financial statements. However, this is not to say that every course will want to devote as much time to financial reporting as this would take. The book is therefore structured into what we believe are separable building blocks.

Part One covers material that is often not taught as such in a course on accounting and financial statement analysis. It is about the environment within which financial reporting takes place – how it is regulated, what an accounting department in a company does, how the accounting records are checked. It also includes the main material on the International Accounting Standards Board. We think this is useful background, not least because students come to the course with different previous exposure to accounting and pre-conceptions as to what it is. However, it can be dispensed with, or can be set as pre-course reading.

Part Two is the core introduction to financial accounting. We examine the basic accounting techniques used by a reasonably simple individual company and the preparation of annual financial statements from the accounting database. This presentation is based on using worksheets to show what is happening in the company's accounting database, rather than the formal book-keeping techniques which involve the famous debits and credits. Most courses require this fundamental knowledge of the accounting equation, the iteration between the Statement of Profit or Loss (Income Statement) and the Statement of Financial Position (Balance Sheet) and accruals accounting.

Part Three then provides a discussion about how financial statements are interpreted. Chapter 8 provides a thumbnail sketch of some of the finance theory that informs interpretation. Most accounting books do not contain such a chapter but we have included it on the basis that accounting is often taught before finance in an MBA or management course and this may help students get to grips with the purposes of analysis as opposed merely to the techniques. It can easily be dispensed with. Chapter 9 contains the basic material on accounting ratios, and Chapter 10 introduces the Statement of Cash Flows as a statement that analyses the changes in opening and closing financial position. In our view Parts Two and Three constitute a basic introduction to accounting for non-financial managers.

However, we are aware that most sets of published financial statements that a manager will want to review are likely to be consolidated financial statements, and our preference in our own teaching is to include some material, however limited, on group accounts. In Part Four, we show how groups of companies prepare consolidated financial statements to enable them to present a worldwide picture of their economic situation. Chapter 11 provides a little contextual analysis about the annual reports of multinational companies and their use and introduces the

Statement of Comprehensive Income. Chapter 12 provides the basics of how a consolidation is done.

A course could certainly stop there, but we provide two chapters with further technical issues. Chapter 13 aims to show that the consolidated statements are a confection of statements drawn up in different currencies and dealing with different activities. The chapter addresses segment reporting and foreign currency translation issues. Chapter 14 analyzes a selection of current technical issues, including a discussion of fair value and financial instruments. We think this may go beyond what some teachers are aiming to achieve at entry level but we also think students may find it useful to have such a discussion. Chapters 15 and 16 are offered in the general spirit of trying to address all major issues that intersect with financial reporting in order to provide a complete guide for the non-financial manager. Again, many courses may not want to spend time on this, but on the other hand the student who buys and keeps the book will be able to refer back to it should the need arise.

Part Five goes further into techniques of financial statements analysis and reviews those such as Z scores, shareholder value and growth calculations. It could be dropped entirely or be taught with Chapter 9. The final chapter takes a look at the changing priorities of the IASB since its inception and analyses the likely changes in standards up to 2015.

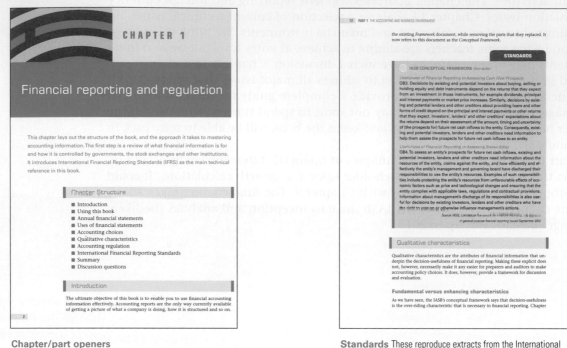

Chapter/part openers
Describe the contents of the chapter in outline and how it fits into the 'big picture'.

Standards These reproduce extracts from the International Financial Reporting Standards (IFRS) and other sources of information published by the IASB.

Company reports These are extracted from the reports of well-known companies that report in IFRS GAAP to give a concrete, real-world dimension to the text.

Between the lines These highlight additional discussion points throughout the text.

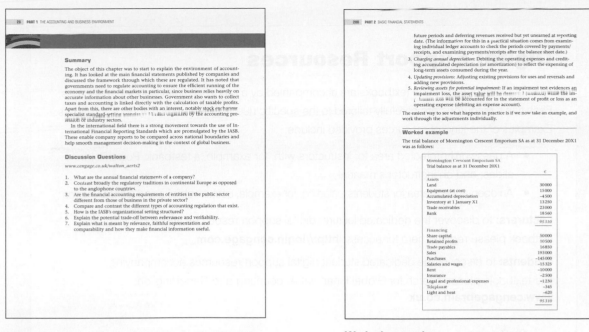

Summary Each chapter ends with a comprehensive summary that provides a thorough recap of issues in each chapter, helping you to assess your understanding and revise key content.

Worked examples
These clearly apply the principles covered in the book to illustrate the meaning clearly.

Discussion Questions These appear in some chapters and help to reinforce and test your knowledge and understanding providing a basis for group discussions and activities.

Assignment Questions These appear in some chapters and test the application of principles covered – the answers are provided on the password-protected part of the website.

Digital Support Resources

All of our Higher Education textbooks are accompanied by a range of digital support resources. Each title's resources are carefully tailored to the specific needs of the particular book's readers. Examples of the kind of resources provided include:

- A password protected area for instructors with, for example, a testbank, PowerPoint slides, and an instructor's manual
- An open-access area for students including, for example, useful weblinks and glossary terms

Lecturers: to discover the dedicated lecturer digital support resources accompanying this textbook please register here for access: **http://login.cengage.com**.

Students: to discover the dedicated student digital support resources accompanying this textbook, please search for Global Financial Accounting and Reporting on: **www.cengagebrain.co.uk**

PART ONE

The accounting and business environment

This first section of the book is intended to provide context and background to the world in which financial reporting takes place. Many management students may never previously have come across accounting nor have any idea of the structures within which it takes place. This section tries to provide background information that should help students understand the subject better in a real world setting. Chapter 1 introduces financial statements and the institutional framework within which International Financial Reporting Standards are developed. Chapter 2 talks about accountants and their different functions.

Financial reporting and regulation

This chapter lays out the structure of the book, and the approach it takes to mastering accounting information. The first step is a review of what financial information is for and how it is controlled by governments, the stock exchanges and other institutions. It introduces International Financial Reporting Standards (IFRS) as the main technical reference in this book.

Chapter Structure

- Introduction
- Using this book
- Annual financial statements
- Uses of financial statements
- Accounting choices
- Qualitative characteristics
- Accounting regulation
- International Financial Reporting Standards
- Summary
- Discussion questions

Introduction

The ultimate objective of this book is to enable you to use financial accounting information effectively. Accounting reports are the only way currently available of getting a picture of what a company is doing, how it is structured and so on.

Photographs can show you the company's physical locations and, if it manufactures or sells physical products, what these look like. Words can describe the company and its products, but only accounting data can tell you about a company's profitability, its size and its financial structure in a format which is more or less comparable with other companies and carries with it an assurance that this is the whole of the company, warts and all, that you are looking at, not just the good looking parts.

Financial accounting is intimately linked with **business** and, as Karl Marx was the first to point out, business cannot exist, except in very primitive forms, without accounting. Accounting data make the business visible, measure its progress and make it possible to manage the business and understand it. Accounting enables the business to work in many locations, directed by a central team. Multinational companies can only work because accounting is there to control what is going on in distant places, to monitor this and to provide information back to centre.

If you look at developing countries and those in transition to a market economy, the lack of accounting skills and of reliable and independent auditors to verify data and ensure that resources are used as intended are major obstacles to economic progress.

On the whole, most managers meet accounting in the form of financial reports, and are rarely concerned with the day-to-day running of the accounting department. However, they do interface with this in areas such as salaries, expense refunds, authorizing payment of invoices and so on. Financial reports and understanding them are the central issue in this book, although we will certainly pass by the accounting department to see what is going on there, as well as review audit, both internal and external. We will focus also on published financial reports. The calculation and dissemination of internal reports is itself a long and complicated subject, usually dealt with as *management accounting* or *managerial accounting*, and calling for adaptation of standard accounting data for internal purposes. In order to understand that, you need to know about standard accounting data, and that is the purpose of this book. What you learn here will enable you to understand the annual **financial statements** published by companies but also the basis of most internal reports as well, since they use the same source data. Externally disseminated financial statements have to be drawn up by reference to a set of accounting rules (sometimes referred to as a 'comprehensive basis of accounting'). This book focuses on the rules issued by the International Accounting Standards Board (IASB) which are used by listed companies in many countries in the world, including the European Union.

Using this book

The book is organized to take you into the accounting world in a series of steps; these do not involve your learning how to be an accountant. In Part One, we will look at the environment within which financial reporting takes place – how it is regulated, what an accounting department in a company does, how the accounting records are checked. In Part Two, we will go on to examine basic accounting techniques used by a reasonably simple individual company and the preparation of annual financial statements from the accounting database. This presentation will be based on using worksheets to show what is happening in the company's accounting database, rather than the formal book-keeping techniques which involve the famous debits and credits. Part Three will then discuss how financial statements are interpreted.

We then move on to look at larger companies. In Part Four, we see how groups of companies prepare **consolidated financial statements** to enable them to present a worldwide picture of their economic situation. We will then go on to consider related issues of international taxation, auditing, corporate governance and dissemination of information to stock exchanges. Part Five will come back to financial statement analysis and review more sophisticated techniques such as growth calculations, integrated ratio analysis, shareholder value and Z scores.

While the structure of the book has been designed to lead you logically through a potential minefield as comfortably as possible, you can, of course, choose to omit some chapters. Our intention is not merely to teach you to understand the nature of accounting information but also to enable you to understand the interactions between accounting and management in a wider sense and to see how intimately accounting links with the life of the company, both internally and in helping manage relations with the outside environment in which the company operates.

Annual financial statements

All commercial companies produce annual *financial statements* (also known as the annual report, the annual accounts). Generally these have to be filed with the **government**, either centrally or in regional offices, and they have to be sent to shareholders. In many countries the government file is available to the public, so the financial statements are in effect public and available to competitors or customers or suppliers, and are regularly consulted by these. Equally there are credit information companies, such as Dun & Bradstreet, Standard & Poor's or Moody's Corporation, which collect financial information and sell it to interested parties.

Many small companies do not like this exposure, but large companies generally welcome it and indeed publish the data widely, including on their websites. Large companies are well aware that this is the only independently confirmed information on the company which is widely available, and is a major tool in engendering confidence in those with whom the company wishes to do business.

The annual financial statements typically consist of the following elements:

- *The statement of profit or loss* (also referred to as 'income statement' or 'profit and loss account') reports on the **revenue**, **costs** and **profit** of the company for the year and consequently is the main **performance** indicator as far as profitability is concerned. The IASB has recently enlarged the scope of this financial performance statement and now calls it the 'statement of comprehensive income' (which is also described as the 'statement of profit or loss and other comprehensive income' referring to its two components).

- *The balance sheet* (the IASB terminology is '**statement of financial position**') gives a picture at a given moment – the last day of the financial year – of how the company has been financed and how that money has been invested in productive capacity (plant, buildings, computers, **inventories** etc.).

- *The notes to the accounts* (in North America these are called 'footnotes') can be anything from two or three pages to 40 or 50 – the **notes** provide detailed analysis of some of the figures in the Statements of Financial Position and Comprehensive Income, such as the dates when loans fall due for repayment, or the different constituents of the total inventory. Importantly, the notes also contain a statement of the **accounting policies** followed by the company. They are increasingly a means of conveying non-accounting information, such as contingent environmental liabilities, to interested outsiders. The notes are subject to audit.

- *The statement of* **cash flows** is an analysis of the main **cash** movements through the company in the previous 12 months – cash created by the company through profitable operations, cash spent on acquiring new capacity, cash repaid to lenders and new borrowings. This statement is obligatory in most developed countries but not all.
- *The statement of changes in equity* is now, under IFRS, a separate report which details **dividend** payments, issues of **capital** and other transactions that change **equity**, including the net profit (net income) for the year.
- *The audit report* is the statement by the independent auditors of their opinion on the other statements.

For a large multinational, these reports are usually bundled together with a lot of voluntary disclosures about **group** activities. Typically the published 'annual report' of a company will start with a chairman's statement, thanking the management team and saying what a good (usually, but just occasionally bad or indifferent) year it has been and so on. This is followed by many pages of photographs of managers, products and plant, as well as lots of charts, graphs and other data which show how individual divisions in the group have behaved. None of this data is subject to independent checking – but it is nonetheless very useful information which no one should neglect. It very often gives a more detailed picture of the deeds behind the numbers, and helps an analyst get a feel for the company.

We will discuss corporate governance issues in more detail in another chapter, but between the operating information and the hard accounting information, many companies put in disclosures, which stock exchanges and other regulators have encouraged or even made mandatory, about company policy in what are perceived as key areas – above all, future prospects, but also things like the company's continuing viability, the risks that it faces, the nature of the control systems which enable the management to believe that they know what is going on in the company worldwide, and how the company deals with sensitive issues such as relations between the management and the auditors, and the award of salary increases to senior management.

If you've never seen the hard copy of a company's annual report, you should have a look at one and preferably several. Generally all you need do is go to the company's website and follow a link to 'investors' or 'investor relations'. In most cases the full annual report is directly downloadable from the company website.

It may have occurred to you that publishing the annual report is an extremely expensive business – it is. Aside from the cost of creating the financial statements in the first place and indeed having them audited, the cost of producing the photo-graphs, artwork and analytical copy, plus running them past your company lawyers and your public relations advisers, is very high before you even get into the cost of printing probably several million copies and having translations made if, like many multinationals, your report is available in several languages. Internally the annual report will involve the accounting managers, the legal and company secretarial specialists, the investor relations staff and public relations – apart from the chief executive, chairman and the board. Also note that companies try to publish their annual report as soon as possible after the financial year end – companies listed in the US often aim at six to eight weeks after the year end. More than 12 weeks is unusual, and the EU specifies a maximum of four months for listed companies.

Uses of financial statements

It is a standard question to ask who uses company financial statements. Broadly, very many people inside and outside the company look at these documents – as we have said already, they constitute the only performance indicator that is publicly available and independently verified. So we can be confident that they are used. What no one has been able to prove incontestably is how financial data are integrated into decision-making and how different accounting scenarios influence users. Accounting data is, or should be, only one of several sources of information about a company and its future prospects. They are concerned with past performance which is not in all circumstances a guide to future performance. Many people prefer to let a specialist (a broker, financial analyst or financial journalist) look at the data and then provide an opinion.

The IASB – of whom more later – says the following:

STANDARDS

IASB CONCEPTUAL FRAMEWORK (extracts)

The objective of general purpose financial reporting is to provide financial information about the reporting entity that is useful to present and potential equity investors, lenders, and other creditors in making decisions about providing resources to the entity.

Source: IASB, Conceptual Framework for Financial Reporting: The objective of General Purpose Financial Reporting, para OB2, issued September 2010

While usefulness for decision-making as an objective of financial statements makes sense, it needs to be put into context. There are two major different traditions in accounting which affect not only how accounting is regulated but also how it is done and how it is used. These are the Anglo-Saxon tradition and the continental European tradition, and we will need to come back to these ideas time and again to explain how accounting works.

Anglo-Saxon accounting

The IASB statement owes more to the Anglo-Saxon than to the continental tradition of accounting. Anglo-Saxon is the term widely used, but 'anglophone' would be more appropriate. In this tradition, countries (US, UK, Australia, Canada, New Zealand, etc.) had in the early twentieth century no free-standing accounting regulations on their statute book (although they had criminal laws, tax laws, etc.). Instead businesses were left to work out their own accounting rules (but alongside disclosure requirements enshrined in company or stock exchange law), and this often took place alongside the development of a powerful accounting profession. You could call this a market solution – to the extent that companies need to communicate understandably, such as to raise finance, they use understandable common measures, but no one obliges them to do so.

What has then happened is that the government has reinforced the market from time to time, so that the **legal obligation** to provide information has grown over time. The regulations have generally been made heavier following on from some market abuse – such as the Enron frauds in the US or, further back, historically the Wall Street crash of 1929. This last was blamed on adventurous accounting, and the Securities and Exchange Commission (SEC), which is the world's leading stock market regulator, was created by the US government as a response.

Accounting regulation in the anglophone countries is a function of the legal vehicle used, not a function of the kind of activity carried on by the business (although there are often special rules for banks and insurance companies, which we do not address in this book). So if you are a US company that wants to be listed on the New York Stock Exchange, you will need to meet stringent SEC accounting requirements, but if you want to run the same business with no public offering of shares, there are hardly any formal accounting requirements which apply in the US. Similarly, if you want to constitute your business as a public limited company (plc – not necessarily listed on the London Stock Exchange) in the UK, you will have to comply with many corporate accounting rules, but if you constitute it as a partnership, there are no statutory requirements for accounting.

STANDARDS

🌐 IASB CONCEPTUAL FRAMEWORK *(extracts)*

Users of financial statements

OB5. Many existing and potential investors, lenders and other creditors cannot require reporting entities to provide information directly to them and must rely on general purpose financial reports for much of the financial information they need. Consequently, they are the primary users to whom general purpose financial reports are directed.

OB10 Other parties, such as regulators and members of the public other than investors, lenders and other creditors, may also find general purpose financial reports useful. However, these reports are not primarily directed to these other groups.

Source: IASB, Conceptual Framework for Financial Reporting: The objective of General Purpose Financial Reporting, issued September 2010

In an Anglo-Saxon accounting context, the financial statements are traditionally a function of the financing of the company. They derive from the Industrial Revolution when technology first transformed business and entrepreneurs started looking for vehicles through which they could raise capital to start industrial ventures. Prior to the Industrial Revolution most business investment was made by owner-managers and was inevitably relatively small scale. But from this point on, the managers of companies were less and less often the source of finance for those companies, and financial reports developed as a means of informing outside financiers (shareholders principally but also banks) as to what had been done with their money. We have the start of a split between management and capital: professional managers started to run 'companies' in which several investors, eventually many, had put money.

The annual accounts were a necessary means of informing the investors (shareholders) and creating an atmosphere of confidence, which in turn would encourage investors to reward the managers – in conditions of uncertainty, the investors would reduce the reward to managers because they could not be sure that it had been earned. At the same time, the idea of independent audit developed as a means of increasing the degree of confidence which shareholders might have in the financial statements. In more recent times, companies have simply extended this principle to customers, suppliers, staff and the general public, as these have become more sophisticated in their understanding of financial data.

Continental Europe

The continental European accounting tradition has its roots much earlier in business history than Anglo-Saxon accounting. The main model for European systems started out in 1673 as a French government statute (known as the 'Savary Ordonnance'), which was borrowed by other countries in this form or in its later form as part of Napoleon's Commercial Code (1807). The French required all businesses (in whatever legal form, but companies as such were rare at that time) to calculate an annual 'inventory' – in effect a statement of financial position (balance sheet). The French model was subsequently borrowed by many countries, one way and another, and in particular by Belgium, Spain, Germany and Italy (this is not to suggest that accounting regulation in those countries is still exactly the same now – regulation is constantly evolving).

The main reason for its introduction in France is believed to have been government regulation of the economy. The government was concerned at the large number of business bankruptcies. Apart from causing people to lose money, bankruptcies also damage confidence in the market, and this, you will appreciate, is essential if the market is to function correctly. Government concern to strengthen the operation of the market, and thus the national economy, is often a key trigger of regulation.

The effect in continental Europe has been to create a tradition where *all* businesses are subject to accounting rules (with extra rules for limited liability companies and listed ones), and where accounting regulation is primarily the concern of the government rather than the accounting profession or companies themselves. This remains broadly the case in these countries still.

Link with taxation

These different historical roots can probably also explain another important aspect of accounting regulation – the link between measuring performance for shareholders and measuring profits for tax purposes. This link is looser in Anglo-Saxon countries than in continental European ones. In the United Kingdom, income tax was introduced first in 1799 – well before there was any accounting regulation as such. There grew up a tradition, therefore, where **measurement** of profit for tax purposes was seen as a legal matter, with its own statutes and jurisprudence which were separate from company regulation. In continental Europe, however, income taxes were mostly introduced in the early 20th century (Germany was a little ahead of this) but well after the introduction of accounting regulation by the State. Not surprisingly, measurement of profit for tax purposes became closely intertwined with other accounting needs, and the formal link between reporting to the tax authorities and reporting to shareholders is much closer than in Anglo-Saxon jurisdictions.

It should be said that the relationship between these two reporting streams is constantly evolving, and that the widespread use of consolidated accounts has introduced a new element into the equation. Consolidated financial statements (or consolidated accounts) are produced by large groups of companies for their shareholders. They consist, as we shall see later, of aggregate figures for all the individual companies making up the group. Tax assessment is done only through the individual companies, and the group financial statements therefore have no tax implications. This means that larger companies, at least, are able to separate out to some degree the measurement of profit for tax purposes, and the measurement of economic performance for shareholders and others. You will appreciate that in theory there should perhaps be no difference between the two concepts, but in practice governments distort economic behaviour through taxation, partly to counter tax avoidance and partly to give companies incentives to behave in a way that the government wishes to encourage (e.g. installing environmentally friendly processes, maintaining employment).

This usually means that tax considerations enter into company strategic choices (or should – individual companies differ quite widely in the extent to which they integrate tax into their planning) and also play a significant role in accounting regulation. For example, tax rules may well fix maximum limits on some **expenses**, and this will encourage companies to charge the maximum in their accounts. The rules may also refuse to accept other types of expenditure as a deduction from **taxable profits**, with the consequence that companies restrict some kinds of activity. We will look at this later in Chapter 15, on taxation.

The extent to which taxation impacts upon company accounting is not only a function of the regulatory environment, but also depends on the ownership of the company, which is in turn an issue frequently linked to size. Many small and medium-sized companies do not operate as a group of companies and their ownership is in the hands of the managers, or of a family. This may mean that the shareholders do not depend upon the annual financial statements as their only source of information about the company – they work in the company, or they can ask or even just go along and have a look.

This means that there is no point in producing sophisticated economic measurements for the shareholders. Annual financial statements of small and medium-sized companies are consequently influenced most heavily by tax considerations – reducing the profit in order to reduce tax becomes the main objective in making accounting choices. This may also mean that managers of small companies have only a hazy idea of their profitability, because they believe the reported figure to be artificially low as a result of tax manipulations yet have no means of knowing the extent of the difference. This is not particularly useful for management decision-making!

Accounting choices

Some people come to accounting believing that it is a set of precise measurement rules which permit the exact measurement of company profit and the value of the company. In fact accounting rules are anything but precise, the measurement of profit can never be anything but an estimate and the accounts do not under any circumstances show what a company is 'worth' (we should also bear in mind that value is a subjective notion and must always be defined when used – for example, the value of something as between buyer and seller is usually different, there are different calculation bases such as economic value, cost, etc.).

You will soon appreciate as you go through this book that accounting measurement is full of choices. We can distinguish between three types of encounter between choice and rules:

1. The rules are quite specific and there is no choice (maybe the law specifies what must be done, or an accounting standard).
2. There are accounting rules, but we have freedom to make a choice between two or more alternative sets of rules, each of which is acceptable to regulators (the most common case).
3. There are no rules so we must decide for ourselves how to deal with a problem (maybe by reference to what other people in the same line of business generally do, or after consultation with our auditors).

The existence of these choices is something that makes accounting comparisons difficult within the same jurisdiction, and also leads to different accounting rules

COMPANY REPORT

THE NESTLÉ GROUP
Consolidated financial statements (overview)

■ Principal exchange rates
■ Consolidated income statement for the year ended 31 December 2011
■ Consolidated statement of comprehensive income for the year ended 31 December 2011
■ Consolidated balance sheet as at 31 December 2011
■ Consolidated cash flow statement for the year ended 31 December 2011
■ Consolidated statement of changes in equity for the year ended 31 December 2011
■ Notes
■ Report of the Statutory Auditor on the Consolidated Financial Statements
■ Financial information – five year review
■ Companies of the Nestlé Group

Source: Nestlé Group, Consolidated Financial Statements 2011 (Nestlé website)

being used in different countries. Companies are generally required, therefore, to state clearly in their annual financial statements what choices they have made in key areas. Large companies typically have several pages devoted to 'accounting principles' alongside their financial statements.

The variability of accounting principles is often criticized by the financial press, and it is one reason why those who design MBA courses insist upon a significant accounting component in the degree. As we advance through the accounting territory we will highlight areas where there are choices and show how these impact measurement.

Profit as estimate

The 'real' profit of a company can only be measured absolutely when the company has ceased operations, all the company resources have been sold, its debts have been paid off and all its money has been distributed to its **owners**.

To illustrate, suppose a company builds a factory, equips it with sophisticated machinery and then uses it to manufacture a product which it sells. Say the factory and equipment cost €100m, and the factory closes down after ten years and is sold for €10m; we can say that, in addition to raw materials, staffing, power and so on, the company had a net infrastructure cost of €90m (€100m to set up, less final exit receipt of €10m) for the factory, which should be taken into account in measuring profit for each of the ten years in which the factory was operating. We only know this net cost for sure when the factory has been sold (when the **residual value** of the factory facilities is realized). If, though, we ignore the cost of the factory in measuring profit in the years when the factory is operating, we will be overstating the profit. Overstating the profit will mislead those who lend to or invest in the firm, and potentially lead to paying out too much in tax and dividends so that the company eventually fails. To avoid this we are obliged to include an estimate of this expense, so the annual profit during those years is necessarily based in part on an unprovable estimate.

IASB's conceptual framework

The IASB's conceptual framework is a high level document that sets out the objectives of financial information, its qualitative characteristics, the elements that make up financial statements and issues of this kind. In its original form it was issued in 1989 as the *Framework for the Preparation and Presentation of Financial Statements*. It is currently being revised as a joint project with the US standard-setter, the Financial Accounting Standards Board and re-issued as the *Conceptual Framework for Financial Reporting*. The revision is unlikely to be completed for several years, but the IASB is aiming to bring in to force individual chapters as they are completed. Chapters One and Three, which we cite here, have been published in final form but other chapters are still being worked on.

We should also say that although the revision process is long, for most of the chapters this only involves some fine-tuning of what existed beforehand. More time is being spent developing areas that were not covered adequately or at all in either the IASB's or the FASB's original frameworks on issues such as measurement and the **reporting entity**. In 2010 the IASB added the new chapters to the existing *Framework* document, while removing the parts that they replaced. It now refers to this document as the *Conceptual Framework*.

STANDARDS

🌐 IASB CONCEPTUAL FRAMEWORK *(extracts)*

Usefulness of Financial Reporting in Assessing Cash Flow Prospects

OB3. Decisions by existing and potential investors about buying, selling or holding equity and debt instruments depend on the returns that they expect from an investment in those instruments, for example dividends, principal and interest payments or market price increases. Similarly, decisions by existing and potential lenders and other creditors about providing loans and other forms of credit depend on the principal and interest payments or other returns that they expect. Investors', lenders' and other creditors' expectations about the returns depend on their assessment of the amount, timing and uncertainty of (the prospects for) future net cash inflows to the entity. Consequently, existing and potential investors, lenders and other creditors need information to help them assess the prospects for future net cash inflows to an entity.

Usefulness of Financial Reporting in Assessing Stewardship

OB4. To assess an entity's prospects for future net cash inflows, existing and potential investors, lenders and other creditors need information about the resources of the entity, claims against the entity, and how efficiently and effectively the entity's management and governing board have discharged their responsibilities to use the entity's resources. Examples of such responsibilities include protecting the entity's resources from unfavourable effects of economic factors such as price and technological changes and ensuring that the entity complies with applicable laws, regulations and contractual provisions. Information about management's discharge of its responsibilities is also useful for decisions by existing investors, lenders and other creditors who have the right to vote on or otherwise influence management's actions.

Source: IASB, *Conceptual Framework for Financial Reporting: The objective of General Purpose Financial Reporting, issued September 2010*

Qualitative characteristics

Qualitative characteristics are the attributes of financial information that underpin the decision-usefulness of financial reporting. Making these explicit does not, however, necessarily make it any easier for preparers and auditors to make accounting policy choices. It does, however, provide a framework for discussion and evaluation.

Fundamental versus enhancing characteristics

As we have seen, the IASB's conceptual framework says that decision-usefulness is the over-riding characteristic that is necessary in financial reporting. Chapter

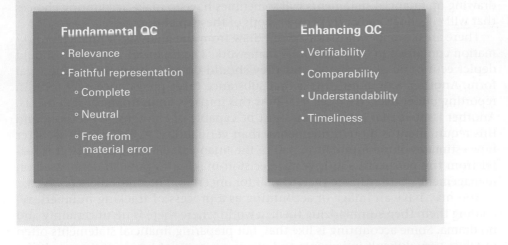

Figure 1.1
Qualitative characteristics

Three of the conceptual framework addresses 'qualitative characteristics' (see Figure 1.1).

The qualitative characteristics of useful financial information . . . identify the types of information that are likely to be most useful to the existing and potential investors, lenders and other creditors for making decisions about the reporting entity on the basis of information in its financial report, *The Conceptual Framework for Financial Reporting: Qualitative Characteristics of Useful Financial Information, issued September 2010.* The document goes on to state that the fundamental qualitative characteristics are relevance and faithful representation.

The conceptual framework adds that information is relevant if it is capable of making a difference in the decisions of capital providers. It says that relevant information could have *predictive value* if it helps form expectations of the future. It has *confirmatory value* if it confirms or changes expectations of the future made in the past.

Financial reports represent economic phenomena in words and numbers. To be useful, financial information must not only represent relevant phenomena, but it must also faithfully represent the phenomena that it purports to represent. To be a perfectly faithful representation, a depiction would have three characteristics. It would be *complete, neutral* and *free from error*. Of course, perfection is seldom, if ever, achievable. The Board's objective is to maximize these qualities to the extent possible.

The IASB conceptual framework identifies four 'enhancing' qualities. These are comparability, verifiability, timeliness and **understandability**.

There is a conundrum in accounting which is that the most reliable information (meaning information that is not subject to uncertainty) is necessarily old information, since all the facts can be established incontrovertibly only after the elapse of some time. Of this, the most relevant information is that which concerns the immediate past because we use it to understand what we need to improve or change in managing the future. Relevant information is timely and has predictive or feedback value. To be useful, accounting information should be both verifiable and relevant. Timely information is likely to include estimates and other uncertainties and this creates a tension. Some would argue that timely information is most useful for prediction, whereas verifiable, certain, data is most useful for stewardship purposes (i.e. judging performance retrospectively). People drawing up financial statements will sometimes have to make accounting choices that will engender trade-offs between both of these qualities.

There are a number of issues we can draw from the analysis of financial information contained in the conceptual framework. The financial statements should depict economic phenomena, but they should do so irrespective of the legal form. Another way to put this is that substance takes precedence over form in reporting under IFRS. We'll see later how this impacts upon financial statements. Another issue is that information must be capable of changing a decision, and this requirement is more fundamental than verifiability. Again we will see later how estimates of the future form part of the financial reporting process. It is better from the perspective of investor decision-making to publish data based on management's best estimate than to wait for uncertain outcomes to be resolved.

You may have an image of accounting as a process of tracking numbers, recording them then summarizing them; a world where there is no uncertainty and no drama. Some accounting is like that, but preparing financial statements often involves very difficult judgments and many estimates of future outcomes. It is a risky business, as the SEC's compliance division will confirm.

Accounting regulation

The existence of choices in accounting is one very good reason to have regulation. Of course, choice is not of itself necessarily a bad thing: it is only a problem in accounting where some people use accounting choice to deceive others. This explains why governments become involved in accounting regulation. As tax collectors they naturally want reliable figures for (taxable) **income**. As managers of the national economy they want that economy to function efficiently and produce wealth. The economy's functioning, and particularly that of the capital markets, is at least slowed down – if not stalled entirely – if investors, customers and suppliers do not know whether they can rely on the financial statements of companies with which they wish to do business. Investors either do not invest or demand much higher returns to compensate for the uncertainty, clients may go elsewhere or be prepared to pay only a low price, while suppliers may refuse to supply on credit. If the financial stability of a company cannot be judged reliably, others are reluctant to deal with it.

This leads to another argument which is that, given that the markets cease to function without reliable information, market pressures surely will force competitive companies to adopt reliable, comparable accounting in order to reduce financing costs and help business relations generally. This argument is also valid, and is supported by the way in which many large companies in the past have voluntarily adopted international accounting standards for their group financial statements and use an international audit firm to attest the validity of these. However, the market is not necessarily that efficient, and there are failures which in part derive from unclear accounting causing people to make wrong decisions.

The world functions on a complex mixture of regulation and market forces. Given that this book is intended to be used outside of any one specific legal environment, we propose to present below the different types of regulation which are to be found. You should note that regulation can exist at an international level (for example **International Financial Reporting Standards**), at a regional level (for example European Union directives and regulations) and at a national level. International managers should make a note that there will be a different mix of regulators in different countries and they may need to familiarize themselves with the local situation.

Types of regulation

It may be worth pointing out that the reasons why a change in regulation takes place are a fruitful field of **research** in accounting. The model that we will use here suggests that, starting from an equilibrium position where there is no obvious pressure for change, there is a cycle:

1. equilibrium
2. shock (which destroys the equilibrium)
3. search for an acceptable solution
4. articulation of regulation
5. new equilibrium
6. unexpected consequences of the change.

The shock to the system could come from any one of a multitude of sources. Individual financial scandals have in the past been a common source of disequilibrium (the Enron failure brought about significant changes in American and European regulation), but other possibilities are economic changes such as the introduction of new techniques (e.g. **derivatives** and **financial instruments** generally), legal changes in the national economy (e.g. joining the European Union, moving from a communist regime to a market economy), economic phenomena (such as the sub-prime crisis and the credit crunch that followed) and so on. The search for a solution often involves seeking consensus, which will involve different people on different issues, leading to some inconsistencies in regulation. The method of articulating the solution is also subject to local cultural differences – some countries prefer legal regulation, others like codes of best practice and so on. The result of all this is that accounting rules are different in different countries in some of their details, even if the main lines tend to converge.

We would distinguish the following types of regulatory body:

■ government – for economic management

■ government – for tax purposes

■ stock exchange

■ private sector body

■ professional accountants

■ specialist industry organizations.

We should also point out that the regulation of the financial statements of banks and insurance companies, while typically linked to that of commercial companies, is nonetheless usually subject to separate rules, because governments wish to control the financial health of banks much more closely than that of commercial companies, and impose limits on their activities based on balance sheet figures. This book does not address the financial statements of banks and insurance companies.

Government

As we have discussed, the government is interested in the efficient functioning of the economy, and this leads to regulation designed to ensure that the markets can operate as far as possible free from fraud and misrepresentation. This form of regulation may be articulated through laws which address accounting, through commercial codes and also government regulatory agencies. An example of this kind of approach would be France, where there are laws governing accounting but also government-sponsored committees which operate under the aegis of the Ministry of Finance and issue detailed regulations on specific accounting issues.

The government is also active in regulating accounting for tax purposes. This is often done through individual measures contained in annual finance laws or similar instruments. In some countries jurisprudence, the decisions of tax courts on specific cases, can also be very important in determining some accounting issues. This is notably the case in Germany and to a lesser extent in the UK.

The stock exchange usually regulates the financial information that has to be provided by companies listed on it. In some countries there is a government regulator that does this, such as the Securities and Exchange Commission (SEC) in the US, while the exchange itself is run by private sector bodies. In other countries there is no split between those who run the stock exchange on a day-to-day basis (generally the members of the exchange) and those who regulate admission to it. This is the case, for example, in Switzerland, where the private sector regulates listed companies (although subject to a limited legal framework). In the EU there has been a move to establish national regulators that are separate from the stock exchange. These are co-ordinated through the European Securities and Markets Authority (ESMA).

Private sector

In most countries there is some input into accounting best practice from the private sector in the form of standard-setting committees of one kind or another. In the US, although the SEC controls listings on the various stock exchanges, and is therefore responsible for specifying what accounting rules they should use, in practice it leaves the task of writing detailed rules (accounting standards) to a private sector body, the Financial Accounting Standards Board (FASB). The FASB is financed by a levy on companies that are registered with the SEC and is a free-standing body without any special rights other than those it derives from the SEC's endorsement of its standards.

This is typical of the modern form of detailed rule-making – the rules do not have to go through a long drawn-out statutory process, and can be changed at any time if they appear to be ineffective or become irrelevant. The flexibility and rapidity of this form and the high level of technicality of its pronouncements are the major argument for using a private sector body rather than relying solely on statutes or government agencies, where accounting regulation would have to compete for parliamentary time with other important issues and be debated by those with no knowledge of accounting.

In many countries that have this kind of private sector regulatory body, it developed from advisory committees run by the accounting profession, and most developed professional accounting bodies have technical committees which make recommendations as to best practice. Such a committee may be the only private sector source of national standards in a particular country but, even so, it does not necessarily command the automatic acceptance of its pronouncements. An example would be the technical committee of the Ordre des Experts Comptables in France.

Another source of private sector rules is industry associations. Their activity varies very much from sector to sector and country to country, but sometimes such organizations agree special rules which apply to their members and are intended to address accounting for transactions which are specific to their industry, or lead to a higher comparability in presentation or valuation of balance sheet and profit or loss items. Evidently such arrangements are voluntary but in some countries they may also be endorsed by official regulatory committees – the UK standard-setter approves 'statements of recommended practice' which are prepared by industry groups such as banks or insurers, and France's Autorité des Normes Comptables confirms industry-specific applications of its accounting plan.

Different combinations of these kinds of regulatory organizations exist in each developed country, and the diverse sources of regulation are one reason why expert local advice is needed.

International

Apart from the national regulators, there are also international bodies which provide important rules. The most well known is the International Accounting Standards Board (IASB). The IASB is the world's leading accounting standard-setter. Since 2002 when its standards were adopted by the European Commission for use by all listed companies in Europe (from 2005) there has been a rush in all major and many minor economies to use its standards. The IASB itself says that its standards are either compulsory or allowed in more than 100 countries. Australia and South Africa also moved to IFRS in 2005, followed shortly afterwards by New Zealand. Canada, Korea and Brazil moved in 2011. China issues its own standards modelled closely on IFRS, Japan allows companies to adopt IFRS voluntarily and may make this compulsory soon. IFRS are accepted by the SEC as the equivalent of US Generally Accepted Accounting Principles (GAAP), and the SEC is considering whether to allow US companies the option to use IFRS instead.

What is the big attraction? Well, if we look at the European Commission's decision in issuing the Regulation 2002/1608, the main issue was that a fundamental objective of the EU is to create a single market with no barriers to movement within it. The Commission perceived that the slightly different financial reporting in each member state was an obstacle to the free flow of capital. If investors could compare one company with another, irrespective of where the **parent** company's main office was based, they could invest more efficiently and companies could raise finance more easily.

A second issue with the Commission was that if IFRS were widely used outside the EU, this would also make it much easier for European companies to raise money on markets outside Europe. The big prize was access to the US markets. When the Commission made its decision, non-US companies using IFRS but listed on an American stock exchange had to provide additional information, including a reconciliation of their equity and earnings to what they would have been under US GAAP. In 2007 AXA, the European insurer, told the SEC that it estimated that preparing this cost them $20m a year, not including internal staff time. One of the IASB's objectives from the start was to achieve parity with US GAAP and this happened in 2007. From 2008, companies using IFRS as issued by the IASB have not needed to provide this expensive reconciliation.

Generically then, we can say that using IFRS means that companies can be directly compared with each other, irrespective of national origins. This should help the investor make better choices. It also helps companies to get more exposure than they otherwise would. They can more easily be listed on different stock exchanges and their financial statements are directly comparable. Using IFRS is part of participating in a global investment market.

One piece of background we should also mention concerns how the standards are labelled. You will see later in the book that some are called International Financial Reporting Standards while others are called International Accounting Standards (IAS). The explanation is history. The IASB was originally named the International Accounting Standards Committee (IASC). The IASC was launched in 1973 by the accounting profession as a recognition that there was much diversity in accounting rules and that the globalization of commerce meant that some of this diversity should be removed. The IASC gradually became accepted as an international source of best practice. In 2001, the IASC was replaced by the IASB. The IASC rules were called International Accounting Standards (IAS). Pronouncements issued by the IASB (since 2001) are known as International Financial Reporting Standards (IFRS). The IAS issued by the former IASC remain in effect unless and until the IASB amends or replaces them. The term 'IFRS' should be understood to include both the older IAS and the more recent IASB standards. We shall use IFRS as the main source of reference in this book and discuss them in more detail below.

Just to add to the problem, there are also things known as Interpretations. These have the same force as IFRS, and are included in the generic term IFRS. They are issued by a special body, now the IFRS Interpretations Committee, but previously the International Financial Reporting Interpretations Committee (IFRIC), and prior to 2002 the Standards Interpretations Committee (SIC). The Interpretations Committee receives queries as to how IFRS should be applied in circumstances that are not specifically covered by a standard, or is asked to resolve apparent conflicts between standards.

For regulators a problem is that some jurisdictions have been tempted to modify IFRS slightly when adopting them. This results in there being slightly different versions in use. Notably the European Union modified IAS 39 on financial instruments. EU companies have to state that they use 'IFRS as endorsed by the EU' (or a similar formula). The SEC only accepts the original IFRS as a substitute for US GAAP when used by a foreign issuer.

There are no other bodies writing international accounting standards for private sector companies, but we should mention that the United Nations supports an intergovernmental working group devoted to accounting and auditing issues at the corporate level. This takes place under the auspices of the UN Conference on Trade and Development (UNCTAD) and is called the Intergovernmental Working Group of Experts on International Standards of Accounting and Reporting (ISAR for short). The ISAR group commissions research reports into current accounting problems. These are debated at an annual conference and recommendations are made to help governments develop their regulatory and professional structures. ISAR supports the IASB and helps involve governments, particularly of developing countries, in discussions about the utility and implementation of IASB standards.

There is also an international representative of the accounting profession: the International Federation of Accountants (IFAC), based in New York. We will come back to it in Chapter 2, on the accounting profession. It has committees which publish recommendations on auditing, education and other matters. It issues auditing standards through its International Auditing and Assurance Standards Board, and these are increasingly being used in Europe to give uniform audit alongside international accounting standards. However, the IFAC also hosts the International Public Sector Accounting Standards Board (IPSASB) which focuses on the accounting and financial reporting needs of national, regional and local governments, related governmental agencies and the constituencies they serve.

Public sector

This is probably a good point to mention that accounting in the public sector is generally very different from that in the private sector, although governments are beginning to turn to private sector techniques. Basically, private sector accounting is concerned with measuring profit and the financial position of and related sources of finance for an enterprise. It produces annual reports which are in effect a series of **interim reports** on a business which is intended to have long or limitless time horizons.

Public sector accounting on the other hand has traditionally had short horizons where the object is primarily to explain what has been done with the money available to spend in any one year. Reports typically focus on a particular source of **revenue** (e.g. **government grants** for road improvement) and explain how it has been spent, or on a particular activity (e.g. primary school education). Any particular public sector unit, say a municipality or a government ministry, does not therefore present a single coherent report on its activities for the year, but rather a whole series of individual reports. Equally, the public sector makes little or no distinction between short-term (sometimes known as current) and long-term (sometimes called capital) expenditure – money in one particular year might be spent on building one hospital, and other money on paying the running costs of another hospital, but for traditional public sector accounting these are just two 'funds' like any others. The hospital is in effect treated as a current year expense and does not appear on any kind of government 'balance sheet' as an asset.

In the 1990s the desire for performance evaluation measures in the public sector caused a number of countries, led by New Zealand, to move towards private sector techniques where long-lived purchases remain on the books, and where 'revenues' are determined or, to put it another way, outputs are assigned financial values, so that the efficiency of the use of resources can be measured. It would be a mistake to think that such a revolution in public sector accounting will be either widespread or rapid. First, it involves a desire on the part of government for transparency in their financial dealings, which is not something too many governments necessarily see as a policy objective. Second, the change-over involves massive re-education, not only of accounting staff but also all those who use financial information, and also a complete reform of accounting systems, which is both costly and time-consuming.

For the moment it would be better to think of public sector accounting as a different subject from that of the private sector (and one which will not be taken further in this book), although changes can be expected. The International Public

Sector Accounting Standards Board (IPSASB) of IFAC plays an important catalyst role by issuing and promoting benchmark guidance, conducting educational and research programmes, and facilitating the exchange of information among accountants and those who work in the public sector. It develops International Public Sector Accounting Standards (IPSAS) for financial reporting by governments and other public sector entities. In general, IFRS are used as the starting point in developing these standards.

International Financial Reporting Standards

The International Financial Reporting Standards (IFRS), established by the IASB, are increasingly recognized as a mature and rigorous set of rules for the preparation of the financial statements of many large and multinational companies and are accepted by most security market authorities. IFRS are also used as the basis for national accounting requirements (partially or in full) or as an international benchmark for countries which develop their own requirements.

The IASB is a private sector body and is not responsible to any governmental organization.

The IASB's objectives are set out in a constitution, the ultimate goal being the development and rigorous application of a single set of global accounting standards, which will produce high-quality financial information to help participants in the world's capital markets to make economic decisions. The IASB has, however, no enforcement authority.

Table 1.1 gives an overview of the IFRS as of January 2012. The table comprises both the main standards (IAS and IFRS) and the interpretations of the successive Interpretations Committees. We will refer to these IASB rules in this text in chapters covering the appropriate topic.

Table 1.1

List of IASB pronouncements as of January 2012

Conceptual Framework	
CF	Framework for the Preparation and Presentation of Financial Statements (being progressively replaced by the joint *Conceptual Framework for Financial Reporting*)

Main standards	
IAS 1	Presentation of Financial Statements
IAS 2	Inventories
IAS 7	Statement of Cash Flows
IAS 8	Accounting Policies, Changes in Accounting Estimates and Errors
IAS 10	Events after the Reporting Period
IAS 11	Construction Contracts
IAS 12	Income Taxes
IAS 14	Segment Reporting
IAS 16	Property, Plant and Equipment
IAS 17	Leases
IAS 18	Revenue

IAS 19	Employee Benefits
IAS 20	Accounting for Government Grants and Disclosure of Government Assistance
IAS 21	The Effects of Changes in Foreign Exchange Rates
IAS 23	Borrowing Costs
IAS 24	Related Party Disclosures
IAS 26	Accounting and Reporting by Retirement Benefit Plans
IAS 27	Separate Financial Statements
IAS 28	Investments in Associates and Joint Ventures
IAS 29	Financial Reporting in Hyperinflationary Economies
IAS 30	Disclosure in the Financial Statements of Banks and Similar Financial Institutions
IAS 32	Financial Instruments: Disclosure and Presentation
IAS 33	Earnings per Share
IAS 34	Interim Financial Reporting
IAS 36	Impairment of Assets
IAS 37	Provisions, Contingent Liabilities and Contingent Assets
IAS 38	Intangible Assets
IAS 39	Financial Instruments: Recognition and Measurement
IAS 40	Investment Property
IAS 41	Agriculture
IFRS 1	First-time Adoption of International Financial Reporting Standards
IFRS 2	Share-based Payment
IFRS 3	Business Combinations
IFRS 4	Insurance Contracts
IFRS 5	Non-current Assets Held for Sale and Discontinued Operations
IFRS 6	Exploration for and Evaluation of Mineral Resources
IFRS 7	Financial Instruments: Disclosures
IFRS 8	Operating Segments
IFRS 9	Financial Instruments
IFRS 10	Consolidated Financial Statements
IFRS 11	Joint Arrangements
IFRS 12	Disclosures of Interests in Other Entities
IFRS 13	Fair Value Measurement

Interpretations

SIC 7	Introduction of the Euro (IAS 21)
SIC 10	Government Assistance – No Specific Relation to Operating Activities (IAS 20)
SIC 13	Jointly Controlled Entities – Non-Monetary Contributions By Venturers (IAS 31)
SIC 15	Operating Leases – Incentives (IAS 17)
SIC 25	Income Taxes – Changes in the Tax Status of an Enterprise or its Shareholders IAS (12)
SIC 27	Evaluating the Substance of Transactions involving the Legal Form of a Lease
SIC 29	Disclosure – Service Concession Arrangements
SIC 31	Revenue – Barter Transactions Involving Services
SIC 32	Intangible Assets – Web Site Costs

IFRIC 1	Changes in Existing Decommissioning, Restoration and Similar Liabilities
IFRIC 2	Members' Shares in Co-operative Entities and Similar Instruments
IFRIC 4	Determining Whether an Arrangement contains a Lease
IFRIC 5	Rights to Interests arising from Decommissioning, Restoration and Environmental Rehabilitation Funds
IFRIC 6	Liabilities arising from Participating in a Specific Market – Waste Electrical and Electronic Equipment
IFRIC 7	Applying the Restatement Approach under IAS 29 Financial Reporting in Hyperinflationary Economies
IFRIC 10	Interim Financial Reporting and Impairment
IFRIC 12	Service Concession Arrangements
IFRIC 13	Customer Loyalty Programmes
IFRIC 14 IAS 19	The Limit on a Defined Benefit Asset, Minimum Funding Requirements and their Interaction
IFRIC 15	Agreements for the Construction of Real Estate
IFRIC 16	Hedges of a Net Investment in a Foreign Operation
IFRIC 17	Distributions of Non-cash Assets to Owners
IFRIC 18	Transfers of Assets from Customers
IFRIC 19	Extinguishing Financial Liabilities with Equity Instruments

The structure of the IASB

The IASB operates under the IFRS Foundation (IFRSF), an independent organization with 22 trustees representing all regions of the world and all groups interested in corporate financial reporting. The IFRS Foundation raises funds and has oversight of the IASB. The Trustees are subject in their turn to the oversight of the IFRS Monitoring Board. The Monitoring Board consists of representatives of the world's capital markets and is intended to provide additional public accountability to the organization.

The current IASB structure has the following components:

- the IFRS Monitoring Board
- the Trustees of the IFRS Foundation (IFRSF)
- the International Accounting Standards Board (IASB)
- the IFRS Advisory Council and
- the IFRS Interpretations Committee.

The structure of the IASB is outlined in Figure 1.2.

The trustees appoint the Board members (as well as the members of the Interpretations Committee and the Advisory Council), exercise oversight and raise the funds needed. As an organization of an international scope, the geographical balance of the trustees is a sensitive issue. The current geographical balance is as follows: six from North America, six from Europe, six from the Asia/Oceania region and four from any area, subject to establishing overall geographical balance. There is also an appropriate balance to the professional backgrounds of the

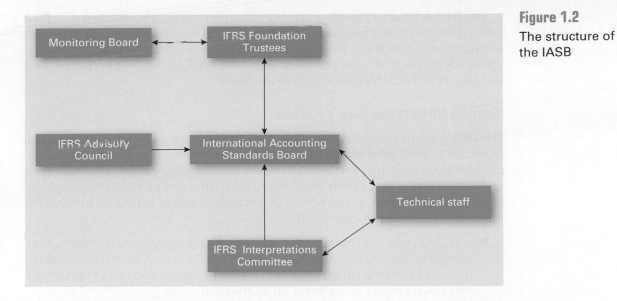

Figure 1.2
The structure of the IASB

trustees, which include auditors, preparers, users, academics and other officials serving the public interest. Two will normally be senior partners of prominent international accounting firms.

All the appointments made by the Trustees are subject to the approval of the Monitoring Board. The Monitoring Board was created in 2009 and includes representatives of the SEC, European Commission, International Organization of Securities Commissions (two members), and the Japanese Financial Services Agency. The Basel Committee (bank supervisors) has observer status. The Monitoring Board is likely to be expanded from 2012 to include stock exchange representatives from emerging markets.

The IASB has sole responsibility for setting accounting standards. It develops and issues International Financial Reporting Standards and approves interpretations developed by the IFRS Interpretations Committee. It comprises 16 board members, each with one vote. The primary qualification criterion for membership is technical expertise. There is a balance of professional backgrounds (auditors, preparers, users and academics). Since 2009 there has been a geographical requirement in addition to that of technical expertise.

Although the IASB has full discretion over its technical agenda, it would normally form working groups or other forms of specialist advisory groups to give advice on major projects. It can outsource detailed research or other work to national standard-setters. A key element of its strategy has been to converge its standards with those of the United States. This process involves significant change to US rules as well as an evolution of IASB rules.

The IFRS Interpretations Committee complements the formal standard-setting process of the board. It reviews, within the context of existing International Financial Reporting Standards and the IASB Framework, accounting issues that are likely to receive divergent or unacceptable treatment in the absence of authoritative guidance, and issues interpretations on these matters. Normally, the Interpretations Committee addresses issues of reasonably widespread importance, and not issues of concern to only a small set of enterprises. Its Interpretations are submitted to the IASB for approval.

The IFRS Advisory Council provides a forum for organizations and individuals with an interest in international financial reporting to participate in the standard-setting process. The board has to consult the Advisory Council on major projects, agenda decisions and work priorities. The Advisory Council is expected to meet three times a year at meetings open to the public.

Standard-setting due process

The IASB's standard-setting procedures have to ensure that resulting International Financial Reporting Standards (including Interpretations) are of high quality and are developed only after giving IASB's constituencies opportunities to make their views known at several points in the standard-setting due process.

The process for the development of a standard would normally involve the following steps (see also Figure 1.3):

■ A project proposal emerges after an idea coming from board members, the Advisory Council, national standard-setters or others. A formal proposal is discussed with the trustees and the Advisory Council and has to satisfy several criteria before being voted on by the IASB.

■ During the early stages of a project, the IASB may establish an advisory committee, or working group, to give advice on the issues arising in the project. The IASB may commission research by national standard-setters or others. Consultation with the working group and the IFRS Advisory Council occurs throughout the project.

■ The IASB may develop and publish discussion documents for public comment. Over time it has become accepted practice that the IASB does routinely issue what it calls a 'preliminary views' discussion paper on all but minor projects. (Constituents perceive that they can have greater input at the discussion document stage, whereas the exposure draft of the standard represents pretty much the IASB's decision as to what the final standard should be.)

Figure 1.3

Standard-setting due process of the IASB

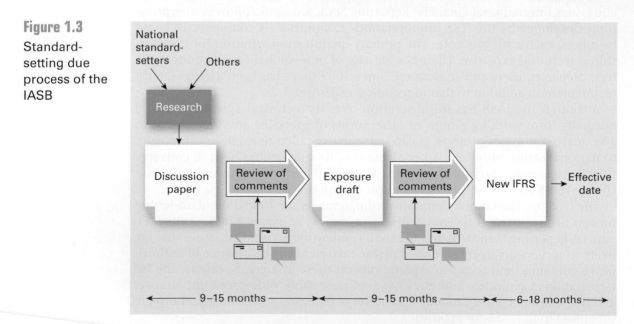

■ Following the receipt and review of comments, the IASB would develop and publish an Exposure Draft for public comment.

■ Following the receipt and review of comments, the IASB would issue a final International Financial Reporting Standard.

Publication of an exposure draft, a main standard or an Interpretation requires approval by ten of the 16 members of the board. A full-blown due process including a preliminary views paper would likely take at least four years and often considerably more. When the IASB publishes a standard, it also publishes a 'basis for conclusions' to explain publicly how it reached its conclusions (including dissenting opinions) and to give background information that may help users of the standards to apply them in practice.

IFRS in Europe

Since 2005 all listed companies have had to use IFRS (apart from a few exceptions which came on stream in 2007). Historically, however, European accounting standards were established through company law directives, which aim at harmonizing company law across member states. Table 1.2 provides an overview of the main developments regarding financial accounting and reporting rules in the European Union. Accounting rules are stipulated in the Fourth and the Seventh Company Law Directive (which are also referred to as the Fourth and the Seventh Accounting Directives). The Fourth Directive (1978) comprises the accounting rules for the preparation and presentation of financial statements of individual legal entities (individual accounts). The Seventh Directive (1983) sets the ground rules for the preparation and presentation of the financial statements of a company as an economic entity, usually a group of individual but economically interdependent legal entities (group or consolidated accounts). Member states were required to incorporate these directives into national legal requirements. Although this succeeded in achieving a considerable degree of comparability between financial statements prepared in different member states, many differences remain. This is due to the fact that the accounting rules of the directives are not very detailed (only minimum rules which may be strengthened by national requirements), do not cover all relevant topics (for example **foreign currency** translation issues or deferred taxation) or leave choices to member states (alternative rules giving member states options).

Sometimes the harmonization effects of the directives are counteracted by discretionary national requirements. Instead of reinforcing the European accounting standards, the European Commission decided in 1995 on an accounting strategy change by adhering to the IASB standards to strengthen European reporting requirements. In June 2000, the European Commission proposed the requirement of the use of IFRS for the consolidated financial statements of all European listed companies. This proposal culminated in the IAS Regulation (2202/1608) in June 2002.

IFRS are, however, not automatically applicable in the EU when issued by the IASB. An endorsement mechanism has been installed to ensure that the IFRS conforms with EU public policy concerns and meet the needs of European listed companies. The endorsement mechanism relies on a two-tier structure: a regulatory level (the Accounting Regulatory Committee, ARC) and an expert level (the European Financial Reporting Advisory Group, EFRAG). ARC decides whether to recommend to the European Commission that it should adopt or reject a standard for application in the EU. EFRAG advises the European Commission on the technical assessment of individual IFRS for application in the EU. Additionally, EFRAG is expected to play a proactive role in interacting with the IASB.

Table 1.2

Financial reporting in the European Union – main developments

1978	Fourth Company Law Directive (individual financial statements)
1983	Seventh Company Law Directive (consolidated financial statements)
1995	Decision on new accounting strategy (adhering to IAS instead of further development of specific European accounting rules)
2000	Announcement of plan to require IAS for consolidated financial statements of listed companies by 2005
2001	Fair Value Directive [requiring/allowing for fair value measurement of specific balance sheet items (mainly financial instruments)]
2002	IAS Regulation
2003	Modernization Directive (reflecting IFRS developments in the Fourth and Seventh Directive)
2005/2007	IFRS mandatory for listed companies in European Union 2011 Proposal to replace Fourth & Seventh Directives

Meanwhile, initiatives were taken in 2001 (Fair Value Directive) and in 2003 (Modernization Directive) to amend the Fourth and Seventh Company Law Directives in order to eliminate incompatibilities between European accounting rules and IFRS and to set a level playing field between European companies that apply IFRS and those that do not. The Commission proposed in 2011 to modernize and merge the Fourth and Seventh Directives.

Table 1.3

Effects of the IAS Regulation (EU)

	Individual financial statements	Group/consolidated financial statements
Listed companies	Member state option	IFRS mandatory
Unlisted companies	Member state option	Member state option

The IAS Regulation applies only to listed companies, and the Commission left to member states the decision as to whether to extend IFRS to non-listed companies. Most states allow unlisted companies a choice, although Germany requires national GAAP for all individual company statements and for the group statements of unlisted companies. This situation is likely to evolve in different ways. National rules are likely to change to become more like IFRS anyway. The IASB has issued in 2009 an *IFRS for Small and Medium-sized entities*. This is a simplified form of IFRS that is intended for use with companies in which there is no 'public interest' (primarily are not listed on a public stock exchange). The Commission will not require adoption of this standard by member states, and different Member

States view it with differing degrees of enthusiasm. The UK plans to adapt it for use by medium-sized private companies.

As mentioned above, a particular issue that impacts European companies is that the EU has not in fact endorsed all the IFRS as issued by the IASB. As a result of pressure from French banks, the Accounting Regulatory Committee 'carved out' part of IAS 39 on the measurement of financial instruments. In stating the basis on which their accounts are prepared, European listed companies are required to specify that they have followed 'IFRS as endorsed by the EU'.

This creates a number of problems, not least with the US. The SEC has approved for use in the US without a reconciliation only IFRS as issued by the IASB. To qualify as equivalent to US GAAP the company must state that it follows IFRS as issued by the IASB, and the audit report must confirm this. UK companies are quite relaxed about this, they just say that their statements comply with IFRS as endorsed by the EU and IFRS as issued by the IASB, and they do not apply the EU carve out (which mostly only affects banks anyway). Their auditors confirm this. However, other member states are not always comfortable with this solution.

IFRS worldwide

As discussed above, a number of developed and developing countries have already moved to IFRS or are intending to do so. In addition to countries that adopt directly a number of states have standards that derive from IFRS. Hong Kong and the Philippines have adopted national standards that are identical to IFRS, including all accounting options, but in some cases effective dates and transition are different. In the case of Hong Kong, companies that are based in Hong Kong but incorporated in another country are permitted to issue IFRS financial statements rather than Hong Kong GAAP statements. Singapore has adopted nearly all IFRS, but has made changes to the **recognition** and measurement principles in several IFRS when adopting them as Singapore standards.

In South Africa IFRS are mandatory for all domestic listed companies. In Japan listed foreign companies can use IFRS (or any other national GAAP for that matter), but domestic companies are not allowed to use IFRS. Canada, Brazil and South Korea have adopted IFRS. Japan has a convergence programme with the IASB and is planning to move to IFRS.

China is still in a stage of developing a representative set of national accounting standards. Most accounting standards published to date are similar to the corresponding IFRS.

Since October 2002, the FASB and the IASB have been committed to the convergence of US rules and IFRS. Different initiatives have been taken, such as a short-term convergence project aimed at removing a variety of individual differences between US GAAP and IFRS, joint projects on significant accounting issues such as business combinations, revenue recognition and leasing. However, because of the volume of differences and the complex nature of some issues, the FASB anticipates that many differences between US and IFRS standards will persist well into the future. The present convergence programme is expected to end in 2013, with joint work after that likely to depend on the SEC's decision whether or not to adopt IFRS.

Summary

The objective of this chapter was to start to explain the environment of accounting. It has looked at the main financial statements published by companies and discussed the framework through which these are regulated. It has noted that governments need to regulate accounting to ensure the efficient running of the economy and the financial markets in particular, since business relies heavily on accurate information about other businesses. Government also wants to collect taxes and accounting is linked directly with the calculation of taxable profits. Apart from this, there are other bodies with an interest, notably stock exchanges, specialist standard-setting agencies and bodies organized by the accounting profession or industry sectors.

In the international field there is a strong movement towards the use of International Financial Reporting Standards which are promulgated by the IASB. These enable company reports to be compared across national boundaries and help smooth management decision-making in the context of global business.

Discussion Questions

1. What are the annual financial statements of a company?
2. Contrast broadly the regulatory traditions in continental Europe as opposed to the anglophone countries.
3. Are the financial accounting requirements of entities in the public sector different from those of business in the private sector?
4. Compare and contrast the different types of accounting regulation that exist.
5. How is the IASB's organizational setting structured?
6. Explain the potential trade-off between **relevance** and verifiability.
7. Explain what is meant by relevance, faithful representation and comparability and how they make financial information useful.

CHAPTER 2

Accounting and accountants

This chapter discusses the work of the company accounting department and the system called 'internal control' which is used to provide reasonable assurance regarding the reliability of the corporate financial statements. It will also introduce independent accountants and the auditing profession, as well as discussing the external audit.

Chapter Structure

- Introduction
- Accounting function
- Accounting database
- Recording transactions
- Organization of data within the general ledger
- Control and audit
- The accounting profession
- Summary
- Discussion questions

Introduction

We are going to start off this chapter by looking at the accounting system within a company and how it maintains its records. If you want just to be able to read financial statements, you may prefer not to learn about the processes through which the data in them are collected. On the other hand, a successful manager in a multinational is bound to have responsibility at some point for a free-standing operating unit and therefore for oversight of its accounting system. In addition, understanding where the information comes from is always going to help understand the information itself, and this is of course true of that provided by financial statements.

This chapter introduces the systems such as internal control and internal audit that are there to safeguard the company's **assets** and underpin the accuracy of the records. It then looks at the audit performed by external independent accountants and introduces the wider field of corporate governance. A more detailed review of audit, internal control and corporate governance is to be found in Chapter 16.

Accounting function

All businesses need a financial accounting system that tracks all the economic transactions that the business undertakes, records them logically in a database, and provides reporting tools to communicate information useful to decision makers. This system is a prime resource of the business and should provide:

- controls to ensure that only legitimate expenses are paid;
- systems to ensure that debts to suppliers are well tracked and paid when due;
- systems to calculate salary payments to employees and deduct social security and other charges;
- controls to ensure that all customers are correctly invoiced, and that customers in turn pay what they owe;
- controls to safeguard the company's assets;
- information to management on a regular basis to enable them to run the business efficiently;
- information to the authorities to support payment of taxes;
- information to shareholders on the health of the company and to help determine dividends;
- information and measurements to others with whom the company has performance-related contracts (debt covenants, employee bonus schemes, **joint ventures**, franchises, licences, etc.);
- information to those who lend money to the company and to suppliers;
- information that represents the company to all outside interests and all stakeholders.

Notice that while the first six objectives are wholly internal to the operation of the company, the other five involve providing information to those who are external to the company. We could describe the first six functions as being those of financial control and the others as those of financial reporting.

The accounting department of a company needs to meet these objectives, and this is mostly done through feeding the company's database, and then using the aggregate data to prepare reports about the company's activities. The nature of

BETWEEN THE LINES

Different companies have different needs – in a large, publicly held company the shareholders will usually be remote from the management, whereas in a small, family company, the managers are often also major shareholders. We will generally assume that the typical company we are dealing with is a large multinational, but will point out differences for smaller businesses as we go along. In this case, a small, family business will often want to keep information secret, while a multinational will generally be keen to give information (accounting reports are normally on the group's website).

the accounting department will vary enormously depending upon the size of the company. A very small business may simply use a part-time book-keeper to process transactions and maintain the database, or use an outside accounting firm to do this. The largest global groups will have enormous accounting departments in each operating unit, together with a large head office unit to gather together data from throughout the group. In an international group, the management of the group is controlled mostly through uniform accounting systems which involve subsidiaries in sending data regularly to head office (or via regional offices) to enable central and regional management to know what is happening. In this sense it would be impossible to manage an international group without accounting.

Usually such a group will have an internal accounting manual which lays out the procedures to be followed in accounting for typical transactions in order to ensure a uniform treatment of operations worldwide, without which management would have difficulty in interpreting the accounting information. The accounting manual may run to several volumes and is usually available in several languages.

In fact global companies have problems because national accounting rules differ from country to country. The national rules should normally be followed for tax purposes, so the group has to have a reporting system which is capable of delivering uniform data worldwide for management purposes and for the group financial statements, while also providing potentially different data in each country to suit local tax requirements. This is one of the reasons that large companies welcome worldwide convergence on IFRS. Potentially, group accounts and individual company accounts can use exactly the same rules. Too much should not be made of the existing differences, since they centre on one or two areas of accounting and generally, therefore, the transition from one set of accounts to the other is not that complicated. At the same time, this is a problem that multinationals have to address, and one that is costly in terms of hiring professionals to deal with it. Very often a multinational will choose to have uniform internal systems, and then ask its accounting advisers in each country, who are familiar with the subtleties of the local regulations, to liaise with the local tax officials and prepare a revised set of accounts for local reporting purposes (see Figure 2.1).

Figure 2.1
Group
reporting flows

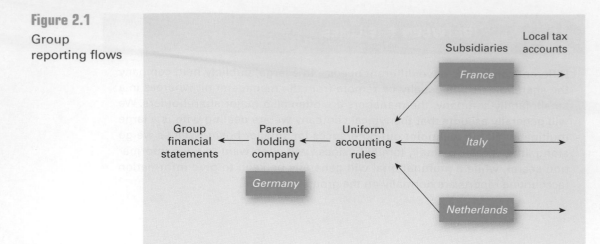

In principle the company's accounting function should provide systems that capture all the transactions that the company undertakes. The main categories of this are:

- sales
- purchases
- payroll
- treasury
- investment in long-term capacity.

These transactions involve an interaction with other departments, and the exact split of responsibility between the accounting function and the operating department will vary according to the nature of the business and the technology used.

In the *sales* area, there are many combinations possible. In a hotel, for example, the reception desk ('front office') generally also operates customer billing and cash collection, and then passes the transactions on to the accounting function ('back office'). In retailing, very often sales representatives call on retailers and take orders in person. The sales person then transmits the order to the company where the system captures it as an instruction to the warehouse and a linked instruction to the accounting department to issue an invoice. Increasingly companies are enabling their customers to access their intranet to place orders directly into the company system, which are then, through the computer, translated into delivery instructions and an invoice.

The accounting department will normally have a data file for each customer, will control credit levels and will send out monthly statements of account to the customer and track payment when that is due. The issue of credit control is occasionally a problematic one which gives liaison difficulties between accounting staff and sales staff. The accounting department will want to make sure that where credit is given, the customer does pay the bills in due course. The sales department on the other hand wants to sell as many units as possible, and easy credit helps them to do this, so they may be less demanding in their assessments of creditworthiness.

The capture of *purchases* has its own problems. Here the company will often have a system of purchase orders or requisitions where a manager with authority to purchase supplies must sign a requisition, a copy of which goes to the accounting department to alert them to the fact that a purchase is in hand. Later, when the goods are received, a delivery document is sent to the accounting department and then the invoice. The accounting department marries all these together and puts them into the system. The supplier data file is then checked with the monthly statement sent by the supplier to ensure that all invoices have been recorded.

Finally the account is authorized and paid. In a small company this is relatively straightforward, but in a big operation it can be very complicated and the potential for error is considerable. This explains why there are specialist companies who review purchases, particularly for large stores, and often recover large amounts of money. Equally, this explains the success of scams where a fraudster sends out invoices for small sums for, say, listing in an internet directory, and some large companies will pay the invoice, although no order was ever placed and the directory does not exist.

The *payroll* is usually a specialist function within accounting. It calls for special knowledge in that in many countries the employer is responsible for deducting social security charges from the employee, sometimes the employee's income tax is deducted by the employer, and then there may be pension schemes and other voluntary schemes, such as savings or membership of a staff social club, to which the employee contributes. This means that each employee's pay file is individual and probably quite complex. Small companies will often subcontract this function to an accounting firm or a specialist service company. The possibilities for error are considerable, and where government deductions are involved, there may be fines for making mistakes. The accounting involved is also quite complex in that the company deducts money from the individual's pay packet and then has to pay this to government departments, pension funds and so on.

The *treasury* function is one where all the others meet up: treasury controls all the receipts and payments into the company's bank accounts, as well as any cash tills that might exist (company accountants do not like cash floating around). Evidently this is the area where authorizations are most stringently required and also where accurate coding of transactions is essential. The treasury unit works very closely with the company's bankers. Accessing the bank's accounting system in real time, the treasury knows exactly how much money is in each of the company's accounts at the close of banking business and then lends out any surplus, perhaps on the overnight market (yes, you can lend money just overnight, provided you have enough of it to do so in large quantities).

The accounting system is organized with separate data files for each bank account, so that the company's information can be checked directly against the statement put out by the bank. This provides a regular control on the accuracy of the company's records – all charges and revenues that have gone through the bank should also be in the company's records. The company regularly (ideally at least once a month) prepares a 'bank reconciliation'. This is a document which compares the balance on the bank account as seen by the bank, with the balance on the corresponding data file within the company. These two will rarely agree because of time lags in transactions going through the bank account, but the differences can and must be identified as a check on the accuracy of both sets of records (in a large company this can involve cross-checking hundreds of transactions). One way of conducting a fraud is to make payments without entering them in the company's accounting records. These payments will show up as differences on the bank reconciliation, but if nobody reviews the reconciliation, they will stay outside the company records.

You can see that the accounting unit has a quite complex set of tasks and objectives. Its prime function is to capture information for the company and to ensure that customers pay their bills and that suppliers are paid – it is a service function to help the company to operate efficiently. However, most company frauds are going to involve obtaining money via the accounting department, so the staff and systems have to be organized to prevent this. Therefore they may seem less than keen on giving a service and rather too inclined to demand bits of paper, and signatures, which appear to be obstacles to the free running of the company.

Accounting database

Coming back to the central issue of accumulating information, a company's financial accounting system is organized to provide data for a central database (the *general ledger*) which is then used as the source of information used by management internally and for external reporting purposes. The accounting database normally looks as shown in Figure 2.2.

Figure 2.2

The financial accounting database

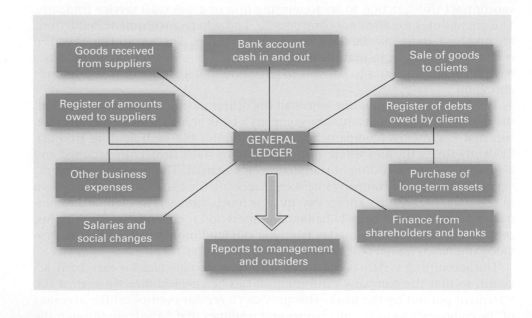

Recording transactions

Information flows into the database through several layers of processing which summarize and resummarize individual transactions to build up to aggregates for the year's activities (Figure 2.3).

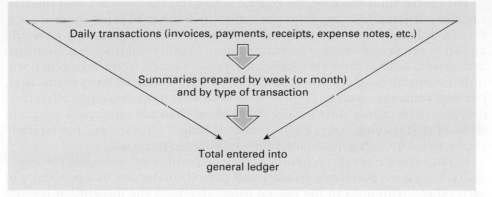

Figure 2.3
Building
aggregates

Journals are used to build up the periodic summaries and feed aggregated data into the general ledger. The general ledger is then used as a source for the preparation of a periodic statement of profit or loss (or income statement) and a statement of financial position (or balance sheet). This kind of approach was particularly useful when all entries in the database were made by hand, and is still used even though virtually all systems in companies are computerized. The essential idea is that while aggregated data are needed in the ledger, to enable management summaries to be prepared, the system must be capable of being interrogated to confirm that a particular transaction has or has not taken place, so it must be possible later to go from the monthly figure in the ledger, for example, back through the journals to the individual transaction. This is both because accounting departments have regularly to deal with queries, and because the transactions are subject to checking by internal or external auditors. There must be what is called an 'audit trail' to show the links and provide evidence that the initial transaction was authorized. Computerized systems may very well carry out the intermediate stage between the individual transaction (known as a 'prime entry' in the trade) and the ledger total. Once the first entry has been keyed in, the system will organize a batch of similar transactions and 'post' this to the ledger, but it is normally organized also to provide a printout of each batch, which becomes the bridge between prime entry and ledger. Of course, there could be several intermediate levels.

Some decisions have to be taken as to what level of detail is going to be useful within an accounting system. At one extreme an accounting system might record every single transaction separately so that its annual profit and loss account is a detailed list of every transaction that has taken place over the year. At the other extreme the profit and loss account could be one figure representing the net difference (profit or loss) of the whole year's revenues and expenses.

The exact point at which one makes a decision about the degree of detail to be kept will vary with the specific circumstances of each company, its size and the nature of the business being carried out. However, as guidelines, the final records should obviously, as a minimum, keep information aggregated for a whole accounting year on each of the separate categories (of the statement of profit or loss and statement of financial position) which will appear in the annual financial statements. Normally, though, the database will be much more detailed. It will need to be capable of delivering information about each individual operating unit within a company, so that an analysis which shows the profitability of each unit for management purposes can be produced without difficulty. This information is aggregated for the purposes of the published financial statements.

The precise form taken by the general ledger and the journals, and the classification of items, will vary from one system to another. In some countries (e.g. France, Belgium, Greece, Spain) there is a State-mandated system, generally known as a *chart of accounts* or accounting plan. In other countries (e.g. Germany, Switzerland, Austria) there are widely used standard charts whose adoption is voluntary. Generally anglophone countries do not use standard charts of this kind, but large companies with uniform systems worldwide must develop in effect their own chart of accounts. A nationally standardized chart has certain advantages in terms of staff training, lower audit costs and cheaper software, but has typically been rejected by anglophone professions as being too restrictive.

In large companies the system may well be partitioned to enable the major operations (sales, purchases, treasury and payroll) to operate independently of each other – with links to the central ledger to ensure the integrity of the system. In this way the specialist functions can operate dedicated systems which not only maintain the ledger but issue invoices or bank transfers, issue monthly statements to customers, provide analysis of outstanding items, etc.

XBRL (eXtensible Business Reporting Language) is set to revolutionize accounting data handling and reporting in this context. Instead of treating accounting information as a block of text, XBRL provides an identifying tag for each individual item of information, such as individual accounts in a chart of accounts. These tags are computer readable and enable automated processing of accounting and related business information by computer software. The specific tags of individual data items are defined in taxonomies. These function as dictionaries. Different taxonomies can coexist and be linked for reporting purposes. This offers a viable solution to link IFRS and national reporting taxonomies. Indeed, national jurisdictions may need their own taxonomies (like a standard chart of accounts and specific reporting formats) to reflect their local accounting regulations, but XBRL could automatically convert them in a generally accepted IFRS taxonomy. Once the appropriate XBRL taxonomies are established and the data are gathered accordingly, different types of reports using varying subsets of the data can be produced with minimum effort. The accounting department could, for example, quickly and reliably generate internal management reports, financial statements for publication, tax and other regulatory filings, as well as credit reports for lenders. XBRL would remove time-consuming and error-prone data-handling processes and improve data accuracy through automated data checks.

The IASB has developed an IFRS taxonomy which it updates regularly. The SEC encourages companies to file XBRL tagged data and offers free software to help investors manipulate the tagged data. An investor can, for example, compare sales in different companies by using this kind of system. They can in effect construct their own analysts' reports comparing companies in the same field.

Organization of data within the general ledger

When the data about the accounting transactions of the company reach the general ledger they will be stored according to a system which has been in existence for hundreds of years: the double-entry system. The first written account of the system appeared in 1494 (by Luca Pacioli) and the fact that the system is still in use today will give you some idea of its practical effectiveness.

First, the general ledger is organized into a series of 'accounts' – data files – each of which is used to record transactions of a particular type. For example, if your business is selling books, you would need one account in which to record sales, another to record the cost of the books sold and a series of accounts to record the various different types of expense incurred in the business (advertising, rent of premises, heat, etc.), as well as accounts for financing and investments in property, inventory, etc. (This is the minimum – if more analysis were useful, then more accounts would be used.)

Each account within the general ledger is organized in a particular way. The account has two columns for figures and some space to write in explanatory remarks and cross-referencing details. The left-hand column is always referred to as the *debit column* and the right-hand column is called the *credit column* (there seems to be no satisfactory explanation for the derivation of these words). Debit and credit are also used as verbs, so one says 'debit insurance expense' to mean a figure should be entered into the left-hand column of the insurance expense account. In formal, manual book-keeping there are no plus or minus signs; the value of an account is the difference between the debit and credit columns, and can be either a debit balance (more left hand than right) or a credit balance (more right hand than left).

A traditional manual ledger account would look as shown in Figure 2.4.

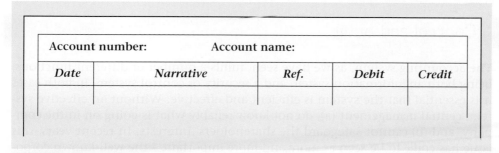

Account number:		Account name:			
Date	Narrative		Ref.	Debit	Credit

Figure 2.4

Layout of a manual ledger account

A computerized printout often preserves the same format, but may also provide a running balance perhaps in a third column out to the right, or elsewhere on the printout.

The exact form in which the accounts are kept is not of essential interest for our purposes – what is important is how the figures are arrived at and what they mean, rather than the detail of the methodology of the data file. However, one normally comes across accounting statements, notably one's bank statement, from time to time, and knowledge of the notation system is useful to that extent. An example of a personal bank statement is shown in Figure 2.5.

If you were looking at a financial accounting textbook intended for accountants, then the whole of the discussion of accounting rules and techniques would involve notation involving debits and credits – making entries in left-hand and right-hand columns. This notation system is largely redundant for our purposes, and we will use non-specialist signs and tools such as worksheets to explain what is going on. Since you are not going to run an accounting system, a detailed knowledge of the notation is not useful and tends to divert attention from the reality of what is actually going on.

Figure 2.5

Example of a personal bank statement

CREDIT SUISSE

Genève

Compte privé

Date	Narrative	In our favour	In your favour	Balance
170709	Balance brought forward			2 726.50
260709	Receipt IIM		348.00	3 074.50
270709	Credit card settlement	1 791.65		1 282.85
280709	Receipt DIP		7 589.70	8 872.55
300709	Monthly payments	3 700.70		5 171.85
90809	Cash – ATM	500.00		4 671.85
160809	Cash – ATM	500.00		4 171.85

Credit = in your favour

Debit – in our favour

Control and audit

The accounting system, as we have seen, fulfils a number of different functions, being both an information system and a security or control system. In both cases it is essential that the system is efficient and effective. Without an effective system, central management (a), do not know reliably what is going on in the company, and (b) cannot safeguard the shareholders' interests. In recent years, this issue has come to be seen as more and more important – the well-known corporate embarrassments, such as the fall of Barings Bank, the large loss at the French Société Générale and the reporting problems of Royal Ahold, would almost certainly not have been possible with tighter systems – in the jargon, tighter internal control. Public concern has grown to the point where many companies publish a statement in their annual report to the effect that the directors are satisfied that they have in place an adequate system of internal control. One of the main objectives of the internal control system is to ensure the integrity of the information system and the security of the company's assets. In that sense it is heavily relied upon by external auditors in assessing the viability of the company's records. In this section we will take a closer look at how a system of internal control operates and its links, through internal audit, to the external audit.

Internal control

Internal control has recently become more important because of the focus on corporate governance and the demands this places on boards of directors and executives to implement and demonstrate control over business operations. One of the most authoritative definitions of internal control comes from COSO (Report of the Committee of Sponsoring Organizations of the Treadway Commission).

Defining internal control

The COSO definition of internal control has become widely accepted and is referred to in other international control frameworks as well. According to COSO, internal control is broadly defined as a process, established, operated and monitored by those charged with governance and management of a company (board of directors, management and other personnel) to provide reasonable assurance regarding the achievement of objectives in the following categories:

- the effectiveness and efficiency of the company's operations
- the **reliability** of its financial reporting and
- its compliance with applicable laws and regulations.

As a process, internal control goes beyond policies and procedures and also includes factors such as corporate culture, systems and organizational structures. The COSO definition underscores the importance of the relationship of control and objectives. Without objectives, talking about control is meaningless. From a broad managerial perspective, the COSO report identifies three categories of control objectives. The first category addresses a company's basic business concerns, including performance and profitability goals and safeguarding of resources (basically an efficiency concern). The second relates to the preparation of reliable financial statements and related financial data derived from such statements. The third deals with complying with those laws and regulations to which the company is subject. Within the COSO framework financial reporting concerns are a basic objective of a system of internal control although not an exclusive one.

Internal control: system components

According to COSO, a system of internal control consists of five interrelated components:

- *control environment* – attributes of the people conducting the company's activities and the environment in which they operate, influencing overall control consciousness;
- *risk assessment* – identification and analysis of relevant risks as a basis for determining ways to manage those risks;
- *control activities* – policies and procedures established and executed that enable management's directives to be carried out;
- *information and communication* – identification, capture and exchange of information for the conduct and control of operations in a form and timeframe that enables people to carry out their responsibilities;
- *monitoring* – assessing of performance of internal control over time and making modifications as conditions change.

These five interrelated components are relevant for each internal control objective. For example, accurate financial reporting builds on a supportive control environment with a strong ethical commitment of corporate management, identification of relevant threats and exposures (erroneous record-keeping, unacceptable accounting rules, unrecognized fraud and embezzlement of assets, loss or theft of data, etc.), efficient information gathering and processing routines and appropriate control policies and procedures to manage financial reporting risks (good document design, accounting manuals, organizational measures, checks and balances, etc.).

COSO – COMPONENTS OF A SYSTEM OF INTERNAL CONTROL
(extracts)

Control environment

The control environment sets the tone of an organization, influencing the control consciousness of its people. It is the foundation for all other components of internal control, providing discipline and structure. Control environment factors include the integrity, ethical values and competence of the entity's people; management's philosophy and operating style; the way management assigns authority and responsibility, and organizes and develops its people; and the attention and direction provided by the board of directors.

Risk assessment

Every entity faces a variety of risks from external and internal sources that must be assessed. A precondition to risk assessment is establishment of objectives, linked at different levels and internally consistent. Risk assessment is the identification and analysis of relevant risks to achievement of the objectives, forming a basis for determining how the risks should be managed. Because economic, industry, regulatory and operating conditions will continue to change, mechanisms are needed to identify and deal with the special risks associated with change.

Control activities

Control activities are the policies and procedures that help ensure management directives are carried out. They help ensure that necessary actions are taken to address risks to achievement of the entity's objectives. Control activities occur throughout the organization, at all levels and in all functions. They include a range of activities as diverse as approvals, authorizations, verifications, reconciliations, reviews of operating performance, security of assets and segregation of duties.

Information and communication

Pertinent information must be identified, captured and communicated in a form and timeframe that enable people to carry out their responsibilities. Information systems produce reports, containing operational, financial and compliance-related information, that make it possible to run and control the business. They deal not only with internally generated data, but also information about external events, activities and conditions necessary to informed business decision-making and external reporting. Effective communication also must occur in a broader sense, flowing down, across and up the organization. All personnel must receive a clear message from top management that control responsibilities must be taken seriously. They must understand their own role in the internal control system, as well as how individual activities relate to the work of others. They must have a means of communicating significant information upstream. There also needs to be effective communication with external parties, such as customers, suppliers, regulators and shareholders.

Monitoring

Internal control systems need to be monitored – a process that assesses the quality of the system's performance over time. This is accomplished through ongoing monitoring activities, separate evaluations or a combination of the two. Ongoing monitoring occurs in the course of operations. It includes regular management and supervisory activities, and other actions personnel take in performing their duties. The scope and frequency of separate evaluations will depend primarily on an assessment of risks and the effectiveness of ongoing monitoring procedures. Internal control deficiencies should be reported upstream, with serious matters reported to top management and the board.

Source: COSO, Internal Control – Integrated Framework, Executive Summary

The internal control system is intertwined with a company's operating activities and exists for fundamental business reasons (see objectives to be accomplished by the system). Internal control is most effective when controls are built into the company's infrastructure and are a part of the essence of the company's operations: internal control should become part of the company's DNA. 'Built in' controls support quality and empowerment initiatives, avoid unnecessary costs and enable quick response to changing conditions. From this perspective, an accounting information system functions as an integral part of an internal control system and is thus more than a bundle of coordinated information flows. In fact, accounting information flows are intertwined with risk assessment processes, hierarchical and horizontal (between different functional departments) communication routines and specific control activities to ensure both the validity, completeness and accuracy of financial reports and the integrity of the resources they report on.

Control activities

Control activities usually involve a *policy component* and a *procedures component*. A policy establishes what should be done, while procedures are the actions to implement procedures. For example, a policy might call for a creditworthiness review before a customer order is formally accepted. The procedure is the actual credit check, performed in a timely manner and with attention given to the factors set forth in the policy, such as financial guarantees, the payment history of the client and the balances of outstanding orders and sales invoices due.

A common and useful way to classify control activities is in relation to the timing of their occurrence – *preventive*, *detective* and *corrective controls*. Preventive controls are policies and procedures designed to prevent an error or fraud from occurring. For example, a creditworthiness check on new customer orders prevents shipping goods and recognizing receivables in the balance sheet for which no full payment will be received. Preventive financial controls, such as validation and edit checks on the input of transactions before they are recorded, will prevent **material** misstatements in accounting records, whether by error or fraud, from occurring during transaction processing in the accounting system. Detective controls are policies and procedures that are designed to detect errors or fraud that might preclude the achievement of specific business or process objectives.

Detective financial controls will be built into the accounting system to spot material misstatements that may occur in processing transactions. Corrective controls are usually linked to detective ones and aim at correcting problems in a timely manner.

Strong preventive controls are essential to support the effectiveness of information and control systems. In an accounting system that processes a high volume of transactions, a lack of preventive controls on the input of transactions before they are recorded can render detective and corrective controls ineffective in detecting and correcting errors in a timely manner. Preventive controls can take a myriad of forms. Within the context of an accounting information system they can be programmed validity and edit checks, file transmission controls, automated posting to ledgers and automated summary checks and reports. These types of preventive application controls are usually accompanied by preventive control measures of an organizational nature, such as an appropriate system of delegation and accountability, linked with a structure of formal approvals and what is known as 'separation of functions'.

While all of the accounting transactions are centralized ultimately on the general ledger, it is good management practice to split up the way the transactions are initiated, recorded and processed into different functional units, partly to allow for the development of specialist skills (division of labour) and partly to provide an environment where fraud becomes difficult. This is known as *separation of functions* or as segregation of duties. It calls for the separation of the four basic functions of transaction processing:

- authorizing transactions
- executing transactions
- recording transactions and
- safeguarding resources resulting from consummating transactions.

A simple example would be that where a payment has to be made, the payment is authorized by one person, the cheque drawn by another person, the cheque signed by a third and the general ledger entry made by a fourth. Each person is responsible for ensuring that they process nothing which is not correctly supported by documents and authorizations, and therefore in theory at least four people would need to be in collusion for a fraudulent payment to be made without a significant risk of detection. Equally, at least four people should have checked that the transaction is valid and has been correctly categorized. Separation of functions is a nice example of an efficient preventive control, in the sense that it simultaneously supports different types of control objectives: safeguarding of assets, ensuring the validity, completeness and accuracy of recorded information and compliance checking.

Separation of functions is obviously easier in a large company than in a small one, and it also has the effect of increasing the costs of each transaction. There is therefore a difficult trade-off between the costs and the level of assurance. But even in small companies with only a few employees it is usually possible to assign responsibilities in a way that achieves the necessary checks and balances. Alternatively, oversight of incompatible activities by the general manager can substitute functional diversification. Recall the payments example. In small companies it is not uncommon that the general manager is the only person authorized to approve outgoing payments and that monthly (or daily) bank statements are to be delivered unopened directly to him or her for review of outgoing payments.

There is, however, the psychological problem that people get used to routines and after a while do not check effectively. Indeed, in a system where everyone knows there are five other people checking the transaction, each link in the chain may start to rely on someone else doing the job properly, leading to a general failure. This is one of the reasons why monitoring activities, involving assessment by appropriate personnel of the design and operation of controls on a timely basis, is a necessary component of an effective internal control system.

Even with strong preventive controls, detective and corrective controls remain necessary. The internal control system will typically include routine checks such as inspection of the monthly bank reconciliation and outstanding customer and supplier accounts, all of which provide areas where fraudulent items can be kept outside the system but also where company records can to an extent be checked against the records of outside organizations with which the company deals. Many companies keep asset registers where lists of computers and desks and so on (to say nothing of cars, plant, etc.) are maintained and these should be checked periodically against the physical existence of these items. Equally, where staff have access to large quantities of goods (supermarket staff, factory workers, etc.) it is usual to have security systems that control what goods the employees are taking in and out of the business.

It should be clear, however, that a good system of internal control can provide only reasonable (not absolute) assurance regarding the achievement of the major control objectives, including the effectiveness of the accounting and reporting systems. Each system of internal control has its inherent limitations. Internal control heavily relies on human judgement in decision-making and this can be faulty. Control activities are bound by cost–benefit considerations due to resource constraints and they can break down as a result of a simple error or mistake. Internal controls can always be circumvented through the collusion of two or more people. Additionally, management usually has the ability to override the internal controls if that suits their personal interests better.

The US Sarbanes–Oxley Act of 2002 (commonly referred to as SOX) made executive management responsible not just for establishing, evaluating and assessing over time the effectiveness of internal control over financial reporting and disclosure, but also for periodically asserting its effectiveness (see Chapter 16 for further details). In the EU, no equivalent of the SOX requirements on internal control currently exists. As to accounting system specifications, the Fourth and Seventh

BETWEEN THE LINES

Why should you check goods being taken *in* to a company? It is not always relevant, but a sophisticated fraud is easy to operate in something like a bar where the barman takes in, for example, a bottle of whisky then, when a customer asks for a measure of whisky, the barman serves the customer from his private inventory and keeps the money. This way the customer is not cheated and the bar owner does not necessarily have any idea anything is wrong. The barman is robbing the business by using its infrastructure, but the main internal controls generally focus on the relationship between the value of sales and the value of the liquor consumed, and the barman is circumventing these controls by bringing in liquor.

Company Law Directives implicitly require companies to maintain accounting records enabling them to prepare financial statements, but explicit requirements on form and content of the accounting records and related controls are left to national legislation. This has led to divergent national requirements in European countries, but none has legal requirements comparable to the SOX requirements to publicly disclose conclusions regarding the effectiveness of internal control with regard to financial reporting.

Internal audit

Most large companies have an internal audit department. The primary task of internal auditors should be to examine and evaluate the adequacy and effectiveness of the company's internal control system and the quality of performance in carrying out assigned responsibilities. In fact, the internal audit function can be considered to be part of the monitoring component of the internal control system. It should be stressed, however, that the primary responsibility for establishing and maintaining the internal control system does not belong to the internal audit function but to the CEO, along with **key management personnel**. The internal audit function's primary responsibility is to evaluate the effectiveness of internal control and thus contribute to ongoing effectiveness.

One of the key issues for a proper functioning of an internal audit function is its independence: the internal audit department should be independent of the activities they audit. The independence of the audit department should be assured through their organizational position and authority within the company and through recognition of their objectivity. Of crucial importance is their reporting line: it is generally recommended that internal auditors report directly to either the (audit committee of the) board of directors, the CEO or a committee of top corporate executives.

The scope of internal auditing potentially covers all activities within the company. In some companies, internal auditors are heavily involved with operational controls, such as periodically monitoring production quality, testing the timeliness of shipments to customers or evaluating the efficiency of production processes (operational internal audit). In other companies the internal audit function will focus primarily on compliance and financial reporting issues (financial internal audit). So, in practice, the scope of the activities of the internal auditors tends to vary considerably, depending on the company's management.

Typically (and we will focus now on responsibilities of the internal auditors that are related to financial reporting) the department consists of a team of several people whose job is to visit the group's different sites and check whether accounting policies and procedures (usually documented in a policies and procedures manual) and related controls are being followed correctly and remain effective. Partly the task is psychological: if people know that at any time in the year the internal audit department may call in to check the accounting transactions and see whether the procedures in the group manual have been followed, they are encouraged to apply the procedures more thoroughly and anyone who was contemplating fraud is discouraged . . . the internal audit department thus acts as a preventive control measure.

The internal audit department can help create a culture within the company that says the accounting function has a vital role to play and that members of it are valued for their technical knowledge and their skill in handling the sometimes difficult interpersonal situations that can arise. Equally, this department can provide important feedback about application problems to those who design and maintain the procedures. A difficulty in operating group-wide systems is that not all operating units are the same size (and therefore may have quite different accounting structures and personnel) and not all have the same type of operations.

By way of example of the problems that can arise when trying to instal uniform systems, here is an actual example taken from a group which had both electronics and entertainment interests. Within the entertainment division was a subgroup which ran London theatres and produced live theatrical shows. The head office internal audit department was conducting an exercise to fix levels of expenditure authority within operating units, as part of the internal control structure. They said that the chief executive of this subgroup could sign contracts only up to an individual value of £500 000. Beyond that he should seek authority from the chief executive of the entertainment division. The chief accountant of the theatrical subgroup said this was not possible because the group did not know the value of many contracts which were signed. The internal audit manager was dumbfounded – how could the chief executive sign contracts without knowing their value? Should he not be replaced at once (and maybe the chief accountant too)?

The chief accountant explained that theatre contracts in the West End of London are usually open-ended. They provide for a minimum weekly rental (generally against a percentage of sales) and, as long as this is exceeded, the **contract** can run indefinitely. Indeed, the object of the exercise is to find a single production that could potentially run for years. So while the minimum weekly rental might be (say) £50 000, the show could run for two or three years, or only two or three weeks, so the value of the contract could be anything from £200 000 to £20m or more. The internal audit manager then understood, but pointed out that the chief executive of the worldwide group could only sign contracts up to £10m without the approval of the board of directors. In the end, they agreed to write a special authority for the theatre subgroup, based on maximum weekly figures.

Getting the 'control environment' right is a very tricky problem in a large group. Ideally you want the accounting departments of the different units to be efficient and useful contributors to the team, who are willing to provide a high quality of service to help with the efficient running of the unit. On the other hand, the integrity of the group system and the necessity to provide inputs whose justification can be demonstrated, if necessary years after the event in a tax investigation, demand that accounting staff insist on the presentation of the appropriate paperwork and the required authorizations. Accounting staff in remote subsidiaries sometimes have a particularly difficult time since they have a line responsibility to the chief executive of their **subsidiary**, but a functional responsibility to the head office accounting managers. Locally employed staff, particularly in areas where unemployment is high, may fear losing their job if they upset the local chief executive, and may therefore not apply systems correctly.

The internal audit team should make frequent but unscheduled visits to subsidiaries to make spot checks on recent transactions but also to reinforce the local accounting unit if there are problems. The internal audit team should have a reporting responsibility within the head office, and not to local managers, although of course they should discuss local problems with operational management on site.

It follows from this that working in internal audit is not a particularly easy job. It is necessary to have a wide knowledge of the group's operations and information systems. A great deal of time is spent away from home visiting remote subsidiaries and often either working in foreign languages or with people who are obliged to use their second or third language, and who, of course, have different cultural backgrounds and therefore different understandings about their role and responsibilities. People in either accounting or operational roles often resent also what they perceive as an intrusion from head office, without understanding that without effective accounting systems the group cannot continue to exist for very long.

The Institute of Internal Auditors (IIA) has played a major role in the development of the internal auditing profession. Established in the US in 1941, the IIA has grown into a highly respected international organization and has taken a leadership role in providing professional guidance for internal auditors. The IIA establishes ethical and practice standards, provides education and promotes professionalism through its worldwide network. It sponsors a certification programme leading to the designation of Certified Internal Auditor (CIA) for those who meet the examination and experience requirements. The IAA's Standards for the Professional Practice of Internal Auditing are divided in attribute standards for the internal auditor and the internal audit department and performance standards for the performance and reporting of internal audit activities.

STANDARDS

🌐 DEFINING INTERNAL AUDITING

Internal auditing is an independent, objective assurance and consulting activity designed to add value and improve an organization's operations. It helps an organization accomplish its objectives by bringing a systematic, disciplined approach to evaluate and improve the effectiveness of risk management, control and governance processes.

Source: Institute of Internal Auditors (www.theiia.org)

External audit

In most jurisdictions the financial statements of medium and large companies must be submitted to an independent audit. This is often referred to as *statutory audit* and is usually carried out by independent firms of auditors. Audit has evolved differently in different countries, and the object of the audit is not uniform. In some countries, the auditor has a quasi-legal role to check for the legality of the company's activities and its annual statements, whereas in other countries the auditor is checking the accounts on behalf of the shareholders. In both cases the audit firm is usually appointed in fact by the management of the company, but the responsibility both for keeping accounts and for preparing the annual financial statements is that of the management of the company, not that of the external auditors.

The external auditor expresses an opinion on the representational fairness of the financial statements in conformity with generally accepted accounting principles. While the company's system of internal control should provide reasonable assurance regarding the reliability of financial statements, the external auditor

STANDARDS

🌐 INSTITUTE OF INTERNAL AUDITORS: STANDARDS FOR THE PROFESSIONAL PRACTICE OF AUDITING

Attribute standards

1000 Purpose, Authority, and Responsibility. The purpose, authority and responsibility of the internal audit activity should be formally defined in a charter, consistent with the *Standards*, and approved by the board.

1100 Independence and Objectivity. The internal audit activity should be independent, and internal auditors should be objective in performing their work.

1200 Proficiency and Due Professional Care. Engagements should be performed with proficiency and due professional care.

1300 Quality Assurance and Improvement Program. The chief audit executive should develop and maintain a quality assurance and improvement program that covers all aspects of the internal audit activity and continuously monitors its effectiveness. The program should be designed to help the internal auditing activity add value and improve the organization's operations and to provide assurance that the internal audit activity is in conformity with the *Standards* and the Code of *Ethics*.

Performance standards

2000 Managing the Internal Audit Activity. The chief audit executive should effectively manage the internal audit activity to ensure it adds value to the organization.

2100 Nature of Work. The internal audit activity evaluates and contributes to the improvement of risk management, control, and governance systems.

2200 Engagement Planning. Internal auditors should develop and record a plan for each engagement.

2300 Performing the Engagement. Internal auditors should identify, analyze, evaluate and record sufficient information to achieve the engagement's objectives.

2400 Communicating Results. Internal auditors should communicate the engagement results promptly.

2500 Monitoring Progress. The chief audit executive should establish and maintain a system to monitor the disposition of results communicated to management

2600 Management's Acceptance of Risks. When the chief audit executive believes that senior management has accepted a level of residual risk that is unacceptable to the organization, the chief audit executive should discuss the matter with senior management. If the decision regarding residual risk is not resolved, the chief audit executive and senior management should report the matter to the board for resolution.

Source: Institute of Internal Auditors, 2007 (www.theiia.org)

brings the assurance to a higher level. It is, however, not the responsibility of the external auditors to detect fraud. While external auditors should certainly report fraud if they spot it and they will normally comment on the adequacy of the internal control system to prevent fraud, their job is not to search for fraud, even if many people think that it is. In a modern multinational, the management are looking to the statutory auditor to provide reassurance to outside stakeholders that the financial statements of the company are a valid representation of the company's financial position and performance. This is part of the very broad role played by financial statements, and the fact that the information is independently verified is probably one reason why the role is so broad.

Nearly all multinationals have their financial statements audited by one of the four international audit networks which dominate the business:

- PricewaterhouseCoopers (PwC)
- KPMG
- Ernst & Young
- Deloitte.

These four firms are probably better known than many of their clients and one of their logos on the audit report (published within the financial statements) carries a high level of reassurance to users in general and the capital markets in particular. As a consequence, any company with ambitions is likely to use one of these firms. In addition, they have worldwide networks and are capable of delivering an audit anywhere in the world. This is quite important in that the multinational generally prefers to have a single firm responsible for all its subsidiaries, not least because this reduces the risk of lack of coordination between countries. This tends to reinforce the dominant position of the 'Big Four', as they are known, since other audit firms cannot offer the global service.

The basic statutory audit consists of two tasks:

1. to check that the accounting database effectively picks up all the company's activities and is correct;
2. to check that the financial statements drawn up from it are a correct representation of what is in the accounting database, use appropriate accounting policies and are a reasonable representation of the company's real state (but this last aspect may not always be part of local audit requirements).

The audit firm maintains a master file on the company and in this is collated all the relevant information necessary for the annual audit. This includes items left outstanding from the previous audit for subsequent management action and an analysis of the company's systems. When starting a new audit, the first requirement is to check the accuracy of the systems chart. Having established the current system and internal controls in place, the next step is to check how well these work. This is done by sampling the transactions of a particular (short) period. If this checking reveals that the internal control system is correctly applied, the auditor can go on to carry out verifications of things like inventory valuations, bank reconciliations (comparing the client's bank records with the statements provided by the bank), customer accounts, supplier accounts and so on. Only if the internal control system is thought to be ineffective will more detailed checking be done.

Once satisfied with the database, the auditor looks at the financial statements and the interpretation of the database which has been made in these. The nature of the company's business does not necessarily change every year, so there need not be any queries at this point, but as new transactions appear, so there may well be disagreement about how these are represented. Such disagreements are usually resolved more or less amicably between the audit staff and the chief accountant, but occasionally there can be substantial disagreement – usually because a change in treatment would diminish profits (we will be looking at cases throughout this book). In such circumstances things can be very tense and large companies have been known to bring in legal opinion, or consult another firm of auditors, when trying to insist on their view of the financial statements. The auditor can, in some countries, even be replaced, but this generally sends a bad signal to the market. The auditor's only threat is to refuse to sign the audit report at all (very extreme) or (more normally) to say that they will be obliged to include a reservation in their audit report which details the matter in dispute.

Although the auditor signs a public report, there is also usually a private report which is given to the management, and is known as a *management letter*. This, unlike the published report, does not follow any prescribed formula but rather comments on the audit findings for the year, highlights potential areas of weakness and makes recommendations. This is something which the following year's audit will revisit to see what action has been taken.

The conduct of the audit is regulated in three ways. Firstly, the statutory audit, by definition, is mandated by a government statute (such as a company law or a commercial code) which will prescribe the objects of the audit and normally specify whether client confidentiality applies or not. In the second place there will normally be a national professional association for auditors which will provide detailed audit regulations. Finally the audit firm itself will have its own internal procedures which all its staff follow – for reasons of efficiency and also to enable the firm's management to assess the degree of risk in the audit and similar issues.

The audit firm has a potentially difficult relationship with its client because, on the one hand, the outside world depends upon the rigour of the audit firm to ensure that the company maintains proper accounts and gives adequate reports while, on the other, the audit firm is in effect appointed by the management, must negotiate with the management and, in many countries, hopes to be able to sell supplementary services such as tax advice and management consultancy to the audit client. This problem is part of the issue of *auditor independence*. Regulators are concerned that, since auditors are at the front line of corporate regulation, they should be independent of management and provide an appropriate control on management. Other aspects of the independence issue include restrictions on employment of former audit firm employees by the client and the necessity of auditor partner rotation over time.

Companies listed on the US stock markets are obliged to appoint an *audit committee* whose members liaise with the statutory auditors. The Sarbanes–Oxley Act requires that all members of the audit committee are independent. The company should also disclose whether or not the audit committee includes at least one member who is a financial expert. The idea is that this committee provides a knowledgeable forum free from the influence of operating management where shareholder representatives can discuss audit problems. SOX even requires that the audit committee appoint the firm of external auditors. The role of the audit committee is growing in a context where society is becoming more and more concerned with corporate governance issues.

NESTLÉ

Report of the Statutory Auditor on the Consolidated Financial Statements to the General Meeting of Nestlé S.A.

As statutory auditor, we have audited the consolidated financial statements (income statement, statement of comprehensive income, balance sheet, cash flow statement, statement of changes in equity and notes on pages 46 to 115) of the Nestlé Group for the year ended 31 December 2011.

Board of Directors' responsibility

The Board of Directors is responsible for the preparation and fair presentation of the consolidated financial statements in accordance with International Financial Reporting Standards (IFRS) and the requirements of Swiss law. This responsibility includes designing, implementing and maintaining an internal control system relevant to the preparation and fair presentation of consolidated financial statements that are free from material misstatement, whether due to fraud or error. The Board of Directors is further responsible for selecting and applying appropriate accounting policies and making accounting estimates that are reasonable in the circumstances.

Auditor's responsibility

Our responsibility is to express an opinion on these consolidated financial statements based on our audit. We conducted our audit in accordance with Swiss law and Swiss Auditing Standards as well as International Standards on Auditing. Those standards require that we plan and perform the audit to obtain reasonable assurance whether the consolidated financial statements are free from material misstatement.

An audit involves performing procedures to obtain audit evidence about the amounts and disclosures in the consolidated financial statements. The procedures selected depend on the auditor's judgment, including the assessment of the risks of material misstatement of the consolidated financial statements, whether due to fraud or error. In making those risk assessments, the auditor considers the internal control system relevant to the entity's preparation and fair presentation of the consolidated financial statements in order to design audit procedures that are appropriate in the circumstances, but not for the purpose of expressing an opinion on the effectiveness of the entity's internal control system. An audit also includes evaluating the appropriateness of the accounting policies used and the reasonableness of accounting estimates made, as well as evaluating the overall presentation of the consolidated financial statements. We believe that the audit evidence we have obtained is sufficient and appropriate to provide a basis for our audit opinion.

Opinion

In our opinion, the consolidated financial statements for the year ended 31 December 2011 give a true and fair view of the financial position, the results of operations and the cash flows in accordance with International Financial Reporting Standards (IFRS) and comply with Swiss law.

Report on other legal requirements

We confirm that we meet the legal requirements on licensing according to the Auditor Oversight Act (AOA) and independence (article 728 CO and article 11 AOA) and that there are no circumstances incompatible with our independence.

In accordance with article 728a paragraph 1 item 3 CO and Swiss Auditing Standard 890, we confirm that an internal control system exists, which has been designed for the preparation of consolidated financial statements according to the instructions of the Board of Directors.

We recommend that the consolidated financial statements submitted to you be approved.

KPMG SA
Geneva, 15 February 2012

Source: Nestlé, Financial Statements, 2011

Corporate governance

In recent years, more and more government and shareholder attention has been given to the question of how management's freedom of action may be limited by outside interests – a topic known as corporate governance. Corporate governance issues arise whenever ownership of a company is separated from its management. There are many issues in this area which cause concern to investors and governments. Abuses by management are not necessarily widespread, but sometimes the remuneration of top executives seems out of all proportion to the effort put in; sometimes managers are either implicated in or unaware of frauds taking place within the company, or indeed of risk-taking by middle management. Some company bosses are thought to be able to operate virtually as dictators, with no effective monitoring of their activity within the company.

Criticism in this area, articulated for example in the financial press, has produced a number of different outcomes. At a general level, most companies are not insensitive to the views of the outside world and make at least a token response by disclosing in their annual report some details of their activities in sensitive areas. Notably, companies are increasingly making voluntary disclosures about their interaction with the environment, their involvement with their employees and the wider community, and their policy on issues such as the use of child labour by subcontractors. In addition, institutional investors such as insurance companies and pension funds increasingly provide a checklist of corporate governance matters to the directors of the companies in which they plan to invest. Only if the board can satisfy them on these points will they go ahead and make an investment.

Many countries have specific rules, regulations and public guidance on corporate governance. Governance regimes tend to differ due to historical, economic and cultural influences. However, with the emergence of global markets national governance structures came under greater public scrutiny and these pressures resulted in a number of government or quasi-official reports (Viénot I and II in France, Cromme in Germany, from Cadbury to Higgs in the UK, OECD) and, more recently, in somewhat converging codes of conduct in most countries which tend to recommend the installation of supplementary controls on management and the distancing of management from the audit. The first plank of such an approach calls for companies to appoint a chairman who is not also the chief executive, and for the board to include 'non-executive' or independent directors who can bring experience and independence to the boardroom. The non-executive directors, aside from normal board meetings, are then called upon to form at least two key committees: the compensation committee (which fixes executives' pay packages) and the audit committee. The audit committee should provide a forum where external and internal auditors can discuss audit issues without line management being present. Sometimes there exists a third committee, the nomination committee, charged with the responsibility of proposing to the board any new executive or non-executive directors. It is generally recommended that a majority of the nomination committee members are non-executive directors.

The basic idea is that the non-executive directors have no role in the day-to-day running of the company, but are there to safeguard investors' interests and to provide ethical controls. Of course, for this to work, the individuals must be experienced in business matters and be willing to take a strong line within the board. It is not clear that this always works, not least because appointment of non-executive directors generally falls to the chairman or chief executive. However, in principle, the non-executives should be in a position to determine what is a fair pay package for senior executives by reference to market conditions. Equally, they should provide some protection for staff who wish to express concerns in the context of internal controls and audit. A frequently encountered problem in large companies is that even if staff are aware that some fraud or abuse is taking place, they are reluctant to report it because they fear that no action will be taken but their position will be made untenable. The existence of an audit committee should make it possible for staff to raise issues which are passed up the audit chain and not discussed with operational management until an investigation has taken place.

In some countries, notably Germany and the Netherlands, large companies have a two-tier board system where a management board runs the company on a day-to-day basis, but this reports to a supervisory board. The supervisory board represents investors and staff, receives regular reports on corporate activity and can replace the management board if they wish.

In the US, the Sarbanes–Oxley Act has been the main initiative to strengthen corporate governance after the Enron collapse. The SOX created the Public Company Accounting Oversight Board (PCAOB), strengthened auditor independence rules, increased accountability of company officers and directors, mandated top management to take responsibility for the company's internal control system, enhanced the quality of financial reporting and considerably increased white-collar crime penalties. We will come back to these developments in Chapter 16.

In Europe, the European Commission plans to modernize company law and enhance corporate governance. In October 2004, the European Commission formally established the European Corporate Governance forum to encourage the coordination and convergence of national codes of corporate governance through regular high-level meetings.

The accounting profession

It is worth spending a few moments to look at the accounting profession as such. In the anglophone world we tend to use the terms 'accountant' and 'auditor' interchangeably, and we tend not to distinguish very clearly between those people who operate independent public accounting firms and those who work for companies or in the public sector. Not the least reason for this is that there is no clear worldwide definition of what an accountant does and, indeed, the training and licensing arrangements and type of work done vary somewhat from country to country. For our purposes we will distinguish between the following categories:

1. independent auditor
2. independent accountant
3. company accountant.

Independent auditors are specialists who work in audit firms and are licensed either directly or indirectly by the government to carry out the *statutory audit* (i.e. independent audit required by company law) of large companies. An individual who works in this way has generally completed a university degree and then studied for professional exams. These exams are typically under the supervision of a professional organization (e.g. American Institute of Certified Public Accountants) and a candidate must also spend at least three years as a student in a public auditing firm. In some countries, such as the UK, success in the professional examination, allied with the necessary practical experience, confers an auditing licence automatically and this is issued by the professional body. In other countries (e.g. Germany) the auditor must register with a government supervisory body.

In fact many auditors leave public practice fairly early in their careers, either to undertake wider management careers or to work full time for a company. In anglophone countries, such accountants may well remain members of their professional body, but in many continental European countries, membership is linked to public practice and anyone leaving public practice leaves their professional body at the same time. This leads to professional bodies being quite different in size and nature. The Institut der Wirtschaftsprüfer (the only body for auditors of public companies in Germany) has approximately 18 000 members, while the Association of Chartered Certified Accountants (one of four bodies in the UK whose members may work as auditors) has more than 100 000 members.

The precise nature of the audit and the relationship between auditor and client vary from place to place. In France, the auditor has a public responsibility to report to the public prosecutor any evidence of a client's failure to comply with the law discovered during the audit. However, in most countries the company's information must be kept confidential by the auditor. There are also differences as to what the auditor is commenting on in the audit report – sometimes it is simply conformity with local accounting rules, while sometimes the auditor is saying that the image of the company given by the annual financial statements is not misleading. This difference is quite important since the user of the financial statements is being offered a different level of reassurance about the information.

It is relatively rare for audit firms to offer only an audit service, although France and Germany in particular say that the auditor, for reasons of independence, may only provide audit services to an audit client, even if they may offer other services to non-audit clients. Anglo-Saxon audit firms generally used to offer a wide range of consulting services to their audit clients and, indeed, provision of the audit was seen by some as the means of access to selling a wide range of consulting services. The Sarbanes–Oxley Act of 2002 put a stop to these practices, by prohibiting audit firms from providing a wide range of non-audit services to audit clients.

Independent accountants are a related branch of the profession. In some countries a network of firms has developed which offer accounting services to (generally small) businesses. In France there are, for example, the Experts Comptables, in Germany the Steuerberater and in the Netherlands the Accountant-Administratieconsulent. These firms specifically do not offer statutory audit for large companies and their principal role is in providing the accounting function for companies that are either too small to have an in-house service or that prefer to outsource the function. They may also provide tax and general business advice.

Company accountant, on the other hand, is a function not necessarily covered by any professional organization, and indeed many company accountants do not have any specific accounting training. At the management end of company accounting, the larger companies tend to engage former auditors or others with specialized professional training to run their accounting function. However, it is commonplace in both North America and continental Europe for people to study business at university, perhaps with an accounting specialization, and then go directly into a company and work in the accounting, internal audit and finance areas, building up a store of practical experience in that way.

Professional accounting bodies exist in most countries, but their nature may vary quite a lot depending on the nature of the economy within which they operate. In the developed world, the standards of professional exams for auditors are comparable, and indeed in the European Union are the subject of a harmonization statute (Eighth EC Company Law Directive), but in the developing world and in countries in transition to a market economy this is not necessarily so. Not all professional bodies have examination requirements for entry and not all are independent associations. For example, the Chinese Institute of Certified Public Accountants is an agency of the Chinese Ministry of Finance.

There are some regional bodies to which national bodies may belong, such as the Fédération des Experts Comptables Européens (European Accountants' Federation) or the Confederation of Asian and Pacific Accountants (CAPA). Finally there is, at a world level, the International Federation of Accountants (IFAC) which represents the profession worldwide and issues auditing standards and public sector accounting standards, as well as providing guidance on education and ethical matters.

Summary

In this chapter we have looked at the functioning of the company accounting unit and seen that its objectives are to provide accurate financial data about the company but also to provide controls which prevent the possibility of fraud. The company runs a permanent accounting database into which all transactions are recorded, processed and summarized, and from which one may at any point produce reports about the company's performance and financial position. The processing of transactions follows the same principles irrespective of whether it is computerized or not, but computerized accounting information systems are widespread and permit efficient accounting and sophisticated analysis.

In larger companies the accounting information system is an integral part of a 'system of internal control' which operates to safeguard assets, improve the reliability of accounting data, ensure compliance with applicable laws and contractual obligations and promote operational efficiencies. This system of internal control is usually backed up by an 'internal audit' function: dedicated staff checking that internal controls are applied and remain effective. Finally all public companies, and many private ones, are subject to independent audit by external auditors. These professionals also rely upon the internal control system and run sample checks on it in order to form an opinion on the accuracy of the company's financial records. They also give an opinion on the validity of the annual financial statements.

The external audit is a major part of a wider system of *corporate governance*, through which investors and other interested parties aim to monitor and control the behaviour of corporate managers, a subject which we will revisit later in the book. This involves the use of disclosures, adhesion to codes of behaviour and the use of board members who represent investor interests. The term 'accountant' or 'auditor' is used fairly freely and there are a number of professional structures and education patterns which occur in different countries. Generally, statutory auditors must be licensed by government and have completed suitable professional training and minimum periods of internship.

Discussion Questions

1. What are the objectives which a company's accounting department should be aiming to achieve?
2. How is the company's accounting database organized and from where does it get its data?
3. How does the COSO report approach a 'system of internal control'?
4. Explain the difference between preventive, detective and corrective controls.
5. What is the relationship between internal control and internal audit?
6. What is the purpose of external audit, and who carries this out?

PART TWO

Basic financial statements

Part Two goes through the main techniques which are used to prepare the basic financial statements – the statement of profit or loss (income statement/profit and loss account) and the statement of financial position (balance sheet) – of individual companies. These are the basic building blocks of financial reporting.

Measurement concepts and the balance sheet equation

Chapter 3 introduces two of the main financial statements. It then goes on to explain the basic assumptions and conventions which are applied to financial accounting and which therefore provide the framework that both limits and informs accounting information. The chapter introduces the balance sheet equation, which represents the fundamental logic on which accounting is based. We will end this chapter with a closer look at how the IASB defines the content of the basic elements of a statement of financial position and profit and loss account.

Chapter Structure

- Introduction
- The balance sheet does not purport to show what the company is worth
- Company characteristics affecting financial reporting behaviour
- Content of financial statements
- The basics of accounting measurement
- Generally accepted accounting principles
- Conventional measurement bases
- Accounting for transactions
- The IASB definition and recognition criteria for elements of the statement of financial position and the statement of profit or loss

- Summary
- Discussion questions
- Assignments

Introduction

In general terms the annual financial statements produced by a business for external consumption (also known as the annual accounts, annual report) are the single public source of economic data on the company and they represent a prime form of communication between the company and its external stakeholders. The statements of larger companies are usually subject to verification by external experts (auditors) and are made available to shareholders. They form the starting point for tax assessment. They are usually of prime interest to all main business partners: banks, other lenders, suppliers of goods and services, major customers. They are often, particularly in large companies, an important device used to monitor contracts (bank covenants, profit shares in joint ventures, employee bonuses, royalties).

In most European jurisdictions there is a requirement for the financial statements to be filed at a public registry so that, even if the company does not provide a copy of the financial statements directly to an interested party, access to them is still available (for example, in the UK there is a single government office which holds all company files; in Belgium they are held by the Banque Nationale de Belgique, but in Switzerland access is restricted; while in Germany many small and medium-sized companies deliberately do not file their financial statements – the fine is minimal). In the US, however, there is no filing system for private companies.

Listed companies also put their financial statements on their website (in html or pdf format) and generally make physical copies of their annual report available to anyone who cares to ask for it – indeed, they see it as a major public relations document – while small, privately owned companies will give up information only when the law or their business interest decrees it.

Historically, the balance sheet and the statement of profit or loss have been the key financial statements, even though a modern corporation is now expected to publish a balance sheet (statement of financial position), statement of profit or loss and other comprehensive income (statement of comprehensive income), statement of changes in equity, statement of cash flows and notes to the accounts. The statement of profit or loss is undergoing a period of change and the IASB prefers to refer to a 'statement of profit or loss and other comprehensive income' (or, alternatively, 'statement of comprehensive income'). This includes not only the results of operations, but also changes in economic values (reported as 'other comprehensive income') We will deal with that in Part Four of this book, and for the time being will refer only to the statement of profit or loss. Indeed, at this point in the book we will concentrate only on the balance sheet and the profit and loss account, since these are at the heart of the reporting system.

The statement of profit or loss sets out the result of the company's business operations for the accounting period (revenues less expenses for the period), while the balance sheet shows, at a given date, the company's financial position: what economic resources (assets) such as factories, equipment, inventory, cash and so on the company owns or controls and where the company's finance comes from (banks, shareholders, etc. – liabilities and equity).

The balance sheet does not purport to show what the company is worth

This issue crops up from time to time in MBA courses and is obviously a key question if one's main interest in looking at the annual financial statements is to form an opinion on the economic health and prospects of the company. Usually, when we ask what a company is 'worth', this means what would we have to pay to acquire the company and this in turn is linked to the value of the future benefits which one would gain by buying the company. If Company X will deliver a dividend (or net positive cash flow) of €10 000 a year for ten years, a first estimate of its total value over ten years is €100 000. Since, if you buy the company, you cannot enjoy all the benefits at once, you would normally be willing to pay less than €100 000 for it – you would deduct a discount to factor in the time value of money and the riskiness of the estimated cash flows. The price agreed is a compromise between the value to the purchaser and what the seller is willing to sell for. In fact, takeover situations typically arise because Company A believes that it can reorganize Company X (maybe there are savings to be made by combining operations) and deliver more than €10 000 a year from it. In this case the owners of Company X will value it on the basis of €10 000 a year but Company A will make a bid at a higher price, so there is a basis for a deal.

The point is that company value, from a market perspective, is (a) based on *future* earnings and (b) these earnings may well be different in different situations. Financial statements give certain economic information about a company's *past* activities, drawn up according to a fairly flexible set of rules. They give partial information, and anyone wanting to make serious use of the statements needs to know (a) what are the rules, (b) to what extent are they flexible, and (c) how this impacts upon interpretation of the information.

On top of that, anyone looking across national boundaries needs to know whether the company uses IFRS and its figures are comparable with other companies internationally, or whether it is using national accounting principles. If the latter is the case, one needs to know how the rules differ from one jurisdiction to another, where different flexibilities arise and so forth (which is much more complicated and is one reason why companies prefer IFRS). Once the analyst has decoded the accounting information, then he or she can make a forecast of future earnings from that information about past performance (and related external factors) and come to a view about the company's worth.

Company characteristics affecting financial reporting behaviour

This brings us to another major point: while the bulk of accounting rules for commercial companies are the same in all developed countries, there are differences at a detailed level from one country to another (as discussed in Chapter 1). Also, the way the rules are applied may differ from one company to another within the same country. While the way companies record and track their transactions in their accounting systems does not vary substantially, the way these are presented in annual financial statements may be subject to significant variations. The rush to use IFRS for listed companies is motivated by a desire to get away from the uncertainties caused by national differences.

However, differences in the accounting rule base used are not the only source of difference in financial statements. Looking first at businesses within one country, there are many differences which impact upon reporting, such as the nature of their ownership, their objectives, their legal form and their size.

Nature of ownership

Most European market economies are in fact mixed economies, with a large slice of activity in the hands of commercial companies but also with a significant element owned by the State. Where a business is owned by the State, its management may have different objectives from those of an ordinary commercial concern, for example, it may not be politically acceptable to show too much profit or the government may want to fatten the company up for privatization. State-owned enterprises may not operate under the same regulations as private sector firms.

In the private sector it is easy to see two extremes: the large, multinational company listed on several stock exchanges and the small company owned entirely by its chief executive. A company whose securities are traded on the capital markets has a major concern in terms of maintaining the buoyancy of the share price and this is likely to lead the company either to release good news as soon as possible and hide bad news as long as possible, or to make an attempt to smooth profits so that the company appears to go from one successful year to another in a reliable progression. For these companies the capital market is a privileged user of their financial information and the rules are likely to be applied by such companies in ways that will influence the market reaction. The management of the company and its owners are separate and distinct from each other, and the financial statements play a significant role in the conduct of that relationship.

The small company at the other extreme has no external shareholders to whom to report. The manager is also the main shareholder and so the reporting pressures are likely to be different. Such a manager might be more concerned about keeping reported profits as low as possible in order to reduce tax **liability**. Or, if it is a family company, the manager may want to keep profits low so that relatives will not demand high dividends and cash can be kept in the business to finance expansion.

These are archetypes and there exist many variants. There are, for example, large, family-owned companies which are not listed on stock exchanges (e.g. Firmenich, Bosch, Mars). There is a particularly large number of these in Germany and Switzerland and this gives rise to another issue, which is the extent to which the community calls for businesses of significant economic size to make financial disclosures purely because their size may cause them to impact upon public interest.

Managerial objectives

The nature of a company's ownership generally impacts upon its objectives. A State or other public sector entity probably has objectives other than profit generation, a listed company may want to angle towards maximizing declared short-term profits (or not – it depends upon the culture of the capital markets where it operates), a privately held company might want to minimize profits in order to minimize tax and dividends. On the other hand, a privately held company that is planning to be listed on the capital markets in the future might choose to maximize profits. A commercial company listed on stock exchanges (a publicly held company) might be looking for long-term growth and be quite willing to take low profits while it builds market share. So while ownership and objectives are often closely interlinked, this is not always the case.

STANDARD PRACTICE

IFRS – WHY GLOBAL FINANCIAL REPORTING STANDARDS FOR SMEs?
(extracts)

BC36 Global financial reporting standards, applied consistently, enhance the comparability of financial information. Accounting differences can obscure the comparisons that investors, lenders and others make. By resulting in the presentation of high quality comparable financial information, high quality global financial reporting standards improve the efficiency of allocation and the pricing of capital. This benefits not only those who provide debt or equity capital but also those entities that seek capital because it reduces their compliance costs and removes uncertainties that affect their cost of capital. Global standards also improve consistency in audit quality and facilitate education and training.

BC37 The benefits of global financial reporting standards are not limited to entities whose securities are traded in public capital markets. In the Board's judgement, small and medium-sized entities – and those who use their financial statements – can benefit from a common set of accounting standards. SMEs' financial statements that are comparable from one country to the next are needed for the following reasons:

(a) Financial institutions make loans across borders and operate multinationally. In most jurisdictions, over half of all SMEs, including the very small ones, have bank loans. Bankers rely on financial statements in making lending decisions and in establishing terms and interest rates.

(b) Vendors want to evaluate the financial health of buyers in other countries before they sell goods or services on credit.

(c) Credit rating agencies try to develop ratings uniformly across borders. Similarly, banks and other institutions that operate across borders often develop ratings in a manner similar to credit rating agencies. Reported financial figures are crucial to the rating process.

(d) Many SMEs have overseas suppliers and use a supplier's financial statements to assess the prospects of a viable long-term business relationship.

(e) Venture capital firms provide funding to SMEs across borders.

(f) Many SMEs have outside investors who are not involved in the day-to-day management of the entity. Global accounting standards for general purpose financial statements and the resulting comparability are especially important when those outside investors are located in a different jurisdiction from the entity and when they have interests in other SMEs.

Source: IASB, IFRS for SMEs, Basis for Conclusions, July 2009

Nature of activity

Company activity is another variable. This is at its most obvious in regulations that affect banks and insurance companies. All jurisdictions have separate regulatory mechanisms for the accounting and disclosure requirements for financial institutions. These may relate to requirements for ordinary commercial companies (the Fourth EC Company Law Directive – a major accounting statute of the European Union – has banking and insurance variants) but usually go beyond them because of the different nature of the assets and liabilities of such companies and the profound effects on society of the failure of financial institutions. In this book we shall concentrate on the financial statements of ordinary commercial companies.

Legal form

Another significant variable in financial reporting within most countries is that of legal form. The major difference is generally between limited liability companies and entities that do not enjoy limited liability. For example, the European Fourth and Seventh Company Law Directives are based on legal form (and then size). Limited liability companies are those whose owners risk only the capital they put into a company – if the company makes a loss, the owners cannot be pursued for more money than they originally agreed to subscribe. Such limited liability vehicles are split in the Fourth EC Company Law Directive between public limited companies (which issue shares of equal value and may be listed on stock exchanges), such as the Aktiengesellschaft in Germany or the Société Anonyme in France, and private limited companies (Gesellschaft mit beschränkter Haftung, Société à responsabilité limitée, etc.) whose capital cannot be publicly traded and which do not necessarily issue shares as such – a Société à responsabilité limitée has 'company parts'.

In anglophone countries, absence of limited liability may also go with absence of regulation in financial reporting terms. In Britain, there are large auditing and consultancy firms employing thousands of people and with sales running into millions of pounds sterling which are constituted as partnerships where partners are personally liable for the full amount of all debts of the partnership, but there is no legal obligation to publish any accounts. The Church of England is probably the biggest landowner in the country, but publishes no financial statements.

Company size

In continental Europe accounting regulations tend to run with the nature of the business (a commercial business follows the same basic accounting rules irrespective of size) but disclosures are modified according to size. The European accounting directives recognize four tiers of size, which are subject to change from time to time. The latest proposals are:

- *micro-entity* – must not exceed two out of the following: sales €0.7m, total assets €0.35m, employees ten
- *small company* – must not exceed two out of the following: sales €10.0m, total assets €5.0m, employees 50;
- *medium company* – must not exceed two out of the following: sales €40.0m, total assets €20.0m, employees 250;
- *large company* – any listed entity, and all that exceed medium-size criteria.

The European Commission introduced the 'micro-entity' reliefs with a 2012 directive. The Commission also announced in 2011 plans to replace the Fourth and Seventh Directive with a single updated directive.

Small companies may benefit from limited public disclosure and freedom from audit. These size criteria are built into reporting regulations within the European Union and outside it. There is nothing self-evidently 'right' about the EU's criteria, but they do give recognition to the idea that small, privately held companies need not disclose as much as large companies, which is a view expressed in many countries, even if the precise cut-off between 'small' and 'not small' is necessarily arbitrary.

In overall terms, it is true to say that published financial statements are aimed at a wide range of potential users, including (actual or potential) shareholders, lenders, trade suppliers, tax authorities, customers, employees, etc. However, the company faces a need to present a different face for different users. It can only provide one, general-purpose set of financial statements but where accounting rules provide any choices (and there are many instances) different companies will choose measurements that give priority to different subsets of users. Some will maximize profit, others will minimize it and so on. These factors have to be considered when evaluating any particular company's financial statements.

Content of financial statements

The core financial reporting process involves preparing an annual statement of profit or loss (or income statement) and a statement of financial position (or balance sheet). The statement of profit or loss brings together aggregated information about a company's performance during a 12-month period (most often the calendar year, but in some countries not necessarily that). The balance sheet shows the state of the company's financial position at the end of that year. Both statements are usually published with comparative data from the previous year (Figure 3.1). The statement of profit or loss might be said to be reporting a 'flow' (business activities during a period) while the balance sheet is essentially a status report – a static inventory of the company's financial position at a given moment (a 'snapshot' of an instant in time).

While the published data usually only show two years (although the Securities and Exchange Commission or SEC asks for three years of income

Figure 3.1

Time periods covered by the statement of financial position and statement of profit or loss

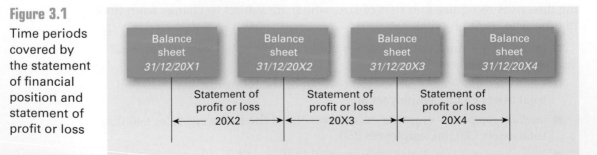

statements for publicly listed companies in the US), analysts need data for a longer time scale and therefore build up collections of annual reports or use inputs from commercial company data services so that they can look at five- and ten-year runs of data and get a wider picture of the progression of a company's economic state.

Obviously, we are going to look in some detail at the content of these statements during this course. However, the intention here is just to introduce them and you should concentrate on the broad lines and picking up the vocabulary.

The structure of a statement of profit or loss is as follows:

Statement of profit or loss for period 20X1

		€'000
Sales		5 356
Raw materials	1 739	
Salaries and wages	783	
Depreciation	462	
External services	873	(3 857)
Profit before interest and tax		*1 499*
Interest		(362)
Profit before taxation		*1 137*
Taxation		(384)
Profit available for shareholders		753

You can see that this format can be split into two different sections, of which the main distinctions are:

1. operating result
2. returns to interested parties other than the owners (providers of loan finance and government).

Looking at the operating result, the approach to expenses shown in this format is known as the *value-added approach*: it shows inputs and outputs and enables the analyst to calculate the value added by the company in transforming raw materials into finished goods (assuming it is a manufacturing company). This is the most common approach in continental Europe.

The alternative approach to presenting operating data is that used more often in the UK and US, which splits expenses not by type of expense, but by the activity to which the expense was assigned (in the technical jargon we refer to a value-added presentation as showing *expenses by nature* while the alternative shows *expenses by function*). The Anglo-Saxon style of format is shown overleaf:

Statement of profit or loss for period 20X1

		€'000
Sales		5 356
Cost of sales		(2 601)
		2 755
Distribution costs	382	
Administrative expenses	874	(1256)
Profit before interest and tax		*1 499*
Interest		(362)
Profit before taxation		*1 137*
Taxation		(384)
Profit available for shareholders		*753*

This kind of disclosure approach involves allocating raw materials, salaries, depreciation and other costs against the three functional areas of cost of sales (manufacturing cost in this case), distribution (marketing, advertising, warehousing and other selling costs) and administration (accounting, legal, general management expenses). In our example, the expenses are being presented in one of two ways:

Nature		*Function*	
	€'000		€'000
Raw materials	1 739	Cost of sales	2 601
Salaries and wages	783	Distribution costs	382
Depreciation expense	462	Administrative expenses	874
External services	873		
Total	3 857	Total	3 857

Opinions differ as to which is the more useful form for analysts. The International Accounting Standards Board (IASB) says there is a case for providing both. Some would say that showing costs by function enables a clearer comparison of efficiency between one company and another in the same industry. For example, if comparing two companies which both manufactured similar forklift trucks, you could compare cost of sales as a percentage of sales revenue to see who was manufacturing more cheaply – or who was making the largest difference (gross margin) between selling price and manufacturing cost. However, many companies do not have just a single product and so the opportunity for extremely precise comparisons does not usually occur. In addition, the allocation of expenses across functions must up to a point be subjective – if a canteen is used by both manufacturing and administrative staff, how much do you allocate to each function? Different companies might have different views.

In any event, this first part of the statement of profit or loss deals with a company's operating activities and provides a basis for comparisons with other years and other companies, irrespective of their financial structure or other consider-ations. The lower part of the statement of profit or loss, on the other hand, shows how the profit generated by the company is split up:

■ interest (payment to those who have provided the company's loan capital);

■ taxation paid to government (society's share);

■ profit retained in the company (to pay dividends to shareholders and to finance future expansion, etc.) and which is in effect the wealth generated by the company in that year.

The taxation identified here is tax on profits or income and does not include elements such as value-added tax (excluded from the statement of profit or loss), import taxes (included under relevant cost headings such as raw materials) and social security charges (included in personnel costs). The level of interest charges is a function of the degree to which the company has been financed by debt.

The statement of financial position presents a picture of the company's finances at the end of the financial year and the assets (factories, machinery, patents, brands, etc.) which it has acquired and which have not yet been consumed within the business. The presentation of information in the balance sheet follows precise rules, although the detail again may vary from one jurisdiction to another. One of two formats offered by the Fourth EC Company Law Directive is known as a horizontal balance sheet and this is probably the format most commonly used in continental Europe. This would look as follows:

Assets		Equity and liabilities	
Intangible assets	943	Share capital	2 455
Tangible assets	1 988	Reserves	982
Investments	213	Retained profit	947
Non-current (or 'fixed') assets	*3 144*	*Shareholders' equity*	*4 384*
Inventory	1 589	Provisions	520
Receivables	973	Financial liabilities	1 500
Cash at bank	881	Trade liabilities	359
Deferred charges	176		
Total	6 763	Total	6 763

Some US companies use the horizontal format, but with the elements presented in the reverse order (note also the somewhat different US terminology):

Assets		Liabilities and equity	
Cash at bank	881	Trade payables	359
Deferred charges	176	Debt	1 500
Receivables	973	Provisions	520
Inventory	1 589		
Non-current Assets		*Equity*	
Investments	213	Ordinary stock	2 455
Tangible assets	1 988	Reserves	982
Intangible assets	943	Retained profit	947
Total	6 763	Total	6 763

The left-hand side of the balance sheet shows the company's assets, split into those which will be used up over a period of more than one year (**non-current assets** or long-term assets) – typically physical plant (tangible assets), patents, brand names, licences (**intangible assets**) and investments (shares or loans to other companies, often made for strategic purposes to cement a business relationship, investments in subsidiary companies). The remaining assets are usually constantly changing and are generated by the company's operating activities. Inventories are being diminished every day as sales take place, but also are being increased as new inventory is bought or manufactured. Amounts due from customers (receivables) would normally also be changing day to day: a company will normally always have inventories and receivables, but the individual items which make up the total are constantly changing.

The amounts stated for each asset are expressed in currency units. As such, they reflect only those matters that can be measured in monetary terms. The balance sheet shows the assets (and liabilities) of the business rather than of the individuals associated with it.

The right-hand side of the balance sheet shows the company's financing. This is split into *capital* (which is a word to be wary of in accounting because it has different meanings in different contexts, but here means money put into the company by the owners: *shares* or, in the US, *stock* and we will call it equity), **provisions** (the company has a liability to pay something in the future, although the precise amount or timing may be uncertain), financial liabilities (loans made by banks, the financial markets, etc.) and trade liabilities (in the US, *payables*, debts due to suppliers – of raw materials, finished goods, etc.).

An alternative balance sheet format is the *vertical balance sheet*. This shows the same information but presents it in a different way: liabilities are shown as a deduction from assets, and are split according to when they are due for payment, while the horizontal format shows them according to whether they are financing or for trade.

The balance sheet data presented in the vertical format would look like this:

	€'000	€'000
Intangibles	943	
Tangible assets	1 988	
Investments	213	
Non-current assets		3 144
Inventories	1 589	
Receivables and prepaid	1 149	
Cash at bank	881	
Current assets	3 619	
Creditors due in less than one year	(359)	
Net current assets		3 260
Creditors due in more than one year		(1 500)
Provisions		(520)
		4 384
Equity		
Ordinary shares		2 455
Reserves		982
Retained profits		947
		4 384

In a published set of financial statements, the shareholders (and other users) receive not only this information but several pages of explanatory notes which amplify the information and analyze certain categories such as non-current assets. Part of this extra detail is sometimes included in the basic statements themselves ('on the face of the accounts', as accountants would say). This additional information is regulated and many of the insights that an analyst wants from the annual financial statements are gained from a thorough review of the notes rather than the primary statements.

For the most part the same information is given in the balance sheet whichever way it is presented. The horizontal presentation gives a picture of the whole company: total assets and the total financing which has been used to acquire those assets. This is sometimes called an *entity* approach, treating the company as an economic whole and not distinguishing between different providers of finance. This is summed up as:

Assets = Equity *and* Liabilities

This contrasts with the vertical presentation which focuses on the interest of the owners, and is known as a *proprietary approach*. This second approach says the owners' interest is measured by starting with the value of the assets and deducting loans and other payables from this amount:

$$\text{Assets } less \text{ Liabilities} = \text{Equity}$$

What is left is the owners' equity. This approach is often used in measuring personal wealth, but using a current market value: a family who bought a house with a loan might calculate (a) the current value of the house and (b) the amount of loan outstanding, and would arrive at the current value of their interest (equity) by deducting (b) from (a). Traditional accounting does not use current values, of course, so the value of the 'equity' number in the balance sheet does not equate to a current or market value of the company.

The IASB Conceptual Framework includes definitions of assets, liabilities and equity. These definitions are important because an item should meet the criteria contained in the definitions to be eligible as an IFRS balance sheet item. We will go into the details of these definitions later on in this chapter, but of specific relevance here is that the IASB defines equity as the residual interest in the assets of a company after deducting all its liabilities.

At present neither the IASB nor the FASB prescribe the format of the financial statements, they specify what minimum information must be given, but not how it is presented. However, they did start a joint project (*Financial Statement Presentation*) whose aim is to provide new formats. This project has been set aside at the time of writing and is unlikely to be finalized any time soon (see Chapter 18).

The basics of accounting measurement

In the next sections of this chapter we are going to review the basic accounting principles by which financial statements are prepared. We will do this in the following stages:

- a consideration of the underlying accounting assumptions and conventions;
- a review of the data recording process within companies;
- an analysis of the balance sheet equation;
- a practical exercise in tracking transactions using the balance sheet equation;
- preparing simple financial statements.

Some knowledge of the accounts preparation process is essential for any sensible interpretation of the end product: the financial statements. The reason for this is that the statements are today highly technical documents which make many assumptions about the state of knowledge of the reader. It is quite impossible for an untrained reader to make much sense of the accounts; for example, just the technical terms (accruals? reserves? provisions?) immediately put the general reader at a disadvantage.

In fact the problems go a lot further than that. Accounting measurement does not purport to provide a total measurement system which gives a rounded economic picture of the company, even if the general public is inclined to believe that it does. The measurement system is based on a series of conventions which automatically limit the information taken into it, and which then demand that accounts preparers use many estimates in allocating revenues and expenses to one year rather than another. Accounting measurement is a very subjective process, giving a partial picture.

In a sense the only absolutely accurate measure of profit is not available until the company has ceased to exist and its assets have been sold and its liabilities paid off – at that point you can calculate all the inputs to the business from its start-up to its final liquidation and arrive at a precise profit for its whole life. This, however, is not very useful in managing the company, and accounting is the art of estimating what proportion of the life profit of the company has been earned in a particular (usually 12-month) period. In order to arrive at this estimate the accountant has to make many assumptions about the future of the company and the uncertainties that surround it. While most accounting information is clear and exactly quantifiable, the profit measure also includes allocations of expenses (and less frequently revenues) between years. No allocation is incontestable, and the published profit figure is therefore an estimate, not a matter of fact, and is subject to correction in subsequent years.

This does not mean that the information is of no use – quite the contrary – but it does mean that the user needs to be clear about what exactly is the nature of the information given in financial statements and therefore needs to understand the essentials of the measurement process. It is rather like driving a car: you look most of the time at the road immediately ahead of you, because that is where the most important decisions lie. It is a convention that traffic driving in the opposite direction to you will use the opposite side of the road, so you need not watch that side so intently, even if to have a complete picture you should be looking at both sides, as well as behind you.

Accounting information is subject to constraints, which you need to know in order to interpret it, but it is also subject to estimate, which makes it flexible and open to manipulation.

Generally accepted accounting principles

The foundation of financial accounting consists of a set of assumptions, conventions and rules referred to as _Generally Accepted Accounting Principles_ (or GAAP). According to the authority which establishes the principles, different GAAP sets can be discerned, like European GAAP (EC Accounting Directives) and related national GAAP, US GAAP and IFRS GAAP. Although different GAAP sets have a lot of principles in common, significant degrees of freedom still exist. In this section we will focus on IFRS GAAP.

Most accounting regimes specify some general qualitative objective of accounting: in France this was that the accounts should be sincere and regular, while in Germany they should conform to the principles of good book-keeping. The European Fourth Company Law Directive specifies two objectives: the accounts should conform to GAAP and should give a true and fair view of the financial state of the company. IFRS, however, require that the financial statements 'present fairly the financial position, financial performance and cash flows'. There is a UK legal opinion that says for the purposes of company law the IFRS 'fairly present' means the same as 'give a true and fair view'.

The idea of a 'true and fair view' delete is a fundamental requirement of the European Accounting Directives. It is referred to in the audit opinion and derives from British accounting, but there is endless discussion about what it actually means – it has not been defined in law or by standard-setters. The unwary reader of financial statements might think that it means the accounts are both true and fair, or perhaps that the financial statements are not misleading. This would be a dangerous position.

The safer assumption is that the term merely means that the financial statements have been prepared by respecting all the technical rules in force at the time of their preparation. In theory, if application of the rules does not give a clear picture (or perhaps would be positively misleading), further explanation should be given in the notes.

If you think about it, for financial statements to be useful and comparable, they need to follow some kind of generally agreed rules. However, as soon as you start to measure according to pre-specified rules, you automatically limit what can be shown in the financial statements.

STANDARDS

The IASB's *Conceptual Framework for* Financial Reporting (introduced in Chapter One) specifies the following:

OB2 The objective of general purpose financial reporting is to provide financial information about the reporting entity that is useful to present and potential equity investors, lenders and other creditors in making decisions about providing resources to the entity. Those decisions involve buying, selling or holding equity and debt instruments, and providing or settling loans and other forms of credit.

Source: IASB Conceptual Framework for Financial Reporting, Chapter One The Objective of Financial Reporting September 2010

For our purposes, you should be sceptical as to whether the existence of the true and fair view principle improves the quality of financial statements, and rely rather more heavily on the other European Fourth Directive requirement that the financial statements should use generally accepted accounting principles. The auditor's report will normally confirm that these have been followed. In the US, the expression 'present fairly in accordance with GAAP' is to be interpreted in this sense.

The IASB rules actually confirm this pragmatic view. According to IFRS, the general objective of financial statements is to give a fair presentation of the (changes in) financial position and performance of a company. The old IASB *Framework* suggested that fair presentation could also be referred to as giving 'a true and fair view', but IAS 1, *Presentation of Financial Statements*, puts forward the main premise that the application of IFRS, with additional disclosure if necessary, is presumed to result in financial statements reflecting a fair presentation. Only in extremely rare circumstances in which management concludes that compliance with IFRS requirements would be so misleading that it would conflict with the objective of financial statements, is a rebuttal of the basic full compliance assumption justified.

At a more applied level, financial accounting follows some key basic conventions, which can be found in the Fourth Company Law Directive:

- *consistency*
- *accrual basis:* accruals and related matching
- *prudence*
- *going concern*.

While **prudence** is a primary measurement convention in the European Fourth Directive, its application in IFRS is much more debated. The earlier standards (IAS) will often reflect it but the IASB tends to the view, set out in the revised joint *Conceptual Framework* and cited above, that accounting information should be **neutral**.

STANDARD

🌐 **IAS 1-PRESENTATION OF FINANCIAL STATEMENTS** *(extracts)*

Fair presentation and compliance with IFRSs

15 Financial statements shall present fairly the financial position, financial performance and cash flows of an entity. Fair presentation requires the faithful representation of the effects of transactions, other events and conditions in accordance with the definitions and recognition criteria for assets, liabilities, income and expenses set out in the *Framework.* The application of IFRSs, with additional disclosure when necessary, is presumed to result in financial statements that achieve a fair presentation.

Source: IAS 1, Presentation of Financial Statements

The significance of these conventions is not conveyed merely by reciting what is understood by them – that is something which comes out in the context of looking at their application to particular accounting problems. However, we need to start somewhere, so we will look at the meaning of these conventions as applied to financial reporting.

Consistency

Consistency is fairly straightforward. It means that accounting measurement practices should be used by a company consistently both from one year to another, and within the same year in relation to similar transactions. It could be argued that from an analyst's point of view, consistency is the most important characteristic needed in financial accounting. If the analyst is looking to put together several years' data to produce a forecast of future performance, each year needs to be prepared on a basis consistent with that in the other years. For predictive purposes the rate and direction of change of the indicators is more important than their absolute values, so a set of indicators, even if only partial in terms of the overall economic picture, if it is produced consistently will provide useful information.

The extent to which financial statements actually are consistent is open to question. Most jurisdictions require companies to explain any change in accounting methods in the notes to the accounts and to provide, where a change takes place, alternative figures showing the effects of the change. However, there is often a grey area between changing estimates or assumptions upon which allocations were based and actually changing the accounting method.

For example, suppose it has been assumed that a certain piece of plant, costing €10m, will last for ten years and therefore its cost should be allocated against profits on the basis of €1m a year. After four years the company decides that the plant will really last 20 years, so the annual charge goes down from €1m to €0.375m (spreading the remaining book value of €6m over the remaining **useful life** of 16 years). The retrospective annual charge of €0.5m goes further down to a prospective annual charge of €0.375m, since €4m have already been expensed in the first three years, while only €2m was appropriate under the new estimate. Generally this manoeuvre would not be classified as a change in accounting policy, but only a change in estimates, and would not call for any explanation in the notes, even though the profit in year five (and the following years) is inflated by the adjustment.

Consistency evidently has an important presentational dimension as well. IAS 1, *Presentation of Financial Statements*, para 45, explicitly states that the presentation and classification of items in financial statements should be retained from one accounting period to the next. However, a significant change in the nature or scope of the operations of the company (for example through an acquisition, disposal or reorganization of operations) may justify a presentational change. In that case comparative information must also be adapted on a consistent basis. Consistency in measurement is only covered indirectly in the IASB rules, where the IASB Conceptual Framework extends the qualitative characteristic of comparability to recognition and measurement issues.

Accrual basis

Accruals is the name of the approach which distinguishes accounting from a simple record of cash transactions. The accruals convention is that accounting aims to measure business transactions at the time they take place, rather than when cash changes hands. For example, a department store offers credit to its regular customers and is given credit by its suppliers. Suppose that the store agrees to take a special consignment of video cameras from a manufacturer. The cameras are delivered on 15 December. The store runs a special advertising campaign at 1 January. You go into the store on 10 January and buy a camera, charging it to your account. On 31 January the store pays its camera supplier, and bills you. You settle your account on 26 February (see Figure 3.2).

Figure 3.2
Sequence
of trade
transactions

Transactions:	
15 December:	delivery by supplier to store
10 January:	you buy camera
31 January:	store pays supplier
26 February:	you pay store

Under a simple cash recording system there would be an inventory purchase on 31 January and a sale on 26 February, and yet we know that you actually went into the store and took the goods on 10 January. The accruals convention is that transactions are recorded as they take place, not only when there is cash involved. So the accruals system would log the incoming inventory on 15 December, the sale on 10 January and so on. The **accruals basis of accounting** leads to financial statements that reflect not only information of past transactions involving the payment and receipt of cash but also of **obligations** to pay cash in the future (arising when the new inventory is accounted for) and of resources that represent cash to be received in the future (recording a receivable when the sale is recognized on 10 January).

This brings us to the related convention of **matching**. This says that all costs and revenues associated with a particular transaction should be brought together when the sale takes place. This means that, in our example, when the store buys the inventory of cameras, they are treated as an asset (an item of value owned by the company) and shown in the balance sheet as inventory (not taken to the statement of profit or loss account as an expense). Only when the individual camera is sold does it move from being inventory to being an expense. Otherwise in the example the expense would fall into December and the related revenue into January. If the store's financial year ended on 31 December, this would cause the first year's profit to be reduced and the second year's to be inflated. The matching convention requires us to put both revenue and expense in the same financial period (the one where the revenue was earned – see the section below on prudence).

In the example it is clear when each transaction takes place and there is no ambiguity about any of the transactions. However, there can be problems in this kind of area. For example, what if the camera turns out to be faulty and you return it, demanding your money back? Should the store not account for any sale until sufficient time has elapsed to be sure that the customer is satisfied? Ambiguities and uncertainties bring about conflicts with the next convention, that of prudence.

Prudence

Basically the *prudence* convention requires that revenues are only recognized in the accounts when they are certain, while expenses should be recognized if they are **probable**. Related to this, revenues should only be recognized when *realized*, that is, when these are sufficiently concrete to be in cash or a form near to cash (an agreement to pay on which the company can go to court). Unrecoverable expenses, though, should be recognized even if not yet realized – for example, you have spent €5000 working on a contract to design software for a client and you hear that the client may be having financial difficulties. Matching would require that you carry the costs forward (as a **current asset**) until you can invoice the client, but a prudent view would be to treat the work as a loss because the client's situation is open to question. This also has the effect of diminishing current year profit (and therefore tax), with the possibility of higher profit the following year. Tax management is mostly about deferring tax payments for as long as possible rather than escaping them altogether. While everyone would like to escape tax, if the accounts are accurate this is generally not possible (outside sophisticated, often cross-border, sets of linked companies, etc.) and the tax manager's objective is to defer tax as long as possible and thereby conserve the company's cash and reduce its financing needs.

At a theoretical level, there is a clear conflict between the application of matching and that of prudence, and the extent to which the one has priority over the other is one of the major differences in the application of accounting between one jurisdiction and another. Germany and Switzerland are famous for very prudent accounting (anticipating expenses, building secret reserves), while the UK is equally so for giving priority to the matching convention (deferring expenses, building hidden losses …).

At a practical level, the degree to which prudence is given a priority has also something to do with tax regulations. In the UK, tax rules only allow the recognition of an expense when that expense has become concrete – a prudent anticipation of an expense is disregarded for tax purposes, with the result that a company that follows very prudent accounting also appears to pay proportionately higher taxes. In France or Germany some anticipation of expenses in the form of provisions is acceptable for tax, provided that it appears in the company accounts, thereby encouraging companies to be prudent in their accounting because that defers their taxes.

In the IASB Framework the meaning of prudence is restricted to an attitude of caution in the exercise of judgements when these are needed to arrive at estimates under conditions of uncertainty such that assets or income are not overstated and liabilities or expenses understated. In the negative sense, the IASB warns that prudence should not lead to 'income smoothing', for example through the creation of undervalued assets or excessive provisions, because these practices lead to financial statements which are not neutral and, therefore, would not have the quality of reliability and representational faithfulness.

Going concern

The going concern convention specifies that in preparing the financial statements it is assumed that the company will continue in business for the foreseeable future. This is a critical assumption because much of accrual accounting measurement is based on allocating expenses over different future time periods, as we have already touched upon. If the business is unlikely to be there in the future, this approach is not valid and prudence would require many items to be written off at once as valueless. This is, of course, often a bone of contention with auditors when a company whose financial statements they have signed then goes out of business a few months later. People who have relied on the financial statements find the figures become meaningless when the company is no longer in business. The going concern assumption is used to justify the valuation procedures and is therefore a major assumption which should be considered by anyone analyzing the financial statements.

In fact, IAS 1, *Presentation of Financial Statements*, paras 25/26, requires management to make an assessment of the company's ability to continue as a going concern when it prepares the financial statements. If management is aware of material uncertainties related to events or conditions that may cast significant doubt upon the company's ability to continue as a going concern, those uncertainties have to be disclosed. If one concludes that the going concern basis is no longer appropriate, this would have a fundamental impact on the carrying value of assets and liabilities. These would have to be revised considering the need to liquidate or curtail significantly the scale of the company's operations.

The US does not have an equivalent management statement. However, the standard-setter is working on a rule requiring a company to present assets and liabilities on a liquidation basis if it thinks the going concern is in question.

Conventional measurement bases

The observation that the balance sheet as a status report of the company's financial position is not a good representation of company value is intrinsically linked with two measurement principles which still dominate current accounting practice: the **historical cost** principle and the **monetary measuring unit** convention.

Historical cost

Financial accounting, as currently practised, is still mainly based on *historical cost*, i.e. the past cost needed to acquire an asset on the date of acquisition (the **cash-equivalent** acquisition cost). In essence financial accounting works by tracking and recording all transactions of a company which have a financial value (book-keeping) and then categorizing these transactions into different classes (accounting) such as assets, liabilities, revenues, expenses. The categorizing process usually involves allocating the effect of transactions to different time periods.

As we have seen, financial accounting takes a starting statement of financial position (the balance sheet at the beginning of a year) and during the course of the year all financial transactions are recorded and classified. The classification will involve a first choice between the statement of profit or loss (revenues and expenses from operating activities during the year) and the closing balance sheet (statement of items owned and items owed to third parties). Thus the closing wealth is a summary of the effect of financial transactions of the year past rather than any independent valuation. The statement of profit or loss is a summary of business operations, whose net effect will be to increase or decrease the ending wealth.

The relationship between the statement of profit or loss and the statement of financial position is one that you will need to think about as you progress through the book. Under a pure historical cost regime, the statement of profit or loss is the key document where revenues and expenses are stated, while the balance sheet value of assets is a residual of the profit measurement process. From this are deducted claims by third parties (liabilities) and what is left is equity.

This is a long way from an independent measure of value in an economic sense. For example, imagine that you bought shares in a listed company, say IBM, on 1 January for €50000. During the year you receive dividend payments of €1000. Under historical cost accounting, you have made a profit of €1000 for the year, and your ending balance sheet will show assets of €50000 (investment) and €1000 (cash). However, it might be that the stock exchange valued your shares on 31 December at €55000. Using market value as the measurement criterion, you are worth €56000 (investment and cash) and your gain for the year is €6000. Different measurement rules give different results, and historical cost accounting uses initial cost as the fundamental measurement criterion and only takes in 'realized' revenues – i.e. where cash or a reliable undertaking to pay cash has been obtained. In the example, the €5000 gain in market value has not been realized – the shares have not been sold – so historical cost accounting disregards the gain. Of course, if you sold your shares at the end of the year, the gain would be part of your profit for the year – in the jargon the gain had been realized and could therefore be 'recognized'.

The big advantage of historical cost accounting is that historical cost is relatively easy to determine and can be verified. The main disadvantage is that subsequent to the date of acquisition, the continued reporting of historical cost based values does not reflect any changes in market value.

IASB rules (and US GAAP for that matter) are not based exclusively on the historical cost principle. In fact, **carrying amounts** in an IFRS balance sheet are a mixture of historical costs, market values, net realizable values and discounted **present values**. That is why the measurement model underlying an IFRS balance sheet is often referred to as a mixed-attribute model. The mixture of different types of value makes the relationship between the statement of profit or loss and the balance sheet less straightforward than suggested following the historical cost model.

Fair value

In IFRS the most commonly used measurement basis other than historical cost is called **fair value**. This is a term that is used in business to mean current market value. The IASB has defined it more specifically as a current sale price (IFRS 13, *Fair Value Measurement* – we discuss this in detail in Chapter 14). Often it is used in accounting where there is no observable monetary transaction from which the historical cost can be taken. This is the case in barter transactions, for example, which are not uncommon in international trade. A company might offer to exchange so many litres of palm oil against so many tractors. How would you account for this in the books? You would have to look at fair value – what is the market value of that many litres of palm oil or that many tractors?

It is used in a similar way to allocate between different components of a transaction. If you sell a new car with three years' free servicing, you have to allocate the price between the two components, the car itself and the three years' services.

Under IFRS, fair value is primarily used as a measurement basis for **financial assets** and liabilities. The argument is that, as with the IBM shares above, if there is a ready market on which such assets and liabilities can be sold, it is better information to reflect those values in the statement of financial position. Historically the reason fair value accounting was introduced is that organizations were holding financial instruments whose risks and value they did not understand. They notched up sudden unexpected **losses**. Fair value is designed to protect against hidden losses and inform about hidden profits.

Fair value is not typically used for physical assets under normal circumstances. Companies mostly hold physical assets so that they can use them in the business, and their market value is less significant than their ability to generate cash flows from being used in the business. Financial assets and liabilities are not used in the same way, and are very near to being cash flows.

In Part Two of this book where we are dealing with the financial statements of relatively simple companies, the only financial instruments we will account for will be amounts due from customers (receivables) and amounts owed to suppliers (payables) or bank loans. In most cases these would be at historical cost under IFRS and so we will not re-visit fair value until Part Four of the book.

Monetary measurement unit

Financial accounting will record transactions as far as they can be expressed in monetary terms. Most transactions carried out by a company involve money, and therefore can be translated into money values easily, especially if the historical cost principle is applied. The use of money values to record business transactions has the advantage that money provides a common denominator by means of which heterogeneous facts and relationships can be expressed as numbers that can be added and subtracted. In fact, financial accounting uses money values to attach labels to economic events. The event of you buying a laptop computer becomes in accounting terms (from your perspective):

Assets:
Computers + €900
Cash − €900

So the physical item, the specific laptop with its specific design and operating characteristics, becomes asset €900.00.

While at a personal level you might regard the purchase as an 'expense', from an economic perspective, you presumably bought it in order to use it over a longer period (let's say over a three-year period), therefore it has a utility for you in the future and remains part of your wealth during that period. You have simply chosen to convert a cash asset into a computer asset, and under a historical cost convention we say that the initial accounting value of the computer is its cost value. Subsequently, the computer will gradually become an expense as it is used. This is how accounting works and, when the computer has no further use, it should be fully expensed, but not before. This process is akin to that of language in tying word labels to objects and there are numerous analogies between the process of communicating by accounting and that of communicating by language.

The use of money and historical cost as the measurement base poses two problems: what happens to values that cannot be expressed in financial terms, and what happens when the value of the money itself changes?

Here too we can see the language analogy. There are some concepts that cannot be expressed by language, or indeed some concepts for which there is an expression in one language but not another. In accounting there are some values not expressed – for example, a company may spend a lot of money advertising a new product. If the product is successful its trade name can become quite valuable in itself (Coca-Cola? Nestlé?) but the future sales value of an established trade name does not normally appear in the balance sheet since it was not bought. Similarly, efficient production depends to an extent on harmonious labour relations and good staff training, but neither value is expressed in financial accounting. It is difficult to say to what extent these omissions matter, but it is necessary to bear them in mind when reviewing balance sheet values. The measurement bases impose significant limitations on the scope of a balance sheet and a statement of profit or loss account. It is necessary to remember that the financial accounting data are organized on these measurement assumptions and values are not in any sense absolute, but are relative to a framework – change the framework and the values will change too.

The other major problem in financial accounting is that of changes in the value of the measuring unit – inflation. Money is expressed in terms of its value at the time a transaction or event is recorded. The measurement system records a trans-action at the nominal value in currency which is exchanged in that transaction. Subsequent changes in the purchasing power of the currency do not affect that amount. For example, supposing that we were measuring physical size, we could talk about something in terms of centimetres and metres. Two metres of cloth implies exactly the same length of cloth today as it did in 1900, but $5.00 worth of cloth is very much less today than it would have been in 1900 because the purchasing power of a dollar, the measuring unit, is much smaller today than it was in 1900.

This means that the values expressed in historical cost accounting may not always be what they appear to be. For example, supposing a bookseller buys for inventory a book which cost him €37.50 and retails at €55.00 in 20X1. Over the next three years the publishers, reflecting the inflation of prices generally, increase their wholesale selling price to €45.00 and the retail price to €75.00. If the bookseller has not sold the copy he originally bought, it will appear in his accounts as inventory worth €37.50 – the historical cost. But if he wanted to buy another copy it would now cost €45.00. The book itself is virtually the same; it is the underlying value of the measurement unit that has changed (and as a consequence, if the book is sold for €75.00, it is not clear that the difference of €7.50 between the original inventory price and the replacement cost of the inventory should necessarily be treated as 'profit'). Many attempts have been made to deal with this change in the underlying purchasing power of the measurement unit, none so far with any lasting success.

Accounting for transactions

We are now going to focus in on the logic and procedures of accounting with a view to establishing a simple model of how accounting works.

The balance sheet equation

One way of approaching this is to look at the company as an artificial and empty vehicle constructed to carry out a particular project. Finance is put into the vehicle and this is used to buy productive capacity (factories, warehouses, vehicles, computers, retail premises, offices, etc.). The production unit operates, its output is sold and profit is generated. The profit belongs to the owners of the company, and they will either take it out of the company as a dividend or leave it in as additional financing. The accounting unit must track what finance comes into the company and what is done with it and prepare periodic reports to the owners (Figure 3.3).

Figure 3.3

Tracking finance

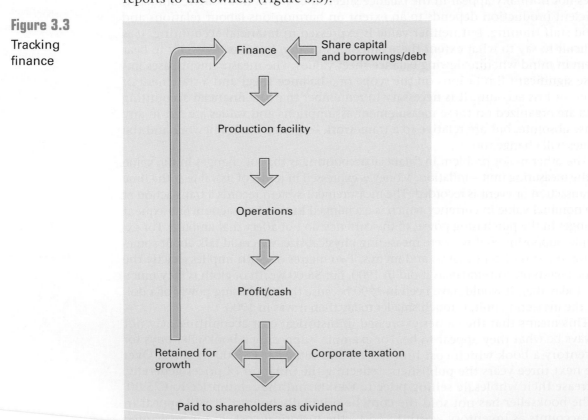

The nature of the vehicle is such that, at the beginning, it can only have as much 'value' as is put into it:

Owners' equity *and* Liabilities (sources of finance) = Assets (uses of finance)

This is called the *balance sheet equation* and is usually stated as:

Assets (uses of finance) = Owners' equity *and* Liabilities (sources of finance)

In this view the left-hand side of the balance sheet equation is said to present the economic resources in which the company has invested the finance or funds available to it as of the balance sheet date. The right-hand side shows the sources of finance or the sources of the funds that are invested in the assets. Every euro invested in the company's assets at balance sheet date comes from either the company's owners (shareholders) or from its creditors (trade and other creditors and lenders), and every euro thus supplied is invested in some asset.

BETWEEN THE LINES

Debt and equity

The sources of finance fall into two major categories: the finance put forward by the owners (equity), and the loans and other finance obtained from outside which do not attract an ownership share (liabilities/debt). The distinction between the two is that the owners take on all the risks of loss from the company's activities and gain from all profits, while loans are made purely in return for interest, which must be paid before arriving at any profit for the owners.

The difference between these two categories is fundamental. The suppliers of a loan are entering into a financial commitment with the company where the return they will receive, and therefore the cost to the company, is fixed in relation to the amount borrowed. The amount borrowed must be repaid at a fixed date and the lenders' risk is simply that the company may not have the means to repay (and bankers try to cover this kind of risk by asking for a legal link to company or shareholder assets – 'security' – in the event of default). The lenders' return is not affected by the company's profitability, except in the extreme of the company ceasing to trade.

The owners, on the other hand, are the people with the last claim upon the company's assets. They take the risk that the company will make a loss, but also reap the rewards if the company makes a profit. (The IASB talks about the 'risks and rewards' of ownership.) We can then recognize two basic categories of sources of finance – that deriving from the owner, and that representing financial liabilities to outside people. The owners' interest is variable, because the owners accept final responsibility (remember, assets – liabilities = equity).

Any business transaction that will be recognized in the accounting system (we will refer to these as *accounting transactions*) will have a dual impact on the numbers in the company's accounting records. Any accounting for a transaction must preserve the equilibrium between sources and uses, and will involve either a change in both or a reallocation within one side of the equation. This is the origin of the term 'double-entry accounting': any transaction must be reflected in (at least) two accounts.

Transactions which involve revenues and expenses fit in this fundamental equation approach, because revenues and expenses have a positive or negative effect on profit, and this belongs to the owners. Profit adds to the 'equity' part of the equation, while a loss will diminish the equity. By way of illustration, sale of inventory will diminish the inventory asset but will increase either cash or receivables assets. There will be a net change in assets, and the counterpart of this is a net change in equity (profit or loss).

Constructing a statement of financial position

The statement of financial position, or balance sheet, is the fundamental accounting statement in the sense that every accounting transaction can be analyzed according to its dual impact on the balance sheet. Let us take a practical example to illustrate how that works out. We will do this using a simple spreadsheet, and we will continue to use this spreadsheet as a means of analyzing accounting transactions. As indicated before, this is not how a book-keeper or accounting software would make the entries; it does, though, reproduce the principles behind the book-keeping, which are what are important. It is intended to simplify the learning process and put emphasis on the substance of the process rather than the form.

Note that the spreadsheet can have as many or as few rows as seems useful, but that overall it must be organized into two parts – assets and finance – and that, as the analysis proceeds, it is probably useful to split the assets side into 'cash' (i.e. bank account in accounting terms) and other assets, while other assets might equally split into short-term trading items and long-term ones (*current* and *non-current assets*). The financing side can also usefully be split between equity and liabilities, with liabilities subdividing into long-term debt (non-current liabilities) and trading liabilities (**current liabilities**), and equity into initial share capital and profits.

> Assets = Equity and Liabilities
> (Cash + Current + Non-current) = (Long-term debt + Trading liabilities)
> + (Share capital + Profit)

Example: supposing three friends decided to form a company (called Reliable Runner SA) which would sell cars. Jane put in €20 000, Alan put in €15 000 and Colin put in €15 000.

1. The initial financing, assuming the money was paid into a bank account, would be accounted for by showing (a) the (historical cost) value of money in the bank, and (b) the (historical cost) value of the shareholders' capital.

2. Next, the company obtained a bank loan for €30 000. Let us assume that this money is put into the company's bank account, so we have a similar

	1	2	3	4	Financial Position
Assets					
Cash	+20000	+30000	−55000	−18000	7000
	+15000				
	+15000				
Receivables					
Inventory				+18000	18000
Property			+55000		55000
Total	+50000	+30000	0	0	80000
Liabilities/equity					
Long-term debt		+30000			30000
Trade payables					
Equity:					
Share capital	+20000				50000
	+15000				
	+15000				
Profit					
Total	+50000	+30000	0	0	80000

transaction, increase in cash assets, increase in financing, but this time it is debt financing. The company now has total assets, all cash, of €80000, while it has equity of €50000 and liabilities of €30000.

3. Its next step is to buy a small office with a car lot for €55000. Up until now we have been looking at transactions which affected both sides of the balance sheet equation, but the new transaction will affect one side only. The company is exchanging one asset, cash, for another asset, property. The total value it owns will remain the same, but the composition of the value will be different. Reliable Runner SA now has assets worth €80000 in the form of property and cash, while it has liabilities of €30000 (loan from the bank) and equity of €50000 (owners' initial capital subscribed).

4. The next move is to acquire some inventory for trading, and the company buys €18000 of second-hand cars for cash (i.e. by issuing a cheque – cash is usually used in accounting to mean liquid funds available immediately at the bank, not necessarily physical cash). Here again there is a swap between cash assets and other forms of asset – this time a current asset, inventory. It is assumed in accounting that inventories (which may be goods for resale, but also raw materials and work in progress) will be sold in less than one year. Of course the longer the inventory turnover period the more financing is required by the company, and hence the emphasis in modern management of 'just in time' inventories.

The company is ready to start trading. If we drew up a balance sheet at this point (drawn from the company's accounting database above) it would look like this:

Assets		Financing	
Non-current assets		Equity	
Property	55 000	Share capital	50 000
Current assets		Liabilities	
Inventory	18 000	LT debt	30 000
Bank	7 000		
	80 000		80 000

Now we are ready to start trading and see what the effect of trading is on the balance sheet equation.

The owners' interest, or equity, represents initially the finance put into the company by the shareholders. That finance can be increased at any time during the company's life by the issue of new shares but, aside from that, it changes regularly as a result of the company's trading activities. The shareholders are the ultimate recipients of the wealth generated or lost by the company. They bear all the risks of the company – if the company fails they will lose their investment – but they are also the people who benefit if the company is successful.

Gains or losses can arise in two main ways: first, through the operating activities of the company (any operating profit or loss will accrue to the benefit or cost of shareholders); second, through changes in the underlying values of the assets. For example, if a company has investments, and the value of these rises, then the shareholders own the increase in underlying values. An important difference between these two types of gain is that classical accounting only recognizes gains when they have been validated by a sale transaction (in the jargon, the gain must have been *realized* in order to be *recognized*). Consequently, many companies have value gains in their assets which are not reflected in the balance sheet (one form of hidden reserve). Operating activities though, by definition, involve a series of completed transactions.

If we concentrate on the trading activities, it follows that as the shareholders are the ultimate recipients of any losses or profits, then trading activities will have the effect of increasing or decreasing the shareholders' equity – in this sense, the statement of profit or loss is simply a summary of the business transactions which have occurred during a period, and is drawn up to explain the net change during a period in the value of the equity. (This linkage between the statement of profit or loss and the balance sheet is known as the *iteration* between the two, and is a central building block of financial reporting.)

Let us now move on to seeing how the trading transaction works in a balance sheet context.

	Financial Position A		5	6	7	Financial Position B
Assets						
Cash	7 000	(a) +5 000				11 750
		(c) −250				
Receivables			(a) 7 000			7 000
Inventory	18 000	(b) −4 000	(c) −5 500	+12 000		20 500
Property	55 000					55 000
Total	80 000		+750	+1 500	+12 000	94 250
Liabilities/Equity						
Long-term debt	30 000					30 000
Trade payables					+12 000	12 000
Equity:						
Share capital	50 000					50 000
Profit		(a) +5 000	(b) +7 000			2 250
		(b) −4 000	(b) −5 500			
		(c) −250				
Total	80 000		+750	+1 500	+12 000	94 250

5. In our example, if a car was sold for €5000 cash, we should be able to re-cord the acquisition of a new asset (€5000 cash) and also show an increase in equity of €5000 (transaction 5a on the spreadsheet).

The sale increases the value of the owners' equity and the cash received increases the assets of the company. However, we have so far failed to record the other aspect of the transaction: the fact that we have given up part of our inventory. We need to record the reduction of our assets by one vehicle. We have gained a cash asset of €5000, but we have given up a car asset, which in this case we had previously bought for €4000 (part of our inventory of €18 000, which amount we need for profit measurement purposes to have allocated across the individual cars concerned – which could bring in an element of subjectivity). The real effect of the transaction is to create a profit of €1000, and this is reflected in the accounts by *expensing* the inventory against the sale. We cancel the inventory value of the car sold by deducting this from the sale. In our balance sheet equation, we reduce inventory by €4000 and reduce profit by €4000 (transaction 5b).

This highlights the relationship between assets and expenses. When a com-pany pays its electricity bill it is easy to see that the expenditure involved relates to something which has already been consumed in the business – the electrical energy. The payment therefore involves an immediate expense in the business operations of the company. It represents a value consumed. However, when a company makes a payment – as in the case of the acquisition of the car inven-tory in our example – the transaction is not always an expense. The car inven-tory represents an economic value which will be consumed in the future by the company and remains in the balance sheet until it is consumed. And that is what has now happened in the case of the car sale above: an asset has been consumed, turned into an expense ('expensed') as a trading transaction by the company.

Many assets represent simply a store of future economic value to be consumed by a business. Clearly an inventory of goods for resale is going to be seen to be consumed relatively quickly. But in the same way, assets such as equipment are used up over a period, albeit several years, and are consumed in the business. Equally, when a company pays in advance for something like insurance or rent, the expenditure is made initially to acquire a future benefit. That benefit expires as the company moves through the time period for which it paid in advance – the asset becomes an expense through the economic benefits being consumed by the company.

We should therefore distinguish between expenditure – where the company simply pays out money – and the classification of that expenditure as an expense of an accounting period or as an asset to appear in the end-period balance sheet and be carried forward to become an expense in a future period.

Returning to the car example, let us also imagine that, as the new owner was driving away, a wing mirror fell off. The company arranged for a nearby repair shop to replace this and carry out one or two other minor repairs. Reliable Runner SA paid the repair shop €250 for this work. That expenditure would also be an expense since the car has been sold (transaction 5c).

During the course of the series of transactions we have just finished describing, the accounting value of the company has changed several times, so any balance sheet which we might have drawn up would also have changed as the transactions progressed. The net change in the equity over the period is, of course, the profit which has been made by the company during that period. Normally this would be analyzed in the statement of profit or loss and only the net change shown in the published balance sheet within equity. A company can draw up a statement of profit or loss as often as it wishes; most companies do this monthly for internal management purposes, as well as annually for official reporting to shareholders and tax authorities.

Credit transactions

All the transactions which we have made so far have involved an exchange of cash. However, in business many transactions are made on credit, with the cash exchange following sometime later. The accounting treatment of such transactions follows exactly the same ideas which we have already explored: if a business sells some goods on credit, it gives up one asset in exchange for another; but where the asset received was cash in the earlier example, in a credit transaction the asset received will be a promise to pay. That promise or debt is just as valuable as the cash, as long as there is an expectation that the person who owes the debt will pay in due course (and why would you give credit in the first place if you were not sure you would be paid?). The account created is known as a receivable.

Suppose that Reliable Runner SA sells another car, this time for €7000, and allows the customer credit. The transaction would appear in the balance sheet equation as an increase in equity and an increase in a new form of current asset, a receivable (transaction 6a in the spreadsheet). Let us say the allocated cost of the car sold was €5500 so we have acknowledged through the balance sheet equation the expensing of another car from our inventory (transaction 6b).

Businesses also receive short-term credit from their suppliers – assets are purchased or other expenses incurred in exchange for a promise to pay in due course. In essence, this is a transaction very similar to the bank loan, with the difference that the finance is normally available only for a short period, so would be presented differently on the balance sheet. A credit supply consists of the receipt by a business of goods or services against a liability to pay later. The supplier and the debt which is owed are described as trade creditors or trade payables.

If our company now decided that it should expand its car inventory and bought two more cars for €12000 but this time on credit, the company should record an increase in assets – the additional car inventory, and an increase in financing – the short-term credit given by the supplier (transaction 7). (There is no limit to the number of rows which might be used – we are constrained slightly by the size of the printed page, but generally one would have as many rows as seemed useful in terms of enabling a relevant and efficient analysis of the figures into a statement of profit or loss and balance sheet.)

If we were to draw up a statement of profit or loss for the whole period since the commencement of the business, it would now look like this:

	€	€
Sales		12000
Expenses:		
Cars	9500	
Repairs	250	9750
Net profit		*2250*

The statement of financial position or balance sheet at the end of the period would look like this:

Assets	€	*Financing*	€
Non-current assets		*Equity*	
Property	55000	Share capital	50 000
Current assets		Profit for the year	2250
Inventory	20500	*Liabilities*	
Receivables	7 000	LT debt	30000
Bank	11750	Trade payables	12000
Total	94250	Total	94250

This series of transactions represents the essence of how accounting tracks and reflects a company's financing and its operations. Essentially, the balance sheet is a financial model of the company – but based on the money value of transactions which have taken place. The statement of profit or loss is an analysis of the wealth-creating (or wealth diminishing!) activities of the company. The statement of profit or loss can be drawn up for any period but is generally drawn up for one year for external reporting purposes and in businesses of any size, at least once a month for internal management purposes. Equally, a balance sheet, or statement of financial position, can be drawn up at any moment, but is published once a year for shareholders and others, while it is produced internally at least quarterly for management purposes.

The spreadsheet represents the company's accounting database. In reality this will consist of potentially hundreds of 'accounts' – data files – which are constantly being updated as the accounting department tracks the company's transactions and indeed participates in them with issuing invoices to clients, paying suppliers and so on. The balance sheet is in fact a highly aggregated summary of the data files in the accounting database and corresponds exactly with that database. The statement of profit or loss is also an aggregation of those data files which deal with the company's operations for a specific period. They represent a more detailed analysis than is provided by the one-line profit entry in the statement of financial position.

You can see in the above example how (a) the balance sheet is a presentation of the latest position in the company's accounting database and (b) how the statement of profit or loss is an analytical document which gives the detail behind the net change in equity over the period (but excluding any new capital introduced by investors or dividends paid to them).

You should also note that the increase in company cash during the trading period (transactions 5–7) was €4750, while the profit was €2250. This is generally the case in accruals accounting, since we are trying to present an economic assessment and while this translates itself into cash flows in the end, there are timing differences. In this case we can reconcile the two as follows:

Profit as calculated	*2 250*
Value of inventory consumed (paid earlier)	9 500
Amount owed by credit customer (will be received later)	–7 000
Change in cash during this period	*+4 750*

We will build on this model in subsequent chapters to see how it deals with more complex transactions and situations. But all the essentials of how accounting tracks company operations are contained in the above example. If you get stuck later on, you should always come back to this introduction to refresh your understanding of how accounting records company activity.

The IASB definition and recognition criteria for elements of the statement of financial position and the statement of profit or loss

Having constructed a basic statement of financial position (balance sheet) and statement of profit or loss (income statement/profit and loss account) from a set of business transactions, we will now turn to some of the formal rules that the IASB has set to delineate the content of the building blocks of these financial statements. These formal rules are important as they sometimes depart from the traditional transactions-based view of accounting. The IASB definitions and overall recognition criteria provide the general setting to which we will refer in later chapters.

Elements of financial statements

The IASB *Conceptual Framework* states that financial statements portray the financial effects of transactions and other events by grouping them into broad categories according to their economic characteristics. These characteristics are the elements of financial statements. Five elements of financial statements are identified and defined: assets, liabilities, equity, revenues and expenses.

Assets, liabilities and equity are the elements that are directly related to the measurement of a company's financial position in the balance sheet and are defined as follows (para 4.4 of the IASB *Conceptual Framework)*:

■ *Asset*: A resource controlled by an entity as a result of past events from which **future economic benefits** are expected to flow to the entity.

■ *Liability*: A present obligation of an entity arising from past events, the settlement of which is expected to result in an outflow from the entity of resources embodying economic benefits.

■ *Equity*: The residual interest in the assets of an entity after deducting all its liabilities.

Income and expenses are the elements of financial statements that are directly related to the measurement of performance in the statement of profit or loss. These elements are defined as follows (para 4.25 of the IASB *Conceptual Framework*):

■ *Income*: Increases in economic benefits during the accounting period in the form of inflows or enhancements of assets or decreases of liabilities that result in increases in equity, other than those relating to contributions from equity participants.

■ *Expenses*. Decreases in economic benefits during the accounting period in the form of outflows or depletions of assets or incurrences of liabilities that result in decreases of equity, other than those relating to distributions to equity participants.

Reading through these definitions, it becomes clear that they are not independent: primacy is given to the definitions of assets and liabilities, whereas the concepts of equity, income and expenses are defined in terms of the level of or changes in assets and liabilities. This is known as the *asset–liability approach* to financial statements.

The IASB *Framework* says (para 4.6) that you should keep the **substance over form** principle in mind when assessing whether an item meets the definition of an asset, liability or equity: the underlying substance and economic reality of the item should be examined and not merely its legal form.

The bulk of the IASB standards contain specific rules with respect to these elements of financial statements. The rules are typically oriented towards three aspects of financial statement elements: recognition, measurement and disclosure.

- *Recognition* is the process of incorporating an item that meets one of the definitions above in the financial statements. An item may meet the definition of, for example, an asset, but fail to meet specific asset recognition criteria and thus be kept off the balance sheet. In other words, meeting the definitions is a necessary but not a sufficient condition for inclusion in the financial statements.

- *Measurement* is the process of determining the monetary units at which the elements of financial statements are to be recognized and carried in the balance sheet and statement of profit or loss. A variety of measurement bases are employed, but the dominating one is still historical cost.

- *Disclosure* refers to the process of additional information dissemination with regard to a financial statement element in the notes to the accounts.

Figure 3.4

Decision stages for inclusion of an item into the financial statements

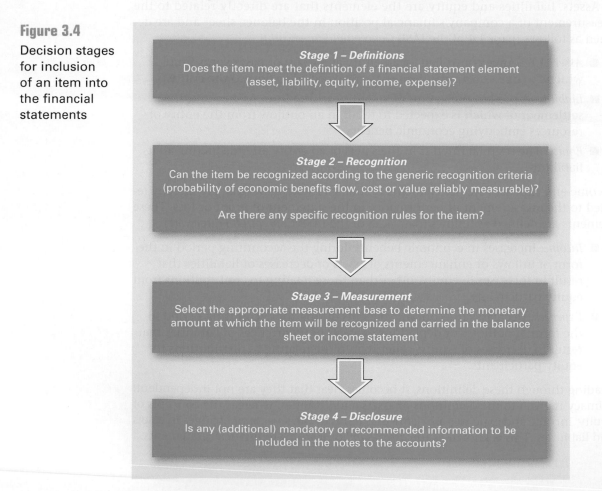

Stage 1 – Definitions
Does the item meet the definition of a financial statement element (asset, liability, equity, income, expense)?

Stage 2 – Recognition
Can the item be recognized according to the generic recognition criteria (probability of economic benefits flow, cost or value reliably measurable)?

Are there any specific recognition rules for the item?

Stage 3 – Measurement
Select the appropriate measurement base to determine the monetary amount at which the item will be recognized and carried in the balance sheet or income statement

Stage 4 – Disclosure
Is any (additional) mandatory or recommended information to be included in the notes to the accounts?

Although specific IASB standards may contain additional and more detailed recognition rules, at a more generic level the IASB *Conceptual Framework* (para 4.38) formulates two generally applicable recognition criteria for an item that meets one of the definitions of financial statement element:

(a) it is probable that any future economic benefit associated with the item will flow to or from the entity, and

(b) the item has a cost or value that can be measured with reliability.

Hence, not all assets and liabilities should be included (recognized) in the statement of financial position. For example, there may be serious doubt that the flow of future benefits will be effectively realized or the value of an asset may be difficult to measure.

The application of these general recognition criteria may imply considerable judgement. The probability assessment refers to the degree of certainty that the future flow of economic benefits will materialize, and should take into account the information available when the financial statements are prepared. In many cases the cost or value of an item is not readily available and must be estimated. The need for estimation as such does not undermine reliability as long as the estimates can be reasonably justified.

Figure 3.4 summarizes the different decision stages in the process of including (information on) an item into the financial statements.

Assets

A company's asset is a resource that it controls as a result of past events and from which future economic benefits are expected to flow to the company. Note that tangibility or physical substance is not an essential characteristic of an asset.

Assets arise from *past transactions* or *past events*. A company would normally obtain an asset through exchanges with third parties, by acquiring them in cash, credit or barter transactions (**property, plant and equipment**, inventory, investments), by selling goods or services (receivables) or by entering into arrangements that provide rights to future benefits (a loan to a third party). There might not always be an expenditure to recognize an asset: an item may be donated to the company free of charge, but if the item has the capacity to generate future economic benefits, it meets the definition of an asset. On the other hand, incurring expenditure may be indicative that future economic benefits are sought, but it is not conclusive proof that an asset has been acquired.

The *future economic benefits* embodied in an asset means the capacity to contribute directly or indirectly to the company's future net cash inflows. These benefits may arise in a number of ways. Economic benefits may result from:

■ the productive capacity of the asset (for example, plant and equipment);

■ the ability of the asset to reduce future cash outflows (for example, renewal expenditure on equipment that results in future production cost savings);

■ the rights incorporated in the asset to receive services in the future (for example, prepayments);

■ direct claims to cash inflows (for example, receivables and short-term investments);

■ cash in hand, because it can be exchanged for goods and services (economic benefits).

In order to meet the definition of an asset these future benefits should be controlled by the company.

Control relates to the company's capacity to benefit exclusively from the benefits embodied in a particular asset. Controlling a resource means that the company can use it to provide goods or services, to settle financial obligations or make distributions to owners. Control usually arises from legal rights of ownership, but an item may satisfy the definition of an asset even where there is no legal ownership. To assess the control issue it is important to analyse transactions in accordance with their substance and economic reality and not merely their legal form. For example, the substance of business arrangements may give a company control over the benefits (and usually at the same time expose it to the risks) that are expected to flow from an asset without specific legal rights. A **finance lease** arrangement is a typical example of a situation where ownership and control do not coincide. Under a finance lease arrangement the owner of, for example, a plant transfers the control over the future economic benefits of using the plant to a lessee, although he or she (the lessor) retains legal ownership. Likewise, possession of an asset will usually indicate control but, even then, a company may hold inventory or cash as agent for another party and be restricted from using it in an exchange transaction, and hence does not control the asset.

Liabilities

A company's liability is a present obligation arising from a past event, the settlement of which will result in an outflow of economic benefits from the company.

A *present obligation* of a company is a present (at balance sheet date) duty or responsibility to act or perform in a certain way. The duty or responsibility obligates the company. The obligation implies the involvement of one or more third parties. Most obligations are legally enforceable and arise under contractual arrangements for amounts borrowed (bank loans, corporate bonds), amounts owed for assets purchased or services obtained (trade payables). When advance payments have been received from third parties, there will be an obligation to provide goods or services. Obligations can also be imposed, such as obligations to pay tax, retirement benefit obligations, the obligation to restore environmentally damaged sites and the obligation to pay damages under a lawsuit.

Obligations can, however, also be constructive. A **constructive obligation** is created or inferred from a company's actions. For example, a company may have a policy of refunding purchases to dissatisfied customers, indicating that it will accept responsibility for faulty goods. The constructive obligation arises when the company has created a valid expectation with the customers of a rebate for anything faulty.

A present obligation arises from a past event known as an **obligating event**. An obligating event arises when the company has no realistic alternative to settling the obligation created by the event. For example, the purchase of goods and the use of services of third parties is an obligating event giving rise to trade payables (unless paid for in advance or on delivery) or the signing of a bank loan contract results in an obligation to repay the loan. In these cases the obligation can be enforced by law. In the case of a constructive obligation to refund faulty goods, the obligating event arises when the goods are actually sold by the company. There is, however, no such thing as 'voluntary' liabilities which are not based on commitments towards third parties, such as planned expenditure on repairs and maintenance of plant and equipment. In that case, the company has the alternative to cancel or postpone the expenditure or to sell the asset before the repairs and maintenance take place and, thus, avoid expenditure.

The liability will lead to a *sacrifice of economic benefits*. The actual settlement of the obligation could involve the payment of cash, the transfer of other assets, the replacement by one obligation with another, the rendering of services etc. Uncertainty about the timing and amount of the future sacrifice of economic benefits is allowable. Liabilities of uncertain timing or amount are known as 'provisions' (see Chapter 6).

A basic distinction is made between financial liabilities and other liabilities. Financial liabilities imply a contractual obligation, while the other category arises from statutory requirements, such as taxes or dividends payable, or from constructive obligations.

Equity

Equity is defined as the residual interest in the company's assets after deducting its liabilities. The residual interest is the ownership interest and represents a claim or right to the company's net assets. The logic of the definition of equity follows the balance sheet equation that assets minus liabilities equals equity. Both equity and liabilities represent (mutually exclusive) interests in a company's assets, but equity ranks after liabilities as a claim to those assets. This means that claims from liabilities must be met before a distribution can be made to equity holders in the event of liquidating the company.

Equity will be usually subdivided as follows:

■ funds contributed by shareholders
■ retained profits
■ reserves representing appropriations of retained profits.

Such subcategories indicate legal or other restrictions on the ability of the company to distribute or otherwise use its equity.

Income and expenses

The IASB definitions of income and expenses rely directly on the asset–liability approach of financial statements. Both are defined in terms of changes in assets and liabilities. *Income* includes both revenue and gains, but these are not separately defined. Similarly, *expenses* embrace both expenses and losses. The subcategories are substantiated in a number of specific IASB standards. The main difference seems to be that gains and losses are presented as net amount, whereas revenue and expenses are usually displayed gross.

Revenue (income) that increases assets is derived from the sale of goods and services, fees, dividends, royalties, grants and rent, whereas gains (income) that increase assets may result from the disposal of assets or from a **revaluation** of specific assets. Examples of expenses that decrease assets are numerous: cost of goods sold (depletion of inventory), advertising costs (use of cash), depreciation (consumption of long-term assets) etc. Expenses may result in an increase in liabilities if, for example, payment is deferred. Losses that decrease assets may arise from the disposal of assets or from a revaluation of specific assets.

Summary

In this chapter we have taken a major step forward in looking at the technical basis of accounting. This has involved looking at the basic conventions of accounting, particularly historical cost as the valuation base, but also conventions such as accruals (accounts try to record all economic events affecting the company when they take place, not just cash movements), matching, going concern (allocations of costs to future periods are only valid if we think the company is going to continue to exist) and consistency (the comparability of data is limited if the basis on which it is prepared changes over time).

We dealt with the accounting database and its fundamental concepts that accounting information records both where finance came from and what was done with it (the balance sheet equation) and that therefore all movements within the database will involve at least two changes, since they must deal with both sources and uses of finance (double entry). We used a spreadsheet as a model of the accounting database and plotted a series of transactions through it. As a result we were able to prepare a statement of profit or loss and a statement of financial position from the database.

Finally, we looked more closely at the IASB definitions and recognition criteria of the elementary building blocks of financial statements. These definitions are governed by the asset–liability approach to financial statements. In order to properly understand the numbers presented in the financial statements, the analyst must be aware of these definitions and the accompanying general recognition criteria.

Discussion Questions

1. Discuss the shortcomings of a statement of financial position as a proxy for company value.
2. Critically assess the usefulness of fair value as a measurement attribute.
3. What is the link between a functional presentation and a presentation by nature of the statement of profit or loss? Provide a number of examples to illustrate your point.
4. Explain what is meant by relevance, timeliness and comparability and how they make financial information useful.
5. Elaborate the link between a statement of financial position and a statement of profit or loss.
6. Explain the difference between expenses and losses.

Assignments

The following questions have answers on the lecturer side of the digital support resources for the book.

1. Jennifer decides that she will go into the tourist industry on Lake Geneva, and buy a concession to hire out canoes on the lake. She borrows CHF40 000 from her parents and puts in CHF20 000 herself. The arrangement with the Canton is that she pays CHF50 000 at the start for the concession, which

runs five years, but must also pay an annual rental of CHF10 000 at the end of the season in October.

She negotiates a deal with a canoe supplier, who sells her 20 canoes for CHF30 000 but agrees that she should pay CHF10 000 on delivery and the rest a year later.

During the season she receives CHF90 000 (cash) in canoe rentals.

Making (and specifying) whatever assumptions you wish, you are asked to draw up a simple statement of profit or loss for the first year and statement of financial position at the end of the year.

2. James, on completing his MBA, sees a possibility to make a profit sell-ing computers. He has the opportunity to buy a job-lot of computers for €50 000, and he can buy a shop lease with two years to run for €5000 and pay an annual rent of €6000. He happens just to have inherited €60 000, so he starts a company and puts the money in as share capital.

    During the first year, he sells €30 000 of computers for €45 000. During the second year he sells no computers at all, and at the end of the year he sells the remaining inventory for €1000 and liquidates the company.

    (a) Calculate his accounting profit for each of the two years of operations.

    (b) Explain why the assumptions made at the end of the first year led to the wrong profit estimate.

    (c) What are the consequences of the assumptions which proved to be incorrect?

3. A&S retail shop. Andy and Stewart met at a training course for young en-trepreneurs. They decide to set up an enterprise to run a retail store at the centre of a small village. Andy recently received £9000 as a donation from his rich aunt. He puts this money and another £3000 of his savings into the business as share capital. Stewart puts in £12 000 of his own savings as share capital as well. A local bank grants them a three-year loan of £6000. Every six months, they repay one-sixth of the bank loan and pay interest at a semi-annual rate of 3 per cent. The interest is recognized on a six-month basis. They rent a fully equipped store with sufficient storage space. They agree to pay a monthly rent of £700 (to be paid at the beginning of each month). Andy and Stewart pay themselves a salary of £600 each at month's end. They decide to use their initials to create the store's name: A&S.

    ■ To announce the opening of the store on the first of April 20X1, A&S launches an advertising campaign which runs during the first week of April. This campaign costs £1000 and is to be paid for on April 7.
    ■ A&S purchases retail goods worth £7000. The supplier agrees to grant a 10 per cent discount if A&S pays immediately on April 1.
    ■ The first month turns out to be a success due to the advertising campaign. A&S is able to sell half its inventory for £4900.
    ■ At the beginning of May, A&S purchases retail goods worth £5000 in cash.
    ■ By the end of the May A&S manages to sell £3500 of goods for £5400.
    ■ In the month of June, A&S decides to provide several shopping carts to improve customer comfort. A&S buys 20 carts for only £1200. The carts are delivered on June 5 and will be paid for mid-July. A&S estimates the expected life of the carts to be five years without any residual value.

- In June, A&S sells £2900 of goods for £4500. A&S also buys retail goods for £5000 and receives a promotional quantity discount of 7 per cent. The goods are paid for when delivered on June 20.
- The availability and convenience of shopping carts attract a broader range of customers. In the month of July, A&S sells £4500 of retail goods for £7200.
- At the beginning of August, A&S buys £4800 of goods and sells £3800 goods for £5800.
- Eager to expand its business, A&S responds to an increasing demand for more customer convenience. In order to provide a home delivery service, A&S buys a second-hand motor van for £15 000 on August 4. A&S estimates that the van will be used for five years, after which the van will have no residual value. A&S pays £12 000 immediately and agrees to pay the remaining balance before August 20X2.
- A&S buy retail goods for £6500 in September. A&S sells £3500 of goods for £5000 at the store. Furthermore, A&S delivers £750 of goods using the van and gets paid £1200.
- At the end of the month, A&S repays part of its borrowings and pays the interest to the bank.
- In October, A&S experiences a slight downturn in sales. A&S manages to sell only £2000 of goods for £3400 at the store and delivers £750 of goods to customers at home for £1200. Given this disappointing decrease in sales A&S buys only a minimum of goods and pays £1250.
- During the month of November, A&S grants promotional discounts to get rid of products near to their expiring dates. A&S sells in total £2400 of goods at a price of £2600.
- At the beginning of December, A&S purchases a considerable quantity of goods to provide for the holiday shoppers. A&S buys £8500 of goods and gets a 5 per cent discount for immediate payment.
- December turns out to be a lucrative month. A&S temporarily hires a student on a part-time basis to help out in the store. A&S pays the student £300 at the end of the month. A&S sells £6500 of goods for £9900 at the store. On top of that, home deliveries (with a cost of £1800) account for £3200 in revenue.
- A&S believes the owners have been working hard and rewards them with a new year's bonus of £300 each.
- In January, A&S replenishes its inventory. A&S purchases £4000 of goods. In January A&S sells £3700 of goods for £6300 all together.
- In February, A&S decides that the store requires a portable computer for administration purposes. A&S buys a portable computer at a price of £1350. The computer is expected to last three years and to have no value afterwards.
- At the beginning of February, A&S purchases £5000 of goods. A&S sells £4500 of goods for £7850 at the store and another £850 of goods by delivery for £1500.
- In March, A&S relies upon an accountant's services to help them with the preparation of their financial statements. A&S pays him £500. During this month A&S purchases another £5000 of goods and succeeds in selling £4600 of goods for £7900.
- At the end of the month, A&S repays part of its loan and pays the interest to the bank.

The fiscal year of A&S runs from April 1 20X1 till March 31 20X2.

You are asked to prepare for A&S a statement of financial position at the end of March 20X2 and draw up a statement of profit or loss for its first fiscal year.

1. George and Val set up a company together to trade as decorators. George owns a three-year-old van which he puts into the company instead of cash for share capital. Val puts in €2000 in cash and they agree the van is worth €2000. They have no premises as such. Materials are stored in their home garage or left in the van. In the first month of business the following transactions take place:

   (a) They get an order worth €600 to decorate a small flat. The customer pays €300 in advance.

   (b) They buy materials worth €125 on credit from Cork Building Merchants which are used in this job.

   (c) When the job is finished the customer pays a further €100 but says they will have to wait another month for the balance of €200.

   (d) They get an order to decorate a large house for €1200 plus materials. They buy €270 of materials on credit from the same builders' merchants.

   (e) At the end of the month they have done 80 per cent of the work on the house-painting order and they pay themselves €500 each as salary.

   Prepare a spreadsheet to show the transactions and then draw up a statement of profit or loss for the month and a statement of financial position as at the end of the month.

   Next month:

   (f) They complete the house job and receive €1200 from the customer plus €270 for the materials.

   (g) They get a job painting some shop premises – the price is €500 including materials. They buy materials on credit from the usual supplier for €80.

   (h) They complete the job and receive €500 cash.

   (i) The next contract is to decorate a flat and they agree to do the job for €800 plus materials. They obtain €180 of materials, but the supplier says that they must clear their outstanding account before he will release the goods. They pay what was due at the end of the previous month.

   (j) The van breaks down and is repaired for €90 which is paid in cash.

   (k) They complete the job and bill the customer for €980. The customer pays €600 and offers to pay the balance plus €20 interest if they will wait two months for it.

   (l) They visit their first client because he hasn't paid the €200 outstanding, but he is not available and a neighbour tells them that he has just gone bankrupt.

   (m) They do no further business that month and pay themselves €500 each as salary at the end of the month.

   Update the spreadsheet and then draw up a statement of profit or loss for the month and a statement of financial position as at the end of the month.

CHAPTER 4

Accruals accounting

In this chapter we go into the detail of how to apply accruals accounting in practice. We will look at credit transactions and the timing of transactions for accounting purposes in general. More specifically, we will address the issues of revenue recognition and of how items of inventory are transferred to the statement of profit or loss.

Introduction

In the last chapter we looked at the balance sheet equation, how that works as the basis of the company's accounting database and how the company's transactions are captured and recorded within that database. In short, we dealt with the basic approach to accounting measurement. In this chapter and the next one, we are going to go into this in more detail with a view to reaching the point where you can prepare basic financial statements, given a listing from the database and information about the surrounding circumstances. It is important that you should know the relationship between the database and the financial statements which are published using its data, and that you should feel comfortable with the contents of the statement of financial position (balance sheet) and statement of profit or loss (income statement/profit and loss account).

Accruals basis of accounting

So far we have largely confined ourselves to looking at transactions in which goods were bought and sold for cash, but the real world of commercial trading includes many transactions where cash changes hands at a different moment from that when the item or service is provided. Also, the classification of an item within a company's accounting system sometimes changes when the item is used up in the company's activities. To be useful, accounting needs to capture all the economic events that occur in a company, when they take place, and the cash movement is usually only a part of the picture. The statement of profit or loss gives a picture of a company's operating performance over a period of time (for published financial statements the relevant period is commonly one year). In essence, that is a simple enough concept, but examined in detail it poses questions as to which transactions of a company are properly taken in as being 'operating' and which transactions belong to which accounting period. In answering this question, accountants may well have to make allocations of expenses and revenues between different accounting periods, which brings in another subjective element in the preparation of financial statements.

To illustrate the point, let us imagine two cases. A company makes up its statement of profit or loss for the year to 31 December.

In example (a) it takes delivery of five washing machines (cost €300 each) on 15 December, and pays the supplier on 31 January. The machines are sold for €400 each during the first week of January.

In example (b) the company obtains the washing machines on 15 December, pays in January, but sells the machines on credit on 20 December and receives payment in January.

Given that the months of December and January fall into different accounting periods, how should we deal with each set of transactions as far as the statement of profit or loss goes?

In example (a) the washing machines were acquired by the company in December, but paid for in January. Should they appear in the company's financial statements in December or January, and in what way should they appear (in accounting terms, how should they be 'recognized')? Should they be recognized as an expense in the statement of profit or loss for the year ended in December?

In example (b) the company received the goods and made the sale in December, but it paid for the goods and received the money for the sale in January. If we tie the goods and the sale together and put them in the same statement of profit or loss, should they go in the December figures or the January ones?

In order to resolve the dilemma we should go back to first principles. What is the purpose of the information given in a company's financial statements? The answer is to provide decision-useful information for investors and creditors. If we put the expense in one statement of profit or loss and the revenue (the sale) in another, we are not actually recording the profit on the transaction within one statement of profit or loss, so the usefulness of both statements is impaired.

The IASB *Conceptual Framework for Financial Reporting* said the following about accruals:

> Accrual accounting depicts the effects of transactions and other events and circumstances on a reporting entity's economic resources and claims in the periods in which those effects occur, even if the resulting cash receipts and payments occur in a different period. This is important because information about a reporting entity's economic resources and claims and changes in its economic resources and claims during a period provides a better basis for assessing the entity's past and future performance than information solely about cash receipts and payments during that period.
>
> *(IASB, Conceptual Framework for Financial Reporting, par.OB17)*

Using these principles we can resolve our two examples. First, the revenue and the expense relating to the same business transaction should be recognized in the same accounting period, and that is the period when the transaction took place. When the washing machines were delivered the company was free to dispose of them in any way it wished up until the point where a customer agreed to buy them. The company possessed the washing machines from the time of delivery, so they should be recognized at the point of delivery, and a debt was owed to the supplier from that time, so that too should be recognized. However, the company had not disposed of the machines, so they would be recognized as part of its wealth, an asset, up to the point of sale. They should therefore appear in example (a) as an asset in the statement of financial position at 31 December (with a corresponding liability to the supplier). In January the sale took place: the machines are no longer available to the company and change status from an asset to an expense at the moment of sale. Payment of the supplier subsequently can be seen as settlement of a balance sheet liability, just like the payment of any kind of debt.

In example (b) the customers agreed to buy the machines in December, but paid in January, so when did the transaction take place? The trading transaction took place at the moment when each customer agreed to buy the machine – legally the machine was theirs, the company selling the machine no longer had the right to dispose of it and the customer had a legal obligation to pay the agreed purchase price. In example (b) the customers did not pay until January, but this did not affect the ownership rights of either party and in economic terms the deferral of the cash settlement is simply the selling company in effect making a loan for a period. The revenue from the sale relates to the moment the sale transaction took place, even though the cash receipt occurred at another time. In short, we can recognize a series of different states:

1. The company acquires the washing machines (an asset). It could exchange another asset (cash) for the machines but is allowed to defer the cash settlement which creates a debt to the supplier (establishes a trade payable – a liability).

2. Some time later the company extinguishes the liability by payment of cash.

3. The company sells the washing machines, but again, instead of taking a cash asset in exchange, it accepts a debt asset (a receivable – the customer's promise to pay).

4. Later the customer settles his debt, cancelling the receivable in the company's statement of financial position in exchange for an increase in cash assets.

Of the four different elements which can be seen above, only part 3 relates to the statement of profit or loss, all the others are changes in balance sheet components. In our example (b) no cash changes hands in either direction when the trading transaction takes place and this is a central element of profit measurement through the accounting system – trading transactions are identified according to when they objectively take place, not according to when cash changes hands.

In this chapter we are focusing on tracking and matching transactions in order to recognize them in the appropriate time period. We shall now go on to review how this problem is handled within the accounting system. We can break this down into four related areas:

1. ordinary trade transactions on credit

2. timing of revenue recognition

3. transactions where invoicing takes place periodically after the goods or services have been consumed and time-based expenses

4. recognition of changed status where an asset is sold and therefore becomes an expense.

Generally speaking, credit transactions are such an integral part of day-to-day trading activities that the data recording system is designed to track these transactions as soon as they occur. On the other hand, the other three types are frequently not built into the data collection system automatically and involve the preparer of financial statements in adjusting the figures produced by the recording system.

Credit transactions

The purchase of goods for resale by a company, and the sale of goods by the company frequently take place on credit, i.e. cash settlement follows after delivery, often with a delay of 30 to 60 days. Any trading company as part of its management of cash resources, will try to obtain the maximum credit from suppliers of goods and give the minimum credit to customers. Of course, the offer of generous credit terms is one of the weapons which can be used in marketing a company's products, and is a point of tension between financial management and marketing. Equally, the correct assessment of the creditworthiness of customers is vital.

This kind of trading generally takes place in an environment where suppliers and customers have a continuing relationship with each other and regularly trade, and is known as trading on 'open account'. That is, a supplier company knows its customer well, knows the customer's reliability as regards ultimate payment and is therefore willing to supply goods on a simple understanding that the customer will pay. No special agreement is necessary for credit to be given on any particular order; there is a continuing flow of orders, goods and payment. In terms of accounting, we need to consider the two separate aspects of this: the purchase of goods on credit and the sale of goods on credit.

Purchases on credit

When goods are purchased on credit, the company buying is gaining a new asset, but instead of exchanging the new inventory asset for a cash asset, the company is acquiring a new liability as the other half of the exchange. In terms of the balance sheet equation the supplier of the goods is making a loan (albeit very short term) to the company.

$$Assets = Liabilities + Equity$$
$$+ Inventory\ 100 = + Payable\ to\ supplier\ 100$$

Later on, when the company settles its debt to the supplier, it will cancel the short-term liability with an exchange for cash:

$$- Cash\ 100 = - Debt\ settlement\ 100$$

	1	2	Final
Assets			
Cash		−100	−100
Inventory	+100		+100
Liabilities			
Trade payables	+100	−100	0

In the long run, the inventory asset is being acquired in exchange for a cash asset, but in the short run there are two stages in the transaction: (1) the acquisition of the asset together with a debt to the supplier, and (2) the cancellation of the debt against a cash payment.

The stage 1 recognition of the inventory and liability to the supplier means that the recording system will always be able to give an up-to-date picture of the amounts owed to suppliers and the amounts acquired for inventory, and will avoid the time delay in recognition which would occur under a system that only recognized cash transactions.

In terms of operating details, of course a company usually has many suppliers, and while for a picture of the company's financial state of affairs the only important number would be the total owed short term to suppliers (representing something which it will shortly be necessary to settle in cash), for internal management purposes the company also needs to know how much is owed to each individual supplier.

What is often done, therefore, is that the general ledger carries an account which aggregates all the amounts owed to suppliers, but the company keeps a separate ledger which duplicates the movements on the total supplier account but holds a separate account for each supplier. The general ledger account then contains summary-level financial data, while the subsidiary ledger is used to record the detailed data for that account. The sum of all the balances of the individual accounts in a subsidiary ledger should equal the amount in the corresponding general ledger account. Each general ledger account that is supported by a subsidiary ledger is called a *control account*. The total supplier account in the general ledger will function as a control account for a subsidiary ledger with all the details of the credit purchase transactions.

Suppliers who provide goods on credit are called *(trade) creditors* and the amounts owed to them *(trade) payables*. So this subsidiary ledger is often called the *creditors' ledger* or *accounts payable ledger*. Again, although we describe this as a ledger, it is unlikely to be a book but rather a computer file storing the details on disk and displaying management information on a screen or printing a hard-copy analysis of balances as required.

Sales on credit

The sale of goods on credit involves exactly the same type of transaction, but viewed from the opposite side. A company which sells on credit similarly needs to recognize the sale and the debt owed to it by its customer. The credit customer is known as a 'debtor' for accounting purposes, because he or she owes a debt to the company. The amount owed by the customer to the company is a 'trade receivable'. The IASB (and US generally accepted accounting principles or US GAAP) uses the term 'receivables' to refer to this type of financial assets, while the EC (European Commission) Accounting Directives typically use the British English terminology and refer to 'debtors' as the corresponding balance sheet item.

Looking at the balance sheet equation, the company wants to recognize a sale (revenue which will increase the value of equity) and an asset (a receivable which is a claim to receive cash from the customer):

$$\text{Assets} = \text{Liabilities} + \text{Equity}$$
$$+ \text{ Receivable } 200 = + \text{ Revenue } 200$$

Subsequently, the debtor will settle the cash owed to the company, and this becomes an exchange between one asset (the claim on the customer) and cash:

$$- \text{ Receivable } 200 + \text{ Cash } 200 = 0$$

BETWEEN THE LINES

What is a creditor?

A creditor is an individual or another company to whom the firm owes money. Another name for it is an account payable. Examples of creditors (or payables):

- *Trade creditors:* Suppliers of raw materials, other inventories, equipment and services which are purchased in the course of business for resale, for which payment has not yet been made.

- *Other creditors:* Amounts owing to outsiders for various other reasons, such as interest payable; usually routine recurring debts for services and supplies ancillary to trading operations.

In a statement of financial position a common distinction is that between amounts due for settlement within 12 months and amounts due for settlement in more than 12 months. Trade creditors (or trade payables) would nearly always be for settlement in substantially less than 12 months.

	1	2	Final
Assets			
Cash		+200	+200
Receivables	+200	−200	0
Equity			
Profit or loss			
Sales	+200		+200

In the general ledger a company would keep an aggregate account of all trade receivables, but here again the operating convenience of managing receivables is best served by a further subsidiary ledger in which all debtors have an individual, personal account. This subsidiary record is called the *accounts receivable ledger* or *debtors' ledger*.

As with the recording of creditors, the system is tracking the daily transactions of the company and therefore reflecting properly the full current financial state of affairs. In other words, the significance of the accruals principle is that the accounts reflect the real changes that have affected the firm's assets, liabilities, revenue and expenses, even though the cash has not changed hands.

The cumulative effect of the entries in the accounts which have just been described is that, at the reporting date, the general ledger shows the total amount owed to suppliers (with supporting detail in the subsidiary accounts payable ledger) and the amount receivable from customers (with detail in the subsidiary accounts receivable ledger).

The accounts receivable ledger function within the financial accounting unit of a company should use the data in its subsidiary ledger to monitor the amount of credit given to customers and the period of credit allowed. In that sense, the data in the subsidiary ledger are useful not only in terms of constantly updating the picture of the company's receivables, revenue and income but also in managing credit effectively and reducing the risk of non-payment. The data in the accounts payable ledger similarly monitors overall trade debts and costs, but also permits of managing supplier accounts to take the maximum period of credit negotiated, making payments at due dates and checking supplier invoices against the delivery information. Both accounts receivable ledger and accounts payable ledger should be exploited to manage the company's short-term finances and to operate internal controls.

One of the crucial internal accounting controls is that the entries on the accounts in the general ledger balance with the summaries of the subsidiary ledgers. The balances of the so-called 'control accounts' in the general ledger for accounts receivable and accounts payable should always equal the total of the balances of the individual accounts in the respective subsidiary ledgers at reporting date. This control is crucial if the entries in the general ledger and in the subsidiary ledger are the result of separate inputs. Separate inputs of the same transaction data can be an important organizational measure to assure the validity, completeness and accuracy of the recording of events.

Recognition of revenue

Revenue is the gross inflow of economic benefits during the period arising in the course of the ordinary activities of a company when these inflows result in increases of shareholders' equity. Put simply, revenue is the money value of goods supplied and services rendered, which is attributable to the current accounting period. The aggregate value for revenue in an accounting period is also described as 'sales' or 'turnover' (in British English). Revenue does not include amounts collected on behalf of third parties such as sales taxes or value added tax (VAT), as these do not result in increases in shareholders' equity (recall the definition of income in the IASB Framework – see Chapter 3).

Revenue is recognized in the statement of profit or loss when it is 'earned', meaning that it is not sufficient merely to have a sale agreement signed, there has to be a certain degree of performance on the part of the supplier as well. The timing of the recognition of revenue is quite important under accruals accounting, as it triggers the matching process where revenues are matched with related expenses to calculate the net effect of a transaction on the profit of the period. Remember that correct profit measurement requires that both revenue and related expenses are recognized in the same period (the matching principle). This also implies that you need to have recognized revenue before a profit can be shown in the statement of profit or loss.

The primary issue in accounting for revenue is determining when the 'earning' process underlying revenue recognition can be considered complete. The procedures normally adopted in practice for recognizing revenue are generally directed at restricting the recognition of revenue to those items that can be measured reliably and represent inflows of economic benefits that can be realized with a sufficient degree of certainty. Revenue recognition will take place when a critical event in the sales process has taken place whereby the uncertainties surrounding the sales transaction (estimates of cost of goods sold, selling price, additional selling costs and the ultimate cash collection) are reduced to an acceptable level and the remaining uncertainties can be estimated with sufficient accuracy.

Timing of revenue recognition

Identifying when the critical event for revenue recognition occurs, is not always straightforward. Let us look at a typical revenue cycle for the sale of goods containing the following stages:

1. customer places order;
2. sales order is recognized after credit approval and inventory check;
3. goods ordered are shipped to customer;
4. customer accepts delivery of goods;
5. sales invoice is prepared and sent to customer;
6. customer pays invoice.

At which stage can the earning process of revenue be considered to be complete? In general, revenue will be attributed to the accounting period in which goods are delivered to the customer or a service is rendered. In other words, revenue is recognized at the point of delivery of the goods or service.

IAS 18, *Revenue*, contains the IASB rules for revenue recognition and measurement and comments on the criteria to identify the critical event that should trigger revenue recognition in different types of sales arrangements. The two most critical criteria to identify an 'earned' sale of goods are (a) the company has transferred the significant risks and rewards of ownership of the goods to the buyer and (b) the company has no longer either managerial involvement nor effective control over the goods. In most cases, fulfilment of these criteria coincides with the transfer of legal title or the passing of possession to the buyer, which normally takes place at delivery and the signing of a delivery note by the customer. Revenue is not recognized when the customer places an order or when the sales order is formally acknowledged. Even though in some companies the amount of revenue that will be earned can be reliably estimated at that time, there has been no real performance of the contract on the part of the seller until the goods have been delivered to the customer. When a payment is received in advance from a customer (before delivery triggers revenue recognition), the company will recognize it as a liability, which is the obligation to deliver goods or render services in the future.

In many cases it is relatively easy to determine what is the point of delivery, but some cases require careful thought – for example, where goods are delivered (or services provided) over a relatively long time period. A ship may take several years to build – does the ship-building company only recognize revenue when the ship is actually handed over to the customer? A legal case may take many months going through the courts – does a solicitor only recognize the revenue in the accounting year when the case is settled? In both examples it would be normal for the client to make payment in a series of instalments, but if the cash value of the instalments were taken to revenue, that would not be an objective assessment of what had been supplied or 'earned'.

IAS 18 requires that for transactions involving the rendering of services over a longer time period (more than one accounting period), revenue should be recognized by reference to the stage of completion of the transaction at the reporting date, provided that revenue, related costs and progress can be measured reliably. This method is often referred to as the '**percentage of completion method**'' (in contrast to the 'completed contract method' which is more common under tax-sensitive accounting regimes). The application of the percentage of completion method in practice will often be based on a professional valuation of the amount of services performed within the single accounting period as a percentage of total services to be performed and using that as a base for allocating revenue, irrespective of cash payments.

Revenue versus gains

Keep in mind that revenue is only one part of income figuring in the statement of profit or loss (although usually by far the most important one). Income encompasses both revenue and gains. The IASB refers to income as an inflow of economic benefits during the period that result in increases in shareholders' equity. Revenue is income that arises in the course of the ordinary activities of the company. Throughout this chapter we assume that revenue is associated with the sale of the company's goods and services, but the company can realize income through other means. For example, if a company sells marketable securities (which figured on its statement of financial position as financial assets) for more than their book value, it realizes economic benefits that increase shareholders' equity, but this is not revenue (unless the company is in the business of selling securities). This type of income is called *gains*, to distinguish it from revenues from selling goods, rendering services or performing other ordinary business activities.

Similarly, decreases in economic benefits during the period that result in decreases of equity (except dividends or other distributions to shareholders) for reasons not associated with the ordinary activities of the company are referred to as 'losses', and these are sometimes distinguished from expenses. Loss of assets through natural disasters as well as losses arising on the disposal of non-current assets, such as buildings or equipment, are typical examples. While revenues and expenses are reported as gross amounts, gains (losses) are often reported net of related expenses (income).

COMPANY REPORT

NOKIA – REVENUE RECOGNITION *(extracts)*

Notes to the consolidated financial statements: 1. Accounting principles
Revenue recognition
Sales from the majority of the Group are recognized when the significant risks and rewards of ownership have transferred to the buyer, continuing managerial involvement usually associated with ownership and effective control have ceased, the amount of revenue can be measured reliably, it is probable that economic benefits associated with the transaction will flow to the Group and the costs incurred or to be incurred in respect of the transaction can be measured reliably.

The Group records reductions to revenue for special pricing agreements, price protection and other volume based discounts. Service revenue is generally recognized on a straight line basis over the service period unless there is evidence that some other method better represents the stage of completion. License fees from usage are recognized in the period when they are reliably measurable, which is normally when the customer reports them to the Group.

In addition, sales and cost of sales from contracts involving solutions achieved through modification of complex telecommunications equipment are recognized using the percentage of completion method when the outcome of the contract can be estimated reliably. A contract's outcome can be estimated reliably when total contract revenue and the costs to complete the contract can be estimated reliably, it is probable that the economic benefits associated with the contract will flow to the Group and the stage of contract completion can be measured reliably. When the Group is not able to meet those conditions, the policy is to recognize revenue only equal to costs incurred to date, to the extent that such costs are expected to be recovered.

Progress towards completion is measured by reference to cost incurred to date as a percentage of estimated total project costs, the cost-to-cost method.

The percentage of completion method relies on estimates of total expected contract revenue and costs, as well as dependable measurement of the progress made towards completing a particular project. Recognized revenues and profits are subject to revisions during the project in the event that the assumptions regarding the overall project outcome are revised. The cumulative impact of a revision in estimates is recorded in the period such revisions become likely and estimable. Losses on projects in progress are recognized in the period they become probable and estimable.

Source: Nokia, Annual Report, 2010

(This is an example of the note to the financial statements of Nokia that illustrates how it applies the accruals and matching principles as regards revenue.)

Period costs

It is worth mentioning here that there are expenses which are time-based and not necessarily transaction-based. Some items of expense are associated with a certain accounting period even though they cannot be traced to any specific revenue generating transactions occurring in that period. Rent of premises is an obvious example where the expense is incurred irrespective of whether any physical use is made of the premises or not. These time-based expenses are called *period costs*. In general, they are the cost of being in business. In a retail chain, for example, the overhead costs of head office activities and the costs of operating the retail stores during the period are costs that cannot be traced directly to the specific merchandise sold.

An accounting recognition issue which is closely related is the recognition within one accounting period of expenses which have not yet been invoiced and where supply is on a continuing basis, such as the supply of electricity and telephone. No physical delivery takes place, and unless invoicing to the company using these facilities coincides exactly with the company's accounting period there will be some adjustment required to ensure that this kind of expense is also properly allocated to the appropriate accounting period. When there is no direct means to connect expenses and revenues, costs should be allocated in a systematic way among the accounting periods in which the business benefits from the costs. However, let us first look at an area where the application of a direct cause-and-effect relationship seems less problematic.

Inventories and profit measurement

An important part of the routine capturing of economic transactions within the system and matching revenue to costs is the treatment of inventories. As we have seen, when a company buys goods to resell (or manufactures goods to sell, which we will also look at in this chapter) their value is treated as an asset by the company (i.e. an item which will generate future positive cash flows for the company). But when the goods are actually sold, this cash flow is realized and the cost of the goods has to be set against it – the inventory has to be 'expensed'.

First we should note that in British English the term used for inventory is 'stock', but in American English 'stock' means shares in a company – quite confusing. As noted before, throughout this book we will use IASB terminology (actually a mix of British and American English) and, thus, the label *inventory*. Let us start just with an assumption that the business buys finished goods for resale, so that we only have one category of inventory which is not processed in any way by the company.

The value of this inventory has a key role to play in the measurement of profit. The cost of goods sold is the amount paid by the retailer to buy the goods which are deemed to have been sold in the current accounting period. The difference between the sales revenue and the cost of goods sold is known as *gross profit* or *gross margin*. It is an important piece of data which can be used by management as a test of a company's efficiency and represents the amount available to a company to meet its operating expenses. The gross margin of two businesses of the same size and selling the same goods should be comparable, and any difference is worth investigation.

Under IFRS, IAS 2, *Inventories*, deals with the recognition of inventory as an asset, specific measurement rules and disclosures about inventories in the notes to the financial statements. Some types of inventories are, however, excluded from IAS 2 and covered by other, more specific standards, such as '**biological assets**', '**agricultural produce**' at the point of '**harvest**' and work in progress on '**construction contracts**'.

Cost of goods sold

The cost of goods sold is the amount paid by the company for the goods it sold to customers in the accounting period. When goods are bought for resale they become an asset – inventory – which is subsequently expensed when the goods are actually sold. For profit measurement purposes a value has to be arrived at for the cost of the goods sold. Of course this might be done by expensing each item when the transaction takes place, and some systems operate that way. But, in practical terms, this is often not worthwhile except where the company sells a very small number of items of high value – say, Rolls-Royce cars, Rolex watches, etc. Usually the measurement may be made just as accurately in terms of the cost for the year (or for a month or a week) by simply calculating the value of goods available for resale during the year and then deducting those which are on hand at the end of the year:

Inventory available at 1/1/X1	XXX
plus goods purchased during year	XXX
Goods available for resale in 20X1	XXX
less cost of inventory on hand 31/12/X1	XXX
= Cost of goods sold during year	**XXX**

Within the data collection system there are various ways of handling the inventory and purchases of goods for resale (or, for that matter, transfers into finished goods from the manufacturing process). The simplest way is to leave the opening inventory account untouched and accumulate new acquisitions of goods for resale in a 'purchases' account. Logically, purchases are made to replenish inventories of goods which have been sold so, in a broad sense, purchases could be expected to approximate to cost of goods sold over a period. At the point where one wants an accurate measure, one measures inventory currently on hand and compares this with the opening inventory value. Any difference is then adjusted against purchases. Supposing opening inventory was €2400, purchases during the period were €5000 and inventory at the end was €2600, the adjustment would be to reduce purchases by €200, which is the increase in inventory, and add that to the existing inventory figure.

A more formal way of doing things is to move the opening inventory into the cost of goods sold or similar account, and then remove the closing inventory at the end of the period. The procedures are not really something you need to worry about. As with many things in accounting there are several different ways of doing it, and the company decides in the light of its information needs. For the purposes of exercises within this book, we will always use the method whereby the inventory remains in a separate account and is adjusted at the end of the measurement period.

Taking a practical example, let us say that a company started the year with an inventory of goods for resale which had cost €3000. During the year it receives further deliveries: April €5000, July €5000 and November €6000. The total value of goods available for sale in 20X1 was €19 000. Supposing that during the year-end stock-take it was recorded that the goods still on hand had an original purchase cost of €4500, the cost of goods sold figure derived (€14 500) will appear in the statement of profit or loss. Supposing that the sales revenue in this case was €25 000, the statement of profit or loss would then show:

	€
Sales	25 000
Cost of goods sold	−14 500
Gross profit	10 500

But note that the published statement of profit or loss might also be presented:

Materials purchased	16 000	Sales	25 000
Gross profit	10 500	Increase in inventories	1 500
	26 500		26 500

In terms of the company's accounting database, the adjustment would appear as follows:

	Closing balances	Inventory adjustment	Statement of profit or loss	Balance sheet
Assets				
Inventory	3 000	+1 500		4 500
Financing				
Sales	25 000		25 000	
Purchases	−16 000	+1 500	−14 500	
Profit				10 500

Calculation of inventory value

You may be able to see at once that the question of the inventory flow and valuation has critical importance in determining the profit of any particular accounting period and has implications for other accounting periods. The closing inventory at the end of the period is a component in determining the cost of goods sold (and therefore gross margin) for two periods: the one ending with that inventory measurement and the one beginning with that inventory measurement.

This can probably best be seen with an example. Let us suppose that a company in its first two years of trading has the following figures:

	Year 1 €	Year 2 €
Sales	20 000	25 000
Purchases	17 000	21 000
Closing inventory value	(a) 2 000	4 000
	(b) 3 000	

As you see, we have included two alternative inventory figures at the end of year 1: figure (a), €2000, is the one the owner has calculated, but the auditor thinks the owner has undervalued the inventory and proposes figure (b), €3000. The company was sold at the end of year 2, with an inventory figure of €4000 agreed by all parties. We have computed the gross profit for the two years, using the owner's and the auditor's inventory figures as at the end of year 1:

Year 1	Using inventory (a) owner's view €	Inventory (b) auditor's view €
Sales	20 000	20 000
Cost of goods sold		
Opening inventory	0	0
Purchases	17 000	17 000
Goods available	17 000	17 000
Closing inventory	(2 000)	(3 000)
Cost of goods sold	15 000	14 000
Gross margin	*5 000*	*6 000*
Gross margin to sales ratio	*25%*	*30%*
Year 2	*(a)* €	*(b)* €
Sales	25 000	25 000
Cost of goods sold		
Opening inventory	2 000	3 000
Purchases	21 000	21 000
Goods available	23 000	24 000
Closing inventory	(4 000)	(4 000)
Cost of goods sold	19 000	20 000
Gross margin	*6 000*	*5 000*
Gross margin to sales ratio	*24%*	*20%*

If you study the figures it will become apparent that where the closing inventory at the end of year 1 has a higher value – column (b) – the gross profit was higher than (a), reflecting the impact of inventory on the cost of goods sold measurement. But the closing inventory is carried forward to become the opening inventory in year 2 and, since it was higher in (b) than (a), the cost of goods sold in year 2 for (b) is higher than for (a), so reversing the year 1 position. By looking at the gross margin percentages you can also see how the inventory figure can distort the measurement of performance.

Of course, if you add the results for the two years together, you will find that the gross profit in aggregate is the same:

	(a)	(b)
	€	€
Year 1	5 000	6 000
Year 2	6 000	5 000
2-year aggregate gross margin	*11 000*	*11 000*

So you can see that, over the complete life cycle of the firm, the inventory measure will have no importance; total profits will be the same. The importance of the inventory measure is that it allocates cost between years and therefore allocates profit between years. Companies trying to minimize profits (say for tax purposes) would be inclined to undervalue inventory, while those trying to maximize profit would maximize inventory valuation.

Your response to this may be that the whole question is irrelevant in that the value of the inventory is surely something which can be empirically proved: you have ten items in inventory and purchase invoices show that these ten cost €X each, so the closing inventory value is €10X. In practice, companies can rarely identify individual items of inventory against the purchase price – nor for that matter would they necessarily find it worth the time and effort to identify individual purchases even if it were possible.

There is also the question of changing prices. In times of inflation, prices are generally changing, although rarely in step with one another, and in a global economy many items are sourced in different currencies. The prices of some items, particularly those reflecting rapid technological change, linked to prime commodities (such as oil, coffee beans, wheat, etc.) or priced in another currency, can fall dramatically or fluctuate quite widely in a short time. It follows that the prices a retailer will pay for items coming into inventory will not normally be level or uniform during any one accounting period.

If identification of individual items is not possible, and prices are not stable, we are left with the major problem of how to ascribe a cost to inventory on hand at the end of the year (or of any other accounting period).

The solution to this problem is that, since individual costs cannot normally be attached to individual items, the accounting measurement can be determined by using assumptions about inventory movements, which need not necessarily coincide exactly with the actual inventory movements since we cannot be certain about the movement of individual items. Indeed, accounting principles such as prudence may call for valuation approaches which differ from physical inventory flow patterns. Later in this chapter we will go on to look at the various methods available to ascribe an accounting cost to inventory using various assumptions about inventory utilization patterns.

Relevant costs

The allocation of purchase price to individual items is not the only problem, though. We must also consider whether the purchase price is in itself the appropriate reflection of the inventory asset. There are two considerations here: on the one hand, prudence demands that we do not use an inventory measure which overstates the value of the inventory and, on the other hand, we should consider whether we have added any value to the goods since they were first purchased.

There is a risk of overstating inventory values when prices fluctuate rapidly. For example, a British importer of a commodity may have ordered 1m tonnes at $28.00, while the £/$ 'exchange rate' was £1 = $1.20, giving rise to a historical cost of £23.33m. Assuming that the commodity was held in stock, but that the £/$ rate moved to £1 = $1.50, although the price of the commodity in dollars might remain fixed, the market value of the 1m tonnes in sterling would drop from £23.33m to £18.67m. Is it then reasonable to continue to value the inventory at £23.33m? Accounting principles usually require that if an asset is held for resale and its historical cost exceeds the market value (this is usually called the 'net realizable value' – that is, what the company could obtain by selling the inventory at the market price, less any selling costs), the value should be *written down* (i.e. reduced) to reflect the unrealized loss. We will come back to this issue later in this chapter.

The other side of the valuation question, additions to value, is perhaps rather more difficult to pin down. It may be that in most cases a retailer, for example, buys goods wholesale, puts them on display and sells them, without in any way changing them. But if the retailer is involved in any costs which improve the product or change it in some way (e.g. a PC hardware supplier buys processors, flat screens, keyboards and DVD devices from separate suppliers and sells them together as a workstation), it could be argued that these costs (repackaging) are part of the inventory asset since they represent an aspect of the cost in bringing the goods to the condition where they can be sold to the customer.

The problem may perhaps be more clearly seen in relation to a second-hand car dealer. Supposing the dealer buys a car in bad condition after a crash but then repairs it, resprays it and generally restores it to a better condition. The item which is finally put on display and sold is not the same item which was bought in the first place. Should its inventory value be the purchase price alone or should it reflect the purchase price and the costs of renovating it or, indeed, should it be valued at what it would cost the dealer to buy a car in renovated condition?

If the inventory value was only the purchase price this would ignore the extra costs associated with bringing the car to a saleable condition so, arguably, it would not match that cost and the subsequent profit on sale, which is what accounting tries to do.

But what about carrying the car at a value based on what it would have cost to buy it already renovated? There certainly appears to be a case for it, since one can argue that it is possible to perceive two stages in the dealer's profit-creating: stage 1 is buying a car and working on it to increase its wholesale value, while stage 2 is simply selling the car. There is a case for recognizing the value gained in stage 1 at a theoretical level but this brings us back to the problem of prudence: the gain has not been realized, i.e. it is purely notional since the car has not been sold. The dealer has increased his or her profit potential but until the car is sold no 'accounting profit' has been made.

The principle should now be clear: all the costs associated with creating a particular asset should be expensed at the same time as the asset is consumed (sold to the customer), in order to match revenues with expenses. Until the item is sold the costs should accumulate as part of the value of the asset, subject to the rule of being carried at the lower of cost or net realizable value.

IAS 2, *Inventories*, requires that the 'cost of inventories' comprises 'all 'costs of purchase', 'costs of conversion' and other costs incurred in bringing the inventories to their present location and condition' (IAS 2, par.10). The purchase cost of inventory comprises the purchase price, import duties and other non re-coverable taxes, and transport, handling and other costs directly attributable to the acquisition of the inventory items. Trade discounts, rebates and other simi-lar items are deducted in determining the purchase price. Conversion costs re-late to manufacturing processes and will be commented on later in this chapter (see the section on manufacturing accounts). The cost of inventories does not include wastage, administrative overheads and selling costs. Storage costs are not included unless those costs are necessary in the production process before a fur-ther production stage.

Inventory accounting techniques

Having reviewed the problems underlying the accounting measurement of inven-tory values, we can now look at the practices employed. In this area we can iden-tify three different categories:

1. continuous inventory, where individual items are identified for accounting purposes;
2. measurement methods that rely on assumptions about inventory move-ments (but do not increase inventory value by adding in any associated costs);
3. methods used where the inventory value of goods for resale includes costs other than the initial purchase price.

Continuous inventory

Although in most industries it is impractical to attach to individual goods the cost of acquiring them, there are some cases where either the nature of the busi-ness or the technology used to control inventory allows this 'actual' valuation.

If a business deals in a small volume of high-value items which are not homo-geneous, as, for example, does a dealer in fine art, it is perfectly possible to keep records of the cost of each individual item of merchandise, so no assumptions need to be made about inventory movements. Each item can have its acquisition cost recorded and this can be expensed individually when the item is sold, leaving a closing inventory value which relates quite specifically to the items still in hand.

Computer technology has also made possible the treatment of individual in-ventory items at their actual purchase price because the ability of a computer to deal with an enormous volume of data means that there is a facility for keeping this information available. However, such techniques are unlikely to be used sim-ply so that inventory can be on an actual basis – generally it is part of the man-agement information system to monitor levels of inventory (for reordering and checking how fast individual items are moving) and to keep a check on buying prices to be sure that selling prices achieve the required gross profit margin on an item-by-item basis.

In short, what is called a *continuous inventory system* has considerable manage-ment benefits in a sophisticated retail business. One advantage may be the ability to calculate an actual cost of goods sold, though the cost of the system is justified not by that, but by the management controls and profit maximization which it provides.

Accounting assumptions

In this area we are taking the cost of each individual item as given, and then using methods based on assumptions about inventory movements to allocate those costs between the cost of sales expense and the inventory asset carried forward to the next year.

These methods would be applicable to any retailing business and to the retailing side of a manufacturing business. For example, going back to our used-car dealer, once cars had been refurbished they would come into inventory at a figure which included initial costs plus refurbishing costs. These systems deal with the subsequent transfer of those costs to expense at the time of sale and are therefore equally applicable whether the company is buying finished goods in from outside and simply reselling them, or whether it is adding value in some way by processing before selling. These systems come into play once the good is ready for resale and enters the retailing system.

There are three generally recognized systems for accounting for inventory within a historical cost framework: LIFO, 'FIFO' and weighted average.

1. *LIFO* (Last In First Out) assumes that the first item of inventory to be sold will be the last item delivered into the stores. It allocates an accounting value to the cost of goods sold which uses the most recent purchase of goods into the stores.
2. *FIFO* (First In First Out) assumes that inventory will be rotated in an orderly manner consistent with good housekeeping: newly delivered items will go to the back of the shelf and the oldest items will be the first sold.
3. *Weighted average*, on the other hand, ascribes a cost to sold units based on the average cost of all the items of that type which were on hand at the time of sale. A new average is computed each time a sale takes place.

Common-sense physical inventory control tends to follow FIFO principles: inventory would be rotated so that the oldest inventory is sold first. But there may be good reasons why, for accounting purposes, we should make the opposite assumption.

In periods of rising prices (and if we disregard temporary fluctuations and goods where technological change has affected their manufacturing cost, the trend for the past hundred years has been for prices to rise), LIFO will provide the lowest inventory value and the lowest profit (making it popular for tax purposes in some countries). FIFO, however, provides a higher inventory value and consequently a higher profit measurement. Weighted average provides a compromise solution to inventory valuation problems in so far as it always produces a final value between FIFO and LIFO. In the UK the vast majority of companies use FIFO for inventory valuation. Practice in other countries is more mixed. Weighted average is popular in continental Europe, whereas a significant number of US companies use LIFO.

When the IASB revised IAS 2, *Inventories* in 2003, the IASB eliminated the use of LIFO to measure the cost of inventories, arguing that it is generally not a reliable representation of actual inventory flows. Consequently, companies obliged to follow IFRS do not have the opportunity to use the LIFO assumption. It has become therefore a noticeable difference with US GAAP that will probably call for attention in the future.

Company policy in this area is much influenced by their tax environment and their profit objectives. A low value ending inventory will reduce current year profits and carry them forward as a kind of hidden reserve in the form of under-valued inventories. If the tax regime permits such practices, a private company will certainly adopt a low inventory value strategy (in the UK, LIFO is not allowed for tax purposes, but in Switzerland, companies are allowed to reduce the account-ing value of their inventory by one-third every year as a tax incentive). Where artificially low values are not allowed, private companies will tend to 'lose' inven-tory, while public companies may prefer anyway to record a higher current profit.

Note that the principle of consistency does not allow a company to switch in-ventory valuation methods from one year to another.

Later, when comparing one company's performance with another, you should check inventory valuation methods used to see that they are equivalent. Note also that US companies, if they use LIFO, are required to state the FIFO value of their inventories in the notes to the financial statements.

Net realizable value

Even when we arrive at a historical cost measure of the inventory on hand at re-porting date using one of the major inventory flow assumptions, our efforts may not end there. In fact, IAS 2, *Inventories*, requires that inventory is valued at his-torical cost, unless its net realizable value is lower. In that case the inventory value should be written down below cost to net realizable value. So the general measure-ment rule is that inventories are measured at the lower of cost and net realizable value. This measurement rule is consistent with the view that assets should not be carried in excess of amounts expected to be recovered from their sale or use.

The net realizable value of inventory items is the net amount that a company expects to realize from the sale of inventory in the ordinary course of business. Writing down the inventory may become necessary for a number of reasons. For

STANDARDS

IAS 2 – INVENTORIES – NET REALIZABLE VALUE *(extracts)*

6. Net realizable value is the estimated selling price in the ordinary course of business less the estimated costs of completion and the estimated costs nec-essary to make the sale.
9. Inventories shall be measured at the lower of cost and net realizable value.
34. When inventories are sold, the carrying amount of those inventories shall be recognized as an expense in the period in which the related revenue is rec-ognized. The amount of any write-down of inventories to net realizable value and all losses of inventories shall be recognized as an expense in the period the write-down or loss occurs. The amount of any reversal of any write-down of inventories, arising from an increase in net realizable value, shall be recog-nized as a reduction in the amount of inventories recognized as an expense in the period in which the reversal occurs.

Source: IAS 2, Inventories

example, the inventory has become damaged, is wholly or partly obsolete or its selling price has declined. Additionally, the costs to complete or the estimated costs to be incurred to make the sale may have increased to levels such that the costs of inventory may not be recovered from sale.

If there are established selling prices for the inventory items, the comparison of cost and net realizable value can be straightforward. In most cases, however, considerable judgement will be necessary to arrive at an accurate comparison. Note that net realizable value is an '**entity-specific value**' and estimates of it have to take into consideration the specific purpose for which the inventory is held. For example, if inventory items are designated to satisfy specific sales contracts, the estimate of the net realizable value should be based on the contract price and not on general selling prices, or if it is an inventory of materials held for use in the production of finished goods, the materials inventory will not be written down below cost if the finished goods in which they will be incorporated are expected to be sold above their cost.

The amount of any write-down of inventories to net realizable value will be recognized as an expense in the period the write-down occurs. The write-down to net realizable value is thus not governed by the revenue matching principle which triggers the cost of goods sold calculation.

Accruals and the working capital cycle

We have seen that the use of accruals in accounting leads to the existence within the statement of financial position of a number of short-term assets and liabilities which are linked to the trading or '**operating cycle**' and, because they are part of a cycle, linked to each other, even if the presentation of the statement of financial position splits the liabilities from the assets. Conventional thinking in this area talks about the concept of 'working capital' and the working capital cycle (Figure 4.1). The working capital cycle models the operating activity of the company as a continuous chain of events:

- Purchase of raw materials for production (or goods for resale) gives rise to trade payables (or creditors) and inventories.
- During production raw materials are converted into finished goods inventories.
- Finished goods are sold to customers, which reduces inventories and creates receivables.
- Customers pay their invoices, which reduces receivables and increases cash.
- Cash is used to pay creditors and a residual cash balance is left, representing the profit (assuming a profit has been made!).

The working capital cycle (or operating cycle) can be defined as the average time it takes to acquire materials, services and labour, manufacture the product, sell the product and collect the proceeds from customers. It is a useful management model for showing the interrelationships within the operating cycle, and some Anglo-Saxon statements of financial position present current assets (inventories, cash and trade receivables in Figure 4.1) and current liabilities (trade payables) together, to emphasize that they are economically linked. However, it does not in all cases explain the cash balance in a company, which is essentially a residual which includes short-term elements of financing and '**investing activities**'.

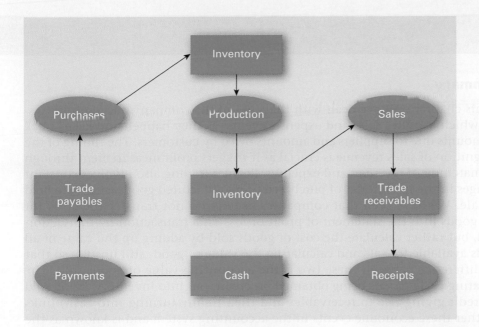

Figure 4.1
The working
capital cycle

You should see that, because accounting tries to capture data when there is an economic event, and not just a cash transaction, the operating cycle involves a series of changes in working capital before a particular cycle is complete and the operation has been completed and a net inflow or outflow of cash has occurred. If a company stopped operating, this part of its statement of financial position would disappear, since it is only concerned with short-term operating events and, equally, when we wish to explain why, over a year, the profit does not equal net cash flow, changes in working capital are a significant part of the answer.

COMPANY REPORT

NOKIA – INVENTORIES *(extracts)*

Notes to the consolidated financial statements – 1. Accounting principles
Inventories are stated at the lower of cost or net realizable value. Cost is determined using standard cost, which approximates actual cost, on a FIFO (First-in First-out) basis. Net realizable value is the amount that can be realized from the sale of the inventory in the normal course of business after allowing for the costs of realization.

In addition to the cost of materials and direct labour, an appropriate proportion of production overheads is included in the inventory values.

An allowance is recorded for excess inventory and obsolescence based on the lower of cost or net realizable value.

Source: Nokia, Annual Report, 2010

Summary

In this chapter we have dealt with that part of the company's accounting system which captures sales and expense 'events' as they happen and keeps track of amounts due to suppliers and amounts owed by customers. The timing of the recognition of sales revenue is crucial as it triggers profit measurement through the matching of revenues and expenses. Regular trading also involves constant changes in the inventories of purchased or manufactured goods which are held for sale. We have seen that companies usually do not transfer the costs for sold goods into the statement of profit or loss on a transaction-by-transaction basis, but rather calculate the cost of goods sold by adding up the value of all goods available for sale and calculating the value of goods still unsold, so that the difference between these two is the accounting value of goods sold. The operating cycle (goods being obtained on credit, put into inventory, being sold on credit giving rise to receivables and then finally turning into cash) links together these economic events in the accounting system and is known as the *working capital cycle*.

Discussion Questions

1. Explain the link between accruals accounting and the concept of working capital.
2. Elaborate how the concept of accruals is applied in accounting for inventory.
3. What is the meaning of a net realizable value test?
4. Describe the issues of revenue and profit recognition relating to construction contracts.
5. What is the primary difference between a periodic inventory system and a perpetual inventory system?
6. A company usually reports on different types of inventory. Elaborate these and explain how they are different.

APPENDICES

1. **Applying LIFO/FIFO and average cost assumptions to inventory**

A detailed knowledge of each basis of measuring inventory is not necessarily useful for non-accounting management, but in order to see how each system works in practice, there follows a very simple set of inventory transactions. You can follow these through, if you wish, to see how they can acquire a different accounting value according to each of the three methods.

Imagine a student who spends his summer selling cold drinks on the beach in the South of France. He buys his inventory from a wholesaler and sells individual cans on the beach. During the summer his inventory turnover works out like this:

	Buys	*Sells*
June	100 crates @ €1.00	90 crates
July	150 crates @ €1.20	120 crates
August	150 crates @ €1.30	160 crates
Total	400 (cost €475)	370

At the end of August, therefore, he has on hand 30 crates of drinks and in order to arrive at an accounting measure of profit he needs to work out a cost of goods sold for the 370 crates sold, and an inventory value for the remaining 30 crates. Notice that:

1. We are not concerned with the selling price of his goods. We are trying to measure the cost of those goods, which is entirely independent of what he received when they were sold. Of course we need to know in due course what the sales revenue was, in order to deduct cost of goods sold and arrive at a profit figure.
2. The wholesale price is rising throughout the period. If the buying price were stable, then the cost of goods sold would be the same under all three methods. It is only under conditions of changing prices that there is a problem about allocating cost in this context.

LIFO

The LIFO model charges out withdrawals from inventory at the value of the most recent invoice, subject to the constraint of quantities. If the inventory withdrawal is for 100 units and the last invoice was for 120, that price is used; but if the last delivery was 80, then the excess of 20 will be costed at the price of the next to last delivery and so on.

Use of the LIFO system has made the following allocations:

	€
Cost of goods sold (€90 + €144 + €207)	441.00
Closing inventory	34.00
Total goods purchased	475.00

Notice that the original inventory at the end of June is still part of the accounting value of inventory, and this is a particular feature of LIFO. Unless a business actually runs out of inventory, the accounting measure of inventory is likely to be at a very old rate (imagine a company which is still selling the same goods after 50 years), while the cost of goods sold will be a recent purchase cost.

	Cost of goods in	Cost of goods sold	LIFO inventory
June			
	100 × €1.00	90 × €1.00 = €90.00	10 × €1.00 = €10.00
July			
	150 × €1.20	120 × €1.20 = €144.00	10 × €1.00 = €10.00
			30 × €1.20 = €36.00
			Total = €46.00
August			
	150 × €1.30	150 × €1.30 = €195.00	10 × €1.00 = €10.00
		10 × €1.20 = €12.00	20 × €1.20 = €24.00
		Total = €207.00	Total = €34.00

Note that in July the delivery was in excess of the withdrawal, so the July price was used for the withdrawal, while in August the withdrawal was greater than the delivery, so was costed at a mixture of the August delivery plus the balance from the July delivery remaining in the inventory valuation.

FIFO

The FIFO model assumes that all transfers out of inventory are made from the oldest goods in store at that time. Using our cold drink figures as for LIFO, this would give us the allocations between cost of goods sold and inventory which are shown here:

	Cost of goods in	Cost of goods out	FIFO inventory
June			
	100 × €1.00	90 × €1.00 = €90.00	10 × €1.00 = €10.00
July			
	150 × €1.20	10 × €1.00 = €10.00	40 × €1.20 = €48.00
		110 × €1.20 = €132.00	
		Total = €142.00	
August			
	150 × €1.30	40 × €1.20 = €48.00	30 × €1.30 = €39.00
		120 × €1.30 = €156.00	
		Total = €204.00	

The system has allocated the cost of the deliveries as follows:

	€
Cost of goods sold (€90 + €142 + €204)	436.00
Inventory at end of period	39.00
Total goods purchased	475.00

Notice that in this case the closing inventory value is at the most recent price. Where prices are rising this means that FIFO will give the highest closing inventory figure – and therefore the lowest cost of goods sold. But if prices are falling, the opposite will hold good.

Weighted average

The weighted average method adjusts the average price of all units in inventory each time there is a new purchase. For example, if the existing inventory is ten units with an average cost of €7.00 and then five more units are delivered at a cost of €8.00 each, any subsequent withdrawal will be costed at:

$$(10 \times €7 + 5 \times €8)/15 = €7.33 \text{ per unit}$$

The allocations made by the weighted average using our original example are:

	Cost of goods in	Cost of goods out	Weighted average inventory
June			
	100 × €1.00	90 × €1.00 = €90.00	10 × €1.00 = €10.00
July			
	150 × €1.20	150 × €1.20 110 × €1.00 = €190	40/160 × €190 = €47.50
		120/160 × €190 = €142.50	
August			
	150 × €1.30	150 × €1.30 + €47.50 = €242.50	30/190 × €242.50 = €38.30
		160/190 × €242.50 = €204.20	

The allocation of the purchases under this method works out as follows:

	€
Cost of goods sold (€90 + €142.50 + €204.20)	436.70
Closing inventory	38.30
Total goods purchased	475.00

The main disadvantage of this method is that it can be quite cumbersome in use, given that the average has to be recalculated every time there is a new delivery of merchandise.

Impact on gross profit

The next stage in considering the use of different inventory valuation systems, is to see what impact the choice of method has on the state of the financial affairs of the company.

If we say that the sales revenue achieved by our student selling cola was €740, his results would look like this:

	LIFO €	FIFO €	Weighted average €
Sales	740.00	740.00	740.00
Cost of goods sold	(441.00)	(436.00)	(436.70)
Gross profit	299.00	304.00	303.30
Balance sheet:			
Value of inventory	34.00	39.00	38.30

The choice of inventory measurement system provides a choice of profit measures. In our particular example the difference between each of the three is not great, but then the quantities involved are not substantial. In a major company the inventory, on hand, could run to several million pounds, therefore a method which has a result 10 per cent different could result in a quite different view of the company's performance.

2. Manufacturing accounts
    We would regard it as beyond the scope of this book to examine in great detail how a manufacturing business (or any business which processes goods before re-sale) accounts for and allocates costs between expenses and the asset value of the finished goods [this is a complex and relatively controversial question normally dealt with in the context of managerial (cost) accounting]. However, a general picture is certainly germane to your understanding of financial accounting.
    As we have discussed, the matching principle calls for revenues and expenses which relate to the same transaction to be recognized in the statement of profit or loss of the same period. It follows that all the costs of manufacturing a product should therefore be expensed at the moment when the product is sold. Typically a manufacturing concern buys raw materials, processes them and then sells them. The actual amount of time taken for the production cycle to be completed will vary from one industry to another, but may last many months between the initial delivery of raw materials and the finished goods moving into the warehouse.
    Until the goods enter the warehouse, all the costs associated with producing them are accumulated and treated as an asset. However, the problems arise in defining exactly what are the costs associated with producing the finished goods.
    We can easily distinguish between two broad categories of cost: direct cost and overhead. Direct costs are those costs which arise directly from the manufacture of the product – for example, the raw materials, the cost of the workers who actually produce the good, packaging, etc. These can be seen quite clearly to form part of the asset.
    Where we run into problems is in the area of overheads where the cost cannot be so easily allocated. Typical overheads might be:

    ■   supervisory production staff;
    ■   cost of machines used in production;

- cost of energy used in production;
- cost of factory building (rent, maintenance, rates, etc.);
- cost of product design team;
- cost of accounting department;
- cost of general management.

As you go down the list, the costs become more remote from the production of the finished good, and it is difficult to pinpoint where exactly the line is drawn between costs which should be allocated to the finished product and costs which should be immediately expensed as part of the general operating expenses.

The answer differs from one company to another, and indeed this is another factor which is influenced by national characteristics and the tax environment. Where tax measurement is linked closely to the company accounts, there is an incentive to carry the minimum of costs in the accounting value of manufactured goods and pass as many costs as possible immediately into expense, to defer tax. As a rule of thumb, expenses such as those of operating the factory (where they can be separated) might be allocated to the asset, while general business operating expenses such as office staff would not be treated as part of the asset. However, some companies may well treat only direct costs such as direct labour and raw materials as part of the asset and expense the rest immediately. One side-effect of this is that where two companies in the same industry make different allocations, their financial statements will not be directly comparable: what is an operating expense in one may be treated as an asset in the other and expensed in the next period.

By way of a simple example, let us suppose that a small factory produces ashtrays. It buys plates of stainless steel which are stamped out by a press into the shape of an ashtray. The factory is operated by four people; three are directly employed producing the ashtrays while the fourth manages the business and handles sales. The monthly payroll is €2800, of which €1000 goes to the manager. The factory is rented and costs €1000 a month; the building includes the offices in which the manager works and these occupy one-tenth of the floor space. During the month of August the electricity bill is €100 and the raw materials consumed were worth €1210. We might allocate the costs as follows:

	Total costs (€)	Production costs (€)	Other operating costs (€)
Payroll	2800	1800	1000
Rent	1000	900	100
Electricity	100	90	10
Raw materials	1210	1210	—
Totals	5110	4000	1110

You can see that even in so simple an example the allocations are problematical: Does the manager not supervise production in any way? Is it reasonable to allocate the electricity bill on the basis of floor area when the machines probably use proportionately more than the office?

The main point though is that €4000 would be treated as costs incurred in producing the finished goods. If the production in the month was 2000 ashtrays, these would appear in the balance sheet at an inventory value of €2 each (€4000 divided by 2000 units) and would pass into the retail part of the business (the equivalent of 'purchases') as being delivered at €2 each. You can see that, if the rent, for example, were treated as a period operating cost and not allocated to the product, the average product cost would decrease to about €1.50: it follows that for internal management purposes it is vital to understand fully how costs are allocated within the company's system; ignorance could lead to wrong decisions, such as how great the unit profit margin is.

The €1110 would be expensed immediately as operating expenses. The ashtrays, however, would be expensed only when they were sold – and at a value which depended upon whether LIFO, FIFO or weighted average was in use.

It is also worth mentioning at this point that a manufacturing business will have a number of different components to its inventory. Aside from the inventory of finished goods, it will also have inventory of raw materials and probably a value for *work in progress* (sometimes 'work in process'). The latter value simply acknowledges that, where the production cycle takes some time, there will at any given reporting date be products which are only part completed.

Assignments

The following questions have answers on the lecturer side of the digital support resources for the book.

1. Allocate revenue between different accounting periods in the following cases:

    (a) Carolyn works as a freelance journalist. In November 20X1 she wrote an article for a magazine. The article appeared in the February 20X2 issue and she was paid in March 20X2. She draws up her financial statements to 31 December.

    (b) Beker Industries manufactures and installs specialized telecommunications equipment at the premises of customers on behalf of Teleworks, a network operator. On 15 December 20X5 Teleworks placed an order with Beker Industries to manufacture and instal 210 specialized equipment items at the plant sites of its customers. Beker Industries had the items on inventory and shipped them to the customers' plants on 28 December 20X5. Beker Industries expects to instal the equipment by 5 January 20X6. Payment is due 14 days after installations of the goods.

    (c) Standard International runs a small chain of bookshops. During the month of December 20X6 it sold books for an amount of €800000. It also sold €100000 worth of gift certificates, 5 per cent of which were redeemed by customers for merchandise in the same month.

    (d) Merseyside Ship-building Inc. receives an order to build a small cargo ship. The work starts on 1 July 20X2. At 31 December 20X2 the ship is 10 per cent complete, at 31 December 20X3 it is 80 per cent complete and the ship finally leaves the yard on 30 June 20X4. During this period Merseyside Ship-building received the following payments from the client: 31 July 20X2 €500000; 1 January 20X3 €500000; 30 June 20X3 €500000; 31 December 20X3 €500000; 30 June 20X4 €750000; 1 January 20X5 €1250000 (final instalment).

(e) Wirral Electrical sells electric appliances wholesale. In November 20X1 it sold 20 fan heaters at €15 each to a retailer (Meols Stores) and in December a further 30 at €15 each to the same customer. In February 20X2 Meols Stores pays its outstanding account, subject to deduction of €30 for two defective heaters which it returned at the same time. In April 20X2 Meols Stores sends back a further heater, demanding a refund because it does not work. How would Wirral deal with this situation in its financial statements?

2. **Review the following revenue-related transactions of Borlo AG with regard to its fiscal year ending on 31 December 20X8.**

■ On 30 June 20X8 the company recognized revenue on a sale of its products for €30 m. The terms of the sale include free after-sales service for a period of two years. The cost to Borlo AG of the after-sales service is estimated to be €2 m per annum and a reasonable profit margin on the service would be 20 per cent.

■ On 20 December 20X8 the company sold goods and recognized revenue on delivery of the goods. The goods had a manufacturing cost of €10 m and were sold at a gross profit margin of 20 per cent. The goods were supplied on a sale or return basis, with a right to return up to and including 31 May 20X9. The customer had returned 50 per cent of the goods by 1 March 20X9. It is uncertain as to how many of the remaining goods will be returned prior to 31 May 20X9.

3. Wirral Electrical had the following statement of financial position as at 31 December 20X1:

	€
Assets	
Inventories	400
Trade receivables	2 500
Cash	1 500
	4 400
Liabilities and equity	
Payables	3 200
Equity	1 200
	4 400

During 20X2 the following business was done:

	€
Cash sales	8 500
Credit sales	14 000
Receipts from clients	13 250
Payments to creditors	17 500
Purchases of goods on credit	18 400
Overheads paid cash	3 000

You are asked to:

(a) Enter the opening statement of financial position and subsequent transactions on a spreadsheet (or any other working paper).

(b) Prepare a statement of profit or loss and statement of financial position as at 31 December 20X2 (closing inventory was €600).

4. The inventory of Lowhill Gravel Company on 30 April 20X4 shows 500 tons of gravel at €7.00 per ton. A physical inventory on 31 May 20X4 shows a total of 600 tons on hand. Revenue from sales of gravel for May 20X4 totals €18 000. All sales took place after the purchases for the month of May were made. The following purchases were made during May 20X4:

Purchase date	Tons	€/ton
5 May	1 000	8.00
15 May	250	9.00
25 May	300	10.00

You are asked to:

(a) Compute the inventory value as of 31 May 20X4, using (i) FIFO, (ii) LIFO and (iii) the weighted average inventory valuation method.

(b) Compute the gross profit using each method.

5. The owner of Mansfield Supply Co. Ltd is considering a change of accounting policy as regards closing inventory valuation. For the first three years of the business the company has used FIFO but the owner is now considering a change to weighted average. Condensed financial statements are given below.

You are asked to provide alternative statements based on the alternative inventory valuations.

The relevant year-end inventory valuations according to the new method would be 31 December 20X1 €7400, 31 December 20X2 €9800, 31 December 20X3 €6900.
Statement of profit or loss for year ended:

	31 Dec. 20X1		31 Dec. 20X2		31 Dec. 20X3	
	€	€	€	€	€	€
Sales		120 000		150 000		110 000
Opening inventory	—		6 300		8 100	
Purchases	68 000		82 900		63 400	
Closing inventory	6 300		8 100		6 700	
Cost of goods sold		61 700		81 100		64 800
Gross profit		58 300		68 900		45 200
Distribution/admin.						
Expenses		59 100		64 800		44 800
Net profit/(loss)		(800)		4 100		400

Statement of financial position as at:

	31 Dec. 20X1 €	31 Dec. 20X2 €	31 Dec. 20X3 €
Non-current assets (net)	36000	32000	28000
Inventory	6300	8100	6700
Cash	2700	10900	13300
Total	45000	51000	48000
Equity			
Share capital	40000	40000	40000
Reserves		−800	3300
Profit/(loss) for year	(800)	4100	400
	39200	*43300*	*43700*
Trade payables	5800	7700	4300
Total	45000	51000	48000

6. The accounting records of RobinHood SA show the following inventory, purchases and sales data for the month of April:

Inventory			
	April 1	90 units @ €4	€360
Purchases			
	April 2	60 units @ €3.50	€210
	April 15	40 units @ €6	€240
	April 27	80 units @ €4.50	€360
Sales			
	April 7	70 units	
	April 18	30 units	
	April 24	40 units	

The company uses a periodic inventory system.

The physical inventory count on April 30 amounts to 130 units of inventory.

Required: Determine the cost of inventory on hand at April 30 and the cost of goods sold for April under (a) the FIFO method; (b) the LIFO method, and (c) the weighted average method

7. Complete the missing figures:

	A	B	C	D	E
Opening inventory	...	236	647	9375	5296
Closing inventory	12200	110	...	8760	5820
Purchases	110500	937	5122	76420	...
Cost of goods sold	108950	...	4928	...	33996

8. The following transactions took place at a wholesale wine merchants during the month of August:

01 Opening inventory	72 crates @ €20
02 Purchase	20 crates @ €21
04 Sale	40 crates @ €30
05 Purchase	60 crates @ €23
09 Sale	60 crates @ €30
12 Sale	35 crates @ €30
13 Purchase	40 crates @ €24
17 Sale	10 crates @ €32
20 Purchase	50 crates @ €25
22 Sale	30 crates @ €32
23 Sale	30 crates @ €32
24 Purchase	45 crates @ €26
28 Sale	40 crates @ €32

You are asked to:

(a) compute the closing inventory according to FIFO, LIFO and weighted average assumptions;

(b) compute gross profit under each assumption.

9. Pino Fabrics manufactures three main products and provides the following data with regard to its year-end inventories:

	Product A	Product B	Product C
Production cost	400	180	240
Selling price	600	240	440
Additional cost to enable sale	—	40	160
Marketing costs	140	40	40
Number of items	20 000	18 000	10 000

You are asked to:

(a) apply a net realizable value test;

(b) propose inventory value adjustments.

CHAPTER 5

Non-current assets and depreciation

In this chapter we are going to look at how the costs of productive facilities, computers and other equipment which are used up by the business are passed through the statement of profit or loss and disappear from the statement of financial position as part of the matching process. The chapter starts with an overview of the general principles of asset valuation. We then consider the main categories of non-current or long-term assets and their specific recognition and measurement characteristics.

Chapter Structure

- Introduction
- General valuation principles of non-current assets
- Expensing non-current assets
- Accounting for depreciation
- Specific valuation principles by type of non-current assets
- Intangible assets
- Tangible assets
- Investments
- Summary
- Discussion questions
- Assignments

Introduction

We have earlier used the model of the company as an empty shell where finance is put in, the finance is used to buy productive capacity and then profits are made (one hopes) by using this capacity. However, the productive capacity (i.e. long-term assets such as buildings or machinery) is used up over time in a company's operations. Accordingly that use must be recognized as an expense in the statement of profit or loss (income statement/profit and loss account), and adjustments made to the value of the assets in the statement of financial position (balance sheet). The profit measure each year would be an over-estimate, if no attempt were made to *match* the using up of the productive capacity with the revenues that are derived from its use.

Just as the inventory of finished goods is consumed and expensed in the course of a company's operations, many other assets are also consumed – although they are frequently consumed at such a slow pace that it may not at first be evident that they should be considered as an expense. Indeed, in the 19th century, early companies such as the railways took the view that their non-current assets had such a long potential life that only repairs required to maintain them at the appropriate level should be expensed – no reduction in accounting value from the original cost was provided.

However, most long-lived assets are eventually consumed. For example, a simple retail operation might take place in a shop on the main street of a town. If the business owns the premises outright, you might ask whether the premises are in any way consumed during business operations. Well, the shop front will deteriorate in condition (wood or aluminium has a finite life) but, perhaps more important, the business may well depend on an attractive, modern presentation to attract customers and therefore it will be necessary to modernize the shop front every five years or so. In either case, there is some limitation on the life of a long-term asset and it will ultimately have to be replaced. If the asset is replaced by a new one, it follows logically that the old asset has been consumed and this expense should be recognized.

For some long-term assets the consumption may be clearer: a business that uses vans for distributing its product or cars for its sales force to visit the customers has assets whose life is limited. Say a van is bought for €30 000, is used in the business for two years and then sold for €10 000: it is quite clear that in those two years the business has consumed €20 000-worth of van. For the accountant there is a problem: there is an expense of €20 000 covering two years which (a) must be recognized in the statement of profit or loss as such, (b) reflects a diminution of asset value which should therefore be reflected in the value of the asset in the statement of financial position, and (c) needs to be matched with the operations to comply with the matching principle and therefore should be allocated across two years of operations.

Looked at from another point of view, every asset is an unexpired expense and at every accounting date a company must review to what extent each individual asset has been consumed during the financial year. The expense must be *recognized* (brought into the accounts), offset against revenue for a more accurate measure of net income and the revised value of the asset shown in the statement of financial position. In principle, all assets can be regarded as a bundle of goods or

BETWEEN THE LINES

IASB FRAMEWORK – DEFINITION AND RECOGNITION OF AN ASSET

Recall that the IASB Framework defines an asset as a resource controlled by a company as a result of past events from which *future economic benefits* are expected to flow to the company. The asset will be recognized if (a) it is probable that *future economic benefits* associated with the element will flow to the entity and (b) the item has a cost or value that can be measured reliably. The point is that assets represent future economic benefits and these will be gradually consumed through the use of the asset.

Applied to a van, this means that, provided that the van is useful in the company's operations and its purchase value is certain, it should be treated as an asset. As the van is used, the amount of future economic benefits is decreasing and the decrease of the economic benefits will be accounted for as an expense.

services which are held by the company for subsequent use in the business. As the goods or services are used, some expense must be recognized and the unexpired expenses carried forward (this is in fact an important point about asset values under historical cost accounting: they are simply expenses of future periods; they do not represent any independent valuation of the asset's 'worth' in any external sense).

We can divide the accounting issues to be considered into two parts:

1. How do we determine the appropriate value of an asset at the point of acquisition?
2. How do we then systematically recognize the using up or expensing of the asset period by period? (The deduction of the expense from the opening value will provide a revised value in the statement of financial position at the end of each period.)

IAS 16, *Property, Plant and Equipment*, addresses these questions both in general and more specifically for tangible assets. Property, plant and equipment are tangible assets held for more than one accounting period (in this sense they are 'non-current' or 'long-term') and used in the production or supply of goods and services, or for administration.

General valuation principles of non-current assets

Non-current assets are initially recorded at cost, which includes all expenditure to get the item ready for use. At first sight there might not seem to be any difficulty about the initial valuation of an asset. When a company buys a van, for example, a price is agreed and paid and that surely is the cost of the asset and the value at which it will initially enter the accounting system. In essence, that argument has much to support it but, if we look a little closer, we will see that there is a need to define more carefully what the asset has cost – or rather what aspect of the cost is an asset, and what an expense.

Supposing the van purchase was invoiced to the company (as is usually the case) at an 'on the road' price of €30 000, the invoice would then be made up of a number of items, as shown below:

Van supply	€
Basic vehicle	29 300
Special gear box	1 300
Petrol	50
Annual vehicle tax	250
	30 900
less Discount	(900)
Net payable	30 000

Should the van enter the books at the invoice price of €30 000? To answer that we have to consider whether all the items paid for on the invoice are really assets, i.e. does everything included within the €30 000 purchase price have a life longer than the end of the current accounting period? In this case, there are two items, the petrol and the annual tax, which are ordinary running expenses which will be consumed within the current accounting year, so we should immediately treat those as an expense for operating the van. The discount may also be a problem. Clearly in this case the amount of discount has been given to arrive at a round sum price, so arguably the expensed element, petrol and tax, should be reduced by some of the discount. Against that, it is unlikely that the dealer intended to offer discounts on petrol or tax, and there is a strong argument for applying the discount to the asset value alone. In this case the costs would be allocated as shown below:

Van asset	€
Basic	29 300
Gear box	1 300
less Discount	(900)
Long-term asset:	29 700
Operating expenses:	
Petrol	50
Annual tax	250
Total invoiced	30 000

Let us consider one further complication: suppose that the company then employs a sign-writer to paint some advertising on the side of the van and this costs a further €500. Should that be treated as an expense or part of the cost of the asset? Is there any difference in nature between what the sign-writer contributed to the final product and what the vehicle manufacturer contributed? The answer has to be 'no', since both are costs associated with providing the van in the form required by the company. The final asset value of the van in the company's books would therefore be €30 200: €29 700 being the cost from the dealer and €500 being other costs associated with reaching the desired final asset.

Would it make any difference to the asset value if the sign-writing on the van had been done by the company's own staff? Suppose the €500 consisted of €100 for paint and €400 for staff wages, would that influence the asset value? Logically the source of the cost should have no bearing, and that is the case here. If a company uses some of its own resources in creating an asset, the cost of those resources becomes part of the cost of the asset. This is the same principle as that applied in manufacturing accounts (see Chapter 4) – just as wage and other costs were allocated to the value of the inventory of manufactured goods, so here the cost of bringing the van to the condition in which it will be used is added to its accounting value.

We can therefore go some way to defining what we understand by the cost of the asset. It consists of all the costs associated with creating the asset in the form required by the company to start productive use.

This principle applies in general to the measurement of all assets in the framework of historical cost accounting. The total asset value recorded can include not only costs paid to a supplier, but also extra items which have all contributed to the bringing into service of the asset. For example, a manufacturing company might well buy some machine tools which are installed in its factory by its own maintenance staff. In that case the asset value at the point where they come into service will include the amount (exclusive of any expenses to do with operations) paid to the supplier, cost of delivery on site, cost of installation including maintenance staff wages and so on.

The basic test in allocating cost between asset value and expense is, was the cost a part of bringing the asset into service? If so, it would be allocated to asset value. Subsequent expenditure is added to the cost of an existing asset only if it will produce economic benefits beyond its originally assessed performance, for example:

- extending the useful life or capacity of a plant;
- upgrading a machine to substantially improve the quality of its output;
- adopting new processes to substantially reduce production costs.

Subsequent expenditure on day-to-day servicing of the long-term asset, including the cost of small repair parts (often referred to as costs of repair and maintenance), is recognized in profit or loss as incurred.

Normally, then, the initial value of an asset will be its cost, but this is subject to a limitation as in the case of inventory valuation. This valuation is subject to the constraint that these costs should not exceed the future economic benefits which will derive from using the asset. Prudence requires that asset values should not be overstated in the statement of financial position. For assets which are held for use in the business (as opposed to being held for resale), the rule is that they should be held at whichever is the lower of cost or **recoverable amount**. Recoverable in this sense is normally taken to mean through use in the business. To use our van example, the fact that the van had been painted with advertising

🌐 IAS 16 – ELEMENTS OF ACQUISITION COST *(extracts)*

15. An item of property, plant and equipment that qualifies for recognition as an asset shall be measured at its cost.
16. The cost of an item of property, plant and equipment comprises:

   (a) its purchase price, including import duties and non-refundable purchase taxes, after deducting trade discounts and rebates.
   (b) any costs directly attributable to bringing the asset to the location and condition necessary for it to be capable of operating in the manner intended by management.
   (c) the initial estimate of the costs of dismantling and removing the item and restoring the site on which it is located, the obligation for which an entity incurs either when the item is acquired or as a consequence of having used the item during a particular period for purposes other than to produce inventories during that period.

17. Examples of directly attributable costs are:

   (a) costs of employee benefits arising directly from the construction or acquisition of the item of property, plant and equipment;
   (b) costs of site preparation;
   (c) initial delivery and handling costs;
   (d) installation and assembly costs;
   (e) costs of testing whether the asset is functioning properly, after deducting the net proceeds from selling any items produced while bringing the asset to that location and condition (such as samples produced when testing equipment); and
   (f) professional fees.

Source: IAS 16, *Property, Plant and Equipment*

on the side would immediately reduce its resale value, but the company was not intending to resell it. The intention was to keep the van and use it in the business for deliveries etc. – so its cost will be recovered through being operated as part of the business.

Nonetheless, non-current assets are subject to special write-downs when there has been some 'permanent impairment' of their value. This might occur if, for example, a company built a factory for manufacturing microchips, only to find that demand falls away – the cost of the factory is unlikely to be recovered through manufacturing the chips and its value should be reduced. We will come back to the issue of impairment testing of assets in Chapter 6.

Expensing non-current assets

Companies acquire assets in order to generate profits by their use. Such operating assets are consumed by the business over a period of time: machines wear out.

The cost of these assets must therefore be expensed in order to match with the revenues produced by using them.

Although that may seem potentially quite a complex operation, in fact systems have been evolved which deal with it pragmatically. In the first place it should be made clear that the problem is again one of allocation. That is, accountants are not concerned primarily with assessing the reducing value of the asset in external terms, rather they are concerned with allocating the original cost of the asset over the period of its use (*depreciating the asset*).

You should note that accounting doctrine distinguishes between two different kinds of reduction in the accounting values of assets: there is (1) systematic expensing of the cost of an asset over the period which benefits from its use – **depreciation** or **amortization** – which takes place routinely every year; and (2) special write-downs where, usually at reporting date, all assets should be considered for 'impairment' and their depreciated accounting value compared with their recoverable value. Any excess must be removed, but this is an unusual event.

The important elements are that the asset has a value at the point where it comes into the company and that, when the company has finished with the asset, it may also have a resale or scrap value at that time. The difference between the acquisition cost and the disposal revenue (**depreciable amount**) is the expense which has to be recognized and allocated in some reasonable way across the financial years when the asset remains in use. This is another significant estimate in the financial statements where we can only say for certain what costs really were when an asset is sold, sometimes many years after it entered service. This allocation of cost has significant effects on measured profitability which in turn may impact upon taxation. In some jurisdictions (the Netherlands, UK, USA) depreciation for tax purposes is calculated separately from that for financial reporting purposes. However, in most mainland European countries the rate of depreciation charged in the financial statements is heavily influenced by tax considerations. In France, for example, the tax authorities will look at what is charged in the annual financial statements as the upper limit of what can be charged for tax purposes. We will discuss below the theoretical basis of depreciation, but you should be aware that there is a strong link with taxation in many countries, and therefore accountants will be likely to look at the agreed tax rates rather than apply accounting standards. Put another way, the accounting standards are sufficiently flexible for it to be possible to comply with both tax and accounting rules, but the possibility of deferring tax by using high depreciation rates will cause a company to be perhaps more prudent in its estimates than might otherwise be the case . . .

STANDARDS

⊕ IAS 16 – DEPRECIATION ACCOUNTING *(extracts)*

50. The depreciable amount of an asset shall be allocated on a systematic basis over its useful life.
53. The depreciable amount of an asset is determined after deducting its residual value. In practice, the residual value of an asset is often insignificant and therefore immaterial in the calculation of the depreciable amount.

56. The future economic benefits embodied in an asset are consumed by an entity principally through its use. However, other factors, such as technical or commercial obsolescence and wear and tear while an asset remains idle, often result in the diminution of the economic benefits that might have been obtained from the asset. Consequently, all the following factors are considered in determining the useful life of an asset:

(a) expected usage of the asset. Usage is assessed by reference to the asset's expected capacity or physical output.
(b) expected physical wear and tear, which depends on operational factors such as the number of shifts for which the asset is to be used and the repair and maintenance programme, and the care and maintenance of the asset while idle.
(c) technical or commercial obsolescence arising from changes or improvements in production, or from a change in the market demand for the product or service output of the asset.
(d) legal or similar limits on the use of the asset, such as the expiry dates of related leases.

60. The depreciation method used shall reflect the pattern in which the asset's future economic benefits are expected to be consumed by the entity.
61. The depreciation method applied to an asset shall be reviewed at least at each financial year-end, if there has been a significant change in the expected pattern of consumption of the future economic benefits embodied in the asset, the method shall be changed to reflect the changed pattern.
73. The financial statements shall disclose, for each class of property, plant and equipment:

(a) the measurement bases used for determining the gross carrying amount;
(b) the depreciation methods used;
(c) the useful lives or the depreciation rates used;
(d) the gross carrying amount and the accumulated depreciation (aggregated with accumulated impairment losses) at the beginning and end of the period;
(e) a reconciliation of the carrying amount at the beginning and end of the period.

Source: IAS 16, *Property, Plant and Equipment*

Reverting to our example of a van, bought for €30 000 and sold for €10 000 two years later, the expense is €20 000 (difference between entry and exit values) and the decision to be made is how to allocate that expense over the two years to match the use of the van with the revenues generated by its use. (It is always a temptation to think that depreciating an asset has something to do with approximating the balance sheet value to a declining second-hand value. This is not the case in traditional historical cost accounting: depreciating is a cost allocation process, which equally is why assets in the balance sheet should be thought of largely as unexpired costs rather than values – even if some of them have substantial resale potential.)

Of course, the accountant cannot know precisely how many years an asset will remain in use, nor its precise scrap value, at the time when a decision has to be made on allocating the expense. These therefore have to be estimated and corrections made (sometimes years later) if the estimates prove to be wrong. (Remember that the process of measuring the annual profit is in any event one of estimation – a question of trying to work out what proportion of the firm's lifetime profit was earned in that 12-month period.)

There are several methods used to calculate depreciation on a systematic basis to match the expensing of the asset with its use. Broadly these fall into one or other of two kinds: those which allocate over time and those which try to match depreciation to use.

With the time-based approach, having arrived at the acquisition value of the asset, an estimate is made both of the likely working life of the asset within the company and of its expected scrap or salvage value at the end of that working life. The difference between the original asset cost and the expected scrap value is called the 'depreciable amount' of the asset – that is, the total expense to be allocated over the working life. One of the methods we shall now consider will then be selected to allocate the depreciable amount over the working life of the asset. We shall look first at these methods, and then at the way in which depreciation is reported in the financial statements.

Straight-line depreciation

This method is the one most favoured by companies, probably because it is the simplest and easiest to use. The straight-line method, as its name implies, assumes that the use of the asset is uniform throughout its working life, and therefore allocates the expense accordingly.

The annual expense (annual depreciation) is found simply:

$$\frac{\text{Depreciable amount}}{\text{Estimated useful life}} = \text{Annual depreciation expense}$$

For example, supposing a company buys desks and other office furniture for €5000, and estimates that they will be used for ten years and have no scrap value. The annual depreciation would be charged as follows:

Depreciable amount: €5000 *less* 0 = €5000

Useful life: 10 years

Annual depreciation charge: $\frac{5000}{10}$ = €500

This method is most appropriate to assets whose consumption takes place in a uniform manner. Examples of this would be assets such as a shop front, a building, a lease premium, furniture and so on.

Diminishing balance method

A method which allocates a high proportion of expense in the early life of the asset is the diminishing balance method (also called reducing balance method). This uses a method which gives a geometric reduction in the charge in succeeding years. A basic difference is that the annual depreciation charge is calculated by applying a percentage not to the depreciable amount but to the asset value after deduction of all previous years' depreciation. The net value of the asset after deduction of the accumulated depreciation might be called the balance of the asset, which diminishes year by year, hence diminishing balance. (The net value after depreciation is also known as *net book value* or *carrying value*.)

There is a mathematical formula for calculating the depreciation rate to be used:

$$d = 1 - \sqrt[n]{\frac{R}{A}}$$

with: d = depreciation rate
         n = number of accounting periods
         R = residual value
         A = acquisition cost

This rate is then applied each year to the balance of the asset at the beginning of the year in order to arrive at the annual depreciation expense.

To take a concrete example, suppose that an asset was acquired for €1050 and was expected to have a five-year useful life and a scrap value of €50; the annual rate would be 45.6 per cent. This is applied to the asset's net value each year as follows:

	Net book value start of year €	Depreciation expense €	Net book value end of year €
1	1050 ×	45.6%	= 479	(1050 − 479 =) 571
2	571 ×	45.6%	= 260	(571 − 260 =) 311
3	311 ×	45.6%	= 142	(311 − 142 =) 169
4	169 ×	45.6%	= 77	(169 − 77 =) 92
5	92 ×	45.6%	= 42	(92 − 42 =) 50

The diminishing balance method allocates a high proportion of expense to the early years of the asset's life. It is therefore suitable for assets whose future service life is subject to uncertainty, such as computer hardware or software, or which have a high maintenance cost in the latter part of their lives. At a practical level, the diminishing balance method is not used very widely by companies and normally, where it is used, the annual depreciation rate is approximated (in the above example a company would probably accept 45 per cent as the rate). Very often, diminishing balance is used when the tax authorities allow it (governments like to collect taxes but they also sometimes use tax to influence behaviour, and high initial depreciation encourages companies to invest and therefore keep up with technology and create employment in the industries which make equipment).

Tax depreciation

As we have noted, tax rules can have a potentially distorting effect on the application of depreciation rules and consequently on comparisons between companies.

LUFTHANSA – TANGIBLE ASSETS *(extract)*

Notes to the consolidated financial statements

Tangible assets used in business operations for longer than one year are valued at cost, less regular straight-line depreciation. The cost of production includes all costs directly attributable to the manufacturing process as well as appropriate portions of the indirect costs relating to this process.

As a result of last year's amendment to IAS 23, borrowing costs are now capitalized if they are incurred in close connection with the financing of the acquisition or production of a qualifying asset. In the reporting year borrowing costs of EUR 2m were capitalized. The useful lives applied to tangible assets correspond to their estimated/expected useful lives in the Group.

New aircraft and spare engines are depreciated over a period of 12 years to a residual value of 15 per cent.

A useful life of between 20 and 45 years is assumed for buildings, whereby buildings, fixtures and fittings on rented premises are depreciated according to the terms of the lease or over a shorter useful life. Depreciation rates are mainly between 10 and 20 per cent per annum. A useful life of up to ten years is fixed for plant and machinery. Operating and office equipment is depreciated over three to ten years in normal circumstances.

Source: Lufthansa, *Annual Report 2010*

Take the following example where the profit after all expenses but before depreciation is €20 000 and the tax rate is 25 per cent. A company buys a vehicle for €30 000; the tax rules say that this may be depreciated at 40 per cent diminishing balance without regard to residual value, and the company estimates it will use the vehicle for four years, when it can be sold for an estimated €10 000. The two approaches would give the following results:

	Profit before depreciation	Annual depreciation	Profit after depreciation	Tax at 25%
Tax method				
Year 1	20 000	(12 000)	8 000	2 000
Year 2	20 000	(7 200)	12 800	3 200
Year 3	20 000	(800)	19 200	4 800
Year 4	20 000	—	20 000	5 000
Totals	80 000	(20 000)	60 000	15 000
Straight-line/economic				
Year 1	20 000	(5 000)	15 000	3 750
Year 2	20 000	(5 000)	15 000	3 750
Year 3	20 000	(5 000)	15 000	3 750
Year 4	20 000	(5 000)	15 000	3 750
Totals	80 000	(20 000)	60 000	15 000

This illustrates fairly well what tax planning is about – both sequences give the same four-year total deductions, but the tax method reduces early profits and pushes tax payments towards later in the life of the asset, so the company is getting the maximum benefit in financing the asset. Of course, from a management perspective, the tax is distorting the quality of the information, turning a stable situation (same before-depreciation profit each year) into the appearance of a company which is becoming more profitable year on year (after-depreciation profit gets bigger over the four years).

This said, the distortion is mitigated in a large company because this will have a portfolio of assets, some of which are changed each year. A company with four vehicles, one of which is replaced each year, will have the same total annual depreciation (€20 000 every year) whichever method is used. Another point is that while in some jurisdictions accelerated methods of depreciation are available to help companies, they must be used for the shareholder accounts. However, as

BETWEEN THE LINES

Special tax method

It may be useful to know that in some countries, notably France and Germany, the tax authorities use a depreciation method which is a combination of diminishing balance and straight-line methods. The problem with diminishing balance is that it cannot, by definition, depreciate an asset to zero, and the method if applied indefinitely leaves a very long tail of small annual charges. The tax authorities get around this by permitting a combination method where the company uses declining balance in the early years and then switches to straight-line once this gives a higher annual charge, and this is applied without regard to any salvage value.

Year	Opening book value	Rate	Annual charge	Closing book value	Remaining life
1	50 000	40%DB	20 000	30 000	4 years
2	30 000	40%DB	12 000	18 000	3 years
3	18 000	40%DB	7 200	10 800	2 years
4	10 800	50%SL	5 400	5 400	1 year
5	5 400	50%SL	5 400	—	0

The depreciation calculation switches from diminishing balance (DB) to straight-line (SL) in year 4 in this case. This is because at that point the diminishing balance calculation would give a lower annual charge (€10 800 × 0.4 = 4320). Applying straight-line to the asset value as it stands at that point (€10 800) gives two years at €5400 and enables the asset to be depreciated to zero, whereas the strict application of diminishing balance would leave the asset with a value of €3888 at the end of the fifth year.

we shall see later in the book, if these companies are part of a group, the group financial statements can be prepared using normal economic methods such as straight-line.

There are other time-based methods, but these are the two which are classically used. There are potentially many usage-based methods. For example, it would be relatively simple to allocate depreciation on a van according to the number of kilo-metres travelled in the year. In practice such methods are rarely used except by companies which extract minerals, particularly oil companies.

Units of production method

Mineral resource companies usually expense the mineral asset as it is extracted for sale – this is called the *depletion method* or the *units of production method*. Supposing a company acquires a quarry for extracting ore, and the acquisition cost is €5m, the unexpired expense represented by this asset would be the un-mined ore available on the site, and it is relatively simple to allocate the acquisition cost on the basis of the amount of ore extracted. If the engineers estimated that the quarry contained 10m tonnes of ore, the cost of the quarry could be divided over the resource:

$$\frac{€\ 5\text{m acquisition cost}}{10\text{m tonnes ore in quarry}} = \text{Depreciation of €0.50 per tonne}$$

As the ore was extracted, the quarry asset could be expensed in direct relation to the ore. So if extraction was as follows:

Year	Tonnes extracted
1	500 000
2	1 200 000
3	1 400 000
	etc.

the annual charge for depreciation would be:

Year	Annual depreciation
1	(500 000 × €0.50) €250 000
2	(1 200 000 × €0.50) €600 000
3	(1 400 000 × €0.50) €700 000 etc.

Clearly the accuracy of the units of production method depends upon the accuracy of the estimate of the ore in the quarry, and this method is only suitable for assets where such estimates of the resource are possible and the utilization of the resource can be monitored in that way. However, it is a method of allocating expense which most closely follows the economic use of the asset, rather than working on an assumed utilization pattern.

Components approach

An asset may be composed of several component parts with different useful lives or providing benefits to the company in a different pattern. This would imply the use of different depreciation rates and methods for each component. IAS 16 requires that the company records its property, plant and equipment in sufficient detail to recognize separately components with different useful lives. Subsequent expenditure that is incurred to replace or renew a separately recognized asset component will be treated as the acquisition of a new asset. The overall useful life of an electricity plant, for example, can be estimated to be 30 years, but one of its major component parts, a steam generator, has to be replaced every ten years. The steam generators will therefore be recognized separately and depreciated over a ten-year period, while the other plant facilities will be depreciated over a 30-year period. When the steam generator is replaced after ten years, the replacement is recognized as a new (component) asset.

Excess depreciation as a hidden reserve

Depreciation is also one of the ways in which companies which wish to follow highly 'prudent' accounting may reduce their profitability. This is done simply by charging excess depreciation against assets and profit. The consequence is that the company appears to have fewer assets than are actually in use, and these are one form of hidden reserve. In fact, accelerated depreciation for tax purposes (offered by governments as an incentive to companies to invest) has the effect of writing off assets while they are still in use, but some companies (rarely if ever those listed on stock exchanges!) go further than that.

Accounting for depreciation

Every year part of the asset cost is expensed in the statement of profit or loss and the statement of financial position shows a reduced net value for the asset. In record-keeping terms, though, the net value of the asset is preserved through two accounts: opening (acquisition) cost and accumulated depreciation. As depreciation is expensed, the asset account is not reduced directly. Rather a separate, linked account is opened to accumulate the value written off. In the published statement of financial position a company must disclose both the original cost of an asset and the cumulative amount written off (this detail is usually found in the notes rather than directly in the balance sheet, but that does not change the principle). This disclosure is facilitated if the information is kept on two separate data files in the records – in a large company it would be impossible to give the information without taking that kind of precaution.

If we take a tangible asset with a gross acquisition cost of €15 000, an expected useful life of five years and no scrap value, it would be depreciated at a rate of €3000 a year on the straight-line basis. The table below shows how the book value of the asset would appear over the years.

Year	Annual depreciation charge €	Gross cost €	Accumulated depreciation €	Net book value €
20X1	3 000	15 000	3 000	12 000
20X2	3 000	15 000	6 000	9 000
20X3	3 000	15 000	9 000	6 000
20X4	3 000	15 000	12 000	3 000
20X5	3 000	15 000	15 000	0

For 20X1, the depreciation charge would be accounted for as follows:

Statement of profit or loss	−3 000 (reduce equity)
Accumulated depreciation	−3 000 (reduce assets)

The net book value of the tangible asset is the sum of the tangible asset account and the accumulated depreciation account relating to that asset at any given point.

Asset – gross cost	15 000
Accumulated depreciation	−3 000
Net book value at end 20X1	12 000

It follows from this that the accounting records are likely to have two accounts involving depreciation in any one year: the income statement expense through which the appropriate part of the asset value is charged against profits in the year, and the reduction of the asset which is accumulated in a separate data file from the asset and accumulates over the life of the asset the total amount by which it has been charged against profits at any given moment.

The accumulated depreciation is simply the reduction of the asset value, but it is held in a separate account in order to facilitate disclosure. It always represents amounts which have already been expensed. Most corporate disclosure rules require that the business shows both the original cost of the assets and the accumulated depreciation.

In some sophisticated accounting systems the regular depreciation expense is recognized on a month-by-month basis and is written into a monthly accounting programme within a computerized system, so that it takes place automatically. However, in general terms it is an adjustment to the financial records which must be made at every balance sheet date to recognize the consumption of some of the unexpired expenses which the company's assets represent.

Note that the management accounts of a company should normally make a deduction for depreciation in arriving at monthly profit and loss figures for operating units. A unit which makes a 'profit' before depreciation, but not enough to absorb the depreciation, is still making some contribution to the company's overheads, but in the long term is obviously not making sufficient money to repay

NESTLÉ – RECONCILIATION DETAILS ON NET CARRYING AMOUNT OF PROPERTY, PLANT AND EQUIPMENT *(extracts)*

Notes to the consolidated financial statements

7. Property, plant and equipment

In millions of CHF　　　　　　　　　　　　　　　　　　　　　　　　　　*2007*

	Land and buildings	Machinery and equipment	Tools furniture and other equipment	Vehicles	Total
Gross value At 1 January 2010	12931	25562	7717	876	47086
Currency retranslations	(961)	(2722)	(670)	(95)	(4448)
Capital expenditure[3]	872	2468	893	151	4384
Disposals	(137)	(688)	(541)	(65)	(1431)
Reclassified as held for sale	(48)	(31)	(5)		(84)
Modification of the scope of consolidation	148	186	(9)	2	327
At 31 December 2010	12805	24775	7385	869	45834
Currency retranslations	(104)	(719)	(187)	(21)	(1031)
Capital expenditure [3]	1022	2643	950	164	4779
Disposals	(140)	(624)	(507)	(65)	(1336)
Reclassified as held for sale	—	5	1	—	6
Modification of the scope of consolidation	526	392	86	14	1018
At 31 December 2011	14109	26472	7728	961	49720
Accumulated depreciation and impairments					
At 1 January 2010	(5014)	(14596)	(5384)	(493)	(25487)
Currency retranslations	434	1461	512	52	2459
Depreciation	(370)	(1319)	(765)	(98)	(2552)
Impairments	(38)	(131)	(17)	—	(186)
Disposals	107	641	492	56	1296
Reclassified as held for sale	30	29	4	—	63
Modification of the scope of consolidation	—	1	10	—	11
At 31 December 2010	(4851)	(13914)	(5148)	(483)	(24396)
Currency retranslations	76	286	125	14	501
Depreciation	(341)	(1263)	(728)	(90)	(2422)
Impairments	(51)	(81)	(17)	(1)	(150)
Disposals	99	525	490	56	1170
Reclassified as held for sale	—	(5)	(1)	—	(6)
Modification of the scope of consolidation	—	3	1	—	4
At 31 December 2011	(5068)	(14449)	(5278)	(504)	(25299)
Net at 31 December 2010	7954	10861	2237	386	21438
Net at 31 December 2011	9041	12023	2450	457	23971

Including borrowing costs.

At 31 December 2011, property, plant and equipment include CHF 1267 million of assets under construction (2010: CHF 802 million). Net property, plant and equipment held under finance leases amount to CHF 194 million (2010: CHF 240 million). Net property, plant and equipment of CHF 323 million are pledged as security for financial liabilities (2010: CHF 112 million). Fire risks, reasonably estimated, are insured in accordance with domestic requirements.

Source: Nestlé Consolidated Financial Statements, 2011 *(Comparative figures omitted for clarity)*

its investment, let alone add to the value of the company. At the same time, the basis on which the depreciation charge is calculated should be checked because, as we have seen, this may not accurately represent the economic consumption of the assets concerned, which therefore distorts the performance measure.

We have dealt with depreciation as simply a question of absorbing the costs of the company's productive capacity as it is used up. This is generally how depreciation is regarded these days, but you may come across alternative notions which are not necessarily incompatible.

For example, in the past some accountants considered depreciation rather as a means of building up a replacement fund to buy new equipment when the old is worn out. This leads to the idea that instead of reducing the cost of the asset year by year in the statement of financial position, you create a provision in the financing side which will be used to buy the new asset. The snags with this are that:

a. The user has no way of knowing how old the assets are because in the asset side of the statement of financial position they are all shown at original cost, no matter how old they are, and there is no direct link with the replacement provisions in the financing side of the balance sheet.

b. Would the company necessarily want to replace a particular asset at the end of its life? Business changes rapidly.

c. Would the same asset still be available?

d. How do you know what it would cost? (This argument also leads to the argument that one should use replacement cost as the basis of depreciation.)

Another argument is that depreciation is the repayment, either to shareholders or to lenders of the money used to buy the equipment. Of course, the depreciation charge does not involve any cash movement – it is purely a paper adjustment of values within the accounting database. However, it should be realized that if no depreciation were charged in calculating profit, and all the profit were paid out in tax and dividend, the original capital would have been lost; so depreciation, by restricting profit, reduces tax and dividends and preserves the original capital.

This question of not involving a cash movement is also important in recognizing the difference between a company's profits for the year and its cash flow – the cash flow will be systematically higher than the profit by the amount of the depreciation charge.

Worked example

The figures below represent the data in the company's accounting database as at 31 December 20X1. As you can see, the company has the following non-current tangible assets: land €120000 (not depreciated, considered to have an infinite life), buildings €80 000 (policy is to depreciate on a straight-line basis over 40 years – i.e. 2.5 per cent per annum) and plant €45 000 (being depreciated at 25 per cent diminishing balance – note that the figure consists of several components bought at different times). We have to update the accounting database for the annual depreciation charges, prior to issuing the annual financial statements. We need to depreciate the buildings and plant:

$$\text{Buildings } €80\,000 \times 0.025 = €2000$$

$$\text{Plant } (€45\,000 - 18\,000) \times 0.25 = €6750$$

(we deduct the accumulated depreciation which has been charged in previous years to find the net book value and then apply the diminishing balance rate)

$$\text{Total charge for 20X1} = €8\,750$$

Database	Adjustment	Statement of profit or loss	Statement of financial position
Assets			
Land	120 000		120 000
Buildings	80 000		80 000
Accumulated depreciation	−14 000	−2 000	−16 000
Plant	45 000		45 000
Accumulated depreciation	−18 000	−6 750	−24 750
Inventory	19 500		19 500
Receivables	17 250		17 250
Cash at bank	8 340		8 340
Totals	258 090	−8 750	249 340
Financing			
Share capital	80 000		80 000
Reserves	62 100		62 100
Profit for the year			16 040
Debt	75 000		75 000
Accounts payable	16 200		16 200
Statement of profit or loss			
Sales	200 000	200 000	
Cost of goods sold	−82 310	−82 310	
Personnel	−61 200	−61 200	
Other expenses	−26 700	−26 700	
Interest	−5 000	−5 000	
Depreciation charge		−8 750	−8 750
Totals	258 090	−8 750	16 040	249 340

Notice that the profit or loss data has been thrown into a separate column to identify it separately from the statement of financial position, but of course the net profit of €16 040 also appears in the statement of financial position.)

Disposal or retirement of a long-term asset

A long-term asset will be derecognized on disposal or when no future economic benefits are expected from its use or disposal. At de-recognition date, the non-current asset item disappears from the statement of financial position and a gain or loss on disposal is included in the statement of profit or loss. The gain or loss from the retirement or disposal is the difference between the net disposal proceeds and the net book value of the asset at the disposal date.

Let us revert again to our example of a van, bought for €30000 and expected to be used for two years with a residual value of €10000. After one year of use we receive a nice offer and decide to sell the van for €23000. On disposal date, the net book value would be €20000 (acquisition cost minus one year depreciation charge), leading to a gain on disposal of €3000 to be included in the statement of profit or loss.

In the accounting records the disposal or retirement will have an impact on both the acquisition cost account and on the accumulated depreciation account. Both accounts will be reduced for the full amount related to the long-term asset disposed of. This will be reflected in the notes to the financial statements where the different types of changes in the net book value of the non-current assets are disclosed (see the Nestlé Report).

Specific valuation principles by type of non-current assets

We did not want to get involved within the general presentation of non-current assets and depreciation with a discussion of particular types of assets. However, we now present a number of different kinds of long-term assets and discuss their particular attributes for accounting purposes.

As we discussed in the early part of the chapter, the value which a company will use for its long-term assets will incorporate the full cost of bringing the asset into service ('bringing the asset to the location and condition necessary for it to be capable of operating in the manner intended by management' according to IAS 16, par.16). We have not examined the implications of this in respect of major categories of non-current assets nor their specific recognition features, and we shall therefore now review some of the more frequently encountered types of non-current assets and the accounting practices normally followed. The EC Company Law Fourth Directive calls for non-current assets to be split between intangible assets, tangible assets and investments, with different valuation rules for each. Although not required, this split also makes sense for non-current assets under IFRS.

Intangible assets

So far discussion of assets has been confined to physical productive assets such as buildings or machinery, but companies also have other assets which are not physical in nature; these are called *intangible assets*. Intangible assets reflect intangible resources such as scientific or technical knowledge, **development** of new processes or systems, intellectual property, privileged customer relationships, etc. Typical intangible assets would be research and development, brand names, copyrights, computer software, licences, patents.

IAS 38 – INTANGIBLE ASSETS (extract)

8. An intangible asset is an identifiable non-monetary asset without physical substance.

12. An asset is identifiable if it either:

(a) is separable, i.e. is capable of being separated or divided from the entity and sold, transferred, licensed, rented or exchanged, either individually or together with a related contract, identifiable asset or liability, regardless of whether the entity intends to do so; or

(b) arises from contractual or other legal rights, regardless of whether those rights are transferable or separable from the entity or from other rights and obligations.

21. An intangible asset shall be recognized if, and only if:

(a) it is probable that the expected future economic benefits that are attributable to the asset will flow to the entity; and

(b) the cost of the asset can be measured reliably.

22. An entity shall assess the probability of expected future economic benefits using reasonable and supportable assumptions that represent management's best estimate of the set of economic conditions that will exist over the useful life of the asset.

51. It is sometimes difficult to assess whether an internally generated intangible asset qualifies for recognition because of problems in:

(a) identifying whether and when, there is an identifiable asset that will generate expected future economic benefits; and

(b) determining the cost of the asset reliably. In some cases the cost of generating an intangible asset internally cannot be distinguished from the cost of maintaining or enhancing the entity's internally generated goodwill or of running day-to-day operations.

52. To assess whether an internally generated intangible asset meets the criteria for recognition, an enterprise classifies the generation of the asset into:

(a) a research phase; and

(b) a development phase.

53. If an entity cannot distinguish the research phase from the development phase of an internal project to create an intangible asset, the entity treats the expenditure on that project as if it were incurred in the research phase only.

Source: IAS 38, *Intangible Assets*

Intangible assets are increasingly important to companies and are a continuing source of accounting problems. It is very difficult to attach a historical cost to some intangibles, such as brand names, which are built up slowly over years. Even if one could attach a cost and therefore have an accounting asset, there is still the question of estimating its useful life and related amortization.

IAS 38, *Intangible Assets*, defines an intangible asset as 'an identifiable non-monetary asset without physical substance' (IAS 38, par.8). This definition contains three essential characteristics of intangible assets:

a. they are assets – resources controlled by the company from which future economic benefits are expected to flow to the entity

b. they lack physical substance; and

c. they are identifiable.

A major problem with intangible assets is that of uncertainty surrounding the future economic benefits which arise from expenditure of this nature. This uncertainty relates to both the amount of future economic benefits and the ability to control the future economic benefits flowing from the intangible items and restrict the access of others to those benefits. For example, if a company spends money training its staff, the object is to improve future operations and, one hopes, profitability. However, the improvement is not certain and the staff may leave at some future point, taking their improved efficiency with them. Similarly, advertising is done to generate future sales, but the long-term effects are generally impossible to estimate and are not under the control of the company.

The identifiability characteristic of the definition of an intangible asset is met when it is separable (capable of being separated from the company and sold, licensed, rented, etc.) or when it arises from contractual or other legal rights. This characteristic is essential to distinguish intangible assets from the more general concept of **goodwill**.

The useful life of an intangible asset can be finite or indefinite. The useful life of the intangible asset is usually assessed based on the expected cash flow streams associated with the asset. According to IAS 38, an intangible asset can be regarded as having an indefinite useful life when there is no foreseeable limit to the period over which the asset is expected to generate net cash inflows for the company. This means that under IAS 38 it is now possible to recognize some intangible assets without having to depreciate them at all.

Intangible assets can be acquired externally or generated internally, although current practice imposes limitations on internally generated intangible resources such as research and development.

Research and development

In some sense research and development (R&D) expenditure is the archetypal intangible asset and raises a number of basic questions when assessing whether the costs incurred in research and development activities qualify for asset recognition. These issues relate to determining whether and when an identifiable asset exists that will generate probable economic benefits for the company and how the cost of such an asset is measured with sufficient reliability.

Where a company has invested in researching and developing new products, it does not seem unreasonable that the cost of creating a new product should be considered an asset, provided that the new product will lead to a commercial exploitation. Very often it is relatively late in the R&D process that one can be reasonably certain that an asset (in the sense of something which will bring a future economic benefits) has been created.

In defining the costs associated with creating the new product, there is the problem of the treatment of the costs of unsuccessful research. For example, supposing a chemist sets out to create a new headache tablet and takes four years, during which he tries five alternative bases, of which only the last is wholly satisfactory. Does the R&D asset include the costs only of the research into the alternative which was ultimately accepted? Or should one consider that the process of defining the unsuccessful alternatives is part of finding the usable alternative, and therefore all the costs should be treated as an R&D asset?

In the US, the difficulty of finding a suitable definition, plus the operation of prudence, have led to a situation where all R&D costs must be expensed as they are incurred. In Europe, the treatment in national accounting rules is generally more flexible: general research must be expensed immediately, but research involved in refining and developing a specific product may be treated as an asset and expensed over its **economic life** (although many companies expense all R&D expenditure immediately anyway, not least because it qualifies immediately as a deduction for tax purposes).

IAS 38, *Intangible Assets*, focuses on the distinction between the research phase and the development phase of an internal project, whereby research costs should be expensed as incurred, but development costs may qualify for recognition. The IASB argues that at the research phase of a project, a company is unable to demonstrate that an intangible asset exists that will generate probable future economic benefits. In the development phase of an internal project, however, activities are focused on the application of research findings or other knowledge to a plan or design of new products or systems and circumstances may enable the company to identify an intangible asset and demonstrate the probable future economic benefits flowing from these development activities. IAS 38 includes specific recognition criteria for development costs (and internally generated intangible assets in general) that expand on the general recognition criteria for intangible assets (see the boxes on IAS 38). If these criteria are met, an intangible asset arising from development should be recognized.

Estimating the useful life of internally generated intangible assets will usually be done on a prudent basis. As with patents, there is a strong economic argument for spreading this over the whole expected commercial exploitation of the project. But again there is the problem of uncertainty – can one reasonably expect that a new headache tablet, for example, might be exploited for as long as 20 years? The amortization method used should reflect the pattern in which the asset's future economic benefits are expected to be consumed by the company. If that pattern cannot be determined reliably, the straight-line method will be used. The residual value of an intangible asset with a finite useful life is generally assumed to be zero.

A detailed analysis of the intangible assets, divided into major classes and showing original cost (or valuation) and accumulated depreciation, has to be disclosed and is usually shown in the notes to the accounts.

Brand names

In many bulk product areas where there are several competing products with very similar characteristics (coffee, chocolate, cars, washing machines, etc.) it has become increasingly understood by management that what is important to the success of a business is not so much its manufacturing capacity (or not exclusively its manufacturing capacity) but also its ability to sell the products. Very often this is associated with the creation and maintenance of brand names. Ownership of a brand name may be described as a right to a future economic benefit (and therefore potentially an accounting asset), but having that brand name appear in the statement of financial position is problematical.

STANDARDS

🌐 **IAS 38 INTANGIBLE ASSETS** *(cont.)*

54. No intangible asset arising from research (or from the research phase of an internal project) shall be recognized. Expenditure on research (or on the research phase of an internal project) shall be recognized as an expense when it is incurred.

57. An intangible asset arising from development (or from the development phase of an internal project) shall be recognized if, and only if, an entity can demonstrate all of the following:

(a) the technical feasibility of completing the intangible asset so that it will be available for use or sale;

(b) its intention to complete the intangible asset and use or sell it;

(c) its ability to use or sell the intangible asset;

(d) how the intangible asset will generate probable future economic benefits. Among other things, the entity can demonstrate the existence of a market for the output of the intangible asset or the intangible asset itself or, if it is to be used internally, the usefulness of the intangible asset;

(e) the availability of adequate technical, financial and other resources to complete the development and to use or sell the intangible asset.

(f) its ability to measure reliably the expenditure attributable to the intangible asset during its development.

71. Expenditure on an intangible item that was initially recognized as an expense shall not be recognized as part of the cost of an intangible asset at a later date.

Source: IAS 38, Intangible Assets

Where a company buys a brand name from another company, there is no problem – a clear historical cost value emerges from the transaction. But where a company creates a brand name – very similar to creating a new product – there are the problems of how early in the expenditure programme does it become reasonable to categorize the costs as being an asset and how to reliably measure the cost of the brand name. Expenditure on internally generated brands (like advertising campaigns) is in most cases indistinguishable from the cost of developing the business in general.

A further issue that has arisen is the question of amortization of brand names acquired in company takeovers. Many large companies which carry brand names argued that the regular advertising and promotion budget maintains the value of the brand, and depreciation is therefore unnecessary and represents a double charge. The IASB has been receptive to these kinds of argument by allowing intangible assets with indefinite useful lives to be accounted for without systematic amortization.

Patents

Patents are in effect a legal protection of an invention which prevents anyone using the invention without permission. As such, they are sometimes costly to establish, but once established they do have a future economic use to the company (either from making or using the product or from licensing others to use it) provided that there is a demand for the particular invention.

Assuming that a patent does represent future economic benefits to the company, it should be recognized at cost and then the cost expensed over the expected useful life of the asset in the normal way. Where a company buys a patent, its historical value is clear, but where it invents the subject of the patent, the problem of identifying the related costs and the application of the specific recognition criteria for internally generated intangible assets come into play. The exact depreciation pattern could be a matter for debate, but unless exploitation can be foreseen with a high degree of certainty, patents are a good candidate for methods which load depreciation into the early years.

Purchased goodwill

Sometimes companies expand by 'buying' customers from other suppliers, and when this happens a company is said to be buying 'goodwill'. For example, a solicitor who was planning to retire could sell the goodwill of her practice to another solicitor. Her clients would presumably still need a solicitor, and although they cannot be forced to move to the alternative selected, she can write to them recommending a specific alternative. The person recommended would have paid a fee for this to happen, and would have an excellent chance of retaining the customers.

Should the figure paid by an entity which acquires customers in this way be treated as an intangible asset? In the absence of legal rights to protect the client relationship or their loyalty, there is usually insufficient ground to establish real control over these items to meet the definition of an intangible asset. Nevertheless, exchange transactions for the same or similar non-contractual customer relationships may provide evidence that the company is able to control the expected future benefits flowing from the customer relationships even in the absence of legal control. The existence of such exchange transactions also provides evidence

STANDARDS

🌐 **IAS 38 INTANGIBLE ASSETS** *(cont.)*

63. Internally generated brands, mastheads, publishing titles, customer lists and items similar in substance should not be recognized as intangible assets.

Source: IAS 38, Intangible Assets

BETWEEN THE LINES

Intellectual capital

Intellectual capital is a relatively new and enigmatic concept, relating primarily to the intangible, highly mutable assets of the firm or, as some have put it, the 'brain power' of the organization. This brain power accounts for an increasing proportion of the capital in traditional industries and forms the backbone of the rapidly growing technology and knowledge-intensive sectors in the global economy.

Microsoft is used as the example of the hidden value of these intangible assets of the firm. In 1996 Microsoft's market value was 11.2 times its tangible asset value. This 'missing' value to a large degree represents the market's estimation of Microsoft's stock of intellectual capital that is not captured in its financial statements.

This is not the exception but rather the rule in financial reporting and illustrates one of the major limitations of the current financial reporting model. The Canadian Institute of Chartered Accountants concludes that accounting for intellectual capital will require developing accounting measures that can differentiate between firms in which intellectual capital is appreciating versus firms in which it is depreciating, and measures that will show the long run return in investment in people skills, information bases and the technological capabilities of organizations.

Source: Extract from 'Buried treasure' by Ramona Dzinkowski, *World Accounting Report,* May 1999

that customer goodwill is separable, a necessary condition to meet the definition of an intangible asset. As such exchange transactions are rare, this kind of goodwill is not frequently encountered in company accounts. However, if recognized, the purchased goodwill must be expensed in the usual way. Views differ as to the appropriate length of the period and the tendency is towards a short economic life on the basis that once the customers have tried the alternative service it is the quality of the alternative which will determine whether they remain customers or not.

IAS 38 explicitly prohibits the recognition of internally generated goodwill as an asset, because it is not an identifiable (separable) resource controlled by the company that can be measured reliably at cost.

There is a third type of goodwill (goodwill arising on consolidation) which is a product of accounting for groups of companies and will be discussed in that context in Chapter 12.

Tangible assets

Historically, tangible long-term assets have been the major assets of companies. IAS 16, *Property, Plant and Equipment*, covers the main non-current tangible assets. Property, plant and equipment are tangible assets held for more than one

AGFA – INTANGIBLE ASSETS *(extract)*

Significant accounting policies

(H) Intangible Assets

Intangible assets with indefinite useful lives, such as trademarks, are stated at cost less accumulated impairment losses. Intangible assets with indefinite useful lives are not amortized. Instead, they are tested for impairment annually and whenever there is an indication that the intangible asset may be impaired.

Intangible assets with finite useful lives are stated at cost less accumulated amortization and impairment losses.

Intangible assets with finite useful lives, such as acquired technology and customer relationships, are amortized on a straight-line basis over their estimated useful lives, generally for periods ranging from 3 to 20 years.

In accordance with IFRS 3 *Business Combinations*, if an intangible asset is acquired in a business combination, the cost of that intangible asset is its fair value at the acquisition date. The fair value of an intangible asset reflects market expectations about the probability that the future economic benefits embodied in the asset will flow to the entity.

Research and development costs are expensed as they are incurred, except for certain development costs, which are capitalized when it is probable that a development project will be a success, and certain criteria, including technological and commercial feasibility, have been met. Capitalized development costs are amortized on a systematic basis over their expected useful lives.

Source: Agfa, *Annual Report, 2010*

accounting and used in the production or supply of goods and services, or for administration.

A detailed analysis of these assets, divided into major classes and showing original cost (or valuation) and accumulated depreciation, has to be shown and is usually given in the notes to the accounts.

Land and buildings

In general terms, a company would recognize such an asset as land or buildings at a value which was based on the acquisition cost and any other ancillary costs. A simple case would be where a company buys a ready-built factory and may only have ancillary costs for professional fees such as for a surveyor and the solicitor who drew up the contract. Both the acquisition price and the fees would be capitalized in the value of the asset – the fees represent an integral part of the cost of bringing the asset to the location and condition necessary for it to be capable of operating in the manner intended by management.

A more complicated case might be where a company buys a plot of land on which there is a derelict building, demolishes the building, clears the site and builds a new factory. The value of the factory in the company's accounting records would include all those costs, as well as perhaps architect's fees and so on.

The aggregation of these elements provides a base cost, but the accounting problems and depreciation approach will depend on the legal means whereby the land is held. A company may either acquire a lease – a licence to use the land for a specific number of years – or it may own the land outright. Under a lease, the problem is that the company's right to use the land will cease after a specified period, but the implications of that depend on the length of the period. If the lease is for a relatively short period, say five years, the asset must be expensed over that period. However, leases are also issued for much longer periods, occasionally as long as 999 years, in which case the cessation of the company's right to use the land is so remote as not to be worth considering. Leased property is usually depreciated over the life of the lease, with a maximum depreciation period for buildings of around 50 years.

Land which is owned outright provides a different problem because of the trend for land prices to rise. This means that in the classic approach to depreciation, the depreciable amount (acquisition cost less estimated residual value) may actually be negative. Supposing you acquired a piece of land for a project limited to ten years and that the land cost €500 000, it could be that with the rise in land prices expected over the ten years the residual value would be (say) €600 000, giving a negative depreciable amount of €100 000.

Land usually has an indefinite useful life and therefore is not depreciated. That still leaves the question of the buildings which may stand on the land. Buildings, on the other hand, have a limited useful life and therefore are depreciable assets. The traditional approach would be to arrive at separate values for the land and buildings (perhaps by asking a professional valuer to give estimates of each and then applying the proportion to the historical cost) and then depreciate the buildings separately from the land – usually over 50 years on a straight-line basis. Here again some companies argue that there seems little justification for depreciating buildings whose value may also rise but which, in any event, sit on land whose value is rising in the long term.

An issue that has not really presented itself very strongly yet is the question of creating provisions for the eventual re-instatement of land to its natural state. This has surfaced, for example, in respect of the decommissioning costs of nuclear power stations. It can be argued that any company which builds a factory should make provisions for the ultimate removal of the factory when its useful life has ended and include the corresponding cost as part of the acquisition cost of the asset. In this vein, IAS 16 requires that when a company incurs an obligation to dismantle and remove the tangible asset and restore the site on which it is located, it should estimate the associated costs and include the initial estimate in the acquisition cost of the asset (we will come back to the issues involved in Chapter 14). The capitalized decommissioning costs will be depreciated alongside the other acquisition costs to match the costs to the asset's revenue-earning period.

Plant and equipment

Here again the purchase price of the plant may well be only a part of the total costs of bringing the plant into service. Ancillary costs to be capitalized might include elements such as site preparation, engineers' time in assembling and testing the plant on site, cost of transport to the site, etc. Sometimes a company's own workforce may be involved in the preparation of the asset. The fact that the company's workforce is involved does not change the basic concept – their wages etc. should be treated as part of the installation cost.

Leased assets

Sometimes a company acquires plant and equipment, or other assets, on a lease agreement rather than buying them outright. The increasing use of this method of financing has highlighted a particular accounting problem. If a company acquires an asset under a lease agreement and in effect has the use of the asset throughout its useful life, should that asset be recognized in the statement of financial position? Should the obligation under the lease to make payments to the lessor be recognized as a liability?

If, for example, a company borrows €100 000 to buy some plant worth €100 000, both the plant asset and the debt liability would appear in the statement of financial position. When a company hires equipment on a lease for substantially the whole of its useful life, the company is in effect acquiring the asset's economic value while incurring a liability to pay for it in instalments. The instalments would include both an element of interest and an element of repayment of the value of the asset. Is this situation different in principle from that where the company borrows the money and buys the asset in two separate transactions?

The US, UK and IASB all have standards requiring that where a company acquires substantially all the risks and rewards of ownership of an asset under a lease, that asset should be recognized in the statement of financial position as well as the liability to the lessor, irrespective of the fact that legal title of ownership to those assets is not transferred to the company. IAS 17, *Leases*, defines a lease as an arrangement whereby the lessor conveys to the lessee, in return for a payment or series of payment, the right to use an asset for an agreed period of time. The type of lease whereby substantially all the risks and rewards of ownership of an asset are transferred is called a finance lease (as opposed to **operating leases**). Accounting for finance leases is a typical example of the application of the 'substance over form' principle whereby the accounting rules act on economic substance and not on legal form.

It is not particularly useful in the context of an introductory financial accounting course to analyze in detail the methods which are used for arriving at a precise value of the asset and splitting the total amounts payable under the lease into repayment of the loan and interest charges. In principle, the asset is valued at fair value (its purchase price if bought on the open market) and this value is recognized as an asset. A balancing liability for the same amount is recognized as an obligation to the lessor. The amount payable over the length of the lease will normally be more than this, since it includes an interest element. The interest element is allocated over the length of the lease, ideally in relation to the outstanding value of the lease liability.

Take a simplified example where a company leases a machine for five years at a rate of €10 000 a year. If the company had bought the machine on the open market it would have cost €35 000. Accordingly the machine will appear in the statement of financial position at €35 000 and there will also be a balancing lease liability of €35 000. This means that the difference between the fair value assumed and the total of the lease payments (€10 000 × 5 years = €50 000) is €15 000 and this represents the implied interest charge on the transaction.

The €15 000 needs to be allocated over the life of the asset in proportion to the amount of the loan outstanding, and this can be done accurately with a computer program or there are simplified approximations to work out the effective rate of interest being charged. If we simplify in this case and say that the implied rate of interest is 10 per cent, then the first annual payment of €10 000 would be split for accounting purposes as €3500 interest charge (€35 000 lease liability × 10 per cent) and €6500 as repayment of the lease liability, leaving €28 500 outstanding at the start of the second year.

In the second year the interest charge is 10 per cent × €28 500 = €2850 and the balance of the annual payment, €7150, is used to further repay the lease liability. This continues until the lease liability is extinguished.

The asset is depreciated in the same way as assets which are owned once a value has been arrived at.

Investments

This is the third category of non-current asset. Companies may make investments on both a short-term and a long-term basis. Short-term investments are often made in liquid securities when a company has a temporary excess of cash. These are sometimes called *treasury investments* and appear as a current asset, often as part of cash at bank (or cash equivalents).

Where a company makes an investment for strategic purposes, which it intends to hold for some length of time, this will appear in the fixed or non-current asset category. Companies may invest in other companies for a number of reasons – to secure a relationship with a major customer or supplier; to participate in a new development but spread the risk with other interested parties; as a forerunner to a takeover. Where a company has a substantial stake in another (less than 50 per cent but large enough, for example, to be given a seat on the board) this is called an investment in an *associated company* (the technique for accounting for associated companies is dealt with in Chapter 12). Where companies set up joint ventures (for example, oil companies sometimes jointly own pipelines) these are often shown as an investment in an associate.

According to the EC accounting directives, such investments are valued at the full cost of acquisition, subject to any permanent impairment of value. If their current value falls below historical cost, then the investment should be written down (and the expense would normally appear in the financial result part of the profit and loss account). In some jurisdictions, if the current value exceeds historical cost, this information would be disclosed as a note to the accounts.

Under IFRS, these investments are measured at fair value (in accordance with IAS 39, *Financial Instruments: Recognition and Measurement*). The IASB defines fair value as 'the price that would be received to sell an asset or paid to transfer a liability in an orderly transaction between market participants at the measurement date' (IFRS 13, *Fair Value Measurement,* para 9). Essentially, fair value is a proxy for current market value. The effect of investments measured at fair value on income will depend on how they are classified. If the investments are classified as **held for trading** (or if the company elects to generically designate the investments on initial recognition at fair value through profit and loss), the changes in fair value are recognized in profit or loss in the period in which they occur. Classification as available for sale would result in recognizing the changes in fair value directly in equity, through the statement of changes in equity, until the financial asset is derecognized; at which time the cumulative gain or loss previously recognized in equity shall be recognized in profit or loss.

BEKAERT – FINANCE LEASES (extract)

Notes to the consolidated financial statements
Finance leases

Leases under which the Group assumes substantially all the risks and rewards of ownership are classified as finance leases. Items of property, plant and equipment acquired by way of finance lease are stated at the lower of their fair value and the present value of the minimum lease payments at inception of the lease, less accumulated depreciation and impairment losses.

In calculating the present value of the minimum lease payments, the discount factor used is the interest rate implicit in the lease, when it is practicable to determine it; otherwise the Company's incremental borrowing rate is used. Initial direct costs are included as part of the asset. Lease payments are apportioned between the finance charge and the reduction of the outstanding liability. The finance charge is allocated to periods during the lease term so as to produce a constant periodic rate of interest on the remaining balance of the liability for each period. A finance lease gives rise to a depreciation expense for the asset as well as a finance expense for each accounting period. The depreciation policy for leased assets is consistent with that for owned depreciable assets.

Source: Bekaert, Annual Report, 2010

Summary

In this chapter we first looked at the question – central to profit measurement – of the treatment of the costs of using up the company's productive capacity. We have seen that where an asset has a determinable life within the company, the cost of using up the asset must be allocated over this life, and impacts upon the estimate of profit for each accounting period. We have seen that there are several conventional bases for measuring depreciation and these do not necessarily reflect their economic consumption when there are tax considerations involved. We have noted that the depreciation charge reduces profit but does not cause any cash flow, thereby introducing another systematic difference between profit and cash flow on a period-to-period basis. When a long-term asset is disposed of, both gross acquisition value and accumulated depreciation are offset against disposal proceeds and a gain or loss on disposal is included in the statement of profit or loss.

We have also considered the accounting treatment and valuation specifics of the main long-term asset categories. Specific recognition and measurement rules with regard to intangible assets, tangible assets and investments have been reviewed.

Discussion Questions

1. Contrast the accounting consequences of financing the acquisition of a building through a bank loan or as a finance lease.
2. What is included in the acquisition cost of a long-term tangible asset? Give examples of at least four costs that would be included in the acquisition cost of a new production line.
3. Discuss the recognition rules for research and development costs.
4. Under what conditions will the disposal of a long-term tangible asset lead to a loss? How will the sale affect the financial statements?
5. What are the most common causes of the depreciation of a long-term tangible asset?

Assignments

The following questions have answers on the lecturer side of the digital support resources for the book.

1. Profit forecasts
    A company is considering investing in a project with a five-year useful life. The project involves paying €75 000 for a licence to manufacture a new product and equipping a production line at a cost of €300 000. The product is expected to have a useful life of five years only, and at the expiry of that time the production line will be sold and should yield a salvage value of €50 000. In order to launch the product the company plans a three-month advertising campaign which will cost €100 000.

    Assuming that in each year the expected sales are €1 000 000 and expenses other than those detailed above are €800 000, draw up two alternative series of statements of profit or loss for the project using (a) straight-line, and (b) diminishing balance depreciation of 30 per cent per annum, for the plant, while treating the other expenses consistently in each set.

    If, for policy reasons, the company wished to maximize profits in the first two years of operation, what accounting choices could be made (within the terms of generally accepted accounting principles) to achieve this?

2. Depreciati Ltd. purchased a truck for long-distance deliveries in Europe on January 3, 20X7. The purchase consideration amounts to €100000. The truck is expected to have a salvage-value of €20000 at the end of its eight-year useful life.

    Required:

    (a) Prepare a depreciation schedule using the straight-line method.

    (b) Prepare a depreciation schedule using the diminishing balance method.

3. On 1 January 20X7, Nyvice Ltd. purchases a specialized machine tool for €20000. The useful life of the machine tool is estimated to be five years. The residual value at the end of its useful life is expected to be zero. On 1 January 20X8, Nyvice purchases another machine tool for €4000. This has an expected useful life of four years and a residual value of €400. On 31 December

20X9, the company sells the first machine tool for €6000. Nyvice Ltd. uses the straight-line depreciation method.

Required:
Show how the statement of financial position and the statement of profit or loss of Nyvice Ltd. are affected by the this purchase for the years 20X7, 20X8 and 20X9.

4. Zetis SA had the following situation in its accounting database at 31 December 20X1:

Assets	
Land	150 000
Buildings	50 000
Accumulated depreciation	−4 000
Plant and equipment	46 800
Accumulated depreciation	−19 300
Vehicles	52 500
Accumulated depreciation	−27 300
Inventory at 1 January	9 400
Receivables	17 300
Cash	24 600
Financing	
Share capital	100 000
Reserves	189 300
Trade payables	5 400
Sales	247 200
Purchases	−69 600
Salaries	−131 000
Other expenses	−41 300

You are asked to draw up a statement of profit or loss and statement of financial position after making the following adjustments:

(a) Provide depreciation on the following assets: buildings, 2 per cent straight-line; plant and equipment, 15 per cent straight-line; vehicles, 40 per cent diminishing balance.

(b) Closing inventory at 31 December was 10 650.

5. A company decides to replace one of its production lines with new machinery. All the costs associated with the exercise are grouped together by the accountant in the same account, pending later analysis. The items appearing in the account after three months are:

	€
Removal of old machinery	2 800
Installation of new power lines	350
Resurfacing factory floor	825
Purchase of new machines	62 100
Transport of machines to factory	3 200
Hire of crane to position new machines	450
Servicing after first month's production	375
Replacement of conveyor damaged in production	580
Engineer's fee to check installation	250

In addition to the above items, the payroll records show that the company's maintenance crew spent 300 hours on installing the machines. The usual charge-out for labour is €5.75 per hour.

Which of the above items should be part of the asset value of the new machinery?

6. Bramen NV, a Dutch engineering company, decided to replace an older machine with a new one because of efficiency concerns and higher quality requirements. The machine was purchased in Canada, transported to Schiphol Airport by plane and subsequently transported to Haarlem by road. The new machine replaces the old one which is dismantled.

   Please indicate which of the following expenditure items will be included in the initial asset value of the new machine.

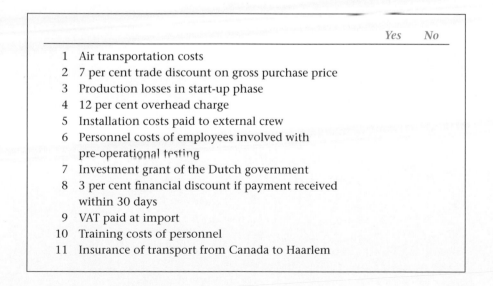

	Yes	No
1 Air transportation costs		
2 7 per cent trade discount on gross purchase price		
3 Production losses in start-up phase		
4 12 per cent overhead charge		
5 Installation costs paid to external crew		
6 Personnel costs of employees involved with pre-operational testing		
7 Investment grant of the Dutch government		
8 3 per cent financial discount if payment received within 30 days		
9 VAT paid at import		
10 Training costs of personnel		
11 Insurance of transport from Canada to Haarlem		

7. On January 2, 20X1, Machinery Unlimited purchased a second-hand trailer at a cost of €63 000. Before placing the trailer in service, the company spent €2200 painting it, €800 replacing tyres, and €4000 overhauling the chassis. Machinery Unlimited management estimates that the trailer will remain in service for six years and have a residual value of €14 200. The trailer's annual mileage is expected to be 18 000 miles in each of the first four years and 14 000 miles in each of the next two years. In deciding which depreciation method to use, Brett Coombs, the general manager, requests a depreciation schedule for each of the following depreciation methods: (a) straight-line and (b) depletion.

You are asked to:

(a) Prepare a depreciation schedule (i.e. for the six year period) for each depreciation method, showing asset cost, depreciation expense, and asset book value.

(b) For income tax purposes, the company wishes to use the depreciation method that minimizes income tax payments in the early years of asset use. Identify the depreciation method that meets this requirement.

CHAPTER 6

Refining the accounting system

In this chapter we are going to look at other areas where the accountant intervenes in the accounting database to refine the information, usually as part of the process of preparing the annual financial statements and with a view to giving a more precise profit estimate and statement of financial position. We are going to look at accruals and deferrals of both expenses and revenues, provisions to anticipate future expenditures related to past events, as well as impairment testing for loss of value in assets. We will end this chapter with a closer look at the components of the equity side of financing.

Chapter Structure

- Introduction
- Accruals and deferrals of expenses and revenues
- Provisions
- Asset impairment
- Bad debts and doubtful debts
- Hidden reserves
- Summary
- Discussion questions
- Assignments

Introduction

The routine accounting system works very well for things like invoices to clients and recording deliveries from suppliers. However, there are transactions that fall slightly outside this convenient framework and need to be brought into it or aligned with it when making accurate profit measurements. For example, we consume electricity and gas, use telephones and are invoiced afterwards; generally company lawyers or auditors do not send in monthly bills, but rather invoice us at the end of delivering a series of services which frequently do not correspond to our accounting year. In these areas the company accountant has to intervene and form a judgement as to what expenses have not been brought into the database, but should be incorporated into the profit estimate. Similarly, some expenses already posted in the database will have to be matched with next period's revenues and, thus, have to be deferred. Such period matching may be necessary for revenues as well.

Accruals and deferrals of expenses and revenues

Accrued expenses and accrued revenues (sometimes called just *accruals*) are previously unrecorded expenses and revenues that need to be adjusted at the end of the accounting period to reflect the amount of expenses incurred or revenues earned during the accounting period. Deferred expenses and deferred revenues (sometimes called *deferrals*) are previously recorded (and probably paid/received) expenses and revenues that have to be adjusted at the end of the accounting period by deferring part of them to the following accounting period.

Accrued and deferred expenses and revenues are the near cousins of payables/creditors and receivables/debtors. These are items where the economic transaction takes place at a different time from the cash transaction, but where the volume or frequency of the transactions does not warrant a continuing record in the basic accounting system, or where the invoice or similar document that is used to record the economic event arrives sometime after the expenses are incurred or the revenues earned – or sometime in advance of this. We have a timing difference between notification of the item and the economic event, so the accountant must make adjustments when preparing the annual financial statements. (Note that a highly sophisticated database which is used for preparing monthly internal accounts may well make monthly adjustments for accruals and deferrals, or use standard charges or some other device to bring these time-based items regularly into the database. For our purposes, the first need is simply to be aware of this type of transaction; later we will need to take these into account when preparing annual financial statements). Figure 6.1 and Figure 6.2 outline the accounting consequences of accruals and deferrals of expenses and revenues respectively.

Accrued expenses

Accrued expenses represent amounts for goods or services that have been received or supplied by third parties, but have not yet been invoiced, paid or formally agreed with the supplier at year-end. Typical transactions in this area would be

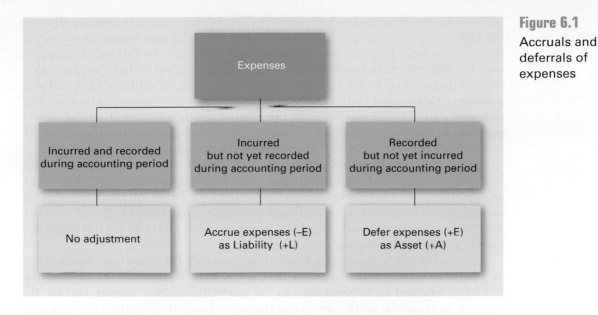

Figure 6.1
Accruals and
deferrals of
expenses

invoices for items such as telephone, gas or electricity, where the bill is received after the service or product has been used. For example, supposing a business prepares financial statements to 31 December each year but receives in February a gas bill for the months of November, December and January. The proportion of the bill which relates to November and December is an expense of the financial year ended on 31 December. Such an expense is called an 'accrued expense' and calls for an adjustment to be made in the financial statements for the year to 31 December to recognize the outstanding charge.

Supposing in this case the invoice referred to was for €1200. In the absence of any specific information about how much related to each month, the accountant will make a straightforward allocation on a time basis: the invoice covers three months, two of those are in the previous financial period, so the accrued expense is 2/3 × €1200 = €800.

	Year- end adjustment	*Following year*
Assets		
Cash		−1 200
Totals	0	−1 200
Liabilities		
Accrued expenses	+800	−800
Equity		
Profit year 1	−800	
Profit year 2		−400
Totals	0	−1 200

This adjustment would be inserted in the accounting system in order to allocate the expense across the appropriate years. The €800 expense would be deducted from the profit, while the corresponding liability would be put in a temporary account and appear in the statement of financial position or balance sheet as a short-term liability. In the following accounting year, when the €1200 bill was paid, only €400 would be treated as an expense, while €800 would extinguish the year-end liability. The operation of the accrual account ensures that the actual payment of the bill automatically expenses the correct portion into the following year operating expenses as well as cancelling the accrual.

Not all accruals fall across two accounting periods. For example, there would be a major accrual each year for the audit fee, which is conventionally treated as an expense of the year being audited (on a matching basis) although the work is carried out in large part in the following year. Accrued vacation pay is another significant accruals category: expensed when personnel services are rendered, but usually paid in the following calendar year.

A further point to note is that not all accruals are for known amounts. That is, when the accountant is drawing up the financial statements, he or she may not have received an invoice such as the gas bill examined above. Part of the exercise in drawing up the annual statements (sometimes called the *year-end exercise*) involves checking expense accounts to see whether all charges for the year have been received. If they have not, the precise details of the charge may not have arrived and the accountant will be obliged to estimate – based on previous year charges or current trends as appropriate (just one of the many instances where the data in the annual financial statements is not a matter of indisputable fact).

Deferred expenses

Deferred expenses (or prepaid expenses) are the opposite of accrued expenses – they are payments made or invoices received in one financial year for expenses which relate to a future financial year. Some items and services, such as rent and insurance (also prepaid mobile phone cards), are paid in advance. As such they are an asset at the time of payment and only become an expense as time elapses and the service or good is used up.

Typically the accounting system does not record such items as assets since in practical terms they start to be used up immediately. Usually such transactions are accounted for as expenses when the invoice or payment enters the accounting records and later on, as a further part of the year-end exercise, the accountant will examine such expense categories to check that the whole of the asset has indeed expired and was properly an expense. Frequently there is an unexpired portion since rental periods, for example, rarely coincide exactly with a company's financial year and, in order to match the transaction to the correct financial periods, the expense needs to be diminished and an asset recognized at balance sheet date, representing the unexpired portion of the expense.

If we take an insurance premium as an example, suppose an annual premium is paid on 1 April and the company's financial year runs to 31 December. Nine-twelfths of the premium should be expensed in the year of payment and three-twelfths recognized as an asset at 31 December – to be expensed in the following year.

Assuming that the premium was €2400 and that it was initially treated as an expense, three-twelfths (€600) should be recognized as an asset at the year-end:

	Original payment	Year-end adjustment	Following year
Assets			
Cash	−2400		
Prepaid expenses		+600	−600
Totals	−2400	+600	−600
Equity			
Profit year 1	−2,400	+600	
Profit year 2			−600
Totals	−2400	+600	−600

The use of the temporary prepaid expenses account allows the part of the expense which relates to the following year to be carried forward to the expenses for that year.

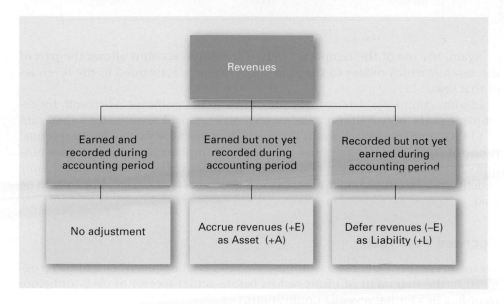

Figure 6.2

Accruals and deferrals of revenues

Deferred revenues

Deferred revenues (also called *precollected or unearned revenues*) are revenues that have been recognized before they are actually earned. At year-end, part of the recorded revenues that have not been earned yet are deferred or carried forward to the following year. These deferred revenues represent a liability that arises because the company has received advance payment for a service it has agreed to render in the future. A typical example from the publishing industry are unearned subscription revenues which represent journal subscription payments received in advance, for which the publishing company agrees to deliver issues of its journal during some future period.

Assuming that a publishing company receives an annual subscription fee of €1400 at the start of the annual subscription period (1 April) and that the subscription fee is initially treated as full revenue, three-twelfths (€350) of the revenue will be deferred and recognized as a short-term liability at the year-end:

	Original receipt	Year-end adjustment	Following year
Assets			
Cash	+1400		
Totals	1400	0	0
Equity			
Profit year 1	+1400	−350	
Profit year 2			+350
Liabilities			
Deferred revenue		+350	−350
Totals	1400	0	0

Again, the use of the temporary deferred revenue account allows the part of the revenue which relates to the following year to be forwarded to the revenues of that year.

In some companies deferred revenue can be quite significant. Microsoft, for example, reports in its 2010 financial statements unearned revenue for a total sum of $14,830 million (see Microsoft Company Report). Note that 'deferred revenue' is one of those peculiar liabilities that does not implyexpected future cash outflows. It meets the definition of a liability in the sense that the future economic benefits to be sacrificed refer to services or goods to be delivered, not cash to be paid.

Accrued revenues

Accrued revenue is the reverse of precollected revenue: revenues will be recognized in the statement of profit or loss before actual receipt of cash (or before recording of a formal revenue notification).

Assume that on 1 September 20X1 the company loans €100 000 to another business which will repay the loan in one year. The company charges interest on the loan at an annual interest rate of 9 per cent to be paid at the end of the loan term. The company prepares its annual financial statements for the period ending 31 December 20X1. In this case the borrower does not actually pay the interest in the year in which the loan was provided. But even if the interest payment is not made until next year, the company has earned interest income this year for a period of four months. The amount earned but unpaid as of the end of 20X1 (one-third of €9000) will be shown on the balance sheet of the loan provider as an asset. The accrued interest income is similar to a short-term receivable.

MICROSOFT – DEFERRED REVENUE *(extract)*

Unearned revenue

Unearned revenue comprises mainly unearned revenue from volume licensing programs, as well as payments for undelivered elements and for other offerings for which we earn the revenue when we provide the service or software or otherwise meet the revenue recognition criteria.

Volume licensing programs – Unearned revenue from volume licensing programs represents customer billings for multi-year licensing arrangements paid either at inception of the agreement or annually at the beginning of each billing coverage period and accounted for as subscriptions with revenue recognized ratably over the billing coverage period.

Undelivered elements – Undelivered elements consist mainly of payments for unspecified upgrades or enhancements of Microsoft Internet Explorer on a when-and-if-available basis for Windows XP, and technology guarantee programs

Other – Also included in unearned revenue are payments for post-delivery support and consulting services to be performed in the future; Xbox LIVE subscriptions; Microsoft Dynamics business solutions products; and other offerings for which we have been paid in advance and earn the revenue when we provide the service or software, or otherwise meet the revenue recognition criteria.

The components of unearned revenue were as follows:

(In millions) June 30	2010	2009
Volume licensing programs	$12 180	$11 350
Undelivered elements	624	1 083
Other	2 026	1 851
Unearned revenue	$14 830	$14 286

Source: Microsoft, Annual Report, 2010

Vodafone

Accrued and deferred revenue (extract)

Revenue for access charges, airtime usage and messaging by contract customers is recognised as revenue as services are performed, with unbilled revenue resulting from services already provided accrued at the end of each period and unearned revenue from services to be provided in future periods deferred. Revenue from the sale of prepaid credit is deferred until such time as the customer uses the airtime, or the credit expires.

Source: Vodafone, Annual Report, 2010

	Year-end adjustment	Following year
Assets		
Accrued income	+3 000	−3 000
Cash		+9 000
Totals	3 000	6 000
Equity		
Profit year 1	+3 000	
Profit year 2		+6 000
Totals	3 000	600\0

The operation of the accrued income account ensures that the actual receipt of the interest cash flow in 20X2 will cancel out the accrual and leads to the recognition of a net interest income for the year of €6000 in the 20X2 statement of profit or loss.

Provisions

A provision is an amount charged against profit or loss and carried forward in the statement of financial position (balance sheet) in anticipation of a future expenditure whose timing or amount are uncertain, but which derive in some way from current circumstances (i.e. the event generating the future expenditure has already taken place). The provision can always be released back to the statement of profit or loss at some future time if it proves not to be needed. Generally, a provision is made where some current event may have future consequences which will create an expense for the company. Prudence and matching both require that this possibility is recognized, but typically neither the exact amount nor the moment when it will crystallize is known, so a provision is created for an estimated amount.

Suppose that a company guarantees the product that it manufactures, under a warranty agreement. Under the terms of the agreement, the company undertakes to repair or replace manufacturing defects that become apparent within one year from the date of sale. On past experience, it is likely that in future periods a material amount of costs will be incurred in replacing or repairing the products sold in the current period. Both the prudence and the matching principles require that the profit of the period in which the revenue is recognized, be adjusted for the future (expected) replacement and repair costs. At the time of the sale, the exact amount of warranty expense is still uncertain. The company can, however, estimate the future repair and replacement costs based on past experience.

Other common examples of this kind of situation are where a company agrees to pay a pension in the future to employees, where a company decides to **restructure** or close down an operation. The adverse impact of business activities on the environment could also create a remediation obligation that has to be provided for.

From an accounting perspective, the provision is created by reducing profits and increasing liabilities:

	Create provision
Equity	
Profit for the year	−15 000
Liabilities	
Provisions	+15 000

Note that the provision is accounted for in the statement of financial position as part of liabilities (although generally separated clearly from debt). Taking into account the estimated timing of the expected future expenditure, it can be a long-term or a short-term liability.

Provisions should be reviewed at each reporting date and adjusted to reflect the current best estimate of the liability amount. When the expenditures for which the provision has been created actually occur, the provision will be used:

	Use provision
Assets	
Cash	−15 000
Liabilities	
Provisions	−15 000

The actual expenditure for which the provision has been set up, does not give rise to an additional expense, but extinguishes (part of) the provision. If it is no longer probable that an outflow of company resources will be required to settle the obligation, the provision should be reversed. The reversal will be credited to income:

	Reverse provision
Equity	
Profit for the year	15 000
Liabilities	
Provisions	−15 000

Provisions can appear, at first sight, to be rather a fluid subject. Students tend immediately to think that provisions must give company accountants a splendid opportunity to manipulate profits, by reducing profits in booming years and boosting them in lean years. This is true to a certain extent. For example, the concept of provisions as introduced by the Fourth EC Company Law Directive gives companies a fair amount of flexibility in deciding how to make use of provisions. However, tax authorities are well aware of this and strictly control what provisions, if any, are accepted in calculating the taxable profit. On the other hand, the IASB has introduced quite restrictive recognition and measurement rules with regard to provisions with the effect of restraining manipulative use of provision accounting.

STANDARDS

🌐 **IAS 37 – PROVISIONS, CONTINGENT LIABILITIES AND CONTINGENT ASSETS** *(extract)*

14. A provision shall be recognized when:

   (a) an entity has a present obligation (legal or constructive) as a result of a past event;

   (b) it is probable that an outflow of resources embodying economic benefits will be required to settle the obligation; and

   (c) a reliable estimate can be made of the amount of the obligation.

If these conditions are not met, no provision shall be recognized.

Source: IAS 37, Provisions, Contingent Liabilities and Contingent Assets

---

IAS 37, *Provisions, Contingent Liabilities and Contingent Assets*, defines a provision as a liability of uncertain timing or amount (IAS 37, par.10). As a liability, a provision should meet the definition and recognition criteria of a liability, but the main difference with an ordinary liability is the uncertainty of the timing or amount. The main characteristics of a provision can be described as follows:

- It reflects a present obligation (at reporting date) as a result of a past event that will probably (i.e. more likely than not) lead to a future outflow of company resources (usually cash) to settle the obligation.

- The timing or amount of the future outflow of resources is however still uncertain.

- The cause of the obligation (the obligating event) lies in the past and should not refer to a future event.

- The obligation can be legal (i.e. enforceable by law) or constructive. A constructive obligation is an obligation that derives from a company's past actions whereby it has indicated to third parties that it will accept certain responsibilities; this may be by a pattern of past practice or by some form of public statement.

- Although the amount and/or timing of future payments are uncertain, it should be possible to arrive at a reliable estimate of the amount of the obligation.

IAS 37 offers a decision tree that is quite helpful in deciding on the recognition of provisions. The decision tree is shown in Figure 6.3. Note that the left-hand side of the decision tree, which leads us to the recognition of a provision in the statement of financial position, reflects in fact the typical IASB criteria for defining and recognizing a liability in the financial statements.

In the case of the product warranty, the obligating event is the sale of the product with a warranty, which gives rise to a legal obligation. A history of claims can be compiled in order to determine the probability of warranty claims and the probable amount of claims related to the sales for a given period can be estimated. In this case, all three recognition criteria have been met and a provision for warranty claims will be recognized in the financial statements. Lawsuits are another area for which provisions can be significant. However, it may not always be clear that a present obligation exists in a lawsuit. Generally one does not wait for the final court decision to recognize a liability, but ponders all available evidence (including the opinion of legal experts) in deciding whether a present obligation exists. If available evidence brings the legal experts to the opinion that it is likely that the company will be found liable, a provision will be recognized for the best estimate of the amount needed to settle the present obligation.

Pensions are often a special case, and we will come back to those later in the book in more detail, but you can see that where, for example, the company gives long service awards, the right to the award is gained by (say) ten years of service and is therefore being earned during the ten years and is strictly a cost of those ten years, but it is difficult to predict how many employees will qualify for these at any given time. This is a classic provision – the company is contractually committed to pay such awards, but does not know how many people will eventually claim them, nor when, so it is a case for a provision.

Figure 6.3 also illustrates the borderline between provisions and contingent liabilities. A **contingent liability** refers to (IAS 37, par.10):

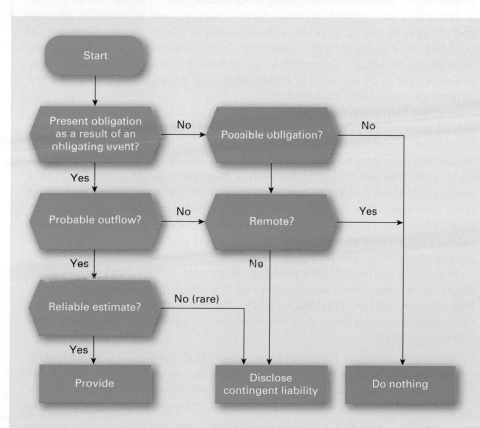

Figure 6.3

Decision tree – recognizing a provision

1. a *possible obligation* that arises from past events and whose existence will be confirmed only by the occurrence or non-occurrence of one or more uncertain future events not wholly within the control of the company, or
2. a *present obligation* that is not recognized because the future expenditure is not probable or the obligation cannot be measured with sufficient reliability.

The difference between a provision and a contingent liability is quite important as to its reporting consequences: a contingent liability is not recognized in the statement of financial position and statement of profit or loss and will only be disclosed in the notes to the accounts.

COMPANY REPORT

NOVARTIS – CONTINGENCIES *(extract)*

A number of our subsidiaries are involved in various government investigations and legal proceedings (intellectual property, product liability, commercial, employment and wrongful discharge, environmental claims, etc.) arising out of the normal conduct of their businesses. For more information, see note 20 to the Group's consolidated financial statements.

We record accruals for contingencies when it is probable that a liability has been incurred and the amount can be reliably estimated. These accruals are adjusted periodically as assessments change or additional information becomes available. For product liability claims, a significant portion of the overall accrual is actuarially determined based on factors such as past experience, amount and number of claims reported, and estimates of claims incurred but not yet reported. We provide for individually significant cases when probable and the amount can be reliably estimated. Legal defense costs are accrued when they are expected to be incurred in connection with a loss contingency and the amount can be reliably estimated.

In some instances, the inherent uncertainty of litigation, the resources required to defend against governmental actions, the potential impact on our reputation, and the potential for exclusion from US federal government reimbursement programs have contributed to decisions by companies in our industry to enter into settlement agreements with governmental authorities. These settlements have had in the past, and may continue in the future, to involve large cash payments, including potential repayment of amounts that were allegedly improperly obtained and penalties of up to treble damages. In addition, matters underlying governmental investigations and settlements may be the subject of separate private litigation.

Provisions are recorded for environmental remediation costs when expenditure on remedial work is probable and the cost can be reliably estimated. Remediation costs are provided for under 'Noncurrent liabilities' in the Group's consolidated balance sheet. They are estimated by calculating the present value of expected costs.

Provisions relating to estimated future expenditure for liabilities do not usually reflect any insurance or other claims or recoveries, since these are only recognized when the amount is reasonably estimable and collection is virtually certain.

Source: Novartis, Annual Report, 2010

Pending litigation for which available evidence does not indicate that it is more likely than not (but still reasonably possible) that the company will be found liable, is an example of a possible obligation to be disclosed as a contingent liability. If the probability of any settlement is regarded as slight (remote), no action is taken. A financial guarantee is an example of the second type of contingent liabilities. If a company guarantees payment of a loan made to a third party, there is definitely a legal obligation. However, as long as there is no available evidence that the borrower has or probably will default, no provision should be recognized in the financial statements. On the other hand, as the granting of a guarantee makes the company contingently liable, the nature and the amount of the financial guarantee must be disclosed in the notes to the accounts.

COMPANY REPORT

PHILIPS – CONTINGENT LIABILITIES (extract)

Guarantees
Philips' policy is to provide guarantees and other letters of support only in writing. Philips does not stand by other forms of support. At the end of 2010, the total fair value of guarantees recognized by Philips in other non-current liabilities was EUR 9 million. The following table outlines the total outstanding off-balance sheet credit-related guarantees and business-related guarantees provided by Philips for the benefit of unconsolidated companies and third parties as at December 31, 2010.

Expiration per period (in millions of euros)	*Business-related guarantees*	*Credit-related guarantees*	*Total*
2010			
Total amounts committed	302	49	351
Less than 1 year	100	22	122
1–5 years	133	8	141
After 5 years	69	19	88

Source: Philips, Annual Report, 2010

Generally speaking, the extent of the use of provisions is one of the areas where Anglo-Saxon practice is noticeably different from practice in continental Europe, and as usual this is driven by tax considerations. Many European tax authorities are more sympathetic to provisions than their anglophone counterparts, which leads to a greater use of them, since they reduce profit. The IASB definition of a provision (see above) requires there to be a **firm commitment** to make a payment, whereas in many other regimes a provision is justified if there is simply a possibility of making a payment.

Finally, it is worth noting that the borderline between provisions and accrued expenses is not always that evident. Recall that accrued expenses are liabilities to pay for goods or services that have been received or supplied but have not yet been invoiced or paid. Sometimes the amount or timing of these accruals has to be estimated, but the uncertainty involved in estimating accruals is generally considered to be much less than for provisions. Moreover, accrued expenses are often not reported separately in the statement of financial position; they may be included in trade or other payables, whereas provisions are reported separately with extensive disclosures in the notes to the accounts.

Asset impairment

Periodically, assets that have already been recognized on the statement of financial position should be reviewed for potential impairment. An asset is considered to have become impaired if its 'economic' value drops below its carrying amount. The general idea is that a company acquires an asset because it believes the expected future economic benefits to be generated by that asset exceed its cost. Subsequently, if the asset's remaining expected future benefits drop below its net carrying value, that asset is considered to have become impaired. In that case, the carrying value of the asset will be adjusted for an *impairment loss*. Like a provision, it is created by making a deduction from profit or loss, but where the opposite entry for a provision for expenses goes into the financing side of the statement of financial position as a liability, the asset impairment adjustment is a deduction from the asset value and is handled just like depreciation.

Asset impairment rules generally prescribe an impairment test in which the carrying value of the asset is compared to some threshold value level to determine whether an impairment has occurred and a write-down must be made. If the threshold level has been triggered, the amount of the impairment loss must be determined and recorded.

These issues are covered by IAS 36, *Impairment of Assets*. IAS 36 requires that assets are not to be carried at values in excess of their *recoverable amount* (the threshold value). An asset is regarded as impaired if its carrying amount exceeds the recoverable amount (IAS 36, par.1). Basically, the recoverable amount of an asset is the amount the company can recover either through using the asset in the future ('**value in use**' – see below) or selling the asset now.

Assets have to be reviewed for indications of possible impairment at the end of each reporting period (IAS 36, par.9). Impairment indicators may relate to either the assets themselves or to the economic environment in which they are used and include both external sources (such as market interest rates, significant adverse changes in technological, market, economic or legal environment in which the company operates) and internal sources (such as internal restructurings, evidence of obsolescence or physical damage of an asset). If there is an indication that an asset may be impaired, a detailed calculation of the recoverable amount is made and the carrying value will be reduced accordingly.

COMPANY REPORT

BAYER

Impairment indicators (extract)

In the fourth quarter of 2003, the Bayer Group considered it necessary to conduct an impairment test on its global assets in accordance with IAS 36. In the industrial business areas in particular, this was triggered partly by the strategic realignment of the Bayer Group, including the plans to place certain of the polymers and chemicals activities into an independent entity, and partly by the deterioration in business conditions in some areas of operation. These conditions mainly consist of an expected accumulation of adverse external factors such as sustained unfavourable price trends, especially higher raw materials prices that cannot be passed on fully to customers, lower volume growth as a result of tougher competition caused partly by global overcapacities, lower economic growth forecasts and continued unfavourable currency trends.

Source. Bayer, Annual Report, 2003

BETWEEN THE LINES

Illustration – impairment of a long-term asset

Assume a company acquired on 2 January 20X1 a specialized machine for €1 500 000, expecting to use it to produce a specific item for 12 years. The equipment was depreciated on a straight-line basis. By the end of 20X4 demand for the specific product has dropped so much that the company expects that the net cash flows the item would generate over the remainder of its product life cycle would be less than the machine's net carrying value (€1 000 000). The value in use was estimated at €800 000, while the estimated net selling price on 1 January 20X5 was €750 000. The equipment is therefore written down to €800 000, its estimated value in use, and the impairment loss is recognized in the 20X4 statement of profit or loss.

Recoverable amount

The recoverable amount is the higher of an asset's 'fair value less costs to sell' and its 'value in use' (IAS 36, par.18) (Figure 6.4).

The IASB defines *fair value* as 'the amount for which an asset could be exchanged or a liability settled between knowledgeable, willing parties in an arm's length transaction'. This fair value definition is very near to market value. This means that the 'fair value less **costs to sell**' essentially equals the net selling price of the asset. However, if the asset is not traded in an **active market**, a reliable estimate should be made of the amount obtainable from an arm's length

Figure 6.4
Recoverable amount

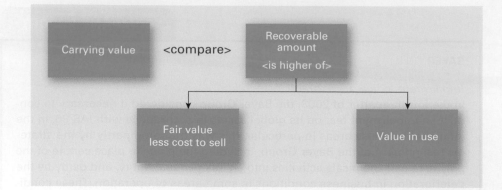

sale between knowledgeable, willing buyers and sellers, less **costs of disposal**. In that case, the outcome of recent transactions for similar assets within the same industry would be considered good evidence. Costs of disposal are the incremental costs that would be directly attributable to the disposal of the asset, such as stamp duty and similar transaction taxes and legal costs, but also costs of removing the asset.

Value in use is to be distinguished from market value or fair value. It typically reflects the value to a particular user rather than to the market in general, recognizing the extent to which the asset contributes to the specific business and performance of the company. IAS 36 defines value in use as the present value of estimated future cash flows from continued use of the asset and eventual disposal at the end of its useful life. Being based on present value calculations, discounting will be an essential part in measuring value in use. Basically, estimating the value in use of an asset involves two essential steps (IAS 36, par.31):

a. estimating the future cash inflows and outflows to be derived from continuing use of the asset and from its ultimate disposal, and

b. applying the appropriate discount rate to those future cash flows.

IAS 36 provides detailed guidance to apply these rules (see box below for some headlines of the calculation guidance).

It is not always necessary to determine both the fair value less costs to sell and the value in use. If either of the values exceeds the carrying amount of the asset, the asset is not impaired and it is not necessary to estimate the other amount. So, in practice, one will probably start with determining the fair value less costs of disposal (or the net selling price). If this value proves to be lower than the asset's carrying amount, the more complex calculation of value in use will become necessary. Figure 6.5 illustrates the typical sequence of steps of an impairment test process.

Individual assets versus cash-generating units

In principle, an asset's recoverable amount is determined at the individual asset level (IAS 36, par.66). However, assets are often used in combination with other assets and not in isolation. Individual long-term assets, for example, usually do not generate cash flows independently. It is their utilization together with other types of assets that generates cash flows. Hence, if the cash flows necessary for

Figure 6.5
Impairment test

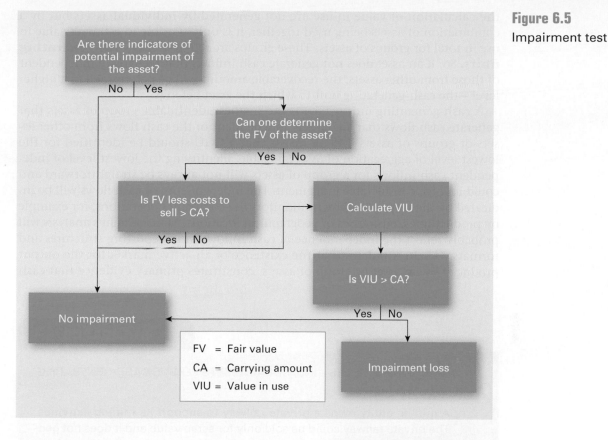

VALUE IN USE – CALCULATION HEADLINES

In calculating an asset's value in use, one should use:

1. Estimates of the future cash flows the entity expects to derive from the asset and expectations about possible variations in the amount and timing of those future cash flows; the estimates should include all estimated future cash inflows and cash outflows except for cash flows from financing activities and income tax receipts and payments.

2. Cash flow projections based on assumptions that reflect the asset in its current condition (without considering future restructurings or improvements) and represent management's best estimate of the set of conditions that will exist over the remaining useful life of the asset.

3. A pretax discount rate that reflects current market assessments of the time value of money and the risks specific to the asset; the discount rate should not reflect risks for which the future cash flows have been adjusted.

Source: Adapted from IAS 36, Impairment of Assets, par.30–57

the calculation of value in use are not generated by individual assets but by a combination of assets being used together, it is only sensible to estimate value in use in total for groups of assets. These groups are referred to as **cash-generating units**. So, if an asset does not generate cash inflows that are largely independent of those from other assets, the recoverable amount will be determined as a higher level – the cash-generating unit to which the asset belongs.

A cash-generating unit (CGU) is the smallest identifiable group of assets that generate cash flows that are largely independent of the cash flows from other assets or groups of assets. IAS 36 insists that a CGU should be identified for the lowest level of aggregation of assets possible. Identifying the lowest level of independent cash inflows for a group of assets will not always be straightforward and could involve considerable judgement. The independence of cash flows will be indicated by the way management monitors the company's operations, for example by product lines, businesses or geographical locations. Management's analysis will probably reflect the independence of cash inflows in its reporting structures and formats. IAS 36 stipulates that the existence of an active market for the output produced by an asset or group of assets, constitutes primary evidence that cash

STANDARDS

IMPAIRMENT RULES – INDIVIDUAL ASSETS VERSUS CASH-GENERATING UNITS *(examples)*

1. A mining entity owns a private railway to support its mining activities. The private railway could be sold only for scrap value and it does not generate cash inflows that are largely independent of the cash inflows from the other assets of the mine. *It is not possible to estimate the recoverable amount of the private railway because its value in use cannot be determined and is probably different from scrap value. Therefore, the entity estimates the recoverable amount of the cash-generating unit to which the private railway belongs, i.e. the mine as a whole.*

2. A bus company provides services under contract with a municipality that requires minimum service on each of five separate routes. Assets devoted to each route and the cash flows from each route can be identified separately. One of the routes operates at a significant loss. *Because the entity does not have the option to curtail any one bus route, the lowest level of identifiable cash inflows that are largely independent of the cash inflows from other assets or groups of assets is the cash inflows generated by the five routes together. The cash-generating unit for each route is the bus company as a whole.*

Source: IAS 36, Impairment of Assets, par.67 and 68

flows are independent. Such an asset or group of assets will therefore be a CGU. Examples of outputs from assets for which an active market exists include oil, electricity, marketable subassemblies, etc.

The recoverable amount of the asset's CGU is determined in the same way as an asset's recoverable amount. The principles to determine the CGU's fair value less costs to sell and its value in use are the same as those applicable for an individual asset. The carrying amount of the CGU should include all assets that generate the future cash inflows at the CGU level. Sometimes it will be necessary to include allocations of the carrying amount of corporate assets (such as a research centre, a central IT department or the corporate head office) when they contribute to the generation of cash inflows of the CGU.

Annual impairment test requirements

IAS 36 (par.10) requires that intangible assets with indefinite useful lives have to be tested for impairment annually, irrespective of whether there is any indication that these may be impaired. The same applies to capitalized goodwill (see Chapter 12 on group financial statements) which is not subject to systematic annual depreciation, but should be tested for impairment annually (according to IFRS 3, *Business Combinations*). An annual impairment test is also required for intangible assets that have not yet been brought into use, due to their higher intrinsic uncertainty.

By their nature, goodwill and intangibles will necessarily be tested for impairment at the level of cash-generating units. These impairment tests can be performed at any time during an annual period, provided that the tests are scheduled at the same time every year.

STANDARDS

ILLUSTRATION – IDENTIFICATION OF A CASH-GENERATING UNIT IN A RETAIL STORE CHAIN

Store Downtown belongs to Alphaline, a retail store chain. Downtown makes all its retail purchases through the central purchasing centre of Alphaline. Pricing, marketing, advertising and human resources policies (except for hiring X's cashiers and sales staff) are decided at corporate level. Alphaline also owns five other stores in the same city as Downtown (although in different neighbourhoods) and 20 other stores in other cities. All stores are managed uniformly.

In identifying a cash-generating unit in this context, one should consider, for example, whether internal management reporting is organized to measure performance on a store-by-store basis and whether the business is run on a store-by-store profit basis or on a region/city basis. Although the stores of Alphaline are managed at a corporate level, they are all located in different neighbourhoods and probably have different customer bases. Downtown generates cash inflows that are largely independent of those of the other stores of the retail chain and, therefore, it is likely that Downtown is a cash-generating unit.

Source: Adapted from IAS 36 – Illustrative Examples

Impairment loss

If an asset's carrying amount exceeds its recoverable amount, it will be written down and an impairment loss recognized as an expense in the statement of profit or loss.

For assets carried at a **revalued amount**, the impairment loss is treated as a re-valuation decrease.

If the impairment loss is determined at the level of a cash-generating unit, the CGU's impairment loss has to be allocated between the assets of the CGU. If goodwill has been allocated to the asset base of the CGU, the impairment loss is allocated first to reduce the carrying amount of goodwill. Secondly, the remaining impairment loss is allocated to the other assets of the CGU pro-rata, on the basis of their carrying amounts in the CGU.

An impairment loss should be reversed (and income recognized) when there has been a change in the estimates used to determine an asset's recoverable

STANDARDS

ILLUSTRATION – IDENTIFICATION OF A CASH-GENERATING UNIT IN A SINGLE PRODUCT COMPANY

Company Unique produces a single product and owns plants A, B and C. Each plant is located in a different continent. A produces a component that is assembled in either B or C. Alternatively, plant A's products can be sold in an active market. The combined capacity of B and C is not fully utilized. Unique's products are sold worldwide from either plant B or C. For example, plant B's production can be sold in plant C's continent if the products can be delivered faster from plant B than from plant C. Utilization levels of plants B and C depend on the allocation of sales between the two sites.

As there is an active market for plant A's products, A could sell its product in that market and, so generate cash inflows that would be largely independent of the cash inflows from plants B or C. Therefore, it is likely that plant A is a separate cash-generating unit, although part of its output is used by plants B and C.

Although there is an active market for the products assembled by plants B and C, cash inflows for B and C depend on the allocation of production across the two plants. It is unlikely that the future cash inflows for plants B and C can be determined individually. This brings us to conclude that plant B and plant C together are the smallest identifiable group of assets that generates cash inflows that are largely independent.

Source: Adapted from IAS 36, Illustrative examples

amount since the last impairment loss was recognized. However, an impairment loss should only be reversed to the extent the reversal does not increase the carrying amount of the asset above the carrying amount that would have been determined for the asset (net of amortization or depreciation) had no impairment loss been recognized.

Bad debts and doubtful debts

Probably the most commonly occurring asset impairment adjustment is that relating to non-collection of company receivables. A company's suppliers will naturally expect to be paid in full, but on the other hand the company may not expect to collect all the debts owing to it. At first sight that might seem a little odd, but there are various reasons why this may be:

1. *A customer may be a bad risk*: it is difficult to assess creditworthiness, so mistakes are made and credit given to those who cannot pay or, on the other hand, a company with a good credit record may suddenly hit bad times.
2. *A customer might be disputing the amount of the invoice you sent*: perhaps he or she thinks the price charged was higher than that agreed or the quantity greater than that delivered.
3. *A customer may have refused to accept some of the goods because they were faulty* or may be planning to send some faulty goods back, but this has not yet been picked up by the accounting system.

There are many reasons why the receivables' balance at any given point is unlikely to be collected in full. If the full accounting value was used in the statement of financial position, it would therefore overstate the value of the asset and of the profit for the period.

There are two separate aspects of assessing a 'prudent' value for outstanding receivables (or 'debtors' in British English). First, there is the case of specific receivables which on the evidence available are not likely ever to be paid and, second, there is a more general assessment of the collectability of all receivables.

In the first case, it is a routine part of credit management to inspect all outstanding receivables and particularly those which have been outstanding a long time. What exact length of time is appropriate depends upon the normal terms of credit in a particular industry – in most cases if a receivable has not been paid within 60 days of the issue of the invoice (or perhaps by the end of the month following the month of issue), the credit manager will regard the receivable as overdue and in need of follow-up. After 90 days the receivable is a source of concern and normally a credit manager would be in touch directly with the debtor at that point to discover why payment has not been made. After six months the credit manager and the accountant should consider the receivable together with whatever information the credit manager has gleaned from the customer (or indeed the sales force) to decide whether the receivable is likely to be settled. It may be that the client is going into liquidation or disputes the bill and refuses to pay and a decision has to be taken about recoverability. If it is decided that the amount is not recoverable, then the receivable becomes categorized as a bad debt and should be removed from the receivables' total. Note that in practice the phrases *bad debts* and *doubtful debts* are quite common, although it would be more accurate to use the labels *bad receivables* and *doubtful receivables*.

The bad debt, although it derives originally from a sale, is considered to be an expense. After all, the original sale took place; it is the settlement of the receivable which has not happened. Accordingly there is a simple transfer to credit

AUSTRIAN AIRLINES

Impairment of aircraft (extract)

Due to the impairment test carried out on the aircraft fleet, there is no requirement for impairment to a lower recoverable value for aircraft employed in the longer term. In detail, calculation is performed on the basis of so-called Cash Generating Units. Since all aircraft are used for all traffic streams according to the transferral concept of the Austrian Airlines Group, the total Group fleet has been included as a single Unit. An interest rate of 5.0 per cent (5.0 per cent the previous year) was set for the purposes of calculation. For the cash flows of the periods from 2012, which lie outside the limits of the calculations of the current corporate plan, the cash flow for the year 2011 was measured and escalated by 2.0 per cent per annum. Because the book values of those aircraft and spare parts specified for disposal but in regular flight operation until that time were below the market values minus disposal costs, no impairments were recognized in the report period (EUR 5.0 m the preceding year). There was also no need for impairment on aircraft not used in own flight operation due to the redimensioning of long-haul.

Source: Austrian Airlines, Annual Report, 2007

the receivable account (and therefore cancel the amount outstanding) and debit the profit and loss account. This evaluation of individual receivables should take place routinely throughout the year, but in any event it will also be a part of the exercise undertaken in preparing financial statements to ensure that no bad debts are included in the receivables' total.

The second consideration is that of taking a prudent view of the likely value to be received from the current receivables' balance at the accounting date when statements are being prepared. As we noted, there are many reasons why the total of accounts receivable may not be ultimately converted to cash, but most of the problems on individual receivables only come to light after the debt has aged a little. Consequently, as the bulk of the receivables outstanding at any one moment will be current, there is no way of knowing which will cause problems.

The prudent response to this is to set aside an 'allowance for doubtful debts'. This is an amount expensed in the statement of profit or loss, but simply held as a credit balance in the general ledger (or nominal ledger) against the day when any of the receivables outstanding at balance sheet date is classified as bad.

The object of making this general allowance for doubtful debts is to show a prudent value of total receivables. Exactly how much should be set aside in the allowance is a matter for consideration in the context of the business of each company. In general terms, a company might be guided by:

- industry practice generally
- average percentage of actual bad debts experienced by the company in previous years
- an estimate consisting of a high proportion of receivables outstanding more than (say) three months plus a low proportion of current receivables.

The precise amount will be a matter of the opinion of the accountant preparing the statements and the auditor.

It may be helpful to look at the impact of such an allowance in the context of a statement of profit or loss and statement of financial position. Let us say that Wholesale Merchants Ltd has total receivables in its general ledger of £115 000 and that in preparing the annual financial statements the accountant has decided that £1000 of receivables should be treated as definitely bad, while a further £1300 should be set aside as an allowance for doubtful debts.

The impact of this will be to create an expense of £2300 and reduce the published balance sheet value of receivables by the same amount. Within the company's records, the transactions would be:

	Write off bad debt	Create allowance
Assets		
Receivables	−1000	
Valuation allowance		−1300
Equity		
Profit for the year	−1000	−1300

The book value of the receivables goes down by £1000 directly and in the published statement of financial position or balance sheet the receivables figure would also be reduced by the valuation allowance, although in the general ledger the allowance will be held in a separate account, and in practical terms all the 'live' receivable accounts will continue to be followed up with monthly statements etc.

Normally, a company will set aside an allowance for doubtful debts each year, and in the next set of statements will simply add to or subtract from the existing allowance to reach the required figure. For example, a company with an unutilized balance on the allowance of £500 brought forward from the previous year would determine the required allowance for the current statement, let us say £750, and then expense the difference (£250) needed to bring the valuation allowance up to the required amount.

It is important to realize that the allowance for doubtful debts is an adjustment made in order that the published financial statements show a reasonably prudent view. Notice that none of the individual accounts of the customers is credited. They still record the full amount due. The allowance will be used during the following year, as the bad debts materialize. This ensures that the bad debts do not affect the expenses (and hence the profit) of the year in which they prove to be bad, but rather the year in which the business was done.

Hidden reserves

Less strict provision accounting rules can lead to significant 'hidden reserves'. Clearly, provisions provide great scope for reducing profits under a prudent accounting regime, even though they are not necessarily considered to be an 'allowable' (i.e. accepted by

COMPANY REPORT

COMPANY REPORT

CHINA SHOTO – ALLOWANCE FOR DOUBTFUL TRADE RECEIVABLES *(extract)*

Significant accounting policies

The Group makes sales on credit. A proportion of the outstanding credit sales may prove uncollectable in due course. An estimate is made of the uncollectable portion of accounts receivables using a percentage based on the ageing profile of the amounts outstanding, and also individually confirmed according to the customers' accrual credit conditions. Historically the Group has not born losses exceeding 1 per cent of gross book value of trade and other receivables but has increased its allowance for doubtful trade receivables during this period to reflect tightening monetary policy, in particular.

There is a degree of uncertainty as to actions the Group is able to undertake to enforce collection of doubtful debts, which may impact the eventual recoverable amounts. Accordingly, the Directors have assessed their best estimate of the recoverability of such debts as nil. More details of the allowance for doubtful trade and other receivables is provided in Note 14.

Source: China Shoto, Annual Report, 2010

---

the tax authorities) expense for calculating the **tax base**. A typical example of provisions that used to be popular for these purposes and that are still allowed under European accounting rules (and under numerous other local GAAP regimes) are the 'deferred maintenance' provisions.

Provisions for maintenance and repairs usually relate to installations and equipment that require substantial expenditure every few years for major refits or refurbishment and the replacement of major components. Suppose a power plant has a useful life of 25 years, but the steam generators need to be replaced every eight years. Utility companies used to account for this type of replacement programme by building a maintenance provision over a period of eight years up to the estimated replacement cost. The provision is used when the steam generator is actually replaced. IAS 37 does not allow this kind of provision, because at balance sheet date there exists no obligation to replace the steam generator independently of the company's future actions. Even the actual intention of the company to effectively replace the steam generator after the eight-year period does not create a present obligation as the company can always decide not to replace the steam generator or avoid the future expenditure by selling the power plant during the eight-year period. In fact, IAS 16, *Property, Plant and Equipment*, clears this point with its guidance on allocating expenditure on an asset to its component parts where these components have different useful lives or provide benefits in a different pattern. Instead of a provision being recognized, the depreciation of the steam generator has to be scheduled over eight years (and not the 25-year periods of the power plant as a whole). The replacement costs of the steam generator then incurred have to be capitalized and depreciated over the subsequent eight years.

It should be clear that, in the aggregate, the 'deferred maintenance' type of provisions (and similar 'intentional' or even more general provisions for potential risks) can be used to even out the trend of profits over several accounting periods or projecting a trend of modestly rising profits over the years (what shareholders generally expect), when true underlying profits may be quite volatile. Provisions which have been created with a view to concealing profits or storing them for the future (the Securities and Exchange Commission talks about 'cookie jar' provisions) could be considered to constitute 'hidden reserves'.

By way of illustration, suppose that in 20X1 a company reported profits of €100m; the position might be:

	20X1 €m	20X2 €m	20X3 €m
Reported profit	100		
Market expectations		120	140

In 20X2 the draft financial statements show a profit of €150m but the company does not expect to be able to sustain that level of profitability, which was caused by unusual trading conditions. If it reports that profit, the situation would be:

	20X1 €m	20X2 €m	20X3 €m
Reported profit	100	150	
Market expectations			225

So it makes a provision:

	20X1 €m	20X2 €m	20X3 €m
Draft profit		150	
Provision		−30	
Reported profit	100	120	
Market expectations			140

The following year is particularly bad:

	20X1 €m	20X2 €m	20X3 €m
Draft profit			110
Release provision			+30
Reported profit	100	120	140

Pressure on immediate profitability in the international field means that such provisions are used less often than they used to be, but it is normal practice for companies to try to even out profit flows a little by matching windfall profits with extra costs (known as *income smoothing*). The SEC says that US companies do this also. Apart from anything else there is a closer correlation between profit and dividend and shareholders look first at the dividend, not the profit, but also check the dividend as a percentage of profit.

The term *reserve* has a specific connotation in technical accounting jargon – it is an amount set aside from profit after tax and will appear in the statement of financial position as a component of owners' equity. Hidden reserves (also secret reserves, silent reserves) are rather different. These are deductions from measured profit, which do not appear separately in the statement of profit or loss when charged and are not visible in the statement of financial position. Historically, such reserves might be created by:

- writing down assets excessively
- creating provisions for fictitious risks
- overstating allowable provisions
- overstating financial liabilities.

The pressures for increased transparency of accounting mean that in many jurisdictions such activity is now illegal and, where it is legal (as in Switzerland) some disclosures have to be made when reserves are released. Clearly, while such reserves may be defended on the grounds of prudence, they provide endless opportunities for disguising the true state of a company's profit and financial position.

Capital structure

Broadly, companies are financed externally either with equity or debt. Equity participates fully in the risks and rewards of ownership – has no guaranteed return, but no upper limit either. Companies have limited liability so the equity-holder's downside risk is limited to the amount of his or her investment. The equity is only ever repaid to the individual investor in the event of liquidation. Ordinarily, an investor realizes the investment by selling the shares they own to someone else, although in restricted circumstances companies can buy back their own shares. (Exact regulation varies quite substantially from one jurisdiction to another.)

Debt is usually advanced to the company for a fixed period, earns a fixed return (although the interest rate may float in line with market rates) and must be repaid at the end of the period. The debt may be for the short, medium or long term, may be in foreign currency and can derive from a variety of sources. Many large companies obtain debt by issuing bonds or debentures which are bought and sold on the international financial markets.

This traditional distinction has broken down somewhat as a result of financial engineering – banks compete with each other for corporate clients by devising ever more complicated debt instruments which incorporate many characteristics of equity.

The decision as to what proportion of debt and equity to use in a company is a major issue. In principle, a company which uses a high proportion of debt (a highly geared company) has the possibility of enhancing the return to shareholders at the cost of making the return more volatile, more risky to the shareholder (discussed in Chapter 17). The ratio of debt to equity is one of the key aspects reviewed by the markets and some companies put a lot of effort into massaging this ratio.

Generally, companies have a target debt/equity ratio around which they operate, but which they do not usually achieve in practice. Issuing new equity can be expensive (professional fees, underwriting etc.) and therefore companies tend to use internally generated funds and debt to finance new projects in the first instance and then every few years issue new equity to move back closer to their target gearing.

Components of equity

The main type of share is the **ordinary shares**. The ordinary shareholders are the ultimate owners of the company and all other forms of finance rank ahead of these for payment. Their interest in the company is called equity – what is left after all other calls have been met.

Equity in a statement of financial position or balance sheet consists of ordinary shares and reserves. Reserves are either capital or revenue in nature. Capital reserves may not be distributed to shareholders (except on liquidation); revenue reserves are usually derived from the company's profit-making activities and may be paid over to shareholders by way of dividend. The archetypal revenue reserve is accumulated or retained earnings.

Ordinary shares have a *face* or *par* or *nominal value*. When companies are created, legal documents are drawn up which specify the upper limit on the number of shares which can be issued. Companies are not obliged to issue all these, and their effective voting share capital is the *issued share capital*. Note that sometimes companies have different classes of ordinary shares – 'A' shares, 'B' shares, etc. – often this is to give different voting rights to different groups of shareholders, a practice not entirely popular with the market.

Ordinary shares are rarely issued at par value and the difference between issue price and par value is also part of equity. It is called *share premium* and is a capital reserve. Costs of issuing shares are offset against share premium.

Preference shares

Preference shares attract a fixed return (hence '7 per cent preference shares') and holders do not routinely have voting rights, so they have the characteristic of debt. On the other hand the preference dividend may not be paid if there are no profits and does not qualify as a deduction before tax. Usually, if no dividend is paid preference shareholders are enfranchized. Typically preference shares are cumulative – if the dividend is not paid, the right to receive it accumulates against future profits. Dividends cannot be paid to ordinary shareholders ahead of preference shareholders. It is a matter of opinion as to whether preference shares should be treated as debt or equity for the purposes of calculating gearing.

Convertibles

Convertible securities – either preference shares or debt which can be converted at some point in the future into ordinary shares – are another form of debt which was particularly popular at the end of the 20th century. The merit of *convertible securities* is that the initial fixed return status means that there is little risk to the lender, while the possibility of converting to equity in the longer term means that if the company does well, the holder can convert to equity and participate in the company's growth. For the issuer it means a finer issue price and, if converted, a relatively cheap way to issue equity. For the analyst there is a problem as to whether convertible debt should be treated as debt or equity for analytical purposes.

In recent years companies have issued all sorts of complex financial instruments which combine both elements of debt and elements of equity.

The earliest instruments were probably convertible debentures or preference shares, where companies might argue that they should be considered to be part of the equity component rather than debt. Variants on this might be debt (sometimes called *mezzanine debt*) which ranked behind other debt for repayment and received a return based on profitability of the company. More recent developments are capital bonds and perpetual loan notes. If a loan is never to be repaid, it can be argued that it is more like equity than debt.

Summary

In this chapter we have dealt with year-end adjustments, including accruals and deferrals (of expenses and revenues) and provisions. We specifically outlined the more subjective aspects of provision accounting and the borderline with contingent liabilities. We have introduced and discussed the concept of impairment testing of asset values which has become a primary procedural issue in preparing financial statements at year-end. The underlying idea of the impairment test requirement is that an asset should not be carried on the statement of financial position at more than the company will be able to recover either from using or selling the asset. Adjusting the carrying amount of receivables for bad or doubtful debts is a specific application of the recoverability analysis of asset values. We have also visited briefly the equity side of financing, looking at how this is made up.

Discussion Questions

1. Accurately accounting for accruals and deferrals is a major issue in preparing financial statements. Discuss what constitutes an accrual and a deferral and give appropriate examples of the main categories one can discern.
2. Explain why and how deferred revenue is recognized in the statement of financial position.
3. In what sense is provision accounting a specific application of the principle of accrual accounting?
4. Explain the meaning of the word 'impairment' within the context of IFRS and discuss why it can be difficult to apply the concept to individual assets.
5. Identify and discuss the main categories of shareholders' equity that you would find in an IFRS statement of financial position. Be sure to enumerate specific sources included in each main category.

6. A company that grants defined pension benefits to its employees usually shows in its statement of financial position a net liability representing the difference between the obligation to pay pension benefits and the fair value of the assets included in the pension fund. Explain why it is not enough to expense the company's yearly contributions to the pension fund and eventually include an overview of the relevant assets of the pension fund (that is a separate entity) as an addendum in the notes.

Assignments

The following assignments have answers on the lecturer side of the digital support resources for the book.

1. The following balances were extracted from the accounting records of Arlington SA as at 31 December 20X1:

100000 ordinary shares	100000
10% preference shares	50000
12% debenture	50000
Premises	130000
Motor vehicles (gross cost €48000)	36000
Purchases	219 700
Administration expenses	73 200
Distribution costs	102 600
Sales	476 900
Receivables	39 250
Trade payables	23 600
Inventory at 1 January 20X1	21 250
Bank balance (asset)	70 420
Investments at cost	45 800
Reserves	48 220
Debenture interest	3 000
Preference dividend	2 500
Ordinary dividend	5 000

You are required to draw up a statement of profit or loss and a statement of financial position for the company as at 31 December 20X1, after taking into account the following adjustments (note that expenses have been analyzed by function, not by type, in this example):

(a) The closing inventory (31 December 20X1) was valued at €19300.

(b) Preference and ordinary dividends were paid halfway through the year, as well as debenture interest, but an accrual should be made for the balance of the debenture interest for the year. The company proposes a final dividend of €8000 on ordinary shares.

(c) The audit fee has been agreed at €5000.

(d) Insurance (included in administrative expenses) has been paid in advance and €950 relates to 20X2.

(e) There are accrued expenses of €480 for telephone (included in administration) and €620 for light and heat (distribution).

(f) The receivables balance includes €1200 of bad debts which should be written off.

(g) Depreciation of 25 per cent on a straight-line basis should be charged on the motor vehicles (which are vans used in distribution).

(h) The market value of the investments at 31 December 20X1 amounts to €44 100.

(i) It is estimated that the tax charge for 20X1 will be €20 000.

(*Comment*: This question is presented in an unhelpful way! You should reorganize the information from the database onto a spreadsheet in a way with which you are comfortable and then deal with the adjustments. You will not have come across one or two adjustments, and should just suggest a way of dealing with them based on what you know so far.)

2. Critically assess the following cases within the context of the IAS 37 requirements for provision accounting.

(a) Company A offers a one year warranty for the products that it manufactures. Yearly revenue subject to product warranties amounts to €3 000 000. In past years between 1 per cent and 3 per cent of the products proved defective. Defective products are replaced.

(b) Company B produces and sells phosphate fertilizers that are used to grow grains. The process of extracting the raw materials from the land the company owns, has a major impact on the natural environment. At balance sheet date, estimates of environmental remediation costs amount to €5 000 000.

(c) A law suit claiming damages has been filed against company C. The company foresees a reasonable possibility of losing the law suit. The company's legal advisers have estimated potential settlement costs at €350 000.

(d)   Company D runs an airline. The company is required by law to overhaul its aircraft once every three years. The future maintenance costs are estimated at €2 500 000.

3. On 2 January, 20X3 Dinasus Ltd purchased a specialized machine tool for £3 000 000. The straight-line depreciation schedule established an annual depreciation charge of £600 000 over a five-year useful life. Changes in market demand brought the company to carry out an impairment test at the end of accounting period 20X6. The impairment test was executed by external valuation experts and they concluded that (a) the machine tool suffered permanent impairment of its operational value, (b) the original useful life was still appropriate, (c) the net present value calculation of the cash flows to be generated by the machine tool amounted to £800 000 and (d) £950 000 is a reasonable estimate of the net selling price of the machine tool at the time of the impairment test.

Required: What are the accounting effects of this impairment test for accounting period 20X6?

4. At 31 December 20X3, Biaz Ltd carries out a review for impairment of a machine shop, acquired at the beginning of 20X1 for £20000. The useful life of the machine shop was estimated at five years with a zero residual value. The machine shop is depreciated straight line. Taking into account the impact of technological advances on operating conditions, the recoverable amount of the machine shop is estimated at £6000, with a remaining useful life of two years.

    Required: Determine if any impairment loss is to be accounted for at the end of 20X3. What would be the book value of the machine shop at the end of 20X4 (no further impairment during 20X4)?

5. The following end-of-year balances (in €) were extracted from Gearcorp's accounting system at 31 December 20X1:

Land	250000
Buildings (acquisition cost)	1 250000
Accumulated depreciation of buildings	−437 500
Equipment (acquisition cost)	595000
Accumulated depreciation of equipment	−178 500
Share capital	650000
Reserves	230000
Debt	960000
Inventory at 1 January 20X1	260 490
Trade receivables	280 300
Bank	1 040000
Trade payables	675 900
Sales	1 810 410
Purchases	−627 360
Salaries	−482 630
Other operating expenses	−120 530
Interest expense	−36000

(a) The value of the closing inventory at 31 December was €320550.

(b) So far, no depreciation has been provided for 20X1. As far as buildings are concerned, the company assumes a zero residual value and applies a 5 per cent straight-line depreciation rate. The equipment is depreciated using the reducing balance method. The equipment has an estimated useful life of five years and a residual value of €100000.

(c) The company rents a building in which the offices of its administrative personnel are located. The monthly rent amounts to €5000. Currently, the trial balance includes the payment of the rent relating to January 20X2, since that rent was prepaid in December 20X1.

(d) The audit fee pertaining to 20X1 is agreed to be €110 000.

(e) The company's tax advisers estimate that Gearcorp will have to pay about €72 3900 corporate income tax on the 20X1 profit.

(f) Included in other operating expenses is a business insurance policy which cost €4800 and which runs for the year from 1 April 20X1.

(g) The company is facing litigation from a former employee and considers it prudent to recognize a provision against legal costs of €30 000.

Required: Use the above information to make the necessary accounting adjustments and draw up Gearcorp's statement of profit or loss for the 20X1 fiscal year as well as its statement of financial position at 31 December 20X1.

6. See assignment Traduct SA in Chapter 12 for an exercise on impairment issues including goodwill.

CHAPTER 7

Preparing financial statements

In this chapter we are going to reach the end of our journey to the first major objective, which is to gain the ability to put together a simple statement of profit or loss and statement of financial position. The techniques we have been using are not those used directly by accountants, but the object is to understand the principles, in order to be able to use financial statements better as managers. This chapter will serve to bring together and review the different allocations and adjustments we have discussed so far, and should consolidate the techniques learned.

Chapter Structure

- Constructing financial statements
- Accounting adjustments
- Uses of financial statements
- Summary
- Assignments

Constructing financial statements

The basic technique for the preparation of a statement of profit or loss (income statement/profit or loss account) and a statement of financial position (balance sheet) consists of taking the aggregate transaction data from the accounting records as at the end of the financial year, quantifying the adjustments necessary to convert the data to reflect generally accepted accounting principles (GAAP), then putting the base data and the adjustments together in the approved statement format.

There is no prescribed way of carrying out this exercise, but most accountants prepare working papers on the basis of what is called an *extended trial balance*. This is not exactly the method we shall use, but we will discuss it here for your information.

The base data with which the accountant starts are the trial balance as at the end of year 2 that is, the listing of all the balances on all the general ledger accounts at the end of the year. The accountant must then refine these data by adjusting for unrecorded bills, revenue invoiced but not yet earned, depreciation, bad debts, provisions, **impairment losses**, etc. This may seem a potentially limitless exercise involving a major investigative activity, but in fact the accountant always starts off with the previous year's adjustments and then checks to see what has changed subsequently, so that the 'year-end exercise' is built up incrementally as the business develops.

The adjustments which are calculated at this stage are put into working papers in the first instance and a draft set of statements is prepared. These will form the basis of discussion with management and auditors, since usually they will involve taking a position about open transactions and other uncertainties (and will also impact on issues like taxation and profit-related bonuses).

The traditional extended trial balance working paper consists of four sets of debit and credit columns which will be added across to give the final picture. You will recall that, formally speaking, the accounting database is constructed with two columns for each account (see Chapter 2) although we have not replicated that presentation, since our object is to understand how the figures work rather than run an accounting function.

Ledger balances	+	Adjustments	=	Profit or loss	or	Balance sheet
D / C		D / C		D / C		D / C
€ €		€ €		€ €		€ €

Mathematically, the ledger balances and adjustments are added together horizontally. Each adjusted balance will have its place in either the statement of profit or loss or statement of financial position (balance sheet) and the adjusted total is entered in the appropriate column. The total debits and credits in the first column will equal each other, as will those in the adjustments column, but the statement of profit or loss and balance sheet columns must be added together to get balancing totals. For our purposes we shall continue to work with single-column spreadsheets, and we will add across to the right as we put in adjustments and so on.

The adjustments consist typically of all the elements we have looked at in the preceding sessions and which are necessary to provide financial statements which fully comply with generally accepted accounting principles. Specifically this involves the following:

1. *Calculation of cost of goods sold*: Insertion of closing inventories to arrive at the measurement of the cost of the goods sold during the period.

2. *Adjustment for accruals/deferrals*: Bringing into the accounts details of expenses and revenues relating to the period but unrecorded at reporting date; carrying forward the unexpired expense for payments made which relate to

future periods and deferring revenues received but yet unearned at reporting date. (The information for this in a practical situation comes from examining individual ledger accounts to check the periods covered by payments/ receipts, and examining payments/receipts after the balance sheet date.)

3. *Charging annual depreciation*: Debiting the operating expenses and crediting accumulated depreciation (or amortization) to reflect the expensing of long-term assets consumed during the year.

4. *Updating provisions*: Adjusting existing provisions for uses and reversals and adding new provisions.

5. *Reviewing assets for potential impairment*: If an impairment test evidences an impairment loss, the asset value will be decreased (credited) while the impairment loss will be accounted for in the statement of profit or loss as an operating expense (debiting an expense account).

The easiest way to see what happens in practice is if we now take an example, and work through the adjustments individually.

Worked example

The trial balance of Mornington Crescent Emporium SA as at 31 December 20X1 was as follows:

Mornington Crescent Emporium SA Trial balance as at 31 December 20X1	
	€
Assets	
Land	30 000
Equipment (at cost)	15 000
Accumulated depreciation	–4 500
Inventory at 1 January X1	13 250
Trade receivables	23 000
Bank	18 560
	95 310
Financing	
Share capital	50 000
Retained profits	10 500
Trade payables	16 850
Sales	193 000
Purchases	–145 000
Salaries and wages	–15 325
Rent	–10 000
Insurance	–2 500
Legal and professional expenses	–1 250
Telephone	–345
Light and heat	–620
	95 310

In reviewing the accounting transactions both before and after the reporting date (date of the statement of financial position), the following information comes to light:

1. The value of the inventory of goods for resale at 31 December 20X1 was €14 150.
2. Rent is payable quarterly in advance and rent for the three months January to March 20X2 was paid in December 20X1.
3. An insurance premium of €1000 was paid in September 20X1, covering the period October 20X1 to March 20X2 inclusive.
4. A telephone account of €120 was received in February 20X2 and related to the three months ending 31 January 20X2.
5. An electricity account (the most recent one paid) for the three months up to the end of November 20X1 for €150 was paid in December 20X1.
6. The financial statements must be audited and the estimated cost of this is €2000.
7. At year-end the company received a notification that a lawsuit was filed against it for injuries due to defects of goods sold. The company's legal counsel believes that an unfavourable outcome is probable and that a reasonable estimate of the settlement is €1000. Settlement is expected to occur at the beginning of May 20X2.

The accountant normally provides depreciation on a straight-line basis for the equipment owned by the company (note there is already accumulated depreciation in the trial balance) on the basis that it will have a nil salvage value and a useful life of ten years. There are no indications that assets might be impaired.

The above details represent the accountant's blueprint for action. She or he will set out the trial balance information on the extended trial balance worksheet we have described, and will then set out to incorporate the adjustments which are required on the worksheet, in order to calculate a draft set of statements.

We will not go through the formalities of the extended trial balance as such but will use a spreadsheet. While managers are unlikely to have to prepare a set of accounts themselves, they need to understand the mechanics of the process, since they may well be involved in making decisions about year-end adjustments and in any event need to know what are the areas of certainty and uncertainty which are concerned with the profit measurement process. Generally, some hands-on practice at drawing up statements fixes the basics more clearly in the mind!

Adjustments

(a) Inventory of goods

The trial balance already contains an 'inventory' figure – the opening inventory at the beginning of the year. The value of the inventory at the end of the year (independently established either by the company or by outside stock-takers) is €14 150. Inventory levels have increased by €900 and this must be reflected in the final statement of financial position. As we have discussed previously, this also fixes the cost of goods sold, and we can adjust the trial balance as follows:

Inventory of goods for resale	+900 (+ assets)
Purchases (becomes 'cost of goods sold')	−900 (+ equity)

(b) Rent prepayment

The information outside the trial balance shows that the €10 000 expenses recorded in the rent account include a payment for the first three months of 20X2. The rent account must therefore be adjusted to show the 20X1 expense only and recognize that at reporting date there is an asset, the unexpired rent expense for three months. From the information given the rent account balance represents 15 months' rent, so the unexpired element must be three-fifteenths, or €2000. Therefore the expense account is reduced by €2000 and a new asset must appear:

Rent expense	−2 000 (+ equity)
Prepaid expenses	+2 000 (+ assets)

(c) Insurance prepayment

The accountant also knows that the last insurance paid (€1000) referred to a six-month period of which only half was in 20X1, so here again he or she has to recognize an unexpired expense. The last payment related half to 20X1 and half to 20X2, so €500 (1/2 × €1000) should be recognized as an asset. Again the expense account is reduced and prepaid expenses increased:

Insurance expense	−500 (+ equity)
Prepaid expenses	+500 (+ assets)

(d) Telephone accrual

The telephone account paid in 20X2 included elements which related to 20X1 and are therefore expenses for 20X1. They must be incorporated in the statement of profit or loss and recognized as current liabilities. The proportion of the bill relating to 20X1 was two-thirds – the months of November and December, so two-thirds of the bill should be accrued (€80). Telephone expenses for 20X1 are reduced and another new balance sheet account opened up, this time accrued expenses:

Telephone expense	+80 (− equity)
Accrued expenses	+80 (+ liabilities)

(e) Electricity accrual

The electricity account also needs adjusting for accrued expenses, but the basis of calculation this time is different. The accountant has discovered from the ledger that the electricity account only includes charges up to the end of November, but no invoice for December charges has yet come in. Notwithstanding, he or she has to make an accrual, and must base the calculation on something else. Sometimes this is done by taking the previous year's figure and making an allowance for inflation, sometimes by taking a proportion of the most recently paid bill. In this case the most recent bill was for three months, so using that as a basis an accrual of one-third of the earlier bill (× €150 = €50) is made. You may think this is a rather crude approximation, which it is, but the amount in relation to overall expenses is not material so a more precise approach is not necessary. As before, the light and heat expense account is reduced and accrued expenses increased:

Light and heat	+50 (– equity)
Accrued expenses	+50 (+ liabilities)

(f) Accrued audit expense

The cost of the annual audit (although the actual work may in part take place after the reporting date) is considered to be part of the operating expenses for 20X1 and this accrued expense should also be recognized. The figure in this case is €2000 and a new expense line is created for it. The adjustment is:

Legal and professional	+2000 (– equity)
Accrued expenses	+2000 (+ liabilities)

(g) Provision for litigation costs

From the advice of the legal experts it is likely that the company will be found liable for the injuries caused by defective products sold in the past. The accountant concludes that there is a present obligation arising from a past event and that a future settlement payment is probable (around May next year). Although the settlement expenditure is still uncertain, the legal experts are able to provide a reliable estimate. All three recognition criteria for a provision have been met and a corresponding liability will be recognized in the statement of financial position.

   An expense line is created for the provision as an operating expense and a new liability account is inserted in the statement of financial position. The adjustment is:

Provision expense	+1000 (– equity)
Short-term provision (liability)	+1000 (+ liabilities)

(h) Depreciation

The company's equipment appears in the statement of financial position at €15000 original cost and must be depreciated over ten years on a straight-line basis. The annual expense will therefore be:

$$\frac{15000}{10} = 1500$$

This is entered by creating a new expense line for the annual charge to operating expenses and crediting the other side of the transaction to the accumulated depreciation account to reflect the reduced value of the asset:

Depreciation expense	+1500 (– equity)
Accumulated depreciation	+1500 (– assets)

The classic problem with the adjustments is to have non-balancing adjustments, with the effect that although one starts from a database where assets equal liabilities and equity, this equilibrium is destroyed by the adjustments. Of course, computerized worksheets build in control of this nature to avoid the problem. MBA students in an exam context have less luck, generally.

Worksheet

	Trial balance	Adjustments	Statement of profit or loss	Balance sheet
Premises	30 000			30 000
Equipment (at cost)	15 000			15 000
Accumulated depreciation	−4 500	(h) −1 500		−6 000
Inventory at 1 January X1	13 250	(a) +900		14 150
Trade receivables	23 000			23 000
Bank	18 560			18 560
Prepaid expenses		(b) +2 000		2 500
		(c) +500		
Totals	95 310	11 900		97 210
Share capital	50 000			50 000
Retained profits	10 500			10 500
Profit for year				(i) 16 730
Trade payables	16 850			16 850
Sales	193 000		193 000	
Purchases	−145 000	(a) +900	−144 100	
Salaries and wages	−15 325		−15 325	
Rent	−10 000	(b) +2 000	−8 000	
Insurance	−2 500	(c) +500	−2 000	
Legal and professional expenses	−1 250	(f) −2 000	−3 250	
Telephone	−345	(d) −80	−425	
Light and heat	−620	(e) −50	−670	
Accrued expenses		(d) +80		2 130
		(e) +50		
		(f) +2 000		
Short-term provision		(g) +1 000		1 000
Provision expense		(g) −1 000	−1 000	
Depreciation expense		(h) −1 500	−1 500	
Profit			(i) −16 730	
Totals	95 310	11 900		97 210

Note
Letters in brackets refer to the adjustments previously discussed.

Since we are splitting out on the worksheet a separate column for the statement of profit or loss, the balance sheet sections will not balance internally – the profit is missing from the equity section. In order to correct this and 'prove' the balance sheet, we need to calculate the profit figure and enter it into the balance sheet [entry (i)].

You have now completed working papers for the statement of profit or loss and statement of financial position as they would appear in the company's books, and all that remains is to set them out in an acceptable format for publication.

Mornington Crescent Emporium SA

Statement of profit or loss for the year ended 31 December 20X1 (format for use internally)

	€	€
Sales		193 000
Cost of goods sold		(144 100)
		48 900
Salaries and wages	15 325	
Rent	8 000	
Insurance	2 000	
Light and heat	670	
Depreciation expense	1 500	
Provision expense	1 000	
Legal and professional	1 250	
Telephone	425	
Audit fee	2 000	(32 170)
Net income		16 730

Statement of profit or loss for the year ended 31 December 20X1 (published format)

	€	€
Revenue		193 000
Cost of goods sold		(144 100)
		48 900
Personnel costs	15 325	
Other operating costs (excluding depreciation and provisions)	14 345	
Depreciation expense	1 500	
Provision expense	1 000	(32 170)
Profit before interest and tax		16 730

Statement of financial position as at 31 December 20X1		
	€	€
Non-current assets		
Premises		30 000
Equipment (at cost)	15 000	
less accumulated depreciation	(6 000)	9 000
		39 000
Current assets		
Inventory	14 150	
Trade receivables	23 000	
Prepaid expenses	2 500	
Bank	18 560	58 210
Total assets		97 210
Equity		
Share capital		50 000
Retained earnings	10 500	
	16 730	27 230
		77 230
Current liabilities		
Short-term provisions		1 000
Trade payables		16 850
Accrued expenses		2 130
Total equity and liabilities		97 210

Accounting adjustments

In preparing annual financial statements we have so far dealt only with the operating result. We now need to add to that adjustments for interest payments and taxation, and consider the dividend.

Interest is usually paid in arrears (sometimes monthly, or quarterly or every six months – customs differ between countries and types of borrowing) and will often need to be considered when calculating year-end accruals.

Taxation also varies from country to country. Tax on company profits may be levied at a national level only, or at both national and regional level. It is rarely found at local municipality level. In some countries it is paid after the accounting year, once annual profits have been determined; in many countries, companies make payments on account based on their own estimate of the profit for a quarter year or half year. At the year end there will normally be an amount to be accrued.

The deduction of interest and **tax expense** normally figures separately in the statement of profit or loss.

Profit before interest and tax	XXXXX
Finance costs (interest expense)	(XXXX)
Profit before tax	XXXXX
Income tax expense	(XXXX)
(Net) profit for the period (Net income available to shareholders)	XXXX

There remains after that the question of dividends to shareholders. Large listed companies will usually pay a dividend every six months and this will be charged directly against accumulated profits in shareholders' equity (companies listed on the New York Stock Exchange have to produce figures every quarter and some pay a dividend every quarter as well). The amount of the final, year-end dividend has to be approved by the shareholders in a general meeting, which takes place when the financial statements have been finalized, as they too are approved at that meeting.

In some countries this final dividend is also shown within the statement of profit or loss as a deduction from the profit for the period and in the balance sheet as a liability, but treatment varies from country to country. More often the dividend is shown simply as a deduction from retained earnings once it has been paid. The IASB rules, however, are very explicit on this point: in accordance with IAS 10, *Events after the Reporting Period,* dividends declared after the reporting date may not be recognized as a liability because they do not constitute a present obligation yet at the date of the statement of financial position – they will be disclosed in the notes to the accounts.

Worked example

In order to demonstrate how the adjustments would look, let us return to the financial statements we prepared in the last session and rework them on the basis of a different capital structure. We can also include an allowance for doubtful receivables and a current income tax accrual.

The share capital in the original example was €50 000. Let us now substitute a different structure:

	€
Ordinary shares	40 000
5% long-term debenture	10 000
Total sources	50 000

The company would need to make the following adjustment:

Debenture interest (5% × €10 000)	−500 (reduce equity)
Accrued expenses	+500 (increase liabilities)

The total trade receivables outstanding was €23 000. If the company wanted to take into account an allowance for doubtful debts of 1 per cent, this would involve a charge of €230 against profits and a reduction of the asset value, in this case, by the same amount:

Doubtful debt expense	−230 (reduce equity)
Trade receivables	−230 (reduce assets)

Assuming an income tax rate of 30 per cent, the company would also need to set aside €4800 as an income tax accrual (original profit was €16730; deduction of €230 doubtful debt allowance and €500 debenture interest would leave €16000, 30 per cent of which is €4800).

Assuming that you are using the same working papers as before, the adjustments are entered into the adjustment column and then extended across horizontally into the statement of profit or loss and statement of financial position.

Current tax expense	−4800 (reduce equity)
Taxes payable	+4800 (increase liabilities)

The adjusted financial statements are as follows:

Mornington Crescent Emporium SA
Statement of profit or loss for the year ended 31 December 20X1

	€	€
Revenue		193000
Cost of goods sold		(144100)
		48900
Personnel costs	15325	
Other operating expenses	14345	
(excluding depreciation, impairment and provisions)		
Depreciation expense	1500	
Provision expense	1000	
Allowance for doubtful debts	230	(32400)
Profit before interest and tax		16500
Interest expense		(500)
Profit before tax		16000
Income tax expense		(4800)
(Net) Profit for the period		11200

Statement of financial position as at 31 December 20X1

	€	€
Non-current assets		
Premises		30000
Equipment (at cost)	15000	
less accumulated depreciation	(6000)	9000
		39000
Current assets		
Inventory	14150	
Trade receivables	23000	
less impairment allowance	(230)	
Prepaid expenses	2500	
Bank	18560	57980
Total assets		96980
Equity		
Share capital		40000
Retained earnings	10500	
	11200	21700
		61700
Non-current liabilities		
Long-term debenture		10000
Current liabilities		
Short-term provisions		1000
Trade payables		16850
Accrued expenses		2630
Taxes payable		4800
Total equity and liabilities		96980

Uses of financial statements

This is by way of recapitulation of some of the issues which we considered at the start of the course. It is a major problem of financial reporting that a single set of numbers is expected potentially to satisfy all manner of diverse objectives:

- measure how much dividend might be paid
- provide reassurance of a company's financial strength to creditors
- provide a basis for measuring future growth for stock market analysis
- measure management performance in a principal/agent context
- provide the basis of taxation of the company
- give employees an idea of the company's strength.

It will be clear to you that (a) some of these objectives are contradictory and (b) accounting leaves open some choices which can affect how the company looks.

It needs also to be understood that the large, listed company which has operations in many parts of the world sees its annual report as a public relations document for trumpeting the group's strength and viability.

A private, family-controlled company may see its financial statements as something secret, to be disclosed to as few people as possible, and where profit is minimized in order to keep taxation low and to retain as much cash as possible in the company.

Summary

In this chapter we have demonstrated the technique used to prepare annual financial statements from the ledger. This involves extracting a trial balance and then using that as a working paper in which we incorporate adjustments for revenues and expenses that fall either side of the year end. The objective is to assign revenue and expense to the appropriate year. We have also discussed how different capital structures are treated in the financial statements.

Assignments

The following questions have answers on the lecturer side of the digital support resources for the book.

1. The trial balance of Arénières Inc. at 31 December 20X4 was:

	€
Land	82 100
Buildings (at cost)	120 000
Accumulated depreciation buildings	−36 000
Equipment (at cost)	89 500
Accumulated depreciation equipment	−53 700
Bank account	83 200
Trade receivables	91 300
Inventory at 1 January	214 300
Share capital	100 000
Reserves	185 600
7 per cent debenture	50 000
Trade payables	184 800
Sales	942 700
Purchases	−398 100
Salaries	−343 600
Other operating expenses	−102 200
Interest expense	−3 500
Interim dividend	−25 000

The following additional information is provided:

(a) The closing inventory at 31 December 20X4 was €216 300.

(b) No depreciation has been provided for 20X4. The company assumes zero residual values and uses the following straight-line rates: buildings 2 per cent and equipment 20 per cent.

(c) The audit fee for 20X4 is expected to be €20 000.

(d) The company estimates that it had phone costs of €1200 and energy costs of €1350 outstanding at the year-end.

(e) Included in 'other operating expenses' is a business insurance policy which cost €3000 and which runs for the year from 1 April 20X4.

(f) The company decides, on the recommendation of its auditors, that it would be prudent to create a provision of €10 000 against a claim for damages resulting from faulty merchandise.

(g) Corporate income tax for 20X4 is estimated at €15 000.

Please draw up a statement of profit or loss and a statement of financial position for the year ended 31 December 20X4.

2. The trial balance of Ansermet SA at 31 December 20X6 was:

	€
Land	155 000
Buildings (at cost)	560 000
Accumulated depreciation buildings	−112 000
Plant (at cost)	1 890 200
Accumulated depreciation plant	−1 039 610
Share capital	750 000
Share premium	220 000
Retained earnings	254 790
Long-term debt	600 000
Inventory	619 300
Trade receivables	414 700
Bank	208 100
Payables	336 800
Sales	2 740 500
Purchases	−1 247 000
Personnel expenses	−691 300
Other operating expenses	−268 100

Supplementary information:

(a) The closing inventory was valued at €584 600.

(b) The audit fee with regard to the 20X6 financial statements is agreed at €50 2800.

(c) The company paid outstanding December 20X6 travel expenses for various staff in January 20X7 – total value €2750.

(d) No interest had been paid at 31 December 20X6 on the long-term debt, which was contracted on 1 January 20X6 at 7 per cent.

(e) Depreciation should be provided at a rate of 2 per cent straight-line for the buildings (assuming no residual value) and 30 per cent diminishing balance for the plant.

(f) The company is facing litigation from an employee who has left and considers it prudent to make a provision against legal costs of €20 000.

(g) The tax advisers suggest that the company will have to pay about €60 000 tax on the 20X6 profit.

Please draw up a statement of profit or loss and a statement of financial position for the year ended 20X6.

3. You are asked to prepare the statement of financial position and statement of profit or loss of Agrestic Corp. for the year ended 31 December 20X4.

The trial balance of Agrestic extracted from the company's accounts at 31 December 20X4 is shown below (all amounts in €).

	€
Land	200 000
Buildings (at cost)	630 000
Accumulated depreciation buildings	–84 000
Equipment (at cost)	108 000
Accumulated depreciation equipment	–27 610
Trade receivables	253 800
Cash and cash equivalents	120 730
Inventory at 1 January 20X4	685 260
Share capital	800 000
Reserves	65 000
Trade payables	95 420
Long-term debt	300 000
Provision (liability)	50 000
Sales	2 465 300
Purchases	–1 258 000
Salaries	–420 800
Other operating expenses	–210 740

You receive the following information:

(a) The value of the inventory on hand at 31 December 20X4 was €558 460.

(b) No depreciation has been provided for 20X4. The company uses the following depreciation rates: 30 years straight-line for the buildings and 30 per cent diminishing balance for the equipment. Residual values are assumed to be zero.

(c) The provision (liability) in the trial balance has been used to pay for legal damages. The company received the court decision on 28 December 20X4. The original estimate of the legal damages amounted to €50 000.

The final court decision set the indemnification at €46 000 and is to be recorded under the heading of 'Other payables'.

(d) The company decides to create a provision of €80 000 for decontamination of land.

(e) The audit fee for the 20X4 financial statements has been agreed at €20 000.

(f) At 31 December 20X4 the interest of 5.5 per cent on the long-term debt has not been paid yet. The long-term debt was contracted on 1 September 20X4.

(g) The company assumes that 2 per cent of the total amount of the trade receivables will be irrecoverable.

(h) The company paid rent in December 20X4 relative to the period December 20X4 to February 20X5: total amount €3000.

(i) The tax adviser estimates the company's 20X4 income taxes to be €120 000.

(j) The Board of Directors proposes a dividend of 50 per cent of the 20X4 net profit to be distributed in May 20X5.

4. The trial balance of Mare's Nest from the company's books at 31 December 20X4 is shown below (all amounts in €).

	€
Land	450 000
Buildings (at cost)	1 320 000
Accumulated depreciation buildings	−640 000
Equipment (at cost)	1 652 000
Accumulated depreciation equipment	−495 600
Trade receivables	489 000
Long-term receivables	65 000
Cash and cash equivalents	365 200
Inventory (raw materials and consumables)	896 600
Share capital	1 500 000
Retained earnings	185 000
Trade payables	854 000
Long-term debt	1 000 000
Provision (liability)	250 000
Sales	4 638 500
Cost of sales	−2 805 000
Other operating income	126 500
Distribution costs	−897 800
Administrative expenses	−690 800
Interest expenses	−58 200

Supplementary information:

(a) On 25 October 20X4 the company booked and paid tuition fees (€10 000 – 100 per cent administration) for an in-house course on the new financial accounting system. The course will be equally spread over the period from 1 November 20X4 to 28 February 20X5.

(b) The audit fee pertaining to 20X4 is negotiated at €125000.

(c) Depreciation should be provided straight-line at a rate of 10 per cent for the equipment, while the buildings have an estimated useful life of 33 years (no residual values assumed). Buildings, land and equipment are allocated as follows: 60 per cent production, 20 per cent distribution and 20 per cent administration.

(d) The closing inventory at 31 December 20X4 was €1 133 800.

(e) The company paid a consultant €3200 for a review of the production cycle administrative controls. The consultant's invoice has been accounted for as 20X4 expenses, but the invoice was in fact an advance invoice for review services to be performed during 20X5.

(f) Mare's Nest received €24 000 of advance fees ('other operating income') from concessionaires on 1 July 20X4, covering marketing services to be delivered over a one-year period (ending on 30 June 20X5).

(g) The company granted a loan of €60 000 to an employee for a five-year period at an annual interest rate of 4 per cent. The employee has to pay the interest every six months. The agreement started at 1 December 20X4. Interest received will be accounted for as finance income.

(h) The tax adviser estimates the company's 20X4 income taxes to be €100 000.

Please draw up a statement of profit or loss and a statement of financial position for the 20X4 period.

PART THREE

An introduction to financial statement analysis

The object in this part of the book is to start to develop some ideas about what financial statement analysis is for and how it is done. Up until now we have been looking at the nuts and bolts of preparing financial statements, essentially so that you understand the fairly strict framework within which accounting data are produced. Now we move on to ask why analysts look at financial statements (Chapter 8) and then we start to use some of the traditional tools (Chapter 9).

A framework for interpretation

In this chapter we look at the fundamental questions an analyst is asking and review some of the management models that guide companies and against which we measure their performance. This section of the book is intended to deepen your understanding of financial statements in terms of interpreting the data disclosed in them, rather than, as previously, in terms of understanding the rules of recognition and measurement. However, it should be remembered that the material in this chapter is usually addressed much more fully in a corporate finance course. The chapter is provided as a link between the two subject areas.

Chapter Structure

- Introduction
- Financial structure
- Sources of finance
- Dividend policy
- Working capital management
- Performance measurement
- Summary
- Discussion questions

Introduction

In interpreting financial statements it is necessary to make assessments of how a company has behaved in relation to how it might have been expected to behave. In order to have a framework of expectations it follows that one must have theories about how companies should behave, and it is that area which we will discuss in this chapter. You will, of course, have your own views about how companies should behave, and other courses within your programme will also have provided many other insights. The reason for raising the issue of company behaviour is that you cannot make assessments of a company's performance without some idea of how you expect it to perform. Inevitably, the treatment here will address first principles: the objective is to provide a basic set of ground rules against which to judge company behaviour, rather than giving any detailed discussion of the theoretical background. You should extend this yourself. You need to bring to financial analysis a mixture of accounting, finance and strategy.

Financial analysis mainly concerns itself with two areas: evaluation of the financial structure and policy of a company, and evaluation of corporate management's performance. A potential lender to the company will be assessing slightly different aspects from those assessed by a potential investor, or perhaps the same aspects but with a different weighting.

The first question to evaluate is that of **financial risk**. The more borrowing a company already has, the more risky it is to lend more. As we discussed earlier, the level of borrowing also impacts upon the variability of profit. A potential investor will need to assess the degree of financial risk in order to decide whether the profit prospects of the company are sufficiently attractive. Business is about taking risks, so investors (and lenders) do not shun 'risky' investments, but they do expect a higher potential return as **compensation** for a higher degree of risk. For the investor, therefore, there is a link between financial structure (risk) and management performance (future potential profits). The return which an investor wants should be sufficient to:

a. compensate for inflation

b. equal the return available from no-risk investments

c. provide compensation for the risk.

This can be represented graphically (Figure 8.1).

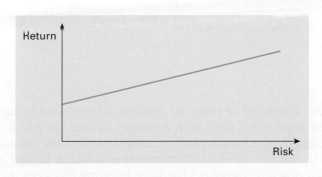

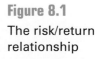

Figure 8.1

The risk/return relationship

This risk/return relationship holds good for both investors and lenders, and is behind the analytical approach which looks at financial structure and management performance: the first to assess financial risk, the second as a basis for forecasting future returns so that the financial decision can be made. We will now take a look at considerations in financial structure (including dividend policy and working capital management) and management performance.

Financial structure

It is worth revisiting the statement of financial position or balance sheet of a company to re-examine it from a point of view of analysis. You remember that the company is simply a legal vehicle into which investors have put money. This in turn has been used to buy productive capacity which is used to generate profits.

Figure 8.2
Financial
structure

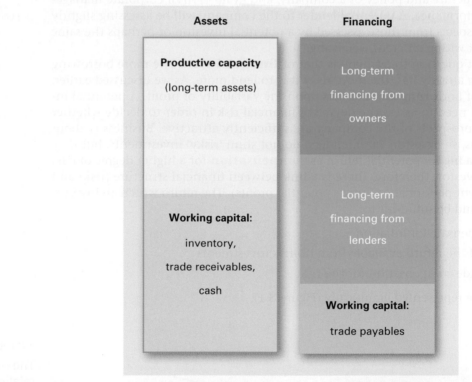

In Figure 8.2 the statement of financial position is structured in such a way as to show how the company has dealt with a number of strategic issues. It enables the analyst to see clearly the long-term financing structure, the investment in productive capacity and the different components of working capital and their relationship to each other. In Figure 8.3 the same building blocks of the statement of financial position are labelled according to accounting terminology.

The issues in relation to the basic structure are, first, that of the proportion of debt to equity (often known as *gearing*) and then, within debt, the term structure or maturity mix (when does the debt fall due for repayment?). Other questions which arise are the security ranking of different debt sources, and, in the case of a multinational, the currency make-up.

As regards the basic gearing of a company, there is no satisfactory guide as to what is a 'good' debt/equity mix. Of course, in general terms higher debt may both increase the return and increase the risk of a company. What one tends to find is that there are industry patterns which reflect other aspects of risk. For example, high-technology companies have a high operational risk and tend to have little financial gearing as a result.

Size and ownership are also factors in explaining the debt structure. Family-held or director-controlled businesses typically try to avoid issuing equity to outsiders because of the loss of management control that this might bring, so they tend to prefer to borrow. Small and medium-sized companies therefore often have higher gearing than their larger competitors.

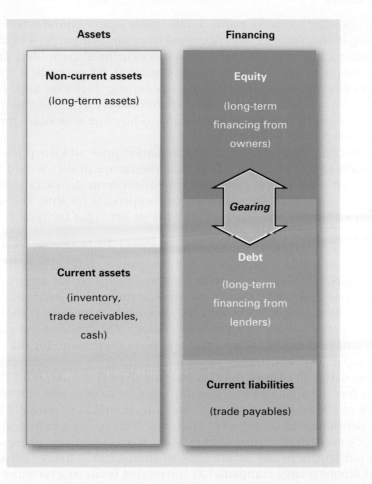

Figure 8.3

Gearing

Gearing has the additional benefit that, under tax law, interest is deductible as an expense in arriving at taxable profit, while the return to the shareholder is after tax. Therefore, given a tax rate of 30 per cent, the real net cost of a 10 per cent interest rate is 7 per cent when compared with the return to equity.

There are no real guidelines as to the appropriate ratio between debt and equity in any industry. Gearing varies enormously from one industry to another and in assessing the gearing in any one company the safest approach is a comparison with the gearing in similar companies. An examination of the statement of financial position of a company will reveal its gearing, and comparison of several balance sheets over a period of time will reveal the trend of that particular company.

Most companies work to a notional debt/equity target ratio. But when raising new finance, they do not automatically split the financing requirement between equity and debt. Normally they borrow for specific needs and then every few years have a major share issue to restore the debt/equity ratio.

Sources of finance

Share issue

When an existing company wants to raise more equity capital it will usually ask its existing shareholders to subscribe more (companies listed on a stock exchange are generally obliged to offer new shares to existing shareholders first). This is done by means of what is called a 'rights issue'. If, for example, a company has 1m shares already issued, the current price on the stock exchange is $3.00 per share and the company wants to raise approximately $1.25m in new finance, it could give existing shareholders the right to buy one new share for every two held, and at a price of $2.50 a share.

The reduction (discount) between the market price and the price of the new share would reflect an expectation that the future profits would have to be split between more people, albeit in the longer term the extra profits created by the expansion of the company would compensate for this. The shareholder may then either buy the shares or sell his or her right to them on the stock exchange.

Normally a company would have the share issue *underwritten*, that is, specialist institutions would guarantee to the company to buy all unsold shares at a predetermined price. The underwriter receives a large fee for accepting this risk, and this is one reason why share issues are not undertaken frequently. Any share issue has to be accompanied by detailed statements (a *prospectus*) about the company's past performance and future expectations. This involves the use of experts to check and confirm the information and is another reason for the high cost of raising equity.

An alternative to issuing rights is to issue shares on a different capital market. This has the advantage of opening up new sources and not obliging the company to sell the new shares at a discount, as well as potentially bringing in finance denominated in a foreign currency. This is not a common tactic and most stock exchanges require that existing shareholders are at least given the right to participate in any future issue of shares, but is likely to become more frequent amongst large companies as the market becomes ever more global and companies want to have the many strategic advantages of being listed on several stock exchanges. It is evident that companies with multiple listings tend to be strong supporters of IFRS (International Financial Reporting Standards) as global reporting standards.

Loans

Loan finance can be obtained in a number of ways, either through financial institutions or directly through the public markets. Typically, many small and medium-sized companies arrange long-term loans from their commercial banks or from merchant banks, in a single direct transaction. However, very large companies can also arrange 'syndicated loans' where the finance is provided by a group of banks or other lending institutions. Syndicated loans are commonly arranged by governments or state agencies for financing development or budget deficits, but they are also sometimes provided for special transactions by commercial companies such as the purchase by an airline of a new fleet of aircraft.

The rate of interest chargeable on such loans is usually a 'floating rate' which goes up and down in accordance with a market interest rate indicator. Central banks fix a minimum lending rate and loans are usually expressed as X per cent over minimum lending rate – in Europe the European Central Bank's interest rate is considered to set the basis for commercial borrowing and lending rates. Although actual rates offered to a customer are fixed individually by the banks, there is usually no difference in rate between banks.

Bonds

Companies also raise large blocks of finance by issuing debt directly to the capital market, known as *bonds*. Frequently such bonds are issued at a fixed interest rate. Bonds, like shares, can be taken up in small quantities by individuals: so bond debt could be raised from a large number of sources. Medium-sized family companies in Europe are often quite active in raising finance on the bond market since that offers public financing and a stock exchange listing but without dilution of control, since only debt is listed and not equity.

Leasing

Another possible source of finance is *leasing*. Here the company in effect rents an asset with finance often supplied by the supplier of the asset. This has the advantage of avoiding the need to raise finance separately when buying new assets. As discussed in Chapter 5, the accounting requirements now ensure that theoretically liabilities under finance leases appear in the statement of financial position in the same way as other sorts of finance.

Other methods

Other aspects of debt management are maturity mix, currency and interest rates. The *maturity mix* is the scheduling of repayment of debt – has the company borrowed in such a way that all its borrowings will fall due at the same time? It may be expensive to carry out a massive refinancing in one exercise and it is usual to spread out the maturity dates of debt.

This also impacts upon interest rates – raising long-term debt at fixed interest rates means locking the company into a high interest charge for a long period if such a manoeuvre takes place when the market rates of interest are high. Borrowing on floating rate agreements can be expensive if made when the market is low but then it subsequently rises. The ideal is to borrow long-term on fixed rates when the market rates are low, and to borrow on floating rates when the market is high.

Hedging

For a continental European company that wishes to raise finance in another currency than the euro, a further element of financial strategy is involved. This is the question of *hedging* foreign investments. The existence of the euro may well reduce the amount of borrowing done in foreign currencies by European companies, but the currency mix can be an important issue and is something normally to be disclosed by companies.

When a French company buys a US subsidiary, if it provides the cash from its home resources, it has debt raised in euro and an investment denominated in US dollars. There is therefore a transactional exchange exposure: the exchange rate between the euro and the US dollar fluctuates regularly. A company investing in a foreign currency risks two things: (a) that the investment will of itself yield a suitable return and (b) that the exchange rate will not vary so widely as to make the loan finance more costly over a period of time.

To illustrate the problem with our USA/France example, suppose a French company buys for US$100m a small US company which subsequently achieves annual profits of a steady $15m – an acceptable return of 15 per cent. The purchase is financed by a domestic loan and at the time of purchase the exchange rate was $1.00 = €1.00. The French company would therefore have borrowed €100m, and let us say that the interest rate was 7 per cent. To illustrate the exchange risk, if we ignore the commercial risk of the investment itself and assume profits remain steady at $15m, the euro outturn of the investment will also depend on the exchange rate. Table 8.1 shows the situation at the time of the initial investment, and the impact of rate changes in both directions.

As you can see from Table 8.1, the result in terms of the French parent's receipts can vary widely as a result of the exchange exposure. The exposure, of course, extends to the value of the investment as well: if the exchange rate went to $1 = €0.80, the euro equivalent of the original investment drops from €100m to €80m, giving an additional balance sheet 'loss' of €20m.

Table 8.1

Impact of exchange rate changes

Investment = $100m

Annual return = 15%

Exchange rate $1 = €1 (at date of acquisition of subsidiary)

French loan €100m – interest rate = 7%

US profit ($)	Rate 1$ = (on reporting date) (€)	French profit (€) (pre-tax)	Interest (€)	Net result (€)
15m	1	15m	7m	8m
15m	0.80	12m	7m	5m
15m	1.30	19.5m	7m	12.5m

> ## BETWEEN THE LINES
>
> ### Run a risk or plant a hedge?
>
> Every time there is a currency 'shock' the spotlight inevitably falls on the management of foreign currency exposures – a complex art due to the many subtle interactions of trading and international capital flows between different economies. Mastering this art begins with exploration of the origins of currency exposure and the risks which flow from it. It is usual to group these risks into three main types depending upon whether the exposure is transactional, translational or economic.
>
> *Source:* Extract from 'Run a risk or plant a hedge' by Martin Scicluna, Deloitte & Touche,
> *Accounting & Business,* May 1998

This kind of problem was a major contributor to the South-East Asian financial crisis of the late 1990s. A number of indigenous companies borrowed heavily in US dollars to finance expansion in the area. When their exchange rates started to slide, this meant that the local currency value of their debt increased enormously, as also did the relative cost of interest. At a stroke the companies became loss-making and had rapidly worsening debt/equity ratios at the same time.

A decision has to be made as to whether a company wishes to accept both the commercial risk and the exchange risk, and usually the answer will be negative. The exchange risk can be minimized by raising the finance in the country where the investment is made. So, in our example above, if the French parent company had borrowed $100m on the US capital market, both the investment and the associated loan and interest would be denominated in the same currency, thereby cancelling one risk with another. The company would have *hedged* its investment and the exposure would be limited to the difference between the US return and US interest payment.

A look at the debt analysis provided in the annual financial statements and the investment analysis will give some indication of the extent to which any particular company hedges its foreign investments with foreign borrowing – although precise details of the investment in subsidiaries are rarely provided as such.

Dividend policy

If it is assumed that the major preoccupation of the managers of a company is to maximize the gain for their shareholders, a major question will be how, in practice, this is best achieved. A shareholder gains from the investment in two ways: (a) through the receipt of dividends and (b) through the increase in the stock market price of the shares (and note in passing that although the creation of profit should help in both these aims, it is not the creation of profit in itself which is the objective).

Following on from the identification of these two types of gain, there arises the question of what importance to give each aim in relation to the other. Is the shareholder indifferent as to whether the gain comes from dividend or market appreciation, or does he or she prefer dividend at the expense of growth in price or vice versa?

One school of thought is that the dividend is unimportant – if a company retains the bulk of its profits in order to finance new profit-making opportunities, the market price of the shares should rise in anticipation of the higher levels of profit to be earned in the future (remember, as we have discussed before, that the market price of shares is determined by expectations of future performance). The shareholder benefits by an increase in market price. If the shareholder needs cash flow from the investment, then he or she can independently convert the market gain into cash flow by selling some of the shares.

However, other theorists say that shareholders give a priority to receiving an assured cash flow from dividends. They hold the shares, not for long-term price appreciation, but for short-term, continuing cash flows. Therefore if the company does not pay a dividend these shareholders are disenchanted, sell the shares and the share price falls because expectations of future dividend cash flows are low. Management is therefore failing in both aspects of maximizing shareholder wealth.

In practice, some companies apparently see a need to pay a continuing cash flow to shareholders irrespective of profit, while others are influenced in determining the amount of a dividend by the current profit. In looking at published financial statements, a comparison of net income after tax with the dividend payments will show whether the dividend is determined independently of the profit level.

Some theorists point out that in all probability it is incorrect to assume that all shareholders are looking for the same type of return – some may want dividends, others prefer price appreciation. Consequently there may be no discernible pattern in shareholder preferences: those who want high dividends will invest in companies that offer high dividends, while those who want price appreciation will invest in the companies which offer that possibility. This is called the *clientele effect* – companies acquire the clientele which prefers their particular approach to the question.

There is no overall best practice in this area against which to evaluate individual companies, but the question of dividend policy is an integral element of financial management because of its potential effect on shareholder wealth (the main objective of management) and subsequently because of the effect on the company's cash flows and its financing. A company with high dividends will have that much less cash available from internal operations – but, depending upon which theory you prefer, may find it easier to issue new shares. In any event, internally generated cash flows are an important part of a company's financing and dividend payments a major use of that finance.

Working capital management

The working capital cycle consists of a continuous flow of values (value-relevant items). We have already reviewed working capital movements and their impact on cash flows in Chapter 4. Their essential nature in many companies is represented in the simplified diagram shown in Figure 8.4. The company has a cash position that it has obtained from shareholders, lenders or from past profitable operations. These funds are used to acquire inventories, either by purchasing goods from third parties or by producing them itself. Other operating costs are also incurred. Trade payables (and other types of current liabilities) intervene between the incurrence of these costs and the actual outgoing cash flows (payments). The company sells the goods to customers, who either pay cash or buy on credit. If the company sells on credit, trade receivables intervene between the recognition of the revenue and the incoming receipts. When the customer pays, the cash position is replenished.

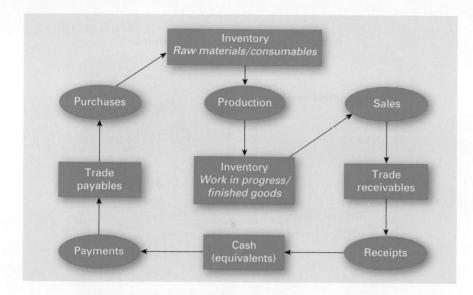

Figure 8.4

The working capital cycle

Basically, in a manufacturing company the working capital affects the following components of the statement of financial position (see rectangles in Figure 8.4):

1. Raw material inventory
2. Work in progress inventory
3. Finished goods inventory
4. Trade receivables (debtors)
5. Cash (equivalents)
6. Trade payables (creditors).

Working capital needs demand a net investment of funds: *net working capital*. The net investment in working capital amounts to the difference between working capital assets (current assets) and working capital liabilities (trade creditors/ current liabilities). It is the net investment of funds needed to get the working capital cycle going.

Financial management in this area consists, on the one hand, of keeping to a minimum the cash tied up in working capital, while, on the other hand, preserving sufficient cash or readily convertible current assets to meet payment needs. In general terms, cash flows are benefited by withholding payment to creditors for as long as possible, while keeping inventories at the various stages of production and debtors to a minimum. However, restriction of cash outflows is not the only objective of management, and there are interactions between the commercial success of a company and these working capital elements (Figure 8.5):

1. *Inventories of raw materials.* The unit cost of raw materials may be reduced by bulk buying, and maintenance of inventory at very low levels risks the possibility of production being halted by a late delivery of an essential item.

2. *Inventories of finished goods.* High inventories of finished goods allow sales always to be satisfied quickly – a sudden increase in sales can be supplied instantly. Sales may be lost because of delays in supply to the customer.

Figure 8.5a

Gross working capital

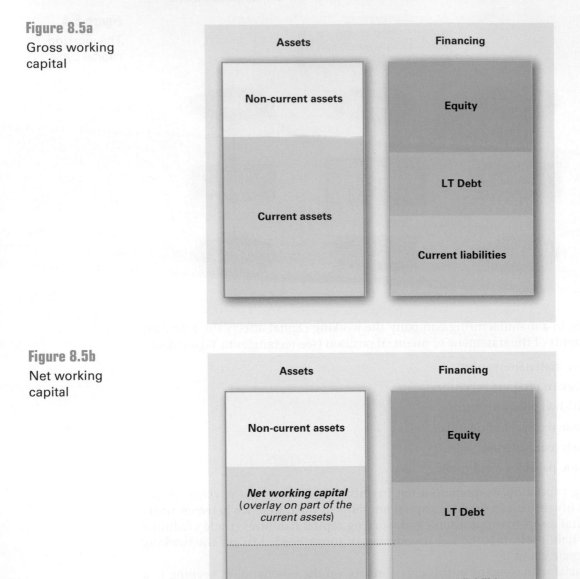

Figure 8.5b

Net working capital

3. *Receivables*. Every company, in the interests of cash management, wishes to buy on credit and have as long a credit period as possible. Customers therefore will take into account the credit available from each supplier when deciding between competing supplies of uniform products.

4. *Payables*. When buying supplies it may be that the supplier who offers the best unit price or the best value for money in terms of product quality is also the supplier who offers the least credit (since they have a competitive edge).

It follows that each company has to determine its working capital management in the light of the trade-offs between the ideal financial management policy and the ideal commercial policy. What exactly these trade-offs amount to will depend on the circumstances of each company and the nature of the industry within which it operates. *Just in time* inventory management, developed in particular by Japanese manufacturers, says that tight management control of inventory levels should eliminate production stoppages or failure to supply customers, while keeping inventories at a minimal level and reducing capital requirements. Suppliers are expected to maintain inventories and deliver to the customer 'just in time'.

It is impossible to suggest any general guidelines as to what is appropriate. In evaluating the working capital policy of any particular company it is essential to compare its policy with that of other companies in the same field or industry norms. The only overall guidelines are that companies should, on the one hand, keep their working capital levels at a minimum consistent with commercial policy while, on the other hand, ensuring that they are generating sufficient short-term cash flows (from inventory and receivables) to meet their requirements for settling amounts due to creditors and other payments (i.e. that they are sufficiently 'liquid').

Liquidity is the other aspect of working capital management and as a concept it is easy to grasp – simple domestic management proceeds smoothly as long as cash is available to meet bills as they fall due for payment. Liquidity as applied in a particular company is a rather more difficult matter to grasp because of the extreme variability of circumstances for each company.

In essence, each company needs to plan its cash outflows and its cash inflows and try to time them so that they coincide with each other. If inflows are large but at infrequent intervals (for example, in large-scale civil engineering contracts), the company is likely to need to maintain high inventories of cash or overdraft facilities, whereas if inflows are regular (for example, in food retailing), cash balances may be kept low and surplus funds invested in the short-term money market.

We can sum up the factors which affect working capital management as follows:

1. *Length of production cycle*. If it takes a long time to move from delivery of raw materials to completion of the finished product, inventories of raw materials and work in progress will be high.

2. *Variability of demand/flexibility of production*. If demand levels fluctuate, high inventories of finished goods may be required, except where the production cycle is short and the volume of production can be changed rapidly.

3. *Scale of credit sales*. In some industries all sales are on credit, in others virtually none. The length of credit demanded will also vary. A high proportion of credit sales and long credit periods will mean a high volume of trade receivables.

4. *Frequency of sale transactions.* A company which sells a high volume of units, each having a relatively low unit price, will tend to have a regular cash inflow. One selling a small number of high-value objects will have an irregular cash inflow. Cash levels will be low where there are regular inflows, but higher where inflows are irregular.

5. *Frequency of payments.* Where outflows are high and infrequent, cash levels may be kept low between outflows, but this pattern is relatively rare since basic running expenses such as wages and overheads form a fairly large and regular component of outflows.

By way of example, one would expect a company in the heavy capital goods industry, say, one which manufactured turbines to order, to have a long production cycle and infrequent cash inflows. It could therefore be expected to have a high level of inventories, receivables and cash, and therefore a high proportion of current assets to current liabilities.

At the other extreme, a retail organization such as a hypermarket would experience frequent, high-volume sale transactions and no credit sales (although the trend towards retailers issuing in-store credit cards is changing that pattern slightly). Its inventories, trade receivables and cash balances would therefore be very low. The relationship between current assets and current liabilities would be in a completely different proportion.

Generally, however, this relationship should be stable. As sales increase or decrease, the absolute value of inventories, trade receivables and trade payables should normally fluctuate in proportion to sales but remain constant in their relationship towards each other. Any marked shift in this relationship means that something has changed in the way the company is managed. One would also expect the relationship between the elements of working capital to be broadly comparable as between companies which work in the same business sector.

In the next chapter we shall be looking at financial statement analysis, and one of the measures used for evaluating a statement of financial position is the proportion of current assets to current liabilities (known as the *current ratio*). You will realize from the discussion of working capital that the nature of the current ratio can be expected to vary from one industry to another and care should be exercised in evaluating it!

Performance measurement

While the financial statements provide considerable information about the financial position of the company, they do not really do the same for a wider appreciation of performance. Of course, one major measure of performance is profitability, and the statements will give that in a number of different forms, but there are other areas not mentioned. By way of example, a particular UK company published its business objectives in the annual report and these were:

1. Maximize use of existing assets (rather than diversify).

2. Increase market share.

3. Build on strong personnel traditions.

Only the first objective can be related to the financial statements as such, although the company includes data in its annual report about the other aspects.

Evaluation of performance involves many considerations other than those which are visible from the annual financial statements. However, our concern here is the information available in the published financial statements.

In its financial objectives the same company stated that its target return is 25 per cent on the assets used and this, of course, can be evaluated from the financial statements themselves. The financial objectives are also expressed as a 5 per cent increase in real terms in earnings per share, and this too can be evaluated by reference to the financial statements.

But notice certain characteristics of the targets for evaluating performance: the absolute profit measure, for example, is not mentioned – the important measures are profit in relation to assets, and net earnings in relation to the individual share (after adjusting for inflation). You cannot judge performance in an absolute sense, but only in relation to another aspect of the company's structure. So a target of (say) profit before tax of €200m is meaningless, whereas a target of 25 per cent return on assets can be compared usefully with other companies.

Improving shareholder value is one possible target for company management to aim for. We will come back to the subject later and look at what this means, but it can be taken to be not only making current profits but ensuring that future profits are better as well. The target of increasing market share cited above is one example of a strategy which should yield not only current profits but future profits as well. For example, increased marketing expenditure is probably necessary to boost market share, causing a short-term decline in profitability; but, once that share has been achieved, it can probably be maintained with less marketing, and the higher volume of business should reduce average unit costs, thereby increasing profit both by increasing sales and by reducing average costs.

Summary

Corporate finance and its management is a very wide subject, and in this chapter we have made a very short examination of some of the major areas. Within such confines it is impossible to be other than superficial, but at the same time a total ignorance of corporate finance issues makes analysis and interpretation of financial statements a less productive exercise.

We have examined the structuring of company finance between debt and equity: this will influence both the volume and variability of the return to the shareholders. Equity is normally raised through the home stock exchange, although flotation on foreign exchanges is both possible and increasingly popular. Usually equity on the home market will be raised by first offering new shares to existing holders. However, issuing shares is an expensive exercise and is not, therefore, done at short intervals.

Debt finance may be obtained from a variety of sources, both individual lenders and capital market issues. The possibility of raising debt on foreign markets allows companies making foreign investments to hedge their investment – to limit their exposure to exchange rate fluctuations.

A major policy decision for companies is their approach to dividend payments to shareholders. Theorists are not agreed as to the best policy and some companies try to maintain a steady flow to shareholders irrespective of profit performance, while others gear their dividend to profits. The effect on share price of the dividend policy is not certain and it is possible that different shareholders have different preferences, buying shares in those companies whose policy most nearly satisfies their preference.

Working capital management is an important aspect of finance, but the composition and best policy towards working capital will be influenced by commercial considerations and the actual circumstances of the individual company within an industry. Some industries require very high levels of current assets, while others need very little. Policy therefore has to be evaluated in relation to the individual company.

Performance measurement has implications wider than purely assessing profit, although profitability is clearly an important measure. Profitability can most easily be stated by expressing it in relation to another aspect of the company's structure, such as assets employed in the business.

Discussion Questions

The following questions have answers on the lecturer side of the digital support resources for the book.

1. Why does an analyst need to take a view about the riskiness of a company as well as its profitability?
2. Distinguish between debt and equity and explain the importance of this ratio in financial statement analysis.
3. What is the working capital cycle, and what are the likely conflicts in managing this from a financial point of view as opposed to a sales or production point of view?
4. Explain why net working capital tends to be industry-specific.
5. How does high liquidity affect the risk/return relationship?

CHAPTER 9

Financial statement analysis I

This is the first chapter to address the tools for conventional financial statement analysis. It introduces the ratio, the classical working tool, and explains how the ratio facilitates comparisons and what key ratios are particularly useful in gaining a quick insight into company performance and financial position.

Introduction

Although this chapter is entitled 'Financial statement analysis', to an extent that is misleading because of course the whole book is about financial statement analysis. The preceding chapters which dealt with the preparation of financial statements are intended to give insights into the recognition and measurement framework within which financial statements are prepared and the limitations of that framework. The chapters that follow will look at more variables in statement preparation and how these impact upon interpretation of financial statement information.

Given that framework, we are now going to look at some technical elements used in the process of evaluating the financial statements of individual companies in order to arrive at conclusions about the company. We are going to examine financial statements through the eyes of users of financial information and, in particular, look at the tools which are used to aid analysis and extract useful information about the company.

The purpose of analysis

We have identified a wide range of potential users of financial statements, but for the purpose of analysis we are going to focus primarily on the needs of equity investors (or potential investors) and to a lesser degree those of suppliers of credit. Such users will each be interested in different aspects of the company and will also have differing levels of technical expertise available to them to interpret what they see. This is an underlying problem in the preparation of financial statements – they should contain information to enable sophisticated users to make good investment decisions, while at the same time they should not obscure the broad picture with so much detail that the less sophisticated user cannot understand them. However, financial statements are becoming increasingly complex and it is doubtful whether they are at all meaningful to those with no special training. Many companies include a section in the report (usually entitled 'Highlights from the year' or something similar) which gives a synopsis for the user who is not equipped to undertake a detailed analysis of the figures.

The tools of analysis which we are going to examine in this chapter are those used by the sophisticated user, and we should consider their objectives in making the analysis to see the relevance of the tools to that purpose. Stockbrokers and investment analysts examine financial statements in order to advise on investments in the shares – or bonds – of commercial companies. The investment might be made by a private individual or an institutional investor such as a pension fund, insurance company or unit trust. The trend in most markets is away from individual investors and towards institutional investors. Many people prefer to make their investments by way of a collective investment vehicle, such as a mutual fund or a policy with a life assurance company, so stock exchange investment is increasingly professionalized. However, the internet offers an alternative approach through the use of online brokers by individuals. Some people apparently like to get up early in the morning, check what the financial reports on television, radio or Internet are saying, and then buy and sell shares. They then go to work, and when they get home in the evening check out the Internet to see how their investment plays have worked out.

As we discussed in Chapter 8, users are primarily interested in answering two questions:

1. How well did the company perform?
2. How strong is the financial position of the company?

BETWEEN THE LINES

Value of accounts

(The annual report) provides an essential service whose key features must be preserved. That essential service is of relatively increased importance in the case of smaller listed companies. The main features may be summarized as:

- acting as a significant landmark in the cycle of business information;

- prompting questions and indicating trends;

- providing a basis for decision-makers to create their own model of the company;

- giving reassurance because the financial statements are subject to regulation and to audit and there is awareness that auditors at least cast an eye over the non-statutory sections of the annual report; and

- providing progressively greater detail, such as segmental information, for those who wish to probe the various aspects of the business.

Source: ICAS, *Corporate Communications: Views of Institutional Investors and Lenders* (Research Committee, Institute of Chartered Accountants of Scotland, 1999)

Their purpose in posing these questions, however, will differ, as will the relative importance of the one question to the other. Investment analysts are mainly interested in assessing future performance of the company. They are therefore only interested in the financial statements as a predictor of the future. The information about what the company did last year has no value of itself; its only relevance is as to whether it will do better or worse next year and whether the expected return is adequate for the expected level of risk.

Typically such analysts are specialists in a particular industry and their investment advice is based on an assessment of the likely performance of the industry in the future, combined with an appreciation of which company within the industry is most likely to perform well within the anticipated economic environment. The performance of any individual company will be affected by the economic environment within which it operates: it is affected by general levels of economic activity, changes in exchange rates, commodity prices, the introduction of new technology, inflation levels, etc.

Management cannot control these external forces which will affect all companies within a particular industry in the same way. But the best management will be able to minimize the impact of negative external forces and maximize the impact of positive external forces. Financial statement analysis provides one method of assessing how well managements perform from one company to another in the same industry.

The emphasis for the lender making a credit decision is likely to be different. Lenders do not participate in success in that the return they receive is not geared to profit. In addition, payment of interest will take place irrespective of the level of profit, so the lenders' concern in future performance is merely that there should be sufficient cash flow for the company to stay in business and pay the interest (*interest cover*).

The greater concern for lenders is the financial strength of the business. The lenders' main risk is that the company should fail and be unable to repay the loan (*default risk*). Future performance will of course have an impact on this, but the stability of the company's finances is the first concern, the marketability of the company's assets the second. The debt/equity gearing will therefore be a key issue, as will the relationship of the company's assets to its liabilities and the external value of the assets. For example, if it costs €100m to open a microchip factory, this asset is useful while there is a profitable market for microchips, but if the company failed following a slump in demand for microchips, a lender would find it difficult to raise €100m on the factory. Recall that the asset impairment rules touch this external value issue through the notion of the recoverable amount of assets.

If we look at the nature of the questions themselves (performance, financial position), it can be seen that each is the sum of a number of different issues. Management performance might be measured according to growth in assets, profit generated in relation to assets used or success in reducing tax liability, or extent of cash inflows, etc. The relevance of each detailed question will vary from one company to another, since no two companies are exactly the same and no two industries require the same proportion of long-term (non-current) assets to current assets, current assets to liabilities, debt to equity, etc.

What may be a useful and relevant measure of success in one industry may be totally irrelevant in another industry. For example, the ratio of sales to assets may be useful when comparing one retail company to another since it says something about the efficiency with which their premises are employed. But such a ratio would be meaningless in relation to an advertising agency, where perhaps a better measure of efficiency would be sales in relation to staff numbers or staff cost. This point should be borne in mind when considering the application of the analytical tools.

Traditional analysis

Financial statement analysis has been carried out ever since financial statements existed, but the methods of analysis have become more sophisticated over the years and, in particular, the development of computers has permitted the use of complex statistical analysis and the development of financial models. In this chapter we shall look at the longer-established methods and review recent developments later in the book.

The basis of traditional analysis is comparison. An absolute number has little information value: to say that Nestlé made €995m last year means very little. If we say Nestlé made €995m but a similar company (say Danone) made only €750m then the information begins to fit into a framework and have more use. But an important point in analysis is the relevance of the comparison. To say Nestlé made €995m but British Airways lost €500m tells us nothing about either company, merely what we already know: that their operations and objectives are quite different.

The framework for comparison may be either the company's own performance in other years, the performance of another company in the same industry or an industry average. Comparison over a period of years is known as a *time series analysis* (or *intertemporal comparison*), while that with a different entity or an industry average is called a *cross-sectional analysis* (or *interfirm comparison*).

Time series analysis

At a simple level, time series analysis (also referred to as *horizontal analysis*) would compare for a single company the figures for one year with those of the preceding year. But this is not very sound from a statistical point of view because such a short period may not reveal trends or may have been distorted by individual events. Analysts therefore, and particularly when making predictions, use at least a five-year base and often prefer a ten-year base. Companies usually provide a five- or ten-year summary of principal figures within their annual report. Such a time frame allows trend analysis.

Trend percentages can be used to follow changes in financial statement items over a longer period. They are computed by selecting a base year and set the amounts of the items of the financial statements of that base year equal to 100 per cent. The corresponding amount for each following year is stated as a percentage of the base amount. Trend percentages of total sales for a five-year period will be computed as follows:

Trend percentages of total sales (20X3 = 100%)						
	20X8	*20X7*	*20X6*	*20X5*	*20X4*	*20X3*
Sales (€m)	617	583	492	413	627	445
Sales – trend %	139	131	111	93	141	100

A long time base may raise questions about the impact of inflation – a 5 per cent inflation rate will lead to a 40 per cent loss of value in the measuring unit over ten years. The impact of inflation on the numbers must therefore be considered in time series analysis. If it is thought to be significant, a simple remedy is to convert the measurement unit to a common value by use of the retail price index – although where property revaluations have taken place during the series, care should be taken in the interpretation.

Cross-sectional analysis

Cross-sectional analysis involves making a comparison with other companies in the same industry for the same year. Potentially this may yield insights if the companies have very similar products, since differences will be the result of different management strategies in the face of the same problems.

Useful comparisons can still be made even if the companies are not exactly similar in their product line, but in evaluating the figures produced it is necessary to make allowances for the differences between the companies. This can become particularly difficult in relation to comparisons with companies which have diversified activities. For example, if one was doing an analysis of listed international media companies, one would find Walt Disney, News Corporation and Pearson. However, while Walt Disney and News Corporation (Twentieth Century Fox) both make films, and all three have significant television activities (but Disney owns the ABC network in the US), only Pearson and News Corporation publish newspapers. They also both publish books, but Pearson has a wide educational range (e.g. Prentice Hall) whereas News Corporation is mainly a producer of bulk fiction (HarperCollins) and Walt Disney, of course, has theme parks and resorts.

Useful comparisons can still be made, but the interpretation must take account of the differences between the companies. A general point to remember is that analysis rarely offers very exact comparisons: you can often only say 'X is worse than (better than) Y as regards such and such an attribute', not 'X performed 22.58 per cent worse (better) than Y'.

The other possibility in cross-sectional analysis is the use of industry averages. Many industries have trade associations which collect and publish such data, and some specialist financial data companies also compile this type of information for sale. These can provide some useful comparisons but here again interpretation must be cautious because the 'average' may be distorted by a number of factors. Because many companies have peripheral activities or more than one product, they may be included in an industry average for their main product, but their accounts will include the results of the other operations, leading to some distortion. Again the definition of the industry grouping may be so wide as to make comparison useless. Sometimes the grouping is dominated by one or two large companies, as would be the case with media companies in Germany, dominated by Bertelsmann, so it may be that the national 'industry average' reflects heavily the structure of one or two companies.

Tools of analysis

A simple approach to analysis would be to compare one component of the statement of financial position (balance sheet) or statement of profit or loss (income statement/profit and loss account) of a company with the same component of the statement of financial position or statement of profit or loss of another company. However, in cross-sectional analysis this would not be very helpful if the two companies being compared were of different sizes. The size problem is overcome by standardizing financial statements and by the use of financial ratios. Moreover, financial ratios, as we will see, are a powerful tool to measure and compare fundamental aspects of the risks and returns which drive investor decisions.

Common-size financial statements

Common-size financial statements allow the comparison of companies with different levels of total assets or sales by introducing a common denominator. In a common-size balance sheet each component of the statement of financial position is expressed as a percentage of total assets. For example, a company's statement of financial position could be restated as follows:

	Published €m	Common size %
Assets		
Non-current assets		
Tangible assets	113.9	22.4
Investments	8.6	1.7
Current assets		
Inventories	53.2	10.5
Receivables	218.6	43.0
Bank	114.3	22.4
Totals	508.6	100.0
Liabilities and equity		
Trade and related liabilities	111.6	22.0
Short-term borrowing	201.3	39.6
Long-term borrowing	3.1	0.6
Provisions	24.1	4.7
Equity	168.5	33.1
Totals	508.6	100.0

In a common-size statement of profit or loss each item is expressed as a percentage of sales. This might look like the following:

	Published €m	Common size %
Sales	5 356	100.0
Cost of sales	(2 601)	(48.6)
Gross margin	2 755	51.4
Distribution costs	(382)	(7.1)
Administrative expenses	(874)	(16.3)
Profit before interest and tax	1 499	38.0
Interest	(362)	(6.8)
Profit before taxation	1 137	21.2
Taxation	(384)	(7.1)
Net profit for the period	753	14.1

Common-size financial statements are not only useful to cross-sectional analysis (comparing operating and financing characteristics of two companies of different size in the same industry), but also for (internal) structural or vertical analysis of the financial statements of a company. A common-size statement of financial position reveals the relative magnitude of the major categories of assets, equity and liabilities. The same proportioning procedure can be repeated within the major asset, equity and liabilities categories to reveal the relative importance of subcategories, for example inventories relative to total current assets, the capital structure of the company (debt relative to equity) and the debt structure (long-term relative to short-term borrowing). If multi-period common-size financial statements are available, the structural perspective can be usefully combined with horizontal analysis for pointing out important changes in the relative weight of financial statement components from one year to the next.

Use of financial ratios

Financial ratios standardize financial statement data in terms of mathematical relationships expressed in the form of percentages or times. Instead of comparing absolute amounts from financial statements, a ratio is used to express the relationship between two elements of financial data that are logically linked, and compares that relationship with the same relationship in the other company. That is more easily understood in relation to an example.

Suppose we wished to compare the profit performance of two companies and had the data shown on the next page about each company.

	Company A €	Company B €
Sales	100 000	200 000
Net profit	10 000	15 000

Assuming that their products and activities are similar, a straight comparison would yield the information that company B had more sales than A and made more profit than A. In other words, company B is bigger than A – but that is easy to see and tells us very little about their relative efficiency.

However, a test of efficiency would be possible if we converted the information given to a ratio of profit to sales which would then tell us which company had the lower costs per unit of sales. This ratio is commonly used, and is sometimes called the 'net profit margin ratio':

$$\text{Net profit margin ratio} = \frac{\text{Net profit}}{\text{Sales}}$$

Applied to our example companies this yields:

$$\text{Company A} \quad \frac{10\ 000}{100\ 000} \times 100 = 10\%$$

$$\text{Company B} \quad \frac{15\ 000}{200\ 000} \times 100 = 7.5\%$$

By using a ratio we eliminate the size difference (the ratio expresses a relationship internal to each company) and are then able to make a meaningful comparison.

We can see that company A has a better performance than B; it makes a higher profit from its sales, so is more efficient than B, although smaller. Note that common-size financial statements are a form of ratio analysis, with total assets as a common denominator for balance sheet categories and sales for income statement items.

A practical point to bear in mind here is that the comparison is warped if the content of the numbers used is not exactly the same. For example, if in the above comparison the company A net profit was before tax, and the company B net profit was after tax, the comparison of ratios would not be valid. The golden rule is that *like must always be compared with like*.

The use of just the one ratio would not be sufficient to make a final assessment of either company; we should certainly look for other ratios to indicate other perspectives on performance, such as sales to capital employed. It could be that A is more capital intensive than B, so that would qualify the efficiency assessment in the first ratio. In essence, a good analyst will look for as many ratios as are meaningful, in order to build up a complete picture of the companies being examined.

Ratio analysis permits many comparisons, depending on the degree of detail available from the source data, and in general the analyst should always be free to construct whatever ratios seem appropriate in the context of the companies under review. However, some ratios are more commonly used than others and the ratios we will review in this chapter are generally useful for most companies. Note that many companies include a selection of ratios in their annual report. For example, Ericsson publishes ratio data in a five-year summary section (see Company Report).

COMPANY REPORT

ERICSSON

Financial highlights – five year summary (extracts)

Five-year summary

SEK million	2011	Change	2010	2009	2008	2007
Income statement items						
Net sales	226,921	12%	203,348	206,477	208,930	187,780
Operating income	17,900	9%	16,455	5,918	16,252	30,646
Financial net	221	–	-672	325	974	83
Net income	12,569	12%	11,235	4,127	11,667	22,135
Year-end position						
Total assets	280,349	–1%	281,815	269,809	285,684	245,117
Working capital	109,552	4%	105,488	99,079	99,951	86,327
Capital employed	186,307	2%	182,640	181,680	182,439	168,456
Gross cash	80,542	–8%	87,150	76,724	75,005	57,716
Net cash	39,505	–23%	51,295	36,071	34,651	24,312
Property, plant and equipment	10,788	14%	9,434	9,606	9,995	9,304
Stockholders' equity	143,105	–1%	145,106	139,870	140,823	134,112
Non-controlling interest	2,165	29%	1,679	1,157	1,261	940
Interest-bearing liabilities and post-employment benefits	41,037	14%	35,855	40,653	40,354	33,404

SEK million	2011	Change	2010	2009	2008	2007
Other information						
Earnings per share, basic, SEK	3.8	9%	3.49	1.15	3.54	6.87
Earnings per share, diluted, SEK	3.77	9%	3.46	1.14	3.52	6.84
Earnings per share (non-IFRS), SEK	4.72	–2%	4.8	2.87	4.24	7.53
Cash flow from operating activities per share, SEK	3.11	–63%	8.31	7.67	7.54	6.04
Cash dividends per share, SEK	2.5[1]	11%	2.25	2	1.85	2.5
Stockholders' equity per share, SEK	44.57	–2%	45.34	43.79	44.21	42.17
Number of shares outstanding (in millions)						
end of period, basic	*3,211*	–	*3,200*	*3,194*	*3,185*	*3,180*
average, basic	*3,206*	–	*3,197*	*3,190*	*3,183*	*3,178*
average, diluted	*3,233*	–	*3,226*	*3,212*	*3,202*	*3,193*
Additions to property, plant and equipment	4,994	35%	3,686	4,006	4,133	4,319
Depreciation and write-downs/ impairments of property, plant and equipment	3,546	8%	3,296	3,502	3,105	2,914
Acquisitions/capitalization of intangible assets	2,748	–	7,246	11,413	1,287	29,838
Amortization and write-downs/ impairments of intangible assets	5,490	–18%	6,657	8,621	5,568	5,459
Research and development expenses	32,638	3%	31,558	33,055	33,584	28,842
as percentage of net sales	*14.40%*	–	*15.50%*	*16%*	*16.10%*	*15.40%*
Ratios						
Operating margin excluding joint ventures	9.60%	–	8.70%	6.50%	8%	12.50%
Operating margin	7.90%	–	8.10%	2.90%	7.80%	16.30%
EBITA margin	9.90%	–	11%	6.70%	9.40%	18%
Cash conversion	40%	–	112%	117%	92%	66%
Return on equity	8.50%	–	7.80%	2.60%	8.20%	17.20%
Return on capital employed	11.30%	–	9.60%	4.30%	11.30%	20.90%
Equity ratio	51.80%	–	52.10%	52.30%	49.70%	55.10%
Capital turnover	1.2	–	1.1	1.1	1.2	1.2
Inventory turnover days	78	–	74	68	68	70
Trade receivables turnover	3.6	–	3.2	2.9	3.1	3.4
Payment readiness, SEK million	86,570	–11%	96,951	88,960	84,917	64,678
as percentage of net sales	*38.10%*	–	*47.70%*	*43.10%*	*40.60%*	*34.40%*
Statistical data, year-end						
Number of employees	104,525	16%	90,261	82,493	78,740	74,011
of which in Sweden	*17,500*	*–2%*	*17,848*	*18,217*	*20,155*	*19,781*
Export sales from Sweden, SEK million	116,507	16%	100,070	94,829	109,254	102 486

---

[1] For 2011, as proposed by the Board of Directors

Source: Ericsson, Annual Report, 2011

Management performance ratios

Assessments of management performance will usually start with a focus on profitability measures and, in a second stage, extend profitability analysis to asset utilization ratios. We have grouped the common management performance ratios in Table 9.1. To an extent these ratios are self-explanatory. They all answer different aspects of the question as to how well management has performed.

Profitability is a primary measure of the overall success of a company. Earning a satisfactory profit is the fundamental goal of most businesses. The *net profit margin* is a first candidate measure of overall profitability. The net profit margin is also referred to as *return on sales* (with the term 'return' used as a synonym of 'profitability'). It shows (in its change from year to year, or compared to another company) how successful the management is in creating profit from a given

A. Profitability ratios

$$\text{Net profit margin} = \frac{\text{Net profit after tax}}{\text{Sales}}$$

$$\text{Gross operating margin} = \frac{\text{Sales less Cost of sales}}{\text{Sales}}$$

$$\text{Net operating margin} = \frac{\text{Net profit before interest and tax}}{\text{Sales}}$$

$$\text{Return on equity (ROE)} = \frac{\text{Net profit after tax}}{\text{Equity}}$$

$$\text{Return on assets (ROA)} = \frac{\text{Net profit before interest}}{\text{Total assets}}$$

$$= \frac{\text{Net profit after tax} + (\text{Interest} \times (1 - \text{tax rate}))}{\text{Total assets}}$$

$$\text{Return on capital employed (ROCE)} = \frac{\text{Net profit before interest on long-term debt}}{\text{Equity} + \text{long-term debt}}$$

$$\text{Earnings per share (EPS)} = \frac{\text{Net profit after tax}}{\text{Number of shares outstanding}}$$

B. Asset utilization ratios

$$\text{Total asset turnover} = \frac{\text{Sales}}{\text{Total assets}}$$

$$\text{Long-term asset turnover} = \frac{\text{Sales}}{\text{Long-term assets}}$$

$$\text{Inventory turnover} = \frac{\text{Cost of sales}}{\text{Inventories}}$$

$$\text{Receivables turnover} = \frac{\text{(Net credit) Sales}}{\text{Receivables}}$$

quantity of sales. *Net* and *gross operating margin* ratios narrow down the analysis to operating profitability. Gross operating margin shows control of manufacturing or purchasing costs (depending upon the activity of the company). It is the preferred ratio to measure operating efficiency. Margin ratios are very useful for trend analysis and intra-industry comparisons. It is, however, very difficult to compare margin ratios for companies in different industries, as they tend to be industry-specific. For example, food retailers operate with low profit margins, while profit margins are generally high in the clothing industry. Both types of business can generate nice profits, because a high sales volume can compensate for a low profit margin.

Net (operating) profit, considered by itself or as a percentage of sales, does not take into account the investment needed to generate the profit. A return on investment ratio (ROI) does. Depending on what is meant by 'investment', different ROI ratios can be used: return on equity (ROE), return on assets (ROA) and return on capital employed (ROCE).

Return on equity (*ROE*) measures how much the company has earned on the funds invested by its shareholders. Funds invested by shareholders are set equal to equity and thus imply both directly invested funds and funds invested indirectly through retained profit. Obviously, the ROE ratio reflects a shareholder perspective. ROE is a slightly dangerous figure in that it is not a 'real' return and should not be compared with, for example, the rate of interest paid on a bank deposit account. It can be used in time series analysis to show whether profitability is improving or declining, viewed from the equity perspective, as opposed to all finance.

Return on assets (ROA) reflects how much the company has earned on the investment of all the financial resources committed to the company. In this ratio the investment base is set equal to the sum of equity and all liabilities – the total sources of funds invested in the company's assets. The ROA shows how well the company has used its funds, irrespective of the relative magnitudes of the sources of those funds (current liabilities, LT liabilities, equity). As the ROA ratio brings in the debt element of the company as well, it affords a comparison between the efficiency of companies with different debt/equity ratios The ROA ratio is used to evaluate management performance both at corporate level and at individual business unit level (divisions within the company). The business unit manager usually has significant influence over the assets used in the business unit, but has little control over how those assets are financed. The business unit manager usually has no impact on the relative roles of external creditors and shareholders in financing his or her assets, because financing decisions are in most cases taken at corporate level and not at business unit level.

Taken in conjunction with the ROE ratio, the ROA ratio shows whether the return to shareholders is changing better or worse than the return on overall financing.

Return on capital employed (ROCE) shows how much the company has earned on invested long-term funds (also called *permanently employed capital*). Shareholders' equity and long-term debt (or non-current liabilities) are funds entrusted to the company for a relatively long period of time and can be considered quasi-permanent capital. Figure 9.1 shows that capital employed (or permanent capital) is also equal to net working capital plus non-current assets. In fact, the statement of financial position equivalency indicates that capital employed is expected to finance non-current assets and the portion of current assets that is not financed by current liabilities (or net working capital).

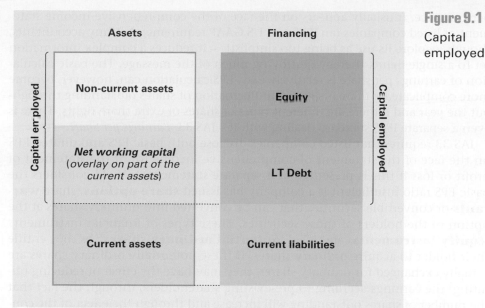

Figure 9.1
Capital employed

The three ROI ratios differ not only with regard to the denominator (the investment base), but also in the calculation of the numerator (the profit figure retained). The calculation of the ROE ratio is straightforward: net profit after tax is by definition the residual net income attributable to the funds invested by shareholders. In arriving at this net profit figure, part of the cost of finance – the interest on debt financing – was subtracted as an expense. Using the same net profit figure in calculating ROA or ROCE would in fact understate the earnings generated by total funds or long-term funds available. Thus, when including interest-bearing debt in the investment base, the interest expense should be added again to the net profit figure to arrive at an earnings level which is not affected by the relative use of equity or debt financing.

Because the interest expense is tax deductible, it also affects taxation in the statement of profit or loss. This means that the amount of the adjustment of the net profit figure in the calculation of ROA or ROCE should be the after-tax interest expense. The after-tax interest expense is the interest expense multiplied by the complement of the tax rate. For example, if the corporate tax rate on income is 30 per cent and the gross interest expense amount to €10000, the after-tax interest expense would be €10000 × (1 – 0.3) or €7000.

The different ROI measures each reflect the earnings generated by a specific pool of funds, excluding the costs of the specific funds considered. In practice, the interest adjustments are sometimes ignored by analysts because they add complexity to calculating the ROA and ROCE ratios.

Earnings per share (EPS) is another way of checking whether profitability is growing from a shareholder-only perspective. EPS is calculated as net profit for the period (net income or net earnings) divided by the average number of shares outstanding during the period. It shows how much of a period's net profit has been earned by each ordinary share. This ratio is given great importance by Anglo-Saxon companies and analysts. It has taken on a major significance in the investment industry and is the single most commonly used measure to compare companies' performance. It usually appears on the face of the comprehensive income statement of listed companies (an IFRS and US GAAP requirement). Many accountants, though, deplore its use as being too simplistic – it reduces a complex information set to a single figure, thereby destroying much of the message. The basic calculation of earnings per share is relatively easy. EPS calculation can, however, become more complicated if there is significant fluctuation of shares outstanding throughout the year and if there are different types of shares or extra share rights. There is even a separate IFRS standard dealing with it – IAS 33, *Earnings per Share*.

IAS 33 requires that listed companies disclose both basic EPS and diluted EPS on the face of the statement of comprehensive income (or of the statement of profit or loss if this is presented as a separate statement). IAS 33 considers the basic EPS ratio insufficient if a company has issued **share options**, share **warrants** or convertible securities that can be converted into ordinary shares at the option of the holders of those securities. These types of financial instruments (**equity instruments**) are called '**potential ordinary shares**', as they entitle their holder to acquire ordinary shares. If these potentially ordinary shares are actually exchanged for ordinary shares, they may have the effect of reducing (diluting) the earnings accruing to pre-existing shareholders, through the fact that the number of shares outstanding will increase and through the effect of the conversion on net income available to ordinary shareholders. IAS 33 sets the rules for calculating both basic and **diluted earnings per share** and provides a basis for quantifying the impact of the conversion of issued equity instruments into ordinary shares in the future.

Analysts also talk about 'quality of earnings' as well as the absolute number as being important (how sustainable are the profits? What activities are they derived from?). This is a question which needs further consideration in the light of accounting and other devices which are discussed later. The key question is the extent to which current profits are affected by special circumstances (e.g. asset sales) and to what extent they can be expected to continue for the foreseeable future.

The EPS number is used as an input to a market ratio, the *price/earnings* or *P/E ratio*:

$$\text{Price/Earnings} = \frac{\text{Market price per share}}{\text{EPS}}$$

The P/E ratio involves an amount not directly controlled by the company: the current market price of an ordinary share. It reflects how the market judges the company's performance. The P/E ratio is another form of rate of return ratio, albeit inverted. The numerator is today's market price and the denominator the EPS for the most recent 12 months. Thus, the P/E ratio varies throughout the year and the major financial newspapers usually display a company's P/E ratio along with the daily market prices of its ordinary shares.

The P/E ratio is also called the *earnings multiple*. It reflects the market's expectations about the company's performance and measures how much the market is willing to pay for a share in the company's potential future earnings. Basically, a high P/E ratio indicates that investors expect that the company's earnings will grow rapidly. Growth expectations will be linked to the industry to which the company belongs. As the relative rate of expected growth in earnings differs significantly among industries, so will the typical P/E ratios for industries tend to vary. In this vein, it makes more sense to compare the P/E ratio of Peugeot SA to the P/E of Volkswagen AG than to the P/E of Microsoft Inc. A decline of the predictions of general economic conditions generally has a negative effect on the overall level of P/E ratios, because the market takes it as an indication that the earnings of virtually all companies will be affected. We will come back to the P/E ratio later.

Investors generally expect two kinds of return: appreciation of the market price of a share and dividend income. Investors who like to receive dividend income will look at the *dividend yield ratio*. It reflects the relationship between the dividends per share paid to shareholders and the current market price of a share. The ratio measures the percentage of a share's market value that is returned (annually) in cash to the shareholders.

$$\text{Dividend Yield} = \frac{\text{Dividend per share}}{\text{Market price per share}}$$

Dividend yields vary widely, from 0 per cent to 5–6 per cent. Young, high growth companies usually are reluctant to pay cash dividends, as they need the funds to finance further growth. Companies with high dividend yields are usually older, established companies. The major financial newspapers publish dividend yields of listed companies daily.

Asset utilization ratios measure how efficiently management uses the company's assets. The concept of a turnover ratio can be explained best with regard to inventory turnover: if the company keeps an inventory of only one unit and sells 50 units during the accounting period, the inventory must completely turn over and be replaced 50 times (assuming we want to keep the ending inventory equal to beginning inventory). If the inventory were 50 units and 50 units are sold, the inventory must turn over and be replaced only once.

Total asset turnover shows how efficient a company is in using its total asset base. It measures the company's success in keeping the total asset base active, with sales as the activity measure of reference. But again, the absolute ratio has little meaning; it is the comparison from one year to another or one company to another similar company which yields the interesting measure of efficiency. For example, does the company make less and less use of capacity? If so, it might indicate a dying market for the product, even if inflation were pushing up the sales price and the profits.

Long-term asset turnover focuses only on the use of non-current assets. The ratio is usually even narrowed down to the turnover of property, plant and equipment. It shows the level of sales the company was able to generate for each euro invested in property, plant and equipment. The long-term asset turnover ratio is often referred to as (the inverse of) the *capital intensity ratio*. This label better reflects the industry-specific nature of the ratio. A steel company is a typical example of a company with a high level of long-term tangible assets (highly capital intensive) and, thus, a low long-term asset turnover ratio. Companies with low long-term asset turnover tend to have a lot of fixed costs which makes them particularly vulnerable to cyclical fluctuations in business activity. When business activity declines and sales drop, they may be unable to cover the fixed costs. Conversely, companies that are not capital intensive, like many service companies, usually have much more flexibility to reduce their costs when sales decline.

IAS 33 – EARNINGS PER SHARE
(extract)

Presentation of basic and diluted earnings per share

66. An entity shall present in the statement of comprehensive income basic and diluted earnings per share for profit or loss from continuing operations attributable to the ordinary equity holders of the parent entity and for profit or loss attributable to the ordinary equity holders of the parent entity for the period for each class of ordinary shares that has a different right to share in profit for the period. An entity shall present basic and diluted earnings per share with equal prominence for all periods presented.

67. Earnings per share is presented for every period for which a statement of comprehensive income is presented. If diluted earnings per share is reported for at least one period, it shall be reported for all periods presented, even if it equals basic earnings per share. If basic and diluted earnings per share are equal, dual presentation can be accomplished in one line on the statement of comprehensive income.

67A. If an entity presents items of profit or loss in a separate statement as described in paragraph 10A of IAS 1 (as amended in 2011), it presents basic and diluted earnings per share, as required in paragraphs 66 and 67, in that separate statement.

68. An entity that reports a discontinued operation shall disclose the basic and diluted amounts per share for the discontinued operation either in the statement of comprehensive income or in the notes.

68A. If an entity presents items of profit or loss in a separate statement as described in paragraph 10A of IAS 1 (as amended in 2011), it presents basic and diluted earnings per share for the discontinued operation, as required in paragraph 68, in that separate statement or in the notes.

69. An entity shall present basic and diluted earnings per share, even if the amounts are negative (i.e. a loss per share).

Source: IAS 33, Earnings per Share

The *inventory turnover* ratio is based on the relationship between the inventory and the volume of goods sold during the period. It shows how many times on average the inventory was acquired and sold during the period. A high inventory turnover indicates that the company is able to sell its inventory quickly. This suggests efficient inventory management, but it can also be troublesome if it means that the company does not keep enough inventory on hand, which could lead to fewer sales if the company cannot fill incoming customer orders. Note that we use cost of sales as the numerator in the ratio and not sales revenue as such, because both inventory and cost of sales are measured at cost.

The *receivable turnover* ratio reflects the relationship of receivables to (credit) sales during the period. A high receivable turnover ratio suggests that the company efficiently manages the funds tied up in credit-granting and is effective in its credit collection activities. In practice, the amount of credit sales is not always known and, if so, total sales will be used as a rough approximation. While a low receivable turnover ratio suggests that significant funds are tied up in unproductive assets, a very high receivable turnover could mean that the company has an overly stringent credit policy that could lead to lost sales.

Inventory turnover and receivable turnover are important indicators of working capital management. They are measures of both operating efficiency and liquidity (see next section). Tensions between operating efficiency and liquidity needs are typical for the trade-offs to be made in working capital management.

In this section we have covered the major management performance ratios, albeit not the only ones. The definitions given are ones commonly found, but are not the only definitions possible – when discussing ratios it is sensible to check exactly what definition is being used. The need to check ratio definitions before comparing is never more true than with the debt/equity or gearing ratio (see next section).

Financial strength ratios

Financial strength ratios indicate the strength of the company's financial position from different points of view. While profitability ratios highlight the return side of the basic risk/return relationship, financial strength ratios mainly focus on the financial risks associated with the company's financial position. Basic financial risk concerns are typically assessed using **solvency** ratios and liquidity ratios.

Solvency refers to the long-term ability to generate cash internally or from external sources in order to meet long-term financial obligations. Solvency ratios mainly focus on the relative size of debt in the financial structure of the company. *Liquidity* refers to the company's ability to generate cash to meet its short-term obligations (essentially working capital needs and immediate debt repayment needs). Liquidity tests focus on the size of, and relationships between current assets and current liability (working capital components). The most common financial strength ratios are shown in Table 9.2.

The *debt/equity ratio* is the solvency ratio found most frequently in the financial press and reflects the relationship between loan finance and shareholders' funds. Recall that debt financing introduces risk because debt implies fixed commitments in the form of interest payments and principal repayment. Recall that default risk refers to potential failure to satisfy the fixed payments associated with debt which will ultimately result in bankruptcy. A lesser financial risk is that a heavily indebted company will have difficulty in obtaining additional debt financing when needed or will have to pay significantly higher interest rates.

A high debt/equity ratio indicates high financial risk because it implies substantial interest charges and an exposure to interest rate movements: if interest rates are rising, this will imply lower profitability in the future. The existence of debt means that ultimately repayment must take place and a glance at the schedule of outstanding debt given in the notes to the accounts will indicate how early this may take place. Most agreements for the provision of long-term finance include stipulations as to the maximum debt/equity ratio the company may have (*loan covenants*) – and this sort of covenant has been the driver of a certain amount of creative accounting designed to improve the debt/equity ratio.

Table 9.2

Financial strength ratios

A. Long-term solvency risk ratios

Gearing (Debt/equity ratio) $= \dfrac{\text{Debt}}{\text{Equity}}$

This ratio is also frequently computed on the basis of debt to total finance:

Gearing (Total finance) $= \dfrac{\text{Debt}}{\text{Debt} + \text{Equity}}$

Interest cover $= \dfrac{\text{Profit before interest and tax}}{\text{Net interest charges}}$

Dividend cover $= \dfrac{\text{Earnings per share}}{\text{Dividend per share}}$

B. Short-term liquidity risk ratios

Current ratio $= \dfrac{\text{Current assets}}{\text{Current liabilities}}$

Acid test (or quick ratio) $= \dfrac{\text{Current assets} - \text{Inventories}}{\text{Current liabilities}}$

Days outstanding of working capital components (see below)

The debt/equity ratio is sometimes computed in slightly different ways, for example debt as a proportion of total capital employed. Sometimes the computation of debt will include all liabilities, both short- and long-term. Occasionally, debt repayable within one year is mixed in within short-term trade and operational creditors, thereby mixing a financing element with working capital. When computing the liability ratios, it is logical to look at the analysis of short-term creditors and include the pure financing element (normally indicated as 'borrowings' or debt in the note which analyses short-term creditors) in the debt/equity ratio and the rest of short-term creditors (trade creditors, taxes payable, dividends payable, etc.) as part of working capital.

Although debt financing implies financial risk, it also holds the potential for an additional return to shareholders. When debt is used successfully – if the company is able to earn more on the external funds provided than the cost of debt – the return to shareholders is magnified through financial leverage. Thus, the impact of debt financing on the trade-off between risk and return is not that straight-forward. We will elaborate on the subject of financial leverage in Chapter 17.

The *interest cover ratio* is often used as a surrogate for the debt/equity ratio, or in addition to that ratio. This is partly as a response to creative accounting schemes which have reduced the reliability of the debt/equity ratio. Interest cover indicates the safety margin between profits and interest charges. In good times, bankers and others like to see interest 'cover' of five times, but it is not unusual to see cover drop to as low as three times.

Short-term liquidity problems arise because current cash inflows don't match current cash outflows. Take another look at Figure 8.2 in the previous chapter. The working capital cycle runs on a proper matching of cash receipts and cash payments. Liquidity problems arise when cash receipts from sales lag behind the cash payments to suppliers, employees, tax creditors, etc. Additionally, the working capital cycle should be able to generate sufficient cash to service short-term debt payments. The main liquidity ratios focus on the make-up of working capital and the activity level of its components.

The *current ratio* and *acid test ratio* (called the *quick ratio* in the USA) are the most common liquidity tests. They measure in a crude way the relationship between assets which will shortly mature to cash, and liabilities which will require cash settlement within one year or one operating cycle. The acid test excludes inventory on the basis that in some industries inventory turns over very slowly and therefore should not be looked to for very quick maturity into cash. Inventory is indeed the least liquid current asset and the most likely to suffer from losses if it has to be liquidated at short notice.

As we discussed in Chapter 8, when looking at working capital management, interpretation of these ratios should be done with care since the working capital structure of companies varies considerably from one industry to another. Hotels and retail businesses often have acid test ratios of less than one (i.e. their short-term **monetary assets** are smaller than their short-term monetary liabilities), because (a) they have very few credit sales, so few receivables and (b) they generate immediate cash from sales and have no need to keep large amounts of cash available at the bank to pay creditors.

As so often in ratio analysis, what is important is not the absolute number, but the direction and rate of change from one year to another. If a company's activity does not change, its working capital ratios should not change either. A sudden move in the working capital ratios means that something in the company's structure has changed, and further questions should be asked as to why this is – for example, an increase in the current ratio may be generated by an increase in inventories, so one should ask: why have inventory levels risen? Has there been a sudden fall-off in demand for the company's products?

Another way of examining individual components of working capital is to compare the balance sheet value with the related annual sales figure (gross margin component). For example, for a retail company, the ratio of inventory on hand at the year-end to annual cost of sales will tell you how many days' business would be required to sell the inventory:

$$\text{Days inventory outstanding} = \frac{\text{Inventories}}{\text{Cost of sales}} \times 365 \text{ days}$$

Similarly:

$$\text{Credit given} = \frac{\text{Receivables}}{\text{(Credit) Sales}} \times 365 \text{ days}$$

$$\text{Credit obtained} = \frac{\text{Trade payables}}{\text{Cost of sales}} \times 365 \text{ days}$$

'Credit given' tells you how many days' credit are given to customers (but note that you need to know either that all sales are on credit or that a substantial proportion of them is on credit). Where a company is buying goods for resale, the ratio of trade payables to cost of sales will show the days' credit obtained or taken from suppliers.

These ratios can also be useful even if you do not know that there is a high proportion of credit sales, or where most of the company's products are manufactured (so purchases from suppliers are only a small part of cost of sales), because while the absolute number of days is no longer a meaningful figure, a significant (say, more than 10 per cent) *shift* in the figure from one year to another will indicate a change in credit arrangements.

It is not uncommon for ratios including balance sheet figures to be calculated by using an average of the balance sheet element during the period. This is usually done by taking one half of the sum of the beginning and ending balance of the item, although it could be meaningful to take into account the timing of specific movements in the balance sheet items over the period. In the illustrations and examples in this books we will, however, use ending balance sheet amounts which can be more easily traced down to the figures on the face of the balance sheet.

Analyzing financial statements

It is very easy for people approaching ratios for the first time to go through a series of reactions, initially seeing the calculation of the ratios as an end in itself and then later asking what use the ratios are. Essentially analysis is about decoding the messages which are built into financial statements and using them to 'tell the story' of the company. Ratios are a means of throwing light upon certain aspects of a company, but not all ratios will be important for all companies and often the calculation of ratios leads to a question rather than an answer. You must remember that ratio analysis is only part (even if important) of the investment appraisal process, and investors need to look at economic variables, information about the company's future plans, etc., as well as decoding the information in the financial statements.

So how does one set about analyzing a set of financial statements? The first question you must ask yourself is why you are making the analysis – is it for lending purposes or for investing? Is it for a long-term involvement or short-term? In short, what is the nature of the decision which you need to make?

Having identified your analysis objective, you should gather what general information is available to you about the nature of the company and its activities – this will depend on whether you have a full annual report which will include much non-financial information and under what circumstances you are carrying out the analysis.

Only then can you look at the financial statements and start work on calculating ratios. A normal process would be to compute a number of standard ratios which we have discussed above, for as long a time series as you have information available. Any one set of financial statements will include previous year comparative figures, but in an ideal situation you would have more than one set of statements so that you could compile a longer time series.

Having computed your ratios, you should look to see if there are any patterns – which ratios are stable, which changing? If ratios are changing, you need to ask why they are doing so. This may be obvious from the financial statements. For example, if the return on equity ratio increases, this might be because of an increase in profit, an increase in sales or a reduction in equity. If the net profit margin ratio (net profit/sales) has gone up (say from 10 to 12 per cent), and you see that sales have remained static, this means that the amount of profit per euro of sales has increased, which probably means that the company is controlling its costs more efficiently but, on the other hand, that poses questions as to why sales have not increased.

It may be that a picture gradually emerges of the activities of the company, and what you have to do is attempt to 'tell the story' of the company based on what is available from its figures.

The next step is to do some cross-sectional analysis, if you have the necessary information – either data from another company in the same field or industry data. You can then compare ratios and there may be further insights into your company from this process. If company A has a gross operating margin of 35 per cent, why does company B, in the same year and carrying out the same activities, have a gross margin of 40 per cent?

Worked example

In order to help put the use of ratios into some context, we will carry out basic analysis on a three-year time series of company data – note that we are not given any background information about the company's activities, so that will limit how far we can make deductions about what is going on, and we do not have any material for cross-sectional analysis. Also, the financial statements are simplified to the extent that we do not have a breakdown of non-current assets and all debt is long term. The company pays a dividend of 20 (unchanged over the years). Interest relates to long-term debt. The applicable tax rate is 30 per cent.

Financial statements:	20X7 €'000	20X8 €'000	20X9 €'000
Statement of profit or loss:			
Sales	620.0	745.0	762.0
Cost of sales	−217.0	−245.8	−266.7
Gross margin	*403.0*	*499.2*	*495.3*
Distribution costs	204.6	260.7	266.7
Administrative expenses	−95.1	−97.2	−101.4
	103.3	141.3	127.2
Interest	−10.0	−30.9	−37.5
	93.3	110.4	89.7
Taxation	−32.7	38.9	−31.4
Statement of financial position:	60.6	71.5	58.3
Non-current assets (net)	312.0	532.0	495.0
Inventories	43.4	49.2	66.7
Receivables	62.0	74.5	91.4
Cash	67.0	70.3	58.0
Total assets	**484.4**	**726.0**	**711.1**
Ordinary shares (€1)	120.0	120.0	120.0
Reserves	195.5	267.9	315.2
	315.5	*387.9*	*435.2*
Debt	100.0	250.0	200.0
Trade payables	36.2	49.2	44.5
Taxes payable	32.7	38.9	31.4
Total equity and liabilities	**484.4**	**726.0**	**711.1**

Before starting on the ratios, let us just see if there are any trends visible from the financial statements as such. We can see that sales increased substantially from 20X7 to 20X8 (20 per cent) but the increase dropped to 2 per cent from 20X8 to 20X9. Profits increased in 20X7/X8, as you would predict from the sales, but dropped off in 20X9. An obvious explanation of this is the rapid increase in interest costs: from €10 000 in 20X7 to €30 900 in 20X8 and €37 500 in 20X9. Looking at the statement of financial position, you can see debt going from €100 000 to €250 000 and then dropping to €200 000 (given the rising interest cost, it may well be that interest rates rose steeply during this period). We can see that long-term assets rose sharply as well, so already we can see some sort of story here: a company seems to have expanded capacity substantially in 20X8, leading to borrowing but also higher sales. In 20X9 sales growth has not continued at the same pace and interest rates have risen, causing the company's profits to fall.

Let us calculate the key ratios and see how this story is fleshed out:

Interpretation

Overall, this looks like a company which has gone for a major expansion/replacement of capacity in 20X8 (long-term assets increased by 70 per cent), financed

	20X7	20X8	20X9
Management performance ratios			
A. Profitability ratios			
ROE	60.6/315.5 = 19.21%	71.5/387.9 = 18.43%	58.3/435.2 = 13.40%
ROA	(60.6+(10×(1–0.3)))/ 484.4 = 13.96%	(71.5+(30.9×(1–0.3)))/ 726 = 12.83%	(58.3+(37.5×(1–0.3)))/ 711.1 = 11.89%
ROCE	(60.6+(10×(1–0.3)))/ (315.5+100) = 16.27%	(71.5+(30.9×(1–0.3)))/ (387.9+250) = 11.55%	(58.3+(37.5×(1–0.3)))/ (435.2+200) = 13.31%
EPS	60.6/120 = 50.50	71.5/120 = 59.58	58.3/120 = 48.58
Gross operating margin	(620–217)/620 = 65.00%	(745–245.8)/745 = 67.01%	(762–266.7)/762 = 65.00%
Net operating margin	103.3/620 = 16.66%	141.3/745 = 18.97%	127.2/762 = 16.69%
Net profit margin	60.6/620 = 9.77%	71.5/745 = 9.60%	58.3/762 = 7.65%
B. Asset utilization ratios			
Total asset turnover	620/484.4 = 1.28	745/726 = 1.03	762/711.1 = 1.07
Long-term asset turn over	620/312 = 1.99	745/532 = 1.40	762/495 = 1.54
Inventory turnover	217/43.4 = 5.00	245.8/49.2 = 5.00	266.7/66.7 = 4.00
Receivables turnover	620/62 = 10.00	745/74.5 = 10.00	762/91.4 = 8.34

	20X7	*20X8*	*20X9*
Financial strength ratios			
A. Long-term solvency risk ratios			
Gearing	100/315.5	250/387.9	200/435.2
	= 31.70%	= 64.45%	= 45.96%
Gearing (Total finance)	100/(100+315.5)	250/(250+387.9)	200/(200+435.2)
	= 24.07%	= 39.19%	= 31.49%
Interest cover	103.3/10	141.3/30.9	127.2/37.5
	= 10.33	= 4.57	= 3.39
Dividend cover	60.6/20.0	71.5/20.0	58.3/20.0
	= 3.03	= 3.58	= 2.92
B. Short-term liquidity risk ratios			
Current ratio	(43.4+62167)/	(49.2+74.5+70.3)/	(66.7+91.4+58.0)/
	(36.2+32.7)	(49.2+38.9)	(44.5+31.4)
	= 2.50	= 2.20	= 2.85
Acid test	(62+67)/	(74.5+70.3)/	(58.0+91.4)/
	(36.2+32.7)	(49.2+38.9)	(31.4+44.5)
	= 1.87	= 1.64	= 1.97
Days inventory out standing	(43.4/217)×365	(49.2/245.8)×365	(66.7/266.7)×365
	= 73.00	= 73.06	= 91.28
Credit given	(62/620.0)×365	(74.5/745)×365	(91.4/762)×365
	= 36.50	= 36.50	= 43.78
Credit obtained	(36.2/217.0)×365	(49.2/245.8)×365	(44.5/266.7)×365
	= 60.89	− 73.06	= 60.90

Growth:	*20X7/X8*	*20X8/X9*
Sales	20.16%	2.28%
Profit	19.47%	−7.04%
Capital employed	53.53%	−0.42%
Net long-term assets	70.51%	−6.95%

largely by an increase in debt. This has resulted in increased sales and improved operating margins in 20X8, but in 20X9 the expansion of sales has not continued and the company has also been hit by higher interest costs.

The effect of the heavy investment is to reduce return on assets from 13.96 to 12.83 per cent, and reduce asset turnover from 1.28 to 1.03 although a return to sales growth would easily correct this in the following year. The impression is that the market for the company's product slowed down in 20X9, causing an increase in unsold inventory (days inventory outstanding up from 73 to 91 days). Receivables turnover has also slipped, suggesting that the company may be chasing sales with extended credit offers (or its customers may be similarly hit by slowdown). Gross operating margin has also slipped, which suggests that the company may have cut sales prices in order to boost business.

The company has sensibly used its internal cash flow to contribute to financing the 20X8 investment (debt increased by €150 000 while long-term assets increased by €220 000 – although credit obtained moved from 61 days to 73) and subsequently to reduce borrowing in 20X9. The gearing ratio (on total finance) moved from an unremarkable 24 per cent (ten times the interest cover) to a rather more risky 39 per cent, although interest cover remained reasonable at 4.6. In 20X9 the repayment of €50 000 brought gearing down to 31 per cent but the higher interest rates and lower profits caused interest cover to decline further to 3.4. If the market does not drop further the company should be able to continue to reduce borrowing and diminish the exposure to interest costs, showing an improved return.

Overall, this looks like a company which has set out on a relatively ambitious expansion plan, financed by borrowing and internal cash flows, which has hit some difficulties with a slowdown in demand. While its gearing rose quite sharply in the expansion phase, the company looks as though it has a sensible policy of retrenching and reducing debt. It should be able to continue to trade satisfactorily and generate further cash to further reduce gearing.

Summary

Financial analysts, lenders and other users of financial statements are concerned to measure both the efficiency of a company's management and the financial strength of the company. They do this by extracting data from the published financial statements and either making comparisons or feeding the data into financial models.

The traditional approach to financial analysis involves making comparisons of a company's results over several years (time series) or comparisons between one company and another (cross-sectional). In order to make the analysis more meaningful, various devices are used to take away the disparity in size between companies.

The chief of these is the use of financial ratios, which express one accounting number in relation to another (economically linked) number. When making comparisons using ratios it is necessary to be sure that the ratios being compared have been calculated from the same basis, and that the companies being compared do indeed have broadly similar characteristics.

An examination of the patterns of ratios and the financial statements themselves can lead the analyst to deduce what the company has been doing without any further non-financial information, although investors would normally take into account not only the results of financial statement analysis but also any other available information about the economy generally, the industry in which the company works etc.

Assignments

The following questions have answers on the lecturer side of the digital support resources for the book.

1. The following is the statement of profit or loss and statement of financial position of a company. Please calculate four accounting ratios (e.g. return on equity, return on assets, gross operating margin, net operating margin, current ratio, gearing ratio) and supply the definition you have used with your answer. Tax rate = 30 per cent.

Statement of profit or loss	
Sales	145 600
Cost of sales	–64 200
Other operating costs	–49 400
	32 000
Interest paid	–17 500
Taxation	–4 500
Net profit	10 000

Statement of financial position			
Assets		Financing	
Tangible assets	149 000	Share capital (€1)	50 000
Accum. depreciation	–17 500	Reserves	63 000
Inventories	82 300	Debt (long-term)	100 000
Cash at bank	56 300	Trade payables	57 100
	270 100		270 100

2. The following figures are drawn from the statement of financial position of Medmove:

	20X1 €'000	20X2 €'000	20X3 €'000
Long-term assets (net)	2 350	2 900	3 800
Current assets			
Inventories	150	160	160
Receivables	310	300	310
Cash	55	0	235
Total assets	2 865	3 360	4 505
Financing			
Trade payables	220	600	200
Debt (LT)	0	0	1 500
Total liabilities	220	600	1 700

No fresh shares were issued during the period. The industry has an organization which publishes average financial data.

The industry average statement of financial position is:

Long-term assets	75	Equity	70
Inventories	10	Debt (long-term)	20
Receivables	10	Payables	10
Cash	5		
	100		100

You are asked to:

(a) calculate whatever ratios you think may be useful in analyzing Medmove's figures (but including current ratio, debt/equity); tax rate = 30 per cent

(b) using the analytical data which you have just computed, and the industry average statement of financial position, comment on the company's position and development.

3. Company RATIS had the following financial statements:

	20X2 €'000	20X3 €'000	20X4 €'000
Statement of profit or loss			
Sales	620.0	745.0	762.0
Cost of sales	–217.0	–245.8	–266.7
Gross margin	403.0	499.2	495.3
Distribution costs	–204.6	–260.7	–266.7
Administrative expenses	–95.1	–97.2	–101.4
	103.3	141.3	127.2
Interest	–10.0	–30.9	–37.5
	93.3	110.4	89.7
Taxation	–32.7	–38.9	–31.4
	60.6	71.5	58.3
Statement of financial position			
Net long-term assets	312.0	532.0	495.0
Inventories	43.4	49.2	66.7
Receivables	62.0	74.5	91.4
Cash	67.0	70.3	58.0
Total assets	484.4	726.0	711.1

	20X2 €'000	20X3 €'000	20X4 €'000
Ordinary shares (€1)	120.0	120.0	120.0
Reserves	195.5	267.9	315.2
	315.5	387.9	435.2
Trade payables	36.2	49.2	44.5
Taxes payable	32.7	38.9	31.4
Debt (long-term)	100.0	250.0	200.0
Total equity and liabilities	484.4	726.0	711.1

(a) You are asked to compute whatever ratios you think will be useful in analyzing the above figures (but including EPS, ROCE, gearing, current ratio, total asset turnover, gross operating margin, net operating margin). Tax rate = 30 per cent.

(b) You are asked to comment on the company's development and activity during the period covered by the financial statements.

4. Gunge AG and Guntzel AG are both wholesale companies working in the same business segment. Given the information embedded in a number of ratios that we collected (see table below), they seem, however, to take a different customer approach to their business.

Ratio	Gunge AG	Guntzel AG
Return on capital employed (ROCE)	14%	15%
Credit given	59 days	19 days
Credit obtained	50 days	47 days
Gross operating margin	42%	17%
Current ratio	2.4	1.3
Net operating margin	11%	11%
Days inventory outstanding	50 days	21 days

Required:
Explain what the ratios reveal with regard to the operating approach of Gunge AG and Guntzel AG. Take into account price competitiveness and customer service level.

5. The managing director of Bavarian Hypermarkets has been approached by the chief executive and majority shareholder of Black Forest Supermarkets, a medium-sized supermarket chain operating in southern Germany. Black Forest is looking for a partner: it feels it cannot grow any further without

outside capital, and would like to sell 40 per cent of its shares to a larger super-market operator who could inject more capital and provide management expertise to expand the chain further. Black Forest is quite willing to contemplate selling a majority stake in due course.

Bavarian Hypermarkets is quite interested in the deal, because they think that the two businesses would be a good fit in operational terms. They hire

Black Forest Supermarkets			
	20X6 €'000	20X5 €'000	20X4 €'000
Statement of profit or loss			
Sales	3674	2987	1643
Cost of sales	–2718	–2151	–1133
	956	836	510
Distribution costs	–412	–392	–242
Administrative expenses	–183	–190	–86
	361	254	182
Interest	315	243	0
	46	11	182
Taxation	–15	–3	–65
Net profit	31	8	117
Statement of financial position			
Non-current assets			
Intangible assets	2100	2200	0
Tangible assets	4446	4220	2085
Investments	0	0	240
Current assets			
Inventories	301	255	105
Receivables	38	42	29
Cash at bank	68	54	73
Total assets	6953	6771	2532
Financing			
Ordinary shares (€1)	1200	1200	1200
Retained profit	1241	1210	1202
	2441	2410	2402
Long-term debt	4000	4000	0
Trade payables	512	361	130
Total equity and liabilities	6953	6771	2532

your firm to carry out an analysis of Black Forest, and you are given the following financial statements, on which you are asked to comment:
Your report should identify and comment on all strengths and weaknesses of the company as revealed by its figures. The tax rate = 30 per cent.

	20X3 €m	20X4 €m	20X5 €m
Statement of profit or loss			
Sales	589.4	601.2	604.1
Cost of sales	−206.3	−222.4	−235.6
	383.1	*378.8*	*368.5*
Distribution costs	−22.7	−18.5	−32.1
Administration expense	−241.9	−254.0	−266.7
	118.5	106.3	69.7
Interest expense	−49.5	−63.0	−72.0
Profit/(loss) before taxation	69.0	43.3	−2.3
Taxation	−22.8	−14.3	0.8
Profit/(loss) after tax	46.2	29.0	−1.5
Statement of financial position			
Non-current (tangible) assets			
Land and buildings	620.0	620.0	620.0
Fittings and equipment	72.4	72.4	72.4
Accumulated depreciation	−37.2	−44.4	−51.6
	655.2	*648.0*	*640.8*
Current assets			
Inventories	143.9	152.0	179.5
Receivables	5.7	6.1	5.9
Bank	12.7	7.3	
Total assets	817.5	813.4	826.2
Ordinary shares (€1)	120.0	120.0	120.0
Retained profits	166.4	165.4	133.9
	286.4	*285.4*	*253.9*
Long-term debt	450.0	450.0	450.0
Trade payables	58.3	63.7	95.4
Taxes payable	22.8	14.3	0.0
Bank overdraft	0.0	0.0	26.9
Total equity and liabilities	817.5	813.4	826.2

6. You work for the financial analysis section of a merchant bank and are asked to prepare a report on the following figures, which relate to a clothing retailer, who is looking to the bank to take a share stake:
    You are asked to prepare:

    (a) eight key ratios which are relevant to the analysis of this company; tax rate = 30 per cent.

    (b) a report which attempts to explain what has been happening to the company over the last three years, using ratios and trends as appropriate, makes recommendations as to the desirability of becoming involved and makes suggestions for the future management of the company.

7. Who is who?
    The following six ratio sets refer to real-life listed companies (consolidated statements). These are:

    (a) An investment company (venture capital)
    (b) A brewery
    (c) A supermarket chain
    (d) A restaurant chain
    (e) A publisher (weekly publications and printing business)
    (f) A steel company

	A	B	C	D	E	F
Debt/equity ratio	0.21	0.90	1.52	3.46	0.26	1.74
Current ratio	2.6	0.95	1.06	1.38	0.63	0.91
Acid test ratio	2.57	0.90	0.39	0.58	0.63	0.86
Inventory turnover	25.12	63.39	11.73	3.33	N/A	185.32
Credit given	70.00	79.00	8.00	38.00	73.00	3.00
Asset turnover	0.94	0.87	2.35	0.97	0.01	3.25
Return on equity	0.11	0.05	0.04	0.01	0.16	0.02

Required:
Identify which company is represented in columns A to F.

CHAPTER 10

Statement of cash flows

Financial analysts make considerable use of cash flow information in their evaluation of companies. This chapter introduces the statement of cash flows and its preparation. It starts out by reviewing the relationship between profits and cash flow, then introduces the format, structure and content of the statement of cash flows and finally shows how to construct one.

Chapter Structure

- Introduction
- Usefulness of cash flow information
- Cash flow cycles
- Format and structure of the statement of cash flows
- Cash flows from investing and financing activities
- Cash flows from operating activities
- Direct method for reporting operating cash flows
- Constructing a statement of cash flows 1
- Disposal of long-term assets
- Constructing a statement of cash flows 2
- Interpretation
- Presentational differences
- Summary
- Discussion questions
- Assignments

Introduction

Our focus so far has been on the preparation of the statement of financial position (balance sheet) and the statement of profit or loss (income statement/profit and loss account), but in this chapter we are going on to consider another essential component of annual financial statements, the statement of cash flows. We first introduced this statement in Chapter 1 – it analyzes the company's cash flows during the period covered by the statement of profit or loss. It presents information about the cash flows associated with the period's operations (with the statement of profit or loss reporting on the economic results of those operations), but also about the cash flows associated with the company's investing and financing activities of the period. The statement of cash flows shows, for example, the cash generated by the company from its operating activities during the year, the company's investment in new non-current assets (increase in or renewal of its productive capacity) and the changes in the company's external financing from one statement of financial position to the next. The statement of cash flows complements the other primary statements and functions in conjunction with both the statement of profit or loss (performance dimension) and balance sheet (financial position).

Although company law generally does not require the disclosure of a statement of cash flows, many accounting standards do. Internationally, corporate practice has settled more or less on what was originally the US model of presentation and which served as the main source of inspiration for IAS 7, *Statement of Cash Flows*.

Usefulness of cash flow information

Financial analysts have long used cash flows as a useful indicator of company performance to complement profit measures, and not least when making comparisons between companies operating in different countries. One of the advantages of a cash flow measure is that it disregards charges such as non-cash depreciation or provisions, which may be applied differently by different companies, and focuses on actual revenue flowing in and costs being paid out. In this sense it filters out some of the differences which arise from accounting practices rather than operating practices.

The statement of profit or loss concentrates on measuring the economic result of the company's operations irrespective of whether the associated cash changed hands during the accounting period or not. The statement of cash flows shows what cash transactions did take place and what the net cash effect of the company's operations was. This information is important to investors, whose return (dividends) is in part dependent on cash flows, and to various creditors who depend on the company's ability to generate adequate cash flows to fulfil its financial obligations.

While the balance sheet shows the financial position of a company at a specific instant of time, the statement of cash flows reflects the change in financial position between two balance sheet dates. It provides information that enables users to evaluate the changes in the company's assets and in its financial structure. Whereas liquidity and solvency tests are mainly based on static financial position information, cash flow information may be used to highlight the dynamics of the short-term liquidity and long-term solvency characteristics of the company: a statement of cash flows offers details to explain why liquidity and solvency ratios have changed between consecutive statements of financial position.

At a more generic level, cash flow information is also important as an essential input for economic decision models, which require an evaluation of a company's ability to generate cash and the timing and certainty of the cash flows. In that context, historical cash flow information is used as an indicator of the amount, timing and certainty of future cash flows. Bankers, when lending to any size company, generally ask for a cash flow projection as part of any loan proposal.

Cash flow cycles

In discussing the structure of a statement of financial position we have treated cash as being part of working capital, but of course the cash in the bank is simply the residual of a great number of different types of cash flows, not only operating cash flows but also purchases and sales of long-term assets, receipt of financing, reimbursement of old debt, etc. In the statement of cash flows, the net change in cash balances is the figure we are trying to explain, in terms of different types of cash flow cycles that generate or use cash. In fact, cash flows through the company continuously in a number of short-term and long-term conversion cycles. Figure 10.1 shows the short-term and long-term cash flow cycles and their interaction with the company's cash position.

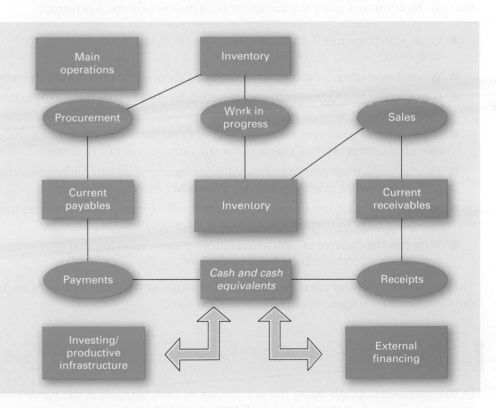

Figure 10.1
Long-term and short-term cash flow cycles

During the course of a year a company will be generating cash flows from its main business operations, which will be used not only for materials, labour and other periodic costs but also for purchasing new productive assets or to pay off debt. It might also borrow fresh funds, sell off old assets and so on. The working capital cycle or operating cycle is the main short-term cash conversion cycle, while the investing and financing cycle are typically longer term (they relate to non-current sources and uses of funds). The investing cycle relates to the acquisition, renewal and disposal of intangible and tangible productive infrastructure, while the financing cycle refers to the long-term sourcing of funds through share capital issuance and borrowings. The investing and financing cycles set the framework, which supports a smooth functioning of the operating cycle. Like the working capital cycle, the long-term cash conversion cycles are both a source and a user of cash.

The different cash conversion cycles all bring about a change in the cash position of the company (and in the various components of the statement of financial position for that matter), and the statement of cash flows specifically analyzes the changes in the company's cash position according to the main drivers of the changes.

The cash flow analysis gives important insights into the company's success and strategy. It shows what cash has been created (or used) by the company's operations in a year – an important measure of performance, in an absolute sense, but also key to the company's potential for internally generated growth. What the company does with its cash (investing in productive capacity, paying off debt, paying dividends, etc.) provides useful indicators of corporate strategy. Some of the questions that can be addressed using the statement of cash flows are the following:

- From which sources did the company raise cash last year? How was the cash used?
- Was the operating cycle capable of satisfying its need for cash during the year?
- If not, is the shortage of cash compensated by new borrowings, issuing new share capital or selling long-term assets?
- Is a surplus of cash used for repayment of debt, for investments in productive assets, retirement of shares or for the distribution of dividends?
- To what extent are new investments being financed by internally generated cash and to what extent by new loans or other external sources?
- Are dividend payments supported by internally generated cash or does the company have to borrow to maintain dividend payments?
- Why has the balance of cash available decreased, knowing that the company's operations have been profitable?

These kinds of question are difficult to answer with only a statement of financial position and/or a statement of profit or loss on hand.

Format and structure of the statement of cash flows

In the statement of cash flows, the net change in cash balances is the figure to be explained. The net change in cash will be aggregated from cash flows regrouped in three major categories: operating activities, investing activities and financing activities. The basic structure of the statement, according to IAS 7, *Statement of Cash Flows*, looks like the following:

> Cash flows from operating activities
> + Cash flows from investing activities
> + Cash flows from financing activities
> _____
> Net change in cash during period
> + Beginning cash balance
> _____
> Ending cash balance

Operating activities are defined (in the negative) to be all transactions that are not investing or financing activities. They are primarily the revenue-producing activities of a company. Operating cash flows include the cash inflows associated with sales revenues and cash outflows associated with operating expenses. IAS 7 provides the following examples of cash flows from operating activities:

a. cash receipts from the sale of goods and the rendering of services;

b. cash receipts from royalties, fees, commissions and other revenue;

c. cash payments to suppliers for goods and services;

d. cash payments to and on behalf of employees;

e. cash receipts and cash payments of an insurance entity for premiums and claims, annuities and other policy benefits;

f. cash payments or refunds of income taxes unless they can be specifically identified with financing and investing activities;

g. cash receipts and payments from contracts held for dealing or trading purposes.

Operating cash flows of a period generally result from transactions and other events that enter into the determination of profit of that period.

Investing activities relate to the acquisition and disposal of long-term assets (tangible and intangible) and other investments (not included in cash equivalents). Note that changes in current receivables and inventory are not treated as investment activities – changes in these current assets are included in operating activities.

Financing activities are activities that result in changes in the size and composition of the contributed equity and borrowings of the company. Again, changes in current payables are part of operating activities and are not included in financing activities. Note also that changes in equity reflect financing activities only to the extent that they relate to the issuance or retirement of share capital. Changes in equity that result from retained profits are part of the profit generating operating activities.

In a statement of cash flows the change in cash balances to be explained covers a concept of cash which is somewhat broader than cash on hand and demand deposits. Many companies, when they have any temporary excess cash, lend this out short term on the money market or buy short-term securities for periods of as few as one or two days. These short-term investments are sometimes called 'treasury' investments and are regarded as being so liquid as to be the same as cash (they are referred to as *cash equivalents*). For purposes of the statement of cash flows, 'cash' means the sum of actual cash and *cash equivalents*. IAS 7 defines cash equivalents as 'short-term, highly liquid investments that are readily convertible to known amounts of cash and which are subject to an insignificant risk of changes in value' (IAS 7, par.6).

IAS 7 – CASH AND CASH EQUIVALENTS *(extracts)*

7. Cash equivalents are held for the purpose of meeting short-term cash commitments rather than for investment or other purposes. For an investment to qualify as a cash equivalent it must be readily convertible to a known amount of cash and be subject to an insignificant risk of changes in value. Therefore, an investment normally qualifies as a cash equivalent only when it has a short maturity of, say, three months or less from the date of acquisition. Equity investments are excluded from cash equivalents unless they are, in substance, cash equivalents, for example in the case of preferred shares acquired within a short period of their maturity and with a specified redemption date.

8. Bank borrowings are generally considered to be financing activities. However, in some countries, bank overdrafts which are repayable on demand form an integral part of an entity's cash management. In these circumstances, bank overdrafts are included as a component of cash and cash equivalents. A characteristic of such banking arrangements is that the bank balance often fluctuates from being positive to overdrawn.

Source: IAS 7, *Statement of Cash Flows*

In this chapter we will look first at the more straightforward issues of investing and financing activities and then look at cash flow from operations, before going on to preparing a statement of cash flows.

Cash flows from investing and financing activities

In discussing the statement of financial position, we have pointed out that it is a basic tenet of financial management that long-term assets should generally be bought with long-term finance, in order to match the expected cash inflows from use of the asset with the outflows to repay the finance. Sometimes companies borrow short-term and arrange new finance when the short-term debt expires (*roll over* the borrowing), but this involves two risks: first, that finance may be difficult to obtain in the second phase and, second, that interest rates may have increased, making the cost of borrowing uneconomic in relation to the asset purchased. The cost of capital is normally an important factor in evaluating an asset purchase and companies expose themselves to an **interest rate risk** if they do not match the borrowing to the investment cash flows. Matching investment with the borrowing is known as *hedging* the interest rate risk, and the decision whether to do this or not is part of the company's financial strategy.

A company will generate long-term finance by retaining cash generated by its operations (increasing its equity through retained profits), but it would not necessarily wish to restrict its investments in new activities (or expanding existing ones) to the rate at which cash is generated internally. It will therefore often borrow outside finance or issue new shares.

Typically, a company will wish to preserve a balance between the amount of funds borrowed and that obtained by issuing shares. That is, it will have a target balance between debt and equity. However, as we mentioned in Chapter 8, issuing shares is a costly business, so what companies often do is finance new projects purely from internal cash flows and borrowing and then once every few years issue a major block of shares which reduces the debt/equity ratio and enables them to pay off (*retire*) some existing debt. Equally, a company might sell off part of its operations which it no longer wants, as part of a rationalization programme.

A company which is expanding will also be buying new long-term assets regularly, as well as selling off old ones which are worn out or which have been superseded by new technology. There will therefore be a pattern of regular change.

The long-term changes to be expected can be summarized as follows:

- Uses of finance:
    Purchase of new long-term assets
    Retirement of existing debt
- Sources of finance:
    Issue of new shares
    New long-term borrowing
    Sale of long-term assets.

In a statement of cash flows, these would be presented as:

- Cash flow from investing activities:
    Purchase of long-term assets (*outflow*)
    Sale of long-term assets (*inflow*)
- Cash flow from financing activities:
    Issue of new shares (*inflow*)
    Payment of dividend (*outflow*)
    New borrowing (*inflow*)
    Retirement of debt (*outflow*).

Note that we have slipped in the payment of dividends here in the financing section. We will discuss this below, but IAS 7, *Statement of Cash Flows*, sees payment of dividend as an adjustment of equity, although some jurisdictions prefer it to be presented elsewhere in the statement of cash flows, such as in cash flow from operations, as a distribution of the cash generated. (Where exactly it appears in the statement of cash flows is not as important as checking when making comparisons that it is treated the same way in all statements being compared.)

Cash flows from investing and financing activities are usually identified indirectly through an analysis of changes for the period in the non-current balance sheet categories. Direct identification of these cash flows through an analysis of the movements (transaction by transaction) in the cash (equivalent) accounts would be a more direct way, but the accounting database usually lacks the detail to proceed in that fashion.

STANDARDS

🌐 **IAS 7 – INVESTING AND FINANCING ACTIVITIES** *(extracts)*

16. The separate disclosure of cash flows arising from investing activities is important because the cash flows represent the extent to which expenditures have been made for resources intended to generate future income and cash flows. Only expenditures that result in a recognized asset in the statement of financial position are eligible for classification as investing activities. Examples of cash flows arising from investing activities are:

(a) cash payments to acquire property, plant and equipment, intangibles and other long-term assets. These payments include those relating to capitalized development costs and self-constructed property, plant and equipment;

(b) cash receipts from sales of property, plant and equipment, intangibles and other long-term assets;

(c) cash payments to acquire equity or debt instruments of other entities and interests in joint ventures (other than payments for those instruments considered to be cash equivalents or those held for dealing or trading purposes);

(d) cash receipts from sales of equity or debt instruments of other entities and interests in joint ventures (other than receipts for those instruments considered to be cash equivalents and those held for dealing or trading purposes);

(e) cash advances and loans made to other parties (other than advances and loans made by a financial institution);

(f) cash receipts from the repayment of advances and loans made to other parties (other than advances and loans of a financial institution);

(g) cash payments for futures contracts, forward contracts, option contracts and swap contracts except when the contracts are held for dealing or trading purposes, or the payments are classified as financing activities; and

(h) cash receipts from futures contracts, forward contracts, option contracts and swap contracts except when the contracts are held for dealing or trading purposes, or the receipts are classified as financing activities.

17. The separate disclosure of cash flows arising from financing activities is important because it is useful in predicting claims on future cash flows by providers of capital to the entity. Examples of cash flows arising from financing activities are:

(a) cash proceeds from issuing shares or other equity instruments;

(b) cash payments to owners to acquire or redeem the entity's shares;

(c) cash proceeds from issuing debentures, loans, notes, bonds, mortgages and other short or long-term borrowings;

(d) cash repayments of amounts borrowed; and

(e) cash payments by a lessee for the reduction of the outstanding liability relating to a finance lease.

Source: IAS 7, Statement of Cash Flows

CAPGEMINI GROUP

Consolidated statements of cash flows for the years ended December 31, 2008, 2009, 2010

6.5 Consolidated statement of cash flows

In millions of euros	Note	2008	2009	2010
Profit for the year (Group share)		451	178	280
Non controlling interests		—	—	(2)
Impairment of goodwill	12	24	12	—
Depreciation, amortization and impairment of fixed assets	10–11	213	164	176
Net charges to provisions		(62)	(54)	(2)
Gains and losses on disposals of assets		3	4	5
Expenses relating to share subscriptions, share grants and stock options	5	22	19	16
Net finance costs	6	(2)	43	54
Income tax expense	7	116	61	124
Unrealized gains and losses on charges in fair value and other		(17)	18	(23)
Cash flows from operations before net finance costs and income tax (A)		748	445	628
Income tax paid (B)		(94)	(56)	(52)
Change in accounts and notes receivable and advances from customers and amounts billed in advance		(158)	309	(85)
Change in capitalized costs on projects		5	(15)	(16)
Change in accounts and notes payable		12	(73)	3
Change in other receivables/payables		35	(115)	25
Change in operating working capital (C)		(106)	106	(73)
NET CASH FROM (USED IN) OPERATING ACTIVITIES (D=A+B+C)		548	495	503
Acquisitions of property, plant and equipment and intangible assets	10–11	(134)	(119)	(144)
Proceeds from disposals of property, plant and equipment and intangible assets		20	24	11
		(114)	(95)	(133)
Cash outflows on business combinations net of cash and cash equivalents acquired	2	(267)	(11)	(218)
Net proceeds on disposals of companies and operations		–	3	1
Net proceeds/payments relating to deposits and long term investments		(16)	(5)	(13)
Cash outflows on cash management assets		–	–	(71)
Dividends received from associates		1	–	1
		(282)	(13)	(300)
NET CASH FROM (USED) IN INVESTING ACTIVITIES (E)		(396)	(108)	(433)
Proceeds from issues of share capital		10	225	46
Dividends paid		(143)	(143)	(122)
Net proceeds/payments relating to treasury share transactions		(75)	8	(1)
Proceeds from borrowing	17	10	569	10
Repayments of borrowings	17	(130)	(310)	(367)

In millions of euros	Note	2008	2009	2010
Interest paid	6	(39)	(26)	(32)
Interest received	6	68	22	21
NET CASH FROM (USED) IN FINANCING ACTIVITIES (F)		(299)	345	(445)
NET INCREASE (DECREASE) IN CASH AND CASH EQUIVALENTS (G=D+E+F)		(147)	732	(375)

In millions of euros	Note	2008	2009	2010
Effect of exchange rate movements on cash and cash equivalents (H)		(185)	60	85
CASH AND CASH EQUIVALENTS AT BEGINNING OF YEAR (I)	17	2 137	1 805	2 597
CASH AND CASH EQUIVALENTS AT END OF YEAR (G+H+I)	17	1 805	2 597	2 307

Cash flows for the period are discussed in Note 18= Cash flows.

Source: Capgemini Group, Consolidated Financial Statements, 2010

Cash flows from operating activities

The statement of profit or loss and the statement of financial position are based on the accruals principle, which could be summed up as trying to present an economic analysis of profit by recording transactions when any relevant economic event takes place (sales, expenses, using up of assets, etc.). Cash flows are only one type of event recorded and, while a company must manage its cash flows, it cannot manage the business just on cash flow information – it needs to know about economic profit and profitability. For example, a company might have more cash coming in from sales than going out on expenses, but if it is not also recording the consumption of its non-current assets (depreciation), it could be making an economic loss even though generating a cash surplus in the short to medium term. Consequently, management focus has traditionally been on profits but, in a healthy company, the reinvestment of cash generated is the main source of internal growth and management should be looking at how best to allocate this resource to increase the profitability of the company. The statement of cash flows helps to show what wealth is being generated. Of course, over the life of the company the total of profits will equal the total of cash flows generated, but on a period-to-period basis this is not the case because of allocations of asset costs (depreciation) and timing differences from credit operations.

Again, the simplest way to get at the operating cash flows for the year would be to look at the company's cash (equivalent) accounts or the cash book (a journal which records all receipts and payments) and remove cash flows relating to long-term assets and financing. This can be done if the accounting records keep details on the types of activities involved, and in the jargon this is known as the 'direct' way of calculating cash flows. However, while this probably is easy enough for a small company, and may be the easiest way also for the small entrepreneur to envisage cash flows, in large companies it is arguably easier and more efficient to calculate the operating cash flow by manipulating the statement of profit or loss and statement of financial position. This is known as the 'indirect' method. In fact, most companies present the information using the indirect method, so that is the one we will use.

The indirect method of calculating operating cash flows consists of taking the net accounting profit for the year and then making three types of adjustments:

1. adjustments for non-cash income and non-cash expenses
2. timing differences arising from the working capital cycle
3. adjustments for non-operating items.

Non-cash income and non-cash expenses are items that enter into the determination of profit or loss, but do not imply a cash flow (e.g. depreciation, provisions, impairment adjustments, etc.)

Non-cash profit or loss items

As we have seen above, the process of preparing annual financial statements involves several kinds of adjustments: refinements to the profit to anticipate revenues and expenses which have not been included in the accounting database (such as accrued expenses and accrued revenue) and to defer previously recorded revenues and expenses to the following period (deferred revenues and deferred expenses), recognition and de-recognition of provisions and periodic and *ad hoc* adjustments to asset values (reflecting the using up of productive assets and extraneous value changes in assets). In the case of accruals and deferrals, these are short-term timing differences between profit or loss items and cash flows but, in the case of asset value adjustments, the associated cash flow (purchase of an asset) has already taken place and we are simply showing that economically it has lost some value which should be taken into consideration when estimating the economic position of the company. From a statement of cash flows perspective, the cash outflow on non-current assets appears under 'investing activities' and is reported when the asset is acquired. Therefore, when depreciation is charged, the investing cash flow has by definition already been reported. There is no operating cash outflow associated with depreciation or impairment charges for loss of value. Consequently, any charge to the statement of profit or loss for the year for these items should be added back to arrive at the underlying cash flow.

Provisions may turn into cash flows in due course, but their fate is uncertain and they too are added back here. Equally, where a provision is released, this will have the effect of increasing profit without increasing cash flows. Such releases must therefore be deducted from profit in calculating operating cash flow.

We can summarize as follows. The statement of profit or loss includes some items which do not reflect current cash outflows or cash inflows. These non-cash income and non-cash expenses should be used to adjust the accounting profit in order to arrive at a first, although rough, approximation of the net operating cash flow:

Net profit or loss after tax	Xxxx
Add back:	
Depreciation charge for the year	xxx
Provisions created in year	xxx
Deduct:	
Provisions released in year	(xxx)
'Cash flow proxy'	Xxxx

If no statement of cash flows is available, analysts frequently calculate this proxy figure which is relatively easy to derive from the basic financial statements. It does not reflect the short-term timing differences which derive from credit operations, nor does it filter out investment and financing related items, but it is often used as an approximation of cash flows from operations. In the absence of directly available cash flow information it has the advantage, in making comparisons between companies and particularly across national boundaries, that it excludes the most subjective elements of annual profit estimations, thereby providing more directly comparable figures.

Working capital movements

Working capital is generated by the operations of a company (see discussion in Chapter 4) and builds on a short-term cash conversion cycle in that a company buys materials (creating inventory and creditors), processes the materials (in a manufacturing environment), pays the creditors, sells the finished goods on credit (creating receivables) and finally the debtors settle in cash, completing the cycle. The exact needs of any business for working capital are dependent on the nature of the business. Some retailers, particularly supermarkets, keep very low inventories and have little or no credit sales, so their net working capital could even be negative. On the other hand, a manufacturing concern may have a long production cycle that takes many months for raw materials to progress through manufacturing and be sold as finished goods. Such companies will have extensive inventories as well as receivables and payables.

Movements in working capital items other than cash will affect cash flow from operating activities: increased trade receivables will mean that the cash from those sales will be received in the next accounting period; increased trade payables means that the cash outflow to suppliers has been deferred to the next period. The statement of cash flows will therefore need to take account of changes in working capital (excluding cash, which is the pivotal figure around which the statement of cash flows is organized and whose changes we are trying to explain) in order to show the cash generated during the year from operations.

Let us just look at an example of how that works. Supposing that in its start-up year a company had no initial share capital but had sales of €10 000, and had purchased €8000 of goods for resale. Its inventory at the year end was worth €1000, it owed €5000 to its suppliers and its credit clients owed €2000. The business had, therefore, the following statement of profit or loss:

	€
Sales	10 000
Cost of sales	−7 000
Profit	3 000

Its statement of financial position at the end of the period was:

Assets	€
Inventory	1 000
Receivables	2 000
Cash	5 000
	8 000
Financing	
Equity – Profit	3 000
Payables	5 000
	8 000

The business has made a profit of €3000, but its cash generated was €5000. How was this possible? The answer is in the movements in non-cash working capital:

	€
Cash owed to suppliers	5 000
Cash held in inventories	−1 000
Cash not yet paid by clients	−2 000
Non-cash working capital	2 000

The €2000 difference represents timing differences and, if the business stopped trading and disposed of its inventories, its cash position would in a few weeks equal its profit as clients paid their accounts and the company paid its suppliers.

If we now move forward into the second accounting period, we can show how the change in net working capital affects cash flows. Let us say that the business has grown by 50 per cent and that the statement of profit or loss for period 2 gives the following result:

	€
Sales	15 000
Cost of sales	−10 500
Profit	4 500

Assuming that credit sales and purchases had grown proportionately, receivables at the end of period 2 would be €3000, inventory €1500 and payables €7500. We can display the statement of financial position at the ends of periods 1 and 2 alongside each other and see not only how the cash position has changed, but also how the other balance sheet components have moved at the same time.

	End period 1 €	End period 2 €	Uses of finance €	Sources of Finance €
Assets				
Inventory	1 000	1 500	500	
Receivables	2 000	3 000	1 000	
Cash	5 000	10 500	5 500	
	8 000	15 000		
Financing				
Payables	5 000	7 500		2 500
Equity				
Accumulated profit	3 000	7 500		4 500
	8 000	15 000	7 000	7 000

In the two right-hand columns we have analyzed the change in each balance sheet component that has taken place during the second year. If you look at the changes, you can see that the inflow of cash is related to the accounting profit through the changes in the other elements of working capital.

	€
Accounting profit	4 500
less uses of finance:	
■ increase in receivables	–1 000
■ increase in inventory	–500
plus sources of finance	
■ increase in payables	2 500
Increase in cash	5 500

The example given is much simplified in order to highlight the changes in working capital – in many companies the increase in payables would not be so high as to finance the increase in receivables and inventory entirely, and there would of course be some share capital subscribed to start with. Accrued or deferred expenses and revenue (or similar items) have been ignored, but would be included here.

Non-operating items

Transactions and events that enter into the determination of profit are not exclusively limited to operating activities. Investing and financing activities may affect the statement of profit or loss as well. For example, when a company sells an item of plant or equipment, this will give rise to a gain or loss which is included in the statement of profit or loss, to the extent that the selling price is different from the net carrying value of the item sold. Such non-operating items affecting the profit figure should not be included in the net operating cash flow. Let us assume that the company sells an item of equipment with a net book value of €60 000 (acquisition cost €100 000 and accumulated depreciation of €40 000) for €90 000. This sale will give rise to a gain on disposal of €30 000 that is included in the operating result. From a statement of cash flows perspective, the transaction is an investing activity (a disposal of a long-term asset) and the inflow from the sale proceeds (€90 000) is to be accounted for in full as an investing cash flow. The gain on disposal is part of the cash flow from investing activities and should therefore be excluded from the net operating cash flow.

After the three types of adjustments, the indirect calculation model of the net operating cash flow would roughly look like the following:

Net profit after tax	Xxxxxxxxx
Add back	xxxxx
Depreciation for the year	xxx
Provisions created	(xxxx)
Deduct	(xxxxx)
Provisions released	(xxxxx)
Gain on asset disposal	Xxxxxxxxx
Net change in non-cash working capital	Xxxxxxxxx
Cash flow from operating activities	Xxxxxxxxx

Direct method for reporting operating cash flows

Although most companies use the indirect method for calculating and reporting operating cash flows, IAS 7 encourages companies to use the **direct method.**

Under the direct method, major classes of gross cash receipts and gross cash payments relative to operating activities are presented. This kind of information could be extracted from the cash books (not very feasible for most companies) or constructed by adjusting sales, cost of sales and other items in the statement of profit or loss for (1) changes during the period in inventories and operating receivables and payables, (2) other non-cash items and (3) non-operating items. The direct method results in a more straightforward presentation that is intuitively understandable by users with little accounting knowledge. The information it provides (and which is not available under the indirect method) may also be useful in estimating future cash flows. On the other hand, the indirect method (also referred to as the reconciliation method) has the advantage that it helps the analyst to understand the reasons for the difference between the period net profit figure and the period's net operating cash flow. If the direct method of presentation is used, IAS 7 does not require to present such a reconciliation.

STANDARDS

IAS 7 – DIRECT METHOD STATEMENT OF CASH FLOWS (extract)

		20X2
Cash flows from operating activities		
Cash receipts from customers	30 150	
Cash paid to suppliers and employees	(27 600)	
Cash generated from operations	2 550	
Interest paid	(270)	
Income taxes paid	(900)	
Net cash from operating activities		1 380
Cash flows from investing activities		
Acquisition of subsidiary X, net of cash acquired	(550)	
Purchase of property, plant and equipment	(350)	
Proceeds from sale of equipment	20	
Interest received	200	
Dividends received	200	
Net cash used in investing activities	(480)	
Cash flows from financing activities		
Proceeds from issue of share capital	250	
Proceeds from long-term borrowings	250	
Payment of finance lease liabilities	(90)	
Dividends paid*	(1 200)	
Net cash used in financing activities		(790)
Net increase in cash and cash equivalents		110
Cash and cash equivalents at beginning of period		120
Cash and cash equivalents at end of period		230

* This could also be shown as an operating cash flow.

Source: IAS 7, Statement of Cash Flows, Illustrative examples

On the previous page and below are two models of a statement of cash flows as exhibited in IAS 7. The two models (direct method and indirect method) refer to the same raw accounting data. Note that the method chosen does not affect the presentation of investing and financing cash flows and that both methods necessarily result in the same net operating cash flow figure. IAS 7 does also require that interest and dividend paid and received and taxes paid should always be disclosed separately on the face of the statement of cash flows (in both presentation models).

STANDARD PRACTICE

IAS 7 – INDIRECT METHOD STATEMENT OF CASH FLOWS (extract)

		20X2
Cash flows from operating activities		
Profit before taxation	3 350	
Adjustments for:		
Depreciation	450	
Foreign exchange loss	40	
Investment income	(500)	
Interest expense	400	
	3 740	
Increase in trade and other receivables	(500)	
Decrease in inventories	1 050	
Decrease in trade payables	(1 740)	
Cash generated from operations	2 550	
Interest paid	(270)	
Income taxes paid	(900)	
Net cash from operating activities		1 380
Cash flows from investing activities		
Acquisition of subsidiary X, net of cash acquired	(550)	
Purchase of property, plant and equipment	(350)	
Proceeds from sale of equipment	20	
Interest received	200	
Dividends received	200	
Net cash used in investing activities		(480)
Cash flows from financing activities		
Proceeds from issue of share capital	250	
Proceeds from long-term borrowings	250	
Payment of finance lease liabilities	(90)	
Dividends paid*	(1 200)	
Net cash used in financing activities		(790)
Net increase in cash and cash equivalents		110
Cash and cash equivalents at beginning of period		120
Cash and cash equivalents at end of period		230

* This could also be shown as an operating cash flow

Source: IAS 7, *Statement of Cash Flows, Illustrative examples*

Constructing a statement of cash flows 1

Let us now do a practical example. The working method is to take two consecutive statements of financial position, calculate the difference between them and analyze these into inflows and outflows of cash. The scheme shown in Figure 10.2 can be used as a rule of thumb to designate balance sheet movement as cash outflows or cash inflows.

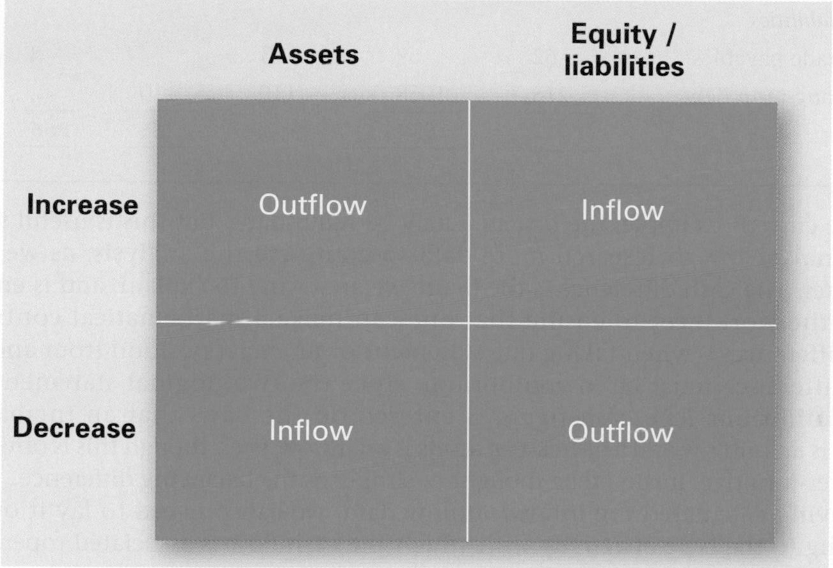

	Assets	Equity / liabilities
Increase	Outflow	Inflow
Decrease	Inflow	Outflow

Figure 10.2
Classifying balance sheet movements as inflows or outflows of cash

An increase of assets (for example buying a car or inventory) and a decrease of equity or liabilities (for example paying a dividend to shareholders or retiring debt), generally imply a use of cash. An increase of equity or liabilities (for example selling new shares, making a profit, getting a new bank loan) and a decrease of assets (for example depreciating long-term assets, selling inventory), imply a source of funds.

	X2	X1	Δ	Outflow	Inflow
Assets					
Non-current tangible assets (at cost)	980	740	240	240	
Acc. depreciation	−350	−265	85		85
Inventories	180	171	9	9	
Trade receivables	115	98	17	17	
Cash	92	110	18		18
	1017	*854*			

	X2	X1	Δ	Outflow	Inflow
Financing					
Equity					
Share capital	600	600	—		
Reserves	90	90	—		
X2 profit	50	—	50		50
Liabilities					
Trade payables	62	69	3		3
Long-term debt	215	1058	110	110	
	1017	854		266	266

In the current example, the first step may be redundant, but this is useful where the analyst has to research more data to complete the analysis, as we shall see later. The cash difference is the figure we are trying to explain, and is entered onto the worksheet to ensure that one can make a mathematical control of the differences – when taking one statement of financial position from another, the difference must be in equilibrium, since the two original statements are in equilibrium. The cash figure is entered on the basis that an increase in assets is an outflow and a decrease of assets is an inflow, even though this is obviously counter-intuitive. It should be thought of simply as the balancing difference.

Having calculated the inflow/outflow data, we can proceed to lay it out according to the type of activity with which the cash flow is associated (operating, investing and financing activities), as follows:

Operating activities	
Net profit after tax	50
Add back depreciation	85
	135
Changes in non-cash working capital	–23
Net cash flow from operations (A)	112
Investing activities	
Purchase of tangible assets (B)	–240
Financing activities	
New long-term debt (C)	110
Net change in cash (A+B+C)	–18
Cash balances	
At beginning of year	110
At balance sheet date	92
Difference	–18

Taking the statement of cash flows line by line, the net profit figure is the profit for the year in the statement of financial position (and in the statement of profit or loss, of course). The depreciation charge for the year is the difference between accumulated depreciation at the beginning and end of the year. The change in non-cash working capital is:

Increase in inventories	–9
Increase in trade receivables	–17
Increase in trade payables	+3
Net change in non-cash working capital	–23

All that is left after that is the increase in non-current tangible assets of 240 and the increase in long-term debt of 110. You should check off the differences identified in the work-sheet against the statement of cash flows to be sure you see where the information comes from.

Having drawn up the statement of cash flows, the next question is: what useful information does that give us about the company?

Essentially here the message is simple – the company has acquired a substantial new non-current tangible asset, and has financed it approximately half by the cash flow it has generated in the year and half by increasing its long-term debt.

The increase in productive capacity is a good sign indicating increased future profits (provided the company can manage the tangible asset successfully, of course). The degree of debt financing is out of line with the company's prior debt/equity ratio. In 20X1 the ratio was 105/690 or 15 per cent, and the financing of a new long-term asset 50 per cent by long-term debt must change this significantly. In fact, the new debt/equity ratio is 215/740 = 29 per cent. Of course, the company may be planning to reduce the debt in 20X3 when it has generated more cash from operations, or may simply have decided to adopt a more aggressive financing stance.

Disposal of long-term assets

The use of raw balance sheet data in constructing a statement of cash flows is more complicated when there are both inflows and outflows under the same caption of the statement of financial position in the course of the year. This is frequently the case with long-term assets, like property, plant and equipment (PP&E), where companies are not only expanding capacity, but are replacing old equipment with new. As regards the statement of cash flows, long-term asset disposals lead to two adjustments: (1) to separate out the disappearing book value of the old long-term asset from the newly acquired assets and (2) to remove the gain or loss on disposal from the operating profit and put it into the investing section, since all non-current asset acquisitions and disposals should appear there.

Suppose that a company had non-current tangible assets at cost of 540 and accumulated depreciation of 235 at the beginning of the year. During the year it sold for 135 some equipment which had cost 275 and had accumulated depreciation of 160. It replaced this with a tangible asset which cost 400. The depreciation charge for the year was 132.

The analysis of the statement of financial position would give the following picture:

	X2	X1	Δ	Outflow	Inflow
Non-current tangible assets	665	540	125		
Acc. depreciation	-207	-235	28		

On the face of it, the company has acquired a new tangible asset which cost 125, and there was a depreciation credit for the year instead of a charge. This is of course hardly likely and would send the analyst immediately to the notes to the accounts for an analysis of movements on tangible assets, where it would quickly be discovered that there had been a disposal and an acquisition. Consequently the analysis can be completed more fully:

	X2	X1	Δ	Outflow	Inflow
Non-current tangible assets	665	540	125	400	275
Acc. depreciation	-207	-235	28	160	132

On the tangible assets line, the 125 represents the difference between the acquisition at 400 and the original cost of the asset disposed of, 275. For the purposes of the analysis we will put both the gross cost and the accumulated depreciation of the asset which has been sold into our worksheet, so that it is clear what is happening. The accumulated depreciation on this asset was 160 which, taken with the difference of 28 between balance sheet dates, means that the charge for the year was 132 (160 − 28 = 132).

The analysis therefore now includes all the elements which have intervened during the year: sale of a long-term tangible asset, acquisition of another one and depreciation charge for the year. In the statement of cash flows the depreciation charge of 132 will be added back to profit in the calculation of operating cash flows. The purchase of the new tangible asset at 400 will appear under investing activities, and there too we must put the asset sold. The book value of (275 − 160) 115 should go there, but it should be adjusted by the amount of the gain or loss. In this case it is a gain of 20 (135 − 115), which we should remove from operating cash flows and add to the book value of the asset in investing activities. We would therefore have 'asset disposal 135' (115 + 20) which is the cash flow arising from the sale of the long-term asset.

Had the resale price received been (say) 100, this would have resulted in an accounting loss of 15. This loss of 15 should be removed from the operating result and be deducted from the disposal under investing activities: 'asset disposal 100' (115 − 15).

We can restate our checklist for operating cash flow as:

Net profit after tax	Xxxxxxxx
Add back	
Depreciation	xxxxxx
Provisions created	xxxxxx
Loss on disposal of assets	xxxxxx
Deduct:	
Provisions released	xxxxxx
Gains on disposal of assets	xxxxxx
+/– Change in non-cash working capital	xxxxxx
Net cash flow from operating activities	xxxxxxxxx

Constructing a statement of cash flows 2

Unlike the preparation of the statement of profit or loss and statement of financial position, there is no one tried and tested way of preparing a statement of cash flows any more than there is a unique format for presenting the data. We shall continue to use the system of comparing opening and closing statements of financial position. This direct comparison has the merit that it produces a table of differences where (given that the two statements of financial position do balance to start with) the differences in outflows will equal the differences in inflows. It gives a good starting point by providing a framework of change for that particular company. Let us do a new example. The statement of profit or loss follows and the statement of financial position has been laid out as a working paper.

Connecticut River Co. Ltd
Statement of profit or loss

Sales		500
Materials used	148	
Salaries	105	
Depreciation	116	
Other expenses	95	−464
		36
Gain on disposal of asset		3
Interest cost		−9
		30
Taxation		−11
Net profit after tax		19

Connecticut River Co. Ltd

Statements of financial position

	X2	X1	Δ	Outflow	Inflow
Land	105	105	—		
Buildings	235	235	—		
Acc. depreciation	−113	−107	6		
Plant	441	397	44		
Acc. depreciation	−356	−282	74		
Inventory	82	75	7		
Trade receivables	243	216	27		
Cash	73	62	11		
Trade payables	190	195	5		
Debt	160	150	10		
Share capital	200	200	—		
Reserves	141	156	15		
Profit for the year	19	—	19		

The worksheet shows the crude differences between the two years' statements of financial position, and the next step is to go in search of explanations of these differences.

The first one is an increase of accumulated depreciation on buildings. There is nothing inherently unusual in this – presumably this is the depreciation charge for the year, which we can verify in a real-life situation from the analysis of non-current assets given in the notes. The statement of profit or loss shows us that the total charge for the year was 116, so there remains another 110 to explain. This 6, anyway, can be put into the inflow column as part of cash flow from operations.

Moving on to plant, there is a net difference of 44. However, there is an asset disposal in the statement of profit or loss (gain on disposal of 3). As there is no change in any non-current assets other than plant, this disposal must occur here, so the difference of 44 must be the difference between an acquisition and a disposal. The non-current asset analysis in the notes to the accounts will reveal that the company bought a new plant asset for 85, and disposed of one whose original cost was 41, which enables us to reconcile the difference:

Plant acquired	85
Plant sold	–41
Balance sheet difference	44

We will therefore complete the plant assets line by showing an outflow of 85 and inflow of 41. Of course, this sale will impact upon the depreciation line for plant as well, since the accumulated depreciation on the plant which has been sold must be removed. The net difference on depreciation is 74, but we know from the other depreciation lines that the depreciation charge for plant during 20X2 was likely to be 110 (116 in statement of profit or loss, less 6 depreciation on buildings). This would give the following:

Depreciation for the year on plan	110
Balance sheet difference	74
Depreciation on plant sold	36

We should be able to verify this from the non-current assets analysis in the notes, in a real-life case. We would show 110 as an inflow, being part of the net cash flow from operations, and 36 as an outflow. Of course the 36 is not an 'outflow' in a real sense, but it is a deduction from the book value of the asset which was sold and it is arithmetically convenient to note it here in this way, bearing in mind it is a deduction from an inflow. The 41 gross cost less 36 accumulated depreciation represents the accounting disposal value of the plant which has been sold (5) to which we will eventually add the gain of 3 (from the statement of profit or loss) to arrive at the sale proceeds which must have been 8.

After that we have routine increases in receivables and inventories, analyzed as outflows. The difference in cash is 11, and we will analyze this as an outflow, to preserve the balance sheet equilibrium (in effect it is the difference between the inflows and the outflows, of course).

If you are unhappy with this treatment of the cash difference, another way to deal with it is just to leave it out. If you do that, when you add up the inflows and outflows you will obviously have a difference, which will be the amount of the cash difference. If these two differences agree, your analysis is arithmetically correct, if not there is a problem.

The trade payables have actually reduced from 20X1 to 20X2, which is fairly unusual (but not impossible) where the inventories and trade receivables have increased, since these three are all linked in an operational sense to the same variable – sales – and therefore should tend to move together. From an analytical perspective a decrease in trade payables is a decrease in financing and therefore an outflow.

The debt line shows an increase of 10. A review of the notes to the accounts will in many jurisdictions show a breakdown of debt, and in this case we understand that a new debt has been taken out for 70. This means therefore that an old debt has been retired, if the net variation is only 10:

New debt	70
Retirement of old debt	–60
Net movement on debt	10

The new debt is an inflow, repayment of the old debt an outflow.

There is no change in share capital, but reserves have gone down by 15. The most obvious explanation for this would be the payment of a dividend, which in most jurisdictions flows directly from retained profit reserves. A review of the analysis of movements on equity in the notes would confirm this. This is then analyzed as an outflow.

The final difference is the profit for the year of 19. This will start off our statement of cash flows, but we must bear in mind that it includes a disposal gain of 3 which must be reallocated in the statement of cash flows to the investment section. The completed worksheet with the analyses on it is reproduced overleaf.

Connecticut River Co. Ltd Statements of financial position	X2	X1	Δ	Outflow	Inflow
Land	105	105	—		
Buildings	235	235	—		
Acc. depreciation	–113	–107	6		6
Plant	441	397	44	85	41
Acc. depreciation	–356	–282	74	36	110
Inventory	82	75	7	7	
Trade receivables	243	216	27	27	
Cash	73	62	11	11	
Trade payables	190	195	5	5	
Debt	160	150	10	60	70
Share capital	200	200	—		
Reserves	141	156	15	15	
Profit for the period	19	—	19		19

We can now proceed to layout the statement of cash flows in the formal way:

Connecticut River Co. Ltd

Statement of cash flows for the year ended 31 December 20X1

Operating activities

Net profit for the year	19	
Add back		
Depreciation	116	
Deduct		
Gain on asset disposal	–3	
	132	
Net change in non-cash working capital	–39	
Net cash flow from operating activities		93
Investing activities		
Purchase of plant	–85	
Disposal of plant	8	
Net cash flow from investing activities		–77
Financing activities		
Loan received	70	
Retirement of debt	–60	
Dividend paid	–15	
Net cash flow from financing activities		–5
Net change in cash during year		11
Cash balance 1 January 20X2		62
Cash balance 31 December 20X2		73

Notes:
1. The net change in non-cash working capital is the total of inventory (outflow 7), trade receivables (outflow 27) and trade creditors (outflow 5).
2. The figure for disposal of fixed assets is the book value of the plant sold (gross cost 41 less accumulated depreciation 36) plus the gain on disposal of 3 moved down from operating activities.

Interpretation

The statement of cash flows is an interesting summary of a company's changes in financial position during the course of a year and can often give clues to business strategy which are not so readily apparent from the statement of financial position or the statement of profit or loss. The format of the statement of cash flows with the basic distinction between operating, investing and financing activities is intended to aid in this type of analysis.

Different elements will have more or less importance from one company to another, but major considerations which should be taken into account when interpreting company statements are:

1. How successful is the company at generating cash from operations? To what extent does this internally generated cash flow provide finance for expansion and to what extent is it used up in providing dividends for shareholders?

2. Is the company disposing of many long-term assets? If so, does this mean a run-down of the business? Are assets being renewed or are new assets being acquired for expansion?

3. Is the company borrowing extensively and, if so, for what purpose? Is it restructuring its debt by replacing old debts with new; is it borrowing for new expansion; is it issuing new equity?

4. Is there any hidden message in the changes in working capital? For example, is a company acquiring higher inventories and higher receivables without any corresponding increase in trade payables? Or, conversely, are payables growing very quickly while other working capital elements are stable (possibly implying a cash shortage or at least an attempt to delay outflows)? Has there been a sudden drop in cash?

The statement of cash flows can potentially provide a useful picture of the structural changes which a company is undergoing and it should be examined with care for any hidden messages.

If we look at the statement of cash flows we have just constructed, the messages there are relatively simple.

Most of the company's operating cash flow comes from depreciation; the profit is relatively small in percentage terms. The main outflow has been on the purchase of new long-term assets, but these – at 85 – are less than the depreciation of 116. In a crude sense this means that the company's total assets are getting smaller. This would prompt an analyst to ask the company if this is significant. It may not be. The company may depreciate its assets very quickly, for tax or prudence reasons, but it is curious.

The increase in working capital is relatively high in relation to profits as well, and one should check (the figures are not given here) whether there has been a substantial increase in sales to justify the change in working capital or, if not, what is going on. The increase in working capital is twice the net profit, which means that profits are being swallowed up to finance expansion. This may be a good thing which will give a better return the next year, but at this point it looks a bit doubtful.

The company seems to have 'rolled over' debt by repaying some but replacing it. Again this is perfectly normal. On the whole, the statement of cash flows reveals that the company is investing in working capital more than long-term assets. This may be a good sign, meaning higher sales the next year and more efficient use of plant, but an analyst would be looking for further information to explain this. Aside from the growth of working capital, the picture is one of little change.

Some analysts will want to know the amount of *free cash flow*. The concept of free cash flow refers to the operating cash flow that can be freed up for new investment initiatives. Free cash flow can be calculated as the net operating cash flow minus three items:

1. cash needed for planned investing activities (like replacements of long-term assets to maintain existing productive capacity)
2. scheduled debt repayments, and
3. normal dividend payments.

A large amount of free cash flow means that there is a lot of discretionary room for expansion and new opportunities, extra retirement of debt or dividend increases. If free cash flow is negative, it would indicate that extra financing is needed just to maintain the current level of business activity (and the related commitments). If a negative free cash flow continues for several years, this becomes troublesome if sources of extra cash (new debt, new share issues, selling assets) dry up. Note that some analysts will only take into account net operating cash flow and planned net capital expenditures to calculate free cash flow.

Additionally, analysts will use cash flow information to construct some extra liquidity and solvency ratios, such as net operating cash flow to current liabilities (*liquidity test*) or net operating cash flow to current liabilities plus long-term debt (*solvency test*). This last ratio is typically used by credit officers in evaluating a company's creditworthiness for long-term debt.

Presentational differences

There are sometimes differences at the level of detail as to how a statement of cash flows is presented. In particular, our model here assumes that interest payments and taxation are part of the net operating cash flow (as they are included in the net profit measure), while dividends are treated as a financing item. Not everyone agrees with that presentation. IAS 7 allows some choice in this matter. It suggests that interest paid can be classified under either operating or financing activities, and interest and dividends received can be included in either operating or investing cash flows. Dividends paid can be interpreted as a cost of obtaining external finance and included in the financing cash flow or they can be treated as a component of the net operating cash flow.

Some companies start from the net operating result instead of from the net profit before or after taxes in the indirect net operating cash flow model. This is not prohibited, but it will naturally affect the content of the different types of adjustments that have to be made to arrive at the net cash flow from operating activities.

A cash flow statement will be accompanied by a significant number of extra disclosures in the notes to the accounts. IAS 7, *Statement of Cash Flows*, contains a lot of specific requirements in this matter. These notes are cross-referenced in the statement of cash flows. Some investing and financing activities do not imply cash flows at all (or only in part), such as the conversion of convertible debt into ordinary shares or acquiring an item of equipment through a finance lease. These non-cash transactions should be excluded from the statement of cash flows, although additional disclosures in the notes would be expected.

In all cases the analyst should either make or adjust his or her own statement of cash flows on a uniform base, or read the notes to the accounts carefully to see how the company has been constructed and take care over items such as dividends so that the statement can be adjusted to be comparable with others.

Summary

Most companies produce a statement of cash flows as well as the statement of profit or loss and statement of financial position. The statement of cash flows analyzes the changes in financial position from one balance sheet to the next for their effect on the company's cash position. The IASB formats of a statement of cash flows which analyzes cash flows between operating, investing and financing activities, have become generally accepted.

Companies generate funds internally from their profit-making activities, but the extent of these funds differs from accounting profit in so far as the accounting profit includes non-cash adjustments such as depreciation and provisions and to the extent that there have been changes in the working capital of the company derived from trading.

Companies' finances are also affected by the acquisition of new long-term assets, the sale of old assets, the borrowing of funds and the issuing of new shares. The payment of dividends and taxes is another drain on company cash flows. The statement of cash flows regroups all these elements of change for the information of shareholders and other financial statement users. The statement of cash flows provides useful information about the company's financial management and under-ly-ing changes in financial position and strategy.

There are no special rules for the workings necessary to construct a statement of cash flows, but we have approached this using one specific method. The method used depends upon an analysis of the net change in position between one statement of financial position and the next. This basic analysis provides a framework from which one may systematically extend the full outflows and inflows by correcting for net movements in each of the important balance sheet categories.

Discussion Questions

1. Explain briefly the incremental utility of the statement of cash flows to external users of financial statements.
2. The statement of cash flows contains three major sections. What are these sections and what information is contained in each?
3. Why does only a small minority of companies use the direct method to elaborate the statement of cash flows?
4. Discuss the different types of adjustment needed to derive a net operating cash flow figure from net profit. Provide an example of each type of adjustment.
5. What is the logic of analyzing components of the statement of financial position when constructing a statement of cash flows?

Assignments

The following questions have answers on the lecturer side of the digital support resources for the book.

1. Seurat AG commenced business on 1 January 20X1, having acquired an existing trading concern. The company's opening statement of financial position was:

	€
Property, plant and equipment	5 000
Inventory	1 200
Cash	1 800
	8 000
Share capital	8 000

During the year it traded successfully and had the following statement of profit or loss:

	€
Sales	25 000
Cost of goods sold	−17 500
	7 500
Other operating expenses	−4 500
Net profit after tax	3 000

Its statement of financial position as at 31 December 20X1 was as follows.

	€	
Property, plant and equipment	5 000	
Acc. depreciation	−1 000	
	4 000	
Inventory	1 800	
Trade receivables	2 300	
Cash	4 300	8 400
Total assets		12 400
Share capital		8 000
Retained profit		3 000
		11 000
Trade payables		1 400
Total financing		12 400

Calculate the company's cash flow for 20X1, and reconcile this with the profit (assuming there is no taxation or dividend for 20X1).

2. During 20X2 Seurat AG (see question 1) continued to trade successfully, and also expanded. It acquired new equipment for €8000, and borrowed €5000 in order to help finance the transaction. Its statement of profit or loss for 20X2 is shown below and its statement of financial position as at 31 December 20X2.

You are asked to prepare a statement of cash flows for 20X2.

Statement of profit or loss 20X2	€
Sales	57 500
Cost of goods sold	−36 300
	21 200
Other operating expenses	−11 000
Profit before tax	10 200
Taxation	−3 000
Net profit after tax	7 200

Statement of financial position at 31 December 20X2	€	€
Property, plant and equipment		13 000
Acc. Depreciation		−2 800
		10 200
Inventory	4 400	
Trade receivables	2 900	
Cash	11 900	19 200
Total assets		29 400
Share capital		8 000
Retained profit		10 200
		18 200
Trade payables		3 200
Taxes payable		3 000
Long-term borrowing		5 000
Total equity and liabilities		29 400

3. Seurat AG (see questions 1 and 2) continued to develop in 20X3. It acquired new equipment for €15 000 and sold its original equipment for €3500 (the equipment sold had a net book value of €3000 at the time of sale). The company also paid off its bank loan and paid a dividend of €2000. Its trading results for 20X3 are given below and its statement of financial position as at 31 December 20X3.

You are asked to:

(a) prepare a statement of cash flows for 20X3
(b) comment on the company's financial position.

Statement of profit or loss 20X3	€
Sales	69 700
Cost of goods sold	−41 300
	28 400
Other operating expenses	−13 500
	14 900
Gain on sale of equipment	500
Net profit before tax	15 400

Statement of financial position at 31 December 20X3	€	
Taxation	−4620	
Net profit after tax	*10 780*	
Property, plant and equipment		23 000
Acc. Depreciation		−3 100
		19 900
Inventory	4 800	
Trade receivables	3 200	
Cash	7 400	15 400
Total assets		35 300
Share capital		8 000
Retained profit		18 980
		26 980
Trade payables		3 700
Taxes payable		4 620
Total equity and liabilities		35 300

4. You are given below successive statements of financial position for a
    company (as at 31 December 20X6 and 20X7) and are asked to prepare a
    statement of cash flows for 20X7.

	20X6 €'000	20X7 €'000
Property at valuation	2 350	3 850
Plant and equipment	980	1 560
Acc. depreciation	−423	−572
	2 907	*4 838*
Inventories	841	923
Receivables	1 213	1 297
Cash	106	73
Total assets	5 067	7 131
Share capital	430	460
Share premium	802	892
Revaluation reserve	435	935
Retained profit	551	771
	2 218	3 058
Trade payables	1 432	1 675
Taxes payable	217	198
Long-term creditors	1 200	2 200
Total equity and liabilities	5 067	7 131

You are advised that no long-term tangible assets were disposed of during
20X7 and that taxation (€217 000) and dividends (€105 000) which related
to 20X6 were paid out during 20X7.
(*Comment:* you should note that this case includes long-term assets held at
valuation rather than historical cost. A valuation change does not involve
any cash flows.)

PART FOUR

The financial statements of multinational companies

In Part Four we switch from an approach anchored in the financial statements of individual companies to one where the focus is the multinational group of companies as a reporting entity, whose shares are listed on one or more stock exchanges. In the remainder of this textbook we will refer to such a multinational group of companies which operate under a unified management structure, as a multinational company (MNC). While all the accounting and reporting rules which we reviewed in the earlier parts of this textbook hold good, there are additional factors which need to be taken into account to understand the content of the financial statements of a multinational company. In particular, being the result of aggregating the financial position and activities of a group of individual companies, knowledge of additional accounting and disclosure rules is necessary to appropriately analyse and understand the figures of a multinational company. Equally, there are public interest issues such as transparency and controls on management behaviour which come into play when looking at a group which employs thousands of people and whose actions affect many different economies.

CHAPTER 11

The annual report

This first chapter of Part Four reviews briefly the annual report of the multinational company. It summarizes its main components and considers its use as a publicity document. Additionally, this chapter elaborates on the notion of comprehensive income and on how it relates to the traditional statement of profit or loss (income statement/profit and loss account).

Chapter Structure

- Introduction
- The corporate report
- Publicity document
- Statement of comprehensive income
- Analyzing the annual report
- Summary
- Discussion questions

Introduction

As we discussed in Chapter 1, it is widely recognized now that there are at least two quite different types of company in any developed economy: small and medium-sized enterprises (SMEs) and large, listed multinationals (MNCs). Where exactly one draws the line between the two is not clear and, in any event, probably varies from economy to economy, but we can identify two models which represent the contrasting poles. First, the SME is a company whose shares are held by a small number of individuals and are not publicly traded. The managers of an SME are usually shareholders. The SME employs relatively few people, its financing is oriented towards bank loans and the main users of its annual financial statements are the tax authorities, the management and the bank.

The second pole is the MNC, which may be listed on several stock exchanges. The MNC has no one shareholder with a significant proportion of its equity, has professional managers, is active in many countries and employs thousands of people. Its main objective is to generate returns for shareholders which it does by generating ever larger profits and trying to push up the share price. Generally, its annual financial statements will have to satisfy a wide range of users: the analysts in the financial markets, so that they can encourage institutional funds to buy the shares; the general public, in the sense of creating a public image of responsibility; and governments, to reassure them that the company is honest and meets its commitments (and does not need further statutory surveillance). Transparency in reporting is essential because uncertainties lead investors to demand higher returns and generate tensions with governments and the general public.

From a financial reporting perspective, the two are quite different animals. The SME has narrow reporting needs, closely linked to taxation, and rarely if ever enters into complex transactions, while the MNC has a wide audience and needs to use the annual report as a major publicity tool both to inform and reassure the world about the activities of the company. Equally, the scope of activities is different: the SME typically has few or only one line of business, its scale of activity is small and it is usually based in one country; and therefore it is relatively easy to see what is going on from its financial statements. The MNC, on the other hand, has many different activities, works in many different currencies and many languages and may well have extremely complex financial and other transactions. A kind of report is needed which can make some attempt to bring together all these different elements and convey some impression of them to users – technically a very demanding challenge!

In terms of regulations, the difference between SME accounting and MNC reports is usually most visible through the difference between individual financial statements and group financial statements (although you should not forget that many small or micro-businesses are not organized as limited liability companies and may only have the most rudimentary of accounts, while some SMEs may operate as groups and have to produce group financial statements). An MNC is usually a combination of very many individual entities, often in a range of product areas and in different countries, operating under some kind of unified management structure. Typically, such a group has sophisticated accounting systems which are capable of providing detailed internal information on a timely basis for management purposes, while maintaining all the usual functions of a financial reporting system as well.

Each individual company in a group has to prepare single company or statutory financial statements which are used, amongst other things, for tax purposes, and then the group prepares what are called 'consolidated' or group financial statements which aggregate the data from the individual companies. These consolidated financial statements are what we shall look at from here on. They reflect the financial position, performance and cash flows of an economic entity, not of a legal one. Consolidated financial statements serve the purpose of giving an economic picture of the reporting entity, which is not used for taxation and is therefore free of constraints imposed by tax rules. In many countries the rules for drawing up consolidated financial statements are separate from those for individual financial statements (although they build on these). In international circles, the accounting rules used are now primarily those of the International Accounting Standards Board (IASB) – which we use here – although there are, of course, many American MNCs and foreign companies listed in the US that use those of the US capital markets (the Financial Accounting Standards Board or FASB – US GAAP).

The consolidated financial statements are published each year, generally in a glossy document often running to 100 pages or more. They are usually reproduced on the corporate website as well, sometimes as a complete pdf document but also sometimes as individually accessible sections. This document includes both legally required information and public relations material. It is often known as the *annual report* or the *corporate report*.

The corporate report

The contents of the annual report will differ from one company to another – as a result of the non-regulatory parts – but, in general, and you should make sure you study some examples to see this, the average annual report contains the following:

1. *Corporate publicity material.* This is not statutory and not checked by the external auditor. Often this is described as a review of operations and contains a chairman's statement or president's letter. It might run to 50 or more pages, will have lots of photographs and is designed to present a good image of the company. This information should not be discarded by the user – much of it is highly informative and relevant – you should just not expect it to contain too much bad news, even though some companies do try to be much more transparent than others.

2. *Management report.* This can be very confusing, because the publicity material may also include items which are described as a management report. The IASB refers to this type of narrative reporting as 'Management Commentary'.

   One should take into account, however, that different countries have different regulations and different traditions about narrative disclosures alongside the financial statements. Companies listed in the US have to provide a 'Management's Discussion and Analysis' (MD&A) which discusses the year's results in relation to the previous year and future prospects. Similarly, the UK Accounting Standards Board recommended that large companies prepare an 'Operating and Financial Review' (OFR).

   In 2010, the IASB issued the IFRS practice statement *Management Commentary*, providing a broad, non-binding framework for the presentation of this type of reporting. It is seen as a narrative report that offers a context within which to interpret the performance, position and progress of the company. Management should provide its perspective on the business and its analysis of the interaction of the elements to help users to understand the company's financial statements and to understand management's objectives and strategies for achieving those objectives. The management commentary report should supplement and complement the financial statements with explanations of the financial statement figures and the conditions and events that shaped that information. The IFRS practice statement suggests that the management commentary should cover the following essential areas:

    a. the nature of the business

    b. management's objectives and related strategies

    c. its key resources, risks and relationships

    d. its results of operations and prospects

    e. its critical performance measures and indicators that management uses to evaluate progress in meeting its objectives.

It should be noted, however, that the practice statement is not an IFRS standard. Consequently, companies are not required to comply with the practice statement, unless specifically required by their jurisdiction.

The EU Accounting Directives also require companies to publish a formal management report, including a narrative review of the development of the company's business and of its position, together with a description of the principal risks and uncertainties that it faces. Where appropriate, the EU management report should include non-financial key performance indicators relevant to the particular business, including information relating to environmental and employee matters.

The European Commission's Transparency Directive has extended these disclosures for listed companies with a corporate governance statement in which companies disclose information about their corporate governance practices. Auditors have to verify that the information provided in the management report is consistent with the annual financial statements for the same financial year. However, some EU member states have gone beyond this requirement and made the management report subject to a full audit requirement.

3. *Statement of financial position.* This is as you would expect from your studies to date, but when we extend the concept of financial position of an individual company to that of an international group of companies, a layer of additional issues arises. We will examine these additional issues in the next chapters.

4. *Statement of comprehensive income (or Statement of profit or loss and other comprehensive income).* We are already familiar with the statement of profit or loss (income statement/profit and loss account), but there are extra ramifications of this which are relevant to large companies with a portfolio of subsidiaries and more complex transactions. We will elaborate the extension of the statement of profit or loss later in this chapter.

5. *Statement of changes in equity* Although this statement is not formally required in all jurisdictions, it is under IFRS. It is a bringing together of information from different places to help the shareholder better understand the changes in equity over the years. IAS 1 *Presentation of Financial Statements* specifies that an analysis should be provided of changes in equity during the year, to include payment of dividends, details of all classes of equity and any changes in these, the net profit or loss for the period and any expenses or income taken directly to equity without passing through the statement of profit or loss. Note that the latter are also included in the statement of comprehensive income (statement of profit or loss and other comprehensive income). Figure 11.1 documents changes of equity and

presents them as originating either from transactions with shareholders in their capacity as owners [new share issues, dividend payments, buy-back of shares (**treasury shares**)] or from transactions with others than shareholders in their capacity as owners (wealth creation by the company operations). Both transaction types bring about changes in the different classes of equity (share capital, share premium, retained earnings, reserves or accumulated **Other Comprehensive Income**) and these changes are detailed in the statement of changes in equity. There is a definite link with 'comprehensive income' which we will elaborate in the next section.

6. *Statement of cash flows.* As introduced in Chapter 10, this statement shows how the company has generated cash during the period and where that cash has gone. The statement of cash flows is a very useful analytical tool and is required as a primary statement by IAS 7, *Statement of Cash Flows*. In a multinational group the statement of cash flows will report incoming and outgoing cash flows at the group level.

7. *Summary of significant accounting policies.* Actually a statutory note to the financial statements, but often placed separately by large companies, usually in close proximity to the statement of profit or loss and statement of financial position. Essential first reading when an analyst looks at a set of financial statements because this specifies what set of rules (e.g. IFRS, US GAAP, etc.) have been followed in preparing the financial statements.

8. *Notes to the accounts.* The notes provide essential further analysis of main statement items (including those of the statement of cash flows). For large companies a lot of very useful information is to be found in the notes and they should always be read very carefully.

9. *Auditor's report.* This is sometimes found at the beginning of the financial statements, sometimes at the end, but should always be checked first in case there is anything unusual.

Figure 11.1
Changes in equity

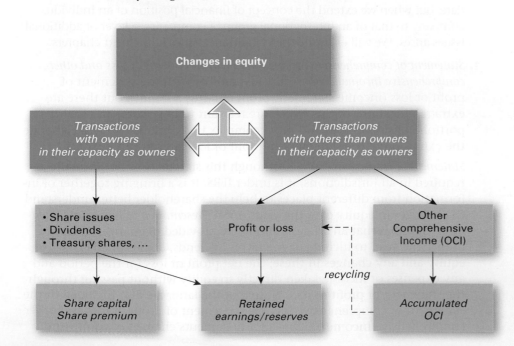

It would be a good idea to look at some examples of corporate reports and try to split them up into these categories – identify the different components – just to make sure you can do so. If you are able to locate the annual report of an SME, this would be a helpful comparative tool. In many countries the SME has much lighter disclosure requirements than the MNC and most SMEs prefer not to show their financial statements to anyone. In France, Belgium and the UK any limited company has nonetheless to file a copy of its annual financial statements with a public registry, and so they are in theory available to anyone who wants to look (although late filing is endemic amongst SMEs). In Germany, SMEs are supposed to file but many do not, while in Switzerland the file is not open to the public. Generally, therefore, SME financial statements are much more difficult to find and, when you have them, contain much less detail than the financial statements of multinationals.

Publicity document

For the MNC, however, the annual report fulfils a quite different role. As far as statutory and contractual requirements are concerned, the MNC has obligations to publish because of its economic importance and usually because it is listed on one or several stock exchanges. These obligations are typically very stringent. Thereafter, the MNC wishes to influence investors and any signs of opacity or failure to disclose what is regarded as key information will cause investors to become suspicious. When they get suspicious they either do not invest or demand a higher return for their money to compensate the increased risk which is attached when there is uncertainty surrounding the company. For example, if an MNC has potentially polluting manufacturing activities but says nothing about its pollution control in the annual report, investors may fear that there is bad news awaiting in the future with, say, a big bill to clean up a polluted river or compensate a poisoned community.

The annual report of an MNC has come to be a major publicity document. It has great authority as the major formal communication between the group and the outside world, and MNCs build on that to use it to present the company in as positive a light as possible and to explain what the company is doing. In some ways it represents the company's passport. Aside from its statutory and investor role, the annual report is widely used when making major sales pitches to potential clients, when talking to governments, even when taking on new staff – it is a way of establishing the company's identity, its size, its range of activities, its financial strength.

The annual report is a key document and many large companies automatically include it on their website. This last is potentially a trap for the analyst or student. For the moment there is no regulation as such of financial information on corporate websites. While company law usually requires that, say, income statements and balance sheets are never published without the audit report and the accompanying explanatory notes about accounting policies and so on, it is not always clear that these constraints apply to the Internet. Some companies may put only extracts of key financial data on the Internet and the analyst should be wary of missing information; and, if in doubt, obtain the published hard copy. That said, of course, the Internet is a great way of obtaining corporate data rapidly. You can even access MNCs' filings with the SEC (Securities and Exchange Commission) in the US which are all made available on the SEC's EDGAR database (www.sec.gov). This gives access not only to the annual report information but also all other data required by the SEC, including MD&A. For a detailed review of a US listed company, this is a good tool.

Statement of comprehensive income

As we have discussed earlier in this book, there are potentially two ways of approaching the articulation between the statement of financial position and the statement of profit or loss. In what we will call the 'operating' approach, you measure the company's revenue and deduct from that the expenses incurred (including using-up of assets), and that gives you net income (or net profit/net earnings) and the statement of financial position consists of the historical cost of the assets less the amounts deemed to have been used up, and the liabilities incurred to finance them.

In the other approach, which we will call the asset–liability approach, you measure the assets and liabilities in the balance sheet, and the sum of all the changes from one balance sheet to the next (other than transactions with shareholders in their capacity of owners, e.g. to issue new shares or pay dividends) is set equal to the income for the period (also called *comprehensive* income). Note that the resulting income figures under both approaches will not be the same. While the comprehensive income yielded by the asset–liability approach will include the net income under the operating approach, it will also include changes in value of the assets and liabilities that are not derived from operations. For example, if a company owned shares in say Yahoo which at the earlier balance sheet date were worth $10m at their market price, and at the subsequent balance sheet date the market price had gone up to $12m, this would give an increase in balance sheet values of $2m. This would appear under comprehensive income, but not in net income under the operating approach.

You should be aware also that when using an asset–liability approach, a measurement basis such as fair value will indeed likely give rise to valuation changes from one balance sheet to the next. IFRS use fair value for some financial instruments which we will look at in Chapter 14.

In the past it had come to be the practice to allow some changes in value not to pass through the statement of profit or loss, but rather to go straight to equity. A significant example of this is the foreign currency translation difference. We will look at this in detail in Chapter 13, but the issue is that when you prepare consolidated financial statements, you have to add together the financial statements of companies that may be using different currencies. They all have to be converted ('translated') to a single 'reporting' currency. If exchange rates have moved during the year, this means that there will be a value difference that has nothing to do with the underlying assets and liabilities, and is essentially temporary and a product of the financial reporting process. These differences were placed directly in equity.

Over time, standard-setters came to feel that although these differences were visible in the financial statements, they were not presented clearly nor necessarily in the same place. IFRS now requires that value changes that do not pass through profit or loss should be shown immediately after the traditional statement of profit or loss, by adding a section called 'Other Comprehensive Income' (OCI) so that the two together would add up to **total comprehensive income**. Figure 11.2 presents the basic structure of a statement of comprehensive income and highlights its link with the statement of changes in equity. The components of 'Other comprehensive income' are enumerated in the extract from IAS 1, *Presentation of Financial Statements* (see below).

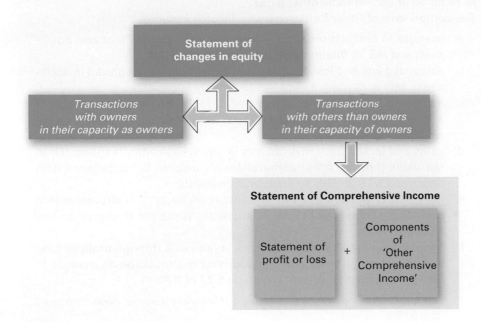

Figure 11.2
Statement of comprehensive income

IAS 1, *Presentation of Financial Statements,* allows a presentation option for the statement of comprehensive income (renamed in 2011 as the statement of profit or loss and other comprehensive income, although the use of the new terminology is not mandatory): (a) a single continuous statement presentation method, and (b) two separate but consecutive statements presentation method.

Whichever presentation is chosen, the distinction is retained between items recognized in profit or loss and items recognized in other comprehensive income. The only difference is that, for the two-statement approach, a total is struck in the separate statement of profit or loss at 'profit for the year' (this is the same amount as is presented as a sub-total under the one-statement approach). This 'profit for the year' is then the starting point for the statement of profit or loss and other comprehensive income, which needs to be presented immediately following the statement of profit or loss.

From 2013 on, IAS 1 additionally requires to group and present items in other comprehensive income on the basis of whether they might at some point in time be reclassified from OCI to profit or loss. Note that Figure 11.1 refers to this reclassification issue as 'recycling'. So, irrespective of which presentation method is selected, the items of other comprehensive income should be classified by nature and grouped into those that, (a) will not be reclassified subsequently to profit or loss; and, (b) may be reclassified subsequently to profit or loss when specific conditions are met (in

OTHER COMPREHENSIVE INCOME

Definition:

Other comprehensive income comprises items of income and expense (including reclassification adjustments) that are not recognized in profit or loss as required or permitted by other IFRSs.

The components of Other Comprehensive Income include:

a. changes in revaluation surplus (see IAS 16 *Property, Plant and Equipment* and IAS 38 *Intangible Assets*);

b. actuarial gains and losses on defined benefit plans recognized in accordance with paragraph 93A of IAS 19 *Employee Benefits*;

c. gains and losses arising from translating the financial statements of a foreign operation (see IAS 21 *The Effects of Changes in Foreign Exchange Rates*);

d. gains and losses from investments in equity instruments measured at fair value through other comprehensive income in accordance with paragraph 5.7.5 of IFRS 9 *Financial Instruments*;

e. the effective portion of gains and losses on hedging instruments in a cash flow hedge (see IAS 39 *Financial Instruments: Recognition and Measurement*).

f. For particular liabilities designated as at fair value through profit or loss, the amount of the change in fair value that is attributable to changes in the liability's credit risk (see paragraph 5.7.7 of IFRS 9)

Source: IAS 1, *Presentation of Financial Statements, extract from para 7*

accordance with other IFRSs). This additional presentation requirement makes the potential effect of items of OCI on profit or loss in future periods clearer. The extracts below provide illustrative examples of the alternative presentation formats. They include the split in presentation of OCI according to the reclassification issue.

PRESENTATION OF PROFIT OR LOSS AND OTHER COMPREHENSIVE INCOME IN ONE STATEMENT

XYZ Group – Statement of profit or loss and other comprehensive income for the year ended 31 December 20X7

(illustrating the presentation of profit or loss and other comprehensive income in one statement and the classification of expenses within profit or loss by function)

(in thousands of currency units)	20X7	20X6
Revenue	390000	355000
Cost of sales	(245000)	(230000)
Gross profit	145000	125000
Other income	20667	11300
Distribution costs	(9000)	(8700)
Administrative expenses	(20000)	(21000)
Other expenses	(2100)	(1200)
Finance costs	(8000)	(7500)
Share of profit of associates	35100	30100
Profit before tax	161667	128000
Income tax expense	(40417)	(32000)
Profit for the year from continuing operations	121250	96000
Loss for the year from discontinued operations	—	(30500)
PROFIT FOR THE YEAR	121250	65500
Other comprehensive income:		
Items that will not be reclassified to profit or loss:		
Gains on property revaluation	933	3367
Investments in equity instruments	(24000)	26667
Remeasurements of defined benefit pension plans	(667)	1333
Share of gain (loss) on property revaluation of associates	400	(700)
Income tax relating to items that will not be reclassified	5834	(7667)
	(17500)	23000
Items that may be reclassified subsequently to profit or loss:		
Exchange differences on translating foreign operations	5334	10667
Cash flow hedges	(667)	(4000)
Income tax relating to items that may be reclassified	(1167)	(1167)
	3500	5000
Other comprehensive income for the year, net of tax	(14000)	28000
TOTAL COMPREHENSIVE INCOME FOR THE YEAR	107250	93500
Profit attributable to:		
Owners of the parent	97000	52400
Non-controlling interests	24250	13100
	121250	65500
Total comprehensive income attributable to:		
Owners of the parent	85800	74800
Non-controlling interests	21450	18700
	107250	93500
Earnings per share (in currency units):		
Basic and diluted	0.46	0.30

Alternatively, items of other comprehensive income could be presented in the statement of profit or loss and other comprehensive income net of tax.

Source: IAS 1, *Presentation of Financial Statements, Extracts from Implementation Guidance*

PRESENTATION OF PROFIT OR LOSS AND OTHER COMPREHENSIVE INCOME IN TWO STATEMENTS

XYZ Group – Statement of profit or loss for the year ended 31 December 20X7

(illustrating the presentation of profit or loss and other comprehensive income in two statements and the classification of expenses within profit or loss by nature)

(in thousands of currency units)

	20X7	20X6
Revenue	390 000	355 000
Other income	20 667	11 300
Changes in inventories of finished goods and work in progress	(115 100)	(107 900)
Work performed by the entity and capitalized	16 000	15 000
Raw material and consumables used	(96 000)	(92 000)
Employee benefits expense	(45 000)	(43 000)
Depreciation and amortization expense	(19 000)	(17 000)
Impairment of property, plant and equipment	(4 000)	–
Other expenses	(6 000)	(5 500)
Finance costs	(15 000)	(18 000)
Share of profit of associates	35 100	30 100
Profit before tax	161 667	128 000
Income tax expense	(40 417)	(32 000)
Profit for the year from continuing operations	121 250	96 000
Loss for the year from discontinued operations	–	(30 500)
PROFIT FOR THE YEAR	121 250	65 500
Profit attributable to:		
Owners of the parent	97 000	52 400
Non-controlling interests	24 250	13 100
	121 250	65 500
Earnings per share (in currency units):		
Basic and diluted	0.46	0.30

XYZ Group – Statement of profit or loss and other comprehensive income for the year ended 31 December 20X7

(illustrating the presentation of profit or loss and other comprehensive income in two statements)

(in thousands of currency units)

	20X7	20X6
Profit for the year	121,250	65,500
Other comprehensive income:		
Items that will not be reclassified to profit or loss:		
Gains on property revaluation	933	3 367
Investments in equity instruments	(24 000)	26 667
Remeasurements of defined benefit pension plans	(667)	1 333
Share of gain (loss) on property revaluation of associates	400	700
Income tax relating to items that will not be reclassified	5 834	(7 667)
	(17 500)	23 000
Items that may be reclassified subsequently to profit or loss:		
Exchange differences on translating foreign operations	5 334	10 667
Cash flow hedges	(667)	(4 000)
Income tax relating to items that may be reclassified	(1 167)	(1 667)
	3 500	5 000
Other comprehensive income for the year, net of tax	(14 000)	28 000
TOTAL COMPREHENSIVE INCOME FOR THE YEAR	107 250	93 500
Total comprehensive income attributable to:		
Owners of the parent	85 800	74 000
Non-controlling interests	21 450	18 700
	107 250	93 500

Alternatively, items of other comprehensive income could be presented, net of tax.

Source: IAS 1, *Presentation of Financial Statements, Extracts from Implementation Guidance*

Analyzing the annual report

Generally speaking, when you first look at a company's report with a view to analyzing the financial statements, we would suggest that you follow this routine:

1. Read the publicity material to get an idea of the company's activities and how it sees them.
2. Check the auditor's report to see if there are any warnings. There are not usually any, because disagreements have been worked out before finalizing the financial statements or the auditors have made sure that adequate information is available elsewhere.
3. Read the summary of the significant accounting policies to see which set of accounting principles has been used and whether there is anything special you should note about the methods used. If you are looking at a European company, remember to check if the company uses IFRS as issued by the IASB or as endorsed by the EU.
4. Look at the main statements: Statement of Profit and Loss and Other Comprehensive Income, Statement of Financial Position and Statement of Cash Flows to get the overall accounting picture.
5. Look at the statement of changes in equity and the notes to the statements to get more detail.

Figure 11.3 wraps up the relationships between the primary financial statements and related concepts.

Figure 11.3

Relationships between primary financial statements

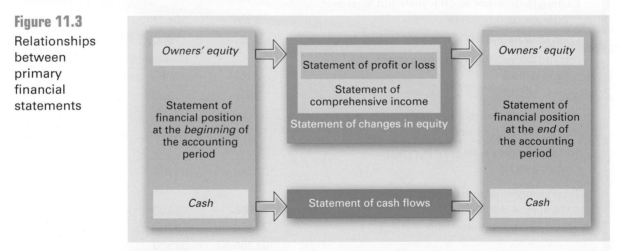

What the IFRS practice statement *Management Commentary* recommends as essential areas of management discussion of the company's situation (see earlier in this chapter) is quite a good guide to what the analyst is trying to do – to flesh out the company's strategy, the risks it faces, its investment stance, etc. The analyst should be trying to provide this kind of strategic overview by analyzing the financial statements and related material.

Summary

This chapter is a short introduction to the world of the financial information of large, multinational companies listed on the main stock exchanges. These companies use the annual report as a major publicity document; it also has to satisfy many legal disclosure requirements. While the basic financial statements that you already know are still at the core of their financial information package, the MNC publishes 'consolidated' figures – which bring together the sum of all its subsidiaries – to give a world overview. We will look at the techniques for putting these together in the next chapter. Their annual reports include a statement of comprehensive income which comprises value changes that have not passed through the operating earnings statement. The reports also include much more supplementary information both by way of detail behind the financial statements and of other matters concerning company strategy and activities.

Discussion Questions

1. Identify the users and uses of a multinational group's financial statements as opposed to those of a small company.
2. Explain how a management report supplements and complements a company's financial statements.
3. Explain how the concept of comprehensive income is related to profit of the year.
4. Provide some examples of 'other comprehensive income'.

CHAPTER 12

Consolidated financial statements

This chapter introduces the concept of consolidated financial statements – also known as group accounts or group financial statements – which are the basis of figures published by multinational corporations. The chapter deals successively with issues such as consolidating wholly owned subsidiaries, goodwill and its measurement, non-controlling interest and the accounting treatment of associates and joint arrangements.

Chapter Structure

- Introduction
- Rationale for consolidated financial statements
- Control as the basis for consolidation
- Consolidation basics
- Acquisition method
- Goodwill and its subsequent measurement
- Non-controlling interest
- Consolidated statement of profit or loss
- Associates and joint arrangements
- Disclosure requirements
- Summary
- Discussion questions
- Assignments

Introduction

As discussed in Chapter 11, multinational companies (MNCs) publish an annual report whose accounting numbers are consolidated financial statements, often known as *group accounts* or *group financial statements*. These are an attempt to represent the whole economic entity which is the MNC. In effect, they are based on the assumption of an Anglo-Saxon pyramid style of management structure. That is to say that there is a 'head office' management team at the top of a chain of command which extends to the furthest subsidiary. The central management's authority must be respected in all the companies owned by the group. In practice, modern group structures do not always correspond to this model in all their arrangements. In individual operations they may have all sorts of shifting arrangements with other companies. There are often alliances with other groups in particular areas. For example, oil companies may form alliances with each other to exploit oil wells or build pipelines, while fighting it out with each other in the high street for retail sales of petrol. These kinds of involvement mean that, at the margin, group financial statements have some difficulty in reflecting the economic realities, but they are still the best implement we have for measuring MNC activities.

Your strategy and economics courses will, if they have not already done so, give you ideas about why companies are organized in groups. However, it is worth just reviewing quickly the main practical reasons. Traditional theory notes that companies tend to develop on either a horizontal or vertical basis. Companies with a vertical basis typically have a production chain for a product that involves:

1. extraction of raw materials
2. transport to manufacturing centres
3. manufacture of products
4. distribution through wholesale outlets
5. retailing to consumers.

The description 'vertical' relates to the progress from basic raw materials to final retailing to the consumer. In theory, a company in the manufacturing sector might well expand its activities up and down to control both its raw materials and its retailing, and this would be called a *vertical group*. Examples of this are the major oil companies, who not only extract the oil but also own tanker fleets, refineries and filling stations.

A *horizontal group*, by comparison, expands into different industries united by some similar process or product. For example, a company might manufacture plastic mouldings for motor manufacturers and thus might expand sideways by moving into the manufacture of plastic mouldings for the toy industry. Oil companies may sprout chemical offshoots to exploit the by-products of the oil refining process.

These two directions are natural lines of development for companies that wish to expand. However, there is a third type of group, the *conglomerate*. The conglomerate diversifies into non-related fields, with the aim of building up a profitable group which draws strength from the fact that it consists of many diverse elements operating in different economic environments. (Finance theory has the concept of a *portfolio* where diversification across a minimum number of different investments reduces the overall risk of the total holding.)

The advantage to a group of being in several different areas is that when one product is having a bad year, other products should not be so badly affected. A particular disadvantage of the vertical group is that if demand for its final product is depressed, it follows that the whole chain of production is similarly depressed. However, it should be noted that while the diversified conglomerate looks like a good idea on paper, there are few managements that have been equally successful at managing all parts of such groups. But again, this is a question to pursue within your strategy courses.

If a company is going to expand, there are three main ways in which the group may be built up: the development of new subsidiaries by a company, the acquisition by takeover of other companies and mergers between companies. Expansion by takeover has long been a common practice amongst Anglo-American companies and is also much more common now in Europe, even if the rules in different countries are sometimes an obstacle. There has for some time been a polarization of business with large companies needing to become gigantic in order to compete on a global scale. The 'global' business can command lower costs than smaller, national businesses, through economies of scale.

It does also happen that companies form joint ventures with other companies. For example, Sony Ericsson Mobile Communication AB was a joint venture established in 2001 by the Japanese consumer electronics company Sony Corporation and the Swedish telecommunications company Ericsson to produce and market mobile phones. The stated reason for this venture was to combine Sony's consumer electronics expertise with Ericsson's technological leadership in the communications sector. The joint venture operated for more than a decade, but ceased to exist when Sony acquired Ericsson's 50 per cent stake in the joint venture in February 2012. A joint venture like this provides a different kind of vehicle and has its own special accounting rules.

Companies have a need to find new products – business theory suggests that products and businesses have a life cycle. When a company's main product is at a 'mature' stage (when the market is static or beginning to decline, and margins have been pared to the limit) it is time for the company to use the cash the product has generated to look for new products or it will decline and disappear. Large, international companies are therefore constantly buying new companies which either help to build global market share or represent an attempt to find growth products.

COMPANY REPORT

THE ACQUISITION OF JAGUAR LAND ROVER BY TATA MOTORS: ACQUISITION RATIONALE *(extract)*

We anticipate that our acquisition and operation of Jaguar Land Rover will result in benefits to us, including (i) immediate entry to the luxury performance car and premium all-terrain vehicle segments; (ii) an improvement in our global market position through a combination of resources and strengths; (iii) strengthening of technological and product development/ innovation capabilities to address changing market trends; (iv) sharing of best practices in manufacturing and quality assurance systems and processes; (v) enhanced human capital and managerial talent; and (vi) potential operational synergies.

The acquisition of Jaguar Land Rover enabled us to acquire internationally recognized brands with a strong heritage and global presence, and increases our product and market diversity. Jaguar Land Rover, which recorded more than 75 per cent of its sales in the US, UK and the rest of Europe for the year ended December 31, 2007, will expand and diversify our international sales market, allowing us to reduce our reliance on the Indian market.

Land Rover provides us an opportunity to broaden our existing portfolio of UV, SUV and crossover offerings. Land Rover's products in the all-terrain vehicle segment are complementary to our products in terms of features, technology and price positioning and as such, allow us to offer a wide range of vehicles that satisfies various consumer needs. Additionally, Jaguar's premium product offerings will provide us with immediate entry into the luxury performance car segment.

The acquisition of Jaguar Land Rover also enables us to leverage Jaguar Land Rover's technology and engineering expertise. For example, Jaguar Land Rover's technological capabilities in petrol engines, Four Wheel Drive technology and Aluminium BIW (Body in White) technology will help us further develop and strengthen our existing engineering capabilities. Through the acquisition, we also gain research and development capabilities of Jaguar Land Rover's strong engineering workforce and its two advanced design centres in the UK.

We believe Jaguar Land Rover will benefit from the acquisition because we will be able to leverage our low cost engineering and sourcing capabilities in favour of Jaguar Land Rover and thereby support Jaguar Land Rover in its cost reduction initiatives and improve profitability. Similarly, in advanced technology areas, we will be able to leverage Jaguar Land Rover's expertise and supply chain.

Source: Tata Motors, Filing 6-K, 2008, p.69

The simplest case of group expansion is where a company forms a subsidiary to expand its operations. This may be done for a variety of reasons. For example, it may be that the holding company wants to take on borrowing specifically for a project, and that can most easily be done by putting the project's assets and the associated lending within a separate subsidiary. It gives the lender a clearer sight of the project independently of the rest of the group.

It is often quite useful for management purposes to organize business operations into separate subsidiaries, since one can delegate management responsibility by making the manager of a specific project a director of that subsidiary, thereby giving him or her the legal power to operate the subsidiary effectively; whereas, if there were no subsidiary, the manager would have to be a director of all the group's activities, extending his or her legal authority beyond the required point.

Once a company extends its operations beyond its home country base there are other powerful reasons for forming new subsidiaries in foreign countries. Where a company has a foreign operation it will be subject to foreign tax on the earnings of the foreign operation. That in itself is a highly complex issue but, if there is no local subsidiary, the question of the profit attributable to that operation is even more complex. In a foreign environment, the limitation of liability is still more important and, since the operation is likely to be more remote than a domestic subsidiary, the necessity for clear lines of management responsibility is even stronger. A foreign operation will have to keep records of its transactions in the local currency, and this is sometimes more easily done through a chain of subsidiaries.

The more noticeable development of groups occurs when one company takes over another pre-existing operation. The reasons for a company to do this are also many and various. If a company is bent on rapid expansion, and has the finance available, there are obvious advantages in acquiring another company which is already trading in the field rather than starting up a totally new company. By takeover, the expanding company gains in one stroke an established market position, working assets and experienced management in that field. Against that it may have to pay a premium to persuade the shareholders of the acquired company that they would benefit from the takeover. An established public company with a good profit record can frequently take over another company simply by offering to give the shareholders of the acquired company shares in the public company in exchange for their existing shares. If it succeeds in persuading them that this is worthwhile, it has only to issue more shares rather than actually raise additional finance – a very effective way of expanding.

The third form of expansion is that of a merger. Since this is the least common form we will not devote a great deal of time to considering it, but it differs in an essential way from acquisition. Under an acquisition, company A buys company B. In effect, it is simply acquiring a new asset in the same way as it might buy a new factory, but at the same time this raises all the usual questions about the valuation of the asset. Under a merger, company A and company B are combining their assets to form, in effect, a new, expanded company whose assets and liabilities are the sum of A and B. It should be mentioned already that, for accounting purposes, IASB (but also the FASB) do not accept the existence of a true merger – they claim that it is always possible to identifiy an **acquirer** and an **acquiree**.

We have implied so far that when a company expands, the new companies it acquires will be fully under its control. However, this is not necessarily the case. A company may have different levels of influence over another company in which it has invested. If company A buys more than 50 per cent of the shares of company B, the implication is that, since the shareholders elect the directors and the directors run the company, company A can fully control company B by exercising its majority vote. It follows from this that 'control' can exist well short of having 100 per cent ownership of the shares in a subsidiary.

It also follows, however, that if company A has only 40 per cent of the shares in company B and the remaining 60 per cent are owned by company C, company A may well have no influence at all, since company C has a voting majority. By contrast, if company A had 40 per cent, but the remaining 60 per cent was widely dispersed with no one having more than 2 or 3 per cent, company A would have effective control except where all the other shareholders joined together to frustrate A, which rarely happens in practice.

At the other extreme, Company A might have only a token shareholding of 10 per cent and have no effective influence whatsoever on Company B. You can see that outside a situation where an investor company owns a clear majority of the shares in a second company, the question of the degree of influence exerted by one company over another is difficult to assess.

ROCHE GROUP

Accounting policies *(extract)*

Consolidation policy

These financial statements are the consolidated financial statements of Roche Holding Ltd, a company registered in Switzerland, and its subsidiaries ('the Group').

The subsidiaries are those companies controlled, directly or indirectly, by Roche Holding Ltd, where control is defined as the power to govern the financial and operating policies of an enterprise so as obtain benefits from its activities. This control is normally evidenced when Roche Holding Ltd owns, either directly or indirectly, more than 50 per cent of the voting rights or currently exercisable potential voting rights of a company's share capital. Special Purpose Entities are consolidated where the substance of the relationship is that the Special Purpose Entity is controlled by the Group. Companies acquired during the year are consolidated from the date on which operating control is transferred to the Group, and subsidiaries to be divested are included up to the date on which control passes from the Group. Inter-company balances and transactions and resulting unrealized income are eliminated in full. Changes in ownership interests in subsidiaries are accounted for as equity transactions if they occur after control has already been obtained and if they do not result in a loss of control.

Source: Roche Group Annual Report 2011

Rationale for consolidated financial statements

If we take the basic case of a group which has wholly owned subsidiaries – the most common situation – the question arises: 'What is the purpose of producing group financial statements?' The main argument for consolidated financial statements is that, although a group may operate through a whole network of theoretically independent legal entities, the fact of real control by a central holding company means that, economically, there may well be only one real entity. (Note, though, that the rationale for consolidated financial statements depends upon the pyramid concept of management structure where there is centralized control. It does not work for groups of linked companies with no central economic control, such as Japanese Keiretsu.) It follows that to appreciate the strength of this economic entity it is not sufficient to look only at the holding company: one must look at the total assets and liabilities under the unified control and disregard the legal entities.

A potential investor who looks only at the holding company financial statements might very easily be misled as to the strength of the group. To take a very simple case, company H, a holding company, might be constituted so that all its trading operations are channelled through a single subsidiary, company X, which also contains all the operating assets and liabilities. The statement of financial position below shows how the balance sheet of the two companies might look.

	Co. H €'000	Co. X €'000	H Group €'000
Non-current tangible assets	500	1 000	1 500
Investment in subsidiary	500	—	—
Current assets	250	350	600
Total assets	1 250	1 350	2 100
Share capital	500	500	500
Retained earnings	300	(50)	250
	800	450	750
Long-term debt	300	700	1 000
Trade payables	150	200	350
Total equity and liabilities	1 250	1 350	2 100
Debt/equity ratio	37.5%	155%	133%

If a potential investor looks only at company H's statement of financial position, he or she could have no idea of the underlying asset and liability structure. The company has a 37.5 per cent debt/equity ratio, so the potential investor would probably regard it as a relatively low-risk company. However, if the financial statements are consolidated (and in essence this just involves adding together the statements of all the companies in the group: the investment cost of the subsidiaries in the parent company statement of financial position is replaced by the assets and liabilities actually acquired), and the 'investment in subsidiary' of €500000 is replaced by the assets and liabilities of company X, the statement of financial position looks very different. From the consolidated financial statements, the investor could see that in fact the group is very highly geared; that is, it has a large amount of debt outstanding, and the losses made by company X are reflected in the group profit and loss.

The view which an investor might have of company H is quite different according to whether it is the consolidated financial statements or simply those of the holding company which are seen, and this is the reason for preparing consolidated financial statements. They give a picture of the economic entity rather than the legal entity: they provide information which is more useful in investment decision-making.

The technique of consolidated accounting for groups was not put forward until the early part of the 20th century, by contrast with much of basic accounting which stems from the second half of the 19th century. In the EU, consolidated financial statements are the subject of the Seventh EC Company Law Directive (1983). Consolidated financial statements have become the norm for large companies in the EU. One now commonly finds that the annual report of a European company includes two sets of financial statements: the consolidated financial statements and the parent company's statutory financial statements, with the latter still largely influenced by tax rules.

Meanwhile, with the spread of IFRS, consolidation practices of listed companies have become globally harmonized to a large extent. The main IFRS rules governing the preparation of consolidated financial statements are covered in IFRS 10, *Consolidated Financial Statements*, and in IFRS 3, *Business Combinations*.

Control as the basis for consolidation

IFRS 10, *Consolidated Financial Statements,* identifies control as the basis for consolidation. A reporting entity (investor) is required to consolidate an investee, if the investor controls the investee. IFRS 10 provides the following definition: 'An investor controls an investee when the investor is exposed, or has rights, to variable returns from the involvement with the investee and has the ability to affect those returns through its power over the investee' (IFRS 10, par.6). Control gives rise to a parent-subsidiary relationship.

The IFRS 10 definition of control comprises three essential criteria (see also Figure 12.1):

1. Power to direct – Does the investor have the current ability to direct activities that significantly affect an investee's returns?

2. Exposure, or rights, to variable returns from an investee, and

3. Linkage between power and returns – Ability of the investor to use its power to affect its returns of the investee.

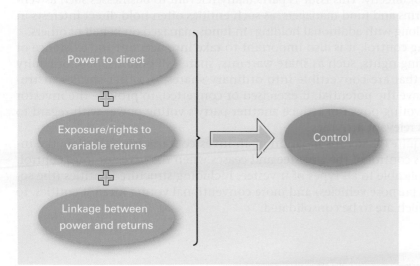

Figure 12.1
Elements of the definition of control

Power – An investor has power over an investee when the investor has existing rights that give it the current ability to direct the so-called 'relevant activities', i.e. the activities that significantly affect the investee's returns. Power arises from rights. Assessing power can be straightforward, such as when power over an investee derives directly and solely from the voting rights granted by shareholdings (control will exist when an investor holds > 50 per cent of an investee's voting rights). In other cases, the assessment will be more complex and require more than one factor to be considered, such as when power results from contractual arrangements. For example, a contractual agreement may enable an investor to direct enough other shareholders on how to vote in order to obtain relevant power. In another context, an investee could be designed so that voting rights are not the dominant factor in decision-making, such as when any voting rights relate to administrative tasks only and the relevant activities are directed by means of contractual arrangements. Large minority holders may also engender power when other shareholdings are widely dispersed, and an investor holds significantly more voting rights than any other shareholder or group of shareholders.

Returns – An investor is exposed, or has rights, to variable returns from its involvement with the investee when the investor's returns from its involvement have the potential to vary as a result of the investee's performance. The investor's returns can be positive or negative. Returns can be synergistic as well as more direct such as dividends or changes in the value of an investment.

Linkage – An investor controls an investee if the investor not only has power over the investee and exposure or rights to variable returns from its involvement with the investee, but also has the ability to use its power to affect the investor's returns from its involvement with the investee.

An investor with decision-making rights regarding an investee also needs to determine whether he/she acts as a principal or as an agent – does the investor exercise his power for its own benefit or on behalf of others (a concept sometimes referred to as 'fiduciary control'). An investor acting as an agent does not control an investee when it exercises decision-making rights delegated to it. Conversely, an investor should always consider whether another entity is acting as an agent for the investor, in which case the decision-making rights delegated to the agent are to be considered as held by the investor directly. This issue is particularly relevant to businesses such as venture capital firms and fund managers, as such entities often hold direct interests in an investee, along with additional holdings in funds managed on behalf of others.

In assessing control, it is also important to take into account the existence of potential voting rights, such as share warrants, share call options, debt or equity instruments that are convertible into ordinary shares, or other similar instruments that have the potential, if exercised or converted, to provide the investor incremental voting power or reduce another party's voting power with regard to the investee's relevant activities.

IFRS 10 requires that consolidation of an investee starts from the date the investor obtains control of the investee and ceases when the investor loses control. IFRS 10 is applicable to all types of investee, including structured entities (the so-called special purpose vehicles) and more conventional voting interest entities, to determine which are to be consolidated.

Consolidation basics

The essence of the accounting treatment is that the assets and liabilities of the holding company and its subsidiaries should be treated as though they were a single entity. The rationale is that, if the holding company controls the assets and liabilities of other companies, then the difference between the individual legal entities should be set aside and the economic whole should be treated as though it were a single company.

This means that instead of showing in the holding company's statement of financial position the amount invested in subsidiaries, we substitute the assets and liabilities of the subsidiary companies. In essence, this is simple enough, but it gives rise to certain problems where the holding company's investment is different in value to the net worth (net value of assets less liabilities) in the subsidiary, or where the holding company owns less than 100 per cent of the shares in the subsidiary.

We will illustrate the accounting solutions in a series of examples which will deal with the individual aspects of different situations and will concentrate on the balance sheet effects (and deal with the consolidated profit or loss later). First, let us look at the basic case, where the holding company's (Holding) investment in the subsidiary (Sub) exactly coincides with the value of the net assets (or equity) in the subsidiary. This would happen where the holding company has formed a subsidiary and subscribed to the shares at par (i.e. paid the nominal value of the shares exactly).

In order to prepare consolidated financial statements the investment by the holding company is eliminated and replaced by the assets and liabilities of the subsidiary. In the example below, a parent company (Holding) has an investment of €25m in a subsidiary (Sub). This investment is represented by €30m of assets and €5m of current liabilities which are in Sub's statement of financial position. For consolidation we put Sub's assets and liabilities into Holding's statement of financial position to replace the investment asset. We look through the investment to the assets and liabilities it represents. In calculating consolidated statements of financial position this is usually done by putting the balance sheets alongside each other, eliminating the parent company's investment against the subsidiary company's equity, and then adding the remaining balance sheet items across (see below).

	Holding €m	Sub €m	Elimination €m	Group €m
Non-current tangible assets	100	20	—	120
Investment in subsidiary	25	—	(25)	—
Current assets	30	10	—	40
Total assets	155	30	(25)	160
Share capital	70	25	(25)	70
Retained earnings	30	—	—	30
	100	25	(25)	100
Current liabilities	15	5	—	20
Long-term liabilities	40	—	—	40
Total equity and liabilities	155	30	(25)	160

The elimination column shows how the investment in Sub has been cancelled out against the net worth of the subsidiary (in this case entirely represented by the share capital of the subsidiary) and then the assets and liabilities have been added across – thus effectively substituting the assets and liabilities of Sub, which have a net value of €25m, for Holding's investment in Sub of €25m. This kind of working paper is classic for consolidation – of course it lends itself easily to a computer spreadsheet application.

Presenting a financial picture of a group as if it were a single entity, also means that intra-group transactions and intra-group balances need to be eliminated (cancelled) as part of the consolidation process. For example, if one company within the group sells it products to another company of the same group, the seller will record the sale in its revenue and the same amount will end up in the cost of sales of the buyer. Moreover, if the invoice has not been paid yet, the buyer will have a trade payable and the seller a trade receivable in its statement of financial position. Another example would be where a parent company provides an interest-bearing loan to a subsidiary. In this case the parent will treat the loan as a financial investment with any interest received accounted for as income, whereas the subsidiary will show the loan as a **financial liability** and interest paid as a finance cost. From the point of view of the group as a single entity, these transactions do not exist and have to be eliminated: intra-group balances at reporting date of receivables and liabilities will be eliminated in the consolidated statement of financial position and related income, expenses and profits in the consolidated statement of profit or loss (see more later in this chapter).

These consolidation basics have been further developed in a set of rules known as the acquisition method. The IFRS acquisition accounting rules are covered in IFRS 3, *Business Combinations*. These complement the IFRS consolidation requirements as found in IFRS 10, *Consolidated Financial Statements*.

Acquisition method

The acquisition method (or purchase method of accounting) is the method to be used to account for a business combination, defined as an event in which an acquirer obtains control of another business (the acquiree). Because a business combination always subsumes an acquirer and an acquiree, it is accounted for as the acquisition (or purchase) of a set of net assets. Note that these net assets do not necessarily have to constitute a legal entity, but they have to represent an economically viable bundle of assets and related activities.

An essential element of a business combination is the transition of control (as defined in IFRS 10, *Consolidated Financial Statements* – see above). A business combination implies the transition of control over a business from one party to another, with the acquirer being the one who obtains control. The timing of the transition of control is also essential in establishing when exactly the acquisition takes place.

The core principle of IFRS 3 is that the acquirer of a business recognizes the assets and liabilities of the acquired business at their fair values at acquisition date and discloses information that enable users to evaluate the nature and the financial effects of the acquisition. We will explain the main recognition and measurement rules of the acquisition method building on a basic example.

Consolidation difference at acquisition date

The primary example of a business combination is the classic takeover, where one company buys the shares of another and takes over the management of the acquired company. From a consolidation perspective, this may lead to a technical issue when eliminating the acquisition cost of the shares in the parent accounts. In the example above the value of the 'investment in subsidiary' in the parent company agreed with the initial capital of the subsidiary, because the parent started the subsidiary and supplied its share capital. However, when a company buys the shares of an existing company, it is usually paying the existing shareholders to hand over their shares – the money does not go to the acquired company and there is no link between the value of the investment as it appears in the parent's statement of financial position and the book value of equity in the subsidiary. They will be different amounts, and that leaves us with a difference between the two which is a core issue in preparing consolidated financial statements.

When one company takes over another, it usually pays a price for the shares which is related to its expectations of future profit potential and not to the book value of the shares. Consequently, the book value is usually different from the purchase price and an adjustment is required when preparing group financial statements to deal with this difference. It is known as *consolidation difference*, or goodwill arising on consolidation.

The acquiree's equity value has to be assessed at acquisition date, including reserves and accumulated profits until that date. When a holding company buys another company which has accumulated reserves at the acquisition date, these reserves (even though they may be retained earnings within the subsidiary) are no longer available for distribution. They are known as *pre-acquisition reserves* and must be offset against the investment in the subsidiary in preparing the consolidated financial statements.

In the following example, we have the statements of financial position of the Holding company and its subsidiary Sub at the acquisition date. Holding has paid €38m for 100 per cent of the shares in Sub whose net assets value (or equity value) is €25m. The consolidation adjustments are as follows:

	Holding €m	Sub €m	Elimination €m	Group €m
Non-current tangible assets	100	20	—	120
Investment in subsidiary	38	—	(38)	
Goodwill	—	—	13	13
Current assets	17	10	—	27
Total assets	155	30	(25)	160
Share capital	70	20	(20)	70
Retained earnings	30	5	(5)	30
	100	25	(25)	100
Current liabilities	15	5	—	20
Long-term liabilities	40	—	—	40
Total equity and liabilities	155	30	(25)	160

Note that the €13m 'goodwill' figure is simply the difference between the investment in the subsidiary at its worth in the parent company's financial statements and the carrying value of the equity of the subsidiary in its statement of financial position at the time of acquisition. Note also that the €5m of retained earnings included in equity at acquisition date are frozen for group accounting purposes at that moment as pre-acquisition reserves. Retained earnings generated later from profits of the subsidiary after acquisition will flow through to the consolidated statement of financial position and increase group retained earnings, but the €5m at the moment of acquisition will always disappear in the consolidation adjustment.

STANDARD PRACTICE

IFRS 3 – THE ACQUISITION METHOD *(extracts)*

4. An entity shall account for each business combination by applying the acquisition method,

5. Applying the acquisition method requires:

   (a) identifying the acquirer;
   (b) determining the acquisition date;
   (c) recognizing and measuring the identifiable assets acquired, the liabilities assumed and any non-controlling interest in the acquiree; and
   (d) recognizing and measuring goodwill or a gain from a bargain purchase.

6. For each business combination, one of the combining entities shall be identified as the acquirer.

8. The acquirer shall identify the acquisition date, which is the date on which it obtains control of the acquiree.

10. As of the acquisition date, the acquirer shall recognize, separately from goodwill, the identifiable assets acquired, the liabilities assumed and any non-controlling interest in the acquiree. (...)

18. The acquirer shall measure the identifiable assets acquired and the liabilities assumed at their acquisition-date fair values.

32. The acquirer shall recognize goodwill as of the acquisition date measured as the excess of (a) over (b) below:

   (a) the aggregate of:

      (i) the consideration transferred measured in accordance with this IFRS, which generally requires acquisition-date fair value;

      (ii) the amount of any non-controlling interest in the acquiree measured in accordance with this IFRS; and

      (iii) in a business combination achieved in stages, the acquisition-date fair value of the acquirer's previously held equity interest in the acquiree.

   (b) the net of the acquisition-date amounts of the identifiable assets acquired and the liabilities assumed measured in accordance with this IFRS.

   Source: IFRS 3, Business Combinations

Recognition and fair value adjustments of acquired assets and liabilities

At this stage of our basic example, we calculated goodwill based on the carrying value of the acquiree's net assets as they figure in the individual financial statements of the acquired company at acquisition date. IFRS 3 does however demand some preliminary adjusting of the acquiree's net asset position before the consolidation process can effectively take place. When first preparing the accounts of the new subsidiary for consolidation, the parent must review the individual assets and liabilities of the acquired company and make two kinds of adjustment of the acquiree's assets and liabilities:

1. recognize any additional assets and liabilities that are not carried on the acquiree's statement of financial position but represent economic substance to the acquirer (IFRS 3, par.10); and
2. adjust the carrying amounts of the acquiree's assets and liabilities to their fair value at acquisition date (IFRS 3, par.18).

Through these additional adjustments, parts of the consolidation difference that we determined in the previous section will be allocated to identifiable assets and liabilities of the acquired company.

Recognizing additional assets and liabilities

Part of the consolidation difference may relate to intangible assets, such as a brand name, a patent or a customer relationship, that the acquiree did not recognize as assets in its financial statements because it developed them internally and charged the related costs to expense. Recognizing an additional intangible will, however, affect goodwill. For example, company Alfa pays €200m for company Beta whose book value of net assets at acquisition date is €100m. Company Beta has a single product, HHH, which is a household name. As a first approximation, the goodwill might be set at €100m. However, if Alfa recognizes the HHH brand as an asset in the consolidated statement of financial position at €75m, this means goodwill becomes €200m less net assets €100m less brand €75m or €25m. In determining whether, at the acquisition date, an item not previously recognized by the acquiree but deemed to have economic substance, has to be recognized as part of the business combination, one should first check whether the item meets the definitions of assets and liabilities in the IASB's Conceptual Framework. For example, reorganization expenses that the acquirer expects to incur in the future to effect its plan to exit an activity of an acquiree or to terminate the employment of or relocate employees, is a typical item that tends to pop up in acquisitions. However, if the acquirer is not obliged to incur such reorganization expenses, there is no present obligation at acquisition date and thus no extra liability. Therefore, the acquirer cannot recognize those expected costs as an additional reorganization provision in the business combination.

Adjusting acquired assets and liabilities to their 'fair value' at acquisition date

What this remeasurement requirement means is that the bundle of acquired assets and liabilities is valued as at the date of the takeover, and that only the remaining difference between the revalued identifiable net assets and the investment by the parent will finally be accounted for as goodwill. The rationale for revaluing the acquired assets and liabilities is that they are being purchased by the new parent company and historical cost, viewed from the parent, runs from the date the parent acquired them, not the date at which they were acquired by the company which the parent has acquired. This seems perfectly reasonable. Recall that fair value is a concept near to market value.

Note that both kinds of consolidation adjustment can only appear in the consolidated financial statements; they are not entered into the accounting records of the subsidiary. This means that they have to be reassessed and re-entered whenever after the acquisition subsequent consolidated financial statements are prepared. Moreover, some of these adjustments need a close follow-up in time. For example, if a new intangible with a useful life of five years has been recognized as part of the business combination, the intangible (existing only in the consolidation files) has to be amortized over its useful life, with the periodic amortization expense to be accounted for as an extra consolidation adjustment. As another example, assume that one of the fair value adjustments relates to a depreciating tangible asset (like PP&E). In the post-acquisition period the depreciation of the acquired tangible asset must be based on its fair value at acquisition date. However, in the subsidiary's own (individual) financial statements, depreciation will go on based on the original historical cost of the asset. So, in the consolidation files both the fair value adjustment and a fair value depreciation adjustment are required.

To pursue the mechanics of this with our basic example, let us assume that the consolidation adjustments at acquisition date involve recognizing an intangible asset worth €8m and increasing the value of the non-current tangible assets to a fair value of €22m. This would give the adjustments shown below.

	Book value of Sub €m	Adjustment €m	Fair value balance sheet €m
Non-current assets			
– intangible	—	8	8
– tangible	20	2	22
Current ass	10	—	10
Total asset	30	10	40
Share capit	20	—	20
Retained ea s	5	10	15
	25	*10*	*35*
Current lia s	5	—	5
Total equity and liabilities	30	10	40

When the revised figures are built into the consolidated financial statements with the holding company, this will give rise to an adjusted goodwill value. It is this figure that will finally end up in the consolidated financial statements as goodwill.

	Holding €m	Revised Sub €m	Elimination €m	Group €m
Non-current assets				
– goodwill	—	—	3	3
– other intangibles	—	8	—	8
– tangible	100	22	—	122
Investment in subsidiary	38	—	(38)	—
Current assets	17	10	—	27
Total assets	155	40	(35)	160
Share capital	70	20	(20)	70
Retained earnings	30	15	(15)	30
	100	35	(35)	100
Current liabilities	15	5	—	20
Long-term liabilities	40	—	—	40
Total equity and liabilities	155	40	(35)	160

Goodwill and its subsequent measurement

Being a residual, the question remains as to whether the goodwill figure can really be regarded as an asset (i.e. does it meet the definition of an asset and the generic recognition criteria?) and, if it is an asset, whether it should be systematically depreciated or periodically tested for impairment. One could even take the view that there is no relationship between the cost of the investment (the cost which the new parent incurred in buying the subsidiary) and the accounting value of the subsidiary, so that goodwill is a meaningless figure. It is almost as though you said the distance from Zurich to Vienna is 600 kilometres, while the distance from Zurich to Geneva is 400 kilometres, so what is the difference of 200? Whatever it may be, it is not the distance between Geneva and Vienna. If goodwill is just a meaningless difference, then it should be labelled as such in the statement of financial position, perhaps, and left alone.

However, the standard rationale for accounting for goodwill is that the purchase price of the new subsidiary's shares represents the cost of acquiring a bundle of assets and liabilities. This cost should be allocated over all identifiable assets acquired and liabilities assumed and, if there is an excess, this is goodwill and represents 'intangible' assets such as know how, client goodwill, etc. to which no accounting value can be reliably attributed. In this vein, IFRS 3, *Business Combinations*, defines goodwill as future economic benefits arising from the acquired assets that are not capable of being individually identified and separately recognized. Its value stems mainly from the synergies of the net assets of the acquiree and from the expected synergies and other benefits from combining the net assets of the acquired company with those of the acquirer. This 'core goodwill' represents resources from which future economic benefits are expected to flow to the entity.

The second question is whether, having identified goodwill as an intangible asset, it should be subject to a systematic amortization scheme or to a periodic impairment test. Initially, IFRS opted for an amortization approach, with acquired goodwill to be amortized on a systematic basis over the best estimate of its useful life. There was a rebuttable presumption that its useful life did not exceed 20 years from initial recognition. However, systematic amortization of goodwill has been an annoying accounting rule for companies with an aggressive acquisition strategy. Clearly, if goodwill is capitalized and amortized, an aggressive company will find that its measured profits from an acquisition are being reduced by the amortization charge. This is not popular with managements who are trying to justify a takeover by showing enhanced profitability (research into takeovers actually shows that practically all acquirers pay too much money and the people who gain most are the original shareholders in the acquired company). The amortization approach has the advantage of being a well-understood practice, due to its simplicity and transparency but, on the other hand, it has the awkward side-effect of creating too much rigidity in subsequent accounting for the effects of goodwill on profit or loss.

IFRS 3, *Business Combinations*, abandoned the amortization requirements and introduced an impairment approach – goodwill is to be tested for impairment annually or more frequently if events or changes in circumstances indicate that it might be impaired. Consequently, goodwill is measured at cost less any accumulated impairment losses. Note, however, that the Seventh EC Company Law Directive and related national GAAP have not been affected by these changes and still require goodwill to be amortized over its useful life.

The impairment approach for goodwill introduces quite a fastidious and recurrent impairment testing process. We introduced impairment testing in Chapter 6. Under IFRS, impairment testing requirements are covered by IAS 36, *Impairment of Assets*. They call for a comparison of the carrying value of the asset with its recoverable amount. Where the carrying amount of the asset is higher than its recoverable amount, the asset is impaired. Because goodwill, by its nature, does not generate cash flows independently from other assets or groups of assets, the recoverable amount has to be determined at the level of the cash-generating unit (CGU) to which it belongs. This means that goodwill should first be allocated to particular CGUs. If this cannot be done on a consistent and reasonable basis, the goodwill will be identified with a group of CGUs. The goodwill will then be part of the total carrying amount of the group of CGUs, which will be compared with the recoverable amount at the same organizational level. An impairment charge should be recognized if the carrying value (including the allocated goodwill) is higher than the recoverable amount of the group of CGUs. An impairment charge calculated at the CGU level will first be allocated to the goodwill associated with the CGU (or group of CGUs) and, second, to the other non-monetary assets existing at that level in proportion to their carrying amounts.

For example, a CGU for which the recoverable amount has been estimated at €48m, comprises the following (allocated) assets:

	Carrying value €m
Goodwill	10
Property	40
Plant and equipment	20
	70

After impairment testing the net carrying values of these assets will become:

	Goodwill €m	Property €m	Plant and equipment €m	Total €m
Carrying value before impairment	10	40	20	70
Impairment loss	(10)	(8)	(4)	(22)
Carrying value after impairment	0	32	16	48

The impairment loss of €22m (i.e. the difference between the recoverable amount of the CGU and its carrying value) is first allocated to goodwill (reduced to zero) and next to the carrying amount of the other assets pro rata the relative carrying value of each asset. The reductions in the carrying amount of the individual assets is treated as an impairment loss. However, the carrying amount of any individual asset should not be reduced below the highest of its fair value less costs to sell, its value in use and zero. If this is the case for an individual asset, the impairment loss not allocated to the individual asset will be allocated on a pro rata basis to the other assets of the CGU.

The costs of such impairment reviews are likely to be high compared to a relatively straightforward amortization procedure. Especially determining the recoverable amount and, more specifically, the value in use of a CGU may be an extensive and time-consuming exercise. While the amortization method is quite successful in targeting the acquired goodwill and making management accountable for its expenditures on goodwill, the impairment-only method is more a valuation approach rather than an accountability approach. The impairment approach is arguably inconsistent with IAS 38's general position that internally generated goodwill should not be recognized. Across the impairment test, it will be quite impossible to separate the acquired goodwill from the internally generated goodwill of the acquiring company at the acquisition date and from the internal goodwill of the business combination built up after the acquisition date. Also, acquired activities are often reorganized and combined into existing activities of the acquiring company, making any distinction difficult. If a clean separation is not possible, different kinds of goodwill will be mixed, probably leading to cushions against recognizing impairment losses that have in fact occurred in respect of the acquired goodwill. If the consumption of the acquired goodwill is not accounted for, this engenders a situation where in fact internally generated goodwill is recognized as an asset up to the amount of the initially recognized acquired goodwill. Moreover, if a business combination is so successful that the recoverable amount of a CGU to which goodwill has been allocated continues to exceed its carrying amount, the goodwill allocated to that unit will continue indefinitely to be recognized at its fair value at the acquisition date.

On the other hand, if the impairment test of goodwill proves positive, the impact of the impairment on the consolidated statement of profit or loss has to be taken at once. At the time of the bursting of the Internet bubble, some groups had to take massive write-offs. After impairment testing of the goodwill that had arisen when AOL and Time Warner combined, the company had to take a $100 billion impairment loss against its goodwill account, basically admitting that the acquisition had been severely overpriced and that AOL had nearly no value.

Non-controlling interest

In preparing our consolidations so far we have used an example where the holding company owns 100 per cent of the shares of its subsidiary (company Sub). Although this is often the case, it is not always so – companies may sometimes have less than 100 per cent of the shares in the subsidiary. The reason might be political: in some foreign countries the government insists that where a multinational wishes to set up a local operation it should be done in partnership with either the foreign government or with local business people. Another reason might be operational – the company wishes to work in partnership with someone else in order to have access to their technical expertise etc.

As far as accounting treatment goes, ownership of less than 100 per cent of the shares presents a problem. If the basic idea is to present an economic picture which gives an overview of the group activities, consolidating 60 per cent of a factory where one owns 60 per cent of the company which runs it, does not really give the whole picture. Showing that the factory is part of the group but is financed in part by outside shareholders gives a more complete picture of the situation.

The accounting standards take the view that where a company has control of another, then it has effective control of all the assets and liabilities, even though the ownership of some part of the company is in other hands. Accordingly, the procedure is that the holding company consolidates all the assets and liabilities, but acknowledges the outside interest with a separate component of group equity, called **non-controlling interest** or **minority interest.**

But then the question pops up whether the non-controlling interest should affect goodwill or not. In this respect, IFRS 3, *Business Combinations*, allows two alternatives: the 'partial goodwill' method and the 'full goodwill' method. Under the partial goodwill method, the non-controlling interest is recognized at its share of the identifiable net assets and does not include any goodwill. The non-controlling interest isv recorded by reference to its share of the fair value of the assets and liabilities of the acquired entity at acquisition date. If any recognition or fair value adjustments are booked in the consolidation process, the non-controlling interest takes part in these adjustments. On the other hand, the full goodwill method will recognize goodwill for the non-controlling interest in a subsidiary as well as the controlling interest. The full goodwill method implies that the non-controlling interest and the goodwill are both increased by the goodwill that relates to the non-controlling interest.

Let us first apply the *partial goodwill method* (which has been the standard method in the past). Assuming that the acquiring company L had bought only 80 per cent of the subsidiary M, paying €600 000 and no additional fair value adjustments, the consolidation would be:

Pre-acquisition equity in the subsidiary is worth €400 000, so L company's share is €320 000 (80 per cent) and the non-controlling interest is worth €80 000 (20 per cent), based on the split of share ownership. L company actually paid €600 000, so it must recognize goodwill of €280 000 (€600K – €320K). In the consolidation adjustments we cancel the pre-acquisition equity of M company as usual, but the counter-adjustment is to create a new line called non-controlling interest of €80 000, as well as offsetting L's part of the equity against its investment.

Under the *full goodwill method*, one would add the difference between the fair value (at acquisition date) of the non-controlling interest and the amount established under the partial goodwill method to goodwill and to the value of the

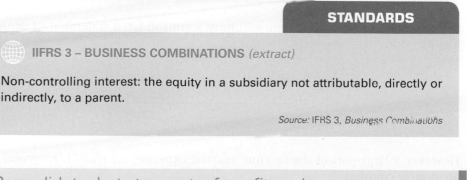

	L Co. €'000	M Co. €'000	Elimination €'000	Group €'000
Goodwill	—	—	280	280
Non-current tangible assets	1 200	300	—	1 500
Investment in M	600	—	(600)	—
Current assets	550	225	—	775
Total assets	2 350	525	(320)	2 555
Share capital	800	300	(300)	800
Retained earnings	1 150	100	(100)	1 150
Non-controlling interest			80	80
	1 950	400	(320)	2 030
Current liabilities	200	125	—	325
Long-term liabilities	200	—	—	200
Total equity and liabilities	2 350	525	(320)	2 555

non-controlling interest. Measuring the non-controlling interest at fair value may prove difficult in practice. It does not suffice to extrapolate partial goodwill to 100 per cent of the outstanding shares, as the fair value of the controlling interest usually includes a control premium whereas the fair value of the minority interest does not. Sometimes an acquirer will be able to measure it on the basis of active market prices for the equity shares not held by the acquirer. In other situations, however, an active market price for the equity shares will not be available and other valuation techniques will have to be used.

Note that under US GAAP, the non-controlling interest must always be measured at fair value, and full goodwill is always recognized.

STANDARDS

IIFRS 3 – BUSINESS COMBINATIONS *(extract)*

Non-controlling interest: the equity in a subsidiary not attributable, directly or indirectly, to a parent.

Source: IFRS 3, Business Combinations

Consolidated statement of profit or loss

We have so far concentrated primarily on the statement of financial position, since this is perhaps the more difficult aspect of consolidated financial statements to understand, but the consolidated statement of profit or loss (consolidated income statement/consolidated profit and loss account) also has its own technical challenges. You will have seen that the consolidated statement of profit or loss includes charges such as depreciation of fair value adjustments or impairment losses on goodwill which do not appear in the financial statements of the individual companies which make up the group. At the same time, the consolidated statement of profit or loss excludes a number of expenses and revenues which are to be found in the individual companies – essentially all those which involve trading with another group company.

Most groups have quite a large number of transactions which are with other members of the same group. If these were not eliminated, the consolidated financial statements would potentially include the same transaction many times over. Imagine a vertically integrated company which grows cocoa beans in subsidiary A, manufactures chocolate in subsidiary B and then sells this through wholesaler C in another country. You might have the following figures:

	Expenses	Revenue	Profit
Subsidiary A			
Expenses	1 200	—	—
Sales to B	—	1500	—
Profit	—	—	300
Subsidiary B			
Purchases from A	1 500	—	—
Other expenses	5 000	—	—
Sales to C	—	7500	—
Profit	—	—	1 000
Subsidiary C			
Purchases from B	7 500	—	—
Other expenses	500	—	—
Sales to retailers	—	8500	—
Profit	—	—	500
Totals	15 700	17 500	1 800

If you aggregate the figures, you will have a consolidated statement of profit or loss like this:

Revenue	17 500
Expenses	15 700
Profit	*1 800*

However, a large part of the revenue and the expenses are within the group and are double counted:

Sales from A to B	1 500
Sales from B to C	7 500
Total	*9 000*

These appear both in the aggregate expenses and the aggregate revenue, so are artificial from the perspective of the group as a single economic entity. Had the group been a single legal entity, the internal transactions would have no meaning. It is only the external transactions which should be retained in the consolidated statement of profit or loss. This should be:

Revenue (outside the group)	8 500
Expenses (outside the group)	6 700
Profit	*1 800*

Notice that this does not change the profit, just the revenue and expenses. From the perspective of an outsider, the internal transactions have no meaning and result in a false set of figures. For example, the profit margin before eliminations would be:

Profit	1 800
Sales	17 500
Margin	10.3 per cent

After elimination of intra-group transactions:

Profit	1 800
Sales	8 500
Margin	21.2 per cent

The intra-group transactions only exist because of the group structure, and they cause the double-counting problem. If they were not eliminated, they would mislead investors (some famous frauds have been engineered this way) and analysts would have difficulty comparing figures between groups.

Note that for the financial statements of the individual companies the revenue and expenses are valid and for tax purposes, the profits are still dealt with as part of the individual companies. Subsidiary A would be taxed on 300, subsidiary B on 1000 and subsidiary C on 500, which is a factor we shall come back to in relation to taxation of groups later (see Chapter 15).

You can see that the group financial accounting system must be able to distinguish between transactions with fellow subsidiaries and transactions with outside parties, so that the internal transactions can be included in the individual company accounts but excluded from the group financial statements.

Another adjustment which should be made is to ensure that the accounting policies used for the consolidated financial statements are reflected in the financial statements of the individual companies which make up the group – the consistency principle applies to group financial statements. When a group has subsidiaries in different countries, they will be subject to different tax rules, which may in turn influence policies such as depreciation or provisions. Equally, all the subsidiaries in the same country may not necessarily follow the same rules, although they usually do. This sometimes results in a situation where, in the consolidation process, the depreciation rates and other aspects of measurement in individual companies have to be adjusted so that the same accounting principles are applied consistently throughout the group. To keep this process as simple as possible and ensure comparable figures for management purposes throughout the group, some companies apply uniform accounting rules worldwide, and then prepare local variants for tax purposes.

In broad terms, the preparation of the consolidated financial statements (which can be done on a spreadsheet) involves the stages shown in Figure 12.2.

Figure 12.2

Process of preparing consolidated financial statements

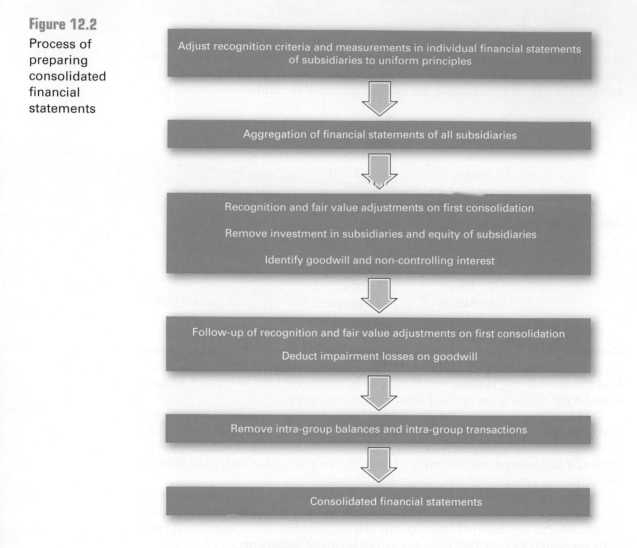

The accounting principles used in the consolidated financial statements are traditionally those of the parent company. This aligns with the idea that the consolidated financial statements have the effect of treating all transactions as though they have been carried out within the parent. However, the influence of taxation and the pressure to align group accounting on the principles used in the major financial markets means that in many countries a multinational may in fact draw up the consolidated financial statements on principles different to those used in the parent; in that case the measurement adjustments ('restatement' of figures in the jargon) may be substantial and sophisticated information systems are required to permit the collection of the necessary data.

Associates and joint arrangements

At the beginning of the chapter we pointed out that there are different kinds of relationship possible between an investor and a company it has invested in (the investee). The different types of inter-company relationship are presented in Figure 12.3. Accounting regulation recognizes three different categories:

1. The investor has a 'controlling' or dominant influence: i.e. the investor can dictate the strategy of the investee, appoint its management and so on. In this situation, the investee is consolidated, as we have just examined.

2. The investor is not able to determine strategy, but has **significant influence**: i.e. the investor's views are considered in determining the investee's strategy. This could, for example, be effected through representation on the investee's board of directors

3. The investor is not able to determine strategy and has no influence whatsoever.

	Type of inter-company relationship	Amount of voting rights	Qualification of shareholdings
1	Control	> 50%	Subsidiary
2	Significant influence	≥ 20%	Associated company
3	No real influence	< 20%	Financial investment

Figure 12.3

Inter-company relationships

The second column of Figure 12.3 indicates the relative amount of voting rights which are presumed to lead to a specific type of inter-company relationship. It should be noted, however, that the distinctions between these categories are not always very clear cut, and depend a lot on the surrounding circumstances. As we have discussed, a shareholding representing 40 per cent of the outstanding voting rights could put the investor in a dominant position if there are no other major concentrations of ownership. However, it would be more likely to put the company in a position of significant influence. It could even leave the company with no influence – for example, in 1999 LVMH, the French luxury goods company, made a contested takeover bid for Gucci. The bid was foiled by concerted action by the other shareholders which eventually left LVMH with a large minority holding but no participation whatsoever in the management of the company.

The type of relationship between the investor and the investee will determine the way the shareholdings are accounted for in the investor's financial statements. The link between the type of inter-company relationship and the accounting method used is documented in Figure 12.4.

Figure 12.4

Inter-company relationship and accounting consequences

	Type of inter-company relationship	Qualification of shareholdings	Accounting method
1	Control	Subsidiary	Full consolidation/ Acqusition method
2	Significant influence	Associated company	Equity method
3	No real influence	Financial investment	Fair value (or at cost)

The case of a financial investment where the investor has no real influence is the easiest to account for, although the accounting treatment can be different according to the applicable accounting regime.

■ Under IFRS, these investments are treated as financial instruments and measured at fair value. IAS 39, *Financial Instruments: Recognition and Measurement,* covers the appropriate accounting rules. The effect on income of measuring these investments at fair value will depend on how they are classified. If they are classified as 'held for trading' (or if the company elects to generically designate the investments on initial recognition at fair value through profit and loss), the changes in fair value are recognized in profit or loss in the period in which they occur. Classification as 'available for sale' would result in recognizing the changes in fair value directly in equity, through the statement of changes in equity, until the financial asset is **derecognized**, at which time the cumulative gain or loss previously recognized in equity should be recognized in profit or loss.

COMPANY REPORT

ROCHE GROUP

Associated companies (extract)
Investments in associates are accounted for using the equity method. These are companies over which the Group exercises, or has the power to exercise, significant influence, but which it does not control. This is normally evidenced when the Group owns 20 per cent or more of the voting rights or currently exercisable potential voting rights of the company. Balances and transactions with associates that result in unrealized income are eliminated to the extent of the Group's interest in the associate.

Source: Roche Group, Annual Report, 2011

■ The Seventh EC Company Law Directive still endorses the **cost method** for investments without significant influence, whereby the financial asset is held in the investor's books at historical cost. If its current value falls below historical cost, then the investment should be written down (and the expense would normally appear in the financial result part of the statement of profit or loss). In some jurisdictions, if the current value exceeds historical cost, this information would be disclosed as a note to the accounts. If the investor receives a dividend from the investee company, then this is treated as financial income.

The case of associated companies where the investor has 'significant influence' over the investee, has historically been more controversial with regard to its accounting consequences. For example, suppose you are a French company that sells bottled non-alcoholic beverages and you want to expand in Russia. The market is difficult, the risk high, so you decide to go into a joint venture with another soft drink company and a Russian entrepreneur. You each take a one-third stake in a new bottling plant in Moscow which will be managed by the Russian partner with technical assistance from the two multinational partners. How is this going to appear in your consolidated financial statements?

Since you do not own or run the plant, it will not be consolidated. On the other hand, you have a significant input into the decision-making and a significant investment which impacts upon the future expansion of your company in that market. You could certainly just treat the investment as a financial asset, but this does not convey the much closer economic relationship you have in it. What can you do?

Essentially, there are two basic methods, known as the **equity method** and the proportionate consolidation method. Under the equity method, the investor shows its investment in its consolidated financial statements at the accounting value of that investment in the investee's books. If, for example, the investor has 25 per cent of the shares in the investee, it shows that investment at 25 per cent of the book value of equity in the investee's financial statements and not at historical cost to the investor or at fair value. Under the proportional consolidation method, the investor takes a proportion of all assets and liabilities of the investee into the consolidated financial statements.

These two different approaches are probably best understood through a detailed example. Suppose that company A buys 20 per cent of company C, whose statement of financial position at the moment of acquisition is as follows:

	€m
Assets	
Non-current tangible assets	600
Current assets	300
Total assets	900
Financing	
Shares	400
Retained earnings	50
	450
Debt	250
Payables	200
Total equity and liabilities	900

The book value of C's equity in C's accounting records is €450m; A owns 20 per cent of that, which is therefore worth (450 × 0.2 =) €90m. Under the equity method, the investment in C which appears in A's consolidated financial statements should therefore be €90m, and any difference between that and the historical cost of the investment is considered as goodwill. The adjustments to bring C into A's consolidated financial statements at equity value would be as follows:

	Company A	Company C	Group
Assets			
Goodwill	—	+60	60
Non-current tangible assets	1 050	—	1 050
Cost of investment in C	150	−150	—
Equity value of investment in C	—	+90	90
Current assets	420	—	420
Total assets	1 620	—	1 620
Financing		—	
Shares	300	—	300
Retained earnings	420	—	420
	720	—	720
Debt	600	—	600
Payables	300	—	300
Total equity and liabilities	1 620	—	1 620

Again, under IFRS, the goodwill should be reviewed for impairment in the normal way. On subsequent consolidations, the book value of C would normally have changed, and all changes must also be reflected in the A's financial statements. So if, for example, C made a net profit of €50m in the year after A had acquired its 20 per cent stake, A would show 'income from associates' of €10m as a separate line item in its statement of profit or loss and would increase the carrying value of its investment in C in its statement of financial position by €10m. Any subsequent dividend would decrease the carrying value and increase cash at bank.

If, on the other hand, C were dealt with on a proportional basis, the consolidation would look like this:

	Company A	Company C (20%)	Adjust	Group
Assets				
Goodwill	—	—	+60	60
Non-current tangible assets	1 050	120	—	1 170
Cost of investment in C	150	—	150	—
Current assets	420	60	—	480
Total assets	1 620	180	−90	1 710

Financing				
Shares	300	80	–80	300
Retained earnings	420	10	–10	420
	720	90	–90	720
Debt	600	50	—	650
Payables	300	40	—	340
Total equity and liabilities	1 620	180	290	1 710

Under the proportionate consolidation method, a part of the underlying assets and liabilities of C appears in A's statement of financial position, as in a normal consolidation, and in future years any profits or losses post-acquisition will flow through to the consolidated statement of profit or loss.

Both methods have their critics. Critics of the equity method point out that only the book value of the equity is shown, and this may conceal a company which is heavily indebted. Indeed, associated companies have been used as a means of shifting debt off the main balance sheet. In addition, the method involves recognizing income from the associated company which has not been paid to the investor and over which the investor does not exercise control – something an analyst would be wary of (see 'quality of earnings' in Chapter 17). Critics of proportionate consolidation, on the other hand, say that a mathematical fraction of assets and liabilities has no economic significance – an investor cannot sell 20 per cent of a factory in case of difficulty, for example – and that the resulting consolidation is meaningless.

It is clearly a difficult issue because the relationship between the investor and its investment may be highly significant (e.g. the **investors in a joint venture** may draw significant economic benefit from that relationship but none has a majority holding) and should therefore not be missing from the group financial statements. From an analyst's perspective, the equity method is easier to decode because profits and losses are separately identified ('income from associates') in published financial statements and can therefore be considered on their own merits in relation to the particular company. Evaluating the effect of proportionate consolidation on the financial statements is not usually possible.

STANDARDS

IAS 28 – INVESTMENTS IN ASSOCIATES AND JOINT VENTURES
(extracts)

Significant influence

5. If an entity holds, directly or indirectly (e.g. through subsidiaries), 20 per cent or more of the voting power of the investee, it is presumed that the entity has significant influence, unless it can be clearly demonstrated that this is not the case. Conversely, if the entity holds, directly or indirectly (e.g. through subsidiaries), less than 20 per cent of the voting power of

the investee, it is presumed that the investor does not have significant influence, unless such influence can be clearly demonstrated. A substantial or majority ownership by another investor does not necessarily preclude an investor from having significant influence.

6. The existence of significant influence by an entity is usually evidenced in one or more of the following ways:

   (a) representation on the board of directors or equivalent governing body of the investee;

   (b) participation in policy-making processes, including participation in decisions about dividends or other distributions;

   (c) material transactions between the investor and the investee;

   (d) interchange of managerial personnel; or

   (e) provision of essential technical information.

Source: IAS 28, *Investments in Associates and Joint Ventures*

IFRS, however, does not leave a choice and requires the use of the equity method for associated companies. The corresponding accounting rules are covered by IAS 28, *Investments in Associates and Joint Ventures*. Associated companies are defined as those where the investor has 'significant influence', which is assumed to be the case where the investor holds at least 20 per cent of the voting rights of the investee. However, the IASB also has a standard which specifically addresses joint ventures – IFRS 11, *Joint Arrangements* – and the provisions of that intersect with those for associates.

Joint arrangements

The IASB defines a joint arrangement as 'an arrangement of which two or more parties have joint control' (IFRS 11, par.4). The parties involved are bound by a contractual agreement that provides joint control of the arrangement to two or more of those parties. Joint control is 'the contractually agreed sharing of control of an arrangement, which exists only when decisions about the relevant activities require the unanimous consent of the parties sharing control' (IFRS 11, par.7). Joint arrangements are quite common in companies operating in the extractive industries, property and construction sectors. This might be the case, for example, where two or three oil companies build a pipeline for shared use.

Joint arrangements take many different forms and structures. IFRS 11, *Joint Arrangements,* recognizes two kinds of joint arrangement:

1. *Joint operations.* A joint operation is a joint arrangement whereby the parties that have joint control of the arrangement (i.e. **joint operators**) have rights to the assets, and obligations for the liabilities, relating to the arrangement. Here the joint operators each devote certain assets (and related liabilities) to a joint exploitation but retain direct ownership of those assets and liabilities. In most cases no special legal vehicle is created. Revenues from the sale of the joint product and any expenses incurred in common, are usually split – for example, when two airlines both operate on the same route and agree to share revenues. A joint operator recognizes and measures

the assets and liabilities (and the related revenues and expenses) in relation to its interest in the arrangement in accordance with relevant IFRS applicable to the particular assets, liabilities, revenues and expenses.

2. *Joint ventures*. A joint venture is a joint arrangement whereby the parties that have joint control of the arrangement (i.e. **joint venturers**) have rights to the net assets of the arrangement. Joint ventures are usually structured through a legal entity. But the existence of a legal structure in a joint arrangement does not automatically means that it qualifies as a joint venture. They will have to be assessed to determine whether the venturers' rights and exposures are to the entity's net assets, or to its underlying (gross) assets and liabilities. The latter category will be classified as joint operations because this better reflects the economic substance of the arrangement. A joint venture intersects with associates – a company or other legal vehicle is created, the venturers make investments in this entity which in turn owns assets and undertakes operations. A joint venturer recognizes its investment in a joint venture and accounts for it using the equity method. IFRS 11 does no longer allow the option of using proportionate consolidation for joint ventures as in the former IASB rules.

Disclosure requirements

IFRS 12, *Disclosure of Interests in Other Entities*, specifies minimum disclosures with regard to interests in subsidiaries, joint arrangements, associates and unconsolidated structured entities. The required disclosures aim to provide information in order to enable users to evaluate (1) the nature of, and risks associated with the reporting entity's interests in other entities, and (2) the effects of those interests on the group's financial position, financial performance and cash flows.

Special attention will go to structured entities (or special purpose vehicles – see also extract from standard below). It should be clear what a structured entity is in the context of the operations of the group and how judgement is applied in assessing whether the group is 'involved' with a structured entity. Material involvement in structured entities may broaden the transactions and relationships to which the disclosures may apply, especially for those who sponsor, or perhaps even transact with, but do not consider to have control over the structured entities.

STANDARDS

IFRS 12 – DISCLOSURE OF INTERESTS IN OTHER ENTITIES *(extracts)*

Structured entities

B21 A structured entity is an entity that has been designed so that voting or similar rights are not the dominant factor in deciding who controls the entity, such as when any voting rights relate to administrative tasks only and the relevant activities are directed by means of contractual arrangements.

B22 A structured entity often has some or all of the following features or attributes:

(a) restricted activities.

(b) a narrow and well-defined objective, such as to effect a tax-efficient lease, carry out research and development activities, provide a source of capital or funding to an entity or provide investment opportunities for investors by passing on risks and rewards associated with the assets of the structured entity to investors.

(c) insufficient equity to permit the structured entity to finance its activities without subordinated financial support.

(d) financing in the form of multiple contractually linked instruments to investors that create concentrations of credit or other risks (tranches).

B23 Examples of entities that are regarded as structured entities include, but are not limited to:

(a) securitization vehicles.

(b) asset-backed financings.

(c) some investment funds.

B24 An entity that is controlled by voting rights is not a structured entity simply because, for example, it receives funding from third parties following a restructuring.

Source: IFRS 12, *Disclosure of Interests in Other Entities*

Summary

In this chapter we have reviewed the techniques of preparing consolidated or group financial statements. A core theme is the determination, and measurement of goodwill arising on consolidation, with related issues such as the bringing into the statement of financial position of intangibles such as brands which are typically missing from individual company balance sheets, the fair valuing of newly acquired assets and liabilities and the incorporation of non-controlling interests. We have noted the necessity of removing transactions within the group since these will distort performance figures and ratios and the necessity of ensuring that accounting policies are harmonized. The consolidated financial statements give a wider economic picture than separate company financial statements. The financial statements of a single subsidiary of a group are always open to distortion.

Group structures may also include associated companies, joint arrangements and financial investments without significant influence. These types of investment require a different kind of accounting treatment to subsidiaries which are under control of a group's parent company.

Discussion Questions

1. Discuss the differences of the concepts of company, business and business combination within the context of IFRS 3.
2. Does a controlling interest always imply majority ownership? Does one need to know the exact level of a ownership in a subsidiary in order to prepare consolidated financial statements?
3. In order to account for investments in other companies it is common to distinguish different degrees of ownership or influence. Describe these and explain the reasoning for the distinctions made. What are the related accounting consequences?
4. At acquisition date, the net assets of the acquired subsidiary are included in the consolidated financial statements at their acquisition date fair value. However, most of the parent's assets and liabilities are measured on an historical cost basis. Is this consistent?
5. Describe the different types of joint arrangements and their respective accounting treatment.

Assignments

The following assignments have answers on the lecturer of the digital support resources for the book.

1. Dickens Enterprises formed a new subsidiary in March 20X4, called Great Expectations (GE). At 31 December 20X4 the statements of financial position of the two companies were as shown below. During 20X4 no intra-group transactions have been recorded.

   You are asked to prepare a work sheet for the consolidated financial statements as of 31 December 20X4.

	Dickens	GE	Elimination	Group
Property, plant and equipment (net)	5 200	750		
Investment in GE	500	—		
Inventories	700	49		
Trade receivables	800	60		
Cash	1 200	25		
Total assets	8 400	884		
Share capital	3 000	500		
Retained earnings	1 900			
Profit for 20X4	700	31		
Subtotal	5600	531		
Long-term borrowings	1 000	300		
Short-term liabilities	1 800	53		
Total equity and liabilities	8 400	884		

2. Company Alpha has set up a subsidiary to deal with the distribution of its products by mail order. At 31 December 20X6 their respective statements of financial position were:

	Parent	Subsidiary
Property, plant and equipment (net)	980	340
Investment in subsidiary	180	—
Loan to subsidiary	50	—
Current assets	360	195
Total assets	1 570	535
Share capital	800	180
Retained earnings	360	—
Loan from parent	—	50
Long-term borrowings	300	250
Current liabilities	110	55
Total equity and liabilities	1 570	535

Draw up a consolidated statement of financial position at 31 December 20X6.

3. Earduster Company acquired 50 per cent of the share capital of Talebearer Company on January 20X6. These shares were acquired at the foundation of Talebearer Company.

During the first year after the acquisition there have been no transactions between Earduster and Talebearer.

The condensed statements of financial position and income statements of both companies at 31 December 20X6 are as follows (all amounts in €):

	Earduster	Talebearer
Assets		
Property, plant and equipment (net)	100 000	300 000
Investment in Talebearer	250 000	—
Other financial assets	100 000	—
Inventories	250 000	900 000
Trade receivables	900 000	400 000
Total assets	600 000	1 600 000
Share capital	000 000	500 000
Retained earnings	000 000	—
Profit for the year	400 000	60 000
Short-term debt	—	400 000
Trade payables	300 000	440 000
Other payables	900 000	200 000
Total equity and liabilities	600 000	1 600 000

	Earduster	Talebearer
Revenue	11 000 000	3 600 000
Cost of sales	–10 000 000	–3 000 000
Gross profit	*1 000 000*	*600 000*
Other operating income	1 000 000	300 000
Other operating expenses	–1 600 000	–840 000
Profit for the period	*400 000*	*60 000*

Required: Prepare the consolidated financial statements of Earduster group as at 31 December 20X6:

(a) using the full consolidation method (combined with the partial goodwill method);

(b) using the proportionate consolidation method;

(c) using the equity method.

4. On July 1, 20X5, Omega Company purchased 90 per cent of the outstanding shares of Beta Company for 1 000 000. Immediately after the acquisition, the separate statements of financial position of both companies appeared as follows:

	Omega	Beta
Property, plant and equipment (net)	1 500 000	880 000
Investment in Beta Company	1 000 000	—
Other financial assets	50 000	160 000
Inventories	900 000	520 000
Trade receivables	650 000	240 000
Cash	263 200	48 000
Total assets	4 363 200	1 848 000
Share capital	2 000 000	800 000
Retained earnings	563 200	48 000
Long-term debt	1 000 000	600 000
Current payables	800 000	400 000
Total equity and liabilities	4 363 200	1 848 000

Beta's other financial assets represent a long-term investment in Omega's long-term debt. The debt was purchased for an amount equal to Omega's carrying amount of the debt. On July 1, 20X4 Omega owes Beta 100 000 for services rendered.

Required:

(a) Prepare a consolidated statement of financial position as of the acquisition date (using the partial goodwill method).

(b) What is the effect on the consolidated statement of financial position if, on the acquisition date, the fair value of the property, plant and equipment of Beta Company were 980 000?

5. On 1 January 20X5 Invigilator Enterprises acquired 100 per cent of the shares of Lemma Company.

    The separate condensed statements of financial position immediately after the acquisition appeared as shown below (all amounts in €):

	Invigilator	Lemma
Assets		
Intangible assets	—	2 000
Property, plant and equipment (net)	490 000	80 000
Investment in Lemma	600 000	—
Inventories	230 000	360 000
Trade and other receivables	400 000	240 000
Total assets	1 720 000	682 000
Financing		
Share capital	1 000 000	200 000
Retained earnings	140 000	100 000
Provisions	20 000	30 000
Current liabilities	560 000	352 000
Total equity and liabilities	1 720 000	682 000

Additional information (at acquisition date):
(a) Lemma owns a patent for the production of a new product. Lemma did not recognize the patent in its financial statements. The estimated fair value of the patent amounts to €80 000.
(b) The fair value of Lemma's main corporate offices is €130 000 (net book value of €50 000).
(c) The fair value of Lemma's inventories amounts to €320 000.
(d) On 1 January 20X5, Invigilator Enterprises still has to pay an invoice (€100 000) for services rendered by Lemma Company in December 20X4.

Required:

(a) Prepare the consolidated statement of financial position of the Invigilator Group as at 1 January 20X5.

(b) Prepare the consolidated statement of financial position of the Invigilator Group as at 1 January 20X5, assuming that the investment in Lemma represents only 90 per cent of the outstanding shares of Lemma Company (apply the partial goodwill method).

6. On 1 July 20X4 Dabster Company acquired 100 per cent of the share capital of company Saltus.

    At the date of acquisition the balances of the equity accounts of Saltus were as follows:

Share capital	400 000
Retained earnings	300 000
Profit for the year (interim)	40 000

The condensed statements of financial position of both companies at 31 December 20X4 are as follows (all amounts in €):

	Dabster	Saltus
Assets		
Property, plant and equipment (net)	1 550 000	500 000
Investment in Saltus	800 000	—
Inventories	300 000	200 000
Trade receivables	150 000	200 000
Cash and cash equivalents	50 000	100 000
Total assets	2 850 000	1 000 000
Share capital	1 500 000	400 000
Retained earnings	500 000	300 000
Profit for the year	100 000	100 000
Current liabilities	750 000	200 000
Total equity and liabilities	2 850 000	1 000 000

Additional information:
(a) At acquisition date the fair value of Saltus' corporate offices (with a re-maining useful life of 20 years) implies a surplus value of €50 000 over the carrying amount.
(b) During the fourth quarter of 20X4 Dabster sells some of its inventory to Saltus for €125 000, which represents cost plus a mark-up of 25 per cent. Half of these goods are still in the inventory of Saltus at the end of 20X4.
(c) At 31/12/20X4, goodwill recognized on the acquisition turns out to be im-paired. An impairment loss of 10 per cent should be taken into account.

Required:
(a) Prepare the consolidated statement of financial position of Dabster Group as at 31 December 20X4.
(b) Prepare the consolidated statement of financial position of Dabster Group as at 31 December 20X4, assuming that the investment in Saltus represents 80 per cent of the outstanding shares. Apply the partial goodwill method.
(c) What would be the impact on the consolidated statement of finan-cial position if the full goodwill method is applied for the 20 per cent non-controlling interest?

7. You work in the mergers and acquisitions department of a merchant bank and have spotted what you consider to be an attractive acquisition. Northeast Foods plc is a small, listed food manufacturer based in Leeds. It has for many years sold a well-established range of tinned speciality foods. The market regards it as rather sleepy and lacking the management edge necessary to convert to modern tech-nology, bring in new products and compete generally. The company is slowly losing market share as supermarkets bring in own-label products of the kind which were Northeast's strength. The €1 ordinary shares currently trade at €5.25.
   You have also identified Wearside Products plc, a relatively young com-pany which grew rapidly as a result of the success of its tortilla chips. It has

broadened its product range but is hungry for more brands and needs to grow to be able to compete more effectively in international markets. Northeast would be a good fit for Wearside, and is reasonably cash rich.

You are about to have a meeting with the chairman of Wearside to discuss mounting a takeover. You are going to suggest that Wearside offers one of its €1 ordinary shares (market value €4.50) plus €1.50 cash for each Northeast share, giving Northeast shareholders a profit of 75cts at present prices. You are prepared to take less than 100 per cent if necessary but would regard a 60 per cent stake as the minimum acceptable.

For 60 per cent you would be willing to offer one Wearside share plus €1.20 cash.

€m	Wearside	Northeast
Non-current assets		
Intangible	200.1	—
Tangible	180.2	67.1
Investments	—	10.5
Current assets		
Inventories	37.4	20.2
Receivables	41.8	19.3
Cash	5.9	39.2
Total assets	**465.4**	**156.3**
€1 ordinary shares	68.5	24.0
Retained earnings	123.9	79.7
	192.4	*103.7*
Current liabilities	48.3	21.6
Non-current liabilities	224.7	31.0
Total equity and liabilities	**465.4**	**156.3**

(a) You are asked to draw up a post-takeover statement of financial position for the group in order to illustrate the effects of the proposed takeover, assuming that Wearside would borrow short-term to meet the cash element of the bid (and subsequently repay from Northeast's cash reserves). You should draw up alternative statements of financial position on the basis of:

  (i) no extra recognition or fair value adjustments

  (ii) recognizing a brand worth €40m;

  (iii) recognizing a brand worth €20m and fair value adjustments of tangible non-current assets worth €20m

(b) You are also asked to draw up a statement of financial position on the basis of taking only 60 per cent of the shares, without additional asset recognition, using historical cost as fair value and applying the partial goodwill method.

(*Note*: this is a fairly tough case and is designed to introduce you to the realities of mergers and acquisitions thinking.)

8. Traduct SA produces dictionaries of ancient languages (Latin, Greek, etc.).
    The company has two divisions, Uno and Duo, which constitute two sepa-
    rate cash generating units. Uno operates as a legal entity and was acquired by
    Traduct SA at the beginning of 20X4.

    Near the end of 20X4, a flooding destroys the paper inventory of Uno and
    damages its 'Machinery and Equipment'. At 31 December 20X4, the directors of
    Traduct SA decide to carry out a review for impairment of the net assets of Uno.

    The net assets of Uno immediately before the impairment review (which
    took place on 31 December 20X4) consisted of the following:

Net assets of Uno	Carrying value prior to impairment test €m
Goodwill arising on acquisition	25
Land	40
Buildings	90
Machinery and Equipment	18
Inventory – paper	10
Inventory – other	30
Net current assets (other than inventory)	65
Total	**278**

The following information is relevant to the impairment review:
- ■ Discounted cash flow calculations (budgeted future cash flows expected
  to arise from the continuation of Uno's activities) show that the value in
  use of Uno can be estimated at 228.
- ■ Uno could be sold on 31 December 20X4 for 190.
- ■ The recoverable value of the paper inventory of Uno is zero.
- ■ The recoverable value of the machinery and equipment of Uno amounts
  to two thirds of its book value.
- ■ Due to rising land prices, the market value of the land is higher than its
  book value.
- ■ The net current assets (other than inventory – paper) are stated at the
  lower of cost and fair value less costs to sell.

Required:
(a) **Compute the amount of impairment of the net assets of Uno
    arising from the impairment review.**

(b) **Allocate the impairment loss between the components of the
    net assets of Uno.**

(c) **Show the values of each of the components of the net assets
    of Uno after the necessary adjustments resulting from the im-
    pairment review.**

CHAPTER 13

Operating segments and foreign operations

This chapter looks into problems arising from multinational operations, including the issues of segment reporting and foreign currency translation. Segment reporting complements consolidated financial statements in that it disaggregates group level data into information by business line, geographical area and/or customer type. Company segments often reflect different risk and return profiles, which cannot be determined from the aggregated consolidated financial statements. In this chapter we also address the special accounting problems of working in several currencies. Up until now we have assumed that the financial statements of a group's subsidiaries were all kept in the same currency, but this is rarely the case for a multinational. The analyst does not necessarily need to be able to convert financial statements for consolidation purposes and in any event cannot break out conversion effects from published financial statements. However, conversion or translation from several currencies potentially brings in a number of distortions, of which the analyst should be aware. In addition, year-on-year comparisons are likely to be affected by value shifts in currencies in which a multinational has major operations, assets and liabilities. Often companies will bring these to the attention of the analyst.

Chapter Structure

- Introduction
- Stock exchange requirements
- Segment reporting

- Foreign currency transactions and foreign operations
- Primary translation – translating foreign currency transactions in the functional currency
- Secondary translation – translating foreign currency financial statements in a group's presentation currency
- Alternative accounting methods for secondary translation
- Functional currency and type of foreign operation
- Hedging a net investment in a foreign currency
- Summary
- Discussion questions
- Assignments

Introduction

The modern multinational corporation typically is present in many countries of the world, often operates different lines of business and trades in many currencies. While consolidated financial statements have the advantage of measuring and presenting the economic group as a whole, they also have the disadvantage of providing highly aggregated data which may be difficult to interpret when a group has several disparate types of business activity and works in several different economies. This problem is addressed by segment reporting requirements – requiring companies to disclose information by **operating segments**.

Usually a multinational will have subsidiaries in many foreign countries and will also have raised finance outside its national base. Quite often multinationals not only borrow money outside their home market, but are also listed on several stock exchanges in different parts of the world. When preparing consolidated financial statements it is obviously necessary that all items are expressed in a single **presentation currency**. Given that the values of a group's assets and liabilities may be stated in foreign currencies, and that the exchange rates between currencies are changing constantly, there is therefore a considerable accounting problem in converting (*translating*) amounts expressed in foreign currencies into the presentation currency. In addition, different stock exchanges may have different reporting rules.

Clearly, this situation is bound to pose a number of problems, both in interpreting such aggregated data and in expressing annual consolidated financial statements in a single currency. We shall look first at the problems of being listed on several stock exchanges, then at the provision of further analysis of company activities and finally at the accounting problems of converting to a single currency.

Stock exchange requirements

Multinational companies increasingly see a stock exchange listing on all major markets as a strategic issue, not necessarily connected with the company's financing. A listing gives local credibility, increases awareness of the company and its products and enables it to make takeover bids which involve share exchange rather than necessarily cash.

Over time the effect of internationalization has been to drive both markets and then companies to attempt to harmonize the kind of financial statements which they use and the information disclosures. IFRS, which we are using in this book, are accepted by most stock exchanges and are as a consequence used by many multinational companies.

However, the major exception to this harmonization still is the United States. Although the Securities and Exchange Commission (SEC) no longer requires that foreign companies reporting under IFRS and that wish to be listed on any of the US exchanges either prepare additional financial statements according to US GAAP or reconcile their IFRS financial statements (net income and shareholders' equity) to US GAAP, domestic US companies are still not allowed to use IFRS for US filing purposes. Analysts, when making international cross-sectional comparisons, need to check whether companies are using IFRS or US GAAP for their financial statements, and decide whether to use a US GAAP-based or an IFRS-based comparison.

Segment reporting

Multinational companies usually carry a group of products or business lines, operate in diverse geographical areas and serve different customer classes. They manage different operating segments and these may vary significantly in terms of rates of profitability, growth opportunities, risks and future prospects. For example, PSA Peugeot Citroën (see Company Report) is well known for its passenger cars but the company actually operates in five distinct business segments: Automotive (the passenger cars and light commercial vehicles), Automotive Equipment (vehicle interiors, automotive seating, etc.), Transportation and Logistics (goods transportation), Finance companies (retail financing to customers and wholesale financing to dealers) and Other (e.g. holding company activities). While consolidated financial statements aggregate accounting data bottom-up to present a picture of the financial position, performance and cash flows of the economic group as a whole, they tend to disguise differing risk and return profiles of group components and, thus, may be difficult to interpret when a group has several disparate types of business activity and works in several different economies. This problem is addressed by requiring companies to disclose information by operating segment.

The core principle of IFRS 8, *Operating Segments*, is that an entity should disclose information to enable users of its financial statements to evaluate the nature and financial effects of the types of business activities in which it engages and

COMPANY REPORT

PSA PEUGEOT CITROËN

Note 3 – Segment information (extracts)

■ Note 3 – Segment information

In accordance with IFRS 8—Operating Segments, segment information is presented in line with the indicators used internally by management to measure the performance of the Group's different business segments. The disclosures below are derived from the internal reporting system and have been prepared in accordance with the IFRSs adopted by the European Union. The Group's main performance indicator is recurring operating income.

3.1. Business Segments

The Group's operations are organized around five main segments:

■   The Automotive Division, covering the design, manufacture and sale of passenger cars and light commercial vehicles under the Peugeot and Citroën brands.
■   The Automotive Equipment Division, corresponding to the Faurecia group and comprising Interior Systems, Automotive Seating, Automotive Exteriors and Emissions Control Technologies.
■   The Transportation and Logistics Division, corresponding to the Gefco group comprising Logistics and Vehicle and Goods Transportation.
■   The Finance Division, corresponding to the Banque PSA Finance group, which provides retail financing to customers of the Peugeot and Citroën brands and wholesale financing to the two brands' dealer networks.
■   Other businesses, which include the activities of the holding company, Peugeot S.A. and Peugeot Motorcycles.

Balances for each segment, as shown in the table below, are on a stand-alone basis. Faurecia and Banque PSA Finance publish consolidated financial statements and segment information for these two businesses is therefore presented down to the level of net profit. For the other segments, as cash positions and taxes are managed jointly in some countries, only operating income and share in net earnings of companies at equity are presented by segment. All intersegment balance sheet items and transactions are eliminated and, for the purposes of reconciliation with the Group's financial statements, are shown under the heading 'Eliminations and reconciliations' together with unallocated amounts.

All intersegment commercial transactions are carried out on an arm's length basis on the same terms and conditions as those applicable to the supply of goods and services to third parties.

3.2 Geographical segments

In the table below, sales and revenue are presented by destination of products sold, and investments and assets by geographic location of the subsidiary concerned.

In accordance with IFRS 8, the Group's geographical segment analysis presents all non-current assets other than financial instruments, deferred tax assets and external pension plan assets.

2010 (in million euros)	Western Europe	Central & Eastern Europe	Latin America	Rest of the World	Total
Sales and revenue	40 775	4 067	4 770	6 449	56 061
Non-current assets (excl. deferred tax assets and financial instruments)·	16 237	1 024	1 141	604	19 006

Source: PSA Peugeot Citroën, Financial Statements, 2010

the economic environments in which it operates. Information about the different types of products and services provided, possibly in combination with different geographical areas in which it operates and/or different customer types, should help users of financial statements better assess the company's risks and returns and make more informed judgements about the company as a whole.

A disaggregation of financial statement data by lines of operations can indeed provide significant information on different risk and return profiles, not determinable from the aggregated consolidated financial statements. For example, segment data could reveal that the larger part of net income is earned by a small high performing product group, that only one out of three business lines is profitable and thus subsidizes the other two, or that important geographical areas have not yet been penetrated, hinting at continued growth opportunities.

Operating segments

Disaggregation of consolidated financial statements into operating segments should follow the way that management segments the company to make operating decisions. IFRS 8, *Operating Segments,* requires operating segments to be identified on the basis of internal reports about components of the company that are regularly reviewed by the chief operating decision maker (CEO, Chief Operating Officer or a group of executive officers) in order to allocate resources to the segment and to assess its performance. Disaggregated performance appraisal (implying the existence of segment revenues, expenses and assets) drives the identification of operating segments. Although segmentation would usually be organized by business or product lines, management can also organize it by geographical area, by customer type, by legal entity, or on another basis. For example, internal management reporting may be structured solely by legal entity,

2010 (*in million euros*)	Automotive	Automotive equipment	Transportation & logistics	Finance companies	Other	Eliminations & reconciliations	Total
Sales and revenue							
— third parties	41 386	11 760	1217	1559	139	—	56 061
— intragroup, intersegment	19	2036	2134	293	79	(4561)	—
Total	41 405	13 796	3351	1852	218	(4561)	56 061
Recurring operating income	621	456	198	507	11	3	1796
Non-recurring operating income	249	87	13	27	—	—	376
Restructuring costs	(77)	(117)	(1)	—	(1)	—	(196)
Impairment losses on CGUs	(230)	—	—	—	(4)	—	(234)
Other non-recurring operating income and (expenses), net	—	(6)	—	—	—	—	(6)
Operating income	563	420	210	534	6	3	1736
Interest income	8	8		—		78	86
Finance costs	(99)	(99)		—		(356)	(455)
Other financial income	5	5		1		223	229
Other financial expenses	(31)	(31)		(3)		(255)	(289)
Net financial expense	(117)	(117)	—	(2)	—	(310)	(429)
Income taxes	(90)	(90)		(140)		(25)	(255)
Share in net earnings of companies at equity	184	19	—	2	(1)	—	204
Consolidated profit for the year	232	232		394			1256
Capital expenditure (excl. sales with a buyback commitment)	2375	460	26	24	4		2889
Depreciation and amortization	(2482)	(496)	(49)	(16)	—		(3043)

NESTLE GROUP

Operating segment displays (extracts)

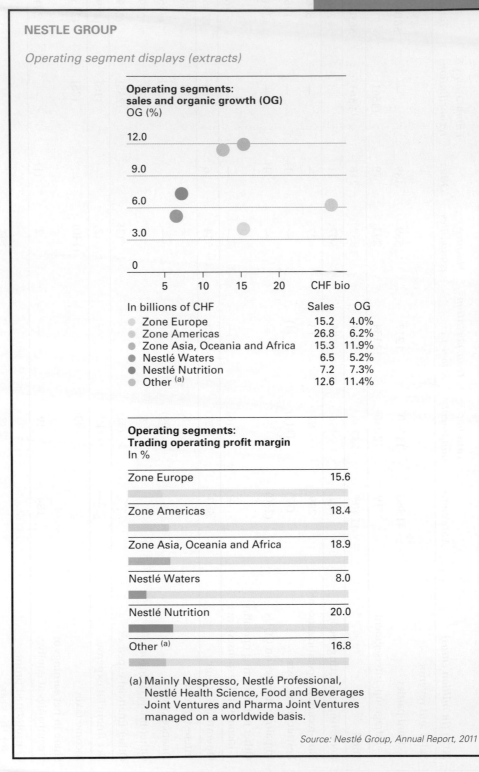

**Operating segments:
sales and organic growth (OG)**
OG (%)

In billions of CHF	Sales	OG
Zone Europe	15.2	4.0%
Zone Americas	26.8	6.2%
Zone Asia, Oceania and Africa	15.3	11.9%
Nestlé Waters	6.5	5.2%
Nestlé Nutrition	7.2	7.3%
Other [a]	12.6	11.4%

**Operating segments:
Trading operating profit margin**
In %

Zone Europe	15.6
Zone Americas	18.4
Zone Asia, Oceania and Africa	18.9
Nestlé Waters	8.0
Nestlé Nutrition	20.0
Other [a]	16.8

(a) Mainly Nespresso, Nestlé Professional,
    Nestlé Health Science, Food and Beverages
    Joint Ventures and Pharma Joint Ventures
    managed on a worldwide basis.

Source: Nestlé Group, Annual Report, 2011

resulting in internal segments composed of groups of unrelated products and services. The Nestlé Group (see Company report) applies a combination of a geographic and a product perspective, through three geographic zones and several globally managed businesses. Nestlé's reportable operating segments are: Zone Europe, Zone Americas, Zone Asia, Oceania and Africa, Nestlé Waters, Nestlé Nutrition, Other (mainly Nespresso, Nestlé Professional, Nestlé Health Science, Food and Beverages Joint Ventures and Pharma Joint Ventures managed on a worldwide basis). As some operating segments represent geographic zones, information by product (powdered and liquid beverages, water, milk products and ice cream, nutrition and health care, prepared dishes and cooking aids, confectionery, petcare) is also disclosed.

The management approach to identify operating segments has the advantage that it builds on the company's internal organization, highlighting the risks and opportunities that management believes are important. The internal reporting focus probably enhances a user's ability to predict actions or reactions of management that can significantly affect the company's prospects.

Operating segments can be vertically integrated (think of, for example, highly integrated international oil companies). According to IFRS 8, operating segments are not limited to those that earn (a majority of) their revenue from external customers. An operating segment can be a component of a company that sells primarily or even exclusively to other segments of the company. Different stages of vertically integrated operations can become separate reporting segments if the company is managed that way.

Not all operations of a company will necessarily be part of an operating segment. For example, the corporate headquarters or some functional departments may not earn revenues or they may earn revenues that are only incidental to the activities of the company. These would not be operating segments.

STANDARDS

IFRS 8 – OPERATING SEGMENTS *(extracts)*

5. An operating segment is a component of an entity:
   (a) that engages in business activities from which it may earn revenues and incur expenses (including revenues and expenses relating to transactions with other components of the same entity);
   (b) whose operating results are regularly reviewed by the entity's chief operating decision maker to make decisions about resources to be allocated to the segments and assess its performance; and
   (c) for which discrete financial information is available.

An operating segment may engage in business activities for which it has yet to earn revenues, for example, start-up operations may be operating segments before earning revenues.

Source: IFRS 8, Operating Segments

Reportable segments

Not all operating segments have to be reported, however. To be reportable, an operating segment must be significant; that is, it must meet at least one of the following quantitative thresholds (IFRS 8, par.13):

■ its reported revenue, from both external customers and inter-segment sales or transfers, is 10 per cent or more of the combined revenue, internal and external, of all operating segments;

■ the absolute measure of its reported profit or loss is 10 per cent or more of the greater, in absolute amount, of (i) the combined reported profit of all operating segments that did not report a loss and (ii) the combined reported loss of all operating segments that reported a loss;

■ its assets are 10 per cent or more of the combined assets of all operating segments.

If the total external revenue reported by operating segments constitutes less than 75 per cent of the company's revenue, additional operating segments must be identified as **reportable segments** (even if they do not meet the quantitative thresholds set out above) (IFRS 8, par.15). Two or more operating segments may be aggregated into a single operating segment if the segments have similar economic characteristics and are similar in respect of nature of products and services, nature of production and distribution processes, type or class of customer, and (if applicable) nature of regulatory environment, for example, banking, insurance or public utilities (IFRS 8, par.12).

IFRS 8 grants companies a lot of discretion in determining operating segments, limited only by internal reporting practices. This discretion entails, however, the need to explain to the public how and why reportable segments are identified as they are. In this vein, the company has to disclose the factors driving the segmentation, including the basis of organization (for example, whether management has chosen to organize the entity around differences in products and services, geographical areas, regulatory environments or a combination of factors). Moreover, for each reportable segment, the company has to indicate the types of products and services from which it derives its revenue (IFRS 8, par. 22).

Segment information content

Complete segment financial statements are not required, but for each reportable segment, information must be provided on segment revenue, segment profit or loss, segment assets and other related segment information, such as a split between external and internal revenue, depreciation and amortization, liabilities, etc. if such information is regularly provided to the chief operating officer.

IFRS 8 does, however, not define the segment information items (revenues, expenses, result, assets, liabilities), nor does it require that accounting policies to be used for segment reporting are necessarily the same as those applied in the consolidated financial statements. In the end, internal reporting procedures will determine the measurement basis of segment information. In this vein, segment reporting rules and practices (with regard to both definition/recognition and measurement) may be highly entity-specific, and, thus, jeopardize the usefulness of segment information for cross-sectional (inter-company) analysis. In the case of PSA Peugeot Citroën (see Company Report) 'recurring operating income' is the main performance indicator to assess segment performance. For each of the segments the following information is available: revenue (external and internal), operating income, non-recurring operating items, capital expenditure, depreciation and amortization. There is however no information on segment assets and segment liabilities. Segment assets and liabilities are only required if they are regularly provided to the chief operating decision maker, but are useful for comparative segment ratio analysis (see Chapter 17). The Nestlé Group uses a performance metric labelled 'trading operating profit', that is after restructuring costs, impairment of all assets except goodwill, litigations and onerous contracts, result on disposal of property, plant and equipment and specific other income and expenses that fall within the control of operating segments. Nestlé does provide segment assets information.

Although the format of segment reporting is entity-specific, in the end the segment financials have to add up into the consolidated financial statements. That's why the company has to provide reconciliations of the total of the reportable segments' revenues, measures of profit or loss, assets and liabilities (if applicable) to the corresponding group level figures in the consolidated financial statements.

Finally, IFRS 8 requires companies to present analyses of revenues from external customers and certain non-current assets by geographical area and even to disclose revenues/assets by individual foreign country (if material), irrespective of the identification of operating segments. In addition, information about the

STANDARDS

IFRS 8 – OPERATING SEGMENTS (extracts)

Information about profit or loss, assets and liabilities

23. An entity shall report a measure of profit or loss for each reportable segment. An entity shall report a measure of total assets and liabilities for each reportable segment if such amounts are regularly provided to the chief operating decision maker. An entity shall also disclose the following about each reportable segment if the specified amounts are included in the measure of segment profit or loss reviewed by the chief operating decision maker, or are otherwise regularly provided to the chief operating decision maker, even if not included in that measure of segment profit or loss:

(a) revenues from external customers;
(b) revenues from transactions with other operating segments of the same entity;
(c) interest revenue;
(d) interest expense;
(e) depreciation and amortization;
(f) material items of income and expense disclosed in accordance with paragraph 97 of IAS 1 Presentation of Financial Statements (as revised in 2007);
(g) the entity's interest in the profit or loss of associates and joint ventures accounted for by the equity method;
(h) income tax expense or income; and
(i) material non-cash items other than depreciation and amortization.

> An entity shall report interest revenue separately from interest expense for each reportable segment unless a majority of the segment's revenues are from interest and the chief operating decision maker relies primarily on net interest revenue to assess the performance of the segment and make decisions about resources to be allocated to the segment. In that situation, an entity may report that segment's interest revenue net of its interest expense and disclose that it has done so.
>
> *Source:* IFRS 8, *Operating Segments*

external revenues for each product and service and about the extent of the company's reliance on its major customers, has to be disclosed.

In practice, segment disclosures tend to vary considerably from company to company. Note that national accounting rules are usually much less exigent on segment disclosures than IFRS or US GAAP. Even the Seventh EC Company Law Directive only calls for disclosure of sales by product and geographical area, but many companies used to go beyond that. However, it is one of the obstacles to clear analysis of the financial statements of multinational companies.

When analyzing the financial statements of multinational companies it is well worth trying to assemble as long as possible a time series of segment data to work out growth trends by business. This will then provide a picture of which businesses are expanding, which contracting and so on.

Analysts would like more segment data. They complain that it is very difficult to forecast future profits of companies if they do not know the relative profitability of different product lines, and are unable to judge what proportion of sales is generated by each. Companies on the other hand do not like giving too much detailed analysis because they feel it gives away competitive advantage, and some argue that analysts do not understand the artificiality which can be induced by segment analysis. Where a company trades across the world, there are many transactions between subsidiaries, and these take place at relatively artificial prices which are fixed by the company.

For example, if a new product is developed in the French parent company, but the product is manufactured in South Africa, does the African subsidiary pay a royalty on the development cost to the French parent? How do you allocate worldwide advertising costs? If you have several different product lines, how do you allocate all

STANDARDS

IFRS 8 – OPERATING SEGMENTS *(extracts)*

Information about products and services

32. An entity shall report the revenues from external customers for each product and service, or each group of similar products and services, unless the necessary information is not available and the cost to develop it would be excessive, in which case that fact shall be disclosed. The amounts of revenues reported shall be based on the financial information used to produce the entity's financial statements.

Information about geographical areas

33. An entity shall report the following geographical information, unless the necessary information is not available and the cost to develop it would be excessive:

(a) revenues from external customers (i) attributed to the entity's country of domicile and (ii) attributed to all foreign countries in total from which the entity derives revenues. If revenues from external customers attributed to an individual foreign country are material, those revenues shall be disclosed separately. An entity shall disclose the basis for attributing revenues from external customers to individual countries.

(b) non-current assets other than financial instruments, deferred tax assets, post-employment benefit assets, and rights arising under insurance contracts (i) located in the entity's country of domicile and (ii) located in all foreign countries in total in which the entity holds assets. If assets in an individual foreign country are material, those assets shall be disclosed separately.

The amounts reported shall be based on the financial information that is used to produce the entity's financial statements. If the necessary information is not available and the cost to develop it would be excessive, that fact shall be disclosed. An entity may provide, in addition to the information required by this paragraph, subtotals of geographical information about groups of countries.

Information about major customers

34. An entity shall provide information about the extent of its reliance on its major customers. If revenues from transactions with a single external customer amount to 10 per cent or more of an entity's revenues, the entity shall disclose that fact, the total amount of revenues from each such customer, and the identity of the segment or segments reporting the revenues. The entity need not disclose the identity of a major customer or the amount of revenues that each segment reports from that customer. For the purposes of this IFRS, a group of entities known to a reporting entity to be under common control shall be considered a single customer. However, judgement is required to assess whether a government (including government agencies and similar bodies whether local, national or international) and entities known to the reporting entity to be under the control of that government are considered a single customer. In assessing this, the reporting entity shall consider the extent of economic integration between those entities.

Source: IFRS 8, *Operating Segments*

the costs of running the head office, including preparation of group financial statements, stock exchange listing costs, investor relations, etc.? There are many factors that impinge upon these decisions, including tax, and the resulting allocations of cost are not necessarily economically meaningful (see Chapter 15 on taxation).

Analysts should look closely at the segment data provided by a company, but remember that allocations distort the overall picture and that no two groups necessarily make their allocations in the same way. Segment data are probably more useful for time series analysis than cross-sectional.

Foreign currency transactions and foreign operations

Any group that operates in different countries is likely to operate in several different currencies. Indeed it may be that most of a group's subsidiaries operate in currencies other than those of its parent (e.g. how many of Nestlé's subsidiaries operate using the Swiss franc?). This of course means that there is a foreign currency conversion question to be resolved when preparing consolidated financial statements.

It is worth considering the behaviour of exchange rates briefly in order to understand the environment within which the accounting decisions have to be made. In the early part of the 20th century, exchange rates were relatively stable and governments attempted to reinforce this stability by promoting 'fixed parities' between currencies or against the price of gold. Later, economic pressures, particularly inflation, made it very difficult to maintain such fixed exchange rates. One solution was to go for 'pegged' rates, where currencies were allowed to move within a narrow tolerance, but this too proved impossible in the economic conditions of the 1960s and 1970s.

Today we have a situation where most currencies are allowed to 'float'; that is, they have no fixed exchange rate and can change rapidly from one day to another. This creates a number of severe financial management problems, as well as accounting problems, and these are not the least of the reasons for the introduction of the euro. As we will show in this chapter, having to deal in many currencies introduces very many measurement problems into accounting, quite apart from uncertainties in decision-making because values are not stable.

For example, a German company buys an asset in the UK. The asset can be bought for £10 000 one day when £1 = €1.75, and can be stated at €17 500 in the German accounts, but next day the rate might move to £1 = €1.60. Is the asset then worth €16 000 and if the rate goes to £1 = €1.80 the day after, do you change the asset once more to €18 000? Rates do not normally move quite as dramatically as in the example, but they do move quickly and the movements are not necessarily consistently in one direction. A sharp drop in value one day does not mean that next day or two years later the value will not gain.

Our purpose in addressing these questions is to consider their impact on the financial statements of public companies. This impact can be seen in two different areas:

1. translation of **foreign currency transactions** and related individual assets and liabilities which are denominated other than in the own reporting currency;

2. translation of the financial statements of foreign subsidiaries for inclusion in consolidated financial statements.

IFRS cover these topics in IAS 21, *The Effects of Changes in Foreign Exchange Rates*. We will address the questions above with this standard as our reference, except when noted otherwise.

Primary and secondary translation

When a multinational group, as a reporting entity, prepares consolidated financial statements, each individual entity included in the reporting entity first has to determine its specific measurement currency (the **functional currency**) and measure its results and financial position in that currency. The functional currency is not necessarily the local currency of the individual entity's country of residence, but in most cases it is. A multinational group will probably comprise individual entities with a number of functional currencies and, thus, will have to consolidate a number of individual financial statements in different reporting currencies.

If an individual entity within the group entered into foreign currency transactions (i.e. transactions that are denominated or require settlement in a currency other than the functional currency of the entity), the foreign currency items first have to be translated into its functional currency. This is the *primary translation* process (i.e. translation of transactions).

Once the individual entities within a reporting entity (the multinational group made up of a parent and one or more foreign subsidiaries and investments in associated companies) have prepared their financial statements in their functional currency, these have to be translated into the currency in which the reporting entity presents its consolidated financial statements. If the functional currency of the individual entity is not equal to the presentation currency of the group, a *secondary translation* process (i.e. translation of financial statements) has to be carried out. The sequence of the currency translation processes and their relationship with the consolidated financial statements is presented in Figure 13.1.

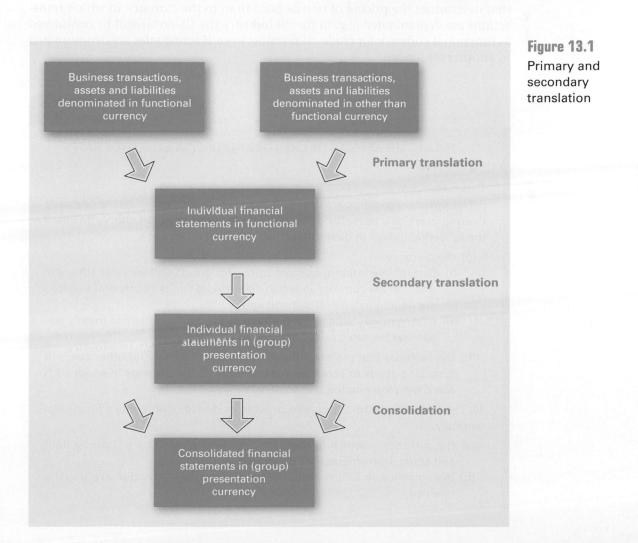

Figure 13.1
Primary and secondary translation

In most cases, the functional currency of the parent will be chosen as the presentation currency of the group financial statements, but this is not a general requirement.

Functional currency

The functional currency concept is central in the translation requirements. Functional currency is defined as 'the currency of the primary economic environment in which the entity operates' (IAS 21, par.8). The primary economic environment in which an entity operates is normally the one in which it primarily generates and expends cash. The functional currency is determined separately for each individual entity within a group. There is no such thing as a 'group functional currency'.

IAS 21 provides specific guidance on how to determine a functional currency (see IAS 21 extracts). It comments on the factors that an entity must consider in determining its functional currency.

It should be clear that determining the functional currency is not a free choice and sometimes will ask for professional judgement when evaluating the relevant indicators. In general, greater emphasis is given to the currency of the economy that determines the pricing of transactions than to the currency in which transactions are denominated (e.g. in the oil industry the US dollar will be considered as functional currency for crude oil revenue, even if actual sales are denominated in another currency).

STANDARDS

IAS 21 – THE EFFECTS OF CHANGES IN FOREIGN EXCHANGE RATES
(extracts)

Functional currency

9. The primary economic environment in which an entity operates is normally the one in which it primarily generates and expends cash. An entity considers the following factors in determining its functional currency:

  (a) the currency:
    (i) that mainly influences sales prices for goods and services (this will often be the currency in which sales prices for its goods and services are denominated and settled); and
    (ii) of the country whose competitive forces and regulations mainly determine the sales prices of its goods and services.
  (b) the currency that mainly influences labour, material and other costs of providing goods or services (this will often be the currency in which such costs are denominated and settled).

10. The following factors may also provide evidence of an entity's functional currency:

  (a) the currency in which funds from financing activities (i.e. issuing debt and equity instruments) are generated.
  (b) the currency in which receipts from operating activities are usually retained.

11. The following additional factors are considered in determining the functional currency of a foreign operation, and whether its functional currency is the same as that of the reporting entity (the reporting entity, in this context, being the entity that has the foreign operation as its subsidiary, branch, associate or joint venture):

(a) Whether the activities of the foreign operation are carried out as an extension of the reporting entity, rather than being carried out with a significant degree of autonomy. An example of the former is when the foreign operation only sells goods imported from the reporting entity and remits the proceeds to it. An example of the latter is when the operation accumulates cash and other monetary items, incurs expenses, generates income and arranges borrowings, all substantially in its local currency.

(b) whether transactions with the reporting entity are a high or a low proportion of the foreign operation's activities.

(c) whether cash flows from the activities of the foreign operation directly affect the cash flows of the reporting entity and are readily available for remittance to it.

(d) whether cash flows from the activities of the foreign operation are sufficient to service existing and normally expected debt obligations without funds being made available by the reporting entity.

Source: IAS 21, *The Effects of Changes in Foreign Exchange Rates*

If the individual entity is a foreign operation, additional indicators have to be considered when determining the functional currency of that entity. A *foreign operation* is defined as 'a subsidiary, associate, joint venture or branch of a reporting entity, the activities of which are based or conducted in a country or currency other than those of the reporting entity' (IAS 21, par.8).

Primary translation – translating foreign currency transactions in the functional currency

A foreign currency transaction is simply a business transaction that is denominated or requires settlement in a foreign currency. Examples include a German company buying or selling goods and services on credit for a price expressed in US dollars, or a Norwegian company taking out a bank loan denominated in euro. On initial recognition of the foreign currency transaction, the transaction will be recorded in the functional currency by applying the **spot exchange rate** at the date of transaction, i.e. multiplying the foreign currency amount by the spot exchange rate between the functional currency and the foreign currency at the date of the transaction. But what happens next at subsequent reporting dates?

The most important single category here is borrowing in foreign currencies – loans may be negotiated for a period of several years and need to be restated in several statements of financial position between initial receipt and final repayment. For example, suppose a UK company borrowed $5m on the eurodollar market for five years, and the current value of the liability moved as shown in Table 13.1. The accounting question that arises is: what value should be given to

Table 13.1

Movements in value

Reporting date	Exchange rate £=	Sterling equivalent
01.01.X1	$1.60	3.125m
31.12.X1	$1.55	3.226m
31.12.X2	$1.40	3.571m
31.12.X3	$1.25	4.000m
31.12.X4	$1.30	3.846m
31.12.X5	$1.40	3.571m

the loan liability in the interim statement of financial position between receiving the loan (1.1.X1) and repaying it (31.12.X5)? In this transaction the company has to repay more than it borrowed and the difference will also need to be recognized as a loss at some point. How and when should the loss be recognized?

In terms of providing useful information for shareholders, the only really useful information is the final repayment value and the total loss over the loan period. However, this information is only available at the end of the period. Should the **exchange differences** be recognized only at that point?

Potentially there could be a number of responses to the question, but IAS 21 takes the view that such items should be translated at the current rate on each reporting date (the **closing rate**) and the resultant difference be taken to the statement of profit or loss. The rationale for this is that the current rate provides the best available (if poor) approximation of the future repayment date and represents the best available information. In fact, accounting for foreign currency transactions according to IAS 21 depends on the type of asset acquired or liability incurred. More specifically, the treatment of foreign currency items depends on whether the item is monetary or non-monetary. *Monetary items* are 'units of currency held and assets and liabilities to be received or paid in a fixed or determinable number of units of currency' (IAS 21, par.8). **Monetary items** such as cash, accounts receivable and loans outstanding derive their value from the number of monetary units into which they are convertible. *Non-monetary items*, such as inventory, equipment, land, buildings and cars, derive their value primarily from supply and demand. In our example, the UK company incurred a monetary liability and will show it in the financial statements at its sterling equivalent using the exchange rate in effect at the reporting date (date of the statement of financial position). Monetary assets (like accounts receivable) are similarly translated using the exchange rate in effect at reporting date. Foreign currency non-monetary assets (and liabilities) are translated using the historical rate of exchange that was in effect at the time the item was acquired or incurred.

A particularly interesting aspect of IAS 21 is that the standard requires that exchange differences arising on translating monetary items at rates different from those at which they were translated on initial recognition during the period, or in previous statements of financial position. shall be recognized in the statement of profit or loss of the period in which they arise, irrespective of whether it is a loss or a gain. Such gains are unrealized until the monetary item is settled (in our example until the loan is repaid), and this recognition of them in profit or loss is one of the few cases where an unrealized gain is taken to the income statement.

(Note that in the rather exceptional case that non-monetary items are measured at fair value in a foreign currency (for example in application of IAS 41, *Investment Property*), these should be translated using the exchange rates at the date when the fair value was determined. Exchange differences resulting from revaluation of non-monetary items carried at fair value will be recognized directly in equity or in profit or loss according to the treatment of the original fair value adjustments.)

Hedging foreign currency transactions

By way of background information in this area, we should also mention other aspects of dealing in foreign currencies which affect profit measurement but which are less immediately germane to an understanding of corporate reports.

One of the ways in which companies minimize the risk of changes in exchange rates causing losses is to take out 'hedges' against individual transactions. For example, where a UK company wants to buy (say) a French machine tool for €10000 and places the order at a time when the exchange rate is £1 = €1 for delivery in six months' time, there is a risk that the rate could move to (say) £1 = €0.8 by the time delivery takes place, with the result that the expected sterling cost rises from £10000 to £12500. The company can avoid the risk by buying euro in advance (*buying forward*) and so fixing the rate actually paid. This sort of technique is known as *hedging*. When such a transaction takes place, the asset would be recognized in the buyer's books at the exchange rate built into the forward contract, not at the rate ruling when the asset was delivered.

In the absence of a hedge, individual transactions are translated at the rate ruling when the transaction took place. Suppose the French machine was delivered on 30 June, when the rate was £1 = €0.8, but three months' credit was allowed. Settlement was made on 30 September when the rate was £1 = €0.85. The accounting transactions would be:

1. Recognize asset 30 June at £12500 and create creditor.
2. Settle creditor 30 September at £11765 and recognize in profit or loss an exchange gain in of £735.

If hedged by a forward exchange contract, the value of the asset would be adjusted for the fair value of the forward contract on delivery date (a value that approximates the difference on the contract amount between the spot exchange rate on 30 June and the forward rate).

COMPANY REPORT

ANGLOGOLD ASHANTI – TRANSACTIONS AND BALANCES IN FOREIGN CURRENCY

Foreign currency transactions are translated into the functional currency using the approximate exchange rates prevailing at the dates of the transactions. Foreign exchange gains and losses resulting from the settlement of foreign currency transactions and from the translation at the year-end exchange rate of monetary assets and liabilities denominated in foreign currencies are recognised in the statement of profit or loss, except for hedging derivative balances that are within the scope of IAS 39. Translation differences on these balances are reported as part of their fair value gain or loss.

Translation differences on non–monetary items, such as equities classified as available-for-sale financial assets, are included in other comprehensive income within equity.

Source: Extract from 'Summary of significant accounting policies', AngloGold Ashanti,

Notes to the Financial Statements, 2010

Secondary translation – translating foreign currency financial statements in a group's presentation currency

The need for secondary translation arises when a multinational group has to consolidate the financial statements of individual entities with different functional currencies. The financial position and results of each individual entity within the group have to be expressed in a common currency (presumably the functional currency of the parent company) so that consolidated financial statements can be presented in the group's presentation currency.

Types of foreign operations

IFRS 10, *Consolidated Financial Statements*, defines consolidated financial statements as the financial statements of a group presented as those of a single economic entity. In other words, we remove the separate legal status of each individual entity in the group and treat them as one company. One implication which we might draw from that is that we should treat all the transactions of the foreign subsidiary as though they had been carried out by the parent company. That would indeed be treating the group as a single entity. If we did that, we should then look at the individual assets and liabilities of the subsidiary as though they were part of the parent and, logically, we should use the exchange rate for each which we would have used if the transactions involved had been carried out directly by the parent. The approach would be something like that shown in Table 13.2.

This arrangement seems quite logical – it treats every element as though the transaction had been carried out by the parent and converted into parent company currency as though the parent had bought foreign currency to meet each

Table 13.2

Consolidation exchange rates

Balance sheet item	Rate
Assets	
Property, plant and equipment	Rate at time of acquisition
Receivables	Closing rate at reporting date (best estimate of likely proceeds)
Inventory	Rate at time of acquisition
Cash	Closing rate at reporting date
Financing	
Equity	
Share capital	Rate at time of subscription
Retained earnings	Rate ruling at successive reporting dates when each slice of retained earnings was added to the statement of financial position
Liabilities	
Equity	
Trade and other payables	Closing rate at reporting date (best estimate of likely payments)
Long-term borrowings	Closing rate at reporting date

transaction. Of course it means that, since different rates are used for different elements of the statement of financial position, this statement will not balance. A new item, *translation difference*, has to be added. That in itself poses a further problem: is the translation difference (gain or loss) something which should flow through the consolidated statement of profit or loss? If the result is a gain, this must be an unrealized gain because the parent still owns the subsidiary and prudence requires that this should not be recognized in the statement of profit or loss. Against that, unrealized gains on long-term liabilities are recognized.

Then again, is this translation adjustment truly a gain or loss? In so far as rates of exchange may fluctuate both up and down, there is no real reason to suppose (on first principles) that the translation difference may not be purely temporary, an accident caused by the timing of the statement of financial position. For example, if the rate of exchange at reporting date is £1 = €1.60 and the next week £1 = €1.70, how valid would it be to recognize a gain or a loss as at reporting date, when the position has already changed at the time the statements are being prepared? If the gain or loss is temporary, then is it useful to include it in the statement of profit or loss? You can see that there are some close analogies here with inflation accounting; both issues pose questions of valuation of assets and liabilities, and whether or not changes in value should be recognized in the statement of financial position and in the statement of profit or loss.

The other question which we must pursue is whether the agreeably logical solution of translating the statement of financial position of the foreign subsidiary as though the assets and liabilities had been acquired directly by the parent provides useful information for investment decisions and for users generally. For example, is it an entirely accurate view of the economic relations between a subsidiary and parent that the transactions of the subsidiary are seen as relating only to the parent and not having their economic basis in the activities of the subsidiary itself?

The answer to that question must depend to a large degree on the facts in any particular case. For example, if a British manufacturing company sets up a Spanish subsidiary whose sole purpose is the marketing of the finished goods manufactured in Britain, there is a strong case for treating the Spanish subsidiary as nothing other than part of the parent's distribution costs. The separate legal status can be seen merely as a convenience, and the entity has no independent existence outside its marketing function. Translation of its statement of financial position (consisting perhaps of a warehouse, inventory of finished goods and receivables, with its main creditor being the UK manufacturing company), as though the transactions were those of the parent, would probably reflect the economic substance.

However, what if the Spanish subsidiary were a rather more complex business which manufactured its own finished goods (under the group brand name perhaps), sold these independently throughout the world (perhaps using other group subsidiaries in countries where these existed) and also sold products manufactured in other countries by other members of the group (a structure used by Philips, for example)? What if, as is often the case, there were local Spanish minority shareholders in the company and if, in order to finance its operations, the Spanish company also borrowed on the local capital market? The situation here is rather more complex, since the Spanish subsidiary is arguably a complete and independent trading entity in its own right and to account for its transactions as though they were carried out by the parent is a denial of that. It would not reflect the economic reality of the situation.

Looking at the mechanics of translation, we can argue a case that the assets and liabilities of the complex subsidiary have an economic relationship with each other, rather than with those of the parent. For example, the inventory does not derive from external manufacturing operations; the manufacturing plant is not an extension of an operation by the parent; the long-term loans borrowed on the Spanish market relate to the Spanish operation and its assets, not to the parent's global financing needs. If we translate the assets at the rate ruling when they were acquired, but the long-term liabilities at the closing rate ruling on reporting date, we are using different rates to translate two items whose economic existence is interdependent. We are arguably distorting the economic relationships and therefore it is questionable whether such an approach does give some approximation of the economic relationship. There seems a good reason here for using the same rate for both assets and liabilities to preserve their interrelationship.

In practical terms, the 'independent' subsidiary could be recognized as a set of interrelated assets and liabilities which were translated for consolidation purposes at the closing rate ruling at the reporting date when consolidation is taking place. In other words, the value used would merely represent a mathematical conversion from one currency to another to enable the group financial statements to be stated in a single currency.

Critics point out, though, that there is a major conceptual flaw in this approach: by consolidating the subsidiary using the current exchange rate, one is importing current values into historical cost accounts and this represents some form of hidden revaluation. According to Purchasing Power Parity theory, exchange rates move in response to inflation, and the use of current rates for fixed assets would mean that an inflation adjustment was automatically being built into the group financial statements. This is not acceptable within the context of pure historical cost, but also it would be inconsistent to revalue some assets and not others; revaluation should be worked out systematically and not on the haphazard basis of currency and differential inflation. The correct rate must be the historical rate.

To illustrate the effect of this, suppose that a German subsidiary of a UK parent bought plant for €300000 on 1.1.20X1 when £1 = €1.5; at that point the asset, if translated, would be worth £200000. During 20X1 inflation is 10 per cent in the UK and 5 per cent in Germany. According to Purchasing Power Parity theory the exchange rate at the end of the year should be £1 × 1.1 = €1.5 × 1.05, or £1 = €1.43. If the asset were translated at the current rate at the year end, it would appear in the group financial statements as £209790.

Alternative accounting methods for secondary translation

Over the years regulatory regimes converged towards a motivated choice of two methods, based largely upon the rationale we have considered above. Typically, two methods are allowed, depending upon the actual conditions under which the foreign subsidiary operates. The method which takes the subsidiary as an extension of the parent is known as the *temporal method*, while that which takes the subsidiary as a whole is known as the *net investment method* (also the *current or closing rate method*). These methods figure in the European Accounting Directives, US GAAP and, historically, in IFRS (although somewhat amended in the 2005 revision of IAS 21).

In order to demonstrate the implications of the choice of method on the picture presented in the group financial statements, we shall now translate the financial statements of a foreign subsidiary using each of these methods.

Temporal method

The temporal method is based on the assumption that the best way of translating the statement of financial position and income statement of a foreign subsidiary is by treating the transactions as though they were carried out by the parent, and thus using rates which relate to the time when the transaction took place (hence 'temporal'). Assets which are carried in the books at historical values are translated at the rate ruling when the asset was acquired, while assets having a current or nominal value (i.e. receivables, cash) are translated at the current rate. The broad lines used are shown in Table 13.3.

Table 13.3

Exchange rates – temporal method

Financial position component	Exchange rate
Non-current assets	
Property, plant and equipment	Historical
Acc. depreciation	Historical
Current assets	
Inventory	Historical
Monetary assets	Current
Liabilities	
Current liabilities	Current
Non-current liabilities	Current
Equity	
Share capital	Historical
Retained earnings	Historical/Average

Current monetary assets will be received after the reporting date, while current liabilities and long-term liabilities will be payable after the reporting date, so all are stated at the closing or current rate as being the best approximation. Other assets are translated at the historical rate which obtained at the time of acquisition. Revenue and expenses are translated at the exchange rates prevailing when the underlying transactions took place. However, in practice the average rate will be used, except for the inventory component of cost of sales and depreciation cost which are translated at historical rates to keep the link with the statement of financial position intact.

Worked example

The European Trading Co. plc invests CHF3m in a Swiss subsidiary. The subsidiary borrows a further CHF2m locally and buys a factory for CHF5m. At the time the subsidiary was set up (1 January 20X1) the exchange rate was £1 = CHF4.00, so the European Trading Co. plc invested £750000 in the share capital of its new subsidiary. During 20X1 the Swiss company traded successfully and achieved profits of CHF500000. The exchange rate had been slipping against the pound during the year and at the end of the year had reached £1 = CHF3.00. The average rate during the year was £1 = CHF3.50. The statements of financial position of the Swiss subsidiary (as expressed in local currency) are shown below.

	1 Jan 20X1 CHF' 000	31 Dec 20X1 CHF'000
Property, plant and equipment	5 000	5 000
less Acc. depreciation	—	–250
Net current assets		
Inventory	—	500
Monetary assets	—	750
Current liabilities	—	–500
		750
	5 000	5 500
Long-term liabilities	–2 000	–2 000
Total net assets	3 000	3 500
Financed by equity		
Share capital	3 000	3 000
Retained earnings	—	500
Total equity	3 000	3 500

During the year the net asset value of the Swiss subsidiary has risen from CHF3m to CHF3.5m. If we now take the financial position of the subsidiary at the beginning and end of the year and use the temporal method to translate it into sterling in order to prepare consolidated financial statements, the relationship of assets and liabilities within the subsidiary will change as shown below:

	1 Jan 20X1 £'000	31 Dec 20X1 £'000	Rate used £ =
Property, plant and equipment	1 250	1 250.00	4.0
less Acc. depreciation	—	–62.50	4.0
Net current assets			
Inventory[1]	—	142.86	3.5
Monetary assets	—	250.00	3.0
Current liabilities	—	–166.67	3.0
	—	226.19	
	1 250	1 413.69	
Long-term liabilities	–500	–666.67	3.0
Total net assets	750	747.02	
Equity			
Share capital	750	750.00	4.0
Retained earnings[2]	—	142.85	3.5
Translation adjustment[3]	—	–145.83	
Total equity	750	747.02	

Notes

1. This rate is assumed: the temporal method requires use of the actual rate at the time the inventory was acquired. For simplicity the example assumes that inventory was acquired uniformly throughout the year.
2. Again to simplify, the depreciation cost in retained earnings is translated at the average rate and not at the historical rate.
3. Under the temporal method the translation adjustment is charged against net income and is only shown separately in this example in order to highlight its existence.

In applying the temporal method, different exchange rates are used for different elements of the statement of financial position, and in this case we can see clearly the dilemma which emerges: in Swiss franc terms the subsidiary has grown by 16.67 per cent in value, but when translated back to sterling using this method the net asset value has fallen slightly. Which is the more useful picture from the point of view of users?

Probably your immediate reaction will be that this translation method must be wrong – but you need to think carefully about it. The major difference between the sterling result and the Swiss franc result derives from the fact that the long-term liability is translated at the current rate, while the major asset is translated at a historic rate. As in this example the rate has moved against sterling, the liability has risen considerably in sterling terms while the asset has remained at its historic sterling value. This is exactly what would happen if the parent had borrowed in Switzerland for repayment ultimately from sterling resources.

The dilemma arises from the fact that the assets and liabilities are being viewed from the parent company standpoint, and the application of the prudence principle requires that the growth in current value of the liability is recognized while the assets are at historical cost. So the question arises as to whether one should ignore the prudence principle and state the liability also at a historical cost, or whether the asset might be revalued. Revaluation of the asset, though, would be inconsistent if other assets owned by the group were not revalued as well.

The strict application of accounting rules designed for accounting within one country and one currency to a multi-currency problem leads to this situation, and one should consider whether such rules can reasonably be extended in that way. The application of the rules ignores the economic reality, which is that the Swiss franc loan was negotiated in order to purchase a Swiss franc asset, and it is expected that the loan will be repaid out of Swiss franc earnings derived from the use of that asset. Does this have anything to do with the parent company other than to the extent of its investment?

This use, in the example, of a local loan to back up the purchase of a local asset is a classic technique in international business. If the parent company had not borrowed any capital but had invested CHF5m, its economic exposure to rate changes would obviously be much greater than for the investment of CHF3m. In effect, it has acquired an asset of CHF5m with a **currency risk** of CHF3m. Economically the loan element is balanced by the asset, since a rate change affects both asset and liability in the same way. This is known as a currency 'hedge'. The major difficulty with the temporal method is that it fails to recognize the economic existence of the hedge – the rate change is reflected in the financial statements only in so far as it affects the liability and not where it affects the asset.

Net investment method

The net investment method (or closing rate method) approximates to the alternative view of the parent/subsidiary relationship. It assumes that the subsidiary should be considered as an entity and the assets and liabilities translated at the same rate, thereby in effect showing the results of rate changes on the parent company's net investment in the subsidiary.

If we apply the net investment approach to the same Swiss subsidiary, the translation would be made at the rate ruling on reporting date (i.e. closing rate on the date of the statement of financial position): in this case therefore the opening statement of financial position would be translated at £1 = CHF4.00, while the closing statement of financial position would be translated at £1 = CHF3.00. Retained earnings are translated at the average rate £1 = CHF3.50.

	1 Jan 20X1 £' 0000	31 Dec 20X1 £' 000
Property, plant and equipment	1 250	1 666.67
less Acc. depreciation	—	–83.33
Net current assets		
Inventory	—	166.67
Monetary assets	—	250.00
Current liabilities	—	–166.67
	—	250.00
	1 250	*1 833.34*
Long-term liabilities	–500	–666.67
Total net assets	750	1 166.67
Equity		
Share capital (initial)	750	750.00
(Translation diff.)	—	273.82
Retained earnings	—	142.85
Total equity	750	1 166.67

Note
The original share capital has been translated at the historical rate, with the difference between that and the closing rate being part of a translation adjustment. The average rate has been used for retained earnings.

Use of the net investment method ties in the rate change to both assets and liabilities, reflecting a current exchange value for both. The precise differences in the results of the two methods may perhaps best be viewed if we now compare the sterling translation of the closing statement of financial position under each method.

The difference in result between the two methods is quite dramatic and emphasizes a point we hope you have now fully realized: that the measurement of profit is subject to all kinds of quite subjective decisions on accounting principles.

	Temporal method 31 Dec 20X1 £'000	Net investment method 31 Dec 20X1 £'000
Property, plant and equipment	1 250.00	1 666.67
less Acc. depreciation	–62.50	–83.33
Net current assets		
Inventory	142.86	166.67
Monetary assets	250.00	250.00
Current liabilities	–166.67	–166.67
	226.19	250.00
	1 413.69	*1 833.34*
Long-term liability	–666.67	–666.67
Total net assets	747.02	1,166.67
Equity		
Share capital	750.00	750.00
Retained earnings	–145.84	142.85
Translation adjustment	142.86	273.82
Total equity	747.02	1 166.67

The essential difference in result derives from the fact that the net investment method has recognized the increase in sterling value of the asset as a result of a rate change, while the temporal method has not done so. Either view of the sterling result of the subsidiary is justifiable, depending upon how you interpret the economic relationship between the parent and the subsidiary.

In the example chosen, the rates of exchange used presented a picture where sterling was weakening against the foreign currency, and the effect of that on the translation was to show up an increased liability under the temporal method. If the rate movements had been the opposite, however, the picture would have been the exact reverse. Under the temporal method, the asset would have remained at its old sterling value while the liability would have diminished, thereby showing a positive translation adjustment. Under the net investment method both asset and liability would have declined, giving a negative translation adjustment. Do not fall into the trap of supposing that the net investment method always gives a more profitable result.

One implication of the differences thrown up by translation methods is that when assessing the performance of a subsidiary from a parent company viewpoint, care must be taken to distinguish the currency effects in the sterling results from the real underlying operating results. Using the relationship which profit bears to the investment in an operation as a yardstick (return on equity), the results for the Swiss operation could be interpreted three different ways:

	Growth in equity	Opening equity	Percentage growth in year
CHF financial statements	500	3 000	16.67%
Temporal method	–2.98	750	–0.40%
Net investment method	416.67	750	55.56%

Precisely the same economic situation can yield three different measures of success or failure, depending on the perspective chosen. This is clearly a problem for the analyst. The effect of translation differences can be highlighted in two ways. First, it will be reflected to an extent in the analysis of non-current assets – when the net investment method is used (and this is standard practice under IFRS – see next section) the translated value of assets will change, as we discussed above. The amount of this change will be reflected in the non-current assets notes, and the analyst can check whether this is material in relation to total assets or whether a portfolio effect applies (what accountants call 'swings and roundabouts') and translation gains on some items are balanced by losses on others. For example, Agfa-Gevaert (see Company Report) shows a negative effect of exchange differences on all property, plant and equipment items in 2010, indicating that, on average, the euro got weaker in 2010 relative to the functional currencies of its foreign operations. The rising value of the US dollar relative to the euro in 2010 probably explains these negative effects to a large extent. Second, the analyst should look at the translation difference taken to equity ('other comprehensive income' accumulated in a separate component of equity) – is this material? If possible, a five-year or more time series should be constructed (back copies of the financial statements would be required) in order to see whether there is a definite trend.

Functional currency and type of foreign operation

IAS 21, *The Effects of Changes in Foreign Exchange Rates*, avoids the difficult choice between alternative secondary translation methods through its guidance for determining the functional currency of a foreign operation. The IASB starts from the premise that the functional currency of a foreign operation that is integral to the reporting unit and the functional currency of the parent will always be the same, because they share the same primary economic environment. It follows that there is no need for specific accounting rules to translate the financial statements of an integral foreign operation for consolidation purposes, as they will already be measured in the parent's functional currency. Consequently, translating a subsidiary's financial statements (in its functional currency) into a different group presentation currency according to IFRS basically follows the net investment method. IAS 21 specifies these basic secondary translation rules in par. 39 (see IAS 21 extracts).

If, for example for regulatory purposes, a company keeps its accounting records and presents its individual financial statements in a currency which is different from its functional currency, the temporal method would, however, still be relevant. For consolidation purposes all amounts would have to be re-measured into the functional currency using the historical rate on initial recognition. Subsequent to this, only monetary items denominated in a foreign currency should be re-measured. This (temporal method-like) procedure produces the same amounts as would have occurred had all transactions been recorded initially in the functional currency.

Consistent with the translation logic of the net investment method, secondary translation differences do not affect profit or loss on initial recognition, but are recognized as other comprehensive income as accumulated in a separate component of equity. They will, however, eventually affect profit or loss on (partial) disposal of the foreign operation. On the disposal of a foreign operation, the cumulative amount of the exchange differences relating to that foreign operation have to be recycled (reclassified) from equity to profit or loss when the corresponding disposal gain (or loss) is recognized (IAS 21, par.48).

AGFA-GEVAERT

Notes to the consolidated financial statements (extract)

Exchange differences in Note 13 Property, plant and equipment

Million euro	Land, buildings and infrastructure	Machinery and technical equipment	Furniture fixtures and other equipment	Construction in progress and advance payments to vendors and contractors	Total
Cost at December 31, 2009	360	1 467	246	18	2 091
Exchange differences	6	22	7	—	35
Change in consolidation scope	1	1	2	—	4
Capital expenditures	3	14	9	22	48
Retirements	(9)	(21)	(15)	—	(45)
Transfers	1	4	0	(11)	(6)
Cost at December 31, 2010	362	1 487	249	29	2 127
Accumulated depreciation and impairment losses December 31, 2009	251	1 293	221	—	1 765
Exchange differences	4	16	5	—	25
Change in consolidation scope	—	1	1	—	2
Depreciation during the year	8	42	14	-	64
Impairment loss during the year	—	1	—	—	1
Retirements	(8)	(21)	(13)	—	(42)
Transfers	—	—	(1)	—	(1)
Accumulated depreciation and impairment losses December 31, 2010	255	1 332	227	—	1 814
Carrying amount December 31, 2009	109	174	25	18	326
Carrying amount December 31, 2010	107	155	22	29	313

Source: Agfa, Annual Report 2010

With respect to the consolidation process, IAS 21 requires goodwill and fair value adjustments to assets and liabilities that arise on the acquisition of a foreign entity, to be treated as part of the assets and liabilities of the acquired entity. As such, they have to be translated at the closing rate.

Both primary and secondary exchange differences must be disclosed, including the amount of exchange differences recognized in profit and loss and the net exchange differences recognized in other comprehensive income and accumulated in a separate component of equity. For the secondary exchange differences a reconciliation of the net amount at the beginning and end of the period has to be provided.

COMPANY REPORT

ANGLOGOLD ASHANTI

Notes to the financial statements (extract)

Financial statements in foreign currency

Group companies

The results and financial position of all group entities (none of which has the currency of a hyperinflationary economy) that have a functional currency different from the presentation currency are translated into the presentation currency as follows:

- share capital and premium are translated at historical rates of exchange at the reporting date;

- retained earnings are converted at historical average exchange rates;

- assets and liabilities for each statement of financial position presented are translated at the closing rate at the date of that statement of financial position;

- income and expenses for each statement of profit or loss presented are translated at monthly average exchange rates (unless this average is not a reasonable approximation of the cumulative effect of the rates prevailing on the transaction dates, in which case income and expenses are translated at the rates prevailing at the date of the transaction);

- all resulting exchange differences are recognized in other comprehensive income and presented as a separate component of equity (foreign currency translation); and

- other reserves, other than those translated above, are converted at the closing rate at each reporting date. These resulting exchange differences are recognised in retained earnings.

Exchange differences arising from the translation of the net investment in foreign operations, and of borrowings and other currency instruments designated as hedges of such investments, are taken to other comprehensive income on consolidation.

For the company, the exchange differences on such monetary items are reported in the company income statement.

When a foreign operation is sold, such exchange differences are recognized in the income statement as part of the gain or loss on sale.

Goodwill and fair value adjustments arising on the acquisition of a foreign operation are treated as assets and liabilities of the foreign operation and translated at the closing rate.

Source: Extract from 'Summary of significant accounting policies', AngloGold Ashanti, 2010

Hedging a net investment in a foreign operation

There is, though, a major loophole in IAS 21 which concerns dealing with currency hedges. A multinational company has investments in many countries which are therefore denominated in many currencies. This potentially creates many exchange exposures and a multinational usually tries to minimize this by borrowing in foreign currencies. So if a British company wants to buy a US subsidiary for $100m it will try to borrow US dollars to finance the deal, rather than sterling. The investment will yield a dollar cash flow which can be used to pay interest and ultimately repay the debt. With a US dollar loan, any move in exchange rates has no effect on this closed circuit; a sterling loan would have fluctuating results.

Companies therefore hedge their investments and borrow in currencies which reflect the currencies of their future expected cash flows. These debts have notwithstanding to be translated into functional currency at reporting date at the closing rate, while the underlying investment is held in the parent at the historical rate. Following normal rules this would mean that the two were not balanced, but IAS 39, *Financial Instruments: Recognition and Measurement*, allows that translation gains and losses on loans which are hedges of investments may be taken directly to equity, without flowing through the statement of profit or loss. This is very rational, but has a flaw in that complex multinationals tend not hedge individual investments, but rather take out a basket of currency loans to hedge

STANDARDS

IAS 21 – THE EFFECTS OF CHANGES IN FOREIGN EXCHANGE RATES
(extracts)

Translation to the presentation currency

39. The results and financial position of an entity whose functional currency is not the currency of a hyperinflationary economy shall be translated into a different presentation currency using the following procedures:

(a) assets and liabilities for each statement of financial position presented (i.e. including comparatives) shall be translated at the closing rate at the date of that statement of financial position;

(b) income and expenses for each statement of profit or loss and other comprehensive income or separate statement of profit or loss presented (i.e. including comparatives) shall be translated at exchange rates at the dates of the transactions; and

(c) all resulting exchange differences shall be recognized in other comprehensive income.

40. For practical reasons, a rate that approximates the exchange rates at the dates of the transactions, for example an average rate for the period, is often used to translate income and expense items. However, if exchange rates fluctuate significantly, the use of the average rate for a period is inappropriate.

Source: IAS 21, *The Effects of Changes in Foreign Exchange Rates*

a basket of investments, so one cannot tie down individual assets to individual debts. Consequently, it is rather in the hands of the treasury department at year-end to say which items are *trading debts* (gains and losses to profit or loss) and which are *hedges* (have no effect on profit), and one does not have to be unduly suspicious to see that this system is open to abuse.

Summary

The analysis of multinational operations faces problems of highly aggregated data and of financial statements denominated in many currencies. Companies are required to provide some analysis of business and geographical segments to help the analyst.

Fluctuating exchange rates pose a major accounting problem when it comes to recognizing transactions denominated in foreign currencies and preparing consolidated financial statements which include foreign subsidiaries.

The notion of functional currency plays a key role in the accounting rules on foreign currency translation. The functional currency of a company is the currency of the primary economic environment in which the company operates. The functional currency is determined separately for each individual entity within a group and each entity has to prepare its individual financial statements in the functional currency.

Business transactions denominated in foreign currency are recorded in the functional currency by applying the spot exchange rate between the functional currency and the foreign currency at transaction date. Subsequently, monetary assets and liabilities must be translated at the rate ruling on each successive reporting date, as providing the best approximation of their ultimate settlement value. Differences arising from translation of such items, whether gains or losses, are taken to the statement of profit or loss.

Accounting regulation has traditionally put forward two methods for translating financial statements of foreign subsidiaries for consolidation purposes. If the subsidiary is translated as though the transactions were those of the parent, its accounts are translated at different rates appropriate to the category of asset or liability concerned. This is known as the *temporal method*. The translation difference is seen as either income or expense for inclusion in the consolidated statement of profit or loss. Alternatively, if the subsidiary is considered to be economically a whole entity in its own right, its financial statements are translated at the rate ruling on reporting date. This is known as the *net investment* (or *closing rate* or *current rate*) *method*. The use of this method preserves the relationships between assets and liabilities within the subsidiary's statement of financial position. It does, however, risk including assets which have, in effect, been revalued, within a historical cost oriented statement of financial position on an unsystematic basis.

IAS 21 sets the functional currency of a foreign subsidiary which is heavily integrated with the operations of the parent and for which the temporal method is more appropriate, equal to the functional currency of the parent. As such, it only refers to the net investment method as the method to be used when translating foreign financial statements to the presentation currency of the group. The translation difference arising on consolidation is not recognized in profit or loss, but is treated as a direct adjustment to shareholders' equity (other comprehensive income accumulated in a separate component of equity).

Discussion Questions

1. Discuss why it is important to complement consolidated financial statements with segment reporting.
2. A central issue in applying IFRS 8, *Operating Segments*, is the determination of which operating segments should be reported. Explain the tests to determine whether or not an operating segment is a reportable segment.
3. Explain the difference between primary and secondary translation issues.
4. In what circumstances can a company's local (national) currency be different from its functional currency? If different, what are the accounting implications?
5. Explain why secondary translation differences are not recognized in profit and loss and deferred (as part of equity) under the net investment method.
6. Discuss the purpose and accounting consequences of currency hedges.

Assignments

The following assignments have answers on the lecturer side of the digital support resources for the book.

1. Norwood Ltd contracts to buy a new machine tool from Illinois Tools Inc. at a price of $85 000 on the following terms of payment: 10 per cent on delivery, 50 per cent after one month and the balance after a further two months. The machine is ordered on 1 September 20X1, leaves the Illinois factory on 1 October and reaches Norwood on 30 November. Norwood makes its payments on 1 December 20X1, 1 January 20X2 and 1 February 20X2. The £/$ exchange rates during this period were:

Date	Exchange rate
1 Sept. 20X1	£1 = $1.20
1 Oct. 20X1	£1 = $1.25
30 Nov. 20X1	£1 = $1.20
1 Dec. 20X1	£1 = $1.20
31 Dec. 20X1	£1 = $1.15
1 Jan. 20X2	£1 = $1.15
1 Feb. 20X2	£1 = $1.10

(a) On the assumption that the invoice was denominated in US dollars, show the balance sheet entries for Norwood at 31 December 20X1 and the income statement items for 20X1 and 20X2 which relate to this transaction.

(b) On the assumption that the invoice was agreed in sterling at £70000, show the same financial statement items for Illinois Tools Inc.

2. Continental Holdings borrows CHF20m on 1 July 20X1 for a five-year term, at a time when £1 = CHF4.00. Show the relevant statement of financial position and profit or loss items relating to this loan for the years 20X1 to 20X6 inclusive, given the following exchange rate information:

Date	Exchange rate
31 Dec. 20X1	£1 = CHF4.25
31 Dec. 20X2	£1 = CHF4.10
31 Dec. 20X3	£1 = CHF3.50
31 Dec. 20X4	£1 = CHF3.25
31 Dec. 20X5	£1 = CHF3.60
30 June 20X6	£1 = CHF4.10

3. Voltaire Industries SA set up a UK subsidiary, Candide Ltd, on 1 July 20X1 with an investment of €17m. The subsidiary borrowed £500000 on the UK market and purchased a leasehold factory for £300000 and plant for £1.0m. The draft statements of financial position of the two companies as at 30 June 20X2 are given below. The exchange rates which applied during the year were:

Date	£ = €
1 July 20X1	1.7
30 June 20X2	1.5
Average for year	1.6

Candide purchased its closing inventories at a time when £1 = €1.55.

Required:

(a) Apply IAS 21's secondary translation requirements in order to prepare consolidated financial statements for Voltaire Industries as at 30 June 20X2.

(b) Comment on how the use of the temporal method (secondary translation) would affect the consolidated financial statements.

	Voltaire		Candide	
	€'000	€'000	£'000	£'000
Non-current assets				
Leaseholds	315 000		3 000	
Acc. depreciation	–75 000	240 000	–300	2 700
Plant	850 000		10 000	
Acc. depreciation	–375 000	475 000	–2 000	8 000
Investment in Candide		17 000		
		732 000		10 700
Current assets (A)				
Inventories	85 000		1 750	
Receivables	120 000		2 500	
Cash	163 000		2 500	
	368 000		*6 750*	
Creditors due in				
less than 1 year (B)	–250 000		–1 250	
Net current assets (A – B)		*118 000*		*5 500*
Creditors due in				
more than 1 year (C)		–100 000		–5 000
Total net assets		750 000		11 200
Financed by equity				
Share capital		400 000		10 000
Reserves		250 000		—
Profit for the year		100 000		1 200
Total equity		750 000		11 200

4. On 1 January 20X1 Flubdub Company set up Yabber Company with a share capital of LC200 million (LC = local currency) and acquired 100 per cent of the outstanding shares of Yabber. At that date the exchange rate was LC1 = €4, so the acquisition cost of the investment in the books of Flubdub amounts to €800 million. LC is Yabber's functional currency.

   During 20X3 Flubdub grants a loan of €600M to Yabber, refundable at nominal value in € after a period of ten years. On granting date, the exchange rate was LC1 = €3. At the end of 20X5 the exchange rate amounts to 1LC = €2. The average rate for 20X5 is LC1 = €2.5.

The condensed statement of financial position and statement of profit or loss of Yabber at the end of 20X5 are as follows (all amounts in LC million):

Statement of financial position at 31 December 20X5	Yabber (LC million)
Assets	
Property, plant and equipment (net)	560
Non-current financial assets	40
Inventories	300
Trade receivables	300
Cash and cash equivalents	200
	1 400
Equity and liabilities	
Share capital	200
Reserves	280
Profit for the year	40
Provisions	40
Long-term liabilities – Flubdub	300
Long-term liabilities – others	200
Short-term liabilities	340
	1 400
Statement of profit or loss of 20X5 – Yabber	
Revenue	1 800
Raw materials and consumables used	–600
	1 200
Staff costs	–800
Depreciation and amortization expense	–80
Profit from operations	320
Other expenses	–280
Profit for the year	40

Yabber's property, plant and equipment were acquired at foundation date and have been financed by the share capital funds and short-term liabilities. These short-term liabilities have been replaced by Flubdub's long-term loan in 20X3. Yabber's non-current financial assets were acquired at the beginning of 20X4, when the exchange rate was LC1 = €3. The historical cost of inventories acquired and used during 20X4 follows the year-average pattern. The reserves reflect the accumulation of retained profits. The historical exchange rate of the reserves corresponds to LC1 = €3 for 20X1 until 20X4.

Required:

Translate the statement of financial position and the statement of profit or loss of Yabber into euro according to:

(a) the net investment method (cfr. IAS 21);

(b) the temporal method.

CHAPTER 14

Issues in financial reporting by multinationals

The object of this chapter is to review what are currently considered to be problems either in understanding corporate reports or in the quality of the information given in them. A financial analyst is likely to encounter some of these in looking at different companies. The subjects are not necessarily related to each other, and you might regard this as a reference section for advanced problems in financial reporting.

Chapter Structure

Introduction

The object of this chapter is to provide a few bridges towards further study of measurement and disclosure in financial reporting. It explores some basic notions of value and how they are related to measurement attributes of assets and liabilities and to the IASB's mixed-attribute model.

Historical cost accounting has been perceived to be inadequate in reporting some transactions and circumstances and has been significantly modified in specific reporting domains . . . the boundaries of the traditional accounting model are moving. Similarly, supplementary disclosures in the notes to the accounts, and in the annual report in general, have been expanding considerably. We will review a number of significant disclosure domains such as contingent liabilities, discontinued operations, pension benefits, and environmental and intellectual capital dis-closures. A financial analyst is likely to encounter some of these in looking at different companies. The disclosure items are not necessarily related to each other, and you might regard this as a reference section for advanced topics in financial reporting.

Values in accounting

We think it is useful first to remind you that the value of anything cannot be stated without some sort of qualification as to the context. For example, what is the value of your computer? First we have to specify: are we looking at its value to you as a tool? As a fashion accessory? As a social symbol? Or some form of economic value? In management, we are usually looking at the economic value of an asset and trying to put a financial measurement on that. But even that needs further qualification: is the relevant value what it cost you to buy the computer originally? Or what it would cost you to buy a new one now? Or how much you could sell it for? (Another way of looking at that is to ask in which market you are making the valuation.)

In thinking about values, it is useful in the first place to distinguish between *entry value*, *exit value* and *value in use*. Entry values are those that relate to acquiring something (how much can you buy it for?), exit values are those that relate to selling or liquidating something, whereas value in use is the incremental firm value from continuing use of the item (which can be seen as a variant of the exit value – an asset can disappear either through being sold, or through being used up within the company). Entry and exit values are both market values, i.e. all similar assets have the same value, whereas value in use is a value specific to the company that uses the item – it is an entity-specific value. An entry value represents a market buying price, while an exit value is a market selling price. When market values are used, they provide comparable information between companies. Value in use, however, incorporates information about management intentions and is therefore subjective and unique to the particular asset. In fact, the company is asked to estimate the future net cash flows expected to arise from the continuing use and ultimate disposal of the asset and then discount these to present value. Different people have different views as to whether the user of accounts finds the comparable market measure more useful than the unique entity-specific measure.

An investor is looking at a company and asking whether the price of the security is justified in the light of the cash flows which will accrue to the owner of the securities. In effect, this is the assessment which the analyst is making – what are the future cash flows which the investment will generate (what is the exit value? What is the value in use?) and do these justify paying the purchase price of the security (entry value)?

The basic accounting model is concerned above all with entry values. Under the historical cost model, the gross value of an asset in the statement of financial position is what it cost to acquire it. This is usually the market value at the time it was acquired (*initial measurement*) and if there is no subsequent remeasurement, this is called *historical cost*. However, in more sophisticated accounting, one may also consider whether it could be useful to remeasure assets at subsequent reporting dates. If this were done, one would have to prescribe a value principle: decide on what basis a new value was to be derived.

Measurement could be a revised entry cost – what would it cost to acquire now an asset in the same age and condition as an existing asset? This is known as 're-placement cost'. Someone who is trying to value a company might approach it on the basis of what it would cost to acquire a similar bundle of assets at today's prices. That might be a current entry value. In an economy where there is rapid inflation, historical cost values soon become irrelevant, and replacement cost might be a more useful measurement approach in some circumstances.

Value in use is based on what benefits can be generated from owning and using the asset. As an entity-specific value, it probably will differ from company to company. Estimating value in use comes down to estimating and discounting the net cash flows that the asset can generate. Accounting uses value in use as a control measure only. Recall that IAS 36, *Impairment of Assets*, demands the calculation of value in use as a threshold value to arrive at an estimate of the recoverable amount of an asset. Long-term assets which are held for use rather than resale are held at cost unless the cash flows which are expected to be generated by their use are lower than cost.

Accounting uses exit values both as a control and as a measurement base for subsequent measurement after initial recognition of a specific set of balance sheet items. Recall that inventories must be held at the lower of cost (normal convention) or net realizable value (the exit value of the inventories). The exit value provides a ceiling for the carrying value of the inventory. However, market exit values could also be used for subsequent measurement of any asset, not just those held for resale.

An interesting additional value concept is the idea of *deprival value* (Figure 14.1). It rests on a comparison of a current entry value (replacement cost) and a recoverable amount which is consistent with IAS 36. Deprival value is known in UK standard setting as value to the business. It is what the loss to the business would be if it were obliged to forfeit the asset in question. Deprival value asks: if the asset were lost, what would the company do? Would it buy a replacement asset? If the answer to that question is yes, then replacement cost is the appropriate value

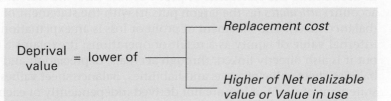

Figure 14.1
Deprival value

to appear in the statement of financial position. If the answer is no (perhaps the asset is no longer used, the product is not profitable, etc.) then the balance sheet value is the present value of the future cash flows from sale of the asset or from remaining use (whichever is the higher).

The application of this rule would normally provide a balance sheet value which is the cost of replacing the company's assets (and liabilities) at reporting date, subject to the proviso that unprofitable assets which would not be replaced are included at a lower value reflecting the economic benefits expected to derive from the asset, either through use or sale. Deprival value was proposed as the valuation approach appropriate in an inflationary situation as providing a current value of an asset, while the recoverable amount limitation is intended to prevent presentation of unrealistic asset values in the statement of financial position. Most assets would therefore still be measured at an entry value (how much to buy the assets, not how much to sell) but at the same (current) value date.

In the past, however, annual income was defined as the change in wealth from the beginning to the end of the year, which could be translated in accounting terms into using the statement of financial position as the measurement focus instead of the statement of profit or loss. As discussed earlier, much of European regulation derives from a 17th-century requirement for businesses to prepare an annual 'inventory' of their worth. There was a period of experimentation as financial reporting evolved in the 19th century when the statement of financial position was the focus of corporate reporting in a number of countries, where, to put it in a simple form, a railway company might have had the following statements of financial position:

	1 Jan 1870	31 Dec 1870
Current value of track, buildings, rolling stock	100 000	135 000
Net current assets	20 000	30 000
Loans	–40 000	–50 000
Net worth	**80 000**	**115 000**
Difference in net worth = 35 000 = profit for year		

This approach uses re-measurement of assets and is consistent with a definition of income which is grounded in economic theory: that a company's income can be objectively determined from the change in its wealth plus what is consumed during the period (Hicks, J., *Value and Capital*, Oxford, Clarendon Press, 1946). Under this approach the measurement issue becomes the valuation of assets and liabilities at a given moment with market exit values as the measurement attribute.

There are a couple of points to bear in mind here. The most important is that in accounting the statement of profit or loss (income statement/profit and loss account) *articulates* (as the jargon puts it) with the statement of financial position (balance sheet). The statement of profit or loss is an explanation of changes in the internal value of equity as a result of operations; it explains a change in equity, but it is also directly linked, through accruals, depreciation and provisions, to the balance sheet value of assets and liabilities. Balance sheet values and values in the statement of profit or loss are not derived independently of each other. Either you measure balance sheet values independently on different dates and the difference is the profit or loss for the intervening period, or you measure income, and the statement of financial position represents unabsorbed costs (assets) and anticipated expenditure (current liabilities) and financing.

In practice, things are less straightforward. Recall the IASB definitions of financial statement elements (Chapter 3): it is clear that at a conceptual level the primacy given to the definitions of assets and liabilities supports only a balance sheet view on income determination. However, financial reporting as it evolved in the 20th century has been oriented around reporting completed transactions, using entry measurement values, without any subsequent remeasurement or much acknowledgement of possible changes in the economic status of assets other than through depreciation.

Measurement attributes

Is the analyst trying to measure future cash flows from the company's operations or the value of the company's assets? We would say that the investor is interested in the future cash flows that she or he is going to receive (dividends plus growth in the market value of the company) and that the company's ability to deliver (increasing) annual profits is the surrogate which is used (it is assumed that if the company produces increasing profits these will generate positive cash flows which will be used for dividends and investment in capacity, which will be reflected in higher market value). The current stock exchange value of a listed company is held, therefore, to represent the present value of the expected future cash flows of the company.

There is a general belief that current accrual-based income measures are a better predictor of future cash flows than are current cash flows. The logic behind this is that in making accrual adjustments, management build in their view of the long-term likely outcomes. This lends to the earnings figures more predictive value than is in the current cash flow figures which include random events. In fact, this general belief is supported by empirical accounting research that shows that current accrual earnings outperform current cash flows in forecasting future cash flows. Moreover, market returns of shares are empirically better correlated with accrual earnings than with actual cash flow measures. These arguments support an analyst's measurement focus on the statement of profit or loss.

Expanding the boundaries of the accounting model

Evolution of the accounting standards of both the IASB and FASB (Financial Accounting Standards Board) has had the effect of challenging the historical cost base. The standard-setters have been expanding the boundaries of the accounting model with the idea that economically significant changes may take place ahead of a completed transaction, sometimes many years ahead, and that more of these changes should be recognized than was previously the case. This is accompanied by the use of economic measurement techniques. This does not change what is ultimately recognized as profit or loss, but rather changes in which accounting periods something is recognized. Some would argue that it is a sufficiently substantial change to imply quite a radical reorientation of financial reporting, to give much more emphasis on representing the current economic status of the entity's assets and liabilities in addition to its completed transactions.

The recognition and measurement rules inherent in any accounting model impose artificial boundaries on what is reported in financial statements. It is a common-place in teaching accounting to acknowledge that there are many aspects of the company, especially intangibles such as customer loyalty, acquired knowledge of a particular business, etc., which escape recognition as they do not meet the definition of balance sheet elements: they have no historical cost or their value cannot be measured with sufficient reliability. In recent years, it has become apparent from financial scandals that the information (economic facts and circumstances) that escapes the historical cost model (based on completed transactions) is more economically important than in the past. This discovered economic significance may derive from changes in circumstances or from changes in understanding of business and business measurement. The effect of the change in perceptions is to drive towards earlier recognition of (changes in) assets and liabilities than takes place under the completed transaction approach.

The most obvious example of a shift in circumstances is the growth in the use of derivatives (such as futures contracts) to manage currency and interest rate exposures and sometimes commodity prices. The rapid rise in this kind of economic activity brought about a situation where companies (and sometimes municipalities) were engaged in contracts whose outcomes were uncertain and which were largely unrepresented in the statement of financial position, because they were incomplete transactions which escaped the measurement model and there was no historical cost to begin with. A number of high-profile losses arising from such contracts (e.g. Orange County, Proctor and Gamble in the US, Metallgesellschaft in Germany) occurred within a relatively short period.

Executory contracts

The recognition issue here is the accounting treatment of *executory contracts*: binding contracts between two parties where performance is not complete. The traditional accounting model largely ignores executory contracts, except in the context of accounting for long-term contracts (and only if the percentage-of-completion method is applied). The problems with financial instruments used in these corporate scandals highlighted that the executory contract has potential value (positive and negative) for the business and challenged accounting to move the boundaries of its measurement model to acknowledge this.

IAS 37, *Provisions, Contingent Liabilities and Contingent Assets* (originally issued in 1998), has the notion of an **onerous contract** ('the unavoidable costs of meeting the obligations under the contract exceed the economic benefits expected to be received from it', par.10), and represents a first step towards bringing executory contracts within the boundaries of financial reporting. The scope of IAS 37 excludes contracts for financial instruments and all executory contracts other than onerous ones. IAS 37 reflects the prudent bias of the traditional model, recognizing executory contracts as significant but addressing only those that are liabilities and not those that are assets. IAS 39, *Financial Instrument: Recognition and Measurement* (first published as a standard in 1999) and its successor, IFRS 9, go much further, however, by recognizing both assets and liabilities that arise from executory contracts that are financial instruments.

Closely related to this is the issue of recognizing changes in economic value in general. The EU Accounting Directives have long had this idea of recognizing value changes both on the downside and on the upside through the possible revaluation of assets. International accounting standards have been equivocal about revaluation. The 1998 crop of IAS also produced IAS 36, *Impairment of Assets*, which calls for assets to be reassessed in the event that some indicator suggests that they might be impaired. Recognition of negative changes in value, not linked to any transaction, were therefore brought into the IASB measurement model. The model was then extended on the upside in 2000 with two industry specific standards: both IAS 40, *Investment Property*, and IAS 41, *Agriculture*, allow for assets to be remeasured at subsequent reporting dates.

Fair value measurement

The change in the boundary of what should be measured has been accompanied by a change in the boundary of how one might measure. This appears to be partly as a result of better measurement models, and partly as a result of established techniques in economics being more fully exploited in accounting. In this vein, recent IASB rules have sometimes required companies to carry assets and liabilities in the statement of financial position at 'fair value'. The IASB defines 'fair value' as 'the price that would be received to sell an asset or paid to transfer a liability in an orderly transaction between market participants at the measurement date' (IFRS 13 *Fair Value Measurement, para 9*). This fair value definition is essentially current market value.

Fair value has been introduced either as a means of putting a value on an incomplete transaction (i.e. simulating a completed transaction by asking what would be the exit value if one quit the transaction at that point) or as the measurement attribute for subsequent measurement in a number of significant accounting standards. In some ways, the use of fair value can be seen as a logical extension of the traditional transaction model: if one wanted to value an executory contract or other asset or liability because the information is necessary ahead of the transaction being complete, fair value in effect simulates a transaction at reporting date. In other words, if the asset were sold or the liability settled, this would be done in the market, so by going to the market for a price, one is staying with the transaction model but applying it in a notional sense.

Measurement hierarchy

Conceptually, fair value is a market-based measurement and as such is not affected by factors specific to a particular company. In that sense, it can be considered to be an unbiased measurement that is consistent from period to period and across companies. The US standard setter believes that this makes it a superior reporting basis to historical cost.

If available, an observable market price in an active market is the best evidence of fair value and should be used wherever possible as the fair value measurement. In an efficient market the market price of an asset or liability at any point in time reflects all available information and represents the market's assessment of all relevant economic factors and events . . . a perfect fair value.

The difficulties that present themselves for accountants in arriving at fair value are what to do when (a) there is more than one market price; (b) the market is very illiquid; (c) there are no recent prices; or (d) there is no market for the specific asset or liability one is trying to measure. Clearly as soon as you move away from a current, liquid market in exactly the same kind of asset or liability, the extent to which the value ascertained can be relied upon starts to diminish. The IASB and FASB intend to provide guidance in 2012 on some of these application issues, especially as concerns emerging markets.

In 2006 the FASB issued a standard, SFAS 157, on making fair value measurements. The IASB issued a very similar standard in 2011 – IFRS 13. Both standard-setters felt that as fair value is used as the measurement attribute in a number of standards, it was simpler to put the guidance on how to calculate it in one place.

IFRS 13 identifies three levels of fair value measurement (see Figure 14.2). Level 1 is where exactly the same transactions can be seen in an active market (using this is sometimes described as 'marking to market'). Level 2 fair value is based on similar but not exactly the same transactions being observable in an active market which can be adjusted reasonably. Level 3, however, is where there are no market transactions and the company must use a financial model to estimate market values (some people refer to this as 'marking to model'). IFRS 13 discusses various accounting models that are available. Since the market price is believed to reflect the market's estimate of expected future cash flows, discounted to present value, then this is an obvious model to use. Clearly Level 3 valuations are more uncertain since they are based on estimates. The standard responds to this by requiring disclosures of assumptions and sensitivities to variations in those.

IFRS 13 specifies that fair value should be an exit price, but also that both entry and exit price are the same. Many people find this peculiar, since they think the price at which you bought something is not the same as that at which you could subsequently sell it. The explanation is that the standard-setters consider these are two different markets. If you buy a new car, the price you pay is the same as the price the dealer will receive (his exit price is the same as your entry price). If you immediately decide to sell it, you enter a different market, that of second-hand cars, which in turn can be segmented into the market at which a dealer might buy a second-hand car, and also the market in which a private individual sells to another private individual. The standard says you have to correctly identify what is the *principal market* for the asset or liability whose fair

Figure 14.2
Fair value measurement hierarchy

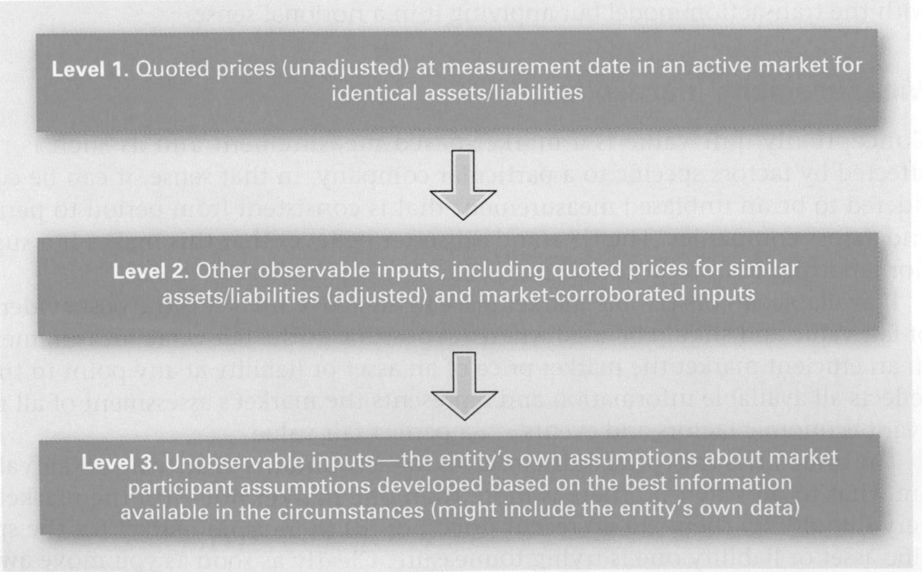

value you are calculating. In the absence of a principal market, you use *'the most advantageous market'*.

Linked to this is the notion of *highest and best use*. Fair value of non-financial assets, for the IASB, is not necessarily the value of the asset in its current use. If there is a use that the market values more highly, then this is the fair value. For example, if you were operating a cinema on a town centre site, it might be that the highest and best use for the asset would be to sell it to a property developer.

A continuing debate on innovation

Fair value has many critics, but the debate is often confused between the issue of (a) whether accounting should recognize assets and liabilities earlier in the transaction cycle and, if so (b) what measurement attribute is appropriate. Recognition earlier in the cycle is much criticized by banks and insurance companies for creating instability in financial statements. The argument seems to be that where there is a long-term transaction (for example a life assurance policy) the important issue is the final settlement values, and recognizing parts of the transaction ahead of final settlement is no guide to the final outcome. Others would say that information about long-term commitments is relevant to current investors.

However, the usefulness of the earlier recognition is also a function of the viability of the current measurement. The 'core deposits' issue on IAS 39 demonstrates this conundrum. Many retail banks use customer deposits as a significant part of their overall financing. While in theory the depositor may withdraw their money at any time, in practice there is a core amount that remains permanently available to the bank. The economic value of the liability is less than face value, because no interest is paid to the depositor, but to recognize this would be to generate a profit every time someone deposits money in their bank account.

Standard-setters claim that fair value is the most relevant measure for some balance sheet categories, especially financial instruments, and that a market-based value is capable of being both objective and consistent. However, critics argue that market prices fluctuate rapidly, and reflecting day-to-day movements in the accounts just creates gratuitous instability rather than reflecting long-term economic value. Given that analysts are trying to value the individual entity, one might have thought that entity-specific values were more useful, but analysts frequently say that they want to make their own entity-specific estimates, based on objective information, so market values are useful and also allow more direct inter-firm comparisons, a mainstay of stock selection.

The standard-setters acknowledge that concerns have been expressed about the reliability of fair value measurements but point out that they are aware that there are problems in its use, which is why it is used only in limited circumstances.

The sub-prime loans crisis that started in 2007 stress-tested fair value measurement for financial instruments. Banks continued to announce regular write-offs from their asset portfolios. These were caused by falling fair values of the assets. This in turn created pressure to abandon fair value measurement, using the argument that what was important was the ultimate outcome of each of the loans, not what you could currently sell them on for.

In response to this the IASB set up a working group to discuss the practical application of fair value in a declining market. Their final report was that the guidance in IAS 39 was satisfactory and the main issue was identifying market prices

BETWEEN THE LINES

How fair is fair value? *(extract)*

We believe that the standard-setters now face a significant dilemma: how can they continue to pursue their mark-to-model approach to asset/liability measurement and, at the same time, promulgate accounting standards that will lead to a style of financial reporting that enables investors to evaluate management performance, assess enterprise value and make sound investment decisions?

Perhaps the answer lies in a return to reality and a limitation on the application of the fair value model to those assets and liabilities that have real and determinable market values. Where reliable fair values are not readily available, ranges of possible fair values (together with assumptions and sensitivity analyses) could be provided in the form of note disclosure. In our view, the IASB has a responsibility to define clearly the boundaries between fair value information that is sufficiently reliable to be incorporated in the primary financial statements, and supplementary fair value information to be provided in the notes to the accounts in the form of ranges of possible outcomes and sensitivity analyses. This is not a difficult path – but is one that the IASB has so far chosen not to follow.

Source: Ernst & Young, IFRS Stakeholder Series, pp.8–9, 2005

when the market had in practice ceased to exist. Their report highlights practical difficulties in making fair value measurements and confusion about appropriate disclosures. The IASB subsequently amended IFRS 7 *Financial Instruments: Disclosures* to clarify the disclosure requirements.

Subsequent analysis seems to suggest that the greater accounting problem in the financial crisis was that provisions for impairment were not applied early enough. IAS 39 calls for impairment to take place only when a particular loan can be seen to be impaired. However, when bankers issue a portfolio of loans, experience suggests that a proportion will fail in some way, and that as economic circumstances change, that proportion will change. IAS 39 meant that these expected losses were not recognized in any way until they took place, creating a cliff effect. The IASB and FASB are now working on a model that anticipates loss.

The IASB's mixed-attribute model

Within the set of IASB standards, fair value accounting has come to complement historical cost accounting mechanisms in several domains leading to what is called a *mixed-attribute* model.

IFRS 3, *Business Combinations*, requires that assets and liabilities acquired in a business combination deal should be measured at fair value at acquisition date. The standard includes guidelines for arriving at fair value which include market value for assets and present value for pension obligations and other financial liabilities. Estimates of market value should be used when no market exists.

IAS 36, *Impairment of Assets*, contains the notion of *recoverable amount*, which it defines as the higher of the asset's fair value less costs to sell and its value in use. The recoverable amount is the value to be used in the statement of financial position if it is lower than the carrying amount. The guidance suggests that the best evidence is a binding sale agreement for a similar asset. Failing that, IAS 36 discusses similar assets trading in an active market and finally the best estimate of the price that could be obtained between a willing buyer and willing seller at arm's length.

The mixed attributes for measurement are also present in IAS 37, *Provisions, Contingent Liabilities and Contingent Assets*. The standard says the amount to be recognized as a provision should be 'the best estimate of the expenditure required to settle the present obligation at the balance sheet date' (para.36). It goes on to specify that this would be the amount required to settle or to pay to a third party to have them accept responsibility. The third party payment suggests a market transaction and therefore a fair value. However, the standard suggests that estimates of outcomes 'are determined by the judgment of the management' and an example in the text makes clear that a provision will be based on expected values – the cost of the different outcomes weighted by the probability of their occurrence.

Financial instruments

A specific problem which has become increasingly important in the past two decades is the ability of companies to enter into forward deals to buy or sell, to borrow or lend, to issue shares or buy back shares, etc. This is the world of financial instruments where the markets are in theory being used to reduce risk because they enable companies to match their risk with a company which has an opposite risk. For example, your company has a US dollar loan to repay in five years, and has revenues in euros. The market matches that with another company which has a euro loan to repay in five years and has revenues in US dollars – you agree an acceptable rate and swap the obligation to repay. This enables both companies to cancel the risk of the exchange rates moving against them. Certainly they lose the potential for gain at the same time, but this is normal – the lower the risk, the lower the potential gain (and the lower the potential loss).

However, this idyllic scenario is an oversimplification and the markets do not always work out the problems correctly. As far as commercial operating companies are concerned, sometimes they receive bad advice and make losses (famously this happened to Procter and Gamble). Sometimes executives look at the upside potential of the currency or commodity markets and are tempted to think they could be making money for their company. They stop trying simply to reduce the company's risk and start trying to bet against the market, occasionally with disastrous results. This happened in the 1990s with Sumitomo Corporation and its copper trader who tried to influence the copper markets by taking major positions, and lost the company millions of dollars in the end (as well as conducting various frauds to obtain the cash resources to pay for the trading). It also happened with Metallgesellschaft and oil futures.

The position is much more serious with banks, although these are fortunately outside the scope of this book. The banks are often the intermediaries in the market-place and sometimes take on risks expecting to be able to find a counter-risk and not doing so, or occasionally just betting on the way the market was moving (e.g. Nick Leeson and the collapse of Barings Bank, or more recently Société Générale).

Fortunately, most commercial companies are not heavily involved in financial instruments, but the publicity given to the major losses which have been run up in this sort of area have caused investors and analysts to call for much more information about company involvement. Unfortunately this has proved very difficult to regulate, not least because companies which make widespread use of commodity markets, for example, see it as unnecessarily onerous and potentially damaging in competitive terms, to disclose their dealings. Equally there are problems about (a) how to value futures contracts and (b) whether a relevant current valuation should be brought into historical cost accounts. Preparers argue that the final settlement value of a futures contract cannot be known until settlement because the markets are volatile. Consequently, potential losses recognized prior to settlement may never be realized and are misleading. The current value of a contract is not necessarily any guide to its future value. (But efficient market theorists say that the current price embodies everything known about the future at that point).

Another problem in this area is the question of whether a financial instrument has been entered into as a hedge for another transaction. For example, if a company has to pay a US dollar sum in two years, it could enter into a forward contract to buy US dollars. This would in effect be a hedge of its exchange rate risk and would enable it to lock into the exchange rate guaranteed by the forward contract. The economic argument is that transactions and their related hedges should be accounted for the same way and balancing gains and losses be offset against each other. This means that in regulating financial instrument disclosures one should potentially have one rule for financial instruments which are either entered into for speculative reasons or as part of general trading policy and another rule for those which are entered into as hedges of specific transactions. Regulators do not like rules which enable corporates to defer accounting for losses, even if there is a related profit due at the end of the contract, but corporates resent recognizing 'paper losses' when the overall arrangement is neutral in profit and loss terms.

IAS 39, *Financial Instruments: Recognition and Measurement* (which is being replaced over a period of years by IFRS 9, but key aspects of IFRS 9 are still being developed. The new standard may be applied voluntarily but its use is unlikely to be mandatory before 2015), covers financial assets, financial liabilities and some commodity contracts (contracts to buy and sell non-financial items like oil, corn, electricity, etc.). Financial instruments include cash, receivables, payables, equity and debt securities as well as financial derivatives. IAS 39 establishes principles for recognizing and measuring financial instruments, whereas IFRS 7 *Financial Instruments: Disclosures* deals with supplementary information disclosure requirements. More specifically, IAS 39 provides recognition and measurement rules for derivative instruments, such as foreign currency options and forwards, commodity futures or interest rate swaps, which were mainly kept off-balance under the historical cost model as their initial cost is often zero or very small. *Derivatives* are defined as financial instruments exhibiting three characteristics:

1. their value changes in response to a change in some market-related underlying variable, such as an interest rate, a commodity price or a foreign exchange rate
2. they require no or a relatively small initial investment
3. they are settled at a future date.

These characteristics make derivatives risky contracts with potentially significant future cash flow consequences. The potential cash flow effects imply future economic benefits or sacrifices and bring derivative contracts within the scope of the asset and liability definitions. Fair value is generally considered to be the most relevant measurement attribute of derivatives. IAS 39 also contains an option for companies to designate a qualified financial instrument (asset or liability) on initial recognition as one to be measured at fair value with fair value changes in profit or loss (the 'fair value option').

IAS 39 defines four categories of financial instrument:

a. *A financial asset or liability at fair value through profit or loss.* This category encompasses both financial instruments held for trading (financial instruments acquired and held with a view to short-term profit taking and derivatives) and designated financial instruments (fair value option).

b. *Held-to-maturity investments* (and liabilities): non-derivative financial assets and liabilities and financial liabilities) that the entity intends to hold to maturity.

c. *Loans and receivables:* non-derivative financial assets with fixed payments that are not quoted in an active market.

d. *Available-for-sale assets:* non-derivative financial assets that are available for sale and not classified as a., b. or c. above.

These different categories of financial instruments (financial assets and financial liabilities) are measured and reported (treatment of fair value changes) differently after initial recognition. Figures 14.3, 14.4 and 14.5 illustrate the main differences.

IFRS 9 reduces this to only two categories: assets that are held for their underlying contractual cash flows (measured using historical cost) and all other financial assets (fair value through profit or loss).

Hedge accounting rules will apply if the financial instrument (usually a derivative) qualifies as an effective **hedging instrument**. The hedge accounting rules will try to match any gain or loss that arises due to movements in the hedged item (the result of a hedged risk) with corresponding (but opposite) movements in the hedging instrument.

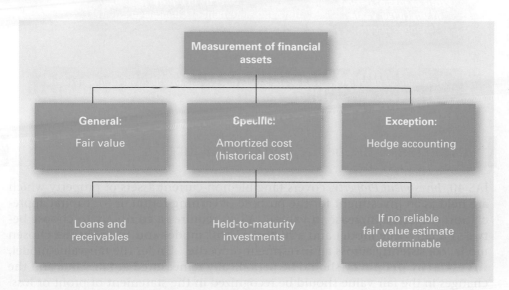

Figure 14.3
IAS 39—
Measurement
bases of
financial
assets

Figure 14.4
IAS 39—
Measurement
bases of
financial
liabilities

Figure 14.5
IAS 39—
Accounting
for changes
in fair value
of financial
instruments

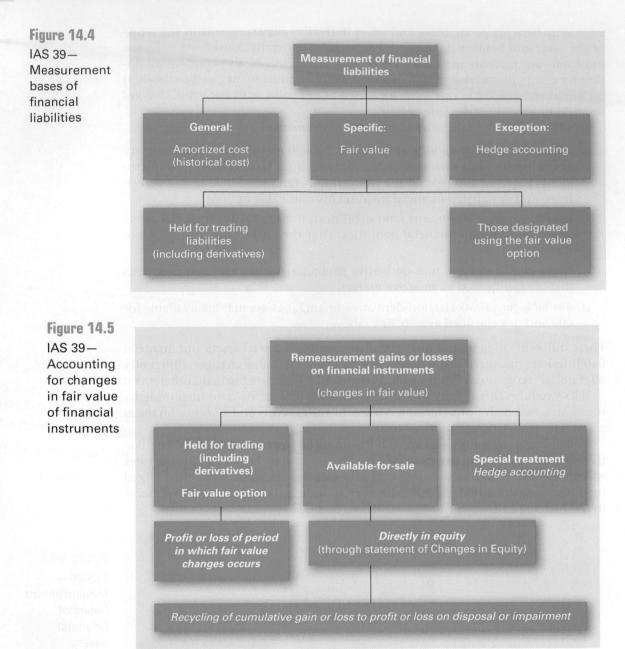

Investment property and agriculture

IAS 40, *Investment Property*, covers tangible non-current assets of property which are held as an investment for the purpose of earning rental or for capital appreciation (expected increase in value). IAS 40 requires a company to choose between a fair value model and a historical cost model and to apply the chosen model consistently across all investment properties. Under the fair value model, **investment property** should be periodically remeasured at fair value and the changes in the fair value should be recognized in the statement of profit or loss.

STANDARDS

🌐 IFRS 7 – FINANCIAL INSTRUMENTS: DISCLOSURES *(extract)*

1. The objective of this IFRS is to require entities to provide disclosures in their financial statements that enable users to evaluate:

   (a) the significance of financial instruments for the entity's financial position and performance; and

   (b) the nature and extent of risks arising from financial instruments to which the entity is exposed during the period and at the end of the reporting period, and how the entity manages those risks.

Source: IFRS 7, *Financial Instruments: Disclosures*

Where the historical cost model is chosen, the fair value of the investment property has still to be established and disclosed in the notes to the accounts.

IAS 41, *Agriculture*, is an industry-specific standard and covers valuation of biological assets and agricultural produce at the point of harvest, but does not apply to products that are the result of processing after harvest. IAS 41 requires measurement at fair value less estimated point-of-sale costs from initial recognition up to the point of harvest. The change in the fair value of the biological assets must be included in the net profit or loss of the period up to harvest. There is a general presumption that the fair value of a biological asset can be measured reliably. If not, the company should apply cost minus accumulated depreciation and minus any impairment losses.

The EU Accounting Directives incorporated these fair value accounting trends through the so-called Fair Value Directive, which is part of the EU's objective of enabling companies to use modern, more transparent accounting practices that are consistent with IFRS, in particular IAS 39. The Fair Value Directive requires member states to permit or require companies to account for some of their financial instruments and a limited number of other balance sheet items at fair value. This directive had to be implemented in national legislation by 1 January 2004. Changes in the value of financial instruments which are fair valued will go to the statement of profit or loss (a change in the current position) or, in certain circumstances, to a specific reserve called the fair value reserve.

COMPANY REPORT

BAYER – NOTES TO THE ACCOUNTS *(extract)*

30. Financial instruments
The system used by the Bayer Group to manage credit risk, liquidity risk and the various types of market risks (interest-rate risk, currency risk and other price risks), together with its objectives, methods and procedures, is outlined in the Risk Report, which forms part of the Management Report.

Carrying amounts and fair values of financial instruments

							Dec.31, 2011
€ million	*Carried at amortized cost*		*Carried at fair value*			*Non-financial assets/ liabilities*	
	Carrying amount Dec.31, 2011	*Fair value for presentation*	*Based on quoted prices in active markets*	*Based on market-derived data*	*Based on individual valuation parameters*		*Carrying amount in the statement of financial position*
			Carrying amount	*Carrying amount*	*Carrying amount*	*Carrying amount*	
Trade accounts receivable	7 061		7 061				
Loans and receivables	7 061	7 053					7 061
Other financial assets	2 920		716	477	35		4 148
Loans and receivables	2 920	2 781					2 770
Available-for-sale financial assets	41		716				757
Held-to-maturity financial assets	109	114					109
Derivatives that qualify for hedge accounting				220			220
Derivatives that do not qualify for hedge accounting				257	35		292
Other receivables	713					1 340	2 053
Loans and receivables	713	712					713
Non-financial assets						1 340	1 340
Cash and cash equivalents	1 770						1 770
Loans and receivables	1 770	1 770					1 770
Total financial assets	12 464		716	477	35		13 692
Of which loans and receivables	12 314						12 314
Financial liabilities	11 149			530			11 679
Carried at amortized cost	11 149	11 661					11 149
Derivatives that qualify for hedge accounting				211			211
Derivatives that do not qualify for hedge accounting				319			319
Trade accounts payable	3 466					313	3 779
Carried at amortized cost	3 466	3 466					3 466
Non-financial liabilities						313	313
Other liabilities	953			167	5	979	2 104
Carried at amortized cost	953	954					953

Derivatives that qualify for hedge accounting		140		140
Derivatives that do not qualify for hedge accounting		27	5	32
Non-financial liabilities			979	979
Total financial liabilities	15 568	697	5	16 270
Of which carried at amortized cost	15 568			15 568
Of which derivatives that qualify for hedge accounting		351		351
Of which derivatives that do not qualify for hedge accounting		346		346

Source: Bayer AG, 2011 Annual Report, Note 30

Pension obligations

Another issue related to financial instruments is that of a company's obligations to pay pensions to former employees. Pension arrangements differ widely between countries and companies. In some countries, such as France, ultimate pension provision is in the hands of the government and is funded by social security charges. Private pension pools are paid out proportionately to those with an interest and there are no guaranteed payments. However, in many countries employers have played a significant role in the past in providing pensions in excess of state benefits. Typically such pension schemes are funded by the company putting money into a separate fund (which accumulates pension assets or **plan assets**), and the fund pays out the pension. The pension schemes are generally classified as either *defined contribution plans* or *defined benefit plans*. Under a **defined contribution** plan, the company pays fixed contributions to the fund and has no obligation to pay further contributions if the fund does not hold sufficient plan assets to pay the pension benefits. The kind of scheme that gives the most difficulty is the defined benefit pension scheme. Defined benefit plans are very common in Europe and North America. The pension scheme guarantees to provide a pension to the retired employee which is a proportion of their final salary or some average of their latter years working at the company. The employee accumulates rights to a bigger and bigger proportion with each year of work.

IAS 19, *Employee Benefits*, sets the rules for pension plan accounting. Defined contribution plans are relatively easy to account for: contributions payable to the plan are recognized as an expense as the employee provides services. For defined benefit plans, IAS 19 requires the company to make an estimate of the pension obligation at reporting date (the **present value of its defined benefit obligations** for current and past service of employees) and to recognize a **defined benefit liability** (a kind of provision), net of the fair value of the funded plan assets. As for the statement of profit or loss effect (pension cost), the underlying principle of IAS 19 is that the cost of providing **retirement benefits** should be recognized in the period when the benefit is earned, not when it is paid. Broadly, the pension cost for the current year is determined as the change in the defined benefit liability for the year and charged to the statement of profit or loss. Pension plans need not be fully funded; they may even be unfunded. The funding rate does affect the defined benefit liability as recognized in the statement of financial position (through the fair value of the plan assets), but not the **defined benefit obligation** (DBO).

There are a number of problems with defined benefit schemes. The central problem is that the defined benefit obligation is estimated based on a set of **actuarial assumptions**. The company (or its actuaries) have to forecast how long employees will work for the company, what their final salary will be and how long they will live after retirement. In assessing how much funding to put aside for this, they similarly have to forecast what the return will be on investments (plan assets) over the expected life of the employee. Obviously, both these areas of forecasting involve some quite distant time horizons and some very significant unknowns, even if the law of large numbers does reduce the forecast risk. The actuarial assumptions encompass demographic and financial assumptions: demographic assumptions about future characteristics of current and former employees (and their dependents), such as mortality during and after employment, rates of employee turnover and early retirement, and financial assumptions dealing with items such as the discount rate (to calculate present value over a relatively long period of time), future salary and benefit levels (defining the target pension) and the expected rate of **return on plan assets**. Defined benefit calculations are quite sensitive for these actuarial assumptions, meaning that if the assumptions prove to be wrong, current shareholders may find themselves making extra provision for employees who stopped work years before. Recent years have proved to be very difficult for companies with defined benefit schemes, precisely because their calculation of the funding requirements has been seriously wrong, leaving a number of schemes acutely underfunded. The primary reasons for this are (a) a considerable increase in life expectancy (50 years ago a European man retiring at 65 would very likely die before reaching the age of 67, whereas he would now probably live to about 75 or 80 years old); (b) the volatile performance of the stock markets in recent years; and (c) the low rates of interest on loans, affecting the discount rate to be used in the present value calculations. This has left some companies facing considerable deficits.

Actuarial assumptions have to be best estimates and financial assumptions must be based on market expectations at the balance sheet date for the period over which the obligations are to be settled. Changes in actuarial estimates (for example for greater life expectancy) will affect the accumulated benefit obligation. These changes in actuarial assumptions, but also unexpected changes in the fair value of the plan assets, result in *actuarial gains and losses*.

IAS 19 is in a transitional phase. An amendment was issued in June 2011 which will be mandatory from January 2013 but which may be applied earlier. The revised standard requires service cost and interest to be reported in the statement of profit and loss with changes in actuarial assumptions being shown in Other Comprehensive Income.

The original standard provided for deferral of changes in actuarial estimates, this allowed for a **corridor** of 10 per cent of the DBO or value of the plan assets

COMPANY REPORT

STORA ENSO – ANNUAL REPORT 2011

Note 1 – Accounting Principles (extract)

Employee benefits

The Group operates a number of defined benefit and contribution plans throughout the world, the assets of which are generally held in separate trustee administered funds. The pension plans are generally funded by payments from employees and by the relevant Group companies, taking into account the recommendations of independent qualified actuaries. Group contributions to the defined contribution pension plans are charged to the Income Statement in the year to which they relate.

For defined benefit plans, pension accounting costs are assessed using the projected unit credit method. Under this method, the cost of providing pensions is charged to the Income Statement so as to spread the regular cost over the service lives of employees in accordance with the advice of qualified actuaries who carry out a full valuation of the plan every year. The pension obligation is measured as the present value of estimated future cash outflows using interest rates of highly rated corporate bonds or government securities as appropriate that match the currency and expected duration of the related liability.

The Group immediately recognizes all actuarial gains and losses arising from defined benefit plans directly in equity, as disclosed in its Statement of Comprehensive Income. Past service costs are however identified at the time of any plan amendments and, where vested, are shown in the income statement, whilst unvested amounts are amortized systematically over the vesting period. In the Group Statement of Financial Position, the full liability for all plan deficits is recorded, as adjusted for any past service costs still to be amortized.

Note 21 – Post-Employment Benefits (extract)

Amounts recognized on the Statement of Financial Position – Defined Benefit Plans

(EUR million)	As at 31 December					
	2011	2010	2011	2010	2011	2010
	Total defined benefit plans		Defined benefit pension plans		Other post-employment benefits	
Present value of funded obligations	807.0	760.3	807.0	760.3	—	
Present value of unfunded obligations	296.0	287.4	275.0	268.5	21.0	18.9
Defined Benefit Obligations (DBO)	1 103.0	1 047.7	1 082.0	1 028.8	21.0	18.9
Fair value of plan assets	773.5	743.1	773.5	743.1	—	—
Effect of asset ceiling	1.9	—	1.9	—	—	—
Net Liability in Defined Benefit Plans	**331.4**	**304.8**	**310.4**	**285.7**	**21.0**	**18.9**
Unrecognized prior service costs	−0.7	−1.0	—	—	−0.7	−1.0
Net Liability	**330.7**	**303.6**	**310.4**	**285.7**	**20.3**	**17.9**

Amounts recognized in the income statement

| (EUR million) | As at 31 December | | | | | |
| | 2011 | 2010 | 2011 | 2010 | 2011 | 2010 |
	Total defined benefit plans		Defined benefit pension plans		Other post-employment benefits	
Current service cost	9.7	10.4	8.6	9.4	1.1	1.0
Interest cost	45.8	47.4	45.0	46.6	0.8	0.8
Expected return on plan assets	−37.9	−34.7	−37.9	−34.8	—	0.1
Past service cost recognized in the year	0.4	0.1	0.2	—	0.2	0.1
Total included in personnel expenses	18.0	23.2	15.9	21.2	2.1	2.0

Defined benefit plans: Country assumptions used in calculating obligations

| | As at 31 December | | | | | |
| | 2011 | 2010 | 2011 | 2010 | 2011 | 2010 |
	Finland		Germany		Sweden	
Discount rate %	4.25	4.75	4.25	4.75	3.50	4.00
Expected return on plan assets %	4.25	w4.60	4.50	4.50	5.00	6.00
Future salary increase %	3.5	3.5	2.5	2.4	3.0	3.0
Future pension increase %	2.1	2.1	2.0	2.0	2.0	2.0
Average current retirement age	63.8	64.0	65.0	65.0	64.9	64.8
Weighted average life expectancy	88.00	88.00	85.00	84.80	87.00	86.84

Source: Stora Enso, Annual Report, 2011

within which such actuarial gains and losses need not be immediately recognized. This provided a sort of cushion against short-term fluctuations. Where a change went outside the corridor, this had to be recognized, but it might be expensed over the remaining service life of the employees concerned. This treatment will be visible in some financial statements for 2012 but will disappear thereafter.

The discount rate which is used to calculate the present value should be the market rate on high-quality corporate bonds. Companies must disclose the discount rate, since use of a high rate has the effect of reducing the present value very significantly. Analysts should compare the discount rate used with that used by other companies.

The disclosures also include the fair value of plan assets. This should be the current market value, where there is one. However, if there is no market, then the fair value has to be estimated by discounting forecast future cash flows. The IASB also introduced extra disclosures calling for a breakdown of the investments included in plan assets by class of investment and a note of the expected rate of return. This too is aimed at allowing analysts to gauge the reasonableness of the assumptions behind the figures.

The IASB and the FASB have agreed a joint project to revise pension accounting, but this is likely to be a long drawn out and controversial project, and has not even been started yet. The standard-setters would like to introduce revised recognition rules to take account of plans where the risks are shared between the employee and the employer. As companies have tended to withdraw from defined benefit plans because the costs are now very high, in light of growing life expectations, they have in some cases introduced schemes where they (and possibly the employee) pay into a fund. The employee receives the fund (or an annuity bought with its proceeds) on retirement, but the employer guarantees a minimum return to the fund while it is accumulating. This is similar to a defined contribution scheme, but with some additional risk for the employer.

Provisions

Provisions and related issues are covered in IAS 37, *Provisions, Contingent Liabilities and Contingent Assets*. IAS 37 refers to a contingency as a condition or situation, the ultimate outcome of which, gain or loss, 'will be confirmed only by the occurrence, or non-occurrence, of one or more uncertain future events not wholly within the control of the entity' (see box below on IAS 37, definitions). In a sense all provisions are contingent because they are uncertain in timing or amount. We have already dealt with the borderline between provisions and contingent liabilities in Chapter 6. Recall that IAS 37 retains a specific distinction between provisions and contingent liabilities. Provisions imply a *present* obligation where an outflow of resources is *probable*, whereas a contingent liability reflects a *possible* obligation or a present obligation where the outflow of resources is not probable or cannot be measured with sufficient reliability.

Generally speaking, any company has an ongoing bundle of obligations, contracts and operations. It is the fact that the company is a continuing business which makes the annual profit of necessity an estimate based on a number of assumptions about the future. IAS 37 in effect says that as long as future foreseeable events are expected to be profitable there is no need to reflect them in the financial statements, and indeed prudence requires that future profits are not recognized in advance. However, future losses are another matter entirely.

If a company has a loss-making division, this would not generally qualify as requiring a contingency note disclosure, but one would expect that the chairman's statement or review of operations would make clear that this is the case and would outline what action is being taken to deal with it. However, the outcome

IAS 37 – PROVISIONS, CONTINGENT LIABILITIES AND CONTINGENT ASSETS (extracts)

Definitions

10. A *contingent liability* is:

   (a) a possible obligation that arises from past events and whose existence will be confirmed only by the occurrence or non-occurrence of one or more uncertain future events not wholly within the control of the entity; or

   (b) a present obligation that arises from past events but is not recognized because:

   (i) it is not probable that an outflow of resources embodying economic benefits will be required to settle the obligation; or

   (ii) the amount of the obligation cannot be measured with sufficient reliability.

A *contingent asset* is a possible asset that arises from past events and whose existence will be confirmed only by the occurrence or non-occurrence of one or more uncertain future events not wholly within the control of the entity.

Source: IAS 37, *Provisions, Contingent Liabilities and Contingent Assets*

of a legal case such as being pursued for anti-competitive behaviour by the European Commission would certainly qualify as something which needs treatment in the financial statements. The question which next arises is, if there is a foreseeable future loss, should we disclose it in the financial statements or do we need actually to recognize the amount of the loss in the accounts?

IAS 37 explicitly states that future operating losses cannot be provided for. Such losses do not meet the IASB definition of liability and, consequently, the recognition criteria set out for provisions in IAS 37. Future operating losses have to be reported in the future in the same way as future operating profits. An expectation of future operating losses constitutes, however, a primary indication that certain operating assets might be impaired and thus could trigger extensive impairment testing of assets. An exception is made for onerous contracts, which could be executory contracts.

An *executory contract* is a contract where the company has entered into an agreement but fulfilment of the terms has not been completed (and perhaps not even started). Most businesses have many of these and, if the business is continuing, you might expect at any given moment that there would be sales agreements, supplier purchase contracts, capital commitments, etc. at varying stages of completion. IAS 37 says that these contracts need no special treatment except if such a contract is particularly 'onerous' – i.e. where the expected unavoidable costs of meeting the contract are greater than the benefits expected to be received from it. In general, if a contract is onerous, the company should recognize the present obligation under the contract as a provision in the balance sheet. An example of an onerous contract could be a **non-cancellable operating lease** for office space which is no longer needed by the company.

Recall that IAS 37 acknowledges the following categories of (potential) liabilities:

4. *Clear liability*, but where the amount and timing of future expenditure is uncertain. Here the company should make a provision – expense an estimated figure in the statement of profit or loss and carry forward a provision in the balance sheet, against which the expense will be offset when it arises.

5. *Possible liability*, or liability where the amount involved is so uncertain as to make a reliable estimate impossible. The company should disclose a contingent liability in the notes to the accounts.

6. A *liability* which is *possible* but *unlikely to cause an outflow of assets* – no disclosure.

Related information is clearly important to the analyst in forming an opinion about the future profitability of the business. At the same time, it is sometimes quite sensitive information whose disclosure may have wider consequences for the company than simply influencing analysts' forecasts. A disclosure that the company is being pursued in the courts for causing environmental damage or infringing other company patents would have a considerable negative public relations impact.

Contingent assets on the other hand arise where events give rise to the possibility of an inflow of economic benefits to the company. Suppose, for example, that the company pursues a claim through legal processes, but the outcome is still uncertain. Prudence considerations prohibit in this case the recognition of an asset in the financial statements since it would probably result in the recognition of income that may never be realized. However, when the inflow of economic resources is probable, the contingent asset (material contingent gains) should be disclosed in the notes. If the inflow of resources is either possible or remote, the contingent asset is not even disclosed. Qualification for disclosure is thus more tight for contingent liabilities than for contingent assets.

The approach with regard to contingent assets and contingent liabilities may, however, change drastically in the future. Indeed, the IASB took the tentative decision (June 2005) to abandon the notion of contingent assets and contingent liabilities altogether. However, many constituents were not happy with the proposals, which included measuring a provision at its fair value. As a result of the financial crisis the project was put to one side but may be revived in the future. A fundamental question is whether the provision should be measured at the value the entity thinks it is most likely to settle, discounted back, or whether the measurement should be based on expected value (the combination of a probability-weighted range of estimates).

Post reporting period events

A more specialist disclosure is events occurring after the reporting period (also referred to as events after the balance sheet date). While multinationals try to publish their financial statements as quickly as possible after the financial year-end, it is difficult to finalize the financial statements of all subsidiaries, obtain auditor approval and then consolidate the statements in under two months, and many continental European companies take up to four months to do this. Potentially

IAS 10 – EVENTS AFTER THE REPORTING PERIOD *(extract)*

Definitions

3. *Events after the reporting period* are those events, favourable and un-favour-able, that occur between the end of the reporting period and the date when the financial statements are authorized for issue. Two types of events can be identified:

(a) those that provide evidence of conditions that existed at the end of the reporting period (*adjusting events after the reporting period*); and

(b) those that are indicative of conditions that arose after the reporting period (*non-adjusting events after the reporting period*).

Source: IAS 10, *Events after the Reporting Period*

this means that events may take place between the financial year-end and the publication date of the financial statements which have a significant bearing upon the future of the company. IAS 10, *Events after the Reporting Period*, addresses more specifically events (both favourable and unfavourable) occurring between the end of the reporting period and the date when the financial statements are authorized for issue.

IAS 10 distinguishes between adjusting and non-adjusting **events after the reporting period. Adjusting events** are those that provide evidence of conditions that existed at the end of the reporting period. These events shall be reflected in the financial statements by adjusting the amounts recognized in the financial statements. Examples are:

■ after the reporting period a court decision confirms that the entity had a present obligation at reporting date – in this case a new provision will be recognized or an existing one will be adjusted

■ the discovery of fraud that shows that the financial statements are incorrect

■ the bankruptcy of a current customer after the end of the reporting period probably confirms an impairment loss on a trade receivable at reporting date – in this case the company will have to adjust the carrying amount of the trade receivable.

Non-adjusting events after the reporting period will not affect the amounts recognized in the statement of financial position or statement of profit or loss but, if material, their nature and an estimate of their financial effect should be disclosed. Examples of such events might be that after the reporting period a fire destroys a major production plant or a restructuring plan is announced. These events could influence the economic decisions of users taken on the basis of the financial statements and thus have to be disclosed. IAS 10 also explicitly states that dividends declared after the reporting period are not recognized as a liability because at the end of the reporting period they do not constitute a present obligation. They should, however, be disclosed in the notes.

'NESTLE - ANNUAL REPORT 2011'

24. Events after the balance sheet date

At 15 February 2012, date of approval of the Financial Statements by the Board of Directors, the Group had no subsequent events that warrant a modification of the value of the assets and liabilities or an additional disclosure.

Source: Nestlé, Annual Report 2011

Discontinued operations

Multinational companies are in effect usually a bundle of businesses that are not necessarily related to each other except by ownership. Often they will sell off parts of the group that they have decided are no longer 'strategic', or they will buy another group and hive off some of its businesses. IFRS require that information about a business that either has already been discontinued or is about to be sold should be shown separately in the financial statements.

STANDARDS

IFRS 5 – NON-CURRENT ASSETS HELD FOR SALE AND DISCONTINUED OPERATIONS *(extract)*

31. A *component of an entity* comprises operations and cash flows that can be clearly distinguished, operationally and for financial reporting purposes, from the rest of the entity. In other words, a component of an entity will have been a cash-generating unit or a group of cash-generating units while being held for use.

32. A discontinued operation is a component of an entity that either has been disposed of, or is classified as held for sale, and
   (a) represents a separate major line of business or geographical area of operations,
   (b) is part of a single co-ordinated plan to dispose of a separate major line of business or geographical area of operations, or
   (c) is a subsidiary acquired exclusively with a view to resale.

33. An entity shall disclose:
   (a) a single amount in the statement of comprehensive income comprising the total of:
      (i) the post-tax profit or loss of discontinued operations and
      (ii) the post-tax gain or loss recognized on the measurement to fair value less costs to sell or on the disposal of the assets or disposal group(s) constituting the discontinued operation.
   (b) an analysis of the single amount in (a) into:
      (i) the revenue, expenses and pre-tax profit or loss of discontinued operations;

> (ii) the related income tax expense as required by paragraph 81(h) of IAS 12;
>
> (iii) the gain or loss recognized on the measurement to fair value less costs to sell or on the disposal of the assets or disposal group(s) constituting the discontinued operation; and
>
> (iv) the related income tax expense as required by paragraph 81(h) of IAS 12.
>
> The analysis may be presented in the notes or in the statement of comprehensive income. If it is presented in the statement of comprehensive income it shall be presented in a section identified as relating to discontinued operations, i.e. separately from continuing operations.
>
> *Source:* IFRS 5, *Non-current Assets Held for Sale and Discontinued Operations*

It is very useful for analysts who are trying to predict future profits to have the profits or losses from businesses that are being sold or have been sold stripped out of the Statement of Comprehensive Income. When that has been done they can see what are the profits from the continuing business. IFRS 5 therefore requires a separate presentation of this as set out in the extract from the standard.

The standard also requires that assets and liabilities that are being sold should be separately identified in the statement of financial position. A bundle of assets and liabilities representing a business to be sold is called a **disposal group**. The accounting for this is another case where prudence is overriding matching. When the multinational has decided to sell this business, it must work out what is the fair value. If this is lower than the book value, then an impairment loss has to be taken, and the disposal group shown in the statement of financial position at fair value less costs to sell. However, if fair value is higher than book value, no gain is recognized at this point.

Environmental disclosures

Part of this change in attitudes involves the company's relationship with society in general and in particular how the company impacts upon the physical environment. Environmental disclosures by companies are still at an early stage, but very few large companies do not make reference somewhere to their environmental policies. Companies exhibit a range of different strategies in pursuing environmental disclosure: from adapting reactive positions in debates on environmentally damaging issues to taking proactive positions, mainly in relatively less sensitive sectors. The less discretionary part of environmental reporting relates to environmental costs being brought into the financial statements.

Accounting standard-setters have so far not addressed the broader issue of corporate environmental reporting, but a number of professional accounting bodies have produced guidelines and the United Nations Intergovernmental Working Group of Experts on International Standards of Accounting and Reporting (ISAR) published detailed recommendations in 1998 which remain the most thorough review of the area but have no regulatory authority. In the EU, environmental accountability and reporting has increased through new initiatives of the European Commission, like the publication of recommendations on the recognition, measurement and disclosure of environmental issues (*Official Journal of the European Communities*, June 13, 2001, L 156/33–42).

The absence of comprehensive regulation leaves companies with a free hand in determining what they publish, with the consequence that information is generally quite specific to the reporting company and is not audited. The majority of the environmental disclosures appear in the directors' report or an equivalent operating and financial review section of the annual report. Alternatives are a stand-alone report or a stand-alone environmental section in the annual report. Financially oriented environmental disclosures figure primarily

COMPANY REPORT

NESTLÉ

Creating shared value Key performance indicators

	GRI	2010	2011
Environmental sustainability			
Production volume			
Total production volume (million tonnes)		43.74	45.21
Materials			
Raw materials used (million tonnes)	EN1	23.27	22.87
Materials for packaging purposes (million tonnes)	EN1	4.59	4.58
Packaging source optimization (kilotonnes saved)	70.8	39.3	
Energy			
Total on-site energy consumption (petajoules)	88.6	90.1	
Total on-site energy consumption (gigajoules per tonne of product)	2.03	1.99	
On-site energy generated from renewable sources (% of total)	12.3	11.6	
Total direct energy consumption (petajoules)	EN3	63.0	64.3
Total indirect energy consumption (petajoules)	EN4	67.6	70.1
Water			
Total water withdrawal (million m3)	EN8	144	143
Total water withdrawal (m3 per tonne of product)	EN8	3.29	3.17
Biodiversity			
Total size of manufacturing sites located in protected areas (hectares) (l)	EN11	44.2	

Source: Nestlé, Creating Shared Value, 2011, extract

in the notes to the accounts and deal mainly with environmental liabilities and contingencies in compliance with financial reporting requirements. The bulk of the environmental reporting is, however, voluntary. The aspects of environmental management that are reported most often include capital expenditures for anti-pollution equipment, recycling and conservation policy, environmental management and audit practices, and the costs of complying with governmental emissions standards.

Should analysts be interested in this information? Well, yes, because viewed from a strictly capitalist standpoint, we are moving further into a political environment where governments are insisting that 'the polluter pays'. This means that any company which has caused pollution, intentionally or otherwise, may become liable to clean up the countryside and compensate people who are badly affected. Hidden pollution is therefore, aside from social considerations, very bad from an investor's point of view because it may mean a severe drain on future earnings. An extreme case in point is the settlements reached in the US between state governments and the tobacco industry for large payments to be made to compensate the government for health care costs caused by treating smoking-related diseases.

Decommissioning liabilities

This brings us back to formal accounting. A potential clean-up or compensation liability should be addressed in compiling the financial statements as either the object of a provision or disclosure of a contingent liability. At a more advanced level, it is worth looking at how companies have to account for decommissioning costs. Decommissioning liabilities arise if a company, when it purchases or constructs an asset, takes on a contractual or statutory obligation to decommission the asset or restore the asset site to certain minimum standards or both, at the end of the asset's life. For nuclear power plants, for example, there usually exists a statutory obligation to dismantle the operational facilities at the end of their useful life. Such future dismantling expenditure and accompanying site restoration costs can be profound. Also oil companies now provide for decommissioning costs alongside the depreciation of mineral resources. In other words, they now recognize that they cannot just close down a well and go away, they need to make good the land as far as possible. Since this cost of using the mineral resource can be estimated, it should be spread over the period when the asset is used. Increasingly we should expect this approach to be applied to factories as well.

There has been some disagreement as to how such decommissioning provisions should be applied. Previous practice was to charge an amount each year to the statement of profit or loss and build up the required provision year on year over the life of the operational facility. However, IAS 37 says that if there is a dismantling obligation, a full provision should be recognized as soon as the obligation exists, usually at construction date or commencement of operations. Additionally, the IASB considers these decommissioning and site restoration costs necessary expenditure in order to access the economic benefits expected to flow from the asset. Therefore, these costs have to be capitalized as part of the acquisition cost of the asset at the date on which the company becomes obligated to incur them.

SIBIR ENERGY

Decommissioning provision – accounting policies (extract)

Oil field and other asset retirement obligations including decommissioning costs

The Group makes full provision for the future cost of decommissioning oil and gas production facilities and related pipelines on a discounted basis upon the installation of those facilities. Provisions for environmental remediation are made when a clean-up is required under the Group's licence obligations, in accordance with Russian state or federal law, or when the requirement is probable and the amount can be reasonably determined

The provision for the costs of decommissioning and environmental remediation of these production facilities and pipelines at the end of their economic lives has been estimated using existing technology, at current prices increased by forecast future Russian inflation and discounted using a real discount rate of 10 per cent (2006: 10 per cent). These costs are expected to be incurred over the next 20 to 30 years. While the provision is based on the best estimate of future costs and the economic lives of the facilities and pipelines, there is uncertainty regarding both the amount and timing of incurring these costs. In addition, there is additional uncertainty regarding the scale of any possible environmental contamination, the timing and extent of future corrective actions and changes in Russian state or federal requirements.

Source: Sibir Energy plc, Annual Report, 2003

However, one of the key differences between decommissioning costs and other costs of acquisition is the timing of the related expenditures. Decommissioning costs will not become payable until some future date, possibly several decades in the future. Consequently, there is likely to be uncertainty over the amount of costs that will be incurred and the issue of the time value of money undoubtedly will be very significant. Management should record its best estimate of the company's obligations and will have to use discounting to address the impact of the delayed cash flows. The amount capitalized as part of the asset's cost will be the amount estimated to be paid, discounted to the date of initial recognition. The related counterpart is recognized in provisions. Thereafter, the asset (capitalized decommissioning costs included) is depreciated over its useful life, while the discounted provision is progressively unwound. With the passage of time the increase in the decommissioning provision is recognized as a borrowing cost. From this, it should be clear that accounting for decommissioning costs will have a profound impact on the statement of financial position and statement of profit or loss as it affects long-term assets, provisions, operating and finance expenses over a long period of time.

If we look further than the financially oriented disclosures on environmental liabilities it becomes, however, apparent that the content and quality of environmental reports varies widely across companies. The heterogeneity of environmental disclosures makes them in fact incomparable. Today, initiatives aimed at converging the practices are being taken by, for example, the Global Reporting Initiative (GRI), which has received considerable support and acceptance worldwide for its guidelines on sustainability reporting. The GRI provides globally applicable guidelines for organizations wishing to report separately on the environmental (as well as social and economic) aspects of their activities. The core issue for most environmental reporting standards is for the reporters to ascertain who the stakeholders of the company are and to adjust the report thereafter. The same goes for other types of corporate social (or societal) reporting.

Intellectual capital

One of the issues the analyst needs to review in addition to assets and liabilities that appear in the statement of financial position is the existence and relevance of the 'intellectual capital' of a group. Essentially the argument is that, while physical assets (such as a city centre sales location or an efficient factory) may be important for the group, intellectual assets (patents, brands, staff know-how, research and development, customer loyalty) are possibly even more so: you can build a new factory in a few months for a finite amount of money, but a brand takes years and the cost cannot be forecast reliably. Intellectual capital is even more important, obviously, in a service industry where it relates to the quality and nature of the service, which in turn is the product you are selling. Increasingly there is a perception that business now changes rapidly, and the ability to develop new products or adapt methods quickly is considered to be part of the intellectual capital of the group. Intellectual capital fits into the framework of analyst's concerns about assessing the quality of the management and the quality of the assets under their control.

How do companies convey this information? We discussed the difficulties of measuring intangible assets in a historical cost framework in Chapter 5. There are several problems. First, a company incurs costs often over several years in product research, staff development and related areas, without being able to tie these costs to an identifiable asset (source of future cash flows) until towards the end of the process, so these costs are taken directly to the statement of profit or loss. Second, where staff development is concerned, the company does not 'control' the asset: a trained person usually has the right to leave the company, so money spent training them cannot be regarded as an asset in accounting terms. Third, a company may hire people who have the skills needed (who have themselves invested in their personal development by doing an MBA) and so there is no acquisition cost available to be capitalized.

Clearly, traditional accounting does not provide the techniques for this kind of asset, and that is not surprising when you remember that financial reporting was developed in the 19th century. So far there is therefore no way of reflecting this through accounting measures in the annual report. However, it is an issue which some companies are trying to address internally and where some discussion should be expected somewhere in the annual report.

BETWEEN THE LINES

The measurement and management of intellectual capital: an introduction

It is recognized that the intellectual capital of a firm plays a significant role in creating competitive advantage, and thus managers and other stakeholders in organizations are asking, with increasing frequency, that its value be measured and reported for planning, control, reporting and evaluation purposes. However, at this point, there is still a great deal of room for experimentation in quantifying and reporting on the intellectual capital of the firm.

Source: IFAC Handbook 1999, extract from summary of study published by the International Federation of Accountants, New York, in October 1998.

Summary

In this chapter we have looked at more advanced measurement issues and at a number of domains of supplementary disclosures. An overview of the IASB's current fair value accounting requirements makes clear that the boundaries of the traditional accounting model are moving. It seems that the age of financial instruments has ushered in incremental changes which tend in the direction of earlier recognition of assets and liabilities in the transaction cycle, as well as remeasurement within the cycle. This change does not change the measurement of profit in an absolute sense – the lifetime profits of the business will still be the same in total – but it does change the period in which profits are recognized.

We also noted that the fashion is for more and more disclosures. In particular, we have looked at the problem of anticipating future costs, both in a general sense as provisions or disclosure of contingencies, and explored the reporting headlines of financial instruments, pension benefits, post reporting period events and discontinued operations. Moreover, we noted that environmental disclosure and intellectual capital reporting has increased over time, but remains largely fragmentary and lacks comparability across companies.

Discussion Questions

1. Explain the differences between the following value concepts: exit value, value-in-use and deprival value.
2. What is meant by an executory contract? Do executory contracts affect financial statements?
3. Discuss why the existence of contingencies is important to the financial statement analyst, making reference to environmental issues and financial instruments.

4. Explain what is meant by intellectual capital and discuss what an analyst can do to make an assessment of the intellectual capital of a particular group.

5. Describe the categories into which IAS 39, *Financial Instruments: Recognition and Measurement*, requires financial assets and liabilities to be classified. For each category, explain how they should be measured in the statement of financial position. If measured at fair value, the explanation should include how changes in fair value of the financial instruments are treated in the financial statements.

Assignments

The following assignments have answers on the lecturer side of the digital support resources for the book.

1. On 31 December 20X8 (fiscal year end), Bruinzee NV is in the process of defending a legal case brought against it for damages caused by the use of some of its products. Bruinzee's legal advisors provided the following estimates of the likely outcome of the litigation:

    ■ 60 per cent probability of defending the case successfully;
    ■ 30 per cent probability of being required to pay €4m in damages;
    ■ 10 per cent probability of being required to pay €6m in damages.

    Given these estimates, a provision of €1.8m (60 per cent × nil + 30 per cent × €4m + 10 per cent × €6m) has been recognized in the 20X8 financial statements. Moreover, the Board of Directors of Bruinzee NV estimate that total legal costs of defending the case will amount to €300 000 (of which €200 000 has already been invoiced by the legal advisors covering fees up to and including 31 December 20X8). The legal fees of €200 000 have been expensed but the remaining expected future legal costs have not yet been provided for at the end of 20X8.

    In the event of successfully defending the litigation case, the legal costs will be recovered, but this has not yet been reflected in the 20X8 financial statements of Bruinzee NV.
    Required
    (a) Evaluate the accounting treatment applied by Bruinzee NV. If you do not agree, propose and explain appropriate adjustments.

    (b) Idem, considering the following revised estimates of Bruinzee's legal advisors and provision amount: '30 per cent probability of defending the case successfully – 60 per cent probability of being required to pay €4 million in damages – 10 per cent probability of being required to pay €6 million in damages. Given these estimates, a provision of €3m (30 per cent 3 nil + 60 per cent 3 €4m + 10 per cent 3 €6m) has been recognized in the 20X8 financial statements.'

2. On 2 January 20X0 Philippo Tist Corporation brought into use an industrial site that had been constructed at a total cost of €50m. The company has the legal right to use the site for a ten-year period, at the end of which the site has to be returned to the legal owner in its original condition. The directors of Philippo Tist estimate that the cost of restoring the site on 31 December 20X9 will be €15m (in 20X9 prices). The construction cost includes the right to use the site without further payment for the ten-year period. The rate to

use in any discounting calculations is 8 per cent. The present value of €1000 receivable in ten years when the cost of capital is 8 per cent is €463.

Required

Show the amounts that will appear in the statement of financial position of Philippo Tist Corporation as at 31 December 20X0 in respect of the site and the amounts that will appear in the statement of profit or loss for the year ended 31 December 20X0. Indicate where in the statement of financial position and where in the statement of profit or loss the relevant amounts should be presented.

(ACCA adapted)

3. Omega follows the cost model when measuring its property, plant and equipment. One of its properties was carried in the statement of financial position at 31 March 20X7 at $6m. The depreciable amount of this property was estimated at $3.6m at 31 March 20X7 and the estimated future economic life of the property at 31 March 20X7 was 18 years. Omega depreciates its properties on a monthly basis. On 1 January 20X8 Omega decided to dispose of the property as it was surplus to requirements and began to actively seek a buyer. On 1 January 20X8 Omega estimated that the market value of the property was $7.1m and that the costs of selling the property would be $80 000. These estimates remained appropriate at 31 March 20X8. The property was sold on 1 June 20X8 for net proceeds of $7m.

Required

Explain, with relevant calculations, how the property would be treated in the financial statements of Omega for the year ended 31 March 20X8 and the year ending 31 March 20X9.

(ACCA adapted)

CHAPTER 15

International taxation

The object of this chapter is to give you a working overview of taxation. Generally speaking, governments have a bigger stake in companies than do shareholders (in terms of receiving cash flows from the company), and yet not all companies pay as much attention to tax minimization as they might, nor do company executives have a clear idea of where tax bites in a company's cost structure.

This chapter will first look at the different kinds of tax and how they are levied within a single jurisdiction and then focus on corporate income taxes and the allocation of income tax expense to accounting periods. The chapter ends with a specific look at tax issues which concern multinationals and cross-border activities.

Chapter Structure

- ■ Introduction
- ■ Corporate income tax and dividends
- ■ Deferred taxation
- ■ International taxation
- ■ Transfer pricing
- ■ Tax havens
- ■ Summary
- ■ Discussion questions

Introduction

The number of taxes to which a company is subject varies considerably from country to country and depends partly upon political structure and partly upon historical precedent. The way in which taxes are collected varies widely as well. From a company perspective, we can identify the main types of taxation which are 'costs' to the company, as follows:

1. social security charges
2. local/regional taxes
3. national corporate income taxes.

Some accountants would say that corporate income-based taxes are not a cost as such because they are not made in exchange of goods and services specific to the company and are only levied when there is profit, so they are a distribution of profit to the government as a priority stakeholder in the success of the company.

However, assuming that we expect a company to be profitable to shareholders, we should try to maximize after-tax cash flows for them, and tax represents a negative flow. In practice, accounting standards-setters do not adhere to the distribution view of corporate income taxation and deal with income-based taxes as a business expense.

Within the European Union, Value Added Tax (VAT) is a major source of tax income and companies collect this for the government, but technically this is a tax on the consumer, not on the company, in the same way as sales taxes are in the US and other countries.

■ *Social security charges*. Here there is a great difference between countries in the extent to which they levy contributions from employers and employees based on the amount of pay. In Switzerland, for example, the deductions are relatively low but the employee is obliged to take out compulsory private medical insurance, whereas in France the deductions are high and relatively little is left to the individual. There is also a great variation in contributions to pension schemes, with some countries preferring a system in which the state plays a major role and others preferring to participate in private sector schemes. This means that in some countries payroll-based charges can amount to an additional 50 per cent on top of gross salaries, whereas in others the employee expects to pay more – and may expect a higher salary. Payroll-based taxes and contributions to pension schemes are generally accounted for in the financial statements as part of personnel cost, and are therefore invisible both to the external analyst and often the internal manager.

■ *Local/regional taxes*. Here again there is a wide variety of taxes and methods of collecting them. In federations, such as Germany or Switzerland, regional political units (Länder, Cantons) are able to levy taxes on cor-por-ate profits, as also are municipalities. This means that corporate income taxes may be split three ways: local municipality, regional political unit and federal government (and they are not necessarily calculated off the same profit base). All of these taxes, since they are profit based, will appear in the financial statements as a deduction from shareholder profit.

However, in other countries there are different ways of channelling money to municipalities. In France they receive the proceeds from annual vehicle taxes, and also levy a tax which is based on the capital structure of the company. In the UK, municipalities receive tax based on the value of property occupied by people in their jurisdiction. These are not income taxes as such and do not therefore normally appear in the statement of profit or loss as a tax but as a cost of property or of running motor vehicles, etc.

■ *National corporate income taxes*. These are the most visible part of company taxation. Governments use this kind of taxation both to raise funds and to encourage (or to penalize) particular kinds of behaviour by companies. The calculation of taxable profit is done according to tax rules, rather than accounting rules, but one of the most important shaping forces in accounting is the relationship between these and in particular the degree to which in any jurisdiction, the calculation of taxable profit is limited by what is in the published accounts.

■ *Value Added Tax* is applied throughout the European Union and the European Commission in fact receives a small proportion (less than 2 per cent) of the proceeds of the national rate. VAT is imposed on customers at each stage of a product's value-added chain, based on the value added at that point. For example, suppose that in a country with a 20 per cent VAT rate, a manufacturer sells its product for €1000 to a retailer. If the seller's cost to manufacture the product is €800, the VAT is 20 per cent of (€1000 – €800) or €40. In practice, companies do not charge the net VAT amount, but charge VAT to their customers on the full amount of the sales and are themselves charged VAT on their purchases. Afterwards the company separates out VAT received from customers and VAT paid to suppliers in its accounting and every month (or three months depending upon jurisdiction) pays the difference between the two to the tax authorities. Consequently, a company's accounts exclude VAT for income reporting purposes, both inside and outside the company. In general, where taxes are simply collected from customers on behalf of a third party, they are not part of the company's revenue and, by implication, are not an expense of the company paying the taxes to its suppliers.

VAT is therefore not a tax as such upon companies, but it does bear upon them to an extent. First, there is the administration of VAT which involves elaborate accounting systems to measure and control VAT payments. Second, there is the cost of maintaining the knowledge of staff and using outside experts to deal with changes and complex transactions. And, third, there is the cash flow problem. A company that sells on credit and is obliged to settle monthly with the VAT authorities will be in effect paying to the authorities VAT from customers which has been invoiced but which the customer has at that time not paid. There is a disguised cash flow effect which can increase a company's capital requirements considerably.

Corporate income tax and dividends

In most countries, even those such as Germany or France which are reputed to have a very close relationship between accounting profit and tax profit, the calculation of taxes on profits is based on an approach where there is a reconciliation statement between accounting profit and taxable profit:

Accounting profit before tax

Add back: disallowed expenses such as entertaining, fines, excess depreciation, excess provisions

Deduct: special allowances for capital investment, environmental protection, etc., non-taxable income

= Taxable profit

A particular problem in corporate taxation is that of the potential double taxation of dividends. Double taxation arises from concurrent corporate and personal income taxation. Suppose a country levies 30 per cent corporate income tax and then the company pays what is left as dividend to its shareholders. Suppose further that personal income tax is 50 per cent. That means that the dividend (70 per cent of the original pre-tax profit) will be subject to a supplementary 50 per cent personal income tax, which amounts to another 35 per cent of the original profit. The pre-tax profit has therefore been taxed in total at 65 per cent. This is a major disincentive to investors and different countries find different solutions to the problem. One way is to tax profits which are to be paid to shareholders at a lower rate than those retained in the company. Another way is to give shareholders a tax credit with their dividend.

A tax credit is intended to remove double taxation and to ensure that only personal income is taxed. Suppose in the above example that the company earns a pre-tax profit of €200 000 and decides that the whole post-tax profit will be made payable to shareholders as a dividend. The government first collects €60 000 as corporate income tax, but gives the shareholders a full tax credit for the same amount. The €60 000 tax credit allows the shareholders to pay no more than an additional €40 000 to comply with their tax obligation of a 50 per cent personal tax rate on €200 000 pre-tax income. In practice, governments will often grant tax rebates equivalent to a partial tax credit and therefore only partially remove double taxation of dividends.

The objectives of measuring (accounting) income for financial reporting purposes are quite different from the basic tax raising motives of measuring taxable profit. Consequently, the income tax expense reported in the statement of profit or loss will probably not be equal to the amount that is actually paid. The topic of deferred taxation arises from these differences. In general, deferred taxation rules will require companies to account for the tax consequences of transactions when the transactions are recognized in the financial statements. To understand the process of recognizing the tax expense in the statement of profit or loss, it is important to realize that the accounting rules that govern the reporting of income taxes in the financial statements, essentially attempt to apply the matching concept, where expenses (income tax expenses included) are matched to the period in which related revenues are reported. In this context specific rules are needed to allocate tax expense between accounting periods.

Deferred taxation

The more advanced sets of accounting rules require that the tax effects of transactions are recognized in the financial statements in the same period as the transactions themselves. Deferred taxes arise in the statement of profit or loss when the amount of taxes paid in the current period does not correspond with the amount of tax expense for the period based on the pre-tax profit reported in the financial statements. Evidently, deferred taxation will also affect the statement of financial position: **deferred tax assets** and **deferred tax liabilities** will reflect the future tax consequences of transactions which were not treated identically for taxation and financial reporting purposes.

Over the years, different sets of rules for accounting for deferred taxation have evolved. The earlier sets of rules were grounded in a statement of profit or loss perspective on deferred taxes. They focused on 'timing differences' or differences between the timing of the recognition of items of income and expenditure for financial reporting purposes (in the statement of profit or loss) and tax purposes. Inconsistencies with the conceptual framework of the IASB (and US GAAP) led in the 1990s to the development of a *temporary differences approach* where the deferred taxation reasoning starts from an analysis of the tax consequences of balance sheet components and not from a tax reconciliation of statement of profit or loss items.

A statement of profit or loss view on deferred taxes

The intuitively most appealing way to illustrate the concept of deferred taxes is, however, still the statement of profit or loss approach. Later we will comment on the balance sheet perspective of deferred taxation which underlies current international reporting rules on income taxes.

Starting from the statement of profit or loss, there are in effect two kinds of differences between the accounting measure of profit and the tax authorities' measure:

1. permanent differences
2. reversing timing differences.

The permanent differences arise because, for example, the tax authorities do not accept some expenses as a deduction from profits. Examples of this would be fines, in some countries bribes, sometimes entertaining or what the authorities consider to be unnecessarily expensive consumption such as supplying managers with luxury cars or holding board meetings in holiday resorts. These are simply 'disallowed', they cause taxable profit for the year to be higher than accounting profit and do not call for any special accounting. Permanent differences can also work in the opposite direction, for example when items of income recognized in the financial statements will never be taxable or where items are recognized as deductible for tax purposes but will never enter the statement of profit or loss as expenses.

Timing differences arise because the timing of the recognition of revenue, expenses, gains and losses in the statement of profit or loss occurs in a different period from taxable profit. Timing differences are differences between taxable profit and accounting profit that originate in one period and reverse in one or more subsequent periods. These timing differences lead to specific presentational issues in the financial statements. For example, some jurisdictions offer high tax depreciation at times, either just to encourage business to invest in general or to encourage a particular kind of investment which the government thinks is important (environmental protection, high technology, etc.). If this tax deductible accelerated depreciation can be claimed without using the high rate in the financial statements, this gives rise to a reversing **temporary difference**. The asset will be fully depreciated over its useful life in the financial statements; however, the tax paid by the company will be artificially low early in the asset's life, but later the asset will be depreciated in the accounts with no tax deduction available.

COMPANY REPORT

PHILIPS

Income taxes disclosures (extracts)
The tax expense on income before tax amounted to EUR 283 million (2010: EUR 499 million, 2009: EUR 99 million).

The components of income tax before taxes and income tax expense are as follows:

	2009	2010	2011
Netherlands	206	952	244
Foreign	292	1007	(753)
Income before taxes of continuing operations	**498**	**1959**	**(509)**
Netherlands:	(17)	(103)	(40)
Current tax income (expense)	(72)	(144)	44
Deferred tax income (expense)	(89)	(247)	4
Foreign:	(201)	(210)	(360)
Current tax income (expense)	189	(52)	149
Deferred tax income (expense)	(12)	(262)	(211)
Income tax expense of continuing operations	(99)	(499)	(283)
Income tax expense of discontinued operations	(2)	(10)	76
Income tax expense	**(101)**	**(509)**	**(207)**

Philips' operations are subject to income taxes in various foreign jurisdictions. The statutory income tax rates vary from 12.5 per cent to 41.0 per cent, which causes a difference between the weighted average statutory income tax rate and the Netherlands' statutory income tax rate of 25.0 per cent (2010: 25.5 per cent; 2009: 25.5 per cent).

Source: Philips, Annual Report 2011 – Note 3

PHILIPS

A reconciliation of the weighted average statutory income tax rate to the effective income tax rate of continuing operations is as follows:

	2009	2010	2011
Weighted average statutory income tax rate	18.1	26.6	55.4
Tax rate effect of:			
Changes related to:			
– utilization of previously reserved loss carryforwards	(0.2)	(0.5)	3.9
– new loss carryforwards not expected to be realized	9.3	2.1	(17.6)
– addition (releases)	(0.4)	0.3	2.9
Non-tax-deductible impairment charges	2.8	—	(98.3)
Non-taxable income	(23.3)	(7.5)	11.1
Non-tax-deductible expenses	23.6	3.9	(22.4)
Withholding and other taxes	4.2	1.2	4.5
Tax rate changes	(0.1)	0.2	(0.1)
Prior year tax results	(28.1)	(1.4)	4.5
Tax expenses due to other liabilities	7.5	(0.4)	(9.0)
Tax incentives and other	6.5	1.0	18.5
Effective tax rate	**19.9**	**25.5**	**(55.6)**

The weighted average statutory income tax rate increased in 2011 compared to 2010, as a consequence of a change in the country mix of income tax rates, as well as a significant change of the mix of profits in the various countries, which resulted in a loss recorded for the period.

Source: Philips, Annual Report 2011 – Note 3

To illustrate the problem let us look at an exaggerated model. Let us say that a company buys an asset in 20X1 for €10 000, intending to depreciate, for financial reporting purposes, over two years, but the tax authorities will allow the whole depreciation in the first year. If the company's profit before depreciation is €25 000 in each year, the accounting profit in both years would be €20 000 (€25 000 less €5000 depreciation on asset). However, the tax computations would be:

20X1	€	
Net profit before tax	20 000	
add back Depreciation	5 000	
deduct Capital allowance	–10 000	
Taxable profit		15 000
Tax due at 50 per cent		*7 500*

20X2	€
Net profit before tax	20 000
add back Depreciation	5 000
deduct Capital allowance	0
Taxable profit	25 000
Tax due at 50 per cent	12 500

Returning to the statement of profit or loss, the figures would be:

	20X1	20X2
Net income before tax	20 000	20 000
Corporate income tax	−7 500	−12 500
Net income after tax	12 500	7 500

The result of the timing difference is that the same net income before tax yields quite different results over the two years. So the question is: should that be reported in the financial statements as given above, or should the tax saving in year 1 (€2500 or 50 per cent of the depreciation difference) be set aside and carried forward to year 2 to **offset** against the year 2 tax charge and equalize the accounting charge for tax?

Deferred tax accounting rules require that the future tax consequences of this difference is recognized in the financial statements. So in the case above, the statement of profit or loss for 20X1 should be constructed:

Net profit before tax		20 000
Taxes due	7 500	
Deferred tax expense	2 500	
Total tax expense		−10 000
Net profit after tax		10 000

The €2500 deferred taxation expense will appear in the balance sheet at the end of 20X1 as a deferred tax liability. The following year the timing difference reverses and the deferred tax liability is released to the statement of profit or loss:

Net profit before tax		20 000
Taxes due	12 500	
Deferred tax expense	−2 500	
Total tax expense		−10 000
Net profit after tax		10 000

For analytical purposes, all you need to know is that a deferred tax liability in the statement of financial position represents the fact that accounting profit for financial reporting purposes has in the past been higher than that for tax purposes and the liability is there to compensate for future taxation on that difference. The tax liability reflects in fact the postponement of tax payments to future accounting periods.

Deferred taxes will normally arise in individual company accounts in jurisdictions where the relationship between accounting profit and taxable profit is reasonably loose. It should also normally appear in group financial statements prepared according to IASB rules. Companies based in jurisdictions like Germany or France where there is a close relationship between accounting profit and taxable profit should restate the individual company accounts for consolidation purposes. Excess depreciation or provisions which have been introduced for tax minimization purposes should normally be corrected during the consolidation process, and deferred tax liabilities introduced if appropriate.

COMPANY REPORT

NOKIA

Income taxes disclosures (extracts)

12. Income taxes

(EURm)	2009	2010	2011
Income tax			
Current tax	−736	−798	−752
Deferred tax	34	355	462
Total	−702	−443	−290
Finland	76	−126	−97
Other countries	−778	−317	−193
Total	−702	−443	−290

The differences between income tax expense computed at statutory rate (in Finland 26 per cent) and income taxes recognized in the consolidated income statement is reconciled as follows at December 31, 2011:

(EURm)	2009	2010	2011
Income tax			
Expense (+)/benefit (−) at statutory rate	−250	464	−311
Permanent differences	−96	4	−22
Non tax deductible impairment of goodwill (i)	236	—	283
Taxes for prior years	−17	−48	−7
Taxes on foreign subsidiaries' profits in excess of (lower then) income taxes at statutory rates	−145	−195	−73
Changes in losses and temporary differences with no tax effect (ii)	577	221	280

Net increase (+)/decrease (–) in tax contingencies	–186	24	7
Change in income tax rates	4	2	39
Deferred tax liability on undistributed earnings (iii)	111	–31	62
Other	–32	2	32
Income tax expense	702	443	290

(i) See note 8.
(ii) This item primarily relates to Nokia Siemens Networks' losses and temporary differences for which no deferred tax was recognized. In 2010 it also includes benefit of EUR 52 million from reassessment of recoverability of deferred tax assets in Nokia Siemens Networks.
(iii) In 2010 the changes in deferred tax liability on undistributed earnings mainly relates to changes in tax rates applicable to profit distributions.

Certain of the Group companies' income tax returns for periods ranging from 2004 through 2010 are under examination by tax authorities. The Group does not believe that any significant additional taxes in excess of those already provided for will arise as a result of the examinations.

Source: Nokia, Annual Report 2011, Note 12

A balance sheet perspective on deferred taxes

IAS 12, *Income Taxes*, deals with the current set of accounting rules for deferred taxation. Although the original IAS 12 required a company to account for deferred tax using the statement of profit or loss approach, IAS 12 (revised) requires the application of a method that is known as the asset–liability approach. The current approach of IAS 12 to deferred taxes (and of the corresponding US GAAP rules for that matter) is balance sheet oriented. Essentially it addresses what it calls 'temporary differences' between the carrying value of assets and liabilities and their tax value. Every asset or liability is assumed to have a tax base, the amount at which the asset or liability concerned is recognized for tax purposes. Temporary differences are differences between the tax base of an asset or liability and its carrying amount in the statement of financial position. Based on these temporary differences, the deferred tax position is calculated as the taxes that would be paid (or received) if the assets of the company were to be realized and its liabilities settled at their current book value.

It is important to note that the timing differences between pre-tax accounting profit and taxable profit do result in assets and liabilities having different valuation bases for financial reporting purposes than for taxation purposes at the end of a given accounting period. Therefore, timing differences will probably be the major source of temporary differences. But the point is that IAS 12 starts from an analysis of carrying values of assets and liabilities to identify temporary differences and not from a detailed review of the eligibility of revenues and expenses for tax purposes. Additional temporary differences may occur because specific tax law rules create different tax bases for taxation purposes to those used for financial reporting purposes. Many of these additional temporary differences, however, relate to more complex taxation issues and are outside the scope of this course. Under the asset–liability approach there is no such thing as a permanent difference. Any difference between the book value of an item in the statement of financial position and its tax base is a temporary difference.

IAS 12 acknowledges two types of temporary differences:

1. **taxable temporary differences** that result in deferred tax liabilities (i.e. taxable amounts in determining taxable profit of future periods), or
2. **deductible temporary differences** that will result in deferred tax assets (i.e. amounts that are deductible in determining taxable profit in future periods).

STANDARDS

🌐 IAS 12 – INCOME TAXES – DEFINITIONS *(extracts)*

5. The following terms are used in this Standard with the meanings specified:

Accounting profit is profit or loss for a period before deducting tax expense.

Taxable profit (tax loss) is the profit (loss) for a period, determined in accordance with the rules established by the taxation authorities, upon which income taxes are payable (recoverable).

Tax expense (tax income) is the aggregate amount included in the determination of profit or loss for the period in respect of current tax and deferred tax.

Current tax is the amount of income taxes payable (recoverable) in respect of the taxable profit (tax loss) for a period.

Deferred tax liabilities are the amounts of income taxes payable in future periods in respect of taxable temporary differences.

Deferred tax assets are the amounts of income taxes recoverable in future periods in respect of:

(a) deductible temporary differences;
(b) the carry forward of unused tax losses; and
(c) the carry forward of unused tax credits.

Temporary differences are differences between the carrying amount of an asset or liability in the statement of financial position and its tax base. Temporary differences may be either:

(a) *taxable temporary differences*, which are temporary differences that will result in taxable amounts in determining taxable profit (tax loss) of future periods when the carrying amount of the asset or liability is recovered or settled; or
(b) *deductible temporary differences*, which are temporary differences that will result in amounts that are deductible in determining taxable profit (tax loss) of future periods when the carrying amount of the asset or liability is recovered or settled.

The *tax base* of an asset or liability is the amount attributed to that asset or liability for tax purposes.

Source: IAS 12, *Income Taxes*

The recognition criteria for deferred tax assets are, however, somewhat tougher than for deferred tax liabilities. A deferred tax asset should only be recognized for all deductible temporary differences to the extent that it is probable that taxable profit will be available against which the deductible temporary difference can be utilized, i.e. there should be a valid expectation of sufficient future taxable profits against which the deductions can be offset. The deferred tax asset or deferred tax liability is measured as the temporary difference multiplied by the tax rate. The tax rate to be used is the rate that is expected to apply when the asset is realized or the liability is settled, based on tax rates that have been enacted by the end of the reporting period.

Returning to the previous accelerated tax depreciation model, we can apply the temporary differences approach as follows:

	20X1	20X2
(a) *Accounting balances*		
Asset carrying amount 1 January	—	5 000
Additions	10 000	0
Accounting depreciation	–5 000	–5 000
Asset carrying amount 31 December	5 000	0
(b) Tax values		
Asset tax base 1 January	—	0
Additions	10 000	0
Tax depreciation	–10 000	0
Asset tax base 31 December	0	0
(c) Temporary differences	5 000	0
(d) Deferred tax balance (50 per cent tax rate)	2 500	0

In 20X1 the accounting depreciation is €5000 (50 per cent of the asset's historical cost or €10000). The tax depreciation amounts to the full historical cost (€10000). At the end of 20X1 the temporary difference between carrying amount of the asset in the financial statements and its tax value is €5000, and the asset has a carrying value that is greater than its tax base. At that time the tax authorities have allowed a bigger tax deduction than recognized for financial reporting purposes. In 20X2 this situation will reverse when the accounting deduction becomes greater than the tax deduction. This means that it is a taxable temporary difference, and therefore this will give rise to a deferred tax liability. The deferred tax liability amounts to €2500, being 50 per cent (tax rate) of the temporary difference. Recognizing the deferred tax liability requires a deferred tax expense in the statement of profit or loss of 20X1. In 20X2 the temporary difference disappears (accumulated accounting depreciation equals accumulated tax depreciation) and the deferred tax liability will be released, implying a deferred tax income (or negative deferred tax expense) of €2500 in 20X2.

This brings us back to essentially the same statement of profit or loss effect as under the statement of profit or loss approach to deferred taxes. It would, however, be wrong to conclude that the statement of profit or loss approach and the asset–liability approach will always produce the same result. In more complex multinational group structures and when we consider the instances where temporary differences are not timing differences, the two approaches can produce quite different results.

The asset–liability approach also implies that every time there is a subsequent change in tax rates, the deferred tax asset/liability will change.

NESTLÉ

Deferred tax assets and liabilities

14.3 Reconciliation of deferred taxes by type of temporary differences recognized in the balance sheet

	Property plant and equipment	*Goodwill and intangible assets*	*Employee benefits*	*Inventories receivables payables and provisions*	*Unused tax losses and unused tax credits*	*Other*	*Total*
At 1 January 2010	(1068)	(1089)	1965	822	307	(139)	798
Currency retranslations	116	87	(149)	(88)	(28)	(18)	(80)
Deferred tax (expense)/ income	(134)	(157)	(98)	101	39	68	(181)
Modification of the scope Of consolidation	(7)	(7)	8	2	—	7	3
At 31 December 2010	(1093)	(1166)	1726	837	318	(82)	540
Currency retranslations	5	(12)	(24)	(24)	(15)	4	(66)
Deferred tax (expense)/ income	(223)	(46)	408	10	62	90	301
Modification of the scope Of consolidation	(36)	(360)	10	14	1	12	(359)
At 31 December 2011	(1347)	(1584)	2120	837	366	24	416

Source: Nestlé Group, Consolidated financial statements 2011

Presentation of deferred taxes in the financial statements

Deferred tax assets and deferred tax liabilities are presented separately from all other assets and liabilities in the statement of financial position. They are classified as non-current items. Tax expense (or income) related to profit or loss from ordinary activities should be presented on the face of the statement of profit or loss. Additionally, a set of supplementary information is to be disclosed in the notes to the financial statements, such as details on the major components of tax expense. One of the more prominent disclosures is an explanation of the relationship between tax expense and accounting profit as a numerical reconciliation between either tax expense and the product of accounting profit multiplied by the applicable tax rate(s) or between the average effective tax rate (i.e. tax expense divided by accounting profit) and the applicable tax rate. In practice, these disclosures can be quite extensive, although not always easily accessible for a multinational group due to aggregation of tax information related to sometimes divergent taxation regimes.

International taxation

The general rule in taxation is that a profit is taxed in the country where the transaction takes place, although this is obviously more complicated for cross-border trading and Internet sales. Generally it is then the country where the buyer resides which determines tax, even if for the moment Internet sales are largely untaxed. From a corporate perspective, tax is administered on a company-by-company basis, and calculated on individual subsidiaries' accounts, not on the group accounts as a whole. This is sometimes an issue that MBA students find bizarre. While the whole point of consolidated financial statements is to look at the company as an economic whole, and from a management perspective one should never lose sight of the overall group, from a tax perspective, the focus is exactly the opposite: tax sees the group as a collection of more or less unconnected activities and deals with it subsidiary by subsidiary.

Consequently, it is useful for a multinational to try to compartmentalize its activities within each tax jurisdiction by forming separate companies and retaining clear records of transactions for discussion with different tax authorities. As noted earlier, many corporations use worldwide systems for uniform internal accounting but then retain local specialists in each country to recalculate the figures in line with local measurement rules and tax needs.

International business presents both threats and opportunities as far as tax is concerned. The fact that national tax authorities cannot go outside their jurisdiction enables the corporation to structure international transactions in the most tax efficient way. On the other hand, mishandling can cause a revenue to be taxed in two different countries, or an expense not to be accepted as a deduction from profit.

Leaving aside tax havens, most countries have entered into double tax treaties with main trading partner nations. These deal with issues like the taxation of international transactions, the rules for withholding taxes on royalties, interest and dividends and similar items. So if a company is thinking about doing business in a country other than its main base, one of the first things to do is check whether there is a double tax treaty and what its content is.

Transfer pricing

The double tax treaty will normally have a section dealing with *transfer prices*. These are the prices, often very difficult to calculate, at which goods and services change hands between subsidiaries of the same group. Artificially fixing the transfer prices is a way of determining where profits are taxed.

Supposing a company makes a machine in country A (corporate income tax rate of 50 per cent) for a cost of €10 000 and sells it to a fellow subsidiary in country B (tax rate 25 per cent) for €11 000. This subsidiary sells it in turn to a subsidiary in country C (tax rate 40 per cent) for €18 000 and that subsidiary sells it to the customer for €20 000. The taxable profit will be distributed over the three countries:

	Taxable profit	Rate	Income tax
Country A	1 000	50	500
Country B	7 000	25	1 750
Country C	2 000	40	800
Total	10 000	30.5	3 050

The group has been able to reduce consolidated tax by artificially fixing the transfer prices and flowing the transaction through a low tax country. Of course, the tax authorities are well aware of this possibility, so the double tax treaty usually states that transfer prices must be 'at arms' length' (i.e. what an independent buyer would have to pay) or at market rates. It is not always easy to prove these prices and companies are well advised to reflect carefully on these issues because most tax jurisdictions can go back many years in a tax investigation and levy penal rates of tax if they do not agree the basis of the transfer price. It remains, for all that, an interesting corner of profit management.

Related to this is the issue of what expenses can be charged by head office or other corporate service centres against subsidiaries. Typically, a multinational has regional management centres which are not themselves revenue generating. Equally, it has research and development activities which probably involve costs being incurred in one jurisdiction and subsequently a new product or process being exploited in other jurisdictions. The same is true of advertising – maintaining a worldwide brand is expensive and has effects everywhere. If your company takes advertising at (say) the World Cup in South Africa which is televised all over the world, does the South African subsidiary pay that, or head office, or who?

This is a problem for internal management purposes in terms of relating costs to revenues, but it is also a problem with the tax authorities. If your R&D is based in the UK but exploited in the US, the UK tax authorities are not likely to accept that the cost should all be offset against UK tax. But the US authority may refuse to accept any expenses either in the sense that the costs were not incurred in the US.

BETWEEN THE LINES

Transfer-pricing: The key international issue?

There is little doubt that (government tax) authorities have become more adept at countering the 'profit-shifting' aspects of transfer-pricing practices and are strengthening their statutory powers with ever more extensive and complex legislation and regulations.

To strengthen the tax authorities' position, regulations typically introduce specific rules to determine arm's length prices and require that taxpayers maintain very extensive records documenting the methods used to determine their transfer prices (which often necessitates the employment of teams of both in-house and outside counsel, accountants and economists). Provision is made as well for the imposition of very stringent penalties in case of non-compliance.

Source: Richard Casna, *'Transfer-pricing: The key to international issue?',*

extract from article in Accounting & Business, February 1998, p.30

Basically, flows between subsidiaries in different countries are easiest when structured according to the tax treaty: transfer prices for goods and services (but may be subject to justification, which is not always easy), royalties for use of intellectual property (brands, product manufacturing processes) and interest (in relation to financing). All of these are, though, with the proviso that the company may need to persuade the tax authorities that the level of charge is justified.

Tax havens

Tax havens have a small place in the corporate world, but they may well be expensive to use (you usually need to work through a local lawyer or accountant) and other tax jurisdictions usually have extensive powers to stop you sheltering profits in a haven. For example, if the UK considers that you have a controlled foreign corporation (CFC) in a jurisdiction which is on its list of havens, it will feel free to tax you in the UK on the profits of that CFC. If you do not provide accounts for the CFC, it will simply estimate the profits and tax accordingly. Tax havens do not generally benefit from double tax treaties with other countries.

Tax havens typically offer low tax or flat rate tax for companies which are resident there but whose activities are external to the haven (hence 'off-shore' companies). These can be used legitimately and effectively by a multinational to provide international services such as finance or insurance to itself. For example, an offshore finance vehicle will borrow on the international markets (guaranteed by the group) and then lend to fellow subsidiaries.

The tax haven lends itself also to the Internet business and it is surprising that more companies such as Internet sales companies or those with international transactions such as tour operators do not site themselves in tax havens. The costs are not negligible and therefore the throughput needs to be substantial to create a saving on tax after professional costs.

In recent years a new kind of tax minimization opportunity has appeared – what are known as 'offshore financial centres'. These are a near relative of the tax haven, but with the difference that they have double tax treaties with major trading countries – they have a foot in both camps, as it were. Like a tax haven, their object is to attract corporate business whose operations take place outside the financial centre. Unlike the tax haven, they levy corporate taxes on income, but these are at a level which is sufficiently high for developed countries not to treat the financial centre as a haven, but sufficiently low so as to still be attractive to companies. Dublin is a financial centre in this sense, and Botswana has just joined the club, hoping to attract business as a regional centre for multinationals operating in sub-Saharan Africa.

Summary

This has been a short tour through the rather strange land of corporate taxation. The principal points to retain are that individual companies pay taxes to governments in a number of different ways. These can impact substantially upon business costs and need to be thoroughly reviewed at the project stage, not left until a new operation is up and running. Corporate income tax is calculated in quite a complicated way and is linked to accounting profit through a reconciliation exercise. Where accounting profit and taxable profit differ, deferred taxes arise.

Deferred taxation for financial reporting purposes relates to the basic accounting question of how to allocate the income tax expense between accounting periods.

Tax is levied on a country-by-country basis, which calls for a good deal of expenditure of resources to compile tax data. The fact that multinationals usually have transactions which run through several subsidiaries and different countries presents tax planning opportunities and some risks in that national tax authorities do not necessarily agree with the company's way of calculating profits, nor with that of other tax authorities. Multinationals can make a limited use of tax havens and offshore financial centres to reduce their taxation.

Discussion Questions

1. Is all the tax which a group pays visible in the financial statements?
2. Contrast the deferred tax concepts of 'timing differences' and 'temporary differences'.
3. On January 3, 20X1 Foldet SA purchased equipment for €1.4m. The equipment has a useful life of four years and will be depreciated using the straight-line method for financial reporting purposes. The residual value is estimated at €200 000. For tax purposes the following tax depreciation amounts are allowed: €450 000 (20X1), €350 000 (20X2), €250 000 (20X3) and €150 000 (20X4). The enacted income tax rate is 20 per cent for 20X1 and thereafter. How would you account for this transaction from a deferred taxation perspective?
4. ZZ consultants have won a contract from the Russian government to advise on small company accounting regulation and to provide training for government officials and educators. Some of the contract will be performed by staff in ZZ's Moscow office, but they will be helped by staff transferred from their offices in Germany, the UK and Switzerland. If the rate of corporate income tax in Russia is 80 per cent, in Germany 60 per cent, in the UK 35 per cent and in Switzerland 25 per cent, how would you advise them to structure their internal transactions? Should all the staff to be used be transferred to the Moscow office or should Moscow be invoiced from other locations with staff flown in and out to meet specific assignments?
5. For what purposes may a tax haven be profitably used by a multinational group?

CHAPTER 16

Auditing and corporate governance

The subject of auditing and auditors was covered in Chapter 2 of this book. The object of this chapter is to set out a little more background information concerning external audit and the framework of corporate governance as they impact upon multinational groups. The chapter does not bear directly on the techniques of financial statement analysis, but is intended to broaden the knowledge base of analysts in respect of the financial statements and the constraints on corporate reporting. It will deal first with the subject of corporate governance, then the audit of group financial statements and related issues of independence, audit committees and finally internal control and risk management.

Chapter Structure

- Corporate governance
- Statutory audit
- Issues in international audit
- Auditor independence
- Internal control and risk management
- Audit committee
- Summary
- Discussion questions

Corporate governance

In a small or medium-sized business, the owners are very often also the managers of the business and prior to the Industrial Revolution most businesses were run this way. It was only in the 19th century that a major change took place, as a result of the Industrial Revolution, and businesses started to become much larger. This had two consequences: large companies were financed by larger numbers of shareholders and so were less and less dominated by individual or family shareholders, and the 'professional manager' started to appear. This gave rise to what is known as an 'agency problem' – the owners of the business (*principals* in the jargon) had to find means to ensure that those whom they appointed to run the business (*agents*) did so in a way that matched with shareholders' needs.

There are a number of ways of addressing this problem. One of the most frequent in the Anglo-Saxon world is to give top managers contracts under which their salaries vary according to how well they meet key shareholder objectives, such as increase in share price or return on equity. However, accounting and audit also play a highly significant role. Historically the accounting statements were a means through which professional managers reported to shareholders on what they had done with the company over a 12-month period, and in many countries audit was introduced as a means whereby a representative of the shareholders checked the accuracy of the financial statements on behalf of the shareholders. It is not clear that this was originally a very effective way of checking on managers, and the evolution of accounting regulation and the audit profession has in part been a response to the need to create transparency in the financial statements and confidence in their accuracy.

In current times the agency problem has been broadened out into the concept of corporate governance. On the one hand, the corporate governance debate puts increased emphasis on the effectiveness and accountability of corporate boards of directors, while, on the other hand, it tends to extend the shareholder perspective to wider stakeholder concerns.

The latter is an important shift in focus and involves a cultural change in what is expected of companies and their management. What it means is that the company can no longer be seen as an isolated unit whose central task is to make money for shareholders and whose other obligations can be summarized as simply to meet legal requirements in all other areas, if they cannot be got round. Increasingly, society is saying that multinationals are extremely powerful and rich entities, many of them more so than the governments of the world's smaller or economically weak states, and they are able to escape control because their structure is international while law is basically constrained to national boundaries. Such companies must be constrained to take into consideration the public interest as well as that of their shareholders, and there must be transparent systems of corporate governance to see that this is done.

Since the beginning of the 1990s many countries have been revising national corporate governance rules or endorsed corporate governance guidance after extensive public consultation and debate (Viénot I and II in France, the Cromme Report in Germany, the Cardon Report in Belgium, the Peters Report in the Netherlands, the early Cadbury Report of 1992 and the Higgs Report of 2003 in the UK and many others). On the international level, the OECD (Organization for Economic Co-operation and Development) has been particularly active in the

BETWEEN THE LINES

Defining corporate governance – OECD Principles of Corporate Governance *(extract)*

Corporate governance involves a set of relationships between a company's management, its board, its shareholders and other stakeholders. Corporate governance also provides the structure through which the objectives of the company are set, and the means of attaining those objectives and monitoring performance are determined. Good corporate governance should provide proper incentives for the board and management to pursue objectives that are in the interests of the company and its shareholders and should facilitate effective monitoring. The presence of an effective corporate governance system, within an individual company and across an economy as a whole, helps to provide a degree of confidence that is necessary for the proper functioning of a market economy. As a result, the cost of capital is lower and firms are encouraged to use resources more efficiently, thereby underpinning growth.

Source: OECD Principles of Corporate Governance, 2004

debate with its report of 2004 on principles of corporate governance. The OECD Principles of Corporate Governance have been widely adopted as a benchmark for achieving good corporate governance in OECD countries and elsewhere. They are intended to assist governments in their efforts to evaluate and improve the regulatory framework for corporate governance, and to provide guidance and suggestions for stock exchanges, investors, corporations and other parties that have a role in the process of developing good corporate governance.

Corporate governance regimes

Different countries have different views about corporate governance. Governance regimes are heavily influenced by the institutional environment. The Anglo-Saxon environment, characterized by large liquid capital markets, a growing concentration of power within institutional investors and an active market for corporate takeovers, has been generally supportive of the development of strong investor protection and of shareholder primacy in the corporate governance debate. On the other hand, for example, the continental European institutional environment is characterized by less liquid markets and greater concentration of power with banks, employees and governments, and stronger family ties. For example, in German companies with their two-tier board system, banks are often represented on the supervisory boards and own large shareholdings in many listed companies. Employee organizations play a significant role in corporate governance through their direct involvement with works councils and, indirectly, in supervisory boards. The stakeholder model of corporate governance in continental Europe tends to give greater attention to the social dimension and the longer term effect of corporate governance issues.

Although those differences in the governance environment and structures have a significant effect on governance practices at company level, economic globalization tendencies and pressures from cross-border investment with investors increasingly seeking opportunities outside their domestic markets, seem to weaken the distinction between governance models and promote convergence, especially on the issue of the effectiveness and accountability of corporate boards.

Reporting on internal control

An effective system of internal control is generally seen as crucial for good governance. The US Sarbanes–Oxley Act (2002) made executive management responsible not just for establishing, evaluating and assessing over time the effectiveness of internal control over financial reporting and disclosure, but also for periodically asserting its effectiveness. To this effect, each annual report filed with the SEC (Securities and Exchange Committee) has to include an internal control report. In this report management should state its responsibility for establishing and maintaining an adequate internal control structure and procedures for financial reporting and assess, as of the end of the company's fiscal year, the effectiveness of the internal control system with regard to financial reporting. Moreover, the company's independent auditors must attest to and report on the assessments made by company management. In this context, the COSO (Committee of Sponsoring Organizations of the Treadway Commission) framework is considered to offer an established set of control criteria to assess the effectiveness of internal control over financial reporting. Related guidance on internal control can be found in the Turnbull (UK) and the CoCo (Canada) frameworks which build on the COSO framework of internal control.

STANDARDS

OUTLINE OF THE SARBANES–OXLEY ACT OF 2002

The Sarbanes–Oxley Act (SOX) affects corporate managers, independent auditors and other players who are integral to capital formation in the United States. This omnibus regulation will forever alter the face of corporate reporting and auditing. SOX titles and key sections are outlined herein.

1. *Title I – Public Company Accounting Oversight Board:* Section 101 establishes an independent board to oversee public company audits. Section 107 authorizes oversight and enforcement of the board to the Securities and Exchange Commission (SEC).

2. *Title II – Auditor Independence:* Section 201 prohibits a CPA Firm that audits a public company to engage in certain non-audit services with the same client. Most relevant to accounting information systems is the prohibition of financial information systems design and implementation services to audit clients. Section 203 requires audit partner rotation in their fifth, sixth, or seventh year, depending on the partner's role in the audit.

3. *Title III – Corporate Responsibility:* Section 302 requires a company's chief executive officer (CEO) and chief financial officer (CFO) to certify quarterly and annual reports. They are certifying the following: they reviewed the reports; the reports are not materially untruthful or mislead-

ing; the financial statements fairly reflect in all material respects the financial position of the company; and they are responsible for designing, establishing, maintaining, and monitoring corporate disclosures, controls and procedures. Section 303 makes it unlawful for corporate officers or directors to fraudulently influence, coerce, manipulate or mislead any independent auditors who are engaged in auditing the firm's financial statements.

4. *Title IV – Enhanced Financial Disclosures:* Section 404 requires each annual report filed with the SEC to include an internal control report. The report shall: state the responsibility of management for establishing and maintaining an adequate internal control structure and procedures for financial reporting and assess, as of the end of the company's fiscal year, the effectiveness of the internal control structure and procedures of the company for financial reporting. The company's independent auditors must attest to and report on the assessments made by company management.

5. *Title V – Analysts' Conflicts of Interests:* Requires financial analysts to properly disclose in research reports any conflicts of interest they might hold with the companies they recommend.

6. *Title VI – Commission Resources and Authority:* Authorizes the SEC to censure or deny any person the privilege of appearing or practicing before the SEC if that person is deemed to: be unqualified, have acted in an unethical manner, or have aided and abetted a violation of federal securities laws.

7. *Title VII – Studies and Reports:* Authorizes the General Accounting Office (GAO) to study the consolidation of public accounting firms since 1989 and offer solutions to any recognized problems.

8. *Title VIII – Corporate and Criminal Fraud Accountability:* Section 802 makes it a felony to knowingly destroy, alter or create records and/or documents with the intent to impede, obstruct or influence an on-going or contemplated federal investigation. Section 806 offers legal protection to whistle-blowers who provide evidence of fraud.

9. *Title IX – White-Collar Crime Penalty Enhancements:* Section 906 sets forth criminal penalties applicable to CEOs and CFOs of up to $5 million and up to 20 years in prison if they certify and file false and/or misleading financial statements with the SEC.

10. *Title X – Corporate Tax Returns:* Section 1001 conveys a 'sense of the Senate' that the corporate federal income tax returns are signed by the CEO.

11. *Title XI – Corporate Fraud and Accountability:* Section 1102 provides for fines and imprisonment of up to 20 years to individuals who corruptly alter, destroy, mutilate or conceal documents with the intent to impair the document's integrity or availability for use in an official proceeding, or to otherwise obstruct, influence or impede any official proceeding. Section 1105 authorizes the SEC to prohibit anyone from serving as an officer or director if the person has committed securities fraud.

Source: Sarbanes–Oxley Act, 107 P. L. 204, § 1, 116 Stat. 745, July 30, 2002

With the passage of the Sarbanes–Oxley Act, company executives in the US must now personally certify the accuracy of the financial statements as well as to the related controls. This requirement has produced a strong incentive for top management to familiarize themselves with the processes underlying financial reporting and to give priority to internal control issues. Applying section 404 – 'Management assessment of internal controls' – of the Sarbanes–Oxley Act of 2002 has been proven to be a challenging experience. Section 404 calls on companies filing with the SEC to identify financial reporting risks, ascertain related controls, assess their effectiveness, fix and control deficiencies, rework documentation and ensure continued monitoring of the controls. This has been a daunting task, especially for companies with complex organizational structures and extensive foreign operations. Practical experience showed that internal control related roles and responsibilities were often poorly defined and not well incorporated into daily business routines. Risk assessment (although an essential component of a system of internal control according to the COSO framework) was generally underdeveloped with the effect that it becomes quite difficult to prioritize control activities: without proper risk assessment control goals remain vague and criteria to assess the effectiveness of control measures arbitrary. Without proper risk assessment it is impossible to discern obsolete or redundant controls from those that mitigate true financial reporting risks. In practice, applying section 404 of SOX has had the effect of dramatically increasing the responsibilities of the average line manager engaged in the processing of transactions that feed the financial statements.

In the EU, no equivalent of the SOX requirements on internal control currently exists, but it can be expected that internal control related requirements will be strengthened in the future.

Independent directors

The role of independent non-executive directors features prominently in recent corporate governance codes. The presence of independent representatives on the board, capable of challenging the decisions of the management, is widely considered as a means of protecting the interests of shareholders and, where appropriate, other stakeholders.

Good corporate governance practices are considered to involve the presence in the central decision-making unit of the company of a number of external or independent directors. In a system such as that of Germany where large companies have two boards, an executive or management board and a supervisory board, this function already exists, with the supervisory board exercising oversight over what the executive directors are doing. In countries where a unitary board is the norm such as France, Belgium and Italy, the recommendation is that a board should include a proportion of non-executive or independent directors whose function is simply to attend board meetings on a regular basis and monitor corporate behaviour. A mixture of executive and non-executive directors has the advantage of combining the executives' in-depth knowledge of the daily operations of the company with the wider experience of non-executive directors. In the best companies the monitoring function of non-executive directors offers an opportunity for the company to emphasize its ethical behaviour by appointing high-profile figures who are completely independent of the business. Independent directors should be selected on their merits and for the greater good of the company as a whole, not to represent concerns of specific interest groups.

However, neither the dual board system nor the unitary board with independent directors is foolproof. Famously, the supervisory board of Metallgesellschaft in Germany were unaware of the dealings of its US subsidiary in oil futures which cost it many millions of dollars to unwind. The supervisory board of Ahold in the Netherlands was not informed on the specifics of revenue dealings of its US operations, leading to the embarrassment of very significant revenue restatements in Ahold's financial statements in 2002/2003. A report on accounting frauds by SEC-registered companies identifies what it calls 'grey' directors which it defines as independent directors who have a business connection with either the company or its executive directors. Although independence is a matter of judgement, it is reasonable to expect that independent directors are free of personal and business

BETWEEN THE LINES

Fraudulent financial reporting: 1998–2007 *(extract)*

A large body of academic research finds that board and audit committee independence affects the effectiveness of board and audit committee oversight. We examined the relation between board independence and fraud. In analyzing board member independence, the following definitions were used to categorize individual members of the board of directors into one of three categories:

- Inside director – A director who was also an officer or employee of the company or a subsidiary or an officer of an affiliated company.

- Grey director – A director who was a former officer or employee of the company, a subsidiary or an affiliate; relative of management; professional advisor to the company; officer or owner of a significant supplier or customer of the company; interlocking director; officer or employee of another company controlled by the CEO or the company's majority owner; owner of an affiliate company; or creditor of the company.

- Outside director – A director who had no disclosed relationship (other than stock ownership) between the director and the company or its officers.

The average percentage of inside directors on the board for fraud firms was 30 per cent as compared to 25 per cent for no-fraud firms. This difference was statistically significant (p-value = 0.010). There was no significant difference in the percentage of outside directors for fraud firms (60 per cent of the board) versus no-fraud firms (63 per cent of the board). There was no statistical difference between the two groups in the average percentage of grey directors. We were able to analyze the types of grey directors serving on the board of directors for 63 fraud and 63 no-fraud firms. The most common types of grey directors were former company officers, consultants and outside legal counsel. Differences in types of grey directors serving on fraud and no-fraud firms were not statistically significant, except for the difference in the percentage of grey directors who were relatives of management. 7 per cent of fraud firm grey directors were relatives of management as compared to 18 per cent for no-fraud firms (p-value = 0.086).

Source: Fraudulent Financial Reporting 1998–2007. An Analysis of US Public Companies, published by the Committee of Sponsoring Organizations of the Treadway Commission (COSO) 2010

connections with the companies of which they are a director. In that sense, former executive (or employee) status, close family relationships with an executive director or representation of a major shareholder would be an indication of an absence of independence.

Aside from generally monitoring what the company is doing, the independent directors are increasingly asked to participate in subcommittees to deal with particular tasks. The most important are the *remuneration committee* and the *audit committee*. The idea of the remuneration committee is that executive directors should not be in a position to fix their own salaries; this should be done by independent directors who make comparisons with other companies and ensure that the package offered is in line with the market and the good of the shareholders and others. It is not clear how well this works either, and the existence of remuneration committees has not stopped major shareholder criticisms of some pay proposals.

The audit committee is responsible for overseeing the financial reporting process and increasingly for monitoring the effectiveness of the system of internal control as well. It acts as an intermediary between the board and the external auditors (and possibly internal auditors as well) on the basis that auditors should not be reporting management failings directly to the managers potentially concerned. The audit committee may need to challenge management decisions or take a position that is not in concert with that of executive directors. That is why independence is an essential quality for audit committee members. We will look at audit committees in more detail later in this chapter.

The European Commission's Action Plan to modernize company law and enhance corporate governance in the EU announced the adoption in the short term of a Commission Recommendation on the role in listed companies of (independent) non-executive or supervisory directors.

Chairman of the board and chief executive officer

Most corporate governance codes recommend a clear division of responsibilities at the top of the company between the chairman of the board of directors and the chief executive officer (CEO) to ensure a balance of power and authority. The running of the board of directors (the chairman's role) should be separated from the executive responsibility of running the company's business (the CEO's role). Concentration of both functions within one person is seen as undermining the accountability of corporate boards.

In two-tier boards (as in Germany and in the Netherlands) the concentration of power issue is less acute. In two-tier boards, the management board is responsible for management of the company while the supervisory board is responsible for overseeing the management board.

Institutional shareholders

It has been argued that part of the need for formal corporate governance frameworks arises from the fact that the major shareholders in large multinationals are typically financial institutions (banks, insurance companies, fund managers, pension funds, etc.). In the US, institutional investors hold more than 50 per cent of all listed corporate shares (about 60 per cent in the largest 1000 corporations), while the largest 25 pension funds accounted for 42 per cent of the foreign equity held by all US investors. Historically this kind of shareholder has considered that they should not intervene in the management of the company directly. They have taken the view that they are making an investment to get a return; if that return is not delivered, they take their investment elsewhere. This kind of passive shareholder approach is blamed for creating an environment where company management felt they could do what they liked as long as the share price held up.

However, this situation is changing, partly because the investment industry has wanted to respond to the criticisms and partly because the individuals who invest in pension funds and collective investment vehicles are increasingly wanting an assurance that their money is not being used to invest in companies with whose behaviour they do not agree. The personal finance press is increasingly vociferous in raising these issues and individuals are increasingly demanding that their money goes into 'ethical' investments. As a consequence, institutional investors are drawing up codes of conduct for companies, and some are now asking company boards to sign up to a code of conduct before the investment fund will buy any shares. This is, of course, another sign of the change in society's values and increases the pressure on companies to address these issues.

Statutory audit

The independent auditor has always had a role to play in corporate governance, and never more so than now when the multinational has subsidiaries all over the world and only the Big Four audit firms have similar organizations which can check on the existence and activities of these vast networks. Essentially, the signature of a Big Four audit firm on a multinational's audit report is taken to be the guarantee of the accuracy and validity of the financial statements, and an assurance that there is nothing nasty hidden behind the bland comments of the chairman. The investment market places a very heavy reliance on the auditor's assurance – the analyst may modify the figures to compare with other companies, may make all sorts of adjustments for forecasting purposes, but the very existence of all the company's assets, its activities and their legality, and the main board's control over these is attested to by the auditor.

In fact the audit of a multinational group is a very difficult task and one which carries with it a great deal of legal and moral responsibility. In essence the audit of a multinational is no different from that of an individual company, since the consolidated accounts are simply a reworking of the financial statements of all the individual companies that make up the group. However, it is more complicated in that the subsidiaries are working in different legal environments, and the more complex the accounting web, the easier it is to 'lose' transactions. The auditor of the group accounts is responsible for any error in the group audit, even if such an error has arisen because of a mistake by the auditor of a subsidiary. Equally, multinationals are under pressure to publish their results as soon as possible after the year-end, which means that the process of auditing and agreeing the accounts of the individual subsidiaries may have to take place within two months of the year-end, leaving a further month to consolidate and agree the consolidation adjustments.

This leads to a situation where the large audit firms like to be the exclusive auditor of a multinational and all its subsidiaries. Critics say this is simply to build up their fee base, which may be true, but it is also true that using several different firms of auditors is necessarily more expensive because they need to have meetings to liaise with each other and necessarily more risky because there is no one with an overview of the whole group. The Bank of Credit and Commerce International (BCCI) is a famous example of a group which operated as two separate but related networks, each network audited by a different Big Four auditor. After the collapse of BCCI it became apparent that there had been a 'black hole' between the two networks which was used to conceal fraudulent or illegal transactions.

Typically the audit of a multinational is a continuing operation where one year's audit leads into the next, and if doubtful issues are identified one year, they may well be subjected to a more intensive scrutiny the following year and so on. The auditor will attempt to identify the areas of the group which have the highest audit risk (operations in a difficult trading and credit environment, such as Russia, high volume of cash transactions, poor control environment, poor local accounting systems, high volume of foreign currency transactions, etc.) and devote most resources to checking these. The auditor will also each year select particular areas for special investigation. These might be selected in response to worries expressed by the group's internal audit or accounting units, or may be selected more or less at random so that even a low-risk part of the group is occasionally subject to an intense scrutiny.

Fortunately the rules for the conduct of an international audit are less likely to be radically different from country to country than for accounting. While audit rules may differ quite radically even between developed countries, there is a set of international audit rules put out by the International Federation of Accountants (IFAC – see Chapter 2) which are often used for multinational audits, and in particular when the accounting rules used are those of the IASB. Analysts should check the audit report carefully, however, to see what rules have been applied. The standard audit report should specify both what accounting rules have been applied by the company and what auditing rules have been used by the auditor in conducting the audit. Beware terms such as 'have been prepared subject to professional standards' which do not specify which professional standards. While auditing standards are much the same in developed countries, they are not uniform and in developing countries may be fairly rudimentary.

Issues in international audit

That brings us to a delicate subject in international audit – how much reliance should you place on the financial statements of companies headquartered in developing or newly industrialized countries? These have been the subject of quite a lot of criticism, mostly as a consequence of the financial crisis in South-East

Asia in the late 1990s. Here it became apparent that a number of companies had had their financial statements audited by Big Four firms, but had either used local accounting standards with a low degree of transparency or used International Accounting Standards while not complying fully with their requirements – using what is known as 'IAS-lite' in the trade.

It became clear that many relevant bits of information had not been disclosed to investors – in particular, issues such as unhedged loans in strong currencies to finance investments which would generate cash flows in weak currencies. This was an important cause of a flight from the Asian markets and the economic depression and collapse of many companies which followed. These deficiencies in reporting and auditing raised a number of questions. First, should the Big Four sign clean audit reports of financial statements which do not conform to high quality international standards? The Big Four pointed out that the accounts made it clear that local standards had been followed and analysts should be reminded that the first thing to do when looking at a company report is indeed to check what rules have been applied. However, the market sentiment was rather that the Big Four should maintain certain minimum standards.

This in turn raises another issue – to what extent is an audit by the same Big Four firm the same the world over? Or, put another way, are the Big Four firms uniformly run and directed? In fact the firms are not multinational companies with pyramid-style reporting and authority chains. They are networks of national partnerships or similar structures which work together through varying mechanisms, but which lack any formal or legal means whereby an international board, as it were, can impose its will on a national partnership on all questions. It is rather like running a franchise operation such as McDonald's where some outlets are directly owned by head office and some are franchises, both regional and local, but without the right to specify in detail what is sold or how it is prepared.

Auditor independence

A perpetual policy issue in audit is the independence of the auditor. Of course, the value of the modern audit depends partly upon the technical skills of the auditor and partly upon the independence and ethical qualities of the auditor. Without the competence and the distance from the management of the company, the audit report is worthless.

In some countries, such as Germany and France, the governments take the view that independence can only be obtained if the auditor performs only audit for the client and has no other relationship with the management. However, in many other countries, including Switzerland, the UK and the Netherlands, the auditor is free to sell other services to the same client, although in the UK the company must publish details of how much it paid for the audit and what other fees it paid the auditor.

There is a good deal of discussion about the effect of this on independence. Audit firms say that independence is a state of mind and does not vary directly

FTSE 100 group Audit Fees – UK top 20				
Company	*Year-end*	*Auditors*	*Audit fee £m*	*Other fees £m*
BP	31 Dec. 05	E&Y	44.2	11.6
HSBC	31 Dec. 05	KPMG	36.5	11.4
Shell T&T	31 Dec. 05	PwC	30.3	3.7
WPP Group	31 Dec. 05	Deloitte	17.9	3.6
Barclays	31 Dec. 05	PwC	17.0	12.0
Royal Bank of Scotland	31 Dec. 05	Deloitte	16.9	7.4
SAB Miller	31 Mar. 06	PwC	13.8	2.9
GlaxoSmithKline	31 Dec. 05	PwC	11.9	2.6
Unilever	31 Dec. 05	PwC	11.7	3.4
Aviva	31 Dec. 05	E&Y	10.0	3.1
Lloyds TSB	31 Dec. 05	PwC	8.9	3.2
Anglo American	31 Dec. 05	Deloitte	8.7	3.7
HBOS	31 Dec. 05	KPMG	7.7	3.7
Rio Tinto	31 Dec. 05	PwC	7.6	1.4
Standard Chartered	31 Dec. 05	KPMG	7.2	1.8
BAT	31 Dec. 05	PwC	6.9	3.9
Prudential	31 Dec. 05	KPMG	6.8	5.6
BT	31 Mar. 06	PwC	6.6	2.6
BHP Billiton	30 Jun. 05	KPMG	6.5	1.7
Old Mutual	31 Dec. 05	KPMG	6.4	4.6
AstraZeneca	31 Dec. 05	KPMG	6.4	0.6

Source: Financial Director, October 2006 pp.43/44

with the commercial relationship. The Big Four also point out that they are bigger than many of their clients, and independence is much more a problem for a single partner firm than one with thousands of partners. However, there is also evidence that over time, audit partners come to identify fairly closely with their clients, and in this connection, the old firm of Coopers & Lybrand, for example, were sanctioned for having been too ready to listen to Robert Maxwell, whose companies they audited for many years.

In France the audit appointment is for six years, and a listed company must appoint two auditors. In Italy the appointment is for three years and may only be renewed twice, leading to a maximum of nine years for the audit engagement. However, auditors point out that statistically the most likely time for a fraud is when there is a new auditor – it takes time for a new firm to understand thoroughly the workings of a large multinational. There is clearly no magic solution to the independence problem.

Following the requirements of the Sarbanes–Oxley Act of 2002, SEC rules further restrict (but do not completely eliminate) the types of non-audit services that an auditor is allowed to provide to audit clients, and the employment of former audit firm employees by the audit client, and provide for audit partner rotation after a period of five years. If an audit firm provides non-audit services that are not prohibited for public company audit clients, such as tax services, these must be pre-approved by the company's audit committee.

Internal control and risk management

The new corporate governance framework generally stresses the role and implications of an effective system of internal control. It sees internal control as part of the accountability of a company's board of directors and management to stake-holders and extends the internal control logic to enterprise-wide risk management. Profitable corporate performance is more and more recognized as the result of successful risk-taking. Corporate activity necessarily involves taking risks and corporate returns are expected to reflect rewards for considered risk-taking. In that sense, effective risk management is essential as good business practice to enable companies to take risks with more confidence and in a rational and informed manner.

Those charged with governance of a company are expected to systematically identify, evaluate and respond to the company's risks. These risks relate to strategy and business operations a well as to compliance with laws and regulations and financial reporting. Stakeholders, and shareholders in particular, expect those charged with governance of the company to inform them about the risks the company faces and also to put the necessary controls in place to deal with these risks. This emphasis on risk control and risk accountability was the result of a number of recent corporate failures where investors were not informed about disproportionate levels of risks incurred by corporate management.

Enterprise-wide risk management and control is particularly important in large multinational groups. In such groups there are many parts that senior executives never see. Decisions are passed up and down the management pyramid, but only an effective internal financial reporting system shows that those decisions are carried out, and only an effective risk management and internal control environment ensures that the risks being taken by the company are being clearly identified, measured and monitored.

In September 2004, COSO published its *Enterprise Risk Management – Integrated Framework*, which in fact extends its internal control framework to risk management and strategic risks. COSO's definition of enterprise risk management is as follows:

> Enterprise risk management is a process, effected by an entity's board of directors, management and other personnel, applied in strategy setting and across the enterprise, designed to identify potential events that may affect the entity, and manage risk to be within its risk appetite, to provide reasonable assurance regarding the achievement of entity objectives.

The COSO ERM Integrated Framework sees internal control as a subset of risk management. Risk management extends the scope of internal control as it is concerned with wider external and internal risks relevant to the determination and execution of a company's strategy to reach the company's objectives than the set of risks focused on within the internal control framework. Nevertheless, internal control is seen as highly instrumental in achieving these objectives. As we have observed before, it is the absence of good internal controls which permits executives to carry out transactions against company policy and without the financial consequences being immediately visible, as Ahold, Parmelat, Enron and others can testify, and hence its importance in corporate governance discussions. There is no point in central management having the right policies in place if they are unable to monitor their application. Internal control is however only one of the means to manage risk exposures. Other devices include transferring risk to third parties, risk-sharing, contingency planning and consciously excluding activities deemed too risky.

A good system of risk management provides the means for central management to effectively deal with uncertainty and associated opportunities, with the ultimate goal of achieving the company's objectives. The ERM framework provides integrated ERM principles, common risk-related terminology and practical implementation guidance to help companies develop and benchmark risk management practices. An effective risk management system will be beneficial to external auditors also as they assess the company's business risks.

In the UK, the Turnbull Report has been quite influential in this respect. It reinforced the awareness of disciplined risk management as being crucial to good corporate governance and UK boards are nowadays significantly more involved in risk management than before.

A logical extension of a governance perspective on risk management is the development of a set of risk disclosure requirements empowering shareholders to use disclosures to bring companies to adopt more elaborate risk management standards. Currently, however, there exist no EU disclosure requirements regarding risk management and internal control. European directives do require disclosure of a company's principal risks, but not how they are managed or controlled. Further risk disclosures could relate to the overall process of risk management and internal control, the management of specific risks and information on the assessment of the effectiveness of risk management and internal control. Moreover, in the EU there is no equivalent to the Sarbanes–Oxley requirements on effectiveness disclosures. Recall, however, that the Sarbanes–Oxley Act only requires the disclosure of opinions about the effectiveness of internal control over financial reporting. It contains no disclosure requirements on compliance risks and operational/strategic risks, although the SEC asks for disclosures of specific risks faced by a company in the Management Discussion and Analysis (MD&A) section of the mandatory filings.

The board of directors is expected to provide oversight of enterprise risk management, but they tend to delegate responsibility and accountability on these matters to one or more committees. The audit committee is a likely candidate. With its focus on internal control over financial reporting, the audit committee is already well positioned to assume this task. Some companies have however established a specific risk committee to focus directly on enterprise risk management.

LUFTHANSA – RISK MANAGEMENT AT LUFTHANSA

Opportunity and risk management system (extracts)

Risk management at Lufthansa

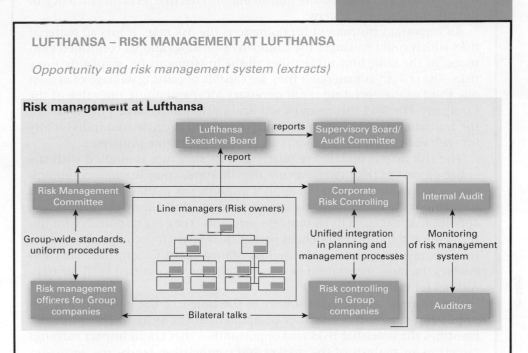

As an international aviation company Lufthansa is exposed to macro-economic, sector-specific and Company risks. Our management systems are constantly updated and enable us to identify both risks and opportunities at an early stage and act accordingly. Our proven risk strategy allows us to take advantage of business opportunities as long as a risk-adjusted return can be realised on market terms.

The calculated management of opportunities and risks is an integral factor in the management of our Company. Our risk management is therefore integrated into our business processes. The system enabling operational risks to be identified and managed at early stage is composed of several modules. These modules are linked systematically with each other – with the exception of financial risk management, for which responsibility is organised centrally. This enables homogenous risks to be identified in their entirety and responsibly managed with the necessary economic competence. The functions of trading, settlement and financial controlling are strictly separated and are based in independent organisational units. The risk management system for financial instruments is part of central financial management. It is described in the section 'Financial opportunities and risks' and in the Notes to the consolidated financial statements under 'Note 47'.

Our Risk Management Committee ensures on behalf of the Executive Board that business risks are permanently identified and evaluated across all functions and processes. The committee is made up of the eight directors of Corporate Controlling, Legal Affairs, Corporate Finance, Corporate Accounting, Corporate Audit (permanent member without voting rights), Corporate IT, Controlling Lufthansa Passenger Airlines and Delvag Group. It is responsible for continuously improving the effectiveness and efficiency of the risk management system.

An important instrument for doing so is the risk map: it lists all material risks which could endanger the Company's earnings and its continued existence. At the same time it identifies all the instruments for managing these risks. Risks count as material if they are capable of causing damage of at least one third of the operating result necessary for maintaining the value of the Company. For 2011 this amount was again determined to be EUR 300m for the Lufthansa Group. The materiality threshold is calculated individually for each of the business segments according to the same principle.

The risk map is updated regularly and its structure is aligned with the entire process of risk management, identification, coordination, communication and control. Lufthansa applies uniform risk management standards throughout the Group. The managing directors of all Group companies also appoint risk managers in all business segments. They are responsible for implementing the Group guidelines within their respective companies and are in close, regular contact with the Risk Management Committee. This also enables the rapid integration of new subsidiaries, as occurred with Austrian Airlines for instance.

Opportunity and risk controlling in the course of the planning and co-ordination processes is a further component of the system. This primarily identifies the potential risks and opportunities that could impact earnings targets in an analysis of the market and competition landscape, evaluates them and initiates steps to manage them.

As both positive and negative departures from plan are covered, this means that the same instruments are used to identify, evaluate, manage and control risks and opportunities.

Over the course of the year we track the opportunities and risks identified in relation to the planned result with the help of the quarterly Opportunity and Risk Report. Potential departures from the planned operating result are quantified by the risk experts in order to focus attention on the most important risks. Both positive and negative variations, i.e. opportunities and risks, are evaluated in the form of a best case/worst case analysis. A discussion of risks and opportunities is also a fixed element of the regular meetings between Group controlling and the managing directors of Group companies.

Additionally, the potential departures from plan are also examined in separate meetings with departments exposed to risk. The focus here is on identifying the action required and the status of steps taken to manage the corresponding opportunities and risks systematically.

The auditors PricewaterhouseCoopers Aktiengesellschaft Wirtschaftsprüfungsgesellschaft (PwC) examined the early risk warning system in place at Deutsche Lufthansa AG in the light of statutory requirements during the annual audit. It satisfies all the statutory requirements made of such a system.

Source: Lufthansa Annual Report, 2011, extract from Combined Management Report

Audit committee

This brings us back to the question of the audit committee. The idea of an audit committee originated in the US more than 30 years ago and initially spread only slowly to Europe. Companies listed on US exchanges were obliged to have an audit committee, and this of itself means that European companies listed in the US needed to have one. However, as the corporate governance movement has gathered pace, so has an indigenous insistence upon the merits of an audit committee in different European countries.

Where an audit committee functions effectively, it has the potential not only to improve the quality of financial reporting as such, but also to reinforce the quality of the control environment and strengthen the position of both the internal audit function and of the external auditor. Essentially, the idea is that the audit committee should provide a quasi-independent forum where those concerned with checking the effectiveness and quality of the company's accounting and control should be able to meet and discuss with shareholder representatives (independent directors) and raise issues of concern. In theory this is a fine idea, and helps encourage an open discussion about the group's effectiveness and protect the 'whistle-blower' from inside the company who is concerned about management fraud, ecological damage, tax fraud or whatever. It also helps preserve the independence of the external auditors from management. However, it depends upon the independent directors being willing to listen and to take action where they think this is necessary. Clearly in practice there is a risk that the audit committee will think it is there to defend the executives, or that it will not follow up the issues raised with the executives. In other words, the success of the audit committee is not guaranteed at all – it depends very much on the quality of the people concerned.

COMPANY REPORT

NOKIA AUDIT COMMITTEE

Committees of the Board of Directors in 2011 (extracts)
The Audit Committee consists of a minimum of three members of the Board who meet all applicable independence, financial literacy and other requirements of Finnish law and the rules of the stock exchanges where Nokia shares are listed, i.e. NASDAQ OMX Helsinki and the New York Stock Exchange. Since May 3, 2011, the Audit Committee consists of the following three members of the Board: Risto Siilasmaa (Chairman), Jouko Karvinen and Isabel Marey-Semper.

The Audit Committee is established by the Board primarily for the purpose of overseeing the accounting and financial reporting processes of the company and audits of the financial statements of the company. The Committee is responsible for assisting the Board's oversight of (1) the quality and integrity of the company's financial statements and related disclosure, (2) the statutory audit of the company's financial statements, (3) the external auditor's qualifications and independence, (4) the performance of the external auditor subject to the requirements of Finnish law, (5) the performance of the company's internal controls and risk management and assurance function, (6) the performance of the internal audit function and (7) the company's compliance with legal and regulatory requirements, including also the performance of its ethics and compliance program. The Committee also maintains procedures for the receipt, retention and treatment of complaints received by the company regarding accounting, internal controls or auditing matters and for the confidential, anonymous submission by employees of the company of concerns regarding accounting or auditing matters. Nokia's disclosure controls and procedures, which are reviewed by the Audit Committee and approved by the Chief Executive Officer and the Chief Financial Officer, as well as Nokia's internal controls over financial reporting, are designed to provide reasonable assurance regarding the quality and integrity of the company's financial statements and related disclosures. The Disclosure Committee chaired by the Chief Financial Officer is responsible for the preparation of the quarterly and annual results announcements, and the process includes involvement by business managers, business controllers and other functions, like internal audit, as well as a final review and confirmation by the Audit Committee and the Board. (...)

Under Finnish law, Nokia's external auditor is elected by Nokia's shareholders by a simple majority vote at the Annual General Meeting for one fiscal year at a time. The Audit Committee makes a proposal to the shareholders in respect of the appointment of the external auditor based upon its evaluation of the qualifications and independence of the auditor to be proposed for election or re-election. Under Finnish law, the fees of the external auditor are also approved by Nokia's shareholders by a simple majority vote at the Annual General Meeting. The Committee makes a proposal to the shareholders in respect of the fees of the external auditor, and approves the external auditor's annual audit fees under the guidance given by the Annual General Meeting. (...)

In discharging its oversight role, the Audit Committee has full access to all company books, records, facilities and personnel. The Committee may retain counsel, auditors or other advisors in its sole discretion, and must receive appropriate funding, as determined by the Committee, from the company for the payment of compensation to such outside advisors.

The Audit Committee meets at least four times a year based upon a schedule established at the first meeting following the appointment of the Committee. The Committee meets separately with the representatives of Nokia's management, heads of the internal audit and ethics and compliance functions, and the external auditor in connection with each regularly scheduled meeting. The head of the internal audit function has at all times a direct access to the Audit Committee, without involvement of management.

The Audit Committee had eight meetings in 2011. The attendance at all meetings was 100 per cent. In addition, any directors who wish to may attend Audit Committee meetings as non-voting observers.

Source: NOKIA, Annual Report, 2011,

In the EU, the Statutory Audit Directive (2006) requires all public interest entities, essentially companies whose securities are trading on a regulated market, to have an audit committee composed of non-executive directors or supervisory directors and/or members appointed by the general meeting of shareholders. At least one of the members of the audit committee should be independent and have competence in accounting and/or auditing. The proposed amendments (published in 2011) to the Fourth and Seventh Company Law Directives include a requirement for all public interest entities in the EU to provide a corporate governance statement in their management report which would contain a description of the company's internal control and risk management systems.

Meanwhile in the US, the Sarbanes–Oxley Act has increased the role and independence of the audit committee. It made the audit committee explicitly and directly responsible for the appointment, compensation and oversight of the work of the external auditor, including resolution of disagreements concerning financial reporting issues between management and the external auditor. Moreover, the audit committee must pre-approve all audit and non-audit services of the auditor.

Summary

The object of this chapter was to give you a certain amount of background information on current corporate governance issues and their relationship with, in particular, the effectiveness and accountability of corporate boards, internal control and external audit. The tenets of recent corporate governance developments are that good governance and internal control must become integrated into the mission, culture and daily operations of the company. This background information should serve to make you better understand the context within which the financial statements have been prepared and some of the information that is published in the annual report. If, as an analyst, you have the opportunity to attend company investor briefings, you should not hesitate to ask companies about the independent directors, the composition and mandate of the audit committee and the functioning and effectiveness of the internal control and risk management system. These are all indications of the transparency of company management and their effectiveness.

Discussion questions

1. What is the current state of the corporate governance debate in the country in which you are based? Try to identify from the different sources of regulation (stock exchange, government, accounting profession, etc.) current guidance in your country.
2. Compare the audit committee disclosures of a US corporation (see SEC EDGAR database) with that of a company based in your country.
3. Do you think that the independence of auditors is an issue about which you should be concerned? What are the rules in your country?
4. Explain the relationship between enterprise risk management and internal control.

PART FIVE

Advanced financial statement analysis

This last section consists of two chapters addressing different issues. Chapter 17 takes up from Chapters 8 and 9 and goes further into the art of financial statement analysis. Chapter 18 looks ahead at what changes are to be expected in IFRS in the short to medium term.

Financial statement analysis II

This is the second chapter to look at how users draw information from financial statements. The first part of the chapter reviews the relationship between the company and its investors, and how information flows from the company to the investors. The second part extends the work done in Chapter 9 on the tools and methods of financial statement analysis.

Chapter Structure

- Introduction
- Investor relations
- Income smoothing
- Why earnings fluctuate
- Professional analysts
- Quality of earnings
- Analytical techniques
- Strategic ratio analysis
- Shareholder value
- Summary
- Assignments

Introduction

In this chapter we intend to take your analytical skills a stage further, introducing some more analytical concepts and tools which provide further insights into a company's financial statements. By the end of it, you should know what other inputs are used by analysts to arrive at their opinions about companies. You should have considered what is implied by the quality of a company's earnings, and learned new methods to use ratios dynamically as a clue to the strategic positioning of a company.

Investor relations

A problem for the financial markets is that, although stock exchanges require companies to publish widely any information that is likely to affect the market price of a share (this is often done by sending a release to the stock exchange itself), in practice not all investors have access to the same information. The bulk of investment in the market comes from collective investment vehicles and not directly from private individuals. Many people save for retirement by buying shares in a unit trust or investing in a life assurance policy or an independent pension scheme. Employer schemes are frequently handed over to professional managers. Consequently, the individual intervenes less and less directly in the market and the vast majority of investment is channelled through different institutional investors. This means that a company seeking investors can address most of the market in effect by talking with professional fund managers and analysts.

This has given rise to the investor relations function. Large companies maintain a department whose job is to communicate, often on a one-to-one basis, with investment organizations. This department is somewhere between a public relations unit and a financial reporting unit. Their job is to maintain continuing relations with market professionals, to respond to their questions and to organize 'road shows': visits to different cities around the world to explain results and usually to enable investors to meet the chief financial officer or chief executive and talk about the company. Company websites often provide their financial data via a link on the home page entitled 'investor relations', rather than (say) financial statements. Analysts are invited to contact the 'corporate communications director', not the finance director.

At the same time, professional analysts will follow individual companies very closely and aim to become a specialist in that company. They will attend company presentations but also make visits to company sites and will constantly be updating their knowledge of the company and their future expectations. Evidently, such analysts have a much more detailed knowledge of the company than the average private individual and this creates an imbalance of knowledge in the market.

That said, the Internet is modifying that a little. Nowadays more and more brokers sell shares to private individuals on the Internet and a market is developing where TV companies will screen business reports early in the morning, often with soundbites from well-known analysts. Private investors then turn to their computer and buy and sell on the basis of that morning's comments. They then check the market regularly through the day to see how their gamble is paying off – all the excitement of betting on horse races or whatever, with the added psychological boost that what you are doing is seriously managing your finances, not amusing yourself. Private investors are coming back to direct buying and selling, but they are taking advice from professional brokers and others. In some ways this is likely to bring further complications to regulating the market because most effort currently goes into ensuring quality information to the professional investor and regulators may yet feel they have to step in to regulate the advice being given to private individuals in order to protect them and preserve confidence in the market.

BETWEEN THE LINES

INVESTOR RELATIONS MEETINGS

The analysts sought to make the best qualitative judgment on the company. Factors of particular interest about the company which were said to make a strong contribution to this qualitative judgment may be summarized as:

- quality of management
- performance indicators
- quality of assets
- verification and assurance.

What was clear from the analysts' comments was that relatively little of this information came directly from the annual report. Company meetings were the key source of qualitative information and the annual report was the confirmation in terms of financial outcomes.

Source: ICAS, Corporate Communications: Views of Institutional Investors and Lenders (Research Committee, Institute of Chartered Accountants of Scotland, 1999)

Income smoothing

There is a basic problem in financial reporting that the net earnings of a company are likely to vary from year to year because they are the result of many different factors, whereas the financial markets want earnings to increase progressively from year to year. This means that company financial executives are under some pressure to 'manage' the reported earnings so that they meet analysts' expectations.

Let us look at this proposition in more detail. First, why are earnings important to analysts? Second, why do they fluctuate? Third, how are they managed?

We talked in Chapter 9 about the price/earnings (P/E) ratio. This is a ratio that reflects the degree of risk which the market considers inherent to a particular company within a particular business sector. The relationship is expressed:

$$\text{P/E ratio} = \frac{\text{Market price of share}}{\text{Earnings per share}}$$

This relationship is fundamental to the stock market. When investment managers are looking for shares to buy, what they are seeking is a share which is *undervalued*, i.e. whose market price is below its real value. The current market price is determined by analysts as a function of the historic P/E for that company, multiplied by forecast earnings per share. If the share is undervalued, that means that the market is either underestimating future earnings or overestimating the riskiness of the company (the higher the risk, the higher the return necessary to compensate investors for running the risk, and so the lower the P/E and price).

BETWEEN THE LINES

The accounts are now so complex that most users need someone else to explain them. But financial analysts are only interested in earnings per share and the price/earnings ratio. Les Cullen, a director of Inchcape, said 'Standard-setters must realize there is a limit to the complexity which preparers can put up with'. He added: 'The City is not using the more complex information. It is still seeing the company as a sort of annuity'. He explained that the markets are more interested in stable earnings patterns and this creates a pressure on preparers to smooth earnings, even though in the modern economy earnings are becoming more volatile. 'There is a disconnection at present between accounting principles and the financial market.'

Source: Accounting & Business, July/August 1999, p.20

The P/E ratios for the sector often fluctuate together (many aspects of risk will affect all companies in the same sector similarly) but the P/E for the individual company within that tends to be fairly stable in relation to other companies in the same sector.

It is changes in expected earnings which are the more frequent cause of fluctuations in price which affect individual companies. During the accounting year, professional analysts will visit the company and will try to obtain information which will give them as good as possible an idea of the likely outcome for the year's earnings. A forecast increase in earnings will cause them to buy more shares (market currently undervalues shares) whereas a drop in forecast earnings will cause them to sell shares (market overvalues the company at current price). There is therefore a direct link between accounting earnings and the market price.

Why earnings fluctuate

The net profit after tax of a multinational is subject to an enormous number of different variables – temporary changes in turnover as a result of local conditions, the arrival of competing products on the market, unexpected losses as a result of, for example, civil unrest, tax changes and so on. A multinational may well be operating in over 100 countries and selling many different types of products, so the number of factors which contribute to the shape of the consolidated statement of profit or loss (income statement/profit and loss account) is inevitably substantial. While there may be a *portfolio effect* (i.e. if you have enough different risk factors they may cancel each other out), there are many circumstances which can influence the final outcome.

Another issue is that net profit after tax is a small percentage of revenues. For example, if you take the results of Amazon for 2007, the revenues were $14 835m (2006: $10 711m) but net profit before tax was $660m (2006: $377m) which is 4.45 per cent (2006: 3.52 per cent). This means that operating expenses and interest amounted to 95.55 per cent of revenues (2006: 96.48 per cent). In this context sales have gone up by 28 per cent but income before tax has gone up 75 per cent. The difference is a one per cent decrease in costs.

You can see that a small shift in costs has a major effect on profits. This has two consequences: first, profits are likely to move up and down, year on year, in an apparently arbitrary fashion but, second, that management can influence profits by relatively small manipulations of costs. If management want the share price to rise steadily year on year, they have to ensure, given the market's dependence upon P/E ratios, that profits rise steadily year on year.

How do managers manipulate profits?

There are a number of classic ways in which this can be done legally and they are all difficult for the analyst to recognize. The most difficult to detect is the management of what are sometimes called *discretionary costs*. These are costs which the group can stop incurring without having any immediate effect on profitability, such as research and development, staff training, advertising. Of course, it is suicide for the company in the medium to long term and also has a bad effect on company morale in the short term, but it is frequently practised. Most groups operate an internal monthly reporting system which compares actual performance with budget and many add to that a forecast for the year-end profit which is updated every month. If this forecast shows that the target profit for the year is unlikely to be achieved, it is possible that the call will go out from head office to abandon advertising campaigns, halt product development or simply defer these until the start of the next accounting year. Any of these tactics will increase short-term profits and there is little or nothing visible on the outside to warn the analyst. Where a company discloses its annual research and development expenditure, this may show a decrease. But even here, the classification as to what is development expenditure and what ordinary running costs is not that clear, and a little creative redefinition could hold the figure up even when real expenditure has dropped.

A second area of action is closure of loss-making divisions. Suppose that a company has five divisions with forecast results as follows:

Division	Profit €m
A	140
B	−120
C	80
D	75
E	50
Group	225

If you close division B, group profit jumps immediately from €225m to €345m. This may or may not be a good idea. It may just hasten the demise of a division which had no future – the product was near the end of its life cycle and could no longer make an adequate contribution. On the other hand, it may cause the company to close a unit which is in a start-up situation. Many operations lose money in their early days – you have only to look at companies like Amazon and other very visible Internet start-ups to see that. The very difficult trick for central management is to decide how long to continue to nurse a start-up (potentially up to five years) and when to decide to cut one's losses and stop the experiment. In this situation, pressure to help the group profit can result in a start-up being abandoned too early because its losses are causing aggregate group profit to suffer. This tactic is usually not all that difficult to spot because there is likely to be some mention of the closure in the notes to the accounts or the management report, but there may be only hints which require interpretation.

A variant on this involves an accounting manipulation: consolidated accounting rules may allow the group to exclude from the consolidation any subsidiary which is to be disposed of. Flagging division B as a disposal would mean that it could be held out of the group result without even closing it down. Until recently this kind of practice was even common for groups applying IAS rules. With the introduction in 2004 of IFRS 5, *Non-current Assets Held for Sale and Discontinued Operations*, however, the exemption from consolidation for subsidiaries acquired and held exclusively with a view to resale has been removed from IFRS.

The third way of smoothing profits is what the Securities and Exchange Committee (SEC) has called 'cookie jar accounting'. This involves using unrealistic assumptions to estimate liabilities for such items as sales returns, litigation costs, product warranty costs, etc. In doing so, they stash accruals (or sometimes unearned revenues) in 'cookie jars' during the good times and reach into them when needed in bad times. Making provisions when profits are higher than expected and releasing them when times are difficult is a classic example. The basic tactic is to create a provision by making a charge against profits and carrying forward a credit in the statement of financial position (go back to Chapter 6 if you want to review the basic technique). This charge will generally not be accepted for tax purposes, but that does not matter since its function is to deceive the market not the taxman. The more difficult problem is to convince the group auditors.

The way this would work might be:

Year 1		
Market expectations of profit		150
Actual revenues		3 400
Actual costs		−3 200
Actual profit		200
Create provision		−45
Reported profit		155

When the results are announced, the slight increase against analysts' forecasts would generate a slight increase in share prices.

Year 2		
Market expectations of profit		170
Actual revenues		3 450
Actual costs		−3 300
Actual profit		150
Release part of provision		20
Reported profit		170

Had the group reported the actual result for Year 1 of €200m and, a year later, the actual result of €150m, the share price would first have rocketed, and the market might have expected profits of €250m in Year 2, leading to a steep decline in the share price once the actual result was announced.

Is this manipulation visible to the analyst? Well, up to a point. In the statement of financial position, the manipulation would show up as a change in the balance for provisions. Provided this is well enough analyzed in the notes to the accounts, the analyst can see whether there has been a net increase or decrease in provisions, without necessarily having enough information to know what exactly has happened – but an analyst attending a road show could ask questions. Equally, the statement of cash flows usually includes a reconciliation between accounting net profit and operating cash flows. The effect on the statement of profit or loss of changes in provisions will also be visible here, because they do not affect cash flows and have therefore to be highlighted in the reconciliation between profit and operating cash flow.

A variant on this technique is known as 'big bath' accounting. This is most frequently applied when a group takes over a new subsidiary but may also occur when there is a change of chief executive. Typically, the company sets up large charges associated with a restructuring operation. These charges help the company to 'clean up' the balance sheet – giving it a so-called 'big bath'. The idea is that the acquiring group or the new chief executive identifies over-valued assets (and under-valued liabilities) and makes a once and for all adjustment for these. This involves major charges and tends to put a crater in the year's profit, but is explained to analysts as an exceptional year where a major cleaning-up exercise (big bath) has been done.

BETWEEN THE LINES

Cookie jar reserves

One of the accounting 'hot spots' that we are considering this morning is accounting for restructuring charges and restructuring reserves. A better title would be accounting for general reserves, contingency reserves, rainy day reserves or cookie jar reserves.

Accounting for so-called restructurings has become an art form. Some companies like the idea so much that they establish restructuring reserves every year. Why not? Analysts seem to like the idea of recognizing as a liability today, a budget of expenditures planned for the next year or next several years in down-sizing, right-sizing, or improving operations, and portraying that amount as a special, below-the-line charge in the current period's statement of profit or loss. This year's earnings are happily reported in press releases as 'before charges'. CNBC analysts and commentators talk about earnings 'before charges'. The financial press talks about earnings before 'special charges'. (Funny, no one talks about earnings before credits – only charges). It's as if special charges are not real. Out of sight, out of mind...

The occasion of a merger also spawns the wholesale establishment of restructuring or merger reserves. The ingredients of the merger reserves and merger charges look like the makings of a sausage. In the Enforcement Division, I have seen all manner and kind of things that ordinarily would be charged to operating earnings instead of being charged 'below the line'. Write-offs of the carrying amounts of bad receivables. Write-offs of cost of obsolete inventory. Write-downs of plant and equipment costs, which, miraculously at the date of the merger, become non-recoverable, whereas those same costs were considered recoverable the day before the merger. Write-offs of previously capitalized costs such as goodwill, which all of a sudden are not recoverable because of a merger. Adjustments to bring warranty liabilities up to snuff. Adjustments to bring claim liabilities in line with management's new view of settling or litigating cases. Adjustments to bring environmental liabilities up to snuff or in line with management's new view of the manner in which the company's obligations to comply with EPA will be satisfied. Recognition of liabilities to pay for future services by investment bankers, accountants and lawyers. Recognition of liabilities for officers' special bonuses. Recognition of liabilities for moving people. For training people. For training people not yet hired. For retraining people. Recognition of liabilities for moving costs and refurbishing costs. Recognition of liabilities for new software that may be acquired or written, for ultimate sale to others. Or some liabilities that go by the title 'other'.

It is no wonder that investors and analysts are complaining about the credibility of the numbers.

Source: Speech by Walter P. Schuetze, Chief Accountant, Enforcement Division,
US Securities and Exchange Commission, 22 April 1999
(www.sec.gov/news/speeches/spch276.htm)

The advantage of this is that future depreciation charges will be lower (and therefore future profits higher) or that excess provisions are available to boost future profits, but at the same time the current share price is often not affected. In fact, if analysts accept the argument they have been given, they tend to look beyond the one-time loss and focus on future earnings. The share price may even rise despite the disastrous immediate effect on profit or loss of the write-offs or accrued expenses, because the market expects even better results in the future.

Is income smoothing a good thing or a bad thing?

This is difficult to say. On the positive side, theorists argue that *clean surplus accounting* (profits after smoothing) is a very good guide to long-term profitability, even if the year-on-year result has been managed. They say that the management have the best grasp of the real underlying capabilities of the group, and they will manipulate the profits to fit into their view of the long-term growth of the group. Consequently the 'managed' profits are a reliable indicator of long-term performance.

On the negative side, people point out that the markets are misled by income smoothing. They claim that often when a company goes broke or is taken over in disastrous circumstances, this follows on a period of profit manipulation which built up market expectations well beyond the capabilities of the company. Some standard-setters work to correct this, saying that the market should have as much information as possible and be allowed to make up its own mind.

Professional analysts

Accounting numbers are not the only input into the assessment of a company's prospects. Analysts use many other factors, mostly economic, about the state of the economies where the company operates, the state of the industry, etc. to help predict future performance. An example of this type of information is provided by Moody's.

Moody's is one of a number of firms that offer a bond rating service – they assess the riskiness of individual companies and then publish their risk rating, which in turn impacts upon a company's cost of borrowing. Moody's use inputs from the following areas (not given in any priority ranking) in order to determine their risk rating:

- industry
- company
- capital structure
- sovereign risk
- bond instrument
- financial flexibility
- capital expenditure
- internal cash flow
- competitors
- use of debt capacity
- customers
- management risk appetite.

Not all the information comes from financial statements! Moody's talk to company management and since they provide ratings for all large companies, talk to all the competing managements too, and therefore have a broad picture of competition and patterns of development. Moody's offer the 'rating pyramid' (Figure 17.1) which shows how they approach the rating decision.

It is our intention within this book to provide some of the skills necessary for quantitative analysis, and you will draw from other books and courses insights into economics, finance, business strategy, etc. which can be used to refine your analysis.

BETWEEN THE LINES

All expert users showed a clear desire to identify what drove cash flow and profits, together with the expert users' application of a mixture of systematic search and intuition for the likely answer. The systematic search followed the route of considering:

- the economy
- product market
- industry
- the business of the company
- quality of management; and
- quality of assets

Source: ICAS, *Corporate Communications: Views of Institutional Investors and Lenders*
(Research Committee, Institute of Chartered Accountants of Scotland, 1999)

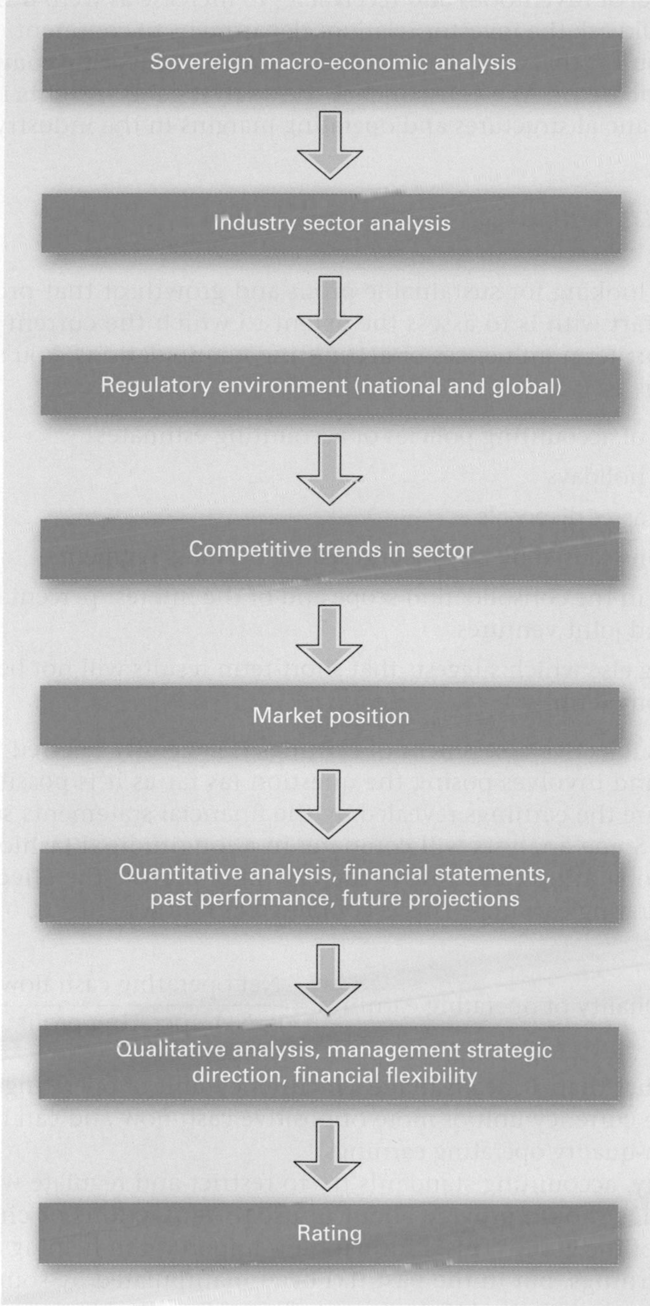

Figure 17.1
Moody's rating
pyramid

```
┌─────────────────────────────────────────────┐
│         Sovereign macro-economic analysis    │
└─────────────────────────────────────────────┘
                        ⬇
┌─────────────────────────────────────────────┐
│             Industry sector analysis          │
└─────────────────────────────────────────────┘
                        ⬇
┌─────────────────────────────────────────────┐
│      Regulatory environment (national and global)  │
└─────────────────────────────────────────────┘
                        ⬇
┌─────────────────────────────────────────────┐
│            Competitive trends in sector       │
└─────────────────────────────────────────────┘
                        ⬇
┌─────────────────────────────────────────────┐
│                Market position                │
└─────────────────────────────────────────────┘
                        ⬇
┌─────────────────────────────────────────────┐
│     Quantitative analysis, financial statements,  │
│       past performance, future projections    │
└─────────────────────────────────────────────┘
                        ⬇
┌─────────────────────────────────────────────┐
│   Qualitative analysis, management strategic  │
│      direction, financial flexibility         │
└─────────────────────────────────────────────┘
                        ⬇
┌─────────────────────────────────────────────┐
│                    Rating                     │
└─────────────────────────────────────────────┘
```

As far as accounting analysis goes, though, you should note the increasing use of investor briefings by companies as a means of obtaining explanations. Investor relations departments in large companies are generally also willing to respond to individual queries, provided that they know the analyst. In this context, the analyst carries out a series of technical measures, calculating ratios and so on, and uses the ratios to form a view about what is going on in the company or to recognize that the expected patterns do not emerge and further information is necessary to explain this anomaly. For example, if sales are increasing, you would expect the level of inventories and receivables to increase as well. If this is not the case, you should ask the investor relations department to comment.

Another point is that analysis frequently involves comparing companies in the same industrial sector. As a consequence the analyst gains insights into what are the typical financial structures and operating margins in the industry.

Quality of earnings

An analyst is looking for sustainable profit and growth of that profit. So a key question to start with is to assess the extent to which the current earnings are subject to short-term influences or accounting manipulations. You should check for such things as:

a. changes of accounting policies or accounting estimates

b. pension holidays

c. unusual asset disposals

d. distortions caused by buying and selling business segments

e. changes in the consolidation scope and of the interest percentages in associates and joint ventures

f. anything else which suggests that short-term results will not be replicated in the long term.

This kind of subjective assessment of earnings is generally referred to as 'quality of earnings' and involves posing the question (as far as it is possible to tell) to what extent are the earnings revealed by the financial statements sustainable in future years? Some analysts will compare, in a longitudinal fashion, operating profit to net operating cash flow to identify and analyze the effect of accruals games on operating earnings. This is computed as follows:

$$\text{Quality of operating earnings} = \frac{\text{Net operating cash flow}}{\text{Net operating profit}}$$

A ratio of higher than 1 means that each currency unit of operating profit is supported by one currency unit or more of positive cash flow and can be considered to reflect high-quality operating earnings.

Increasingly, accounting standards try to restrict and regulate what information companies should provide about unusual transactions or changes in the components of the group. This information is important in helping analysts forecast future earnings, but in the past has been manipulated by some companies to try to mislead analysts. IAS 1, *Presentation of Financial Statements*, prohibits the distinction of ordinary activities and extraordinary items on the face of the statement of profit or loss. The IASB reasoned that extraordinary items are not that special in the sense that they result from the normal business risks faced by the company and, thus, do not warrant presentation in a separate caption of the profit and loss account. Disclosures in the notes to the accounts (and even on the statement of profit or loss) may, however, hold significant information to identify and analyze the effect of special and non-recurrent items and transactions. Indeed, IAS 1 requires that when items of income and expense are material, their nature and amount should be disclosed separately.

STANDARDS

🌐 **IAS 1 – PRESENTATION OF FINANCIAL STATEMENTS** *(extracts)*

Separate disclosure of material items of income and expense

97. When items of income and expense are material, an entity shall disclose their nature and amount separately.

98. Circumstances that would give rise to the separate disclosure of items of income and expense include:

  (a) write-downs of inventories to net realizable value or of property, plant and equipment to recoverable amount, as well as reversals of such write-downs;
  (b) restructurings of the activities of an entity and reversals of any provisions for the costs of restructuring;
  (c) disposals of items of property, plant and equipment;
  (d) disposals of investments;
  (e) discontinued operations;
  (f) litigation settlements; and
  (g) other reversals of provisions.

7. Material Omissions or misstatements of items are material if they could, individually or collectively, influence the economic decisions that users make on the basis of the financial statements. Materiality depends on the size and nature of the omission or misstatement judged in the surrounding circumstances. The size or nature of the item, or a combination of both, could be the determining factor.

Source: IAS 1, Presentation of Financial Statements

Critical accounting judgements and estimates

IAS 1, *Presentation of Financial Statements,* also requires that companies explain critical judgments and estimates that impact the financial statements significantly (see Standards box). These are in effect the IASB's response to Enron.

STANDARDS

🌐 **IAS 1 – PRESENTATION OF FINANCIAL STATEMENTS** *(extracts)*

Judgements and sources of estimation uncertainty

122. An entity shall disclose, in the summary of significant accounting policies or other notes, the judgements, apart from those involving estimations (see paragraph 125), that management has made in the process of applying the entity's accounting policies and that have the most significant effect on the amounts recognized in the financial statements.

125. An entity shall disclose information about the assumptions it makes about the future, and other major sources of estimation uncertainty at the end

of the reporting period, that have a significant risk of resulting in a material adjustment to the carrying amounts of assets and liabilities within the next financial year. In respect of those assets and liabilities, the notes shall include details of:

(a) their nature, and
(b) their carrying amount as at the end of the reporting period.

Source: IAS 1, *Presentation of Financial Statements*

This is very useful information for analysts, assuming that the company has correctly identified and discussed these. The nature of the expenses of each company and those that are subject to major uncertainties will vary considerably, so this is a helpful note pointing the analyst to issues that may help in assessing the quality of earnings and in forecasting future earnings.

COMPANY REPORT

RYANAIR – USE OF ESTIMATES AND JUDGEMENTS

Critical accounting policies (extracts)

The preparation of the Company's financial statements requires the use of estimates, judgments, and assumptions that affect the reported amounts of assets and liabilities at the date of the financial statements and the reported amounts of revenues and expenses during the periods presented. Actual results may differ from these estimates. The Company believes that its critical accounting policies, which are those that require management's most difficult, subjective and complex judgments, are those described in this section. These critical accounting policies, the judgments and other uncertainties affecting application of these policies and the sensitivity of reported results to changes in conditions and assumptions are factors to be considered in reviewing the consolidated financial statements included in Item 18 and the discussion and analysis below. For additional detail on these policies, see Note 1, 'Basis of preparation and significant accounting policies', to the consolidated financial statements included in Item 18.

Long-lived Assets

As of March 31, 2011, Ryanair had €4.9 billion of long-lived assets, virtually all of which were aircraft. In accounting for long-lived assets, Ryanair must make estimates about the expected useful lives of the assets, the expected residual values of the assets, and the potential for impairment based on the fair value of the assets and the cash flows they generate.

In estimating the lives and expected residual values of its aircraft, Ryanair has primarily relied on its own and industry experience, recommendations from Boeing, the manufacturer of all of the Company's aircraft, and other available marketplace information. Subsequent revisions to these estimates, which can be significant, could be caused by changes to Ryanair's maintenance program, changes in utilization of the aircraft, governmental regulations on aging of air-craft, changes in new aircraft technology, changes in new aircraft fuel efficiency and changing market prices for new and used aircraft of the same or similar types. Ryanair evaluates its estimates and assumptions in each reporting pe-riod, and, when warranted, adjusts these assumptions. Generally, these adjust-ments are accounted for on a prospective basis, through depreciation expense.

Ryanair periodically evaluates its long-lived assets for impairment. Factors that would indicate potential impairment would include, but are not limited to, significant decreases in the market value of an aircraft, a significant change in an aircraft's physical condition and operating or cash flow losses associated with the use of the aircraft. While the airline industry as a whole has experienced many of these factors from time to time, Ryanair has not yet been seriously impacted and continues to record positive cash flows from these long-lived as-sets. Consequently, Ryanair has not yet identified any impairments related to its existing aircraft fleet. The Company will continue to monitor its long-lived assets and the general airline operating environment.

The Company's estimate of the recoverable amount of aircraft residual val-ues is 15 per cent of current market value of new aircraft, determined periodi-cally, based on independent valuations and actual aircraft disposals during the current and prior periods. Aircraft are depreciated over a useful life of 23 years from the date of manufacture to residual value.

During the fiscal year ended March 31, 2009, accelerated depreciation of €51.6 million arose in relation to aircraft disposals during the year and an agree-ment to dispose of additional aircraft in the 2010 fiscal year. In particular, this charge arose due to an adverse change in the exchange rate between the US dollar and the euro between the accounting periods in which the aircraft were purchased and March 31, 2009. There was no such accelerated depreciation rec-ognized in the 2010 or 2011 fiscal years.

Source: Ryanair, Annual Report 2011

Analytical techniques

Common accounting base

Moving on to the techniques used to analyze the accounting data, when compar-ing two or more companies it may be necessary to adjust the statements because of accounting differences. Of course, there are often elements for which the ana-lyst is unable to adjust because insufficient information is available, but the more one is comparing like with like, the more useful is the analysis. Many analysts try, when carrying out cross-sectional analysis, to eliminate any major account-ing differences between companies or, for that matter, convert all companies to a common accounting base. The most obvious examples of this are reducing all revalued assets back to historical cost or treating goodwill as an asset instead of writing it off. As discussed before, the first thing to do when analyzing a com-pany is to look at the notes to the accounts dealing with accounting policies. When comparing two different companies, you should compare their policies on major issues such as accounting for goodwill, depreciation rules, accounting for R&D costs, and valuation generally. You should also look at their provisions to see whether they are comparable.

The analyst can often usefully put pro-forma statements on to a spreadsheet, using an adjusted, common accounting base to make comparisons. Indeed this is a technique which is virtually essential when analyzing the financial statements of companies which are based in different countries. This is a subject which is beyond the scope of this book, but it is easy to see that common assumptions – or as near as the analyst can get – are essential to make valid comparisons.

Common size

Ratios have the characteristic that they do away with size considerations so that quite different companies may be compared. You will remember that this may also be done by the preparation of *common-size financial statements* – these consist of a statement of profit or loss and a statement of financial position expressed in percentages (i.e. profit or loss items expressed as a percentage of sales, balance sheet items as a percentage of total assets). Common-size financial statements are usually a good starting point in the financial statement analysis process. They allow a straightforward internal or structural analysis of the company's financial position and performance and can be easily used for comparisons in time or in space (industry comparisons).

EBITDA

EBITDA sounds like some strange mantra, and certainly some analysts can be heard chanting it at times, but this is simply a rough proxy for net operating cash flows. EBITDA stands for 'earnings before interest, taxation, depreciation and amortization'.

While multinational companies have largely harmonized their cash flow reporting and produce statements of cash flows in line with IAS 7, *Statement of Cash Flows*, and therefore provide operating cash flow data, some analysts prefer a measure drawn directly from the statement of profit or loss. The idea is that the analyst is trying to assess operating cash flows before non-cash accounting allocations of cost (depreciation, provisions and amortization) and before returns to lenders and taxation. How much cash is the business generating on a day-to-day basis? This measure may be subject to technical criticism, but it has the advantage that it strips out – as far as possible – subjective accounting adjustments from the income measure and enables a more robust comparison of performance year on year or company to company.

Objectives of analysis

As we have discussed, there are many potential uses and users of annual financial statements, but for the immediate purpose of financial statement analysis we are addressing only the needs of the two main groups for whom the financial statements are formally prepared: investors and creditors. These two groups are concerned with similar but different investment decisions about the company.

Investors (whether actual or potential) face a buy/sell/hold decision. They receive a return on their investment in the form of a flow of dividends and the difference between buying and selling price of the shareholding. There is no established pattern of behaviour amongst long-term shareholders as to whether they prefer income by way of dividends or by way of holding gain. (Clearly short-term holders are only interested in a speculative holding gain.) Finance theory suggests that shareholders should be indifferent, on the assumption that if a company restricts its dividend payments the share price will rise, so shareholders wanting cash flow can realize this by selling a part of their holding.

The evidence suggests that some companies pay high dividends in the belief that their shareholders want this, while others believe that shareholders prefer capital gains and restrict dividends. The way in which unit trusts are sold suggests that fund managers believe these are different markets. Some companies attempt to satisfy both types of shareholder and offer the option of taking the dividend in the form of new shares.

Professional investors have varying points of view. US pension funds often look at dividend flows (over as much as a 50-year time horizon) while many UK brokers sell to institutional investors on the basis of expected holding gains. For example, Ian Hay Davison, chairman of Alexander Lang & Cruikshank, wrote the following:

> At 8.15 each weekday morning the security salesmen and analysts in my firm meet to consider the ideas that will be put to our 300 or so institutional customers during the day. Analysts responsible for following companies in various sectors of the market give their recommendations for specific shares: buy, hold or sell. It is these recommendations, together with similar conclusions reached at 20 or so other security houses, that collectively drive prices in the market. The single most important figure affecting the analyst's – and hence the market's – view is forecasted earnings per share. I know that accountants deplore the fact that judgements about the worth of a share turn largely on one number. Nonetheless that is what happens, and you and I know that it is accounting rules that determine earnings per share.

The way this works is that brokers expect the price/earnings (P/E) ratio of a company to be stable (subject to economic changes, management changes, etc.) and the market price to be a function of the forecast earnings and the P/E ratio (as discussed in earlier in this chapter).

For example, if a hotel company is forecast to have earnings per share of €4 and a P/E of 12, its market price should be €48. If an analyst who follows the hotel sector believes that the company is actually going to achieve significantly better than €4, say €5, this would mean that she or he would expect the price to rise to €60, and the securities house would issue a buy recommendation to its clients. These recommendations can themselves move the market.

The professional investor will look at indicators which are predictors of future performance on the assumption that growth in profits will lead to high dividends or high share price rises. Clearly these indicators may be to do with the state of the economy or may be based on some inside information (investor relations departments of large companies hold special briefings for brokers and institutional shareholders) about new products etc. However, this course is concerned directly only with the information which can be gleaned from the published financial statements, so while acknowledging that investors use many different information sources, we will concentrate on financial statement information.

Growth in profits may be predicted from the financial statements based on a number of factors such as evidence of management skill, or evidence of high investment. Other factors such as a high debt/equity ratio will provide indicators of some aspects of the degree of risk in investing in the company.

The investor wishes (a) to predict the level of future returns and (b) to evaluate these against competing investment opportunities in the light of the riskiness of the investment (the higher the risk, the higher the expected return to compensate for the investment).

The creditor (the supplier of loans rather than short-term trade credit) is also concerned with predicting performance but from a slightly different angle. The creditor's main risk is default risk but ordinarily the creditor will also be concerned to assure themselves that the company's likely future cash flows will be sufficient to meet interest payments and finally repay the debt. The creditor will have more interest in the financial structure and prospective cash flows of the company. But then again, it is earnings that ultimately generate cash flows, bringing us back to earning power or profitability as a fundamental concern for both (prospective) shareholders and creditors.

Broadly, both investor and creditor will use much the same indicators, but the relative importance of specific indicators will be different. The indicators may also serve different purposes at different times. The investor may use indicators which lead to a buy decision. Having already bought a holding, the release of new accounting data will prompt a hold/sell decision. In making this decision the investor will look not only for the indicators of the future, but will also look for feedback into his or her own decision-making process. She or he will examine how the company actually performed during the period an investment was held, as compared with the predictions made at the time of making the investment, to improve future predictions.

Strategic ratio analysis

A further development in financial statement analysis has been the attempt to develop (combinations of) ratios which will give insights to a company's strategic positioning in terms of the kind of analysis proposed by authors such as Porter or Peters. These authors introduced a strategic analysis framework centred around ideas such as the life cycle phases of products and firms, whether the company operates in a market where entry is difficult (margins should be large) or entry is easy (margins are tight), whether its products are specialist, niche products (low volume, high margin) or bulk (high volume, low margin) and many other considerations. Again, detailed discussions of business strategy should be looked for in specialist publications or courses, but our point is that proper analysis of financial statements can provide significant inputs for strategy analysis.

Sustainable growth

Most analysts will start their analysis by looking at growth of key items of financial statements, such as sales, net fixed assets, net profit and EPS (earnings per share). Trend analysis will automatically deliver the necessary data to determine a year-to-year growth rate or an average growth rate over a longer period. Growth rates are often compared with the rate of inflation to determine 'real' growth. Point of departure usually is sales growth, with the co-variation of sales and net working capital, net long-term assets, operating margins, net profit and operating cash flows being primary material for further analysis. It makes sense to try to differentiate organic growth and acquired growth as they tend to have quite different implications for further analysis. *Organic growth* is fuelled by the company's own operations, whereas *acquired growth* is the result of buying the assets and operations of other companies (through mergers and acquisitions). Sales growth is not always an indicator of successful performance and its relationship with operating efficiency and liquidity concerns needs careful attention.

The concept of sustainable growth looks at growth from an overall shareholder profitability perspective and measures the rate at which a company can grow while keeping its profitability and financing structure unchanged. The *sustainable growth rate* ratio is calculated as:

Sustainable growth rate = Return on equity × (1 − Dividend payout ratio)

The dividend payout ratio is:

$$\frac{\text{Dividend}}{\text{Profit attributable to shareholders}}$$

Sustainable growth stands for the internally generated growth potential if the company's profitability, dividend payout policy and level of debt financing are kept constant. Equity is, of course, equal to the net worth of a company, so the ROE (return on equity) ratio would tell you by what proportion the company would grow if it retained its profits and reinvested them. This is then reduced by the dividend payout, since clearly the dividend involves returning cash to shareholders, to show the proportion of net worth retained in the company each year out of that year's earnings. This is described as 'sustainable growth'. It ignores the fact that depreciation has been charged in arriving at this figure because that is regarded as a surrogate for the cash outflow required to sustain the company at its present size.

Put another way, a company which is breaking even after depreciation charges (which reflect the economic life of the assets) should be able to replace its assets and stay the same size; a company which makes a profit (i.e. makes a positive return on equity) but pays it all out to shareholders by way of dividend will similarly stay the same size; but to the extent that a company has profits which are greater than the dividend, it will have internal growth potential.

This potential growth rate can be used as one basis of comparison. Clearly companies can also borrow, but ultimately that increases risk and is subject to fairly finite limits which link back to the company's equity base and the growth of that equity base. It is therefore a useful growth indicator to compare companies. If comparing companies within the same industry, one might predict that a company with a higher than average sustainable growth rate would be able to increase its market share.

ROI decomposition

There is a conventional relationship between management performance ratios which links return on investment, profit margin and asset turnover as follows:

$$\text{Profit margin} \times \text{Asset turnover} = \text{ROI}$$

A ROI (return on investment) ratio can be analyzed as a combination of two factors: overall profitability of sales and asset utilization.

If we apply this reasoning to the ROA (return on assets) ratio, we arrive at the following algebraic equality:

$$\frac{\text{Profit before interest}}{\text{Sales}} \times \frac{\text{Sales}}{\text{Total assets}} = \frac{\text{Profit before interest}}{\text{Total assets}}$$

Each of the terms on the right-hand side of the equation has its own meaning. Profit before interest divided by sales is a variant of the net profit margin (an overall profitability measure). Sales divided by total assets is the total asset turnover ratio. In fact, we decompose the ROA ratio into other financial characteristics that can be examined individually.

The ROA decomposition suggests two ways to improve the ROA: by increasing either the net profit margin or the turnover of total assets (or both). The net profit margin will increase by earning more profit per currency unit of sales. The total asset turnover will increase in either of two ways: (a) by generating more sales volume with the same amount of assets, or (b) by reducing the amount of assets required for a given volume of sales (for example, by disposing of or decreasing less productive assets). The total asset turnover ratio can be analyzed further through the component measures of total assets turnover (inventory turnover, fixed asset turnover, receivables turnover, etc.). Profit margins will improve by (a) reducing cost of sales and other operating costs for a given volume of sales or (b) increasing unit sales prices.

The ROI decomposition logic underscores the fact that an overall ROI measure is the combined effect of a large number of factors and responsibilities. It can be used by external analysts as a guide to drill-down to specific policy areas and identify areas of concern.

To a certain extent the relationships among the decomposed ratios/factors are industry specific. Industries that are capital intensive are likely to have a low asset turnover ratio. However, such an industry is also usually characterized by high margins because it is difficult for new companies to enter the market. A company which is capital intensive but also has low margins will be on a declining trend in its life cycle. Industries that have little capital involved will have higher asset turnover ratios. However, they will normally be highly competitive because of the lack of barriers to entry into the market and will therefore show lower margins.

Financial leverage

Taking the analysis one step further, the ROE can be analytically linked to the return on assets ratio with the introduction of the concept of financial leverage.

$$ROA \times \text{Financial leverage} = ROE$$

Starting with the ROA ratio, we arrive at the following algebraic equality:

$$\frac{\text{Profit before interest}}{\text{Total assets}} \times \frac{\text{Total assets}}{\text{Equity}} = \frac{\text{Profit before interest}}{\text{Equity}}$$

Alternatively, we can start from the original ROE definition and get the following:

$$\frac{\text{Net profit for the period}}{\text{Total assets}} \times \frac{\text{Total assets}}{\text{Equity}} = \frac{\text{Net profit for the period}}{\text{Equity}}$$

In both formulae financial leverage is defined as the proportion of total assets acquired with funds supplied by the shareholders. It measures how many euro of assets are employed for each euro invested by shareholders. Financial leverage will increase if debt financing increases or if part of the shares outstanding are re-purchased. The essential message of the ROE decomposition is that both financial leverage and ROA are drivers of the return to shareholders: debt financing can be used to lever shareholder profitability.

A related, but somewhat different, concept is the *financial leverage coefficient* ratio, defined as ROE divided by ROA:

$$\text{Financial leverage coefficient} = ROE\% / ROA\%$$

Leverage is positive (or financial leverage coefficient greater than one) if the company's rate of return on total assets exceeds the average after-tax interest rate on its debt. In that case, the company lends money at one rate and uses that money productively at a higher rate of return. The excess of the after-tax rate of return on assets and the after-tax interest rate on the borrowed funds, accrues to the benefit of the shareholders. Note that financial leverage can be a disadvantage too: if the company does not succeed to earn a rate of return on assets which is higher than the after-tax cost of debt, the shareholders will have to support the deficit.

Debt financing will increase the financial leverage effect. If leverage is positive, the financial leverage coefficient will increase with gearing. We illustrate this effect in Table 17.1 under three different gearing assumptions with total assets, ROA and after-tax cost of debt being held constant.

The higher the debt/equity ratio, the higher the effect (positive or negative) of debt financing on the ROE. Note that in this scenario analysis we kept the cost of debt constant. In practice, however, increasing gearing will undoubtably have an effect on the cost of debt too. Increased debt financing will bring lenders to demand a higher risk premium and, thus, a higher interest rate, possibly up to the level where leverage becomes negative (financial leverage coefficient 1).

Combining ROI decomposition and financial leverage brings us to the following overall model (also called the DuPont model):

$$\text{ROE} = \text{Net profit margin} \times \text{Asset turnover} \times \text{Financial leverage}$$

or:

$$\frac{\text{Net profit for the period}}{\text{Equity}} = \frac{\text{Net profit for the period}}{\text{Sales}} \times \frac{\text{Sales}}{\text{Total assets}} \times \frac{\text{Total assets}}{\text{Equity}}$$

This model allows an integrated profitability analysis with the three factors as profit drivers and by linking these to underlying competitive mechanisms and managerial coping behaviour.

Table 17.1

Financial leverage effect at different debt/equity ratios

Total assets = 1000
ROA = 10%
After-tax cost of debt = 7%

Debt/Equity	100%	150%	300%
Profit before interest	100	100	100
Cost of debt	35	42	52.5
Net profit	65	58	47.5
ROE	13%	14.5%	19%
Financial leverage coefficient	13%/10% = 1.30	1.45	1.90

Segment data analysis

The analysis of the consolidated financial statements, using ratio analysis and related techniques, is important to evaluate company performance through time and relative to its peers. However, it does not shed light on the inner dynamics of the company's performance. In that sense, examining the performance of the company's operating segments through an analysis of the segment reporting data may deepen the understanding of the factors and operations that drive the group's consolidated performance.

Given the nature of the operating segment information provided, a number of segment ratios can be computed, such as:

$$\text{Segment profit margin} = \frac{\text{Segment result}}{\text{Segment revenue}}$$

$$\text{Segment operating cash flow (EBITDA) margin} = \frac{(\text{Segment operating result} + \text{Depreciation and amortization expense})}{\text{Segment revenue}}$$

$$\text{Segment asset turnover} = \frac{\text{Segment revenue}}{\text{Segment assets}}$$

$$\text{Segment ROA} = \frac{\text{Segment result}}{\text{Segment assets}}$$

$$\text{Segment gearing} = \frac{\text{Segment liabilities}}{\text{Segment assets}}$$

Comparing these ratios through time and across segments will increase the understanding of the factors driving overall company performance. They are useful in comparing risks and returns of different operations within a company and among investment alternatives.

The segment ROA can be further analyzed by performing a DuPont type of analysis in the following way:

$$\text{Segment ROA} = \text{Segment profit margin} \times \text{Segment asset turnover}$$

Taking into account inter-company differences in segment reporting formats, segment data analysis could also be used to analyze and benchmark comparable segments of peer companies within the same industry. This type of comparison probably makes more sense than comparing high-level, aggregated data of peer companies where similarities are usually much less evident than at operating segment level. But then again, one should keep in mind that segment reporting according to IFRS 8, *Operating Segments*, is entity-specific, not only with regard to information items reported, but also in respect of the measurement bases used.

Operational gearing

Another aspect of a company's competitive position is the flexibility of its cost structure: companies with high fixed costs cannot react easily to downturns and generally need to seek high market share to maximize their fixed capacity. Companies in the same industry but which organize themselves with higher variable costs are more flexible, but may need to site themselves in a high price niche rather than look for large market share.

This can be illustrated graphically. The convention in management accounting is that a company's costs are either fixed or variable in the short to medium term (this is an oversimplification, but useful for analytical purposes). Thus a company with high fixed costs would have the relationship between volume and profit shown in Figure 17.2.

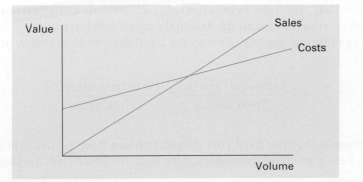

Figure 17.2

The relationship between volume and profit in a company with high fixed costs

Clearly, the higher the volume, the more profit, and such a company has some interest in reducing prices to gain market share, because that will lead to more than proportionately higher profits. Conversely, a company with low fixed costs and high variable costs is not very sensitive to volume changes and has much more interest in increasing prices. Such a company should therefore seek niche products, or highly differentiated products, where a small volume can be sold at high price.

Analytically, the concept of *operational gearing* refers to the volatility of profit as a function of changes in sales while taking into account the company's cost structure. Operational gearing can be interpreted as the percentage change in profit as sales changes 1 per cent. It can be measured as follows:

$$\text{Operational gearing} = \frac{\text{Sales} - \text{Variable costs}}{\text{Profit before tax}}$$

or:

$$\text{Operational gearing} = \frac{\text{Profit before taxes} + \text{Fixed costs}}{\text{Profit before tax}}$$

Let us look at the following illustration with two companies (company A and company B) with identical sales and total costs, but with a different cost structure (mix of fixed and variable costs):

	Sales	Fixed costs	Variable costs	Profit before tax	Operational gearing
Company A	100	20	70	10	3:1
Company B	100	70	20	10	8:1

If sales increase by 10 per cent, net profit of company A will increase by 30 per cent (increase in sales minus proportionate increase of variable costs, or 10 minus 7), while net profit of company B would increase by 80 per cent. Conversely, if sales decline, this would have a much more dramatic impact on the profitability of the company with high operational gearing (company B).

Unfortunately, the split between fixed and variable costs is not transparent from financial statements and the external analyst will have to settle with a rough proxy for operational gearing (a proxy for fixed costs to total costs), or the ratio:

$$\frac{\text{Long-term assets}}{\text{Total asset}} \quad \text{or} \quad \frac{\text{Long-term assets}}{\text{Current assets}}$$

This assumes that the fixed cost element comes from plant costs (labour and materials being relatively variable). The high variable cost operator will buy semi-finished goods, for example, rather than process raw materials in house, so variable costs are higher and the asset base is lower.

Z scores

Some analysts like to use computerized models for assessing company performance. The best known in this kind of area are Altman in the US and Tafler in the UK. Essentially their technique consists of comparing the past financial statements of successful companies with those of similar but unsuccessful companies from which they derive a model against which to assess other companies. To give a simplified example, such a model typically works on a weighted series of ratios such as:

$$0.2 \text{ ROE} + 0.5 \text{ Debt/equity} + 0.25 \text{ Current ratio} \geq 1$$

If a company scores below a certain value, it is deemed to be at risk. These models are known generically as 'Z scores' after Altman's original work. Declining profitability and liquidity ratios typically have a significant effect in business failure models.

Such models may well be useful to audit firms and to banks to assess the viability of clients, and have the merit that they are an objective test. Critics on the other hand point out that the models are derived from statistical relationships which existed between particular companies in the past in particular industry sectors and particular economies and there is no guarantee that other companies at other times and in other circumstances will replicate the same relationships. The method does not, as it were, attempt to harness together data about actual economic circumstances as such.

It is a complex technique which is beyond the scope of this book. A number of proprietary versions are available on the market and there is an extensive research literature.

Shareholder value

An alternative approach to analyzing financial statements is the concept of shareholder value, which appeared in the US during the 1980s, but does not really have a generally agreed rationale or working methodology. Our intention here is to provide an introduction to the subject, which students can take forward when they study the related material in the finance literature. The underlying idea is that instead of looking at earnings per share and the P/E ratio to arrive at the value of a company, the analyst should look at the discounted present value of forecast earnings.

In principle the idea is excellent and in effect simply uses the definition of income which is used in economics. However, in practice the idea is more difficult because it involves forecasting future earnings over at least a ten-year horizon and determining the appropriate discount rate to use.

The basis normally used for imputing value in economics is the discounted value of the future cash flows that a project presents. You will normally cover the concepts of discounting and present values in the context of a finance or business statistics course. The essence is covered below.

BETWEEN THE LINES

Present value

Present value calculations are used in economics, finance and financial management to assign a value to future cash flows after adjusting for the time value of money. The essence of present value is that a rational person will prefer to have a receipt sooner rather than later because the money can be used to generate more money.

For example, if a company has a choice of receiving $1000 now or $1000 in a year's time, it would prefer to have the cash now because it could be invested and earn a return. If the money was put into risk-free securities where it could earn 15 per cent, then $1000 now would be worth $1150 in a year's time.

Extending that, the $1000 to be received after a year is worth $1000/1.15 (or $870) today, because $870 invested today at 15 per cent would yield $1000 in a year's time. Similarly, $1000 to be received in two years' time is worth $1000/(1.15 × 1.15) $756 at present (i.e. compound interest at 15 per cent for two years would be $244).

By way of a simplified example, supposing that a listed company was forecast to have a life cycle of five years, the cost of capital for a company at that level of risk is 10 per cent and it is forecast to generate the following cash flows after meeting its operating costs:

	1 €m	2 €m	3 €m	4 €m	5 €m
Net cash flows	100	250	250	200	50
Discount factor:	0.909	0.826	0.751	0.683	0.621
Present values	90.9	206.6	187.8	136.6	31.0

The present value of the company – or the shareholder value – is €652.9m. Supposing that it has 200m shares in issue, the share price should be (€652.9/200) = €3.26. If the actual share price is €2.70, then the investor should buy or hold, whereas if the actual market price was €3.50, the investor should sell (if holding shares) or simply not buy, on the basis in both cases that the share price will be likely to move towards €3.26.

If the management of the company is performing well, they will be increasing the future net cash flows of the company and therefore *increasing shareholder value*. The concept of shareholder value as a means of evaluating investments is very useful; however, the methodology involves a considerable amount of subjective inputs. These revolve around two key points: (1) the forecast cash flows of the company; and (2) the discount rate.

Forecast cash flows

The cash flow forecast needs to consider both the likely cash flows from existing operations and the capital expenditure necessary to renew existing equipment and expand capacity. The cash flow statement gives cash flows both from operations and outflows to pay interest and tax (the dividend stream is part of shareholder value, since this is being directed to the shareholder), the net after these is in effect the cash available for the shareholder or for reinvestment. In forecasting the future, it is necessary to make assumptions about the rate of inflation and the rate of real growth (which derive partly from observation of economic indicators and partly from an estimate of management's performance).

Estimating the capital expenditure rate is even more difficult. In the future, given a long time series of cash flow statements, it will be possible to produce a long-term average correlation between profit growth and investment growth. At this time, the analyst could take annual depreciation as a surrogate for maintaining existing equipment, and add to that a year-on-year change in net fixed assets and net working capital. The longer the time series, the more reliable an average figure would be.

Discount rate

There is an extensive literature on this subject. The discount rate should reflect the cost of capital as adjusted for inflation and the risk associated with the particular activities of that company. Alternatively, the analyst might use the weighted average cost of capital for the individual company.

There are many different formulations which might be used, both to forecast cash inflows (e.g. starting from forecast sales and using profit margins) and cash outflows, and the question of discount rate is contentious, since a small difference in discount rate usually gives a large difference in present value. However, it is a valuation model which best approximates the real cash flows of the company and is particularly useful in cross-sectional analysis of companies in the same industry, since the same basic assumptions can be used.

Summary

In this chapter we have aimed to expand your knowledge of financial statement analysis and put it in closer touch with the actual practices of securities houses. We have looked at the evaluation model which examines the surrounding economic environment and we have quality of earnings considerations and accounting adjustments which should be considered in making financial information more directly comparable. We have seen that the analyst's forecast of earnings and the market P/E ratio are used to forecast the future share price and make buy/sell/hold decisions by investors.

We then went on to look at how financial statement analysis can give inputs into the strategic analysis of a company. We looked at a ratio for sustainable growth, ROE decomposition as well as indicators of how capital intensive an industry is and its operating gearing. Finally, we looked also at the evolving concept of shareholder value.

Assignments

The following questions have answers on the lecturer side of the digital support resources for the book.

1. Cleaney Inc.
   You are an analyst working for the American venture capital firm Docker Warden (DW). DW has received a request from a company called Cleaney Inc. to provide the latter with additional venture capital. Should DW accept to do so, then Cleaney will issue new shares to which DW will subscribe.

   However, before discussing the terms of the potential transaction, the board of DW wishes to obtain an objective image of Cleaney Inc. Thus, it is your assignment to conduct a preliminary analysis on the basis of the available financial data (including segment information). The board of DW has asked you to prepare a report that includes:

   (a) an analysis of Cleaney's investment and financing policy;
   (b) a review of Cleaney's management as evidenced by the financial statements;
   (c) an executive summary, including your assessment of the situation and recommendations.

   To complete this task, you are provided with the company's annual financial statements from 20X4 to 20X8, as well as with the following additional information: the principal activity of Cleaney, incorporated at the start of 20X0, consists of the production of card- and coin-operated washing machines. These are subsequently sold or leased out either to commercial launderettes or to laundry rooms on the multi-housing market. The latter consists of apartments, condominium units, colleges and universities. Since 20X1, Cleaney has been generating additional revenue from the selling and leasing out of card- and coin-operated reprographics equipment (i.e. mainly photocopiers) to schools, colleges, universities, libraries and government institutions. Up until the end of 20X5, Cleaney simply traded in such reprographics equipment. At the beginning of 20X6, Cleaney's management decided, however, that the company would manufacture the equipment itself in an attempt to strengthen its position in that particular market as well as increase the profitability of that activity segment. As a result, Cleaney now no longer purchases any finished photo-copiers from other manufacturers: all the reprographics equipment that it sells or leases out is own manufacture.

Annual financial statements Cleaney Inc. (in US$'000)

Income statements

	20X8	20X7	20X6	20X5	20X4
Sales	158 268	150 260	134 200	81 400	64 400
Cost of sales	−120 345	−114 926	−102 400	−61 200	−48 600
Gross operating margin	37 923	35 334	31 800	20 200	15 800
Distribution costs	−17 100	−16 863	−10 200	−6 500	−5 300
Administration expenses	−9 230	−8 607	−7 100	−3 400	−2 500
Operating income	11 593	9 864	14 500	10 300	8 000
Interest expense	−8 270	−7 085	−4 000	−2 300	−2 100
Income before tax	3 323	2 779	10 500	8 000	5 900
Taxation	−1 662	−1 727	−5 400	−2 700	−500
Net income	*1 661*	*1 052*	*5 100*	*5 300*	*5 400*
Dividends proposed	−332	−0	−1 020	−1 060	−0

Statements of financial position

	20X8	20X7	20X6	20X5	20X4
Non-current assets					
Tangible assets	82 435	78 440	67 382	35 300	33 250
Intangible assets	59 840	61 516	60 482	22 500	12 850
Current assets					
Inventories	3 391	6 521	3 800	2 900	1 500
Receivables	7 992	8 551	6 500	4 300	1 600
Cash and cash equivalent	13 559	6 047	8 506	7 576	9 700
Total assets	167 217	161 075	146 670	72 576	58 900
Current liabilities					
Loans (interest-bearing)	17 840	9 454	0	0	0
Trade payables	13 932	16 840	15 330	9 776	13 600
Taxes payable	1 662	1 727	5 400	2 700	500
Non-current liabilities					
Long-term debt	88 550	89 482	82 400	20 600	25 300
Equity					
Ordinary shares					
($1 nominal value)	2 000	2 000	2 000	2 000	1 300
Share premium	25 400	25 400	25 400	25 400	11 400
Dividend (proposed)	332	0	1 020	1 060	0
Retained earnings	17 501	16 172	15 120	11 040	6 800
Total liabilities and equity	167 217	161 075	146 670	72 576	58 900

Analysis of non-current assets

	20X8	20X7	20X6	20X5	20X4
Acquisition cost					
Balance 1 January	185470	157450	78380	62260	62470
Additions	22710	29660	89640	16970	130
Disposals	–2630	–1640	–10570	–850	–340
Balance 31 December	*205550*	*185470*	*157450*	*78380*	*62260*
Acc. depreciation					
Balance 1 January	45514	29586	20580	16160	13820
Disposals	–1769	–1120	–7334	–600	–240
Depreciation expense	19530	17048	16340	5020	2580
Balance 31 December	*63275*	*45514*	*29586*	*20580*	*16160*
Net book value					
31 December	*142275*	*139956*	*127864*	*57800*	*46100*

Segment information

	20X8	20X7	20X6	20X5	20X4
Sales					
Laundry services	114251	114186	105822	72015	58965
Reprographics services	44017	36074	28378	9385	5435
Gross operating margin					
Laundry services	27490	26210	23580	16470	13240
Reprographics services	10433	9124	8220	3730	2560
NBV of non-current assets					
Laundry services	93659	95367	85516	46166	40128
Reprographics services	44327	40825	38479	9691	4492
Distribution and administration	4289	3764	3869	1943	1480

2. Gloucester Gardens plc.

   You are an analyst working for an American investment bank, Insecurity International (II). You are called in by a junior associate in the Mergers and Acquisitions department to comment on a particular case.

   II has been approached by a venture capital firm, Kindly Keep Repaying (KKR), which wants to dispose of a small investment in a company (Gloucester Gardens) which runs a chain of garden centres in south-west England. Gloucester Gardens (GG) started out as a nursery growing plants for direct sale to the public and also selling to the trade. Over a period of 20 years it first expanded its retail activities to sell a wide range of garden products beyond its own plants, and then took on more and more new retail units, supplied partly from its own nursery.

   The company is now operated as two divisions: nursery and retail. All the output from the nursery is sold through the GG retail division, although for internal control purposes it is sold at market prices by the nursery division to retail.

The KKR representative says that GG is family run but the founder is nearing retirement and is quite interested in selling out, although his daughter is also involved in managing the business and would like to stay on and participate in the expansion of the business, assuming that some satisfactory package could be worked out. The family knows that KKR is making this approach.

KKR thinks that the GG operation has potential as the basis of establishing a national chain of such centres, but thinks that the existing family management do not have the necessary expertise to grow any further. KKR would like to see their stake bought out by a major national retailer, possibly with the potential to slot the GG operation alongside a chain of out-of-town DIY or similar stores. KKR itself paid £1 400 000 for a 25 per cent stake in GG early in 20X8 and is looking for upwards of £3 000 000 for its stake.

The M&A associate thinks that possible targets would include WH Smith (Do It All), Kingfisher (B&Q), Ladbroke's (Texas) or Sainsbury's (Homebase) and wants you to prepare an analysis of the figures for the last five years for GG for presentation to a potential client.

When the KKR representative has left, the M&A associate provides the attached figures and asks you to prepare a report for her to include:

(a) an analysis of the company's investment and financing policy;

(b) a review of its management as evidenced by the financial statements (including segment information);

(c) an executive summary, including your assessment of the situation and recommendations.

£'000	20X5	20X6	20X7	20X8	20X9
Statements of profit or loss					
Sales	2 220.0	2 941.3	3 537.8	4 573.0	5 584.0
Cost of sales	–1 344.7	–1 766.8	–2 105.0	–2 697.4	–3 262.5
Gross margin	875.3	1 174.5	1 432.8	1 875.6	2 321.6
Distribution expense	–116.0	–130.0	–147.0	–160.0	–171.0
Administration expense	–245.0	–268.0	–304.0	–337.0	–383.0
	514.3	776.5	981.8	1 378.6	1 767.6
Interest expense	–83.0	–146.0	–232.3	–269.0	–332.6
Disposal income	0.0	2.0	–4.0	0.0	3.6
Profit before tax	431.3	632.5	745.5	1 110.6	1 438.6
Taxation	–125.1	–202.4	–246.0	–388.7	–517.9
Profit after tax	306.2	430.1	499.5	721.9	920.7
Dividends declared	–75.0	–100.0	–140.0	–190.0	–240.0

£'000	1995	1996	1997	1998	1999
Statements of financial position					
Non-current assets (A)					
Retail premises	2086.0	3006.0	4478.0	5847.0	6774.0
Acc. depreciation	−208.8	−284.0	−395.9	−542.1	−711.4
Nurseries	3200.0	3200.0	3200.0	4400.0	4400.0
Acc. depreciation	−624.2	−730.9	−837.6	−984.3	−1131.0
Plant and equipment	91.0	109.0	158.0	296.0	278.0
Acc. depreciation	−56.4	−68.0	−82.8	−142.0	−146.4
Vehicles	49.0	65.0	122.0	176.0	194.0
Acc. depreciation	−19.7	28.6	246.9	290.9	296.3
	4516.9	5268.5	6594.8	8959.7	9560.9
Current assets (B)					
Inventories – retail	139.4	233.2	350.3	546.5	799.0
– nurseries	440.0	530.0	588.6	699.8	761.6
Receivables	111.0	147.1	212.3	320.1	446.7
Cash at bank	56.3	101.7	108.4	15.2	13.1
	746.7	1012.0	1259.6	1581.6	2020.4
Short-term liabilities (C)					
Trade payables	−269.0	−353.4	−484.1	−701.3	−880.9
Taxes payable	−125.1	−202.4	−246.0	−388.7	−517.9
Overdraft	0.0	0.0	0.0	−182.2	−182.8
	−394.1	−555.8	−730.2	−1272.2	−1581.6
Sub-total (A+B−C)	4794.5	5624.7	6984.2	9079.1	9759.7
Long-term liabilities (D)	−1500.0	−2000.0	−3000.0	−3200.0	−3200.0
Net Assets (A+B−C−D)	3369.5	3724.7	4124.2	6069.1	6799.7
Equity					
Ordinary shares	1800.0	1800.0	1800.0	2400.0	2400.0
Share premium	784.0	784.0	784.0	1547.0	1547.0
Retained profit	785.5	1140.7	1540.2	2122.1	2852.7
Total equity	3369.5	3724.7	4124.2	6069.1	6799.7

Analysis of non-current assets

20X5

	Retail premises £'000	Nursery premises £'000	Plant and equipt £'000	Motor vehicles £'000	Total £'000
Cost					
Cost: 1 Jan	1369.0	3200.0	82.0	26.0	4677.0
Additions	717.0	0.0	24.0	31.0	772.0
Disposals	0.0	0.0	–15.0	–8.0	–23.0
Cost: 31 Dec	2086.0	3200.0	91.0	49.0	5426.0
Depreciation					
Balance 1 Jan	156.7	517.5	49.2	13.5	736.9
Disposals	0.0	0.0	–11.0	–6.0	–17.0
Additions	52.1	106.7	18.2	12.2	189.2
Balance 31 Dec	208.8	624.8	56.4	19.7	909.1
Net book value 31 Dec	1877.2	2575.8	34.6	29.3	4516.9

20X6

	Retail premises £'000	Nursery premises £'000	Plant and equipt £'000	Motor vehicles £'000	Total £'000
Cost					
Cost: 1 Jan	2086.0	3200.0	91.0	49.0	5426.0
Additions	920.0	0.0	32.0	28.0	980.0
Disposals	0.0	0.0	–14.0	–12.0	–26.0
Cost: 31 Dec	3006.0	3200.0	109.0	65.0	6380.0
Depreciation					
Balance 1 Jan	208.8	624.2	56.4	19.7	909.1
Disposals	0.0	0.0	–10.2	–7.4	–17.6
Additions	75.2	106.7	21.8	16.3	220.0
Balance 31 Dec	284.0	730.9	68.0	28.6	1111.5
Net book value 31 Dec	2722.0	2469.1	41.0	36.4	5268.5

20X7

	Retail premises £'000	Nursery premises £'000	Plant and equipt £'000	Motor vehicles £'000	Total £'000
Cost					
Cost: 1 Jan	3006.0	3200.0	109.0	65.0	6380.0
Additions	1472.0	0.0	83.0	72.0	1627.0
Disposals	0.0	0.0	–34.0	–15.0	–49.0
Cost: 31 Dec	4478.0	3200.0	158.0	122.0	7958.0

20X7

	Retail premises £'000	Nursery premises £'000	Plant and equipt £'000	Motor vehicles £'000	Total £'000
Acc. depreciation					
Balance 1 Jan	284.0	730.9	68.0	28.6	1 111.5
Disposals	0.0	0.0	–16.8	–12.2	–29.0
Additions	111.9	106.7	31.6	30.5	280.7
Balance 31 Dec	*395.9*	*837.6*	*82.8*	*46.9*	*1 363.2*
Net book value 31 Dec	4 082.1	2 362.4	75.2	75.1	6 594.8

20X8

	Retail premises £'000	Nursery premises £'000	Plant and equipt £'000	Motor vehicles £'000	Total £'000
Cost					
Cost: 1 Jan	4 478.0	3 200.0	158.0	122.0	7 958.0
Additions	1 369.0	1 200.0	138.0	54.0	2 761.0
Disposals	0.0	0.0	0.0	0.0	0.0
Cost: 31 Dec	*5 847.0*	*4 400.0*	*296.0*	*176.0*	*10 719.0*
Acc. depreciation					
Balance 1 Jan	395.9	837.6	82.8	46.9	1 363.2
Disposals	0.0	0.0	0.0	0.0	0.0
Additions	146.2	146.7	59.2	44.0	396.1
Balance 31 Dec	*542.1*	*984.3*	*142.0*	*90.9*	*1 759.3*
Net book value 31 Dec	5 304.9	3 415.7	154.0	85.1	8 959.7

20X9

	Retail premises £'000	Nursery premises £'000	Plant and equipt £'000	Motor vehicles £'000	Total £'000
Cost					
Cost: 1 Jan	5 847.0	4 400.0	296.0	176.0	10 719.0
Additions	927.0	0.0	46.0	56.0	1 029.0
Disposals	0.0	0.0	–64.0	–38.0	–102.0
Cost: 31 Dec	*6 774.0*	*4 400.0*	*278.0*	*194.0*	*11 646.0*
Acc. depreciation					
Balance 1 Jan	542.1	984.3	142.0	90.9	1 759.3
Disposals	0.0	0.0	–51.2	–33.4	–84.6
Additions	169.3	146.7	55.6	38.8	410.4
Balance 31 Dec	*711.4*	*1 131.0*	*146.4*	*96.3*	*2 085.1*

Net book value 31 Dec	6 062.6	3 269.0	131.6	97.7	9 560.9

Segment information

	20X5 £'000	20X6 £'000	20X7 £'000	20X8 £'000	20X9 £'000
Sales					
Nursery	1 100.0	1 325.0	1 415.0	1 620.0	1 700.0
Retail	2 220.0	2 941.3	3 537.8	4 573.0	5 584.0
Gross margin					
Nursery	220.0	265.0	283.0	324.0	340.0
Retail	655.3	909.5	1 149.8	1 551.6	1 981.6

CHAPTER 18

IFRS and the future

This chapter will analyze the origins of the IASB, and the rapid global spread of IFRS as the accounting basis of choice in international capital markets, and it will review likely changes in international standards that will arise in the short to medium term.

Chapter Structure

- Introduction
- Strategic evolution
- The IASB's first decade
- The 2007 financial crisis
- The next five years
- Summary

Introduction

This book is based on the financial reporting standards of the International Accounting Standards Board (IASB). We have given you, we believe, enough information about the structure and workings of the IASB to enable you to work with their standards. However, for those who are curious about the organization, its origins, its work and the possible future direction of its standards, this final chapter is offered to provide more depth to your understanding. It falls into three sections. The first deals with the origins of the IASB, as the International Accounting Standards Committee that started work in the 1970s, and its mutation into the IASB. The second section reviews the work of the new organization in the first decade of this century and the effects of the financial crisis and then the final section looks at the IASB's work programme and the likely changes to its standards up to 2015.

Strategic evolution

The International Accounting Standards Committee (IASC), the founder body from which the IASB developed, had its first meeting in June 1973. It was the brain child of Sir Douglas Morpeth (at the time president of the Institute of Chartered Accountants in England and Wales – ICAEW – and a partner in the UK practice of Touche Ross, now Deloitte), and Lord Benson (chairman of the Overseas Relations Committee of the ICAEW and partner in Coopers & Lybrand).

The genesis of the IASC was a telephone conversation in the margins of the five-yearly world congress of accountants which took place in Australia in 1972. Benson was a well-known figure in international circles and played a role in the organization of the world congress. Morpeth was leading the British delegation and was also the deputy chairman of the newly-formed Accounting Standards Committee in the UK. Following a presentation by Benson to the congress, Morpeth remarked to him that it was odd that the world organization in considering its future structure had not thought to establish a standard-setting mechanism. Morpeth later commented that, in a world where standard-setting was in its infancy, it seemed to him that the work of the new British standard-setter could be adapted for international use.

Benson was a highly dynamic figure. He was born into the accounting aristocracy as the grandson of one of the four Cooper siblings who created the firm Cooper Bros in the 19th century. Apart from the Second World War, Benson spent his whole life in the firm (he joined when he was 16 and was a partner at 25) and was one of the principal architects of its overseas expansion, leading ultimately to the merger with Lybrand, Ross Bros and Montgomery, the US firm, to create Coopers & Lybrand (subsequently merged into PricewaterhouseCoopers). Benson had been president of the ICAEW in 1966/67 and had established the Accountants International Study Group to work with Canada and the US to try to harmonize practices. Benson seized on the notion of an international standard-setter and took it forward, becoming its founder chairman. Amongst other things, Benson arranged that the IASC would be based in London, where it has remained ever since.

The IASC was funded and run by national accounting professional bodies, but although people were enthusiastic about the IASC, none of these bodies ever actually used its standards as a substitute for national standards. In the 1970s and 1980s the IASC created a body of standards but these were used by teachers as an illustration of best practice and were also used by developing countries as a template for their own national standards: the IASC lacked a clear role.

This was to change in 1987 when the then Secretary General, David Cairns, started to build a relationship with the International Organization of Securities Commissions (IOSCO). This organization, largely under the influence of the US Securities and Exchange Commission (SEC), was trying to improve and harmonize stock exchange regulation across the world. At that time all major stock exchanges had their own listing requirements, including accounting requirements, that had to be followed by companies that wanted to offer their securities on that market. There were of course many different sets of requirements, and IOSCO wanted to remove some of the difficulties and costs implicit in this. It set out to create a stock exchange 'passport' – an internationally-accepted set of listing requirements that would be used by all IOSCO members for *secondary* listings. In other words, each company had a *primary* listing, usually in its home country, where the national requirements would be followed and the national regulator would be the primary regulator of the company. However, such companies could apply to list their securities in other stock exchanges using the IOSCO listing rules. As long as the company met the IOSCO requirements, regulators in markets being used for secondary listings would not impose additional requirements.

IOSCO needed a set of financial reporting standards as part of its passport and entered into a relationship with the IASC that their standards would be developed for international capital market use. It should be understood that over this time stock exchanges were becoming more liberal about their approach to listing and some already accepted secondary listings using International Accounting Standards, and within the EU there were 'mutual recognition' arrangements that each country accepted financial statements drawn up using other member state's GAAP. The most significant underlying issue was that the SEC did not accept foreign companies' financial reports drawn up under foreign GAAP except with a reconciliation. This is known as the '20-F reconciliation' after the annual report filing required of foreign registrants by the SEC. This reconciliation is a costly item to prepare and involves sometimes quite dramatic differences between the US measure of equity and earnings and those under national GAAP, which in turn provides an awkward platform to explain company performance to analysts. Many non-US companies hoped and expected that if the IASC's standards were accepted by IOSCO, then companies using them would be able to have a secondary listing in the US without a reconciliation. The US capital markets dominate the world's supply of capital to commercial companies and many companies also believe that a US listing is a key component of being regarded as a serious international organization (for a discussion of this see Bay and Bruns discussion of Daimler-Benz's listing in the US, details in Further reading list).

There followed a decade of highs and lows in the relationships between IOSCO and the IASC and the IASC and its supporters. At the end of 1998 the IASC finally delivered a set of much improved and extended standards and submitted them to IOSCO for evaluation. In May 2000, IOSCO delivered its verdict – International Accounting Standards (IAS) would be accepted as the secondary listing requirement, but national regulators could ask for further information if they wanted it. This meant that the SEC was not obliged to abandon its reconciliation and indeed that organization issued a Concept Release (i.e. a discussion paper) asking constituents to comment. It pointed out that having a set of standards was not in itself enough, they had to be applied rigorously and be audited consistently across the world. It would wait for more experience of the use of the standards to emerge before making a decision. People felt that the IOSCO endorsement was a success, but not the success that had been hoped for. More work needed to be done.

However, this was immediately followed by a bombshell from the European Commission (EC), dropped in June 2000. The EC announced that it had decided to adopt IAS for all listed companies in the EU. This radically changed the political framework: by 2005, IAS would be the generally accepted accounting principles of a major slice of the world's economy. IOSCO's limited success paled into insignificance as the IASC gained a major politicalally.

Why did the EC do this? The official explanation was that it was part of the initiative to create an EU-wide single capital market, and it was also intended to give EU companies easier access to world markets (for which read the US market). The EC had been taking initiatives since 1966 to harmonize accounting as part of its objective of creating a market in which there was freedom of movement across national boundaries. Its programme had achieved limited success, and in 1995 it had more or less abandoned the attempt to create EU-wide rules in the face of resistance from companies and governments. The 2000 announcement was a major change of official policy and ultimately gave the EC the power to override national requirements.

So the international standard-setter entered the first decade of the 21st century on a completely different footing. Not only was its status much enhanced by EC endorsement, but the whole structure of the organization was changed. The old IASC, funded by the accounting profession, disappeared (formally agreed at a meeting in Edinburgh in July 2000) to be replaced by a private sector organization funded from a Delaware foundation. The new structure put the IFRS Foundation in overall charge, with a mission to raise funds and appoint Board members. The standard-setter became the International Accounting Standards Board, whose members were professionals hired for their knowledge and experience. The focus was clearly writing high quality financial reporting standards for the international capital markets.

The IASB's first decade

When the IASB sat down to its first public standard-setting meeting in April 2001 its attention was split between several priorities:

- legacy projects from the old IASC
- improving the existing IAS
- preparing the standards for 2005 and application in the EC
- converging with the US
- leadership projects.

The IASB had inherited a draft discussion paper on accounting for insurance contracts. The worldwide insurance industry uses widely divergent standards and the objective was to create something that would introduce a single approach. In retrospect the IASB probably should have shelved this, but in fact it worked on it for many months before accepting that it would take years to resolve and must be put to one side. The IASB continues to work on it, but the technical problems are difficult, and they put stress on cross-cutting issues such as revenue recognition, the measurement of liabilities and the recognition of intangibles. An interim standard authorizing companies to continue to use national GAAP subject to certain constraints was issued in 2004 to smooth the adoption of IFRS. The insurance project became a joint project with the US, but continues to have problems, not least that the FASB and IASB disagree on the precise mechanism to release profit. It is possible the IASB will have a final standard in place for 2015 and likely that this will not be converged with the US.

The old IAS had been prepared over a 25-year period by large, volunteer committees. Despite initiatives to improve the standards for IOSCO purposes, the IASB felt there were a number of inconsistencies that could be picked off quickly and improve the standards further. Consequently many of the old standards were amended slightly, and some quite radically. In particular the IASB introduced into IAS 8 *Accounting Policies, Changes in Estimates and Errors* a hierarchy of actions to be taken when seeking a policy for a transaction that was outside the existing standards.

This improvements process was also linked to the imperative of having workable standards ready for EU adoption. Although the official adoption date was 2005, companies had to publish comparative figures and so the effective date was 2004. Much pressure was in particular brought by the EU to change some aspects of IAS 39 *Financial Instruments: Recognition and Measurement* on the measurement of financial instruments. The IASB introduced the fair value option which allows companies to choose to value any financial instruments at fair value through profit and loss. The European Central Bank intervened because it felt the option was too wide. Overall, the imperative of reaching the adoption deadline (which was not only for the EU but also for Australia and South Africa) dominated the agenda during 2002 and 2003. The IASB produced a new standard, IFRS 1 *First-time Adoption of IFRS*, to address the practicalities of how companies should treat the transition from national GAAP to IFRS.

Nonetheless, the IASB also put some effort into converging with the US. In September 2002, it signed the Norwalk agreement with the Financial Accounting Standards Board (FASB) which set out the basis of future cooperation, including working on joint projects. This was facilitated in all probability by the appointment of Robert Herz as chairman of the FASB earlier that year. Mr Herz, formerly a partner in PricewaterhouseCoopers in New York, had been a part-time member of the IASB prior to his FASB appointment. Curiously, although a US citizen, he had been educated in England, and had first qualified as a member of the ICAEW before returning to the US and becoming a CPA. He had subsequently been very active on international committees, particularly within the International Federation of Accountants.

At the inaugural standard-setting meeting, Sir David Tweedie also talked about the necessity for the IASB to establish credibility for itself as initiating standards that would change national practice. The IASB chose to address **share-based payment**, a subject that had caused the FASB considerable political difficulties in the 1990s. The issue was that management could be paid by granting them options to buy company shares at reduced prices. This just caused cash to come into the company when the shares were issued and equity to be increased by a corresponding amount. However, since the shares were issued at reduced prices, the transfer of value was much greater than that shown in the balance sheet, and no remuneration expense appeared in the income statement. This was very popular, especially in the US, given that the true cost of senior executives' remuneration was not revealed.

The IASB rapidly issued IFRS 2, *Share-based Payment*, which requires the fair value of share options to be calculated at **grant date** and then be expensed over the related service period. The FASB in turn amended its own standard to reflect the tougher IASB standard. Some people, notably Financial Executives International, warned that the sky would fall in. However, in practice Enron and the other financial scandals that burst just after the turn of the century had changed the world's appetite for listening sympathetically to large corporations. The IASB scored an early success.

Once 2005 was out of the way, attention was more clearly focused again on the 20-F reconciliation. While the IASB was busy improving its standards and converging with the US, the EC was also active negotiating with the SEC. In a dramatic development the EC and SEC agreed a 'road map' for removal of the reconciliation requirement for companies using IFRS. A provisional date of 2009 was set for IFRS compliant companies to drop the requirement, and the EC generously agreed that it would not introduce a reconciliation requirement for US companies listed in the EU.

A key part of this road map was not that the IASB had to achieve a given level of convergence but that the SEC needed to be sure that a system was in place that would give continuing convergence, and also milestones were set to be achieved by the beginning of 2008. The FASB and IASB translated this into a document issued in 2006 called the Memorandum of Understanding (MoU) which set targets for what had to be achieved, and in so doing fixed the ongoing work priorities.

In fact, the IASB did not achieve the targets that it had agreed. A significant issue was feedback from constituents that they wanted more projects to start with the issue of a preliminary views discussion paper. In theory, the idea was that the issue of an exposure draft gave people the opportunity to comment and for the standard-setter to respond. However, the perception was that the standard-setter was reluctant to move much away from what had been published in the exposure draft. The IASB members responded more flexibly to comments on discussion papers. The IASB therefore changed its practice to more routinely start the consultation process with a discussion paper. As far as the MoU was concerned this meant that, for example, the FASB standard on fair value measurement was issued as a discussion paper rather than an exposure draft. In general terms this also meant that the process of issuing a standard from scratch would be likely to take at least four years (see Figure 1.3 on standard-setting due process in Chapter 1).

Although the IASB throughput slowed down, the political pace accelerated and the SEC did not even wait for the end of the roadmap period or the MoU deadline. In November 2007, it announced that it would accept IFRS financial statements as the equivalent of US GAAP and there would be no reconciliation requirement. This was a very significant breakthrough, achieved actually after about 20 years of efforts. The SEC did the IASB another favour at the same time by pointing out that this relaxation referred to companies using IFRS as issued by the IASB. It did not refer to those using IFRS subject to a carve-out, as in the EU.

The 2007 financial crisis

The IASB's reasonably steady progress was to be knocked off course by the financial crisis that started in 2007. Jointly with the FASB it had told constituents that it would leave financial instruments alone for a while to give companies time to get used to applying IAS 39, the measurement standard. They also put out a paper discussing the complexities of financial instrument accounting and what might be options for making it more simple.

As the financial crisis started to bite, banks started complaining that using fair values in their financial statements was making them record exaggerated losses as the markets fell away. The standard-setters shrugged and suggested they were just the messenger, the problem was the markets. However, a groundswell of opinion started to form to the effect that using fair value to measure financial instruments had exacerbated the crisis or even maybe caused it. In 2008 the G8 and G20 groups of world leaders started to get onto the case and told the FASB and

IASB they should review their standards, simplify the accounting for financial instruments and get substantially converged by June 2011.

This triggered a crisis period in standard-setting, with the two boards meeting physically or by videolink at least once a month and generally much more often. While the sense of crisis is now past, and the pace is reverting to normal, the FASB and IASB are still working on financial instruments. Under different pressures, the two standard-setters took different paths to revising their standards. The IASB determined to replace all aspects of IAS 39 with a new standard, IFRS 9, which at the moment is due to come into force in 2015. The June 2011 deadline was totally missed and at the moment it is likely that further changes will be made. With the benefit of hindsight, the main failure of the accounting standards was thought to be not fair value, but the method of recognizing loan losses. The standard-setters are still working on this.

The next five years

Looking at technical issues, the two boards have been working on joint standards on leasing and revenue recognition, both of which are likely to come into force in 2015. The leasing standard is intended to reduce the use of leases as a form of off balance sheet financing. It will require all leases (not including real estate) of longer than a year to be capitalized. Revenue recognition aims to provide a single standard to cover all aspects and be applicable to all industry sectors. It will have little impact on many industries but may affect those who provide bundled goods and services and long-term contracts. The seller has to recognize a performance liability when a contract is signed, and an equal and opposite contract asset. The contract is split into separate 'performance obligations' if there are several different parts to it. The IASB also completed IFRS 13, *Fair Value Measurement*, which provides a converged set of rules for measuring fair value when another standard requires that.

The IASB has been conducting an agenda consultation to provide guidance on what constituents think it should be doing once the US convergence projects and financial instruments revisions are finished. The answer seems to be that people think there should be a period of calm, during which the IASB could sensibly concentrate on finishing the revision of its conceptual framework, and looking at taking a more active role in implementation.

The more problematical issues seem to be those of endorsement of IFRS by further countries. The EU, Australia and South Africa adopted the standard in 2005 and China set out to write its own standards closely aligned on IFRS. There has been a second wave of endorsements starting in 2011 with Canada and Brazil moving to IFRS, followed by South Korea and Mexico. India and Japan are still hesitating, although Japan already allows its listed companies to use IFRS if they want to. The 'elephant in the room' is the US. The SEC said it would make a decision in 2011, after it had performed detailed studies of the IFRS world. It missed the deadline, saying it had not yet finished, and no new deadline has been established, although some people seem fairly sure a decision will be made in 2012.

However, as the SEC has worked on the topic, it has advanced the public debate. From these signals, it would appear that the likelihood is that the US will not adopt IFRS in the way the EU did, it will do something nearer to the Chinese approach, which is to maintain its own standards while bringing these very close to IFRS. The SEC calls this 'condorsement', and it appears that they would maintain the 'US GAAP' label as opposed to referring to IFRS, but would set the FASB the task of amending US GAAP to conform to existing IFRS over a five-year period. Thereafter the FASB would look at each new standard individually and decide how to address it.

The big question about this approach is that it is left pretty well to the FASB to decide how close to get. As the current IASB chairman, Hans Hoogervorst, has said, the key issue is whether non-endorsement should be a major exception, or whether it is routine. There are many advantages to the US in going this route, not least that there is no transition moment, and no obvious conversion cost. It also avoids disturbing the many references in the law and elsewhere to US GAAP. It is a low impact way for US companies of getting to global standards. The disadvantage is the impact on the IASB – would the FASB be able to unduly influence new standards by threatening not to endorse? It does seem that a clean endorsement or not decision is unlikely to be made, and it could be years before the effects of the compromises that are reached can be fully understood.

Summary

In this chapter we have tried to give you some insights into the work of the IASB. We have discussed briefly where it came from and where it is going to. The chapter falls into three sections. The first dealt with the origins of the IASB and the work of the IASC. We have shown where it came from and how it ended up in its role today. In the second section we have analyzed the work of the IASB and the objectives it has had in mind in its key formative years. The final section is a discussion of the next decade of the international standard-setter, the growing use of its standards and the possibility of use of IFRS by the US.

FURTHER READING

Adams, C. A. (2004) 'The ethical, social and environmental reporting-performance portrayal gap', *Accounting, Auditing and Accountability Journal* 17(5):731–57.

Aerts, W. (2005) 'Narrative accounting disclosures', in C. L. Cooper (ed.) *The Blackwell Encyclopedia of Management, 1: Accounting*, 2nd edn (pp. 312–318), Oxford: Blackwell.

Aerts, W., Cormier, D. and Magnan, M. (2007) 'The association between web-based corporate performance disclosure and financial analyst behaviour under different governance regimes', *Corporate Governance: An International Review* 15(6):1301–29.

Aerts, W. and Cormier, D. (2009) 'Media legitimacy and corporate environmental communication', *Accounting, Organizations and Society* 34(1), 1–27.

Aerts, W. and Tarca, A. (2010) 'Financial performance explanations and institutional setting', *Accounting and Business Research* 40(5):421–450.

Aerts, W. and Cheng, P. (2012) 'Self-serving causal disclosures on earnings and short-term IPO valuation – Evidence from Chinese initial public offerings', *Accounting and Business Research* 42(1):49–75.

Aisbitt, S. (2006) 'Assessing the effect of the transition of IFRS on equity: the case of the FTSE 100', *Accounting in Europe* 3:117–34.

Alexander, D. and Jermakowicz, E. (2006) 'A true and fair view of the principles/rules debate', *Abacus* 42(2):132–64.

Armitage, S. and Marston, C. (2008) 'Corporate disclosure, cost of capital and reputation: Evidence from finance directors', *British Accounting Review* 40(4):314–366.

Barth, M., Clinch, G. and Shibano, T. (1999) 'International accounting harmonization and global equity markets', *Journal of Accounting and Economics* 26(1–3):201–35.

Barth, M. E. and Landsman, W. R. (2010) 'How did financial reporting contribute to the financial crisis?', *European Accounting Review* 19(3):399–423.

Bay, W. and Bruns, H-G. (2003) 'Multinational companies and international capital markets', in P. Walton, A. Haller and B. Raffournier (eds) *International Accounting*, 2nd edn (pp. 385–403), London: Thomson Learning.

Beaver, W. H. (1991) 'Problems and paradoxes in the financial reporting of future events', *Accounting Horizons* 5(4):22–35.

Benston, G., Bromwich, M., Litan, R. E. and Wagenhofer, A. (2006) *Worldwide Financial Reporting: The Development and Future of Accounting Standards*, Oxford: Oxford University Press.

Bocqueraz, C. and Walton, P. (2006) 'Creating a supranational institution: the role of the individual and the mood of the times', *Accounting History* 11(3):271–88.

Boerner, H. (2005) 'Are corporate accounting systems out-of-date?', *Corporate Finance Review* 10(2):35–41.

Bradbury, M. (2007) 'An anatomy of an IFRIC Interpretation', *Accounting in Europe* 4:109–22.

Brown, P. (2011) 'International Financial Reporting Standards: what are the benefits?', *Accounting and Business Research* 41(3):269–285.

Cairns, D. (2006) 'The use of fair value in IFRS', *Accounting in Europe* 3:5–22.

Camfferman, K. and Zeff, S. (2007) *Financial Reporting and Global Capital Markets: A History of the International Accounting Standards Committee, 1973–2000*, Oxford: Oxford University Press.

Chen, J. J. and Zhang, H. (2010) 'The impact of regulatory enforcement and audit upon IFRS compliance – Evidence from China', *European Accounting Review* 19(4):665–692.

Cheng, P., Aerts, W. and Jorissen, A. (2010) 'Earnings management, asset restructuring, and the threat of exchange delisting in an earnings-based regulatory regime', *Corporate Governance: An International Review* 18(5):438–456.

Colley, J. L. Jr, Doyle, J. L., Logan, G. W. and Stettinuis, W. (2005) *What is Corporate Governance?* New York: McGraw-Hill.

Cooper, S. (2007) 'Performance measurement for equity analysis and valuation', *Accounting in Europe* 4:1–50.

Cormier, D., Ledoux, M. J., Aerts, W. and Magnan, M. (2010) 'Corporate governance and information asymmetry between managers and investors', *Corporate Governance* 10(5):574–589.

Dao, T. H. P. (2005) 'Monitoring compliance with IFRS: some insights from the French regulatory system', *Accounting in Europe* 2(1):107–35.

Daske, H. (2006) 'Economic benefits of adopting IFRS or US-GAAP – have the expected costs of equity capital really decreased?', *Journal of Business Finance and Accounting* 33(3/4):329–73.

Dellaportas, S., Gibson, K., Alagiah, R., Hutchinson, M., Leung, P. and Homrigh, D. V. (2005), *Ethics, Governance and Accountability: A Professional Perspective*, Brisbane: John Wiley and Sons.

Delvaille, P., Ebbers, G. and Saccon, C. (2005) 'International financial reporting convergence: evidence from three continental European countries', *Accounting in Europe* 2:137–64.

Denning, B. (2004) 'Adopting International Financial Reporting Standards: the tax implications', *Accountancy Ireland* 36(4):19–22.

Dick, W. and Walton, P. (2007) 'The agenda of the IASB: a moving target', *Australian Accounting Review* 17(42):8–17.

Erchinger, H. and Melcher, W. (2007) 'Convergence between US GAAP and IFRS: acceptance of IFRS by the US Securities and Exchange Commission', *Accounting in Europe* 4:123–40.

Faux, J. and Wise, V. (2005) 'Financial reporting policy in a dynamic environment', *International Review of Business Research Papers* 1(2):1–9.

Fearnley, S. and Hines, T. (2006) 'Rules are a big problem for small companies', *Financial Times*, 19 January, p. 12.

Gélard, G. (2004) 'What can be expected from accounting standards?', *Accounting in Europe* 1:17–20.

Gorman, J. F. and Hargadon, J. M. (2005) 'Accounting futures: Healthy markets for a time-honored profession', *Journal of Financial Service Professionals* 59(1):74–9.

Hague, I. P. (2004) 'IAS 39: underlying principles', *Accounting in Europe* 1:21–6.

Haller, A. (2003) 'Segmental reporting', in P. Walton, A. Haller and B. Raffournier (eds) *International Accounting*, 2nd edn (pp. 444–470), London: Thomson Learning.

Henderson, S., Peirson, G., Herbohn, K. and Ramsay, A. (2006) *Issues in Financial Accounting*, 12th edn, Sydney: Pearson-Prentice Hall.

Hooghiemstra, R. (2012) 'What determines the informativeness of firms' explanations for deviations from the Dutch corporate governance code?', *Accounting and Business Research* 42(1):1–27.

House, J. (2004) 'Financial reporting: national standard-setters – endangered species', *Accountancy* 133(1327):86–7.

Hunter, L., Webster, E. and Wyatt, A. (2005) 'Measuring intangible capital: a review of current practice', *Australian Accounting Review* 15(2):4–21.

James, S. and Nobes, C. (2006) *The Economics of Taxation*, Harlow: Prentice Hall.

Johnson, L. T. and Petrone, K. R. (1998) 'Is goodwill an asset?', *Accounting Horizons* (September): 293–304.

Kvaal, E. and Nobes, C. (2010) 'International differences in IFRS policy choice: A research note', *Accounting and Business Research* 40(2):173–187.

Lamb, M. (1995) 'When is a group a group? Convergence of concepts of "group" in European Union corporation tax', *European Accounting Review* 4(1):33–78.

Larson, K. (2007) 'Constituent participation and the IASB's International Financial Reporting Interpretations Committee', *Accounting in Europe* 4:207–54.

Leuz, C. (2010) 'Different approaches to corporate reporting regulation: How jurisdictions differ and why', *Accounting and Business Research* 40(3):229–256.

Nobes, C. W. and Parker, R. (2002) *Comparative International Accounting*, 7th edn, Harlow: Pearson Education.

Nobes, C. W. and Schwencke, H. R. (2006) 'Modelling the links between tax and financial reporting: A longitudinal examination of Norway over 30 years up to IFRS adoption', *European Accounting Review* 15(1):63–87.

Penman, S. H. (2003) 'The quality of financial statements: perspectives from the recent stock market bubble', *Accounting Horizons* 17 (supplement):77–96.

Pope, P.F. and McLeay, S.J. (2011) 'The European IFRS experiment: objectives, research challenges and some early evidence', *Accounting and Business Research* 41(3):233–266.

Power, M. (2010) 'Fair value accounting, financial economics and the transformation of reliability', *Accounting and Business Research* 40(3):197–210.

Richard, J. (2004) 'The secret past of fair value: lessons from history applied to the French case', *Accounting in Europe* 1:95–108.

Sarens, G., De Beelde, I. and Everaert, P.(2009) 'Internal audit: A comfort provider to the audit committee', *British Accounting Review* 41(2):90–106.

Schipper, K. (2005) 'The introduction of International Accounting Standards in Europe: implications for international convergence', *European Accounting Review* 14(1):101–26.

Shortridge, R. T. and Myring, M. (2004) 'Defining principles-based accounting standards', *The CPA Journal* 74(8):34–8.

Sloan, R. G. (2001) 'Financial accounting and corporate governance: a discussion', *Journal of Accounting and Economics* 32:335–47.

Soderstrom, N. and Sun, K. J. (2007) 'IFRS adoption and accounting quality', *European Accounting Review* 16:675–702.

Stanton, P. A. and Stanton, P. J. (2002) 'Corporate annual reports: research perspectives used', *Accounting, Auditing and Accountability Journal* 15(4):478–500.

Sunder, S. (2011) 'IFRS monopoly: the Pied Piper of financial reporting', *Accounting and Business Research* 41(3):291–306.

Sutton, T. (2003) *Corporate Financial Accounting and Reporting*, 2nd edn, London: Prentice Hall.

Tarca, A., Street, D. L. and Aerts, W. (2010) 'Improving MD&A: A national necessity', *Financial Executive* 26(10):53–56.

Tarca, A., Street, D. L. and Aerts, W. (2011) 'Factors affecting MD&A disclosures by SEC registrants: Views of practitioners', *Journal of International Accounting, Auditing and Taxation* 20(1):45–59.

Taylor, P. A (2003) 'Foreign currency translation', in P. Walton, A. Haller and B. Raffournier (eds) *International Accounting*, 2nd edn (pp. 405–442), London: Thomson Learning.

Tokar, M. (2005) 'Convergence and the implementation of a single set of global standards: the real life challenge', *Accounting in Europe* 2:47–68.

UNCTAD Secretariat (2003) 'Accounting needs of developing countries', in P. Walton, A. Haller and B. Raffournier (eds) *International Accounting*, 2nd edn (pp. 366–384), London: Thomson Learning.

Van Caneghem, T. and Aerts, W. (2011) 'Intra-industry conformity in dividend policy', *Managerial Finance* 37(6):492–516.

Walton, P. (1993) 'The true and fair view in British accounting', *European Accounting Review* 2:49–58.

Walton, P. (1998) 'Benson's projects take a decisive turn', *Accountancy and Finance Update* (South Africa) 3(5):7–9.

Walton, P. (1998) 'Henry Benson', in M. Warner (ed) *The IEBM Handbook of Management Thinking* (pp. 482–486), London: International Thomson Publishing.

Walton, P. (2003) 'European harmonisation', in F. D. S. Choi (ed.) *International Accounting and Finance Handbook,* 2nd edn (pp. 17.1–17.17), New York: John Wiley and Sons.

Walton, P. (2004) 'IAS 39: where different accounting models collide', *Accounting in Europe* 1:5–16.

Walton, P. (2006) 'Fair value and executory contracts: moving the boundaries in international financial reporting', *Accounting and Business Research* 36(4):337–43.

Walton, P. (ed.) (2007) *The Routledge Guide to Fair Value and Financial Reporting*, Abingdon: Routledge.

Whittington, G. (2005) 'The adoption of International Accounting Standards in the European Union', *European Accounting Review* 14(1):127–53.

Wüstemann, J. and Kierzek, S. (2005) 'Revenue recognition under IFRS revisited: conceptual models, current proposals and practical consequences', *Accounting in Europe* 2:69–106.

GLOSSARY

accounting policies The specific principles, bases, conventions, rules and practices applied by an entity in preparing and presenting financial statements.

accounting profit Profit or loss for a period before deducting tax expense.

acquiree The business or businesses that the acquirer obtains control of in a business combination.

acquirer The entity that obtains control of the acquiree.

acquisition date The date on which the acquirer obtains control of the acquiree.

active market A market in which transactions for the asset or liability take place with sufficient frequency and volume to provide pricing information on an ongoing basis.

actuarial gains and losses The changes in the present value of the defined benefit obligation resulting from (a) Experience adjustments (the effects of differences between the previous actuarial assumptions and what has actually occurred); and (b) the effects of changes in actuarial assumptions.

adjusting events after the reporting period See 'events after the reporting period'.

agricultural activity The management by an entity of the biological transformation and harvest of biological assets for sale or for conversion into agricultural produce, or into additional biological assets.

agricultural produce The harvested product of the entity's biological assets.

amortization (depreciation) The systematic allocation of the depreciable amount of an asset over its useful life.

asset A resource: (a) controlled by an entity as a result of past events; and (b) from which future economic benefits are expected to flow to the entity.

associate An entity over which the investor has significant influence.

biological asset A living animal or plant.

borrowing costs Interest and other costs that an entity incurs in connection with the borrowing of funds.

business An integrated set of activities and assets that is capable of being conducted and managed for the purpose of providing a return in the form of dividends, lower costs or other economic benefits directly to investors or other owners, members or participants.

business combination A transaction or other event in which an acquirer obtains control of one or more businesses. Transactions sometimes referred to as 'true mergers' or 'mergers of equals' are also business combinations as that term is used in this IFRS.

carrying amount The amount at which an asset is recognized in the statement of financial position.

cash Cash on hand and demand deposits.

cash equivalents Short-term, highly liquid investments that are readily convertible to known amounts of cash and which are subject to an insignificant risk of changes in value.

cash flows Inflows and outflows of cash and cash equivalents.

cash-generating unit The smallest identifiable group of assets that generates cash inflows that are largely independent of the cash inflows from other assets or groups of assets.

change in accounting estimate An adjustment of the carrying amount of an asset or a liability, or the amount of the periodic consumption of an asset, that results from the assessment of the present status of, and expected future benefits and obligations associated with, assets and liabilities. Changes in accounting estimates result from new information or new developments and, accordingly, are not corrections of errors.

closing rate The spot exchange rate at the end of the reporting period.

compensation Includes all employee benefits (as defined in IAS 19) including employee benefits to which IFRS 2 applies. Employee benefits are all forms of consideration paid, payable or provided by the entity, or on behalf of the entity, in exchange for services rendered to the entity. It also includes such consideration paid on behalf of a parent of the entity in respect of the entity. Compensation includes: (a) short-term employee benefits, such as wages, salaries and social security contributions, paid annual leave and paid sick leave, profit-sharing and bonuses (if payable within 12 months of the end of the period) and non-monetary benefits (such as medical care, housing, cars and free or subsidized goods or services) for current employees; (b) post-employment benefits such as pensions, other retirement benefits, post-employment life insurance and post-employment medical care; (c) other long-term employee benefits, including long-service leave or sabbatical leave, jubilee or other long-service benefits, long-term disability benefits and, if they are not payable wholly within 12 months after the end of the period, profit-sharing, bonuses and deferred compensation; (d) termination benefits; and (e) share-based payment.

component of an entity Operations and cash flows that can be clearly distinguished, operationally and for financial reporting purposes, from the rest of the entity.

consolidated financial statements The financial statements of a group in which assets, liabilities, equity, income, expenses and cash flow of the parent and its subsidiaries are presented as those of a single economic entity.

construction contract A contract specifically negotiated for the construction of an asset or a combination of assets that are closely interrelated or interdependent in terms of their design, technology and function or their ultimate purpose or use.

constructive obligation An obligation that derives from an entity's actions where: (a) by an established pattern of past practice, published policies or a sufficiently specific current statement, the entity has indicated to other parties that it will accept certain responsibilities; and (b) as a result, the entity has created a valid expectation on the part of those other parties that it will discharge those responsibilities.

contingent asset A possible asset that arises from past events and whose existence will be confirmed only by the occurrence or non-occurrence of one or more uncertain future events not wholly within the control of the entity.

contingent liability (a) A possible obligation that arises from past events and whose existence will be confirmed only by the occurrence or non-occurrence of one or more uncertain future events not wholly within the control of the entity; or (b) a present obligation that arises from past events but is not recognized because: (i) it is not probable that an outflow of resources embodying economic benefits will be required to settle the obligation; or (ii) the amount of the obligation cannot be measured with sufficient reliability.

control of an investee An investor controls an investee when the investor is exposed, or has rights, to variable returns from its involvement with the investee and has the ability to affect those returns through its power over the investee.

cost The amount of cash or cash equivalents paid or the fair value of the other consideration given to acquire an asset at the time of its acquisition or construction, or, when applicable, the amount attributed to that asset when initially recognized in accordance with the specific requirements of other IFRSs, e.g. IFRS 2.

costs of disposal Incremental costs directly attributable to the disposal of an asset, excluding finance costs and income tax expense.

costs to sell The incremental costs directly attributable to the disposal of an asset (or disposal group), excluding finance costs and income tax expense.

currency risk The risk that the fair value or future cash flows of a financial instrument will fluctuate because of changes in foreign exchange rates.

current asset An entity shall classify an asset as current when: (a) it expects to realize the asset or intends to sell or consume it in its normal operating cycle; (b) it holds the asset primarily for the purpose of trading; (c) it expects to realize the asset within 12 months after the reporting period (d) the asset is cash or a cash equivalent (as defined in IAS 7) unless the asset is restricted from being exchanged or used to settle a liability for at least 12 months after the reporting period.

An entity shall classify all other assets as non-current.

current liability An entity shall classify a liability as current when: (a) it expects to settle the liability in its normal operating cycle; (b) it holds the liability primarily for the purpose of trading; (c) the liability is due to be settled within 12 months after the reporting period; or (d) the entity does not have an unconditional right to defer settlement of the liability for at least 12 months after the reporting period.

An entity shall classify all other liabilities as non-current.

current tax The amount of income taxes payable (recoverable) in respect of the taxable profit (tax loss) for a period.

deductible temporary differences Temporary differences between the carrying amount of an asset or liability in the balance sheet and its tax base that will result in amounts that are deductible in determining taxable profit (tax loss) of future periods when the carrying amount of the asset or liability is recovered or settled.

deferred tax assets The amounts of income taxes recoverable in future periods in respect of: (a) deductible temporary differences; (b) the carry-forward of unused tax losses; and (c) the carry-forward of unused tax credits.

deferred tax liabilities The amounts of income taxes payable in future periods in respect of taxable temporary differences.

defined benefit plans Retirement benefit plans under which amounts to be paid as retirement benefits are determined by reference to a formula usually based on employees' earnings and/or years of service.

defined contribution plans Retirement benefit plans under which amounts to be paid as retirement benefits are determined by contributions to a fund together with investment earnings thereon.

depreciable amount The cost of an asset, or other amount substituted for cost (in the financial statements), less its residual value.

depreciation (amortization) The systematic allocation of the depreciable amount of an asset over its useful life.

derecognition (of a financial instrument) The removal of a previously recognized financial asset or financial liability from an entity's statement of financial position.

derivative A financial instrument or other contract within the scope of IFRS 9 (see paragraphs 2.1) with all three of the following characteristics: (a) its value changes in response to the change in a specified interest rate, financial instrument price, commodity price, foreign exchange rate, index of prices or rates, credit rating or credit index or other variable, provided in the case of a non-financial variable that the variable is not specific to a party to the contract (sometimes called the 'underlying'); (b) it requires no initial net investment or an initial net investment that is smaller than would be required for other types of contracts that would be expected to have a similar response to changes in market factors; and (c) it is settled at a future date.

development The application of research findings or other knowledge to a plan or design for the production of new or substantially improved materials, devices, products, processes, systems or services before the start of commercial production or use.

direct method of reporting cash flows from operating activities A method whereby major classes of gross cash receipts and gross cash payments are disclosed.

discontinued operation A component of an entity that either has been disposed of or is classified as held for sale and: (a) represents a separate major line of business or geographical area of operations, (b) is part of a single co-ordinated plan to dispose of a separate major line of business or geographical area of operations or (c) is a subsidiary acquired exclusively with a view to resale.

disposal group A group of assets to be disposed of, by sale or otherwise, together as a group in a single transaction, and liabilities directly associated with those assets that will be transferred in the transaction. The group includes goodwill acquired in a business combination if the group is a cash-generating unit to which goodwill has been allocated in accordance with the requirements of paragraphs 80–87 of IAS 36 or if it is an operation within such a cash-generating unit.

economic life Either: (a) the period over which an asset is expected to be economically usable by one or more users; or (b) the number of production or similar units expected to be obtained from the asset by one or more users.

employee benefits All forms of consideration given by an entity in exchange for service rendered by employees or for the termination of employment.

entity-specific value The present value of the cash flows an entity expects to arise from the continuing use of an asset and from its disposal at the end of its useful life or expects to incur when settling a liability.

entry price The price paid to acquire an asset or received to assume a liability in an exchange transaction.

equity instrument A contract that evidences a residual interest in the assets of an entity after deducting all of its liabilities.

equity interests In IFRS 3, is used broadly to mean ownership interests of investor-owned entities and owner, member or participant interests of mutual entities.

equity method A method of accounting whereby the investment is initially recognized at cost and adjusted thereafter for the post-acquisition change in the investor's share of the investee's net assets. The investor's profit or loss includes its share of the investee's profit or loss and the investor's other comprehensive income includes its share of the investee's other comprehensive income.

events after the reporting period Those events, favourable and unfavourable, that occur between the end of the reporting period and the date when the financial statements are authorized for issue. Two types of events can be identified: (a) those that provide evidence of conditions that existed at the end of the reporting period (adjusting events after the reporting period); and (b) those that are indicative of conditions that arose after the reporting period (non-adjusting events after the reporting period).

exchange difference The difference resulting from translating a given number of units of one currency into another currency at different exchange rates.

exchange rate The ratio of exchange for two currencies.

exit price The price that would be received to sell an asset or paid to transfer a liability.

expected cash flows The probability-weighted average (i.e. mean of the distribution) of possible future cash flows.

expenses Decreases in economic benefits during the accounting period in the form of outflows or depletions of assets or incurrences of liabilities that result in decreases in equity, other than those relating to distributions to equity participants.

fair value The price that would be received to sell an asset or paid to transfer a liability in an orderly transaction between market participants at the measurement date.

fair value less costs to sell The amount obtainable from the sale of an asset or cash-generating unit in an arm's length transaction between knowledgeable, willing parties, less the costs of disposal.

finance lease A lease that transfers substantially all the risks and rewards incidental to ownership of an asset. Title may or may not eventually be transferred.

financial asset Any asset that is: (a) cash; (b) an equity instrument of another entity; (c) a contractual right: (i) to receive cash or another financial asset from another entity; or (ii) to exchange financial assets or financial liabilities with another entity under conditions that are potentially favourable to the entity; or (d) a contract that will or may be settled in the entity's own equity instruments and is: (i) a non-derivative for which the entity is or may be obliged to receive a variable number of the entity's own equity instruments; or (ii) a derivative that will or may be settled other than by the exchange of a fixed amount of cash or another financial asset for a fixed number of the entity's own equity instruments. For this purpose the entity's own equity instruments do not include puttable financial instruments classified as equity instruments in accordance with paragraphs 16A and 16B of IAS32, instruments that impose on the entity an obligation to deliver to another party a pro rata share of the net assets of the entity only on liquidation and are classified as equity instruments in accordance with paragraphs 16C and 16D of IAS32, or instruments that are contracts for the future receipt or delivery of the entity's own equity instruments.

financial asset or liability held for trading A financial asset or financial liability that: (a) is acquired or incurred principally for the purpose of selling or repurchasing it in the near term; (b) on initial recognition is part of a portfolio of identified financial instruments that are managed together and for which there is evidence of a recent actual pattern of short-term profit-taking; or (c) is a derivative (except for a derivative that is a financial guarantee contract or a designated and effective hedging instrument).

financial guarantee contract A contract that requires the issuer to make specified payments to reimburse the holder for a loss it incurs because a specified debtor fails to make payment when due in accordance with the original or modified terms of a debt instrument.

financial instrument Any contract that gives rise to a financial asset of one entity and a financial liability or equity instrument of another entity.

financial liability Any liability that is: (a) a contractual obligation: (i) to deliver cash or another financial asset to another entity; or (ii) to exchange financial assets or financial liabilities with another entity under conditions that are potentially unfavourable to the entity; or (b) a contract that will or may be settled in the entity's own equity instruments and is: (i) a non-derivative for which the entity is or may be obliged to deliver a variable number of the entity's own equity instruments; or (ii) a derivative that will or may be settled other than by the exchange of a fixed amount of cash or another financial asset for a fixed number of the entity's own equity instruments. For this purpose rights, options or warrants to acquire a fixed number of the entity's own equity instruments for a fixed amount of any currency are equity instruments if the entity offers the rights, options or warrants pro rata to all of its existing owners of the same class of its own non-derivative equity instruments. Also, for these purpose the entity's own equity instruments do not include puttable financial instruments that are classified as equity instruments in accordance with paragraphs 16A and 16B of IAS 32, instruments that impose on the entity an obligation to deliver to another party a *pro rata* share of the net assets of the entity only on liquidation and are classified as equity instruments in accordance with paragraphs 16C and

16D of IAS 32, or instruments that are contracts for the future receipt or delivery of the entity's own equity instruments.

financial liability at fair value through profit or loss A financial liability that meets either of the following conditions. (a) It meets the definition of held for trading. (b) Upon initial recognition it is designated by the entity as at fair value through profit or loss. An entity may use this designation only when permitted by IFRS 9 paragraph 4.3.5 (embedded derivatives) or when doing so results in more relevant information, because either (i) it eliminates or significantly reduces a measurement or recognition inconsistency (sometimes referred to as 'an accounting mismatch') that would otherwise arise from measuring assets or liabilities or recognizing the gains and losses on them on different bases; or (ii) a group of financial liabilities or financial assets and financial liabilities is managed and its performance is evaluated on a fair value basis, in accordance with a documented risk management or investment strategy, and information about the group is provided internally on that basis to the entity's key management personnel (as defined in IAS 24).

financial risk The risk of a possible future change in one or more of a specified interest rate, financial instrument price, commodity price, foreign exchange rate, index of prices or rates, credit rating or credit index or other variable, provided in the case of a non-financial variable that the variable is not specific to a party to the contract.

financing activities Activities that result in changes in the size and composition of the contributed equity and borrowings of the entity.

firm commitment A binding agreement for the exchange of a specified quantity of resources at a specified price on a specified future date or dates.

firm purchase commitment An agreement with an unrelated party, binding on both parties and usually legally enforceable, that (a) specifies all significant terms, including the price and timing of the transactions, and (b) includes a disincentive for non-performance that is sufficiently large to make performance highly probable.

foreign currency A currency other than the functional currency of the entity.

foreign currency transaction A transaction that is denominated in or requires settlement in a foreign currency.

foreign operation An entity that is a subsidiary, associate, joint venture or branch of the reporting entity, the activities of which are based or conducted in a country or currency other than those of the reporting entity.

functional currency The currency of the primary economic environment in which the entity operates.

funding (of retirement benefits) The transfer of assets to an entity (the fund) separate from the employer's entity to meet future obligations for the payment of retirement benefits.

general purpose financial statements Financial statements that are intended to meet the needs of users who are not in a position to require an entity to prepare reports tailored to their particular information needs.

goodwill An asset representing the future economic benefits arising from other assets acquired in a business combination that are not individually identified and separately recognized.

government Government, government agencies and similar bodies whether local, national or international.

government assistance Action by government designed to provide an economic benefit specific to an entity or range of entities qualifying under certain criteria.

government grants Assistance by government in the form of transfers of resources to an entity in return for past or future compliance with certain conditions relating to the operating activities of the entity. They exclude those forms of government assistance which cannot reasonably have a value placed upon them and transactions with government which cannot be distinguished from the normal trading transactions of the entity.

grant date The date at which the entity and another party (including an employee) agree to a share-based payment arrangement, being when the entity and the counterparty have a shared understanding of the terms and conditions of the arrangement. At grant date the entity confers on the counterparty the right to cash, other assets, or equity instruments of the entity, provided the specified vesting conditions, if any, are met. If that agreement is subject to an approval process (for example, by shareholders), grant date is the date when that approval is obtained.

group A parent and its subsidiaries.

harvest The detachment of produce from a biological asset or the cessation of a biological asset's life processes

hedged item An asset, liability, firm commitment, highly probable forecast transaction or net investment in a foreign operation that (a) exposes the entity to risk of changes in fair value or future cash flows and (b) is designated as being hedged (IAS 39 paragraphs 78–84 and AG98–AG101 elaborate on the definition of hedged items).

hedging instrument A designated derivative or (for a hedge of the risk of changes in foreign currency exchange rates only) a designated non-derivative financial asset or non-derivative financial liability whose fair value or cash flows are expected to offset changes in the fair value or cash flows of a designated hedged item (IAS 39 paragraphs 72–77 and AG94–AG97 elaborate on the definition of a hedging instrument).

held for trading See 'financial asset or financial liability held for trading'.

highest and best use The use of a non-financial asset by market participants that would maximize the value of the asset or the group of assets and liabilities (e.g. a business) within which the asset would be used.

hyperinflation Loss of purchasing power of money at such a rate that comparison of amounts from transactions and other events that have occurred at different times, even within the same accounting period, is misleading.

Hyperinflation is indicated by characteristics of the economic environment of a country which include, but are not limited to, the following: (a) the general population prefers to keep its wealth in non-monetary assets or in a relatively stable foreign currency. Amounts of local currency held are immediately invested to maintain purchasing power. (b) the general population regards monetary amounts not in terms of the local currency but in terms of a relatively stable foreign currency. Prices may be quoted in that currency. (c) sales and purchases on credit take place at prices that compensate for the expected loss of purchasing power during the credit period, even if the period is short. (d) interest rates, wages and prices are linked to a price index. (e) the cumulative inflation rate over three years is approaching, or exceeds, 100 per cent.

identifiable An asset is identifiable if it either: (a) is separable, i.e. capable of being separated or divided from the entity and sold, transferred, licensed, rented or exchanged, either individually or together with a related contract, identifiable asset or liability, regardless of whether the entity intends to do so; or (b) arises from contractual or other legal rights, regardless of whether those rights are transferable or separable from the entity or from other rights and obligations.

impairment loss The amount by which the carrying amount of an asset exceeds its recoverable amount.

initial direct costs Incremental costs that are directly attributable to negotiating and arranging a lease, except for such costs incurred by manufacturer or dealer lessors.

inputs The assumptions that market participants would use when pricing the asset or liability, including assumptions about risk, such as the following: (a) the risk inherent in a particular valuation technique used to measure fair value (such as pricing model); and (b) the risk inherent in the inputs to the valuation technique. Inputs may be observable or unobservable.

intangible asset An identifiable non-monetary asset without physical substance.

interest in another entity For the purpose of IFRS 12, an interest in another entity refers to contractual and non-contractual involvement that exposes an entity to variability of returns from the performance of the other entity. An interest in another entity can be evidenced by, but is not limited to, the holding of equity or debt instruments as well as other forms of involvement such as the provision of funding, liquidity support, credit enhancement and guarantees. It includes the means by which an entity has control or joint control of, or significant influence over, another entity. An entity does not necessarily have an interest in another entity solely because of a typical customer supplier relationship. Paragraphs B7–B9 of IFRS 12 provide further information about interests in other entities. Paragraphs B55–B57 of IFRS 10 explain variability of returns.

interest rate implicit in the lease The discount rate that, at the inception of the lease, causes the aggregate present value of (a) the minimum lease payments and (b) the unguaranteed residual value to be equal to the sum of (i) the fair value of the leased asset and (ii) any initial direct costs of the lessor.

interest rate risk The risk that the fair value or future cash flows of a financial instrument will fluctuate because of changes in market interest rates.

interim financial report A financial report containing either a complete set of financial statements (as described in IAS 1) or a set of condensed financial statements (as described in IAS 34) for an interim period.

International Financial Reporting Standards (IFRSs) Standards and Interpretations issued by the International Accounting Standards Board (IASB). They comprise: (a) International Financial Reporting Standards; (b) International Accounting Standards; (c) IFRIC Interpretations; and (d) SIC Interpretations.

inventories Assets: (a) held for sale in the ordinary course of business; (b) in the process of production for such sale; or (c) in the form of materials or supplies to be consumed in the production process or in the rendering of services.

Inventories encompass goods purchased and held for resale including, for example, merchandise purchased by a retailer and held for resale, or land and other property held for resale. Inventories also encompass finished goods produced, or work in progress being produced, by the entity and include materials and supplies awaiting use in the production process. In the case of a service provider, inventories include the costs of the service, as described in IAS 2 paragraph 19, for which the entity has not yet recognized the related revenue (see IAS 18).

investing activities The acquisition and disposal of long-term assets and other investments not included in cash equivalents.

investment property Property (land or a building or part of a building or both) held (by the owner or by the lessee under a finance lease) to earn rentals or for capital appreciation or both, rather than for: (a) use in the production or supply of goods or services or for administrative purposes; or (b) sale in the ordinary course of business.

joint arrangement An arrangement of which two or more parties have joint control.

joint control The contractually agreed sharing of control over an arrangement which exists only when decisions about the relevant activities require the unanimous consent of the parties sharing control.

joint operation A joint arrangement whereby the parties that have joint control of the arrangement have rights to the assets, and obligations for the liabilities, relating to the arrangement.

joint operator A party to a joint operation that has joint control of that joint operation.

joint venture A joint arrangement whereby the parties that have joint control of the arrangement have rights to the net assets off the arrangement.

joint venturer A party to a joint venture that has joint control of the joint venture.

key management personnel Those persons having authority and responsibility for planning, directing and controlling the activities of the entity, directly or indirectly, including any director (whether executive or otherwise) of that entity.

lease An agreement whereby the lessor conveys to the lessee in return for a payment or series of payments the right to use an asset for an agreed period of time.

lease term The non-cancellable period for which the lessee has contracted to lease the asset together with any further terms for which the lessee has the option to continue to lease the asset, with or without further payment, when at the inception of the lease it is reasonably certain that the lessee will exercise the option.

legal obligation An obligation that derives from: (a) a contract (through its explicit or implicit terms); (b) legislation; or (c) other operation of law.

lessee's incremental borrowing rate of interest The rate of interest the lessee would have to pay on a similar lease or, if that is not determinable, the rate that, at the inception of the lease, the lessee would incur to borrow over a similar term, and with a similar security, the funds necessary to purchase the asset.

level 1 inputs Quoted prices (unadjusted) in active markets for identical assets or liabilities that the entity can access at the measurement date.

level 2 inputs Inputs other than quoted prices included within Level 1 that are observable for the asset or liability, either directly or indirectly.

level 3 inputs Unobservable inputs for the asset or liability.

liability A present obligation of the entity arising from past events, the settlement of which is expected to result in an outflow from the entity of resources embodying economic benefits.

liquidity risk The risk that an entity will encounter difficulty in meeting obligations associated with financial liabilities that are settled by delivering cash or another financial asset.

losses Decreases in economic benefits and as such no different in nature from other expenses.

market-corroborated inputs Inputs that are derived principally from or corroborated by observable market data by correlation or other means.

material Omissions or misstatements of items are material if they could, individually or collectively, influence the economic decisions that users make on the basis of the financial statements. Materiality depends on the size and nature of the omission or misstatement judged in the surrounding circumstances. The size or nature of the item, or a combination of both, could be the determining factor.

measurement The process of determining the monetary amounts at which the elements of the financial statements are to be recognized and carried in the balance sheet [statement of financial position] and income statement [statement of comprehensive income].

minority interest See 'non-controlling interest'.

monetary assets Money held and assets to be received in fixed or determinable amounts of money.

monetary items Units of currency held and assets and liabilities to be received or paid in a fixed or determinable number of units of currency.

net investment in a foreign operation The amount of the reporting entity's interest in the net assets of that operation.

net realizable value The estimated selling price in the ordinary course of business less the estimated costs of completion and the estimated costs necessary to make the sale.

Net realizable value refers to the net amount that an entity expects to realize from the sale of inventory in the ordinary course of business. Fair value reflects the amount for which the same inventory could be exchanged between knowledgeable and willing buyers and sellers in the marketplace. The former is an entity-specific value; the latter is not. Net realizable value for inventories may not equal fair value less costs to sell.

non-adjusting events after the reporting period See 'events after the reporting period'.

non-cancellable lease A lease that is cancellable only. (a) upon the occurrence of some remote contingency; (b) with the permission of the lessor; (c) if the lessee enters into a new lease for the same or an equivalent asset with the same lessor; or (d) upon payment by the lessee of such an additional amount that, at inception of the lease, continuation of the lease is reasonably certain.

non-controlling interest The equity in a subsidiary not attributable, directly or indirectly, to a parent.

non-current asset An asset that does not meet the definition of a current asset.

notes Notes contain information in addition to that presented in the statement of financial position, statement of comprehensive income, separate income statement (if presented), statement of changes in equity and statement of cash flows. Notes provide narrative descriptions or disaggregations of items presented in those statements and information about items that do not qualify for recognition in those statements.

obligating event An event that creates a legal or constructive obligation that results in an entity having no realistic alternative to settling that obligation.

offsetting See 'set-off, legal right of'.

onerous contract A contract in which the unavoidable costs of meeting the obligations under the contract exceed the economic benefits expected to be received under it.

operating activities The principal revenue-producing activities of an entity and other activities that are not investing or financing activities.

operating lease A lease other than a finance lease.

operating segment An operating segment is a component of an entity: (a) that engages in business activities from which it may earn revenues and incur expenses (including revenues and expenses relating to transactions with other components of the same entity), (b) whose operating results are regularly reviewed by the entity's chief operating decision maker to make decisions about resources to be allocated to the segment and assess its performance, and (c) for which discrete financial information is available.

options, warrants and their equivalents Financial instruments that give the holder the right to purchase ordinary shares.

ordinary equity holders Holders of ordinary shares.

ordinary share An equity instrument that is subordinate to all other classes of equity instruments.

other comprehensive income Items of income and expense (including reclassification adjustments) that are not recognized in profit or loss as required or permitted by other IFRSs.

owners Holders of instruments classified as equity.

parent An entity that controls one or more entities.

party to a joint arrangement An entity that participates in a joint arrangement, regardless of whether that entity has joint control of the arrangement.

past service cost The change in the present value of the defined benefit obligation for employee service in prior periods, resulting from a plan amendment (the introduction or withdrawal of, or change to, a defined benefit plan) or a curtailment (a significant reduction by the entity in the number of employees covered by a plan).

plan assets (of an employee benefit plan) (a) Assets held by a long-term employee benefit fund; and (b) qualifying insurance policies.

post-employment benefits Employee benefits (other than termination benefits and short-term employee benefits) that are payable after the completion of employment.

potential ordinary share A financial instrument or other contract that may entitle its holder to ordinary shares.

power Existing rights that give the current ability to direct the relevant activities.

presentation currency The currency in which the financial statements are presented.

present value of a defined benefit obligation The present value, without deducting any plan assets, of expected future payments required to settle the obligation resulting from employee service in the current and prior periods.

probable More likely than not.

profit or loss The total of income less expenses, excluding the components of other comprehensive income.

property, plant and equipment Tangible items that: (a) are held for use in the production or supply of goods or services, for rental to others, or for administrative purposes; and (b) are expected to be used during more than one period.

protective rights Rights designed to protect the interest of the party holding those rights without giving that party power over the entity to which those rights relate.

provision A liability of uncertain timing or amount.

realizable value The amount of cash or cash equivalents that could currently be obtained by selling an asset in an orderly disposal.

reclassification adjustments Amounts reclassified to profit or loss in the current period that were recognized in other comprehensive income in the current or previous periods.

recoverable amount The higher of an asset's (or cash-generating unit's) fair value less costs to sell and its value in use.

related party A person or entity that is related to the entity that is preparing its financial statements (in IAS 24 referred to as the 'reporting entity'). (a) A person or a close member of that person's family is related to a reporting entity if that person (i) has control or joint control over the reporting entity; (ii) has significant influence over the reporting entity; or (iii) is a member of the key management personnel of the reporting entity or of a parent of the reporting entity. (b) An entity is related to a reporting entity if any of the following condition applies: (i) The entity and the reporting entity are members of the same group (which means that each parent, subsidiary and fellow subsidiary is related to the others). (ii) One entity is an associate or joint venture of the other entity (or an associate or joint venture of a member of a group of which the other entity is a member). (iii) Both entities are joint ventures of the same third party. (iv) One entity is a joint venture of a third entity and the other entity is an associate of the third entity. (v) The entity is a post-employment benefit plan for the benefit of employees of either the reporting entity or an entity related to the reporting entity. If the reporting entity is itself such a plan, the sponsoring employers are also related to the reporting entity. (vi) The entity is controlled or jointly controlled by a person identified in (a). (vii) A person identified in (a)(i) has significant influence over the entity or is a member of the key management personnel of the entity (or of a parent of the entity).

relevant activities For the purpose of IFRS 10, relevant activities are activities of the investee that significantly affect the investee's returns.

reportable segment An operating segment for which IFRS 8 requires information to be disclosed.

research Original and planned investigation undertaken with the prospect of gaining new scientific or technical knowledge and understanding.

residual value (of an asset) The estimated amount that an entity would currently obtain from disposal of an asset, after deducting the estimated costs of disposal, if the asset were already of the age and in the condition expected at the end of its useful life.

restructuring A programme that is planned and controlled by management, and materially changes either: (a) the scope of a business undertaken by an entity; or (b) the manner in which that business is conducted.

retirement benefit plans Arrangements whereby an entity provides benefits for its employees on or after termination of service (either in the form of an annual income or as a lump sum) when such benefits, or the employer's contributions towards them, can be determined or estimated in advance of retirement from the provisions of a document or from the entity's practices. (See also 'post-employment benefit plans'.)

return on plan assets (of an employee benefit plan) Interest, dividends and other revenue derived from the plan assets, together with realized and unrealized gains or losses on the plan assets, less (a) any cost of managing plan assets; and (b) any tax payable by the plan itself, other than tax included in the actuarial assumptions used to measure the present value of the defined benefit obligation.

revenue The gross inflow of economic benefits during the period arising in the course of the ordinary activities of an entity when those inflows result in increases in equity, other than increases relating to contributions from equity participants.

separate financial statements Those presented by a parent (i.e. an investor with control of a subsidiary) or an investor with joint control of, or significant influence over, an investee,, in which the investments are accounted for at cost or in accordance with IFRS 9.

separate vehicle A separately identifiable financial structure, including separate legal entities or entities recognized by statue, regardless of whether those entities have a legal personality.

share-based payment arrangement An agreement between the entity or another group entity or any shareholder of the group entity and another party (including an employee) that entitles the other party to receive (a) cash or other assets of the entity for amounts that are based on the price (or value) of equity instruments (including shares or share options) of the entity or another group entity, or (b) equity instruments (including shares or share options) of the entity or another group entity, provided the specified vesting conditions, if any, are met.

share-based payment transaction A transaction in which the entity (a) receives goods or services from the supplier of those goods or services (including an employee) in a share-based payment arrangement, or (b) incurs an obligation to settle the transaction with the supplier in a share-based payment arrangement when another group entity receives those goods or services.

share option A contract that gives the holder the right, but not the obligation, to subscribe to the entity's shares at a fixed or determinable price for a specific period of time.

significant influence The power to participate in the financial and operating policy decisions of an investee but is not control or joint control of those policies.

spot exchange rate The exchange rate for immediate delivery.

structured entity An entity that has been designed so that voting or similar rights are not the dominant factor in deciding who controls the entity, such as when any voting rights relate to administrative tasks only and the relevant activities are directed by means of contractual arrangements. Paragraphs B22–B24 of IFRS 12 provide further information about structured entities.

subsidiary An entity that is controlled by another entity.

tax base of an asset or liability The amount attributed to that asset or liability for tax purposes.

tax expense (tax income) The aggregate amount included in the determination of profit or loss for the period in respect of current tax and deferred tax. Tax expense (tax income) comprises current tax expense (current tax income) and deferred tax expense (deferred tax income).

taxable profit (tax loss) The profit (loss) for a period, determined in accordance with the rules established by the taxation authorities, upon which income taxes are payable (recoverable).

taxable temporary differences Temporary differences that will result in taxable amounts in determining taxable profit (tax loss) of future periods when the carrying amount of the asset or liability is recovered or settled.

temporary differences Differences between the carrying amount of an asset or liability in the statement of financial position and its tax base. Temporary differences may be either: (a) taxable temporary differences; or (b) deductible temporary differences.

total comprehensive income The change in equity during a period resulting from transactions and other events, other than those changes resulting from transactions with owners in their capacity as owners.

useful life Either: (a) the period over which an asset is expected to be available for use by an entity; or (b) the number of production or similar units expected to be obtained from the asset by the entity.

value in use The present value of estimated future cash flows expected to arise from the continuing use of an asset and from its disposal at the end of its useful life.

warrant A financial instrument that gives the holder the right to purchase ordinary shares.

INDEX